# GREENBERG'S GUIDE TO

# LIONEL TRAINS:  1945 - 1969

# By  Bruce  C.  Greenberg,  Ph.D.

# Edited  By  Roland  LaVoie

*Cover  Photograph:  The  Seaboard  6250,  H.  Powell  Collection.*

Copyright 1987

**Greenberg Publishing Company**
7543 Main Street
Sykesville, MD 21784
(301) 795-7447

Manufactured in the United States of America

Greenberg Publishing Company offers the world's largest selection of Lionel, American Flyer and other toy train publications as well as a selection of books on model and prototype railroading. Our catalogue is available for $2.00 refundable with your order.

Greenberg Publishing Company also sponsors the world's largest public model railroad shows. The shows feature extravagant operating model railroads for N, HO, O, Standard and 1 Gauges as well a huge marketplace for buying and selling nearly all model railroad equipment. The shows also feature, a large selection of dollhouses and dollhouse furnishings. Shows are currently offered in metropolitan Boston, Long Island in New York, Philadelphia, Pittsburgh, Baltimore, Norfolk, New Jersey and Florida. To receive our current show listing, please send a self-addressed stamped envelope marked "Train Show Schedule" to the address below.

# TABLE OF CONTENTS

# INTRODUCTION

**Greenberg's Guide for Lionel Trains, 1945-1969**, Sixth Edition, is our most comprehensive report on the toy train marketplace. This edition records a very uneven pattern of price changes. At the present time, however, in the spring of 1987, prices are rising slowly for more desirable items.

## PURPOSE

The purpose of this book is to provide a comprehensive listing with current prices for Lionel locomotives, rolling stock and accessories, in O and O-27 Gauges, produced from 1945 through 1969. We include those variations which have been authenticated. In a few cases we ask our readers for further information where information is missing or doubtful. Values are reported for each item where there have been reported sales.

## DETERMINING VALUES

Toy train values vary for a number of reasons. First, consider the **relative knowledge** of the buyer and seller. A seller may be unaware that he has a rare variation and sell it for the price of a common piece. Another source of price variation is **short-term fluctuation** which depends on what is being offered at a given train meet on a given day. If four 773s are for sale at a small meet, we would expect that supply would outpace demand and lead to a reduction in price. A related source of variation is the **season** of the year. The train market is slower in the summer and sellers may at this time be more inclined to reduce prices if they really want to move an item. Another important source of price variation is the relative strength of the seller's **desire to sell** and the buyer's **eagerness to buy.** Clearly a seller in economic distress will be more eager to strike a bargain. A final source of variation is **the personalities** of the seller and buyer. Some sellers like to quickly turn over items and, therefore, price their items to move; others seek a higher price and will bring an item to meet after meet until they find a willing buyer.

Train values in this book are based on OBTAINED prices, rather than asking prices, along the East Coast during the winter of 1986-87. We have chosen East Coast prices since the greatest dollar volume in transactions appears there. The prices reported here represent a "ready sale", or a price perceived as a good value by the buyer. They may sometimes appear lower than those seen on trains at meets for two reasons. First, items that sell often sell in the first hour of a train meet and, therefore, are no longer visible. (We have observed that a good portion of the action at most meets occurs in the first hour.) The items that do not sell in the first hour have a higher price tag and this price, although not representing the sales price, is the price observed. A related source of discrepancy is the willingness of some sellers to bargain over price.

Another factor which may affect prices is reconditioning done by the dealer. Some dealers take great pains to clean and service their pieces so that they look their best and operate properly. Others sell the items just as they have received them, dust and all. Naturally, the more effort the dealer expends in preparing his pieces for sale, the more he can expect to charge for them. This factor may account for significant price differences among dealers selling the same equipment.

From our studies of train prices, it appears that mail order prices for used trains are generally higher than those obtained at eastern train meets. This is appropriate considering the costs and efforts of producing and distributing a price list and packing and shipping items. Mail order items do sell at prices above those listed in this book. A final source of difference between observed prices and reported prices is region. Prices are clearly higher in the South and West where trains are less plentiful than along the East Coast.

## CONDITION

For each item, we provide four categories: **Good, Very Good, Excellent and Mint.** The Train Collectors Association (TCA) defines conditions as:

FAIR Well-scratched, chipped, dented, rusted or warped

GCOD Scratches, small dents, dirty

VERY GOOD Few scratches, exceptionally clean, no dents or rust

EXCELLENT Minute scratches or nicks, no dents or rust

MINT Brand new, absolutely unmarred, all original and unused, in original box

In the toy train field there is a great deal of concern with exterior appearance and less concern with operation. If operation is important to you, then ask the seller whether the train runs. If the seller indicates that he does not know whether the equipment operates, you should test it. Most train meets have test tracks provided for that purpose.

We have included MINT in this edition because of the small but important trade in pre-1970 mint items. However there is substantial confusion in the minds of both sellers and buyers as to what constitutes "mint" condition. How do we define mint? Among very experienced train enthusiasts, a mint piece means that it is brand new, in its original box, never run, and extremely bright and clean (and the box is, too). An item may have been removed from the box and replaced in it but it should show no evidence of handling. A piece is not mint if it shows any scratches, fingerprints or evidence of discoloration. It is the nature of a market for the seller to see his item in a very positive light and to seek to obtain a mint price for an excellent piece. In contrast, a buyer will see the same item in a less favorable light and will attempt to buy a mint piece for the price of one in excellent condition. It is our responsibility to point out this difference in perspective **and** the difference in value implicit in each perspective, and to then let the buyer and seller settle or negotiate their different perspectives.

We do not show values for Fair or Restored. **Fair** items are valued substantially below Good. We have not included **Restored** because such items are not a significant portion of the market for postwar trains. As a rough guide, however, we expect that Restored items will bring prices equivalent to Good or possibly Very Good. The term professional restoration refers to highly proficient technical work. There is disagreement among restorers as to what constitutes approprate technique and finished product. There are substantial differences in the price that consumers are willing to pay for restored items.

As we indicated, prices in this book were derived from large train meets or shows. If you have trains to sell and you sell them to a person planning to resell them, you will not obtain the prices reported in this book. Rather, you should expect to achieve about fifty percent of these prices. Basically, for your items to be of interest to a buyer who plans to resell them, he must purchase them for considerably less than the prices listed here.

We receive many inquiries as to whether or not a particular piece is a "good value." This book will help answer that question; but, there is NO substitute for experience in the marketplace. WE STRONGLY RECOMMEND THAT NOVICES DO NOT MAKE MAJOR PURCHASES WITHOUT THE ASSISTANCE OF FRIENDS WHO HAVE EXPERIENCE IN BUYING AND SELLING TRAINS. If you are buying a train and do not know whom to ask about its value, look for the people running the meet or show and discuss with them your need for assistance. Usually they can refer you to an experienced collector who will be willing to examine the piece and offer his opinion.

## INFORMATION SOURCES

Seeking advice is especially important because of the danger posed by fakes and frauds. Recently, the Train Collectors Association, the largest train collecting organization in the United States, published the details of a chemical dyeing process which can alter a common plastic locomotive cab or freight car's color into an apparently real and "rare" but spurious color. While it is not the purpose of this book to be judgmental about this matter, we urge our readers to exercise extreme caution in purchasing Lionel postwar equipment purported to be a "factory error" because of a difference in color. The Factory Errors chapter, in Volume 2 of this edition, contains entries which are known to be genuine factory errors. Readers should consult expert opinion before contemplating any such purchase.

The Lionel collector and operator has several additional sources for toy train information. First there is the companion **Greenberg's Guide for Lionel Trains** manufactured before World War II. It presents a comprehensive listing of Lionel O and O-27 from their beginnings in 1915 through 1942, of Standard, from its beginning in 1906 through 1940 when production ceased, and of Lionel 2-7/8 Gauge from 1901-1906.

Also we published, in late 1985, **Greenberg's Guide to Fundimensions Trains: 1970-1985**, providing in-depth coverage of this production.

There are several other volumes of interest to the Lionel enthusiast. Between 1946 and 1966 Lionel issued hundreds of pages of service and instruction sheets for its dealers. These have been skillfully edited and organized into **Greenberg's Repair and Operating Manual for Lionel Trains**. This manual is the ultimate operator's guide. It helps him solve most operating problems; problems often due to design limitations. This book also describes the development of Lionel trains. In addition we offer **Plasticville: An Illustrated Price Guide** which provides a comprehensive photographic record with current prices. These books are available directly from Greenberg Publishing Company or from your local book or hobby store.

## REPORTING POSTWAR VARIATIONS

The first edition of Greenberg's Price Guide to Postwar and Fundimensions Lionel trains was published in 1977 as a response to collector demand for a comprehensive and reliable price guide to the toy train market. In the last seven years the Guide went through five editions and is now in its Sixth Edition. The book has rapidly developed; hundreds of new variations have been added and hundreds of entries have been changed. The Guide is the standard descriptive and price reference for the Lionel trains.

The main reason for the Guide's success has been the response and interest of you, the collector and enthusiast. Over the years, collectors from all over the United States and Canada have written with comments, suggestions and advice. These contacts have enabled the Guide to become accurate and thorough, although it still needs reader input.

In a little over the year between the Fifth and the Sixth Editions, enough data was amassed to provide over 500 new entries, new variations and corrections to previous entries, as well as several new articles of research on various aspects of Lionel postwar production. The sheer volume of contact has been a tribute to your interest, generosity and sincerity.

However, the incoming volume of mail and information, desirable as it is, has created a serious problem: the need to better respond to and organize new data. One approach will be to use computer-based compilation to increase the accuracy of our recording methods. Another approach is explained in this article.

The decision-making process concerning the listing of new items is surprisingly complex—and sometimes quite agonizing. Some-times a variation is difficult to establish, and upon follow-up letters asking for specific information, reveal that the item is not in fact a new variation. At other times, a really odd item may strain one's credibility—yet the variation is genuine. In general, there are three major criteria used by the editors before listing a variation:

(1) **CREDIBILITY**: Obviously, we are not referring to the trustworthiness of the enthusiast! That is something we assume all along. Rather, we are trying to answer the classic question of the skeptic: "How do you know this variation came from the factory?" Two examples will show what is meant. One very experienced and knowledgeable collector reported a 50 Gang Car with light gray bumpers instead of blue ones, and three blue men instead of two blue and one gray, as a rare variation. The problem here is that bumpers and men are easily replaced, so there is no way to tell whether it is a true factory variant or a post-factory alteration. In this case, our listing might read: "Same as (A), but three blue men and gray bumpers. Confirmation requested. NRS" (No reported sales). Perhaps someone else will be able to furnish data to show that this gang car is really a factory variant. For example, a reader may be the original owner of a similar piece with the same characteristics. Another example is a 9134 Fundimensions Virginian covered hopper with a silver cover instead of the normal blue cover. This 9134 came straight out of its factory sealed box, so it was clearly factory production. We have assumed that it is a factory error. The car body had been spray-painted with its cover on. We would like to know how many cars the factory similarly processed. It is most likely only a curiosity, not a rarity, and it is listed as such. Besides, the covers for such hoppers are easily interchanged.

(2) **CORROBORATION**: Many times the type of proof sent along with the report is crucial. Photographic evidence is very helpful. Of greater importance is independent verification by other collectors.

(3) **COMPLETENESS**: Several possibly good variations have fallen victim to incomplete reports. It is not enough to say that one has a 6560 crane car with no smokestack on the cab. There are several different 6560 cranes—which one is being reported? However, if the correspondent says that his crane is "the same as (B), but has no stack", he has given us the proper basis for comparison. Many major variations turn on a minor item—and so does the value. For example, the common variety of the Fundimensions 9737 Central Vermont boxcar and a scarce variation appear identical from the outside. Both are painted tuscan brown. However, the common one is painted over brown plastic, while the scarce one has an orange plastic body. The correspondent would have to look inside the boxcar to see the difference! The common one is worth only $6, the scarce one $35. The more complete your descriptions, the better.

If you wish to report a new entry, variation or correction to us, please use the reporting sheet enclosed with this book. We appreciate very much your cooperation, enthusiasm and good will in helping us document Lionel train production. As has been our custom, we will acknowledge all varieties noted in the Guide as coming from your collection and/or observation. Every letter to us will be answered. Varied sections of the book will help you with types of couplers, trucks, frames, etc.

---

**Cover photograph:** 6250 Seaboard, graciously loaned by Harold Powell, was photographed by Earl Sakowski of Mettee Studio. This mint example came with a horizontal left marker and vertical right one.

# ACKNOWLEDGMENTS

This book represents the bringing together of the knowledge of the train collector community. It is especially true of this, the Tenth Anniversary Edition of the Greenberg Guide to Postwar Lionel Trains. As I continued through the editing for this edition, I surveyed the enormous quantity of new data and the many new articles for it and felt as if I were editing two books instead of one. How little I realized that this would become literally true!

Given the abundance of new information, our first decision was whether or not to include the articles that first appeared in the Fifth Edition of this work. These articles included analyses and discussions of the Berkshires, Steam Turbines, Milk Cars, Flatcar molds and Tank Cars. It was clear that we could not include these fine articles at this time but we have decided to reprint them in a separate volume.

Even after having omitted the articles from the Fifth Edition, we found nevertheless, that with the new information and new articles, the Sixth Edition would have been a mammoth 400 pages. This growth was caused by the enormous increase in our knowledge about Lionel trains. In some chapters, the listings have almost doubled as new variations and explanations have come to light.

Consequently, we have decided to issue a second volume to this edition, which will be available soon. This second volume will contain the following excellent new articles: Linda Greenberg's discussion of the 45, 145 and 2145 Gatemen; Ralph Hutchinson's articles on the 2400 Series passenger cars and the 6362 Flatcars, updated and expanded from their original publication in the LCCA journals; Richard Vagner's history of Lionel's General steam engines and sets; and Tom Rollo's articles on the Madison passenger cars and Lionel's boxes. In addition, the volume will contain a greatly expanded paper section and discussion — well over twice the previous size — by **Robert Osterhoff**. The listings for catalogued sets and substantially expanded listings of uncatalogued sets; billboards; and peripherals, factory errors, and prototypes will also be issued in that edition. **Thomas Rollo**, a Milwaukee-area collector, has written a literate and highly entertaining piece about Lionel's use of light bulbs. Additional information for this article came from another light-bulb scholar, **Bruce Stiles**. Mr. Rollo's deductive reasoning is remarkable; he has managed to reconstruct Lionel's manufacturing cycle from the firm's use of light bulbs! Read the article and see for yourself what a truly skillful writer can do. The book also includes **Joseph Pehringer's** short but important piece concerning the staple-end and bar-end trucks and a brief history of Greenberg Publishing Company.

This 10th Anniversary volume represents the most significant investment of time and energy ever made for the study of Lionel trains. It contains several of the finest articles ever written about Lionel trains and the most complete record of production ever published. The book begins with the feature article by **Robert Swanson** "Order Out Of Chaos", the history of Lionel's 9-1/4" boxcars. In this article the author brings several different perspectives to understanding the development of the car. He considers the consumer catalogues, repair manuals, the boxes, the trucks, the frames and the car bodies. With the insights from this multi-faceted approach, he explains the variations and establishes the chronology. This article marks the first time that such a comprehensive understanding has been published and reflects both the author's skill and the growing body of knowledge on which he could draw. Mr. Swanson has also written an insightful study of Lionel's first postwar set of 1945, the 463W. Not only has Mr. Swanson written two major articles, he also carefully and analytically read the entire text. He made several very important corrections and added substantially to the crispness and sharpness of the text.

**Jim Sattler**, a contributor to this series for many years, spent an extraordinary amount of time reviewing his entire collection and writing several very important short essays. His studies of the Gang Car, Trolley and Crane have created structured and consistent reports. Mr. Sattler also carefully reviewed the manuscript and pointed out a number of inconsistencies and errors as well as clarifying language and concepts. In conjunction with Jim Sattler's review, **Bruce Greenberg** rewrote extensive portions of the boxcar, caboose, crane and searchlight, hopper, and tank car chapters. His purpose was to reorganize the sometimes fragmented and inconsistent data into chronological progression based on our current knowledge.

**Pat Scholes** has written an informative and interesting article about Lionel's radio control set.

**Richard Shanfeld**, with assistance from **Joseph Sadorf** and others, has written the authoritative account of the development of the GG1. He has taken the many disparate pieces of information and organized them into a meaningful explanation. **Richard Lord**, with additional information from **Ray Sorensen**, has contributed a comprehensive study of Lionel's F-3 Diesels. **Richard Vagner** has extended his previous excellent work on Lionel's gondolas. **Dr. Charles Weber**, among many other contributions and comments, has revamped the descriptions and classifications of a subject for which he is the acknowledged authority—the 6464 Series boxcars.

Once we have our articles and listings in text form, our next step is always to make this information run an intellectual gauntlet of readers for mistakes, corrections and additions. No fewer than 23 readers helped us in this task; all made substantial contributions. They are, in alphabetical order: P. Ambrose, J. Breslin, T. Budniak, P. Catalano, R. Griesbeck, L. Hodgson, R. Hutchinson, J. Kotil, M. Ocilka, H. Powell, C. Rohlfing, T. Rollo, G. Salamone, J. Sattler, W. Schmeelk, R. Sigurdson, K. Starke, L. Steuer, Jr., R. Swanson, C. Switzer, I. D. Smith, C. Weber and K. Wills.

In addition **Paul Ambrose** gave us great information on variations throughout the book, and his knowledge of sets, both catalogued and uncatalogued, is most impressive. **Chris Rohlfing** went through his complete collection for his comments and additions; we rely heavily on his reports and the number of contributions bearing his name shows this clearly. Mr. Rohlfing also served as correspondence editor for this volume and devoted many, many hours to answering reader inquiries and writing new entries based on reader comments. This function is critical to the development of our knowledge. **I. D. Smith**, who has assisted us in many ways, gave the manuscript his particular brand of close reading and caught many errors and thought of elements which escaped us all. If we needed to know how something operated, he was the man to call. **Harold Powell** helped us a great deal with prices as well as variations. He has patiently explained many pieces of rolling stock to this editor. Finally he lent us several very fine locomotives from this collection to photograph. The Seaboard on the cover is from his collection. **Glenn Halverson** keeps on finding the rare and the unusual; he sent in data on new factory errors and accessory entries. **Joe Algozzini** has, we believe, cornered the intellectual market on factory errors and prototypes, and he sent us a huge list of these from his own collection. His expertise on fakes and frauds was of great assistance as well. Not to be outdone, **Terrall Klaassen** sent us photos documenting production and prototype pieces we had never seen before. **Skip Carlson** of Washington State sent us a long list of corrections and additions from his own collection. **Dr. Charles Weber** raised important issues for discussion among us, and his revision of his previous work on 6464 Boxcars substantially extended our knowledge. Dr. Weber has been collecting trains since the mid-1960s and was able to offer us insights based on his lengthy experience. **Mike Ocilka** updated his flatcar mold information and sent in new variations throughout the book. **Mike Denuty** sent us a very helpful classification list of Lionel's steam engine tenders and a number of other new variations. **Bruce Stiles** of Lehigh Valley Trains illuminated (if you will pardon the pun) our listings of the Lionel boxed light bulbs and their lamp replacement dealer sets. Finally, **Gordon Wilson** added yet more information on the military and space items, more comments on accessories and other useful additions.

Other contributions were made by the following collectors and operators, ladies and gentlemen all: **J. Abraham, R. Arcara, D. Anderson, O. Anderson, K. Armen, F. Atkins, T. Austern, T. Budniak, L. Bohn, M. A. Brooks, G. Brown, P. Bender, H. Brandt, R. Brezak, L. Barrett, S. Blotner, J. Breslin, P. Catalano, N. Cretelle, R. Cretelle, F. Cieri, F. Cordone, B. Chin, J. Divi, M. Denuty, M. Drousche, R. Davis, F. S. Davis, D. Ely, H. Edmunds, D. Embser and J. Eastman.**

Also: **J. Foss, Jr., D. Fleming, J. J. Frank, Jr., J. Greider, F. Grittani, M. Goodwin, C. Grass, T. Groves, R. Gluckman, R. Griesbeck, M. Gesualdi, H. Holden, S. Hardwell, R. Harbina, M. Harrigan, B. Hudzik, Dr. W. Hopper, E. Heid, J. Hubbard, P. Iurilli, G. Kline, K. Koehler, J. Kotil, J. Keen, T. Ladny, J. Letterese, C. Lang and A. LaRue.**

Also: **B. Michel, J. Merhar, S. Mathis, G. S. Meisel, P. Mooney, T. McLaughlin, P. Murray, B. McLeavy, D. McCarthy, R. Nikolai, M. Nicholas, J. Notine, S. Natoli, R. Niedhammer, D. Orsello, N. Oswald, Sr., S. Perlmutter, T. Phelps, D. Pickard, B. J. Pearce, F. Pendley, M. Rubin, M. Rini, N. Ritschel, R. Rupp, B. Renfrew, M. Rohlfing and G. Romich.**

Also: **R. Schreiner, F. Salvatore, Jr., D. Schwab, A. Staebler, F. Stem, M. Stoken, L. Steuer, Jr., W. F. Spence, Brad Smith, S. Snook, W. Schilling, G. Salamone, T. Stucchio, E. Trentacoste, C. Theis, E. Vieth, B. Weiss, B. Werley, J. West, J. Whittam, K. Wills, V. Weisskopf, L. Wyant, W. S. Weber, R. Young, R. Ziska, E. Zukowski and R. Ziegler.**

This is an extraordinary list of contributors representing a very wide range of interests and expertise. Such a generous sharing of knowledge is very rare in this world. It is possible that I have omitted someone and I would like to apologize if this is the case.

I would also like to extend personal thanks to my two favorite Joes, **Bratspis and Gordon**, of the Toy Train Station in Feasterville, Pa., for allowing me to use their shop as a base for research, conversation and good, old-fashioned comradery among train enthusiasts. That also extends to the notorious **Friday Night Irregulars**, who know who they are! Thanks also to my wife, **Jimmie** and my son, **Tom**, for their encouragement and patience. My colleagues and students at **Cherry Hill High School East** have given me much personal encouragement as well.

This project which spanned two years was managed by **Cindy Floyd**. She organized the correspondence, provided the readers and editors with timely reports, directed the entering of the manuscript in our computers and its typesetting and coordinated the production with the art department. She was assisted by **Maureen Crum**, one of our staff artists who both designed and executed the book's preparation. **Donna Price** edited the book for style and consistency and in addition prepared materials for the editors and readers. **Marsha Davis** entered a large part of the manuscript on a computer and made many of the changes requested by the editors. **Dallas Mallerich, III,** prepared the index and with **MaryAnn Suehle** attended to last minute details.

Extensive new photography was undertaken for this volume. The entire diesel chapter was rephotographed and most of the boxcar chapter. Some of this photography was done by **George Stern**, some by **Tim Parrish** and some by **Bruce Greenberg**. Most of the new black and white prints were made by our staff photographer, **Maury Feinstein**. Several collectors gave very generously of their time to provide equipment for photography. **Larry Nuzzaci** was of great assistance to our photography effort and many of his trains — diesels, boxcars, flatcars and cabooses — grace this volume. **Richard Lord** lent several very unusual items to photograph and **Perry Mohney** assisted by providing Lionel Alcos to photograph.

One final thought: I exhibit a 5 x 8 Lionel layout at the Greenberg Train Shows, and more often than not I run one of my favorite engines, a nicely preserved 675 steam engine. It is forty years old, yet it runs as if it were new. I pick it up and marvel at its workmanship — the precise fit, the nickel tires, the intricate main and side rods, the exact die-casting. When I examine this engine, a little of the pride of workmanship performed so long ago travels down the decades to me, at this moment, in this place. I would like to dedicate this work, with warmth and affection, to the Lionel factory workers and engineers, living and departed, whose desire to make Lionel Trains the best in the world has given me so much pleasure.

Roland E. LaVoie, Editor
Cherry Hill, New Jersey
February, 1987

**PUBLISHER'S NOTE**

Roland LaVoie has just completed the most challenging and difficult editing assignment that he has ever undertaken. He has given unsparingly to this enormous project. The quality of this work reflects his dedication and skill.

Bruce C. Greenberg
Publisher

# FEATURE ARTICLE

## ORDER OUT OF CHAOS:
## A SYSTEMATIC STUDY OF
## LIONEL'S 9-1/4 INCH BOXCARS

### By Robert Swanson

## PART 1: INTRODUCTION

This article speaks for a series of Lionel rolling stock which has not received anywhere near the attention it deserves. In fact, one may make a case that the 2454 Series and its offshoots are Lionel's anticipation of Rodney Dangerfield's comedy routine — they "don't get no respect!" These boxcars, which were manufactured by Lionel from 1946 through 1953, have been neglected far too long by Lionel collectors. On the larger side, they are overshadowed by the popular and more colorful 6464 Series, and on the smaller side, they are outnumbered by the cheaper 6004 / 6014 / 6024 / 6044 Series. Lionel's catalogues from this period did little to stimulate interest in the 9-1/4" boxcars, since they are mostly incomplete or inaccurate concerning the boxcars which were actually produced. (Catalogued sets including these boxcars are listed in Table 12 at the end of this article.) While several books and articles have been published in recent years which correctly identify the major variations, they seem to contain an increasing amount of confusing or conflicting information concerning the dates and details of minor variations.

The objectives of this article are threefold. First, I will try to establish some standard terminology and definitions which will permit consistent and efficient discussion. Second, I will identify and describe the "pieces of the puzzle," the major and minor variations. Finally, I will try to fit all the pieces together into a single consistent "big picture" of the development and production of the 9-1/4" boxcars.

Two basic definitions are necessary to get us started:

● MAJOR VARIATIONS are differences in Lionel's car number, road name, herald or painted body color. These variations were established at the time the car body was painted and heat-stamped. Since there are only two body mold variations (with roof hatch for the operating merchandise cars and without it for all others), this feature plays no part in analyzing the development of the 9-1/4" boxcars.

● MINOR VARIATIONS are car variations due to changes in components such as frames, doors, trucks and couplers and plunger housings. Minor variations can be created or "faked" by interchanging components between two or more cars or by "repairing" a car with service station parts. With this in mind, the collector may find the information in this article useful in determining which minor variations are legitimate cars, which are plausible and which are totally outlandish.

There are several methods of establishing the validity of minor variations. The first is by observing a significant number of absolutely identical cars. Another method is through determining the date of several individual components and then finding a period of common manufacture or availability of these components. Box and set information can be used, when available, to establish dates for cars and components. The greatest validity is established when all methods point to a single consistent conclusion.

Table 8, presented later in this article, represents a summary and consolidation of information gathered over the past 12 years. During this time, I have collected over 100 of the 9-1/4" boxcars and observed the features and variations of perhaps a thousand more. Nevertheless, I am still making new observations and gaining new insights from other collectors. Should any readers have further information, please let us know so that this article can be updated.

## PART 2: MAJOR VARIATIONS

Table 1 contains a listing of the 17 major variations of the 9-1/4" boxcars with a summary description. Color pictures of these cars are shown throughout this article.

### CATALOGUE NUMBERS

The four-digit catalogue number assigned to these boxcars was a natural extension of the Prewar numbering system. The semi-scale boxcar introduced in 1940 was numbered 2954. Most of the cars Lionel introduced in 1945 and 1946 with the new knuckle coupler were numbered in the 2400 Series, so it was natural that the boxcar should be numbered 2454. Operating cars were numbered in the 3400 Series, so the merchandise car was numbered 3454, and the electronic set with its unique radio-controlled couplers was numbered in the 4400 Series; hence, the 4454 boxcar.

In 1948, Lionel changed the non-operating series number from 2400 to 6400 to reflect the introduction of the magnetic coupler, with the boxcar assuming the predictable number of 6454. Some boxcars produced in early 1948 carried the 6454 number even though they were equipped with the older coil couplers. Similar observations have been noted in studies of tank cars, gondolas and hoppers. My own theory as to why this happened is very simple. There was probably a delay in the delivery of the tooling for the magnetic couplers. The coil coupler was still in production in 1948 for O Gauge cars and operating cars. Bodies and boxes for O27 cars had already been stamped with the 6400 Series numbers. When production schedules called for the assembly of O27 sets, the couplers that were available were used to avoid shipping delays and inventory pile-ups in the factory. Since very few of the 6400 Series cars came with coil couplers, the delay in magnetic coupler production was probably very short.

Non-operating 9-1/4" boxcars manufactured from 1948 to 1952 were stamped with five different road names, yet they all carried the same 6454 number. Dash numbers were never added to identify road names or color variations, as was done for the 6464 boxcars. This was because Lionel did not specify which boxcar would be included in which catalogued set. Lionel made the selection of road name from the cars in production at that time, not the customer. Obviously, the Lionel Corporation had not yet realized the potential for a highly differentiated boxcar market. In fact, the 1948 catalogue states on page 24 that the "...Lionel Corporation reserves the right to alter lettering or emblems on sides of its boxcars."

To make the job of identifying and discussing the major variations a little easier, I have added a single letter

FIGURE 1: 9-1/4" Boxcars manufactured in 1946 and 1947. Top shelf: 2454(A)1 Pennsylvania (orange door); 2454(A)2 Pennsylvania (brown door). Middle shelf: 2454(B) Baby Ruth, 4454 Baby Ruth Electronic Control. Bottom shelf: 3454 Automatic Merchandise Car. R. Swanson Collection.

## TABLE 1: MAJOR VARIATIONS OF 9-1/4" BOXCARS

| CATALOGUE NUMBER | ROAD NAME | YEARS MADE | BODY COLOR | LETTERING |
|---|---|---|---|---|
| 2454(A) | Pennsylvania | 1946(early) | Lt. Orange | Black |
| 2454(B) | Baby Ruth | 1946-47 | Lt. Orange | Black |
| 3454 | PRR Mdse. | 1946-47 | Silver | Blue |
| 3464(A) | ATSF | 1949-52 | Orange | Black |
| 3464(B) | NYC | 1949-52 | Tan | White |
| 3474 | Western Pacific | 1952-53 | Silver | Black |
| 4454 | Baby Ruth (Electronic) | 1946-47 | Lt. Orange | Black |
| 6454(A) | Baby Ruth | 1948(early) | Orange | Black |
| 6454(B) | NYC | 1948(early) | Orange | Black |
| 6454(C) | NYC | 1948 | Brown | White |
| 6454(D) | NYC | 1948 | Tan | White |
| 6454(E) | ATSF | 1948 | Orange | Black |
| 6454(F) | SP | 1949 | Lt. Brown | White(1) |
| 6454(G) | SP | 1950 | Lt. Brown | White(2) |
| 6454(H) | SP | 1951-52 | Red-brown | White(2) |
| 6454(J) | Erie | 1949-52 | Brown | White |
| 6454(K) | Pennsylvania | 1949-52 | Tuscan | White |

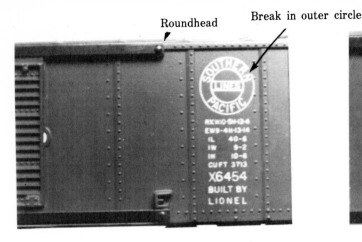

Roundhead    Break in outer circle    Flathead

**Figure 2:** The early Southern Pacific herald (1949) has large letters and a small diameter inner circle. The outer circle almost always has a break between the R and the N.

**Figure 3:** The later Southern Pacific herald (1950-52) has smaller letters than the early one, and a larger diameter inner circle.

designation behind the catalogue number in Table 1. In Table 8, a number will be added behind the letter to identify the minor variation (e.g. 6454(B)-3). Hopefully, this shorthand notation will permit a concise identification of variations without a lengthy description of details.

The operating car introduced in 1949 was numbered 3464, since the 3454 number had already been used for the merchandise car. Again, two road names shared the same catalogue number. The choice for inclusion in sets was still Lionel's, not the customer's. It was not until 1952, when the silver 3474 Western Pacific operating car was introduced, that a boxcar with a specific road name was identified for inclusion within a specific set. While the 3474 was never offered in a consumer catalogue for separate sale, Lionel tried to promote the marketing potential of this car as part of a set and brought specific attention to the road name of this car on page 11 of the 1952 catalogue.

## ROAD NAMES

Road names and heralds will be discussed in the chronology section under the year they were first introduced. However, I would like to pause for a minute here to discuss the "new" or built dates heat-stamped on some of the boxcar bodies. These "new" dates are associated more with the road name than the Lionel number, as the following chart shows:

| TABLE 2: NEW DATES | | |
|---|---|---|
| **ROAD NAME** | **CATALOGUE NUMBER** | **NEW DATE** |
| Baby Ruth | 2454, 4454, 6454 | None |
| PRR Merchandise | 3454 | 6-46 |
| Pennsylvania | 2454, 6454 | 6-45 |
| ATSF | 3464, 6454 | None |
| NYC | 3464, 6454 | 9-44 |
| Southern Pacific | 6454 (both heralds) | 3-42 |
| Erie | 6454 | None |
| Western Pacific | 3474 | 1-52 |

The new dates for two of these cars, the 3454 PRR Merchandise Car and the 3474 Western Pacific, follow Lionel's frequent Postwar practice of indicating when the car was first made and catalogued for sale. However, that is where the pattern ends. None of the Baby Ruth, ATSF or Erie cars ever had new dates, regardless of when they were produced. The Southern Pacific, NYC and Pennsylvania cars all had new dates from the time of World War II, when no trains were produced. Does this mean that Lionel made the heat stamp dies during the Second World War in anticipation of Postwar production? Possibly, but more likely the Second World War new dates represent dates found on the real railroad boxcars which were the prototypes for Lionel's models. In its advertising, Lionel made much of the fact that its "realistic" trains were designed from real railroad blueprints. These blueprints (or associated photographs) were probably the source of all the graphics information — including the built dates. Why were not all the 9-1/4" boxcars done this way? No one knows for sure. This inconsistency shows that Lionel was not always obsessed with complete accuracy.

## COLORS

Another major variation in the 9-1/4" boxcars is the body color. Since all the bodies of these boxcars were painted, we are discussing the paint color, not the color of the molded plastic. Lionel could and did change the colors of the molded plastic, depending upon what plastic was available at the time. Several writers have pointed out that material shortages between 1946 and 1949 affected the body mold color quite a bit. The complex subject of Lionel's body mold colors is best left to its own article.

Before discussing paint color variations, I again feel that standard definitions are necessary for clear understanding. The eight separate and distinct colors used on the 9-1/4" boxcars are listed in Table 3. The objective here is to apply a color name to one and only one color, regardless of the number and road name of the car to which it is applied. In other words, all cars listed as brown should be the same color when placed side by side in the same lighting, no matter if they are NYC or Erie cars. Likewise, the early SP cars should all appear to be a lighter brown when compared with the brown NYC or Erie cars. Interestingly, the later SP cars have a definite red-brown color unlike the brown shade of the earlier SP cars, which show no hint of red. The tuscan color found on the Pennsylvania cars can be described as a red-brown which also contains a trace of purple. The orange used on the 2454 and 4454 cars in 1946 and 1947 should be defined as light orange to distinguish it from the orange used on several 6454 cars in 1948 and on the 3464(A) ATSF cars made from 1949 to 1952. Tan is my name for the color between orange and light brown which has been called burnt-orange by some collectors. Why complicate matters with an 11-letter hyphenated word when one 3-letter word will serve just as well? Finally, silver is just that — silver.

| TABLE 3: COLORS | | | |
|---|---|---|---|
| COLOR NAME | YEAR MADE | CATALOGUE NUMBER | ROAD NAME |
| Light Orange | 1946-47 | 2454 | PRR, BR |
| | 1946-47 | 4454 | BR |
| Orange | 1948 | 6454 | BR, NYC, ATSF |
| | 1949-52 | 3464 | ATSF |
| Tan | 1948 | 6454 | NYC |
| | 1949-52 | 3464 | NYC |
| Brown | 1948 | 6454 | NYC |
| | 1949-52 | 6454 | Erie |
| Light Brown | 1949-50 | 6454 | SP |
| Red-brown | 1951-52 | 6454 | SP |
| Tuscan | 1949-52 | 6454 | PRR |
| Silver | 1946-47 | 3454 | PRR Mdse. |
| | 1952-53 | 3474 | WP |

At this point, I imagine that some collectors may feel that this color list is incomplete. At the least, they will point out that they have seen several orange, brown and tuscan variations that I have not mentioned. There is no question that additional color and gloss variations can be found. However, I raise this question: Did all of these minor paint variations exist at the time these cars were manufactured? I do not think so. Dirt, cleaning agents and fading can cause significant differences in the hue and gloss of the same paint on different cars. Several examples will illustrate this point clearly.

Consider first the question of fading. I have a 6454(K) Pennsylvania car which appears on one side to be a pure brown with no hint of the purple cast usually found in the tuscan color. The opposite side of this car has some damage, but it is otherwise like new, and the paint is clearly the usual shade of tuscan. So is the inside of the car. (Unlike many of the 6464 cars, Lionel painted these bodies both inside and out.) I believe that this car was owned for several years by a collector who placed this car on a shelf with the damaged side against the wall. The brown side faced outward, where it was faded by sunlight or fluorescent lighting. Tuscan Pennsylvania and red-brown Southern Pacific cars seem to be particularly susceptible to fading, which can leave them a nondescript brown color. Opening the doors and looking inside the car will usually reveal the original color.

Dirt and cleaning can also affect the paint hue and gloss. Light orange Baby Ruth or Pennsylvania cars can appear much darker if smudged by newsprint or covered with years of attic dirt. A good cleaning will bring the car back to its original light orange color, but the cleaning agent will determine whether it

is a dull orange or a slightly glossy orange. Cleaning with a mild soap solution will tend to leave a dull finish, while cleaning with furniture polish or any other cleaner containing a polishing agent will leave a shinier finish. If you try cleaning some of these cars yourself, you too can produce some of these reported minor paint variations!

There is, however, another source of minor color variation which deserves more study than is allowed by the scope of this article. This is the influence of the underlying body mold material upon the paint color. I have some cars with thin coats of paint over completely clear molded bodies. Particularly in bright light or with back lighting, these cars look significantly different from cars with opaque or heavily painted bodies. The body mold color which seems to have the most noticeable effect is the orange body molded in 1952. The brown, tuscan and red-brown of the 6454 cars made with the orange body mold are all distorted to some degree by the orange mold material. Additionally, orange-painted 3464 cars which have orange bodies appear brighter than other orange-painted 3464 cars. On the other hand, cars with two coats of paint (a different color for each coat) do not appear to be affected by the color of the first coat! Mold material colors and multiple coats of paint obviously require more study and correlations with other datable features.

There is one final aspect of paint colors which merits some notice. During the four years from 1949 to 1952, Lionel was manufacturing three different, but similar 6454 boxcars. Each road name had its own subtle color difference. The Southern Pacific cars were colored light brown or red-brown, the Erie cars were painted brown and the Pennsylvania cars were painted tuscan. Incredibly, each of these cars came with doors painted exactly the same color as the body. After observing hundreds of these cars, I have never seen a car of one color stamped with the road name usually reserved for another color. Likewise, I have never seen a car in original condition where the door color did not precisely match the body color. This speaks volumes about Lionel's quality control, inspection and general attention to detail. Remember that these three cars were produced concurrently through numerous production runs over a four-year period. It would have been very easy for a tuscan body to be stamped Erie or Southern Pacific. Brown doors could have easily been placed on a red-brown body — or vice-versa. Such "mistakes" would not have necessarily been intentional or due to carelessness, either. One of the most common forms of color blindness or color weakness in human vision is an inability to distinguish between shades of red and brown. Obviously, Lionel kept people with this color deficiency away from the boxcar assembly and inspection lines. As a result, there are very few "wrong" color variations for collectors today. Some variations will be discussed in the last section of this article, Prototypes, Paint and Color Samples, Factory Errors and Altered Cars. However, none of the 6454 cars discussed involve paint color mix-ups.

## PART 3: MINOR AND COMPONENT VARIATIONS

To repeat the definition in the introduction: Minor boxcar variations are those due to changes in components. The components considered in this article are doors, frames, trucks and couplers, plunger housings (operating cars), merchandise car hatch pins and door guide attachment pins.

### DOORS

Four distinct types of boxcar doors are defined in Table 4 and shown in Figure 6. The first three types are die-cast metal

Figure 4: 9-1/4" boxcars manufactured in 1948. top shelf: 6454(A) Baby Ruth and 6454(B) orange NYC. Second shelf: 6454(C) brown NYC and 6454(D) tan NYC. Bottom shelf: 6454(E)ATSF. R. Swanson Collection.

doors originally designed for the prewar scale-detailed 2758 Automobile Car and also used on postwar 2758 and 2458 cars. The fourth type is a molded plastic door designed specifically for the 9-1/4" boxcars. Subcategories of the four major types are also defined in Table 4 to identify color and / or surface treatment. These subcategories arise from applications to specific catalogue numbers and road names (see Table 8).

The highly detailed metal doors were designed and cast as pairs for the double-door automobile car. (In this discussion, when the terms "right" and "left" door are used, we refer to the position of the doors on the sides of the automobile cars, not their positions on the 9-1/4" boxcars.) They look great when placed side by side in their original application. The right door looks fine when used by itself on the single-door boxcars, but the left door does not because it lacks a designation board and a latch handle. When this door appears on the single-door 9-1/4" boxcars, it looks like a mistake! However, since these doors were made in pairs, Lionel used them in pairs. Even when production of the double-door automobile car ended in 1948, Lionel continued to make right and left (wrong) doors for another three years! The three types of metal doors are distinguished by a pin or stud cast on the back side of one or both doors. Type 1 doors have no pins. Type 2 doors have a short hollow stud on the back side of the right door only. A drive pin inserted in this stud was the attachment point for the door-opening mechanism on the 3454 PRR Merchandise Car.

These doors were subsequently used on non-operating cars. Type 3 doors are equipped with longer solid studs on both right and left doors for the door-opening mechanism of the 3464

| TABLE 4: DOORS |
|---|
| **TYPE 1:** Metal, no pin on back, different right and left doors. |
|    1-Y:  Painted light orange - 1946 |
|    1-B:  Painted brown - 1946-47 |
| **TYPE 2:** Metal, short hollow pin on back of right door, no pin on back of left door. |
|    2-S:  Painted silver - 1946-47 |
|    2-B:  Painted brown - 1947-48 |
| **TYPE 3:** Metal, long solid pin on back of both right and left doors. |
|    3-B:  Painted brown - 1949 |
|    3-M:  Painted to match car color - 1949-52 |
|    3-X:  Chemically blackened, unpainted - 1949-52 |
| **TYPE 4:** Plastic, long solid pin on back of all doors, all doors similar to right metal doors, no left doors. |
|    4-M:  Painted to match car color - 1952-53 |
|    4-U:  Unpainted black plastic - 1952-53 |

Figure 5: Operating boxcars manufactured from 1949 to 1953. Top shelf: 3464(A)1 - note brown door and 3464(A) with black door. Bottom shelf: 3464(B) New York Central and 3474 Western Pacific. R. Swanson Collection.

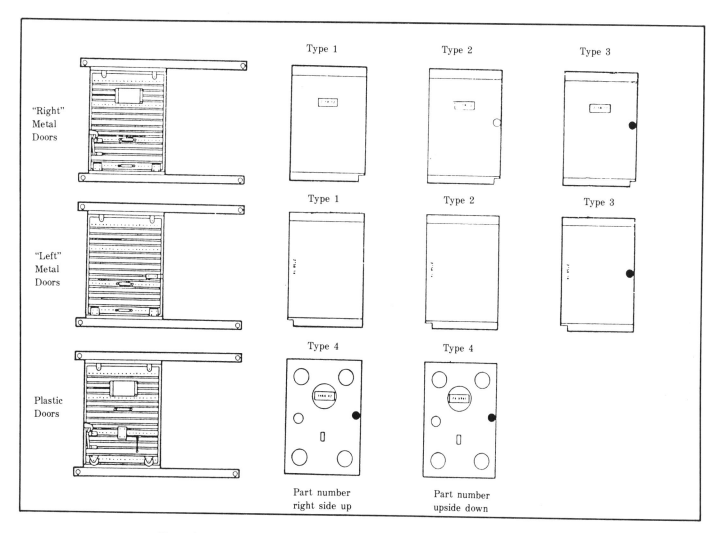

Figure 6: Doors used on 9-1/4 inch boxcars. Drawings by Konrad Koch, Prime Graphics.

operating cars. With pins on both doors, the body could be assembled onto the frame in either direction and the operating mechanism would still open the door.

In 1952, Lionel finally developed new tooling for molding the doors out of plastic. These plastic doors, which are all right-side doors (apparently someone finally noticed the absence of the door latch!), have been designated as Type 4 doors. Notice in Figure 6 that the plastic door has a second smaller designation board which is not present on the metal doors. In addition, the shape of the lower door slide housings has been changed from square to circular. However, the question which begs an answer is: Why did Lionel invest in new door tooling when significant production of the 9-1/4" boxcars would continue for only another year? Was the plastic door associated with the introduction of the 3474 Western Pacific car, which required a painted door on an operating car? The injection-molded plastic doors were undoubtedly cheaper to make than the die-cast metal doors, and they certainly improved the appearance of the boxcars (since the inappropriate left doors were not needed).

## FRAMES

The published information on the frames for the 9/1-4" boxcars has probably been more incomplete and inconsistent than information on any other component of these cars. Table 5 and the drawings in Figure 7 are an attempt to set the record straight, once and for all. As it happens, the frames I have identified for the 9-1/4" boxcars have most of the same characteristics as the tank car frames identified by Bill Schilling. The frames made between 1947 and 1950 also contain some features required by the 3462 and 3472 Operating Milk Cars, as detected by David Fleming. (Editor's Note: See the previous edition of **Greenberg's Guide to Lionel Trains, 1945-1969**, for Mr. Schilling's discussion of postwar tank car frames and Mr. Fleming's article on the operating milk cars.)

All of the boxcar frames have six holes which are always used and whose purpose is well understood: four holes in the corners for screws used to mount the frame to the car body and two holes used for mounting the trucks. It is those mysterious extra holes in the frames which leave collectors perplexed. However,

## TABLE 5: FRAMES

| TYPE | STEPS | HOLE PATTERN | CATALOGUE NUMBER | YEARS MADE | SIDE FLANGE |
|---|---|---|---|---|---|
| 1A, B | yes | A, B (1) | 2454 | 1946-47 | A. Plain |
| | | | 3454 | 1947 | B. Indents (2) |
| | | | 6454 | 1948 | B. Indents |
| 2A, B | yes | A, B, C | 4454 | 1946-47 | A. Plain |
| | | | | 1947 | B. Indents |
| 3 | yes | D | 6454 | 1948 | Indents |
| 4 | yes | D, E | 6454 | 1949 | Indents |
| 4M (3) | yes | D, E | 3464 | 1949 | Indents |
| 5M A, B | no | D, E | 3464 | 1950 | A. Indents |
| | | | | 1950 | B. Cutouts |
| 6 | no | A | 6454 | 1950 | Plain |
| 7 | no | E | 6454 | 1951-52 | Plain |
| 7M | no | E | 3464 | 1951-52 | Plain |
| | | | 3474 | 1952 | |
| 7P (4) | no | E | 3464 | 1952 | Plain |
| | | | 3474 | 1952-53 | |

(1) Hole pattern designations:
    A. Four holes; used for mounting the merchandise car mechanism.
    B. Two holes with slight drawing, probably planned for original mounting of electronic receiver but never used. One or both "B" holes in some early 1948 cars are not drawn and have a much smaller diameter than usual.
    C. Three holes; actually used for mounting and adjustment of electronic receiver.
    D. Four holes (three round, one narrow slot); used in operating milk car frame for mounting operating mechanism.
    E. Four holes (including large center hole); used for mounting operating plunger mechanism.

(2) Type 1B and 2B frames made in 1947 and early 1948 have side flanges with inch-long indentations which were required

for door clearance on operating milk cars. All Type 3, 4, 4M and a few 5M (5A) frames have these same indentations. The majority of the Type 5M (5B) frames have cutout sections in the side flanges which were required by the plastic doors used on milk cars beginning in 1950. Type 6 and 7 frames have neither indentations nor cutout sections.

(3) Frame types with an "M" suffix have been embossed around three of the Type E pattern holes for the mounting of the operating mechanism. The "M" indicates that the large center hole has been embossed to accept the metal plunger housing.

(4) Frame types with a "P" suffix have also been embossed for the operating mechanism, but the center hole has been prepared for a plastic plunger housing.

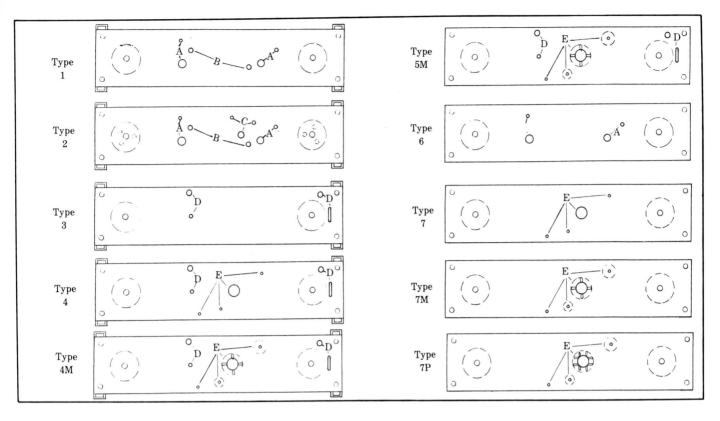

**Figure 7: Frames used on 9-1/4" boxcars as viewed from the bottom. Drawings by R. Swanson.**

the extra holes can be grouped into five distinct patterns of two to four holes each, as explained in Note (1) to Table 5.

In the "A" pattern, the four holes are needed for the 3454 PRR Operating Merchandise Car. The smaller pair of these holes is used for mounting the operating mechanism to the frame, while the larger pair of holes is used for passages bringing the wires from the trucks to the operating solenoid. These larger holes are also used for the same purpose in the 4454 boxcar with its electronic receiver. However, in the electronic boxcar the larger holes are usually lined with rubber grommets to protect the wiring.

It is interesting to note that the two holes of the "B" pattern were not only pierced, but also drawn to accept self-tapping or sheet metal screws. However, to my knowledge these holes were never used on any box, tank or milk car. The spacing and position of the "B" holes suggests that they were intended for mounting the electronic receiver inside the 4454 electronic boxcar. However, none of the 4454 cars I have observed have used these "B" holes. Instead, a Type 2 frame is used which contains an additional three-hole "C" pattern for an L-shaped receiver mounting bracket and access to the receiver tuning screw. Most of the Type 2 frames also have three embossed nubs around each truck mounting hole to insure a good electrical ground for the electronic receiver.

The four-hole "D" pattern, which first appeared on the Type 3 frames, is most often erroneously reported as "two small holes" because the third round hole and the slot are usually obscured by one of the trucks. The slot and the small hole near the center of the car are used for mounting the operating mechanism in the milk cars. The two holes near the side of the frame are used for clearance of two rivets which hold the milk car mechanism together. The round "D" hole located near the

truck mounting embossment is usually egg-shaped instead of circular. This is because the "D" hole is pierced as a perfect circle but is then distorted when the truck mounting dish is embossed.

The four-hole "E" pattern is used for the operating mechanism of the 3464 and 3474 operating boxcars. These holes were punched during the main piercing and forming operation for the frames. Frames actually used in the operating cars required a secondary operation to prepare the large center hole for the plunger housing and to emboss the area around two of the smaller holes. The secondary operation was not required for the non-operating cars, so the areas around these holes are always flat on 6454 cars.

Note (2) in Table 5 discusses the indentations and cutout notches found on the side flanges of some frames. These features were required for the door frames of 3462 and 3472 Operating Milk Cars.

## TRUCKS AND COUPLERS

Postwar die-cast trucks with knuckle couplers are discussed in some detail elsewhere in this book. (Editor's Note: See the discussion of these trucks by Joseph Pehringer in this edition). The only contribution I can add to this area is to point out that the Type 3 and Type 5 couplers can be divided into two easily distinguishable sub-classes.

As shown in Figure 9, the Type 3A couplers made in 1946 had the coupler head attached to the supporting plate by a single peened-over stud. This attachment was a weak point in the design, and the coupler head frequently became loose or separated. In 1947, the Type 3B coupler was introduced with a simple but effective means of strengthening the weak joint.

Figure 8: Non-operating boxcars manufactured from 1949 - 1953. Top shelf: 6454(F) SP with early herald. Middle shelf: 6454(G) SP (light brown), 6454(H) SP (red-brown). Bottom shelf: 6454(J) Erie, 6454(K) Pennsylvania. R. Swanson Collection.

## TABLE 6: TRUCKS AND COUPLERS
### Used for the 9-1/4 inch Boxcars

All of the following are die-cast metal trucks:

**TYPE 1:** Staple-end truck, "whirly", deep-dished or regular wheels with thick axles, early coil coupler design with "flying shoe", 1945 and early 1946. Not known to be used on any 9-1/4" boxcars.

**TYPE 2:** Staple-end truck with regular wheels and thinner constant-diameter axles, early coil coupler design with "flying shoe", early 1946.

**TYPE 3:** Staple-end truck with regular wheels and axles, later coil coupler with sliding shoe supported by metal plate attached to axles.

(A) Coupler head attached to supporting plate by integral stud peened over, 1946.

(B) Coupler head attached to supporting plate as in (A) above, except that the joint is strengthened by staking at four points, 1947-early 1948.

**TYPE 4:** Staple-end truck with regular wheels and axles, magnetic type coupler, no extra hole in activator plate, swaged end of rivet attaching activator plate is visible when observed from bottom of truck, 1948 - 1949.

**TYPE 5:** Staple-end truck with regular wheels and axles, magnetic type coupler, extra hole in activator plate.

(A) Swaged end of rivet attaching activator plate is visible when observed from bottom of truck, early 1950.

(B) Roundheaded end of activator plate rivet visible when observed from bottom of truck, late 1950-1951.

**TYPE 6:** Bar-end truck with regular wheels and axles, magnetic-type coupler, extra hole in activator plate, round head of rivet visible in activator plate as in 5(B), 1952 - 1953.

After the stud was peened, a staking operation was added to produce a mechanical interlocking at four additional points, as can be seen in the right side of Figure 9.

The subdivision of Type 5 couplers is easier to see but harder to explain than the Type 3 subdivision. Production in 1950 began with the Type 5A coupler characterized by the activator rivet with the flared end down and visible from the bottom of the truck plate. For some reason, during the middle of the 1950 production run Lionel changed the assembly of the coupler and the rivet was inserted from the bottom with the round head

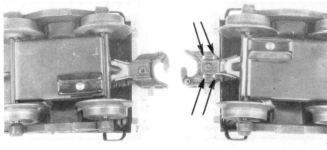

3A without stake marks    3B with stake marks

Figure 9: Type 3 trucks. 1946 production on the left without stake marks. 1947 production on the right had the knuckle attachment strengthened by the addition of four stake marks.

down, resulting in the 5B coupler. Since this change did not alter the operation or reliability of the coupler, one can only surmise that the change increased the efficiency of the assembly. There certainly must have been some advantage, because Lionel never returned to the earlier rivet orientation.

## PLUNGER HOUSING

There was one change in the mechanism of the 3464/3474 operating cars during their production from 1949 to 1953. Early in 1952, the housing supporting the plunger and plunger return spring was changed from metal to plastic. A frame change was also required to accept the plastic housing; compare the center holes of Frames 7M and 7P in Figure 7. This change was probably a cost reduction.

Figure 10: A comparison of a 1946 Merchandise Car without a visible roof hatch pin (left) and a 1947 car with a visible roof hatch pin (right).

## 3454 PRR MERCHANDISE CAR HATCH PIN

The hinge pin which supports the roof of the 3454 PRR Merchandise Car is attached by two completely different methods. Cars manufactured in 1946 have a brass wire hinge pin which is bent at a 90-degree angle at both ends. The hinge pin is attached to the car body by two molded plastic posts which appear to be molded with slots which are heated and

closed after the hinge pin was inserted laterally. This hinge pin is not visible from outside of the car at all.

The attachment method used in 1947 is identical to the method used on the 3462 Milk Car introduced that year. In this method of attachment, a steel or plated pin with a rounded head on one end is inserted through the end of the car body, as shown in Figure 10. The internal plastic posts now have holes instead of slots to support the pin. After the pin was inserted from the end of the car through the roof hatch, it was bent past the second support post to lock it into place. This second method of attachment eliminated the need for heat to close the open slots, but it left the car with an exposed pin head on the car end.

## DOOR GUIDE ATTACHMENT PIN

The metal door guides of the 9-1/4" boxcars were all attached with short fluted drive pins having a head on one end. There are some variations in the length and fluting (straight vs. spiraled), but I have never removed enough pins to know for sure which was used when. However, there is a variation in head shape which is visible without disassembling the car.

Most of the cars have door guide drive pins with round heads. However, for some unknown reason, most of the cars made in 1950 used a flathead drive pin. The differences between these two drive pins can be seen in Figures 2 and 3. The use of the flathead pin in 1950 may have been caused by materials shortages associated with the Korean War, or it may have been the result of a purchasing mistake. Whatever the reason, the round head pins returned with the beginning of 1951 production.

A few 3464 (A) ATSF boxcars have turned up with flathead drive pins, yet these cars have many other components indicative of 1952 production. It is possible that some 1950 body assemblies were stored for use by the service department but later assembled onto frames and trucks in 1952. I have seen four such cars in different parts of the country, so I do not think they are all service station repairs.

## THE MOLDED HUMAN FIGURE

The molded human figure used in the production of the 3464 and 3474 operating cars comes in several variations. The most noticeable difference is that some have flesh-colored hands and faces, while others are entirely blue, as molded. The figures with the painted hands and faces were probably produced in 1949 and early 1950, while the solid blue figures represent 1950 or later production. The great frequency of cars with missing figures, the variety of reproduction figures readily available and the ease in swapping figures between cars leads me to largely ignore the figure as a dating feature for the 9-1/4" operating boxcars.

## BOXES

A study of the boxes used for shipping the 9-1/4" boxcars provides some interesting insights into the development of the series. Obviously, cars and boxes can be and often have been swapped through the years. Boxes cannot be used as a sole or conclusive dating factor for any specific car. However, when large numbers of cars in boxes are observed and careful comparisons between different boxes are made, some definite patterns do emerge. Through the years I have observed and collected 24 different boxes for the 9-1/4" boxcars. These boxes are listed with a brief description in Table 6.

Figure 11: The top two rows of boxes from 1946 - 1947 are much larger than those below. The large boxes were designed to contain a corrugated cardboard inner liner. The third and fourth rows are boxes from 1948 - 1949 except for the right-hand box in the fourth row which is early 1950. All boxes in the third and fourth rows are 10-1/8" long. The fifth and sixth rows contain boxes used from 1950 - 1953. These boxes are all 8-11/16" long.

The boxes designed for the 9-1/4" boxcars in 1946 and 1947 were large enough to contain a corrugated cardboard inner liner to protect the plastic body. I stress the idea of the plastic body because all-metal cars such as the 2458 Automobile Car and the 2457 Caboose were packaged during this same period in smaller boxes with no inner liners. Apparently, Lionel believed that plastic bodies required more protection than metal bodies in these years.

TABLE 7:  BOXES USED FOR THE 9-1/4 INCH BOXCARS

**LARGE SIZE:**  With cardboard inner liner, 1946 - 1947

1. No. 2454 Boxcar, no ATMA logo, 11" x 3-3/4" x 2-5/8"
2. No. 2454 Boxcar, ATMA logo, 11" x 3-3/4" x 2-5/8"
3. No. 2454 Merchandise Car, no ATMA logo, 11" x 3-3/4" x 2-5/8"
4. No. 4454 Boxcar, Electronic Control, no ATMA logo, 11" x 3-3/4" x 2-5/8"
5. No. 3454 Merchandise Car, no ATMA logo, 11" x 4" x 3-1/4"
6. No. 3454 Merchandise Car, ATMA logo, 11" x 3-3/4" x 3-1/4"
7. No. 2454 Boxcar, overstamped on 2458 box, no ATMA logo, no inner liner, 11-1/4" x 3-3/8" x 2-3/8"

**MIDDLE SIZE:**  No liners, ATMA logo, 10-1/8" x 3-1/4" x 2-1/4"

8. No. 6454 Boxcar, 1948
9. No. 6454 S.P. Boxcar, 1 Lionel 1, 1949
10. No. 6454 Erie Boxcar, 2 Lionel 2, 1949
11. No. 6454 P.R.R. Boxcar, 3 Lionel 3, 1949
12. No. 3464 S.F. Boxcar, 1949
13. No. 3464 NYC Boxcar, 1949
14. No. 3464 NYC Boxcar, NYC overstamp of 3464 S. F. box, 1949
15. No. 6454 Boxcar (6454 overstamp of 3464 S.F. box), 1950

**SMALL SIZE:**  No liners, ATMA logo, 8-11/16" x 3-1/4" x 2-1/4"

16. No. 3464, NYC Boxcar, 1950 - 1952
17. No. 3464, S.F. Boxcar, 1950 - 1952
18. No. 3464 S.F. Boxcar, OPS ceiling price $5.50, 1952
19. No. 3464  NYC Boxcar (NYC overstamp of S.F.), 1951 1952
20. No. 3474  W.P. Boxcar, OPS ceiling price $5.50, 1952
21. No. 3474  W.P. Boxcar, 1953
22. No. 6454  S.P. Boxcar, 1950 - 1952
23. No. 6454  Erie Boxcar, 1950 - 1952
24. No. 6454  P.R.R. Boxcar, 1950 - 1952

Figure 12: Two Lionel Boxes. The top shelf has a box originally printed as a 2458 Automobile Car from 1946. The box was overprinted 2454 on all four sides and on both ends as well. The 2458 is a metal car which was packaged without a liner. The 2454 is a plastic car that Lionel, in 1946, usually shipped with cardboard liners. The box came with a 2454-A2 Pennsylvania brown door. Was this a field trial to determine if plastic cars could be shipped without cardboard liners without damage or did Lionel simply run out of the right box and solved the momentary crisis by using another box?

After the Second World War, Lionel continued a practice begun before the war in order to meet shipping demands and / or to adjust the firm's box inventory. Lionel would black out the original car number (and sometimes the description) on the box and then overprint another number and / or description. One box listed as number 7 in Table 7 is a 2458 double-door Automobile Car box which has been re-marked to contain a 2454 boxcar. The car usually found in this box is a 2454(A)-2 brown-door Pennsylvania boxcar, probably made in mid-1946. Notice in Figure 12 that the original number and description have been obliterated, but the O Gauge designation has been left visible and unaltered. Was this reworked 2458 box used with the 2105WS set, the only O Gauge set to contain a 2454 boxcar in 1946? Or was the box used with O-27 sets as well, making the description a misnomer?

Another feature I have observed on some of the large boxes is the presence or absence of the American Toy Manufacturers' Association logo. I presume that the boxes without the logo were printed in 1946 and those with the logo were printed in the following years. All of the small and mid-size boxes used for the 9-1/4" boxcars I have seen carried the ATMA logo.

Figure 13: The case of the shrinking box. The top shelf has a 1947 box with the blue words "LIONEL" and "TRAINS" touching the blue band which surrounds them. This lettering was used in 1945 through 1947. However this box also has the "TOY MF'RS U.S.A" logo which first appears in 1947. This box was designed to accommodate a cardboard liner. The second shelf box is dated from the side view as either 1948 or 1949. Note the blue words "LIONEL" and "TRAINS" no longer touch the blue border. It is smaller because Lionel no longer used inner liners with plastic freight cars. The third shelf is a 1950 through 1952 box. Note that it is significantly shorter than the other two boxes. The reduction in length was achieved by removing the steps from the car frame and turning the trucks with couplers inward when inserted in the box.

The 3454 Merchandise Car came in two different boxes. The 1946 cars came in four-inch boxes which did not have the ATMA logo, while the 1947 cars came in 3-3/4-inch wide boxes which did have the logo.

One of the more curious boxes is box number 3 in Table 7, marked 2454 Merchandise Car. I have a number of these boxes, and I have always found them with 2454 PRR Baby Ruth boxcars inside. The car number on the box was correct; the description was not. The box does not have an ATMA logo, but the cars inside have been both 1946 and 1947 vintages, so I cannot date this box with any certainty.

In 1948, Lionel made a major change in boxes, along with the switch to magnetic couplers. The firm eliminated the corrugated inner liners; this permitted a substantial reduction in the size of the boxes used for the 9-1/4" boxcars. Instead of an inner liner, the box end flaps were cut and folded to create a protective pocket for the coupler which extended past the end of the car body. These intricate end flaps also protected the ends of the cars from damage.

As we will see in the chronology section, there were five major variations of the 6454 boxcar produced in 1948, yet they all came in the same box, number 8 in Table 7. This box contained no hint of the road name or body color of the car packaged inside.

In 1949, the policy of not designating the road name was completely reversed. The non-operating 6454 boxcars came in the same boxes as 1948, except that the end flaps were overstamped in black ink with the road name and a single digit number on each side of the Lionel name. These are Boxes 9, 10 and 11 in Table 7. The 3464 operating boxcars introduced in 1949 had boxes containing the road name as part of the original end flap printing.

Figure 14: Two examples of Box 13 from Table 6. The upper box is an early 1949 box and lists Lionel locations as "NEW YORK ... CHICAGO ... SAN FRANCISCO." The lower box is a late 1949, (still a long box) and lists Lionel locations as "NEW YORK .... CHICAGO". Note that San Francisco is no longer included. R. Swanson Collection.

Road name markings on the boxes meant that the quantity of boxes with a particular name and number had to be coordinated with the quantity of that particular boxcar being manufactured. Since these quantities did not always agree, Lionel was once again forced to re-mark boxes to make them match the products already produced. Boxes 14 and 15 in Table 7 are examples of such reworked boxes.

Box 15 is of particular interest because of the car it contained and the set it was shipped with. As shown in Table 8, frames with footsteps are believed to have been phased out of production in early 1950. I have two Number 15 boxes, and they both contain 6454(K)-2 Pennsylvania boxcars. One of these cars is known to have come from a 1471 WS set headed by a 2035 steam locomotive with Magnetraction catalogued in both 1950 and 1951. The Type 4 frame and the Type 5A trucks together point to early 1950 production. Lionel was probably using up leftover Type 4 frames with footsteps, and evidently the firm had run out of long 6454 boxes of any description. The expedient way to keep the production lines moving was to re-mark leftover long 3464 S.F. boxes, since the trucks of a boxcar with footsteps could not be turned inwards to fit the car into the shorter boxes.

Another change was made in boxes printed after mid-1949. At the suggestion of Tom Rollo, I started looking at the cities printed on the blue band on the box sides. All boxes listed in Table 7 from Nos. 1-11 list the Lionel locations "New York...Chicago...San Francisco". Boxes 14 through 24 list only New York and Chicago, reflecting the termination of the San Francisco showroom agreement. Boxes 12 and 13 come in two variations, some with San Francisco and some without. This indicates two separate production runs, one in early 1949 and the other in late 1949. Boxes printed in late 1949 without the San Francisco entry appear to be the only mid-sized boxcar boxes carried over for early 1950 boxcars.

The elimination of frame footsteps in 1950 brought a second reduction in box size. By rotating the trucks so that the couplers were under the car body, the box could be shortened by about an inch and a half. Considering the quantities Lionel was dealing with, this reduction must have meant a considerable savings to the firm in warehouse space and shipping costs. For the operating boxcars, the change in length was indeed the only change from the earlier boxes. For the non-operating cars, the boxes were shortened and the end flap printing was revised to include the boxcar road name, as shown in Figure 12 (Note the disappearance of the 1, 2 and 3 numbers.) These boxes remained virtually unchanged through the end of the 9-1/4"

Figure 15: Two different 3474 boxes. Lower box has OPS ceiling price of $5.50 while upper box has no OPS price marking. OPS was Office of Price Stability, a Korean War government agency.

boxcar production. Of course, the introduction of the 3474 Western Pacific boxcar in 1952 brought an appropriately marked box at that time.

The only box variation that I am aware of during the 1950-1953 period is the presence of OPS ceiling prices on some 3464 S.F. and 3474 W.P. boxes. The OPS price, when it appears at all, is usually printed directly onto the box. However, occasionally the OPS price was indicated by a white paste-on label. I recently had the opportunity to purchase a complete set of the OPS paste-on labels — 16 pages of them! The labels came in an original Lionel envelope which had a message to dealers printed on its front. It said that the envelope contained OPS labels for all items listed in the 1951 catalogue. This leads me to believe that the OPS price marking was required during 1952. For the first five or six months of 1952, the only items the dealers had in inventory were leftover 1951 production items. These items had to be marked with OPS prices during all of 1952, so the paste-on labels were sent out to dealers. Items produced in 1952 were marked with the OPS price at the factory, usually as part of the original box printing instead of a stick-on label. Still, the curious thing about the OPS marking is that I have observed it only on S.F. and W.P. operating boxcar boxes, not on the NYC or any of the boxes containing non-operating cars. Does this mean that the OPS markings were only required on items meant for separate sale, but not for items included as part of a set, where an OPS marking would have been on the set box? Or, was the OPS marking required on all the individual component boxes within the set? Additional reader information on this subject would be welcomed.

## PART 4: THE CHRONOLOGY
## AN INTRODUCTION TO TABLE 8

Now that we have identified the major variations, component variations and boxes, it is time to fit all the pieces of the 9-1/4" boxcar puzzle together into one integrated picture to explain the development and production of these cars. Table 8 is a graphical attempt to describe and date all the major and minor variations on a single page.

The distinctive component features are listed at the top of Table 8. A time line is then used to indicate the production sequence of the component variations. The identification codes for the doors were defined in Table 4, frames in Table 5 and trucks and couplers in Table 6.

The seventeen major boxcar variations are listed in the lower part of Table 8. A time line to the right of the road name indicates the most likely production dates for that variation. Minor variations are designated by a number indicating the production sequence. Each time there is a change in one or more components, a different minor variation is established. The specific components which comprise a minor variation can be determined by noting which component variations appear directly above the car production time line.

### 1946

Production of the 9-1/4" boxcars began with the 2454(A)-1 orange-door Pennsylvania cars. The orange-door cars are always found with Type 2 trucks and couplers ("Flying Shoe" design with regular wheels and axles). Since the doors were the same as the doors already being produced for the brown 2458 Automobile Car, except for the color, Lionel quickly realized that it could reduce its parts inventory by also using brown doors on these boxcars (2454(A)-2). Next came the abandonment of the "Flying Shoe" coupler design. The introduction of the Type 3A trucks and couplers led to variation 2454(A)-3. At this point, another major change was made. The Pennsylvania road name to the left of the door was replaced by the Baby Ruth logo (2454(B)-1). Curiously, the PRR logo and the printing to the right of the door remained unchanged.

The 4454 Electronic Control boxcar and the 3454 PRR Automatic Merchandise Car were also produced in 1946, with both cars employing Type 3A trucks.

### 1947

Production of the 2454(B) and 4454 cars continued unchanged from the end of 1946, except that the 3B coupler with a stronger coupler head mounting was used instead of the weaker 3A coupler. Several other changes in components were made during the year.

The first mid-year change was the use of Type 2 doors painted brown on 2454 and 4454 cars. The short pin on the back of the right door served no useful purpose on these non-operating cars, but evidently the door mold had been modified in 1946 and Type 1 doors could no longer be made. The fact that this change did not show up until mid-1947 production indicates that a large inventory of doors was produced before the mold was modified.

The next mid-year change was a minor modification in frames (1B). The 3462 Operating Milk Car, introduced in 1947, used a frame which was essentially a boxcar frame with some additional holes and slots. The milk car frame required slight indentations about one inch long in the side flanges. These indentations were required for clearance of the milk car door frames. For some reason, this milk car feature was incorporated into the boxcar frame tooling and not left to the secondary milk car frame tools. This side flange indentation appears on all boxcar frames until 1950, when several other tooling changes occurred.

Production of the 3454 PRR Merchandise Car apparently did not resume until later in 1947, since no early-year variations have been found. All of the 1947 PRR Merchandise Cars I have examined contain all of the typical 1947 features: Type 3B couplers, Type 1B frames, exposed head for the roof hatch pin and the slightly smaller Type 6 box. The current availability of the 1947 cars is substantially less than for the 1946 version and,

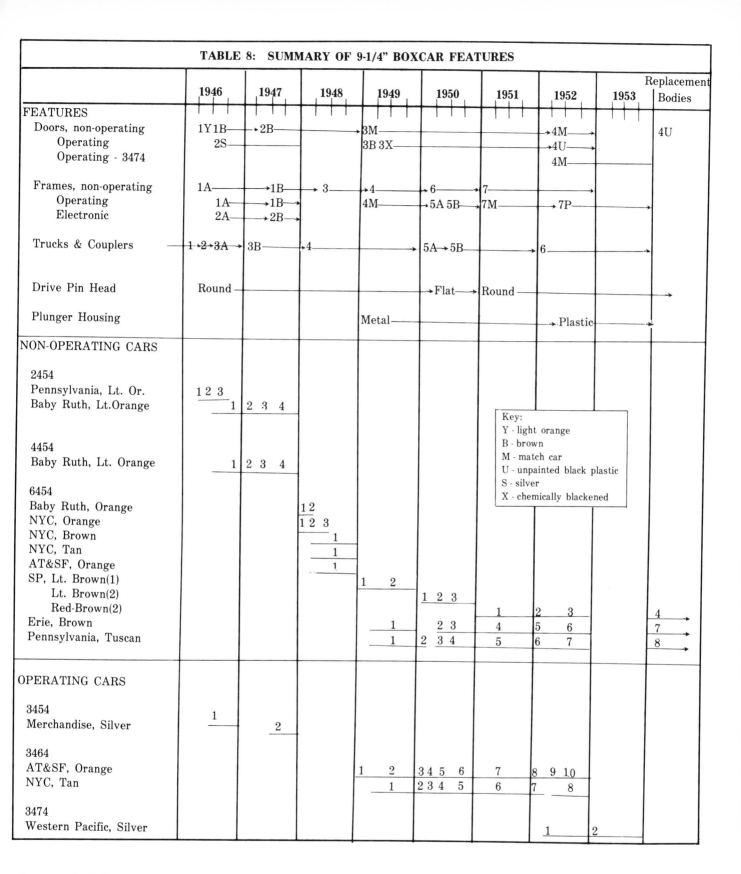

**TABLE 8: SUMMARY OF 9-1/4" BOXCAR FEATURES**

| | 1946 | 1947 | 1948 | 1949 | 1950 | 1951 | 1952 | 1953 | Replacement Bodies |
|---|---|---|---|---|---|---|---|---|---|
| **FEATURES** | | | | | | | | | |
| Doors, non-operating | 1Y 1B | →2B | | →3M | | | →4M→ | | 4U |
| Operating | 2S | | | 3B 3X | | | →4U | | |
| Operating - 3474 | | | | | | | 4M | | |
| Frames, non-operating | 1A | →1B | →3 | →4 | →6 | →7 | | → | |
| Operating | 1A | →1B→ | | 4M | →5A 5B | →7M | →7P | → | |
| Electronic | 2A | →2B→ | | | | | | | |
| Trucks & Couplers | 1→2→3A | →3B | →4 | | →5A→5B | | →6 | → | |
| Drive Pin Head | Round | | | | →Flat→ | Round | | → | |
| Plunger Housing | | | | Metal | | | →Plastic | → | |
| **NON-OPERATING CARS** | | | | | | | | | |
| 2454 Pennsylvania, Lt. Or. | 1 2 3 | | | | | | | | |
| Baby Ruth, Lt.Orange | 1 | 2 3 4 | | | | | | | |
| 4454 Baby Ruth, Lt. Orange | | 1 2 3 4 | | | | | | | |
| 6454 Baby Ruth, Orange | | | 1 2 | | | | | | |
| NYC, Orange | | | 1 2 3 | | | | | | |
| NYC, Brown | | | 1 | | | | | | |
| NYC, Tan | | | 1 | | | | | | |
| AT&SF, Orange | | | 1 | | | | | | |
| SP, Lt. Brown(1) | | | | 1 2 | | | | | |
| Lt. Brown(2) | | | | | 1 2 3 | | | | |
| Red-Brown(2) | | | | | | 1 | 2 3 | | 4 |
| Erie, Brown | | | | 1 | 2 3 | 4 | 5 6 | | 7 |
| Pennsylvania, Tuscan | | | | 1 | 2 3 4 | 5 | 6 7 | | 8 |
| **OPERATING CARS** | | | | | | | | | |
| 3454 Merchandise, Silver | 1 | 2 | | | | | | | |
| 3464 AT&SF, Orange | | | | 1 2 | 3 4 5 6 | 7 | 8 9 10 | | |
| NYC, Tan | | | | 1 | 2 3 4 5 | 6 | 7 8 | | |
| 3474 Western Pacific, Silver | | | | | | | 1 | 2 | |

Key:
Y - light orange
B - brown
M - match car
U - unpainted black plastic
S - silver
X - chemically blackened

of course, the 3454 was completely phased out at the end of 1947.

It is fun to speculate on the decline and fall of the 3454 PRR Merchandise Car, which had been so popular in 1946. I suspect that the major factor in its demise was the introduction of the immensely popular 3462 Automatic Refrigerated Milk Car. The buying public seemed to like the milk car better, perhaps because they perceived it as more realistic. It did have a man to toss out the milk cans and a special platform to receive them. With the merchandise car, there was no all-important human figure, and the little packing boxes came flying out the door at random, seldom falling into the unrealistic dump tray included with the car. Lionel probably liked the milk car better because of its higher profit margin. At $8.95 and ultimately $11.50, the milk car must have been considerably more profitable than the $5.50 Merchandise Car.

## 1948

The year 1948 brought many changes, both major and minor. As mentioned, the merchandise car was dropped from production. As I will explain later, I also believe that production of the 4454 Electronic Control boxcar ended in 1947. This left only plain, non-operating boxcars. Did this mean a dull inventory for Lionel's train sets? Not by a long shot! Almost everything but the size was new with the non-operating boxcars! There was a new number, 6454. The couplers were changed to the new Type 4 magnetic couplers. There was a new frame, the Type 3. There were new colors: orange instead of light orange, brown and tan. Best of all, there were new road names, New York Central and Santa Fe. Even the boxes were new. Most of these changes were introduced at the beginning of the year, but a few were phased in after the inventory of older components was depleted.

Production began with 6454(A) Baby Ruth and 6454(B) New York Central cars, both painted the new shade of orange. The first cars produced in 1948 had Type 3B coil couplers, even though they were marked with 6454 numbers. Even more of the 1948 production had leftover Type 1B frames. By the time production of the Type 3 frames began, production of the Baby Ruth cars had already been phased out. Shortly thereafter, the orange NYC car's color was shifted to brown and tan versions. I must admit that I have no way of telling which color came first, brown or tan, although the presence of the tan color on the later operating NYC cars would suggest that tan was the later color. The orange Santa Fe boxcar was also produced during this period.

The new 1948 box was substantially smaller than the previous boxcar boxes because the cardboard inner liner was no longer used. All of the 1948 boxcars came in exactly the same box. It was only marked "6454 BOX CAR", with no mention of road name or color. Information to date has not shown any correlation between catalogued sets and the boxcars they contained. I have three 1427 WS sets in boxes which contain the following boxcars: Brown NYC, Tan NYC and Orange ATSF. Lionel apparently used whatever boxcar was available when the sets were assembled and packaged.

I mentioned earlier that I felt the production of the 4454 Electronic Boxcar ended in 1947. I will point out two bits of evidence and let the reader draw his own conclusion. First, the use of light orange paint was discontinued on regular boxcars at the end of 1947 and a darker orange was introduced in 1948. It is doubtful that a darker orange 4454 boxcar exists; no one has ever confirmed one. Second, the box size changed in 1948, but I have never seen a smaller 4454 box. Assembly of 4454 boxcars could have continued in 1948 using leftover parts and boxes, but these cars would have been impossible to distinguish from 1947 production (4454-4). (We would like to hear from any reader who has evidence of 4454 component production from 1948 or later.)

There is another possible 1948 car which I have never seen, but have speculated might exist. Has anyone ever seen a 2454 NYC boxcar? If you examine the X6454 number on the NYC cars, you will notice that the "6" seems to be a little larger and lower than the other digits. Was the NYC heat-stamping die originally made with a 2454 number and then modified to 6454

to reflect the new coupler design? If so, were any cars stamped before the "2" was changed to a "6"? It is curious that the 2454 boxcar listed for separate sale on page 28 of the 1948 consumer catalogue has NYC markings! Verrrry interesting...!

## 1949

With all the changes made in 1948, one might expect that some or at least one of that year's cars would have carried over to 1949 production. Wrong! Lionel must have felt that the boxcar line was too bland in 1948 without some kind of an action car, so the major push for 1949 was to overcome this deficiency. The introduction of the magnet in the 6019 and UCS operating tracks opened the possibility for a new series of low-cost operating cars. The 3464 Operating Boxcar was the first of this new series. Using a few stamped parts, wire springs and a molded human figure, Lionel created a low-cost operating car which did not require a solenoid, special trucks or die-cast parts.

Lionel must have been confident that its new operating boxcar would be eagerly accepted by the train-buying public, because the firm not only used the car to spruce up the O-27 sets, but also as a replacement for the "scale-detailed" 2458 Automobile Car in O Gauge sets. Most people consider the 9-1/4" boxcar to be an O-27 product, but between 1949 and 1952 it was the only boxcar made by Lionel, and it was included in no fewer than 11 catalogued O Gauge sets (see Table 12).

Production of the 3464 Operating Boxcar began in 1949 with an orange ATSF car, although it was soon joined by a tan NYC car. Both of these cars must have been planned from the beginning because, for the first time, Lionel put the initials of the road name on the boxcar boxes as part of the end flap printing. Since both cars carried the same Lionel number 3464, how do we know which car came first? The main evidence is the existence of the 1949 brown-door version of the ATSF car, while no legitimate examples of brown-door NYC operating cars from this time have ever been found.

The brown-door ATSF 3464 represented a natural extension of Lionel's earlier policy: Paint all doors brown regardless of body color. The single door color certainly simplified production and parts inventory. However, there was a problem on the operating cars with brown-painted doors. The painted door did not slide very well against the painted plastic body, causing sluggish operation. The chemically blackened metal door was thus introduced as an engineering solution to reduce friction and improve the performance of the operating mechanism. The black door was introduced before the production of the NYC car began, so all of the operating 3464 NYC cars have black doors.

Though the non-operating 6454 boxcar was retained in 1949, it certainly didn't get much promotion. It was not included in any sets shown in the 1949 consumer catalogue. The NYC and ATSF road names used in 1948 were moved to the prolific 3464 Series, and three new road names were introduced on the non-operating 6454 cars: Southern Pacific, Erie and Pennsylvania. (The Pennsylvania name was actually a re-introduction, since it had been used on the 2454 in early 1946.)

Even though the three new 6454 cars are not shown in the 1949 catalogue (only a 1948 NYC is shown), their introduction date can be well established by thorough, detailed examination of specific components. First, these cars always have Type 3 doors, which are distinguished by the long solid pin on the back side. (The 1952 cars have plastic doors, but that will be discussed later.) The Type 3 doors were developed for the 3464 operating cars which were not available before 1949. On the other hand, the earliest versions of the SP, Erie and Pennsylvania 6454 boxcars are all equipped with Type 4 couplers, the earliest magnetic couplers without an extra hole in the activation plate. Type 4 couplers were discontinued at the end of 1949 production.

There are two more pieces of evidence which tie the introduction of the three 6454 cars to 1949: frames and boxes. The Type 4 frame has been identified as 1949 production, since it was specifically designed to accommodate the new 3464 operating boxcars. In 1950, Lionel introduced the Type 5 frame, which lacked the steps of the Type 4. The hypothesis that the three new road names in the 6454 line were in fact introduced in 1949 is strongly supported by the fact that the earliest frame used with these cars is the Type 4. It should be noted, however, that the first 1949 SP 6454 cars were assembled with leftover 1948 Type 3 frames, but these cars still have other characteristics which strongly date them as 1949 products.

In my own mind, the boxes provide the clinching argument for the 1949 introduction of the three 6454 boxcars. The boxes used for the 6454 cars in 1949 were unique to that year. These were actually the same as the 1948 boxes, but the end flaps were overstamped in black ink with a road name and a number: 1-SP; 2-ERIE; 3-PENN. This is the closest Lionel ever came to assigning dash numbers to the 6454 cars, and this practice lasted for only one year. In 1950, the new shorter boxes contained the road name as an integral part of the blue lettering of the box end, and the 1, 2 and 3 numbers were never seen again.

There is one other detail peculiar to 1949 which must be mentioned at this point. There were two clearly different circular heralds used on the 6454 SP boxcars. (See Figures 2 and 3 earlier in the article.) The outer diameter of both heralds is about the same, but the letters are much larger in the 1949 herald, requiring a smaller inner circle. Another distinguishing feature of the 1949 heralds is a break in the outer circle between the letters R and N in the two o'clock position of the circle. This break was undoubtedly caused by a defect in the heat-stamping die, since it appears throughout the entire 1949 production run. The only herald known to be from 1949 which does not have this break appears on the black 6454 SP boxcar which was part of the collection of the late Hank Degano. The defect in the stamping die was most likely the reason for the development of new tooling for the herald in 1950. That herald has smaller letters, no breaks in the circle.

### 1950

The year 1950 can be called a year of many minor variations. Besides the change in the SP heralds discussed above, there were changes in frames (3), trucks (2), boxes and the drive pins used to attach the door guides and brakewheels. These varied component changes were phased in at different times during 1950, creating as many as four different minor variations to a single car in one year!

The truck and coupler changes are probably the easiest to explain. The 1950 production began with conversion to the Type 5A coupler, which included a second small hole in the magnetic activator plate. This second hole permitted an easier, less expensive assembly and repair of the roller pickup version of the magnetic coupler and truck. Around mid-year, production switched to the 5B coupler, which is distinguished by the roundhead of the activator plate attachment pin showing instead of the flared end. This change was probably made to reduce assembly costs, but the specific reason is not known without exact knowledge of the assembly procedure and tooling.

Early in 1950 (but not right at the beginning of production), Lionel made another curious change in a very minor component — the drive pin used to attach the door guides and brakewheel to the plastic body. Instead of the usual roundhead pin used since 1946, a flat-headed pin which looks like a small carpet tack was used for the bulk of production in both operating and non-operating cars. This same drive pin found its way onto other cars in 1950, including stock and milk cars. As discussed previously, the use of these drive pins could have been a result of material shortages due to the Korean War, but the most likely explanation is a purchasing error. Whatever the case, Lionel did not like these pins because the firm returned to the round-headed design in 1951. The Lionel Service Manual, unfortunately, does not help solve the mystery. The 9-1/4" boxcars made from 1946 through 1948 used a door pin carrying the part number 45-70, indicating that this part was first used on the old 45 Gateman made as early as 1935. There is no mention of a flat-headed pin anywhere in the Service Manual.

Let us proceed to a mystery we **can** solve! The most significant change Lionel made to these boxcars in 1950 was the elimination of the steps from the frame. If we can assume that Lionel began its 1950 production with the Type 5A trucks and couplers, then we can find that a few cars were assembled which used leftover 1949 frames with steps (PRR 6454(K)-2, ATSF 3464(A)-3 and NYC 3464(B)-2). Once the leftover 1949 frames were used, the bulk of the 1950 boxcar production used frames without steps.

There is a necessary digression from our chronological narrative at this point. Our analysis of trucks, frames and boxes can be used to solve other dating mysteries. We have observed that some 6454 Pennsylvania cars came with Type 4 frames with steps. We know that these Type 4 frames were superseded in 1950 by Type 5 and Type 6 frames without steps. The 6454 Pennsylvania car in question came in a Type 15 box (see box table), which is a 3464 ATSF medium-sized box overstamped "6454". The box was first made in late 1949 because 1949 was the first year of the 3464 ATSF car and because the box does not have San Francisco listed as a Lionel showroom. The San Francisco entry was dropped from Lionel's boxes in late 1949. The car has Type 5A trucks which were introduced in 1950 and replaced later in 1950 by Type 5B. From these characteristics, we can date this particular car as early 1950 production; no other dating fits all these characteristics. In this case, one might question the unusual combination of features. Our hypothesis is that Lionel had unfilled orders requiring boxcars and had available for assembly most of the components: bodies, trucks and leftover frames. However, these components would not fit the new, shorter Lionel boxes. It is likely that there were unused long 3464 boxes in the warehouse, and Lionel was consequently able to make up a batch of cars using the old frames and box them to fill pressing orders. One Pennsylvania 6454(K)-2 came in one of these overmarked boxes with set 1471 WS shown on Page 15 of the 1950 consumer catalogue.

Lionel had two strong motives for eliminating the steps. The first was the material savings for the frame itself. If the car frames were stamped from coiled sheet metal stock, the width of the coil could have been reduced from 2-7/8" to 2-1/8", a material savings of 25 percent. With the old style frame, the material between the steps was cut out and discarded. The second source of savings came about because Lionel now had the ability to rotate the couplers inward when packaging the cars; this meant that the firm could use smaller car and set boxes and reduce its packaging, warehousing and shipping costs.

Two completely different "step-less" frames with totally different hole patterns were used in 1950. The operating cars used the Type 5A and Type 5B frames, which were essentially 1949 frames with the steps cut off. In fact, close examination of these frames suggests that this is exactly how they were made because the side flanges near the end have some distortion lines caused by the punching of the steps. The A and B versions of this frame relate to the side flange detail associated with the operating milk car doors. The A version has indentations to accommodate the metal doors and their frames used from 1947 to 1949. The B version has cutouts to accept the plastic door frame used on milk cars made after 1949.

The non-operating 6454 cars used an entirely different frame in 1950, Type 6. These frames showed no traces of the steps. The Type 6 frames also contained none of the holes, slots, indentations or cutouts required for operating boxcars or milk cars. Instead, they had four holes which had been required for the 3454 Operating Merchandise Car made in 1946-47! How — or why — did these holes reappear in 1950?

One possibility is that Lionel had two completely separate sets of tooling for stamping these frames. The first set of tooling was used for Type 1 and Type 2 frames made from 1946 to early 1948. These frames, with some off-line modification, were used in 1947 for the 3462 Milk Cars. As milk car production increased dramatically in 1948 (Lionel was to sell two and a half **million** of these cars between 1947 and 1955!), a second, more efficient set of tools could have been developed which was subsequently used to produce the Types 3, 4 and 5 frames. When the step elimination program came along for 1950, the production department may not have been in the position to release the efficient tool set so it could be modified, in view of the tremendous demand for the milk cars. This could have required the tool or engineering department to retrieve the older Type 1 tooling, which was then no longer in service. This tooling could have been modified some time in 1949 to be ready for 1950 production of Type 6 frames without disrupting any production schedules. The 3464 operating car frames could not be produced on the older tooling because there was no provision for the four holes required for the operating mechanism, particularly the large center hole. The experience and benefits gained from the modified tooling in 1950 probably justified the expense in developing a third set of tooling which was optimized for stamping the Type 7 frames which appeared in 1951.

The elimination of the steps in 1950 led to a whole new series of boxes. Since the trucks could be turned with the couplers facing inward, the box length was reduced from 10-1/8 inches to 8-11/16 inches, a saving of almost 1-1/2 inches in space. The boxcar road name always appeared on the end flaps of these shorter boxes as part of the standard printing.

### 1951

Production of the 9-1/4" boxcars settled down considerably in 1951. The five basic cars introduced in 1949, two 3464s and three 6454s, all continued in production for a third year, with the only major variation occurring in the 6454 Southern Pacific. The light brown color used on the SP cars in 1949 and 1950 was dropped in favor of a red-brown color. The new Type 7 and Type 7M frames were strictly boxcar frames. For the first time in almost four years, they contained no milk car features. (However, with the additional punching of four square and two round holes, boxcar frames were still converted into tank car frames.) Doors, trucks and boxes continued unchanged from late 1950 production. The roundhead drive pins for attaching door guides and brake wheels returned in 1951. All in all, it was a rather dull year for boxcar production. The year 1951 turned out to be the eye of a hurricane of change.

### 1952

Four component changes and the introduction of the first new road name and car number in three years made 1952 another year of many variations. The first change was in the trucks, with the bar-end metal truck replacing the staple-end variety. The next change was the replacement of metal doors with plastic ones.

The final component changes only involved the operating boxcars. The housing that supports the activator plunger and its return spring was changed from metal to plastic. Changes were also made in the frame so that the new plastic housing could be snapped into place. These changes obviously saved assembly time and production costs.

From the consumer's perspective, the most notable change for 1952 was the introduction of the colorful 3474 Western Pacific operating boxcar. This silver-painted car with its large yellow feather is quite a contrast to all the other rather drab orange and brown boxcars of the 9-1/4" series. All of the Western Pacific boxcars have plastic doors, though some of the early ones have metal plunger housings. Unfortunately for collectors, the Western Pacific has not held up too well to wear and tear; its silver paint lost its brilliance rapidly and the water-release decals used for decoration often chipped and discolored.

| TABLE 9: CONFIRMED MIXED VINTAGE VARIATIONS | | | | |
|---|---|---|---|---|
| NUMBER | ROAD NAME | CLOSEST CAR IN TABLE 8 | DIFFERENCE FROM CLOSEST CAR | REMARKS |
| 3464(A)-11 | ATSF | 3464(A)-10 | Type 3X doors Flat head drive pins | 1950 body on 1952 chassis |
| 3464(A)-12 | ATSF | 3464(A)-9 | Type 5B frame | Type 5B (1950) frames with Type 6 trucks; also reported by Schilling in tank car article (see previous edition). |
| 3464(B)-9 | NYC | 3464(B)-8 | Type 5B frame and metal plunger housing | Same as 3464(A)-12 |
| 3474 - 3 | WP | 3474 - 1 | Type 5B frame | Same as 3464(A)-12 |

My best estimate of the introduction for the 1952 component changes is shown in Table 8. However, there have been a number of sightings of 1952 operating cars which do not fit the chart. Most of these "misfits" have a majority of components from 1952, but they also have one or two components from 1950. When I saw the first couple of cars with this mixture of components, I assumed that the cars had been repaired or upgraded by mixing parts from two cars. With time, however, I saw more and more cars with exactly the same mix of components, and these cars have been reported by other collectors as well. It could be that these cars were assembled after the decision was made to discontinue the 9-1/4" series. As components ran out in the production area, substitute parts from an earlier year could have been brought in from the service department. The mixed vintage cars which have had several confirmed sightings are listed in Table 9.

### 1953

According to the catalogues, the 3474 Western Pacific was the only 9-1/4" boxcar available in 1953. The availability of even this car was not widespread; the car was included in one inexpensive O-27 set. Perhaps all production of 9-1/4" boxcars stopped in 1952, and the limited 1953 offering was to use up cars and parts already manufactured. It is important to remember that 1953 was the year of introduction for the larger 6464 Series. If any cars were in fact manufactured during 1953, they are indistinguishable from 1952 production. After 1953, no 9-1/4" boxcar appeared in a Lionel catalogue of any kind for 31 years.

### REPLACEMENT BODIES

Some confusion about minor variations has arisen because of the availability of replacement bodies through the service department. Replacement bodies were available as early as

1947 and were still available well into the 1960s. The replacement bodies were painted, marked and had doors and brakewheels installed. In most cases, the replacement bodies were exactly like the regular production. In all probability, they were leftovers or seconds from a regular production run.

However, some 6454 Southern Pacific, Erie and Pennsylvania bodies were assembled, probably in the late 1950s, using black, unpainted plastic doors. I do not believe that black plastic doors were ever used on 6454 cars completely assembled at the factory. I have bodies with all three road names and black plastic doors which have never been mounted to frames. The complete cars with black plastic doors which I have seen always have components of several different years. In fact, several have been mounted on tank car or milk car frames. These cars usually show clear signs of post-factory assembly or repair.

Table 10 shows the part number and description contained in several Lionel replacement parts lists. The page numbers refer to the original pages of the Lionel Service Manual; some equivalent lists can be found in the Greenberg printing of the four-volume Lionel Service Manual pages.

### PROTOTYPES, COLOR SAMPLES, FACTORY ERRORS PART 5: ALTERED CARS AND THE FUTURE

Several references have been made throughout this article to some rare one-of-a-kind cars (or those few in number). These cars were not part of the regular production runs and do not yield significant information concerning the chronological development of the 9-1/4" boxcars. However, I think it is important to identify as many of these cars as possible and point out the possible pitfalls and blind alleys into which collectors may be led by them. These cars will be divided into four categories: prototypes, paint and color samples, factory errors and post-factory altered cars. The article will conclude with a short discussion of the new 9-1/4" boxcar series first produced by Fundimensions in late 1983. For definitions of Prototypes, Paint/Color Samples and Factory Errors, refer to James M. Sattler's definitions in the Factory Errors and Prototypes chapter of this edition.

### PROTOTYPES

Known and verified prototypes, color samples and factory errors of the 9-1/4" boxcars are extremely rare. There are no known large groups or collections of these cars, as is the case with the 6464 boxcars. The prototypes I am aware of are listed in Part I of Table 11. Photographs in the 1946 consumer catalogue and some other Lionel photographs of the same period show some 2454 and 3454 cars painted brown or tuscan with white Pennsylvania lettering. The photos appear to be taken on the Prewar Lionel showroom layout, since the T-rail 072 track is clearly visible. Another car which appears in at least one of these photographs is a silver 2454 with Alcoa markings. I have no information at all concerning the current existence of any of these prototype cars shown in the Lionel catalogue or photographs.

Several years ago, I had the opportunity to examine a boxcar which supposedly came directly from the Lionel factory in Hillside, New Jersey. This was a 2454-type car painted dull gray primer not only on the body, but also on the doors, door guides and frame. The first impression of this car was that it was a sloppy private repaint. However, after close inspection, it was apparent that the gray primer was a rather thin coat over a clear molded plastic body. One could look into the car

| Table 10: 9-1/4" Replacement Bodies | | | |
|---|---|---|---|
| PAGE NUMBER | PART NUMBER | DESCRIPTION | COMMENTS |
| 9/15/47 Parts List: | | | |
| 19 | 2454-9 | Boxcar body, stamped | PRR? |
| 21 | 3454-3 | Body Assembly | |
| 1949 Parts List: | | | |
| 31 | 2454-13 | Boxcar Body, stamped | Baby Ruth? |
| 34 | 3454-3 | Body Assembly | |
| 37A | 3464-18 | Boxcar Body, complete | Metal doors? |
| 4/56 Substitute Parts List: | | | |
| 5 | 2454-13 | Obsolete, use 4454-6 | Electronic |
| 5 | 3464-18 | Obsolete, use 3464-31 | Plastic doors |
| 8/59 Parts List: | | | |
| 52 | 2454-13 | Body ptd., sub. 4454-6 | |
| 57 | 3454-3 | Body assembly | |
| 58 | 3474-2 | Boxcar Body | WP |
| 63 | 6454-6 | Boxcar Body (Brown NYC) | Tan? |
| 63 | 6454-11 | Boxcar Body (Brown PRR) | Tuscan |
| 63 | 6454-26 | Boxcar Body (Brown Erie) | Brown |
| 63 | 6454-51 | Boxcar Body (Brown SP) | Red-brown |

through the open doors and see light in the corners where the paint did not completely cover the body. There was no trace of any other paint under the gray. Detailed examination also revealed no trace of heat-stamped markings which had been overpainted. The very poor condition of the car, along with the poor quality paint job, still left me with serious doubts about the validity of this car. Then, several months after seeing this unmarked gray car, I noticed a striking similarity between this car and a photo of the 2454 Alcoa car. The door guides and the door guide drive pins on both cars had been completely painted. Perhaps this gray car was a legitimate Lionel prototype which for some reason had been discarded before being completely painted and lettered. The 2454 Alcoa car is shown on Page 138 of McComas and Tuohy's **Lionel: A Collector's Guide, Vol. VI.** It is evident from the photo that the name "Alcoa" and the other letters and numbers were placed on the car with decals — a clear indication of a prototype.

Previous editions of the Greenberg Postwar Guides contain a photograph of an unpainted and unmarked clear plastic-bodied 2454 boxcar. I have never seen one of these cars directly, but several reportedly exist. Clear bodies which have not been painted for almost 40 years will surely show signs of yellowing. (That, in fact, has happened with clear-bodied examples of the 2333 Santa Fe F-3 locomotives; these pieces are known to be genuine salesmen's samples.) On the other hand, painted cars which have been recently stripped should appear completely clear; they may also show faint signs of heat-stamped lettering and traces of paint in the corners and crevices.

## PAINT AND COLOR SAMPLES; SALESMEN'S SAMPLES

Cars falling into this category include those cars that were made to allow decisions concerning the proper colors for mass production; they are identical to their mass-produced equivalent except for their color schemes. These cars are extremely rare because they represent color schemes which were ultimately rejected for mass production. Sometimes these cars were used by salesmen as demonstration samples.

Several color samples are shown in the 1946 consumer catalogue. The first is a Pennsylvania boxcar in brown instead of light orange. This may actually be a 3454 operating car since a roof latch seem faintly visible, but Pennsylvania lettering is identical to what was stamped on the early 2454 non-operating boxcars. This car also appears in the same picture as the Alcoa prototype in the McComas and Tuohy Lionel book.

Also, in the 1946 catalogue, a silver Pennsylvania boxcar with black lettering is shown in front of the coal elevator on page 1. The "Pennsylvania" lettering to the left of the door distinguishes this car from the usual silver 3454 cars which are lettered "Automatic Merchandise Car". The current where-abouts of these different colored Pennsylvania cars is unknown.

There are two color variations of the 3454 "Automatic Merchandise Car" which have turned up recently. The first is painted the normal silver color, but all lettering and logos are stamped in red rather than dark blue. Several of these cars have been reported in various parts of the country, providing some evidence that possibly there was a limited production run of the red-lettered cars. Another 3454, which seems to be "one-of-a-kind", is painted brown with white lettering. The "Automatic Merchandise Car" lettering is definitely heat-stamped, but the line width appears somewhat thicker than the normal blue or silver lettering. Both the red-lettered silver and white-lettered brown cars which I have examined exhibited all the attributes of 1946 production (including blue wiring), making them closest to 3454-1 variations in Table 8.

I was also fortunate in being able to examine first-hand a black 6454 Southern Pacific boxcar owned by the late Hank Degano. This car is unique not only because of its black color, but also because it is the only SP car with the early herald that I have ever seen that did not have the break in the outer circle at the 2 o'clock position. The markings on the car were definitely heat-stamped, but evidently this car was stamped before the stamping die was damaged on the outer circle of the herald. Other features of this car included Type 4 trucks and couplers, Type 3M doors (the only **painted** black doors I have ever seen) and, surprisingly, a Type 1 frame. This car is clearly a color sample, not a prototype.

Another car I place into the Color Sample category is a silver Operating Merchandise Car in the C. Adair Roberts Collection which is numbered x2454 and marked "Baby Ruth". This silver Baby Ruth is truly unique, but the most startling feature of this

| **TABLE 11: ONE-OF-A-KIND OR RARE CARS** | |
|---|---|
| **DESCRIPTION** | **SOURCE** |
| **I.  Prototypes** | |
| 1. 2454 Baby Ruth, Orange Door | 1946 Catalogue, p. 1 |
| 2. 2454 Alcoa, Silver | McComas & Tuohy: Lionel: A Collector's Guide, Vol. VI, page 138 |
| 3. 2454 Gray Primer, No Markings | Sold in 1982 by Don Shaw |
| 4. 2454 Clear, No Markings | Formerly in collection of the late Bill Eddins |
| **II.  Paint and Color Samples; Salesmen's Samples** | |
| 1. 3454 PRR Merchandise Car, tuscan with white "Pennsylvania lettering" | 1946 catalogue, inside front cover |
| 2. 3454 PRR Merchandise Car, brown with white "Automatic Merchandise Car" lettering | Sold in 1985 by Ed Prendeville |
| 3. 3454 PRR Merchandise Car, silver with red lettering | J. Sattler Collection |
| 4. 6454 SP, black | H. Degano Collection |
| 5. 2454 PRR, silver with black lettering | 1946 Catalogue, Page 1 |
| 6. Silver Merchandise Car marked 2454 Baby Ruth | C. Adair Roberts Collection |
| 7. 6454 Pennsylvania, orange: black lettering | Unconfirmed to date |
| **III.  Factory Errors** | |
| 1. 3454 Merchandise Car, Silver: markings only on one side | J. Sattler Collection |
| 2. 3464 ATSF, Orange: markings only on one side | R. Swanson Collection |
| 3. Orange body, no markings | Stewart Collection |
| 4. Tan, no markings | R. Swanson Collection |
| 5. 3464 ATSF: Tan body, white lettering | R. Niedhammer, J. Sattler, Stewart, Margulies and Smith Collections |

Figure 16: Top shelf left: 3464(A) Santa Fe Operating Car without printing on one side. Top shelf right: unnumbered, tan 9-1/4" car without printing on either side. See Table 11 Factory Errors 2 and 4. Middle shelf left: 2454 PRR Baby Ruth with orange doors instead of brown doors but not confirmed as factory production. Middle shelf right: 6454J Erie with post factory installed orange painted doors. Bottom shelf left: snow white 2454 Baby Ruth Boxcar which was produced by post factory chemical alteration. Bottom right: post factory custom painted Lancaster and Chester Boxcar.

car is its Baby Ruth lettering. The letters are not solid, as they are on all the other 2454 cars. Instead, the letters are only outlined the way they are on the later 6024 Baby Ruth cars. This car has a Type 1A frame without side indentations, two blue wires and no visible roof hatch pin — all features indicating 1946 production. On the other hand, the car has 3B couplers which are indicative of 1947 production. This car, which must have an awfully interesting history if it could only speak, was obtained as part of a set of trains from its original owner.

I would like to mention one final car in this section. There have been reports of an orange 6454 Pennsylvania car with black lettering. I have heard several unconfirmed reports that such a car exists, but I have never seen one or talked directly with an owner of such a car. One report indicated that this road name and color combination might have been a replacement body which was not shipped as a complete car. I would appreciate hearing from any collector with first-hand information about his car.

## FACTORY ERRORS

Lionel's quality control department must have been very good during the late 1940s and early 1950s because very few production mistakes slipped through the inspectors and ended up with customers. I am aware of only two boxcars in this series where the heat-stamping was left off one side of the car.

One is a 1947 silver 3454 Merchandise Car from the collection of Jim Sattler and the other is a 3464(A)-4 operating ATSF car in my own collection. There may well be others, of course.

Several other odd cars have turned up which have no lettering at all. I classify these as factory errors because they have bodies with very poor paint jobs which should never have left the factory. One tan car and one orange car in the Stewart Collection are known; both have identical features — a very unusual combination of component features, at that. First, they are mounted on Type 1 tank car frames (!) and are equipped with very rare double sliding-shoe trucks used only on the O Gauge 3854 Operating Merchandise Car! Also, the door guides are attached with small, bright-head drive pins which look like the type used on American Flyer boxcars made around 1950. It is quite possible that these rejected bodies somehow got out of the Lionel factory and were assembled into complete cars by another party, using repair parts. These cars do have an unusual combination of features, to say the least!

The tan 3464 ATSF cars with white lettering could be errors or they could be color samples. There are a number of these cars in collections, and there seems to be little doubt that some were included in sets shipped from the Lionel factory. I am aware of at least six of these cars and have unconfirmed reports of several more. The only one I have inspected was clearly manufactured in 1949. It was identical to a 3464(A)-2 ATSF car in every detail, except that the car body was painted the tan color usually reserved for the New York Central cars. The best guess is that someone at the factory, perhaps new to the production line, put some tan bodies through the ATSF heat-stamping patterns before the error was discovered by a supervisor.

## ALTERED CARS

One of the primary objectives of this article, as stated in the introduction, was to help collectors judge whether variations in boxcars which they observed at meets and shows were legitimate or not. I certainly do not claim to be the final authority on this subject, but nevertheless I would like to pass along some examples and suggestions which may be helpful to other collectors as they are forced to wrestle with this question from time to time. Of couse, be warned that the whole area of prototypes and factory errors is very risky, even for the most experienced collectors.

The most common alteration is probably the substitution of one or two components such as trucks and couplers in order to repair a damaged car. If identical original replacement components and the proper tools and procedures are used, the repair should not affect the authenticity of the car. On the other hand, lack of attention to details or the unavailability of exact repair parts may result in a repair job producing a purportedly minor variation. Each collector will have to decide for himself whether these home-made variations affect the collectibility of the repaired car or not.

Some cars have been intentionally altered by operators in order to "improve" their appearance or performance. The 6454 Erie with orange doors and the blue and white Lancaster and Chester (shown in Figure 16) are two examples of cars in this category. The orange doors on the Erie car are repainted Type 3M doors with long pins on their inner sides. The L & C car is an obvious repaint of a tan 3464(B) NYC car. There was no attempt on the part of the seller to suggest that either car was a rare original Lionel variation.

Two other cars in this category are a different matter. An orange-door 2454 PRR Baby Ruth could be an altered car made by taking the orange doors off a 2454(A)-1 made in early 1946 and installing them on a 2454(B)-1 car. If this is the case, whoever made this particular car also changed the trucks to the open-shoe Type 2. On the other hand, since the trucks, doors and all other component features are consistent with early 1946 production, this may be a very rare legitimate variation. It could possibly be the orange-door Baby Ruth car shown in page 1 of the 1946 consumer catalogue, except that in this case the Pennsylvania logo to the right of the door does not seem to match the catalogue illustration exactly.

There is also a white 2454 PRR Baby Ruth car which has raised all kinds of questions — and controversy! Except for the body color, this car has all the component features of a 2454(B)-4 car, which would indicate mid to late 1947 production. The car surface has several small gray dots. When the gray dots were scraped, small amounts of orange paint became visible underneath with a ten-power lens. The gray dots had likely protected the orange paint underneath from chemical alteration. Since the car was purchased from a source known to have sold other chemically altered white cars, it is highly likely that this car was also chemically altered. Moreover, several collectors familiar with chemical and dye processing have shown me 2454 cars they have made in colors such as red, blue, green and (almost) white. (Editor's Note: The Train Collectors' Association has issued a warning about

Figure 17: A comparison of the Lionel 1946 - 1952 boxcar body on top with the 7910 Chessie Boxcar (1985). The Lionel has a large body sprue in the middle of the roof underside for injecting plastic and also has four corner columns for the frame mounting screws. These features were eliminated in the Fundimensions design which has a very small sprue at the brakewheel end (right) and one hole in each end for attaching the screws through the frame. The car has internal stiffening ribs which also serve as stops so that the frame does not go too far into the body.

fraudulent pieces produced by just such a process, including white 3656 stock cars and white 3562-50 barrel cars. Collectors should exercise extreme caution in these matters.) Needless to say, if a collector has the opportunity to buy an odd-color car, he should consider carefully the possibility that this car has been altered from its original factory color.

## THE PRESENT AND THE FUTURE:
### FUNDIMENSIONS

When I first conceived this article in 1983, Lionel had not produced 9-1/4" boxcars for 30 years. Clearly, this was a "closed" series which could be discussed and analyzed without fear that Lionel would ever re-run any of these cars. However, the 1984 Traditional catalogue showed the folly of trying to outguess the makers of Lionel Trains! There, on page 12 of the catalogue, was a 7910 Chessie System boxcar which appears to be a direct descendant of the 9-1/4" boxcars!

When the 7910 Chessie boxcars were finally shipped by Fundimensions in August 1985, I immediately compared the new car with the old. The Chessie car is exactly the same size as the old ones, and the car even uses two metal door guides to hold the doors. However, the similarities end right there. The 7910 is obviously made from a completely new mold which differs from the old one both inside and out. The corner posts molded inside the old bodies which provided the attachment points for four self-tapping screws (and which were so fragile) are gone. The new body is attached to the frame by two sheet metal screws at the car ends. The mounting method and frame appear similar to those first used on the 6656 stock car in 1950.

The side ribs and rivets on the 7910 also have slightly different spacing than those on the original 2454-4 mold. The two rows of rivets immediately to the left of the doors are complete on the new cars, where there had been interruptions on the older cars for the heat-stamping of the road name. That's an ironic reversal of the usual Fundimensions practice!

The doors on the 7910 are also different from any of the previous doors. The new doors are molded plastic, but they

Figure 18: Side view comparison of the Lionel 1946-52 boxcar body and the 7910 Chessie boxcar manufactured in 1985. Note differences in rib spacing and the lack of interuption in ribs to the left of the door on the Chessie boxcar. R. Swanson collection.

have external details similar to the right-hand metal die-cast doors last made in 1951. The new doors have no trace of any pin on the back sides and, like the bodies, they are not painted but are molded out of colored plastic.

The 7910 Chessie System turns out not to be the leader in the revival of the 9-1/4" boxcar series. In late 1983, Fundimensions made a special uncatalogued set for the Toys-'R-Us stores which contained a 7912 Geoffrey's Star Car, a giraffe car which was based on a 9-1/4" boxcar body with a hole in the roof. (Regular giraffe cars are based on the short stock car molds.) In July of 1985, Lionel shipped a second set to Toys-'R-Us; this one contained a 7914 "Geoffrey's Carnival Carrier" giraffe car. Both of these Toys-'R-Us cars have molded white bodies and doors. They are identical to the 7910 boxcar except for the rectangular hole in the roof and the internal giraffe car mechanism. (The 7910 has a center hole in its frame filled with a plastic plug.)

Lionel (under Fundimensions management) has evidently developed new tooling and reintroduced the 9-1/4" boxcars for their smaller, lower-priced Traditional Series. The larger 9200/9400/9700 Series boxcars will probably be kept for the Collector Series. It will be interesting to see if some of the old road names and color schemes are re-run in the 7900 Series. (Editor's Note: Through 1986, no other examples have been catalogued.) Because of the many mold and component differences, collectors need not fear any confusion between the new and the old cars.

| TABLE 12: AVAILABILITY OF 9-1/4 INCH BOXCARS ACHORDING TO LIONEL'S CONSUMER CATALOGUES | | | | |
|---|---|---|---|---|
| YEAR | CAR NUMBER | SEPARATE SALE? | SET APPLICATIONS 027 | O |
| 1946 | 2454 | yes | 1411W, 1413WS | 2105WS |
|  | 3454 | yes | 1409, 1409W, 1415WS, 1421WS |  |
|  | 4454 | no |  | 4109WS |
| 1947 | 2454 | yes | 1435WS, 1437WS | 2125WS |
|  | 3454 | yes | 1439WS |  |
|  | 4454 | no |  | 4109WS |
| 1948 | 2454 | yes |  |  |
|  | 4454 | no |  | 4110WS |
|  | 6454 | no | 1427WS, 1429WS, 1445WS |  |
| 1949 | 3464 | yes | 1451WS, 1453WS, 1445WS | 2139W, 2151W |
|  | 4454 | no |  | 4110WS |
|  | 6454 | yes |  |  |
| 1950 | 3464 | yes | 1457B, 1473WS | 2159W, 2161W, 2167WS, 2175W |
|  | 4454 | no |  | 4333WS |
|  | 6454 | yes | 1471WS |  |
| 1951 | 3464 | yes | 1481WS | 2167WS, 2175W, 2185W |
|  | 6454 | yes | 1471WS |  |
| 1952 | 3464 | yes |  | 2179WS, 2183W |
|  | 3474 | no | 1483WS |  |
|  | 6454 | yes |  |  |
| 1953 | 3474 | no | 1511S |  |

29

A study of the 9-1/4" boxcars is almost the perfect case study in the Lionel manufacturing process for any collector. Very few of these cars are scarce, so any collector can acquire them and study nearly all the variations on a modest budget. These boxcars have been overshadowed by the more popular 6464 Series, but they should not be ignored; they were a commendable attempt at realism when they were produced and they are, if not colorful, very interesting to collect and study.

## PART 6: ACKNOWLEDGMENTS

An article of this length and depth obviously cannot represent the efforts of just one person. Through the years, there have been many people who have helped me acquire these boxcars, given me information and encouraged me with great persistence to write this article. For their help and encouragement, I would like to thank Harold Powell, Bruce Balsley, Tom Rollo, Charlie Pendergast, Barbara and Don Shaw, Ed Prenderville, Rand Washburn, Ralph Hutchinson, John Palm, Ron Niedhammer, C. Adair Roberts, Jack Smith and the late Hank Degano.

Special words of thanks and appreciation are also extended to Barbara Houtsma, June Smith and Nancy Wilczewski, who patiently and efficiently typed and proofread the original manuscript, which must have seemed to be a never-ending saga.

# Chapter I

# DIESEL AND ELECTRIC ENGINES
# AND MOTORIZED UNITS

These F-3 AB combinations were usually catalogued as O-27 units and have only a single motor in the A unit. First shelf: 2240 Wabash AB. Second shelf: 2242 New Haven AB. Third shelf: 2243 Santa Fe AB. Fourth shelf: 2245 Texas Special AB. The 2242 was only catalogued as a Super O locomotive (1958-59) while the 2243 was catalogued as O-27 (1955-56) and O (1957). L. Nuzzaci Collection.

First, last and always, Joshua Lionel Cowen was a steam engine man. To be sure, he thought that electrics like the big GG-1 "sort of slide along, like a big, pretty snake", but he had an instinctive dislike for any locomotive which did not feature the spinning, flashing rods of his beloved "iron horses". Shortly after World War II, however, Cowen realized that he had to modernize his line, just as the real railroads were doing. And so began the long and prestigious run of Lionel's diesels, electrics and charming, little self-propelled auxiliary units.

## DIESELS

One factor which convinced Joshua Lionel Cowen to modernize his line was cost-sharing for the expensive dies used to make the first of the great diesels, the F-3. The Santa Fe and New York Central Railroads, as well as General Motors, the makers of the F-3, knew that Lionel's locomotives were billboards in miniature which would pay off in advertising for them. Therefore, they agreed to underwrite part of the cost for the F-3 dies.

When the F-3 emerged in 1948, it was not prominently displayed in the catalogue, but sales figures soon had Cowen wondering why he had not produced the locomotive earlier. A big, twin-motored double-A unit, the F-3 broke all sales records. It could not be produced fast enough to meet the demand! The Santa Fe version of this locomotive became Lionel's all-time top seller, lasting for 18 years through four different numbers. Many other road names joined the originals in time, and B units were soon produced. When the locomotive was equipped with Magnetraction in 1950, there was not a load the twin-motored giant could not haul. For this edition, Richard Lord has written a comprehensive study of the F-3, along with some extra detail from Raymond Sorensen.

The F-3 series started in 1948 with the 2333 Santa Fe shown on the top shelf and the 2333 New York Central. The 2343 Santa Fe on the bottom shelf was introduced in 1950. Note the differences between the BUILT BY LIONEL and GM decals on the top shelf with those same features on the bottom shelf. L. Nuzzaci Collection.

Other diesels were, of course, produced soon after the F-3 emerged from Lionel's miniature erecting shops. In 1949, a fine model of the NW-2 switcher was produced. Before this locomotive was cheapened in 1955, it had a die-cast frame and, in the minds of many operators, the finest electric motor ever made by Lionel. In 1950, a shortened model of the Alco FA was made to give O-27 railroaders their own powerful diesel. This locomotive also featured the excellent switcher motor and a die-cast base before it was cheapened. (The editor's 30 year old 2023 Union Pacific Alco with this motor pulled 42 Fundimensions freight cars all by itself at a recent Greenberg train show!)

In 1955, production of the GP-7 and GP-9 "road switchers" began to replace the "premium" Alcos and switchers. These were good models of the popular general purpose locomotive made by General Motors, even if Lionel's designation was not totally accurate. Lionel simply turned a GP-7 into a GP-9 by adding a plastic fan shroud to the roofs of the GP-7. In the real world, GP-7 locomotives came both ways.

In 1954, Lionel produced an awesome model of the boxy Fairbanks-Morse Trainmaster diesel. These magnificent locomotives are all highly-prized and sought by collectors and operators - with reason. All these locomotives had two motors and were fearsome pullers. In addition, they were built to scale, which meant that they were the longest single O Gauge locomotives Lionel ever produced.

The only diesel which was out of scale was the strange 44-ton switcher series made only for a few years, beginning in 1956. Lionel apparently wanted an inexpensive switcher engine for its low-end market which would still be of a bit better quality than its least expensive switchers and Alcos. The attempt was not very successful because the 44-ton engine was rather unattractive and far too large to represent its prototype.

The Lionel diesels represent good opportunities for collectors at both ends of the financial scale. All of the Fairbanks-Morse

locomotives and the better F-3 AA pairs command very high prices, even for the more common versions. The better NW-2 switchers and Alcos also are somewhat costly, as well as the GP-7 and GP-9 locomotives. However, the collector operating on a budget can accumulate a fascinating collection of less expensive Alcos and NW-2 switchers at bargain prices, since these were made in huge numbers.

## ELECTRICS

The Lionel Corporation has always been justly famous for its models of electric engines. In prewar years, its models of the Olympian bi-polar electric in Standard Gauge were seldom matched by competitors. It was, therefore, fitting that Lionel should begin its postwar production of electrics with a real thoroughbred — the Pennsylvania Railroad's magnificent GG-1. The handsome prototype, styled by Raymond Loewy, had a service life of half a century and was an excellent subject for a Lionel model. The first GG-1, the single-motored 2332, was produced in 1947. Later models of this locomotive added Magnetraction and a second motor, and they were selected to pull some of Lionel's best passenger consists, such as the Congressional Limited. Although Lionel's model was too short to be a true scale model, it was an excellent "runner", and many operators still use it as their Number One engine today. For a complete survey of the GG-1 variations produced, see Richard Shanfeld and Joseph Sadorf's article in this edition.

The GG-1 was not the only electric produced; others soon followed. In 1956, Lionel produced a good model of the General Electric EP-5 rectifier, which the firm erroneously called a "Little Joe". (The real "Little Joe" was originally built for export to the Soviet Union; hence the nickname for Joseph Stalin. It never got to Russia, but it did serve for many years on the South Shore Line near Chicago and on the Milwaukee Road, where it was a star performer for a long time.) Engineers on the New Haven gave the prototype the nickname

Top shelf: 2344 New York Central F-3 AA. Middle shelf: 2345 Western Pacific F-3 AA. Bottom shelf: 2353 Santa Fe F-3 AA from 1953-55. L. Nuzzaci Collection.

"Jet" because the engine air blowers produced a jet engine sound. The Lionel model had four-wheel trucks instead of the prototype's six-wheel units, but otherwise it was a good model with Lionel's best features. It was made in New Haven, Pennsylvania, Milwaukee and Great Northern markings.

Another electric "brute" was produced in 1958, but it did not meet with public success, so it was only made in Virginian markings. This was the homely but powerful General Electric E-33 or EL-C Rectifier. The prototype was built to haul heavy coal trains over mountain territory — certainly not for beauty! Lionel's model was faithful to its prototype, but in a small model the result was a rather boxy, ungainly locomotive despite its attractive blue and yellow markings. This is now an engine prized by collectors.

One other electric deserves mention — the odd 520 Box Cab electric, made in 1956. This was a model of a General Electric 80-ton box cab which was made without any of Lionel's premium features for the low end of the market. It was not very successful, but can be regarded as a "sleeper" by collectors since it is not too common and there is no real interest in it.

Except for the 520 Box Cab locomotive, all the electrics are sought by collectors, with the GG-1 getting the most attention and the best prices. The common New Haven EP-5 can be a good buy for the collector who is in the right place at the right time.

### MOTORIZED UNITS

Real railroads featured much more than main line locomotives and rolling stock, and so should Lionel Land, in the eyes of its administrators. In the postwar years, Lionel produced a dazzling array of self-propelled auxiliary equipment, featuring clever engineering and great charm. These were first produced in 1955, when the 41 U.S. Army Switcher, the 50 Gang Car and

the 60 Trolley initiated a long and highly successful line of these little wonders. The Army Switcher had a normal three-position reversing switch, but the others changed direction when their bumpers struck an object. A little man sitting atop the Gang Car changed his seating position when the locomotive reversed, and the trolley reversed its pole. Many variations of these units soon followed, among them two snowplows (both plow and rotary types), a stylish station wagon called an "Executive Inspection Car", a "Fire Fighting Car" and a "Ballast Tamper".

Perhaps the most cleverly engineered and certainly the most complicated of these units was the 3360 Burro Crane of 1956-1957. This crane could propel itself and a few cars, just like any locomotive. However, through an ingenious slip clutch, it could also swivel its cab, lower its hook and lift loads.

The Gang Car is very common, easily affordable and a great deal of fun to operate. Beyond that, however, the motorized units are prized by collectors and bring high prices, especially the Mining Switcher and the AEC Switcher, which are true rarities. Other common units are the 41 and 51 Army and Navy Switchers. These units added considerable color and action to the Lionel line, and they are only rivaled by the better accessories for operating fun.

### LIONEL F3s
#### By Richard Lord
#### Additional Information by Raymond Sorensen

The F3s are among the most highly valued of all postwar Lionel trains. Much has been written about the magnificence of the F3s, and I will not venture to add my comments. Instead, it is the purpose of this article to help F3 enthusiasts better understand these trains.

The F3s have "evolved" greatly over the years since their introduction in 1948. Some of the changes were for the

Top shelf: 2354 New York Central F-3 AA. Middle shelf: 2355 Western Pacific F-3 AA. Bottom shelf: 2356 Southern F-3 AA. Note that the grab-rails found on the front of the earlier F-3s were deleted for these models. L. Nuzzaci Collection.

betterment of the product, while others tended to mute the original bold design statement of the first F3s. The mechanical and technological alterations are largely considered to be advancements. The later F3s ran more quietly and functioned better than the early F3s. Some operators feel that the vertical-motored F3s pull better than their horizontal-motored counterparts, though this is open to debate. The first 2333 New York Central and Santa Fe models were issued with rubber-stamped Santa Fe or New York Central lettering, which did not hold up well and was soon replaced by heat-stamped lettering. The early celluloid porthole windows used on the 2333 Santa Fe and the 2333 New York Central models were extremely fragile and difficult to fasten into the window openings; as a result, these were replaced with plastic porthole inserts which were again remodeled for ease of assembly. (The New York Central model also carried a 2333 number, but in the Service Manual its parts carry a 2334 prefix.) The Styrene plastic used beginning in 1951 helped improve the paint adherence qualities of the cabs. On the other hand, there were also changes that were made for the sake of economy and ease of production, and these are seen as "cheapening" the product. These changes are the elimination or reduction in the authenticity of cab detail. It must be noted, however, that the fine paint schemes of the later F3s compensated for the production of these later simplified cabs.

The F3s are also among the most expensive Lionel postwar trains to collect. Even the so called "common" F3s are rising steadily in price as they are getting harder to find in collectable condition. As a result, one must take great care in the purchase of F3s paying close attention to originality and condition. To complicate matters, the F3 market is rife with reproduction parts and cabs, some of which are very difficult to distinguish from the originals. Perhaps because of their high prices, the relatively small (but still quite significant) number of F3 enthusiasts, the competition for the available train dollars or

a combination of all three, the F3s are slow sellers in some markets. Even so, the price rise is still noteworthy.

This article will help the F3 collector as he examines an item for originality, and will also assist in determining the scarcity or desirability of a particular piece. Figure 1 is a handy reference guide by year to the mechanical and trim features of the F3s. The mechanical features are: the motors, horn location, lamp, frame, pilot and trucks. The cab trim features include the GM logo, roof vents, portholes/lens, nose grab-irons, side ladders, ornamental horn, cab fastening technique and type of stamped lettering.

The following is a brief explanation of the mechanical features:

● MOTORS: Two types of motors were used on the F3s - horizontal and vertical. The horizontal motor, as the term

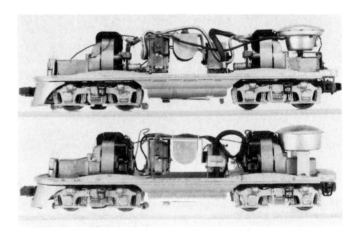

The F-3s came with both horizontal (early) and vertical (later) motors. There are two versions of the horizontal motor: early - top shelf and later - bottom shelf. The early motor has very large brush holders. R. Vagner Collection. G. Stern photograph.

Top shelf: 2363 Illinois Central F-3 AB. Middle shelf: 2367 Wabash F-3 AB. Bottom shelf: 2368 B & O F-3 AB. L. Nuzzaci Collection.

implies, had the power shaft running sideways which in turn powered gears downward to the wheels. The horizontal motor had two types of brushes — an early 1948-type where the brushes protruded in tubes from the brushplate and used coiled brush springs, and a later type where the brushes were integrated into the brushplate and did not extend outward from it, using V-shaped brush springs instead of the earlier coiled variety. Vertical motors had a power shaft that ran down and under the motor to the gears that turned the drive wheels. Some service men believe that these motors are significantly easier to service than the horizontal variety, and they run a great deal more quietly as well.

● HORN LOCATION: The operating horn of the F3 was first placed in the power unit. In the earliest (1948) 2333 models, this horn was fastened to the rear of the frame by a Z-shaped bracket holding a rubber washer at the top where the horn sat. In 1949, this arrangement was replaced by a U-shaped bracket with folded tabs on each end to be mounted across the rear motor from one side of the frame to the other. However, due to motor vibrations the horn did not operate as well as it could have. As a result, the horn was moved to the trailing A-unit in the 1953 and 1954 productions. In 1955, the horn was placed back in the power unit when the less "vibrant" but better pulling vertical motor was introduced. The horn in the single-motor F3s was always in the power unit.

● LAMP: At first, the operating nose lamp of the F3 was a "clip-on" type fastened to the frame by two tabs. In 1953 and thereafter the lamp housing was cast into the frame. Throughout its life, the F3 took a No. 1445 18-volt bayonet-based lamp.

● FRAME: Prior to 1955 the frames on the A units were cast metal with the number 2333-20 and the wording "MADE IN U.S. OF AMERICA THE LIONEL CORPORATION NEW YORK". After 1955, the number did not appear on the frames.

The "B" unit frames were molded plastic with the wording "GENERAL MOTORS TYPE F3 B DIESEL ELECTRIC UNIT MADE IN U.S. OF AMERICA THE LIONEL CORPORATION NEW YORK". The early "B" units also had rubber-stamped numbers on the frame, i.e. "2343B", while later "B" units did not.

Also, before 1955, the battery plate was stamped with the wording in black lettering "TO OPERATE HORN INSERT A SIZE 'D' FLASHLIGHT CELL HERE" and also read, in bolder print, "CAUTION REMOVE CELL WHEN LOCOMOTIVE IS NOT IN USE". Beginning in 1955, a black rectangular-shaped sticker was applied to the battery cover replacing the wording in white which read "TO OPERATE HORN INSERT A SIZE 'D' CELL HERE. REMOVE CELL BEFORE STORING LOCOMOTIVE". The screw on the battery plate prior to 1955 was a slotted flathead screw with ridged edges (for gripping) and beginning in 1955 it had a slotted roundhead without the grip ridges.

● PILOT: The pilot was comprised of several parts screwed together. In 1955 and thereafter the screws were eliminated and the pilot assembly was "staked" together. The pilot also had a "notch" in the bar that ran underneath the coupler. The notch was the result of two "lips" that extended down from the pilot bar. In 1954 the lips and notch were eliminated because the lips tended to catch on switches in turns. This interference with switch boxes was a recurring problem, especially with O-27 track. In 1952 Lionel put out a special service bulletin showing owners how to fix their F3s so they would run through the 1122 O-27 switches. The chief remedy was to bend the tip of the E-unit lever inward where it projects downward from the cab body.

● TRUCKS: Before 1955, the F3 trucks were painted, screwed together, and had footsteps that were fastened by screws. The trucks also had a coil coupler with sliding shoe, and a dual

Top shelf: 2373 Canadian Pacific F-3 AA. Middle shelf: 2378 Milwaukee Road F-3 AB. Bottom shelf: 2379 Rio Grande
F-3 AB. L. Nuzzaci Collection.

pickup roller fastened to one of the trucks. The earliest 2333 models of 1948 had smaller pickup rollers than did the rest of the run. In 1955 and thereafter, the trucks were blackened through an oxidation process, staked together, and the footsteps were eliminated. The coupler was changed from coil to magnetic with no sliding shoe, and each truck had its own pickup roller.

Also before 1955 the A unit pilot truck carried an identification plate that read "LIONEL" accompanied by the Lionel "L" logo. The rear truck was molded with the wording "MADE IN U.S. OF AMERICAN THE LIONEL CORPORATION NEW YORK". The "B" unit used the A unit rear trucks. The truck construction beginning in 1955 was vastly different and had no lettering.

The following is a brief discussion of the cab trim and stamping technique found on F3s:

• GM LOGO: From 1948 through 1952, the GM logo was applied via decal to the Santa Fe, New York Central, and Western Pacific F3. In 1953 and thereafter the logo was heat-stamped. Curiously, the Lionel Service Manual lists three separate GM decals for the 1948-52 F3s. The 2333 and 2343 Santa Fe units used part 2333-104; the 2334 and 2344 New York Central units used part 2334-23, and the 2345 Western Pacific used part 622-126 — the same decal first used on the 622 switcher. Color and size probably account for the differences, but reports have surfaced of F3s with the "wrong" decals. This occurred when Lionel ran out of a specific decal for one model and simply substituted a decal from another model until the correct one was available. Therefore, the type of decal should not affect the value of the piece very much — but among collectors it sometimes does.

• ROOF VENTS: Prior to 1953, the diesel roof vents were an authentic looking wire mesh/screen type. This mesh screen

was attached to the cab by an unusual double speed nut from within the cab. From 1953 on the screen mesh was eliminated and the vents were molded into the plastic cab, beginning with the 2353-54-55 models.

• PORTHOLES WITH LENSES: From 1948 through 1954, the F3s had open portholes with plastic lenses. From 1948 to 1950, the lens was a celluloid contact lens-type cap that was easily lost or broken. From 1951 through 1954, the lens was changed to a plastic snap-in type that stayed in place. There was a slight change in the shape of the plastic lens in 1953 for ease of assembly. In 1955, the portholes with lenses were eliminated, and thereafter there was a filled porthole molded into the cab that was painted over or remained the color of the plastic cab.

Of interest is the fact that the Southern carried over certain features not found on other F3s for a particular catalogue year. For example, in 1955, the portholes with lenses were eliminated, but the Southern still had them. The Southern even had portholes with lenses in 1956 while all other F3s did not. Could it be that Lionel used up old stock on the Southern and continued cataloguing it until it sold what had already been produced? The answer is probably yes. During the same years, the green GG-1 was not made, but it was available to dealers because Lionel had a plentiful back stock of the green cabs. The same could have occurred with the F3 production and the Southern.

Also, in recent years the versions of the Texas Special have been noted. The first was a 1954 version with portholes, silver frame and trucks, and red pilot. The 1955 production had filled-in portholes, silver frame and pilot, and black trucks. The latter version is consistent with the F3 changes that occured in 1955. This is the only time Lionel substantially changed and

The F-3 on the top shelf has nose grab-irons; the F-3 on the bottom shelf does not. R. Vagner Collection, G. Stern photograph.

continued an F3 road name without also changing its catalogue number.

• NOSE GRAB-IRONS: The nose grab-irons were placed on all F3s from 1948 through 1952; thereafter, they were eliminated and the holes in the body were eliminated. The grab-irons would not reappear for 27 years, when the Fundimensions 8952-53 Brunswick green Pennsylvania F3 model reinstated them.

• MOLDED SIDE LADDER: The F3s from 1948 through 1954 had a snap-on simulated black plastic ladder. This was eliminated in 1955. Thereafter, a side ladder was molded into the plastic cab and was painted over or was the color of the plastic shell.

• ORNAMENTAL HORN: Prior to 1955 the ornamental horn was an assembly of two pieces that was locked into place underneath the cab. The die-cast horn piece was attached to a black sheet metal bracket with tabs folded over from the inside of the cab. Beginning in 1955, the horn was a single piece snap-in type, although the piece was still die-cast.

• CAB FASTENING TECHNIQUE: From 1948 through 1952 the cab was fastened by three screws to the F3 frame. Beginning in 1953 the cab nose was fastened to the chassis by a smaller screw, and the rear of the cab had two clips that gripped the end of the frame piece to fasten the rear of the cab. This change was the result of the problem that Lionel had with stripped screw holes in the F3 cab rears. However, one problem was substituted for another in this case. If the rear brackets, which were riveted to the plastic cab, were bent up too sharply because they gripped the frame end too tightly, the cab shell could crack when the cab was removed from the frame for locomotive servicing. Many cabs produced from 1953 onward show signs of such cracking — some beyond repair.

• STAMPING: The principal means of lettering and numbering F3 cabs was through heat-stamping. This process left a depression in the cabs as the heat melted the plastic. Another method was rubber-stamping, which left no such depression under normal stamping conditions. In addition, some F3s had a combination of heat and rubber-stamping. For example, the B & O F3 had heat-stamped lettering and numbers, but the lines were rubber-stamped.

It is necessary to caution the reader about heat-stamping. The first several units of a run each day or the start of each shift period, i.e. after lunch, had a deep depression as the result of a "hot iron". Later units had a shallower depression as the "iron" tool cooled. On some F3s like the B & O, the stamping process appears to have been rubber-stamped while in fact the lettering and numbers were heat-stamped. Some of these units may have been run through the stamping process very fast, not allowing time for the tool to regain its heat between stampings, or perhaps the stamping "iron" was faulty or set too "cool". In any case, the result was that some heat-stamped cabs came out looking rubber-stamped. Of course, without heat or enough heat to make a proper depression in the plastic with the paint, a heat-stamping tool becomes a rubber-stamp of sorts.

Heat-stamping cannot always be determined by feel. One way of detection is to hold the cab sideways so that you look along the surface of the cab in natural light. If you use a magnifying glass, you will see depressions, especially in letter corners and edges. It takes a keen and trained eye to tell heat from rubber-stamping when the touch of the heat-stamping tool is lighter than normal.

To conclude the discussion of Figure 1 and the evolution of F3s, it should be stated that there were also some changes not noted. Lionel experimented with materials and part types from time to time, and some of them appeared on some F3s. For example, Lionel experimented with quieting down or lessening the vibrations caused in F3 motor gears. In 1954 and 1955, a nylon idler gear was used which still was too noisy — the vibration problem was later solved via the vertical motor. This and other harder to detect changes in F3s should be of little or no concern in the examination, as most of the changes occurred at times when major alterations were made — chiefly in 1953 and 1955. Figure 1 is the only guide one needs to determine the date of manufacture and originality of F3s. As usual, there is an exception — the differences in the 1948 and 1949 production runs of the 2333 and 2333 Santa Fe and New York Central models. Look for the smaller pickup rollers in the 1948 models and, especially in the case of the New York Central, larger and less crisp lettering of the New York Central letters on the 1948 cabs.

Figure 2 shows the year of manufacture of F3s, including major variations. This chart, besides its use as an F3 chronology, is also of interest in valuing F3s. In using this guide, one must first understand the economics it represents. It is no surprise to anyone that when an item is in demand and supply is short, that the value of that item increases above that of items in more supply, given equal demand. In terms of F3 values this principle applies. The F3s that were produced in less quantity relative to the production of other F3s have a higher value. Also the number of F3s that have survived in collectable condition is a critical factor in determining collector supply. The number of years of an F3's production is the central element in predicting scarcity. In looking at Figure 2, one may predict which F3 would have the highest value given this economic explanation, even if one knows nothing about F3s. As an example, since the Canadian Pacific, Milwaukee Road and Baltimore and Ohio were made for only one year, one would predict correctly that they would be of the greatest value.

The only intervening factor in this equation is the possibility that there is an unequal demand. That can be true for some F3s. For example, although the Santa Fe is by far the most common of the F3s, it is in demand because people constantly re-discover its attractive "Warbonnet" paint scheme. In addition, since the F3s are such excellent runners, people buy

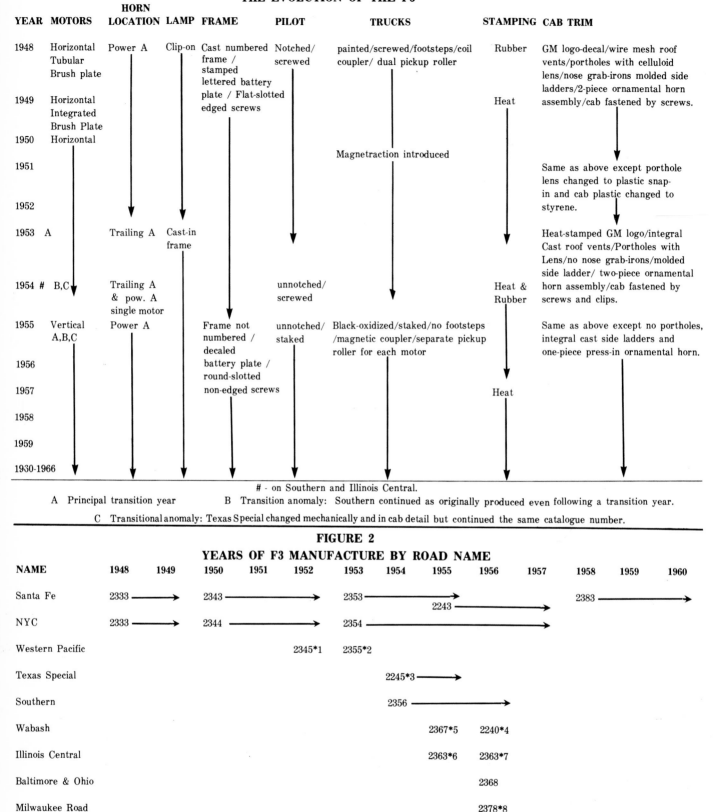

# FIGURE 1
## THE EVOLUTION OF THE F3

| YEAR | MOTORS | HORN LOCATION | LAMP | FRAME | PILOT | TRUCKS | STAMPING | CAB TRIM |
|---|---|---|---|---|---|---|---|---|
| 1948 | Horizontal Tubular Brush plate | Power A | Clip-on | Cast numbered frame / stamped lettered battery plate / Flat-slotted edged screws | Notched/ screwed | painted/screwed/footsteps/coil coupler/ dual pickup roller | Rubber | GM logo-decal/wire mesh roof vents/portholes with celluloid lens/nose grab-irons molded side ladders/2-piece ornamental horn assembly/cab fastened by screws. |
| 1949 | Horizontal Integrated Brush Plate | | | | | | Heat | |
| 1950 | Horizontal | | | | | | | |
| 1951 | | | | | | Magnetraction introduced | | Same as above except porthole lens changed to plastic snap-in and cab plastic changed to styrene. |
| 1952 | | | | | | | | |
| 1953 | A | Trailing A | Cast-in frame | | | | | Heat-stamped GM logo/integral Cast roof vents/Portholes with Lens/no nose grab-irons/molded side ladder/ two-piece ornamental horn assembly/cab fastened by screws and clips. |
| 1954 # | B,C | Trailing A & pow. A single motor | | | unnotched/ screwed | | Heat & Rubber | |
| 1955 | Vertical A,B,C | Power A | | Frame not numbered / decaled battery plate / round-slotted non-edged screws | unnotched/ staked | Black-oxidized/staked/no footsteps /magnetic coupler/separate pickup roller for each motor | | Same as above except no portholes, integral cast side ladders and one-piece press-in ornamental horn. |
| 1956 | | | | | | | | |
| 1957 | | | | | | | Heat | |
| 1958 | | | | | | | | |
| 1959 | | | | | | | | |
| 1930-1966 | | | | | | | | |

# - on Southern and Illinois Central.

A  Principal transition year        B  Transition anomaly:  Southern continued as originally produced even following a transition year.

C  Transitional anomaly: Texas Special changed mechanically and in cab detail but continued the same catalogue number.

# FIGURE 2
## YEARS OF F3 MANUFACTURE BY ROAD NAME

| NAME | 1948 | 1949 | 1950 | 1951 | 1952 | 1953 | 1954 | 1955 | 1956 | 1957 | 1958 | 1959 | 1960 |
|---|---|---|---|---|---|---|---|---|---|---|---|---|---|
| Santa Fe | 2333 → | | 2343 → | | | 2353 → | | 2243 → | | | 2383 → | | |
| NYC | 2333 → | | 2344 → | | | 2354 → | | | | | | | |
| Western Pacific | | | | | 2345*1 | 2355*2 | | | | | | | |
| Texas Special | | | | | | 2245*3 → | | | | | | | |
| Southern | | | | | | 2356 → | | | | | | | |
| Wabash | | | | | | | | 2367*5 | 2240*4 | | | | |
| Illinois Central | | | | | | | | 2363*6 | 2363*7 | | | | |
| Baltimore & Ohio | | | | | | | | | 2368 | | | | |
| Milwaukee Road | | | | | | | | | 2378*8 | | | | |
| Canadian Pacific | | | | | | | | | | 2373 | | | |
| Rio Grande | | | | | | | | | | 2379 → | | | |
| New Haven | | | | | | | | | | | 2242 → | | |

| *1 | Fully detailed | *3 | Two variations | *5 | Dual motor | *7 | Brown letter |
|---|---|---|---|---|---|---|---|
| *2 | Some detail eliminated | *4 | Single motor | *6 | Black letter | *8 | Three variations |

Top shelf: 2383 Santa Fe AA. Middle shelf: 2343C Santa Fe B, 2344C NYC B. Bottom shelf: 2356C Southern B unit. L. Nuzzaci Collection.

the F3 for its operating ability as well as its collector value. Even a battered F3 unit is worth some money because many operators take advantage of a thriving repainting and relettering market — even some custom paint schemes can be observed on weatherbeaten Santa Fe shells. Conversely, the Milwaukee might be a truly scarce F3, but its duller paint scheme may make it less attractive as a buy for a collector who also wants the locomotive for his operating layout. Lately there has been a big resurgence of interest in the New York Central F3 because the current runs of Lionel trains have featured numerous New York Central pieces of rolling stock to go along with the NYC F3 — and, naturally, this has affected the price of that locomotive.

Although production figures of the F3s are not known, one would expect that the number of F3s produced per year declined in later years as consumer demand fell. F3s produced for, say, two years in the late 1950s would therefore be in less supply and hence of greater value than F3s produced for two years in earlier years. One would expect the New Haven and Rio Grande to be in less supply and of greater value than the Texas Special, for example.

One other factor in using Figure 2 is in regard to variations. The Milwaukee Road had three variations and the Illinois Central and Texas Special had two. The Wabash was produced for two years, first as a dual-motored unit and then as a single-motored piece with a different catalogue number. These Wabash F3s may have the same road name and very similar paint schemes except that the 2367 B unit has a white stripe immediately adjacent to each end while the 2340 B unit does not have a white stripe immediately adjacent to the end (J. Sattler comment.) The units are each desired for very different reasons. The dual-motored unit is, of course, a better runner

and has better trim, but the single-motored Wabash unit came in only one O-27 set and does not turn up in excellent condition very often due to paint adherence problems. Finally, the Western Pacifics produced for two years with different Lionel catalogue numbers are different in cab trim and desirability. Both the earlier and later cabs have clear plastic portholes. However, the later Western Pacific has louvered roof and lacks grab-irons.

## A LEGEND BEGETS ANOTHER LEGEND: THE LIONEL GG-1 ELECTRIC

### By Richard Shanfeld and Joseph Sadorf

Additional Material By:
Jerome Butler, Raymond Dennis and James Pauley

The early Postwar period was a boom time for the Lionel Corporation. The desires of the public for toy trains had been unfulfilled for four years because of World War II, and as Lionel began to make trains again in late 1945 consumers were ready to buy. Much depended upon the diversity and appropriateness of the product, and indeed during those years Lionel introduced many of its best and longest-running innovations.

However, by the end of 1946 one glaring flaw was evident in the Lionel product line. All of Lionel's locomotives were steam engines, and with the modernization of the real railroads and Lionel's penchant for realism, this was a situation which demanded a response. Lionel, too, had to modernize. But which way to go? Joshua Lionel Cowen was an avowed sentimentalist when it came to his beloved steam engines, and later on he reluctantly allowed Lionel to enter the age of the

The 2332 was equipped with a single motor and was underpowered. Note the nickel rims on the center wheel of the 2332s. The 2330, (third shelf) was introduced in 1950 and came with two motors and without nickel rimmed drivers as did all later GG1s. R. Shanfeld Collection.

Diesel. There was one area of motive power for which Lionel had a rich tradition and an excellent model to follow — the electric engine. In 1947, that is the path Lionel traveled.

In the first place, Lionel had always made good models of electrics in the Prewar era. Lionel was justly famous for its models of New York Central center-cab electrics and even more so for its magnificent models of Milwaukee Road bi-polar electrics so well exemplified by the 381 and 402 Standard Gauge models. The Milwaukee Road prototypes were so strong that they could outpull any steam engine, even the most powerful compounds. Lionel's problem was that these models could not be updated into the Postwar era because the stamped sheet metal technology which produced them was rapidly being abandoned for die-casting techniques. Even with a tradition of

electric engines, what electric locomotive could lend itself to die-casting and still tap a large potential market?

It was the great good fortune for both Lionel and train collectors everywhere that there was such a prototype for Lionel to model. This was the Pennsylvania Railroad's sleek, streamlined GG-1 Electric, which had already established itself as a legendary performer since it first began running under the Pennsylvania's catenary in 1934. This massive locomotive had twelve drive wheels which supplied awesome tractive effort for the heaviest freight trains. In addition, it could take long strings of passenger cars and maintain high-speed express service better than any steam engine. These engines ran on 11,000 volt, 25-cycle AC current; they were so reliable that it seemed all they needed was an occasional trip to the wash

Top shelf: 2340 GG1. Middle shelf: 2340 GG1. Bottom shelf: 2360 GG1. The 2340 was introduced in 1955. Mechanically it is quite similar to the 2330 with dual motors, Magnetraction and a battery powered horn. The 2360 was introduced in 1956 and initially retained the mechanical features and decorating scheme of the 2340. R. Shanfeld Collection.

racks. Besides, with their sleek, Raymond Loewy design, the GG-1s were a great expression of confidence in the future. (Loewy also designed the streamlined K-4 steam engine, also modeled by Lionel, and such diverse symbols of corporate America as the Exxon logo, the Oreo cookie and the Coca-Cola soda fountain).They sang under their catenary for nearly 50 years before they were retired, and there are quite a number preserved for posterity. (As of November 1986, the Railroad Museum of Pennsylvania in Strasburg, Pa., owns and displays the 4935 and also displays the 4800, the original riveted prototype engine, which ran in service from 1934 to 1980). Obviously, the GG-1 was a great candidate for Lionel to model.

The first Lionel model of the GG-1, the 2332, made its debut in 1947. It immediately became a favorite with toy train enthusiasts. It had a die-cast body shell finished in a rich Brunswick green with gold striping and lettering, just like its prototype. Except for its lack of scale length, a compromise made necessary by the need to negotiate the 30-inch diameter of O Gauge track, Lionel's GG-1 was a very accurate model. The 2332 had a rugged single motor mounted on an angle; even today, it is noted as a smooth runner by collectors, although it cannot pull the heavy trains so easily handled by the twin-engine versions with Magnetraction. The 2332 had trouble pulling its catalogued consist of three Madison cars. It had lights at both ends and two pantographs which were insulated from the body shell by white rubber insulators. The operator could even re-route the wiring so that the motor got its power from overhead catenary! So intent was Lionel on

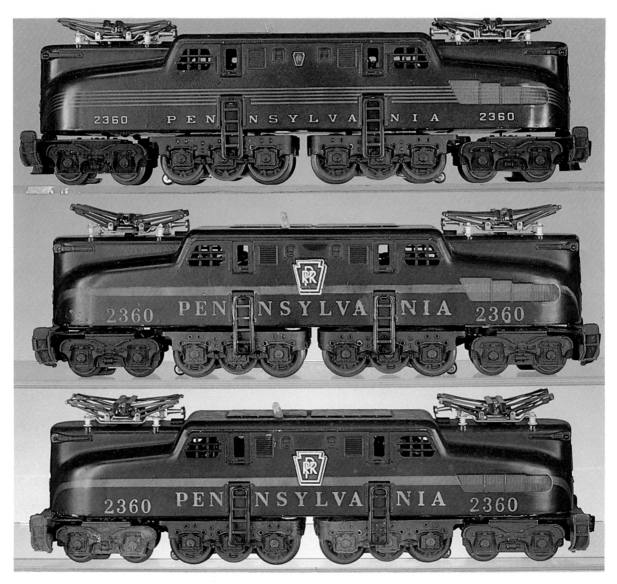

Three different versions of the 2360. The 2360 was introduced in 1956. Initially the 2360 was made with five stripes in both tuscan and green. The green version is shown on the top shelf, the tuscan version on the previous plate. Later, Lionel replaced the five stripes on the tuscan model with a single stripe. This model retained the uneven height air vents. In 1961, Lionel changed the air vents and marker light detail. Compare shelves 2 and 3. R. Shanfeld Collection.

presenting a realistic model that the firm even tried to duplicate the sound of the GG-1's harsh air horn by mounting a vibrator box inside the chassis. If the harsh buzz of the 2332's horn sounds like a stick rattling around inside a plastic box, that is no accident. That's exactly what the vibrator box was!

In many ways, the 2332 was a kind of "test bed" for the models which were to follow it in 1950 and afterwards. There are two persistent production controversies concerning the early run of these engines. A small number of these locomotives were made in flat black instead of dark Brunswick green. These black locomotives had rubber-stamped Keystones instead of the later water-release decals, but the striping and Keystones are not very well applied. The "silver" Keystones on the sides (and their red rubber-stamped counterparts) are usually found badly blurred. To add to the confusion, some early Brunswick green GG-1 examples came with these rubber-stamped Keystones.

Another controversy revolves around striping and lettering which is apparently silver. It may well be that all of the 2332 GG-1 locomotives were originally stamped in gold. According

to one plausible scenario, the ink used in the rubber-stamped striping and lettering had an unfortunate tendency to oxidize over the years into what looks like, at first glance, silver paint. The silver stamping and lettering is probably the result of a chemical reaction. Lionel used a paint shade known as Illinois Bronze and mixed it with real silver to form the ink used on the GG-1. The bronze flake, made from copper and brass, gave the gold appearance and the silver was used to add brightness. Unfortunately for Lionel, contaminants in the vehicle varnish caused oxidation to occur. This oxidation caused the bronze mix to turn black, leaving the silver, which was unaffected by the chemical reaction. This same reaction occurred on Prewar pieces, which did not have the silver added. On such pieces as the 309 and 310 passenger cars, the original gold stamping has turned black. Closer examination in natural light of a 2332 which has been stored in its box since new will show striping and lettering in a color which resembles the color of pale dry ginger ale. A few 2332 locomotives with this paint formulation have recently turned up in their original boxes in like new or mint condition. These examples clearly show the original color

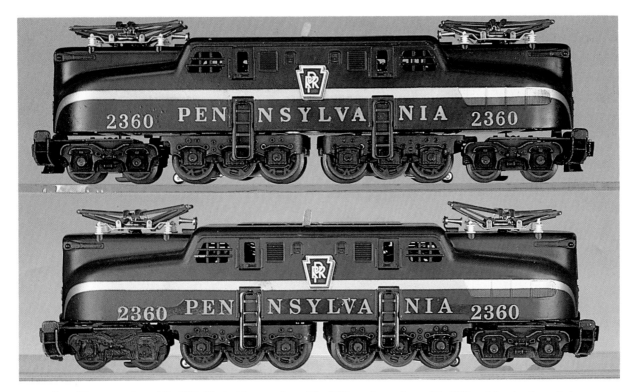

Two different versions of the 2360. The last two versions of the 2360 are shown above. The 1962 model on top has a single gold stripe and heat-stamped lettering and numbers. The lower unit from 1962-1963 has decaled lettering and numbers. R. Shanfeld Collection. B. Greenberg photograph.

to be a pale gold, not silver. Even when new, many examples of the 2332, whatever the variety, show faded central striping.

There are many construction differences between the single motor 2332 and the double motor 2330, 2340 and 2360 models which followed in 1950 and afterward. The front trucks of the 2332 are different from all the double-motor GG-1s in that the area around the mounting screw hole is stamped in a triangular shape. Unlike any later GG-1s, the 2332 had nickel rims on its center truck wheels. The front trucks of the 2332 use electrical coil uncouplers, as did all the later GG-1s (except the revivals by Fundimensions, which use magnetic mechanical uncouplers). The pickup shoes for the uncouplers on the front trucks are close to the coupler ends of the trucks until a transition in 1961 with the 2360 tuscan model, when the pickup shoes were placed closer to the mounting screw away from the coupler itself. The reason for the change was probably related to production costs, since the 3662-1 milk car used the same pickup shoe found on the 2360 models produced in 1961 and afterwards.

A few of the earliest 2332 locomotives have turned up with motor brush plates made of red thermoset compound rather than the usual black. Other such brush plates have been observed on late 1946 and early 1947 examples of the 671/2020 Pennsylvania Turbines and the 726 Berkshire. There has been much speculation about whether these were special models, but the truth about them is a little more prosaic. These examples represent a short period when Lionel was undergoing severe materials shortages due to the demand for trains in the early Postwar period. Other examples of shortages from this period point this out, most notably the 022A switches, special modifications of the usual 022 switches which lacked the metal bottom and were packed with an 1122-100 double controller usually found with O-27 switches. (Thomas Rollo has supplied us with this information).

The harsh vibrator box horn of the 2332 gave way to a 1 1/2 volt battery-operated horn in all the double-motor GG-1 models. The battery horn, which used a "D" size dry cell, was activated by a relay which used the whistle control DC voltage (about 5 volts DC) to close the circuit. Since the battery was comparatively hard to replace (the operator had to disassemble the front truck), many a later GG-1 was stored with the battery still inside the locomotive. When the battery leaked, severe corrosion of the body shell and frame resulted. (None of the Fundimensions GG-1 models possesses a horn).

For the collector, there is a special caution about battery leakage concerning the GG-1. When checking a 2330, 2340 or 2360 for battery damage, the collector should check the window area at the top of the cab in addition to the bottom frame and body cavity. If the GG-1 had been stored wheels-up in its box with its battery still installed — an easy thing to do — any leakage from the battery would drain downward towards one of the window areas, where the metal casting is very thin. Such acid leakage has actually eaten away the entire window area of some unfortunate examples.

The single-motor 2332 had its motor mounted on an angle driving a single axle, and it did not have Magnetraction. All later GG-1 models had Magnetraction and two vertically mounted motors, one for each six-wheel power truck, driving the wheels through spur gears. The 2332 has an E-unit slot on top cut into a half-circle; all other GG-1 models have a straight E-unit slot. In addition, the 2332's single motor is secured at the top of the body shell by a large flat-headed screw; all later models lack this method of mounting. In the early production of the 2332 shells, the cab is shimmed by a brass washer 1/16 '" thick where the motor mounts to the inside of the cab. This was necessary to correct the mounting post for the motor truck, which had been cast too short in early runs.

The 2330 GG-1, made only in 1950, represented a radical departure from its 2332 predecessor. As mentioned before, a better-sounding horn was added, and so were a second motor and Lionel's new Magnetraction. As with the NW-2 switchers introduced that year, Lionel used separately mounted magnets on the power trucks instead of the later magnets mounted inside the drive axles. Occasionally, one of these magnets would rub against the power truck frame and rob the locomotive of some of its performance. On the switchers, this could only be corrected by carefully filing the magnet down, since the magnets were applied with a special baked cement at the factory and could not be moved. The correction was much easier on the GG-1; the magnet could simply be pried out and carefully re-glued to the frame. However, removing and replacing the magnet would destroy some of the magnetic flux, since the magnets were originally magnetized at the factory only after they had been installed. Binding could also occur when one of the bushings on a power truck wheel was pressed too far into the frame. The Lionel Service Manual recommended spacer washers to solve that problem. The mechanical elements of the 2330 ran unchanged through all the later models of the locomotive; the differences were only in the body shells from that point on.

The frame of the new Magnetraction GG-1 was made in two pieces, as opposed to the four-piece construction of the 2332. The 2332 had used a separate plate for each pilot truck, and the motor and non-powered trucks were also separate pieces. The 2330 used a one-piece metal stamping to mount both of its power trucks, one of the pilot trucks, the horn with its relay and the reversing switch. The second part was a small plate which covered the battery and acted as a battery contact. This plate, which also held the other pilot truck, was stamped from steel.

There were some cosmetic changes between the 2330 and the 2332 as well. The five stripes running across the side of the body were slightly lower on most 2330s and were interrupted by the two ladders vertically mounted on the body shell. Although the striping continued to be rubber-stamped, the lettering and numbers were now heat-stamped. Experience had shown that the rubber-stamped lettering and numbering on the 2332 wore off when the locomotive was handled. That is why so many 2332 locomotives are found today which have been re-striped and numbered, most often by silk-screening processes which Lionel seldom used anywhere in its production. The heat-stamped lettering and numbering was much more durable. It should be noted that a GG-1 should never be handled by the lettering or stripes, but rather by its trucks. In addition to avoiding the handling of the stripes and numbers, the collector should avoid using newspaper or other printed paper for storage because the inks will react with the bright coloring and be absorbed into the stripes and lettering, dulling them. Floral paper or Teflon-coated plastic bags are better for storage, especially when a small pouch of water-absorbing silica is added to the box; these pouches are used in photography and electronics.

The graduated-height air vents of the 2332 and the marker lights shaped as squares retreating to rectangles were retained on the 2330. The triangular mounting screw hole on the front trucks of the 2332 gave way to a rounded half-moon shaped plate around the mounting hole of the 2330 and its following models.

The GG-1 was not produced during the years 1951 to 1954 — a curious turn of events, since Lionel enjoyed its greatest sales successes in those years. However, the GG-1 returned in 1955

with the 2340 model, which had the same mechanical features as its 2330 predecessor. This time, the Brunswick green GG-1 had a new tuscan-colored partner to match the new Congressional passenger set offered in that year. The aluminum passenger cars which came with the tuscan GG-1 had flat channels instead of fluted channels; maroon striping was mounted in the channels. The Congressional set represented Lionel at its best; certainly the sight of these cars pulled by the tuscan 2340 would impress any observer of a model train layout. There were no other cosmetic changes between the 2330 and the 2340 models; the Lionel Service Manual listed the body part numbers as 2340-30 for the tuscan version and 2340-31 for the Brunswick green version. The suffix numbers Lionel used for marketing purposes were 2340-1 for the tuscan version and 2340-25 for the green version; the original box part numbers are 2340-27 for the green version and 2340-10 for the tuscan version. These numerical differences can help collectors identify the correct boxes and parts for their particular 2340 locomotives (and, for that matter, the 2360 versions with their own parts nomenclatures).

The last number for the GG-1, the 2360 model, was introduced in 1956. This number was made in several interesting variations. In 1956, the 2360 was catalogued as a five-stripe locomotive in tuscan and green colors, just like its predecessors. However, there were several small but significant changes to the body shell casting. In previous models, the air vents at the front sides had been graduated in height in four distinct steps. With the 2360, these vents became even in height all the way across the body, beginning in 1961. Incredibly, this body change actually followed the practice of the Pennsylvania Railroad, which made the same change to the real locomotives in the late Fifties! This year marked other changes to the casting as well. The marker lights of previous versions had been placed in a square housing coming back into two rectangular boxes. With the 1961 2360, these marker lights became teardrop-shaped, as on the prototype. Finally, the posts into which the pantograph insulators fit were strengthened by being made broader than their predecessors.

However, it is important to note that these changes did not occur right away, and so the differing models of the 2360 can be dated with some precision. The green 2360 model does not show any of the cosmetic changes, although it was catalogued from 1956 to 1958. (The Lionel Service Manual gives the body shell numbers as 2360-7 for the tuscan version and 2360-26 for the green version. Significantly, a parts sheet dated 11/59 lists the 2360-26 body shell as "obsolete"). It is possible that only one run of the Brunswick green 2360 was made, or that leftover 2340 green-painted body shells were simply numbered as 2360 models, although it continued to be available through 1958. The green 2360 never used the body shell which went through its cosmetic changes and differing paint styles.

The tuscan 2360, however, shows many changes which begin in 1957. In this year, the GG-1 was offered in tuscan in only one set; after this, Lionel merely catalogued the GG-1 to help dealers dispose of existing stocks. The earliest tuscan 2360 models used the older style body shell, five stripes and heat-stamped lettering and numbering. Then, the older style cab was given a new lettering and striping job; one large single rubber-stamped gold stripe replaced the five narrow stripes, the lettering in "PENNSYLVANIA" was made much larger and the locomotive number was made larger as well. The Pennsylvania Railroad had introduced this single-stripe and large Keystone scheme on the prototypes in 1955. On the first version of this new decorating scheme, all the striping, was rubber-stamped. The numbers and lettering were large and were heat-stamped. However, in 1961 a second version emerged; the only difference was that the lettering and numbering was heat-stamped, while the single stripe was painted. Usually, Lionel designated a new number for any locomotive which would receive changes such as these. In this case, the firm probably had a large number of leftover body castings after 1955. Therefore, the new number 2360 was put into effect anyway and Lionel painted up the leftover body castings into green or tuscan versions as the market demanded. The new body die was not needed until later on, when the supply of older shells was exhausted. That did not occur until the next model of the GG-1 came out.

In 1957, Lionel catalogued the tuscan single-striped GG-1 as 2360-10. This locomotive was part of set 2293W, a Super O freight set. The green GG-1 was still available; it was listed in the 1957 catalogue as 2360-25. Most likely, these were 1956 green locomotives being depleted. The 1958 catalogues list both GG-1s for sale again, this time with the green 2360-25 locomotive being illustrated. In this case, both versions were probably leftover production. Apparently no GG-1s were made in 1958, although Lionel catalogued the GG-1 to help dealers deplete their stocks. (It must be remembered that 1958 was a severe recession year, and Lionel was cutting back its operations considerably).

Two versions of the 2360 locomotive. The upper locomotive has side ventilator screens which differ in height while on the lower locomotive, the ventilator screens are approximately the same height. R. Shanfeld Collection, B. Greenberg photograph.

As usual, the catalogue illustrations are models of inaccuracy. The 1957 catalogue illustration shows clearly that the older body style was used for the drawing. However, the green GG-1 illustrated in the 1958 catalogue is a curious kitbash of the old and the new body styles! The marker lights appear to be those on the older body shell, but the air vents look like they are all in the same height, as on the newer body shell. The 1961

catalogue illustrations are poorly rendered drawings based on the older body shell; the vents are clearly graduated in height, but the marker lights look like the newer, teardrop-shaped ones.

After a two-year absence, the 2360 GG-1 returned in 1961, this time only in the tuscan single-striped version. Finally, the new body shell features were introduced with these production runs. The lettering and numbering was heat-stamped, as before, and the single stripe was painted onto the body shell. Sometime, in 1962 and 1963, the last years for production of the GG-1, one further change was made. The lettering and numbering was no longer heat-stamped; instead, water-transfer decals were used. These examples represent the last stage of production for the Postwar GG-1.

After a fourteen-year absence from production, Fundimensions revived the tuscan GG-1 in 1977 with its 8753 model; this model lacked the horn of its predecessor and had nylon drive gears - a feature disliked intensely by many collectors. Fundimensions quickly changed that feature back to the original metal gears when it issued the black 8850 Penn Central model of 1978. One more Fundimensions model, the 8150, was made in 1981; this one was done in green and had excellent striping and lettering resembling the 2340 model, but in a glossy Brunswick green which collectors applauded.

Few Lionel locomotives have found more favor — or more controversy — than Lionel's GG-1s. All kinds of variations, some suspect, some no doubt genuine, have turned up in collector circles. Some single-stripe versions have been found with small Keystones on the sides; some five-stripe versions have been found with large Keystones. Many repainted and restriped locomotives exist, due to both wear of the original decor and the popularity of the locomotive. Reproductions of the GG-1 body shells have been made by at least three separate manufacturers or restorers; these can usually be detected by the use of silk-screened stripes, letters and numbers. Lionel seldom used silk-screening as a decorative technique in the Postwar era. Quite a number of paint color variations have turned up, even in the later models. "Odd" versions of the GG-1 should be approached with care by the collector, and expert advice is a must before purchase.

If the GG-1 is a complex area for the collector, at least the aesthetics of the Lionel GG-1 offer great joy. The Lionel GG-1 can outhaul anything on a model train layout in its double-motor version (except perhaps a Fairbanks-Morse twin-motor Diesel), and with its bright lights, its raised pantographs and its air of effortless operation, it is an appropriate model of a prototype which was, and is, a legend by itself.

### DIESEL POWER TRUCK TYPES

Lionel diesels came with four basic motors. The study of these units shows Lionel's continuing concern with cost and quality considerations.

**TYPE I MOTOR**

Die-cast truck frame
Five exposed gears
Lettered: "THE LIONEL CORPORATION NEW YORK"
Four axle depressions
One screw
Axles not visible

**TYPE II MOTOR**

Built-up power truck with attached side frames to suit prototype
Sheet metal bottom
Five external gears

Top Shelf: 41 United States Army switcher, 42 Picatinny Arsenal and 51 Navy Yard. Middle shelf: 53 Rio Grande, 53 Rio Grande and 56 Mine Transport. Bottom shelf: 57 AEC, 58 Great Northern and 59 US Air Force Minuteman. The window struts on these pieces are easily broken and consequently the engines need to be handled with great care. L. Nuzzaci Collection.

Lettered: "LIONEL DIESEL SWITCHER, "OIL",* THE LIONEL CORPOR-ATION NY MADE IN U.S. of AMERICA"
Four axle bearings, all visible
Two axles visible — either one or two magnetic axles
Unpainted side frames
Three-position reverse
Three-part pickup assembly
There are seven subcategories to Type II

### TYPE II SUBCATEGORIES

|  | A | B | C | D | E | F | G |
|---|---|---|---|---|---|---|---|
| Oil hole with valve |  |  |  | X | X |  | X |
| No oil hole |  | X | X |  |  |  |  |
| Oil hole, no valve |  |  | X |  |  | X |  |
| One magnetized axle |  | X |  | X |  | X | X |
| Two magnetized axles | X |  | X |  | X |  |  |
| Round axle bushings | X | X | X |  |  | X | X |
| Axle bushing with swage marks |  |  |  | X | X |  |  |

### TYPE III MOTOR

No bottom plate
Five external gears
Exposed worm and spur gears only, worm is relatively centered between
 axles
No Magnetraction
No axle bearings

---

* It is not clear if "OIL" appears on all Type II motors, particularly Type IIA and IIB.

### TYPE III SUBCATEGORIES

(A) No tires, front spring-mounted motor
(B) Two tires on non-geared side, non-spring-mounted motor, examples: 213, 215

### TYPE IV MOTOR

No bottom plate
Motor has only worm and spur gears; both visible
No axle bearings, axles visible, spacers added to axle on one side
Rubber tire traction with grooved wheels to hold tire (no Magnetraction)
Black motor side frames

**Bold print** indicates that the name appears on the side of the item. When it does not appear on the side or where its name is abbreviated, the item's popular designation, i.e., **HANDCAR**, appears in bold and its omission from the item's side is noted in the text.

LIONEL'S 44-TONNERS, 520 ELECTRIC, 42 PICATINNY ARSENAL AND 51 NAVY YARD SWITCHERS: A BRIEF NOTE

#### By Louis Bohn

Model railroad enthusiasts of the Fifties often wondered where Lionel found the prototypes for its engines. In fact, there has been considerable speculation as to whether any prototypes existed at all. Many people in the Eighties are still curious about this question. All the unusual pieces listed in the title above came from one source — the 1941 issue of the Locomotive Cyclopedia!

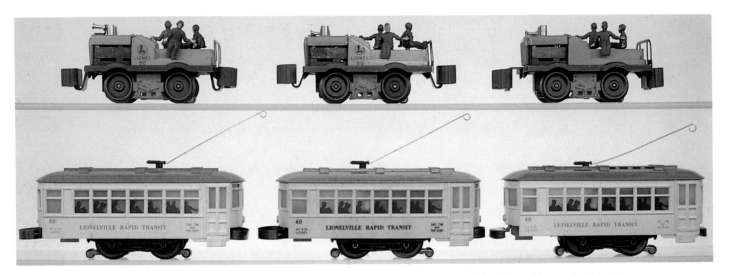

Three different versions of the Lionel Gang Car. The left unit has the centered horn and the U-shaped bumper bracket, the center unit has the right side horn and the U-shaped bumper bracket while the right unit has the right side horn and the L-bumper bracket. On the second shelf are three versions of the 60 Trolley. The left and center trolleys do not have clerestory vents and do have two-piece bumpers. The right hand trolley has the clerestory roof vents and blue lettering and the one-piece bumper. L. Nuzzaci Collection.

The Locomotive Cyclopedia is an annual trade report on motive power. It provides useful technical data and photographs of new equipment. Although the Cyclopedia has been out of print for many years, it was reprinted at one time by the Kalmbach Publishing Company, and hopefully it will be available again one day.

|  | Gd | VG | Exc | Mt |
|---|---|---|---|---|

**41 U.S. ARMY** Switcher, 1955-57, 2-4-2, gas turbine, black with white-lettered "TRANSPORTATION CORPS", three-position E-unit, no light. Several pieces have been reported with a red, white and blue triangle above the center window on both sides. One report says this was a post-factory addition. However, we need to learn if this variety was indeed factory produced. Reports from original owners would be very helpful. Breslin comment. Price for usual variety.                         30    50    70    95

The Lionel 42 Picatinny Arsenal locomotive prototype is shown in the Cyclopedia on page 1053. There is a real Picatinny Arsenal located near Dover, New Jersey where the United States Army conducts experimental artillery tests. Comments by L. Bohn. The photograph is reprinted with the gracious permission of Kalmbach Publishing Company.

**42 PICATINNY ARSENAL** Switcher, 1957, 2-4-2, gas turbine, olive drab with white handrails and lettering, three-position E-unit, no light.
                                                                  80   140   200   275

**44 U.S. ARMY** Mobile Missile Launcher, 1959-62, blue with white lettering, gray missile launcher with four missiles, blue man sits at control panel, red light on roof, three-position E-unit, one fixed die-cast coupler, Magnetraction, Type IIF motor, Type III pickups. P. Ambrose comment.

(A) Dark gray missile launcher, blue man with face and hands painted flesh color. J. Algozzini Collection.                    40    75   100   150
(B) Light gray missile launcher, unpainted blue man.    J. Algozzini Collection.                                              40    75   100   150

**45 U.S. MARINES** Mobile Missile Launcher, 1960-62, olive drab with white lettering, gray center unit on frame, gray launch unit, red light on roof, Magnetraction Type IIF motor, Type III pickups, one fixed die-cast coupler. P. Ambrose Collection.                   50   100   150   200

## THE NO. 50 GANG CAR
### By James Sattler

The No. 50 Section Gang Car was first made in 1954. It provided a new type of "action" on the operating Lionel layout of the time, because rather than having an E-unit for reversing, it was the first Lionel item equipped with a reversing mechanism which is operated by the movement of the bumper slide as it strikes an obstruction. Thus, the No. 50 Section Gang Car could be operated on a siding which had No. 26 Bumpers at each end or, more likely, it would have been placed on the track itself and when it struck either the locomotive or a car or caboose of a train, the Gang Car would automatically reverse its direction without regard to the direction of the train.

The Gang Car had a substantial number of changes over its 11 years of production. Two of the most visible are changes in the bumper and changes in the horn. The earliest bumper was U-shaped and had a blue pad. Later Lionel changed to an L-shaped bumper. The new metal bumper stamping required considerably less material, as it was shorter.

The earliest cars have three-piece metal horns mounted on the center of the hood. The horns consist of a turned metal horn, a rivet and mounting bracket. These horns were also used on the F3 diesels. When Lionel developed a simpler one-piece plastic horn for its diesels, these lower cost units were used with the gang car. When Lionel changed its horn type, it relocated the horn from the center of the brushplate to the right side. At the same time it changed the mounting screw for the brushplate from a flathead Phillips screw to a roundhead screw.

The Lionel Service Manual states on page II-23 (Greenberg reprinting) that "Because the bumper slide must make good

Top shelf: 52 Fire Car, 54 Ballast Tamper and 3360 Burro. Middle shelf: 55 Tie-Jector, 69 Maintenance Car and 68 Executive Inspection Car. Bottom shelf: 3927 Track Cleaning Car and 520 Lionel Lines electric engine. L. Nuzzaci and R. Lord Collections.

| 50 LIONEL Gang Car | | | | | | |
|---|---|---|---|---|---|---|
| Code | A | B | C | D | E | F |
| Year | 1954 | 1954 | 55-63 | 55-63 | 1964 | 1964 |
| Horn location | C | C | R | R | R | R |
| Bumper shape | U | U | U | U | L | L |
| Bumper size | 27mm | 27mm | 27mm | 27mm | 27mm | 30mm |
| Bumper color | bl | gr | gr | bl | bl | bl |
| Lettering color | bl | bk | bk | bk | bk | bk |
| Fixed men clothing | blsh | ol | bl ov | bl ov | bl ov | bl ov |
| Left arm location | out | out | out | out | down | out |
| Color: rotating man | o.g. | bl | o.g. | o.g. | o.g. | o.g. |
| Armature plate cover | m | m | d | d | d | d |
| Screw type | f.h.p. | f.h.p. | r.h.p. | comb.* | r.h.p. | r.h.p. |
| Value: VG | 20 | 15 | 15 | 15 | 15 | 15 |
| Value: Exc | 50 | 55 | 35 | 35 | 50 | 50 |
| Value: Mt | 80 | 90 | 55 | 55 | 70 | 70 |

*The single screw holding the rear portion is a flathead Phillips.

1. Year: this is our best estimate of Lionel production.
2. Horn location: centered or right side
3. Bumper shape: U-shaped or L-shaped
4. Bumper size: measured at greatest width
5. Bumper color: blue or gray
6. Lettering color: blue or blck
7. Clothing: blue shirt, olive shirt, blue overalls
8. Left arm location: out or down
9. Rotating man color: olive green or blue
10. Armature cover color: matches rear section, darker than rear section
11. Armature cover screws: flat head Phillips, roundhead Phillips

electrical contact to the body of the car, portions of the channel in which the slide moves are usually wire-brushed or sand-papered to remove the excess black oxide finish. In latter part of production the axle-grounding spring was redesigned and extended to make direct contact to the slide contact spring..." Another running change in production is also noted on the same page: "In the early part of production a quantity of No. 50 Gang Car was made without axle bushings. In subsequent production 671-248 axle bushings were used on the driving axle only..."

We need to link these characteristics to those noted below and determine how these affect our chronological listing.

NOTE: New letter codes have been tentatively assigned to the observations listed below. These observations were made from items in the collection of James Sattler and from manufacturing variations known to exist. The letter codes from Greenberg's Guide to Lionel Trains: 1945-69, Fifth Edition have been also reported.

**Gd  VG  Exc  Mt**

**50 LIONEL** Gang Car, 1954-64, orange body with blue or gray bumpers, two fixed men, one rotating man, bump reverse, no light.

**51 NAVY YARD** Switcher, 1956-57, 2-4-2, Vulcan, light blue with white lettering, three-position E-unit, no light, window struts often broken.

**45  75  100  150**

**52 FIRE CAR** 1958-61, red plastic body with white lettering mounted on die-cast chassis, gray pump and hose reel, red light. The unit has no precise prototype, but according to Lionel Service Manual it "incorporates the features of several pieces of railroad fire-fighting equipment". Mechanical-

Top shelf: 600 Katy NW-2 (1955) and 601 Seaboard (1956). Middle shelf: 602 Seaboard (1957-58) and 610 Erie (1955). Bottom shelf: 611 Jersey Central (1957-58) and 613 Union Pacific (1958). L. Nuzzaci Collection.

The Lionel 520 Boxcar Electric is the most exotic of the unusual Lionel small motorized pieces. Its prototype is an 80 ton, 600 volt DC-powered engine using a third rail as well as a pantograph. Built for the Chile Exploration Company, this photo appears in Section 16, page 1040, Figure 16.55 of the 1941 Cyclopedia. Comments by L. Bohn. This photograph is reprinted with the gracious permission of Kalmbach Publishing Company which has published a reproduction of the 1941 Cyclopedia.

ly and electrically, it is quite similar to the 50 Gang Car and 60 Trolley. It is powered by a double-wound field motor, and its direction is controlled by the bumper-operated slide which changes the connections of the field winding relative to the armature. A rack and pinion arrangement swivels the fireman sitting on his seat with his "deluge gun" as the car changes direction. The warning light carried by the Fire Car was originally scheduled to be the automatically-flashing lamp No. L-257. However, the lamps

available at that time were not sufficiently bright, so all Fire Cars produced in 1958 were equipped with steadily-burning 57 lamps. However, the flashing lamp was available (both were specified by the Service Manual), and it is likely that some Service Stations used it. When found today, the Fire Car's foam lamp pad is usually deteriorated beyond repair; however, replacement units for this pad are readily available. N. Cretelle and R. LaVoie comments. **80 125 150 225**

**53 RIO GRANDE** Snowplow, 1957-60, 2-4-2, Vulcan, black body and lettering, yellow cab sides, handrails and snowplow, three-position E-unit, no light, one coupler, window struts often broken.

(A) Lettering "Rio Grande" has letter "a" printed backwards.

              **95 150 225 300**

(B) Same as (A), but "a" printed correctly. **120 210 290 440**

**54 BALLAST TAMPER** 1958-61, 1966, 1968-69, yellow with black lettering, blue man in cab, one fixed coupler, shift lever for tamper action, unit is geared to half-speed while tamping, two activator track clips to operate shift lever, no reverse, no light, antenna on rear easily damaged.

              **70 100 155 200**

Two versions of the Tie-Jector. The left one does not have the slot behind the door; the right one does have a slot. The slot provided ventilation for the motor. Early Tie-Jectors without the slot often show evidence of storage bin melting. L. Nuzzaci and R. Lord Collections.

NW-2 Switchers. Top shelf: 614 Alaska Railroad and 616 Santa Fe. Middle shelf: 621 Jersey Central and 622 Santa Fe. Bottom shelf: 623 Santa Fe and 624 Chesapeake & Ohio. L. Nuzzaci Collection.

|  | Gd | VG | Exc | Mt |
|---|---|---|---|---|

**55 TIE-JECTOR** 1957-61.
(A) Red with white lettering, number on side "5511", switch lever for ejector action on side, two activator track clips to operate switch lever, no reverse, one coupler on rear, no light, pulling more than one car could damage gears or cause the motor to overheat.    **70 100 135 180**
(B) Same as (A), but slot similar to savings bank car behind rubber man. J. Algozzini Collection.    **100 130 165 210**
(C) Same as (A), but orange tint to red plastic body. Probable 1957 production. J. Algozzini Collection.    **100 130 165 210**

See also Factory Errors.

**56 M St. L [Minneapolis & St. Louis] MINE TRANSPORT** 1958, 2-4-2, Vulcan, white cab sides and railing, red body and lettering, three-position E-unit, no light, window struts often broken.    **150 225 300 450**

**57 AEC** Switcher, 1959-60, 2-4-2, Vulcan, three-position E-unit, no light, white body, red cab sides, window struts often broken. Many collectors feel that the cream-colored variety is a result of aging or chemical change. The reason for this is that the unit was made from a white plastic which was not resistant to ultraviolet light and, consequently, oxidized in the air. If a deep cream-bodied cab shell is removed from its frame, the portion of the body which was flat against the black frame — and thus shielded from light and air — is white. L. Bohn and G. Salamone observations.
   **175 300 400 600**

**58 GREAT NORTHERN** Rotary Snowplow, 1959-61, 2-4-2, Vulcan, green body and logo, white cab, sides and handrails, snow blower rotates when moving, three-position E-unit, no light, window struts often broken.
   **180 250 375 500**

See also Factory Errors.

**59 MINUTEMAN** Switcher, 1962-63, 2-4-2, gas turbine.
(A) White body with blue and red-lettered "U.S. AIR FORCE", "MINUTE-MAN", three-position E-unit, no light, black handrails. **150 225 300 450**

See also Factory Errors.

This is the two-piece spring bumper used on the 60 Trolley in 1955-57 production. The 1958 one-piece bumper had a plastic piece slipped over the edge of the metal bumper bar. R. Bartelt Photo.

**60 LIONELVILLE** Trolley, 1955-58, four-wheel Birney style, yellow plastic body with red roof, lettered "60 BLT 8-55 LIONEL", "LIONELVILLE RAPID TRANSIT" AND "SAVE TIME HAVE FARE READY". Trolley pole rotates according to direction of operation, bump reverse, interior light. We believe that all these trolleys had two small roof slots towards each end; these slots were centered on the roof. Later models have four additional clerestory vents along the edges of the clerestory. An aluminized paper reflector on the roof underside was added to prevent roof damage due to the combination of bulb and motor heat.
(A) 1955, no aluminized paper reflector, original bulb aluminum-painted, no clerestory vents, metal silhouettes attached to slides simulate changing of motorman's position with car's direction, two-part spring bumper, red roof, square-top trolley pole holder, orange motor brush holder, slotted screw fastens frame to body, black lettering.    **100 175 275 400**
(B) 1955, same as (A), but spline-top trolley pole holder, black motor brush holder, Phillips screw fastens body to frame, six-sided threaded bushing. Came in orange box with lining lettered "NO. 60 TROLLEY". T. Rollo

NW-2 Switchers.  Top shelf:  633 Santa Fe and 634 Santa Fe.  Middle shelf:  635 Union Pacific and 645 Union Pacific.
Bottom shelf:  6220 A.T. & S.F. and 6250 Seaboard.  L. Nuzzaci Collection.

reports that his version was purchased as a Christmas present in 1955, the trolley's first year, at Marshall Field and Company of Chicago. The original bulb was replaced a little more than a month after Christmas of 1955; it is likely that the coating covering the top half of the bulb prevented the dissipation of heat, contributing to the bulb's short life. T. Rollo comments, T. Rollo and H. Powell Collections.          **100  175  275  400**

(C) Same as (A), but aluminized paper reflector, only one metal silhouette for motorman, celluloid silhouettes on both sides of windows. B. Smith Collection.          **100  175  275  400**

(D) 1955, same as (A), but no motorman silhouettes, spline-top trolley pole holder, Phillips screw body fastener, six-sided threaded bushing. M. Denuty Collection.          **60  125  175  250**

(E) 1956, two-piece spring bumper, blue lettering, no clerestory vents, red roof, square-top trolley pole holder, no aluminized paper reflector inside roof, orange motor brush holder, slotted screw holding body to frame, six-sided threaded bushing on frame. R. LaVoie Collection.
          **75  100  125  175**

(F) 1956, same as (E), but with aluminized paper reflector, trolley pole holder with splines on top. This is the most common trolley variety. H. Edmunds Collection.          **75  100  125  175**

(G) 1957, aluminized paper reflector within roof, no clerestory vents, two-part spring bumper, orange-red roof, square-top trolley pole holder, orange motor brush holder, body fastened to frame with Phillips screw, light metallic blue lettering, six-sided threaded bushing on frame. C. Rohlfing and J. Ranker Collections.          **90  120  140  200**

(H) Same as (G), but splines atop trolley pole holder. H. Edmunds and H. Powell Collections.          **90  120  140  200**

(I) Same as (H), but dark red lettering. Very hard to find. D. Brill and J. Ranker Collections.          **NRS**

(J) Same as (I), but regular red roof. G. Meisel Collection.          **NRS**

(K) 1958, early, one-piece bumper, blue lettering, bright red roof without clerestory vents, no six-sided threaded bushing on frame, slotted screw

**All the 60 Trolleys had roof slots, as shown here. Only the late production models had clerestory vents, which would have been along the sides of the long walkway-like structure on the center of this roof. R. Bartelt Photo.**

holds body to frame, black motor brush holder, splines atop trolley pole holder. Appears to be a combination of earlier and later parts, indicating transition piece. J. Ranker and J. Alvatrain Collections.          **NRS**

(L) 1958, one-piece bumper with plastic piece fitted atop metal bumper end; blue lettering, clerestory vents, red roof, aluminized paper insert, black brush holder, six-sided threaded bushing on frame, Phillips screw holds body to frame, splines atop trolley pole holder. J. Abraham Collection.
          **90  125  160  225**

(M) Same as (K), but orange motor brush holder, no aluminized paper reflector, black lettering on one side and blue lettering on other side. This is an unusual piece because of its odd lettering scheme. G. Wilson Collection.          **NRS**

(N) Two-piece bumper, black lettering, people on strips in door, front and back windows, "PERRY ST. - EAST" in one end window on top and "NEAL ST - LOCAL" in other top end window. T. Klaassen Collection.          **NRS**

**65 HANDCAR** 1962-66, "HANDCAR NO.65" appears embossed on side of plastic body, R. Friedman comment. Red pump, two vinyl men pump,

Top shelf: 202 Union Pacific and 209 New Haven. Middle shelf: 205 Missouri Pacific AAs. Bottom shelf: 204 Santa Fe AA.

one in a red and one in a blue shirt; the vinyl often causes a chemical reaction with the plastic body which damages the body where the men stand, no light, no reverse. Two different bodies are found:

**TYPE I:** The five-laminate rectifier is exposed and visible from the underside. It is mounted through a 3/8" x 9/16" slot in the frame end. The rectifier is numbered "G16542". The plastic body base is filled at the end center to cover the rectifier. The middle rail collector passes through a spring and a hole in the collector slide. It is soldered to the slide bottom. R. Griesbeck Collection.

**TYPE II:** The rectifier is not visible from the underside, and a stamped metal clip holds the rectifier in place. The rectifier is thin and mounts inside the frame. There is no slot. The plastic body is open at the end center. The middle rail collector slide has a vertical post through the spring to which the collector wire is attached. R. Griesbeck Collection.

| | Gd | VG | Exc | Mt |
|---|---|---|---|---|
| (A) Dark yellow body. | 75 | 150 | 200 | 275 |
| (B) Light yellow body. | 90 | 125 | 225 | 350 |

**68 EXECUTIVE INSPECTION CAR** 1958-61, DeSoto 1958 station wagon **without** name on side, red with cream side panel and roof, knob on roof is E-unit cutoff switch, two-position E-unit, operating head and taillight.
75  100  150  225

See also Factory Errors and Prototypes.

**69 MAINTENANCE CAR** 1960-62, self-powered signal service car, "MAINTENANCE CAR" does not appear on side, dark gray and black body with light gray platform, blue bumpers, L-shaped bumper bracket, one blue man, sign reverses when direction reverses, "DANGER" on one side and "SAFETY FIRST" on the other.
90  185  225  300

**202 UNION PACIFIC** 1957, Alco A unit, O-27, orange body with black lettering, sheet metal frame, opening where front coupler would be is closed off, dummy coupler on rear, one-axle Magnetraction, two-position E-unit, headlight, Type IID motor, Type II pickups, no horn, no weight.
15  30  50  75

See also Factory Errors and Prototypes.

**204 SANTA FE** 1957, Alco AA units, O-27, Santa Fe freight paint scheme, blue body with yellow cab roof, upper stripe and lettering, red and yellow lower stripe, sheet metal frame, front and rear dummy couplers, two-axle Magnetraction, three-position E-unit, light in both units, Type IIE motor, Type II pickup, no horn, no weight.
30  60  80  135

**205 MISSOURI PACIFIC** 1957-58, Alco AA units, O-27, blue body with white lettering, sheet metal frame, front and rear dummy couplers, two-axle Magnetraction, three-position E-unit, light in powered unit, Type IIE motor, Type II pickup, no horn, no weight.
25  45  75  135

**208 SANTA FE** 1958-59, Alco AA units, O-27 Santa Fe freight paint scheme, blue body with yellow cab roof, upper stripe and lettering, red and yellow lower stripe, sheet metal frame, front and rear dummy couplers, two-axle Magnetraction, three-position E-unit, light in powered unit, Type IIE motor, Type II pickup, horn, no weight.
35  60  90  160

**209 NEW HAVEN** 1958, Alco AA units, O-27, black body with orange and white stripes and lettering, sheet metal frame, front and rear dummy couplers, two-axle Magnetraction, three-position E-unit, light in powered unit, Type IIE motor, Type II pickup, horn, no weight.
65  125  195  300

**210 The Texas Special** 1958, Alco AA units, O-27, red body and lettering with white stripe, sheet metal frame, front and rear dummy couplers, two-axle Magnetraction, three-position E-unit, light in powered unit, Type IIE motor, Type II pickup, no horn, no weight.
30  60  85  155

**211 The Texas Special** 1962-66, Alco AA units, O-27, red body and lettering with white stripe, sheet metal frame, front and rear dummy couplers, two rubber traction tires on drive wheels, weight in body, two-position E-unit, light in powered unit, Type IIIB motor, Type II pickup, no horn, with weight. The two units came in an outside carton marked on the end "NO. 211/LIONEL/TRAINS" and on top "12-87", on bottom "THIS BOX MEETS THE/CONSTRUCTION REQUIREMENTS/OF THE N.M.F.C.". Box has certificate naming St. Joe Paper Company of Hackensack, N.J. as manufacturer. The inner box for the powered unit is marked "NO. 211P/211-7" on the end flap, while that box's maker was the Mead Corporation of North Bergen, N.J. The dummy unit box is marked

**Top shelf: 208 Santa Fe Alco AAs. Middle shelf: 210 Texas Special AAs. Bottom shelf: 211 Texas Special AAs.**

"NO. 211T with a marked-over area/LIONEL/TENDER/218-12" on the end flap. This lettering reflected Lionel's peculiar custom of calling the trailing dummy A or B units as 'tenders." W. Hopper Collection, I.D. Smith comments. **30 50 85 125**

**212 U.S. MARINE CORPS** 1958-59, Alco A unit, O-27. See also next entry.

(A) Blue body with white stripes and lettering, sheet metal frame, opening where front coupler would be is closed off, dummy coupler on rear, one-axle Magnetraction, two-position E-unit, light, Type IID motor, Type II pickup, no horn, no weight. **25 50 75 100**

(B) Same as (A), except slightly lighter blue, much brighter white lettering and trim, die-cast dummy coupler on front, dummy coupler on rear, no reverse unit, Type IIA motor, no tires, no Magnetraction.

**30 60 90 120**

**212T U.S. MARINE CORPS** 1958-59, dummy unit made to match 212 above but apparently sold separately. Came in box stamped "212T". Fixed couplers on front and rear. Locomotive is numbered "212" only; the "T" designation on a Lionel brown Kraft-paper locomotive box was used to indicate a motorless unit of a pair of engines, while the "P" suffix indicated

the unit with the motor. We suspect that this dummy unit was made to match (B) above. P. Ambrose comment. Price quoted must include "212T" box, since a quick cab switch could fake this piece easily. This unusual locomotive is discussed in **Greenberg's Lionel Service Manual**, Vol. I, Chapter II, p. 63. **100 150 225 350**

**212 SANTA FE** 1964-66, Alco AA units, O-27, Santa Fe war bonnet passenger paint scheme, silver body with red cab, nose and stripe; yellow and black trim, black lettering; sheet metal frame, front and rear dummy couplers, two rubber traction tires on drive wheels, two-position E-unit, light in powered unit, Type IIIB motor, Type III pickup, horn, with weight, E-unit lever has slot in roof. I.D. Smith observation. **50 80 125 175**

**213 MINNEAPOLIS & ST. LOUIS** 1964, Alco AA units, O-27, red body with white stripe and lettering, sheet metal frame, front and rear dummy couplers, two rubber traction tires on drive wheels, two-position E-unit, light in powered unit, Type IIIB motor, no horn, with weight. **40 75 100 150**

**215 SANTA FE** Uncatalogued, 1965, Alco AA or AB units, gray plastic body painted silver and red with black and yellow stripes and black lettering, Type IIIB motor, with weight, two-position E-unit.

(A) With powered A Unit and 218C dummy B Unit. **35 50 75 100**

**This unusual 212T locomotive was apparently offered for separate sale. G. Stern photograph.**

53

Top shelf: 212 Santa Fe and 216 Burlington.  Middle shelf: 217 Boston and Maine AAs.  Bottom shelf: 218 Santa Fe AAs.

|  | Gd | VG | Exc | Mt |
|---|---|---|---|---|

(B) With powered A Unit and 212T dummy A Unit in set 19444, tire traction. I.D. Smith and P. Ambrose observations.    **35  50  75  100**

(C) Same as (B) and in same set, but powered unit has black plastic body shell while dummy unit has gray plastic body shell. S. Carlson Collection.

**35  50  75  100**

**216(A) BURLINGTON**  1958, Alco A unit, O-27, silver body with red stripes and lettering; sheet metal frame, front and rear dummy couplers, two-axle Magnetraction, three-position E-unit, light, Type IIE motor, no horn, no weight.    **38  75  100  250**

**216(B) MINNEAPOLIS & ST. LOUIS**  Uncatalogued, lighted, Alco A unit, O-27, gray plastic body painted red, with weight, white lettering, Type IIIA motor, three-position E-unit, open pilot, no front couplers.

**40  75  100  150**

**217 BOSTON & MAINE**  1959, Alco AB units, O-27, letters B and M **only** on unit's side.

(A) Black body with large blue stripe, thin white stripe at roof line, black and white lettering, sheet metal frame, front and rear dummy couplers, two-axle Magnetraction, three-position E-unit, light in A unit, Type IIC motor, Type III pickup, no horn, no weight.    **35  75  100  150**

(B) Same as (A), but blue stripe is teal blue, not the usual sky blue. Some AB pairs do not match colors as a result of this variation, but they are legitimate pairs. G. Halverson and J. Bratspis comments.

**35  75  100  150**

**218 SANTA FE**  1959-63, Alco, O-27, Santa Fe war bonnet passenger paint scheme, silver body with red cab, nose and stripe; yellow and black trim, black lettering, sheet metal frame, front and rear couplers, two-axle Magnetraction, three-position E-unit, light in powered unit, Type IIC motor, Type III pickup, horn, no weight.

(A) Two 218 double A units (Type IIC motors).    **35  50  70  100**

(B) One 218 powered A Unit and one 218C dummy B Unit.

**35  50  70  100**

**218C, 223 SANTA FE**  1963, Alco AB units, O-27, Santa Fe war bonnet passenger paint scheme, silver body with red cab and stripe, yellow and black trim, black lettering, A unit numbered 223; B unit numbered 218, sheet metal frame, front and rear dummy couplers, rubber traction tires on drive wheels, two-position E-unit, light in A unit, horn.    **40  75  100  150**

**219 MISSOURI PACIFIC**  Uncatalogued, c. 1959, Alco AA units, blue with white lettering, sheet metal frame, front and rear dummy couplers, two-axle Magnetraction, two-position E-unit, light in powered unit, Type IIC motor, Type III pickup, no horn, no weight.    **35  50  70  110**

**220 SANTA FE**  1961, Alco A unit, O-27, Santa Fe war bonnet passenger paint scheme, silver body with red cab, nose and stripe, yellow and black trim, black lettering, sheet metal frame, front and rear couplers, three-position E-unit, two-axle Magnetraction light. Corrugated box for power unit. Box for dummy A says "220T Tender". C. Rohlfing and P. Ambrose comments.  Also available with 220T dummy A unit in uncatalogued set X568 in 1960; advance dealer catalogue shows this dummy. P. Ambrose comment. Price for powered A only.    **25  50  70  100**

**221**  Alco A unit, O-27, sheet metal frame, opening where front coupler would be is closed off, dummy coupler on rear, rubber traction tire on one drive wheel, two-position E-unit, no light, Type IVA motor, Type III pickup, no horn, no weight.  Three different locomotives with the same number, as follows:

**221 Rio Grande**  1963-64, yellow with black stripes and lettering.

**20  30  40  60**

**221 U.S. MARINE CORPS**  Uncatalogued, olive drab with white stripes and lettering, two-position E-unit, one-axle Magnetraction.

(A) Light, no weight. Part of uncatalogued set 19334 made for J.C. Penney. P. Ambrose comment.    **60  90  150  200**

(B) Same as (A), but no light. Probably part of uncatalogued set; number and retailer not known. J. Greider Collection.    **60  90  150  200**

**221 SANTA FE,**  Uncatalogued, olive drab with white stripes and lettering, two-position E-unit, tire traction, no light or weight. P. Ambrose comment.    **60  90  150  200**

Top shelf: 225 Chesapeake & Ohio A. Middle shelf: 226 Boston & Maine AAs. Bottom shelf: 227 Canadian National A unit, 228 Canadian National A unit.

**222 Rio Grande** 1962, Alco A unit, O-27, yellow with black stripes and lettering, sheet metal frame, opening where front coupler would be is closed off, dummy coupler on rear, rubber traction tire on one drive wheel, no reverse, light, Type IVA motor, Type III pickup, no horn, no weight.

                                                      15    30    40    60

**223 SANTA FE:** See entry 218C above.

**224 U.S. NAVY** 1960, Alco AB units, O-27, blue body with white lettering, sheet metal frame, front and rear dummy couplers, two-axle Magnetraction, three-position E-unit, light in A unit, Type IIC motor, Type III pickup, no horn, no weight.     40    75    100    150

**225 CHESAPEAKE & OHIO** 1960, Alco A unit, O-27, dark blue with yellow lettering, sheet metal frame, front and rear dummy couplers, two-axle Magnetraction, two-position E-unit, light, Type IIC motor, Type III pickup, no weight.     25    35    50    75

**226 BOSTON & MAINE** Uncatalogued, 1960, only "BM" on sides, Alco AB units, O-27, black body with large blue stripe, thin white stripe at roof line, black and white lettering, sheet metal frame, front and rear dummy couplers, two-axle Magnetraction, three-position E-unit, light in A unit, Type IIC motor, Type III pickup, horn, no weight.   35   60   100   120

**227 CANADIAN NATIONAL** Uncatalogued, 1960, Alco A unit, O-27, green body with yellow trim and lettering, sheet metal frame, opening where front coupler would be is closed off, dummy coupler on rear, no reverse, light, Type IIIA motor, Type III pickup, no horn, made for Canadian market, with weight.   30   45   80   125

**228 CANADIAN NATIONAL** Uncatalogued, 1960, Alco A unit, O-27, green body with yellow trim and lettering, sheet metal frame, front and rear dummy couplers, two-axle Magnetraction, two-position E-unit, light, Type IIC motor, Type III pickup, no horn, made for Canadian market, no weight.   30   45   60   90

**229 MINNEAPOLIS & ST. LOUIS** 1961-62, Alco A unit in 1961 and Alco AB units in 1962, O-27, red body with white stripes and lettering, sheet metal frame and front and rear dummy couplers. A unit has one-axle Magnetraction, two-position E-unit, headlight, Type IIB motor, Type III

pickup, horn, no weight. We do not know if the 1961 A unit differed from the 1962 version. Both have the same catalogue specifications (horn, headlight and Magnetraction), but the 1961 catalogue showed the lettering "M St L" interrupting the side stripe. We do not know if this version was made. Our color photograph shows the 229 as illustrated in the 1962 catalogue. P. Ambrose comment.
(A) A unit only, red body.    25    50    70   100
(B) A and B units.    50    75   100   150
(C) A unit only, olive drab body. Very hard to find. G. Wilson Collection.   125   225   300   500

**230 CHESAPEAKE & OHIO** 1961, Alco A unit, O-27, blue body with yellow stripe and lettering, sheet metal frame, opening where front coupler would be is closed off, dummy coupler on rear, two-axle Magnetraction, two-position E-unit, light, Type IID motor, Type II pickup, no horn.   25   35   50   75

**231 ROCK ISLAND** Alco A unit, 1961-63, O-27, sheet metal frame, front and rear dummy couplers, two-axle Magnetraction, two-position E-unit, light, no horn.
(A) Black body with red middle stripe, white upper stripe and lettering, Type IIA motor, Type III pickup.   35   50   70   100
(B) Same as (A), but without lettering and white upper stripe, motor type not known.   40   60   80   125
(C) 1963, same as (A), but without red stripe, with white upper stripe, Type IIC motor, Type III pickup. Hard to find.   50   75   125   200

**232 NEW HAVEN** 1962, Alco A unit, O-27, orange body with black stripe and black and white lettering, sheet metal frame, opening where front coupler would be is closed off, dummy coupler on rear, Magnetraction, two-position E-unit, light, Type IIE motor, Type II pickup, no horn, no weight, came with set 11232. P. Ambrose comment.   25   30   50   75

**400 BALTIMORE AND OHIO** 1956-58, Budd RDC passenger car, silver body with blue lettering, operating couplers at both ends, Magnetraction, three-position E-unit, lights, horn, single motor.   100   150   175   250

Top shelf: 229 Missouri Pacific AB. Middle shelf: 230 Chesapeake & Ohio A, 231 Rock Island A. Bottom shelf: 1055 Texas Special A, 1065 Union Pacific A.

                    **Gd  VG  Exc  Mt**

**404 BALTIMORE AND OHIO** 1957-58, Budd RDC baggage — mail car, silver body with blue lettering, operating couplers at both ends, Magnetraction, three-position E-unit, single motor, light, horn.

                   **100  175  200  300**

**The 520 Box Cab electric had a prototype! It was a General Electric locomotive built for the Chile Exploration Company. R. Lord Collection.**

**520 LIONEL LINES** Box Cab Electric, 1956-57, GE 80 ton, 0-4-2, O-27, red body with white lettering "LIONEL LINES", sheet metal frame, single pantograph, dummy coupler on one end, operating coupler on the other end, three-position E-unit, no light, no horn, check pantograph for damage. Similar body used for 3535 Security Car, part No. 520-5, and on the Fundimensions Laser Train Security Car of 1983. However, the original 520 cab is wider and higher than on the Security and Laser cars, and there is no extension of the roof line on the 520 cab. This locomotive is a very close model of a boxcab electric engine sold by General Electric to the Chilean Exploration Company for use in its copper mines. The Lionel model is surprisingly accurate, right down to the air tanks atop the cab and the

portholes. The Lionel number 520 was in the same range as the 523 shown on the illustrated prototype. F. Grittani, J. Notine and R. Young comments.

| | Gd | VG | Exc | Mt |
|---|---|---|---|---|
| (A) Black pantograph. | 28 | 48 | 65 | 85 |
| (B) Copper-colored pantograph. | 28 | 48 | 75 | 90 |

See also Factory Errors.

**NW-2 SWITCHERS**

**600 MKT** 1955, NW-2 Switcher, O-27, red body with white lettering, sheet metal frame, operating couplers at both ends, one-axle Magnetraction, three-position E-unit, no light, Type IID motor, Type II pickup, no horn.
(A) Black frame with black end rails, Type IID motor.    50  75  100  150
(B) Gray frame with yellow end rails, Type IIE motor, Type II pickup. Much easier to find in the Midwest and on the West Coast than on the East Coast. This is probably because the earliest production runs were sent the farthest distance from the factory to assure relatively uniform release times for an item. When there was a change in production very early, the items made before the change could be found more quickly in the Midwest and West. Another example of this phenomenon is the 3562-50 yellow operating barrel car with a gray body painted yellow, which is also easier to find in the western sections of the country. T. Rollo and R. LaVoie comments.

                  **60  90  125  175**

(C) Gray frame with black end rails, Type IID motor, Type II pickup. Lower Collection.          **NRS**
(D) Same as (A), but Type IIE motor with two-axle Magnetraction. A. Arpino Collection.         **50  75  100  150**

**601 SEABOARD** 1956, NW-2 Switcher, black and red body with red stripes and white lettering, black sheet metal frame, operating couplers at both ends, two-axle Magnetraction, three-position E-unit, no light, Type IIE motor, Type II pickup, horn.   **50  75  100  150**

**602 SEABOARD** 1957-58, NW-2 Switcher, O-27, black and red body with red stripes and white lettering, sheet metal frames, dummy couplers at both ends, two-axle Magnetraction, three-position E-unit, light, Type IIE motor, Type II pickup, horn. Differs from 601 in its operating headlight and dummy couplers.       **50  75  100  150**

There are three different versions of the 2023 Union Pacific. First shelf: 2023 Union Pacific in silver. Second shelf: yellow and gray with yellow nose. Third shelf: yellow and gray with gray nose. Fourth shelf: a 2033 AA unit in silver. L. Nuzzaci and R. Lord Collections.

**610 ERIE** 1955, NW-2 Switcher, black body, yellow lettering, operating couplers, axle Magnetraction, three-position E unit, light, Type IIE motor, Type II pickup, no horn.

| | | | | |
|---|---|---|---|---|
| (A) Black frame. | 50 | 75 | 100 | 150 |
| (B) Yellow frame. Lebo Collection. | | | | NRS |
| (C) Same as (A), but no light. Lahti Collection. | 50 | 75 | 100 | 150 |
| (D) Same as (B), but no light. Giroux Collection. | | | | NRS |

(E) Same as (A), but early production with two-axle Magnetraction, no light, reportedly only a few thousand made, Yeckel observation. We do not know if this is the same as (C). **NRS**
(F) Black frame, no light, mold part 600-3 with raised number board on side of shell, as on 621 Jersey Central, but no lettering on number board. Reportedly a 1956 factory replacement cab. J. Algozzini Collection. **NRS**

**611 JERSEY CENTRAL** 1957-58, NW-2 Switcher, O-27, orange and blue body with blue and white lettering, sheet metal frame, one-axle Magnetraction, three-position E-unit, light, Type IID motor, Type II pickup, no horn.

| | | | | |
|---|---|---|---|---|
| (A) Dummy couplers front and rear. Weiss Collection. | 50 | 75 | 100 | 150 |
| (B) Dummy coupler on front, operating coupler on rear. Confirmation requested. Possible service repair. | 50 | 75 | 100 | 150 |

**613 UNION PACIFIC** 1958, NW-2 Switcher, O-27, yellow with gray hood top and cab roof, red lettering, "ROAD OF THE STREAMLINERS", sheet metal frame, dummy couplers, both ends, Magnetraction, three-position E-unit, light, Type IIE motor, Type II pickup, no horn, bell.

| | | | | |
|---|---|---|---|---|
| (A) Non-operating couplers. | 75 | 100 | 150 | 225 |
| (B) Operating couplers. A. Arpino Collection. | 75 | 100 | 150 | 225 |

(C) "ROAD OF THE STREAMLINERS" on right side of cab when observer faces front, "SERVES ALL THE WEST" on left side, "NEW 7-58" near nose, two-axle Magnetraction, ornamental horn. S. Carlson Collection.

| | | | |
|---|---|---|---|
| | 75 | 100 | 150 | 225 |

**614 ALASKA** 1959-60, NW-2 Switcher, O-27, blue body with yellow-orange lettering, yellow dynamic brake superstructure on top of motor hood, sheet metal frame, dummy couplers at both ends, one-axle Magnetraction, two-position E-unit, light, Type IIG motor, Type II pickup, no horn, appears to be the only example of IIG motor.

(A) No dynamic brake unit, Niedhammer observation. This is a legitimate variation, not a simple omission. This version came with a plastic bell situated in such a way that the dynamic brake unit could not be installed. P. Catalano observation.

| | | | | |
|---|---|---|---|---|
| | 50 | 75 | 100 | 150 |
| (B) With yellow dynamic brake unit atop hood. | 75 | 100 | 150 | 225 |

**616 SANTA FE** 1961-62, NW-2 Switcher, black body with black and white safety stripes front and rear, white lettering, operating horn uses one C-size battery, decorative horn and bell are omitted, sheet metal frame, three-position E-unit, light. On some bodies, the holes for the ornamental horn and bell are plugged, and on some they are not. A. Arpino comments.

(A) 1961, dummy couplers, Type IID motor, Type II pickup, came with set 2570. The 1961 catalogue and the Service Manual (Greenberg printing, Chapter II, p. 175) indicate that this unit had dummy couplers. C. Rohlfing Collection.

| | | | |
|---|---|---|---|
| | 75 | 100 | 150 | 200 |

(B) 1962, operating couplers, Type IID motor, Type II pickup, came with set 13018. The 1962 catalogue clearly shows this locomotive with operating

All five center cab diesels are shown above. On the top shelf are the red and black 625 Lehigh Valley and 624 Baltimore & Ohio. The second shelf has the all red 627 Lehigh Valley and the 628 Northern Pacific. The lowest shelf has the 629 Burlington diesel. Nuzzaci Collection.

**Gd VG Exc Mt**

couplers on page 19, but the Service Manual in (A) above did not cover 1962 production. A. Arpino Collection. **75 100 150 200**

(C) 1962, late: dummy couplers, no marker lights or radio antenna, two-axle Magnetraction, chromed ornamental bell instead of black; probably a transitional piece between the 616 and the 617. R. Harbina Collection.

**60 80 125 180**

**617 SANTA FE** 1963, NW-2 Switcher, black body with black and white safety stripes front and rear, white lettering, sheet metal frame, operating couplers both ends, dummy horn, bell and radio antenna trim pieces, two-axle Magnetraction, marker lights, headlight lens, three-position E-unit, light, Type IIE motor, Type II pickup, horn. A. Arpino and P. Ambrose comments.

(A) Early sheet metal frame. A. Arpino Collection, P. Ambrose comment.

**75 100 150 225**

(B) Same as (A), but Type IID motor with one-axle Magnetraction. A. Arpino Collection. **75 100 150 225**

(C) Same as (B), but late sheet metal frame. A. Arpino comment.

**75 100 150 225**

**621 JERSEY CENTRAL** 1956-57, NW-2 Switcher, O-27, blue body with orange lettering, sheet metal frame, operating couplers at both ends, one-axle Magnetraction, three-position E-unit, no light, Type IID motor, Type II pickup, horn.

(A) Royal blue plastic body, part no. 600-3. J. Algozzini Collection.

**40 60 100 140**

(B) Same as (A), but navy blue plastic body. J. Algozzini Collection.

**40 60 100 140**

**622 SANTA FE** 1949-50, not catalogued as Santa Fe. Catalogued but never made as Lionel (1949) and New York Central (1950), NW-2 Switcher, first Magnetraction engine, black body with white lettering, die-cast frame, coil-operated couplers at both ends, three-position E-unit, light both ends, Type I motor, Type I pickup, no horn, operating bell, excellent runner, 6220 is similar except numbered for O-27. Magnetraction feature of 1949 models

is often demagnetized and undetectable. 1950 models feature changed design.

(A) 1949, large GM decal on cab. **90 125 175 250**

(B) 1950, small GM decal on lower front side of motor hood, no weight in cab. **75 100 150 200**

(C) 1950 late, same as (B), but weight cast in cab frame.

**75 100 150 200**

(D) "LIONEL" not "SANTA FE", catalogued in 1949 but not made for production; only one example ever observed. See Factory Errors and Prototypes chapter. **Not Manufactured**

(E) "NEW YORK CENTRAL" not "SANTA FE", catalogued in 1950 but not made. **Not Manufactured**

See also Factory Errors and Prototypes.

**623 SANTA FE** 1952-54, NW-2 Switcher, O-27, black body with white lettering, die-cast frame, coil-operating couplers at both ends, Magnetraction, three-position E-unit, Type I motor, Type I pickup, no horn, excellent runner. Suggestion has been made that color variations in the decals are entirely due to aging, since blue is particularly susceptible to fading. Reader comments invited. Weisskopf comment.

(A) Ten stanchions hold handrail to side. **50 75 100 150**
(B) Three stanchions hold handrail to side. **50 75 100 150**

**624 CHESAPEAKE & OHIO** 1952-54, NW-2 Switcher, O-27, blue body with yellow stripe and lettering, die-cast frame, coil-operating couplers at both ends, Magnetraction, three-position E-unit, lights, at both ends, Type I pickup, no horn, excellent runner. Hard to find with yellow stripe and decaled lettering intact.

(A) Ten stanchions hold handrail to side. **75 100 150 225**
(B) Three stanchions hold handrail to side. **75 100 150 225**

(C) Same as (A), but number 624 is centered on the cab side and no round C & O decal is present. Possibly, this cab was mismarked at the factory and no room was left for the decal. M. Drousche Collection. **NRS**

**625 LEHIGH VALLEY** 1957-58, GE 44-ton switcher, O-27, red and black body with white stripe and lettering, black sheet metal frame, dummy

Top shelf: 222 Rio Grande, 2024 Chesapeake & Ohio. Middle shelf: 224 United States Navy A and B units. Bottom shelf: 219 Missouri Pacific. L. Nuzzaci Collection.

couplers at both ends, one-axle Magnetraction, three-position E-unit, light, Type IID motor, Type II pickup, no horn. All other centercab switchers had operating couplers. P. Ambrose comments. Possibly modeled after a 77-ton centercab switcher sold by General Electric to the Chilean State Railways in 1949. R. Young comment. **50 90 130 165**

**626 BALTIMORE AND OHIO** 1959, GE 44-ton center-cab switcher, blue body, yellow lettering and frame, Type II D motor with one-axle Magnetraction, headlight, Type II pickup, three-position E Unit, no horn, disc-operating couplers, O-27. H. Powell Collection, I.D. Smith observation. **75 125 175 250**

**627 LV** 1956-57, GE 44- ton switcher, O-27, Lehigh Valley paint scheme, red body with white stripe and lettering, black sheet metal frame, operating couplers at both ends, three-position E-unit, no light, Type IID motor, Type II pickup, no horn.
(A) One-axle Magnetraction. **40 60 90 120**
(B) Two-axle Magnetraction; I.D. Smith comment. The Service Manual lists this locomotive as having only one-axle Magnetraction. One reporter who has examined hundreds of 627 and 628 engines reports that 99 out of 100 pieces are found with one-axle Magnetraction, but a few two-axle versions exist. Lionel may have misassembled a few of these locomotives, or in a post-factory repair, a different motor was substituted. We find it remarkable how consistent the factory was in its production, considering the vast number of pieces produced, and how few inappropriate repairs have been performed by Service Stations. That fact speaks well for the excellence of the Service Manual itself. **40 60 90 120**

**628 NORTHERN PACIFIC** 1956-57, GE 44 ton Switcher, O-27, black body with yellow stripe, yellow sheet metal frame, operating couplers at both ends, one-axle Magnetraction, three-position E-unit, light, Type IID motor, Type II pickup, no horn. See previous entry for note about examples with two-axle Magnetraction. **35 45 75 100**

**629 BURLINGTON** 1956, GE 44 ton Switcher, O-27, silver body with red stripe and lettering, sheet metal frame, operating couplers at both ends, one-axle Magnetraction, three-position E-unit, light, Type IID motor, Type II pickup, no horn. The silver finish on most pieces is not attractive. Hence a substantial premium for excellent and better.
(A) Black sheet metal frame. **75 125 200 300**
(B) Red sheet metal frame; same paint color as used on 2328 GP-7. E. Zukowski Collection. **75 125 200 300**

**633 SANTA FE** 1962, NW-2 Switcher, O-27, blue body with blue and yellow safety stripes and yellow lettering, sheet metal frame, dummy coupler on rear only, two-position E-unit, light but no lens on light, Type IVA motor, Type III pickup, no horn, traction tires. **40 75 95 150**

**634 SANTA FE** 1963, 1965-66, NW-2 Switcher, O-27, blue body with yellow lettering, sheet metal frame, plastic dummy front coupler, metal dummy rear coupler, two-position E-unit, light, Type IVA motor, Type III pickup, no horn.
(A) 1963, 1965, yellow and blue safety stripes on front of motor hood and on cab, with lens. **25 40 60 100**
(B) 1966, same as (A), but no safety stripes, without lens.
**25 40 60 100**
(C) 1970, very early MPC, used old Lionel number. No safety stripes, but lens. Silver plastic bell and silver plastic brake wheel. Red end marker lights. Listed here for user's convenience. **15 20 40 50**

**635 UNION PACIFIC** 1965, uncatalogued, NW-2 Switcher, O-27, yellow plastic body painted yellow, red striping and trim, red "NEW 7-58", white "U.P." and "635" on front of cab, no bell, no horn, Type IVA motor, Type III pickup, light but no headlight lens, dummy couplers front and rear, weight on underside of hood, came in 1965 uncatalogued set 19440. P. Ambrose and Niedhammer observations. **30 50 70 125**

See also Factory Errors and Prototypes.

**645 UNION PACIFIC** 1969, NW-2 Switcher, O-27, black frame, yellow unpainted plastic body with red heat-stamped lettering and stripes, weight attached to hood underside, headlight with lens, two-position reverse, two fixed couplers, Type IVB motor, Type III pickup.  **30  50  70  110**
See also Factory Errors and Prototypes.

**1055 TEXAS SPECIAL** 1959-60, not shown in the consumer catalogue but listed as part of a special set "To meet the needs of the low-price mass toy market" in the 1959 and 1960 Advance Catalogues. In 1959, it was described as No. 1105 Texas Special set and in 1960 as the No. 1107 Sportsman Diesel set. Although the 1959 catalogue illustrated unnumbered cars such as a 6014-type short boxcar, a short single-dome tank car, an SP-type caboose and a 6012-type short gondola with canisters, W. F. Spence reports that the set came with the following numbered and lettered cars: 6045 two-dome tank car, 6044 Airex blue boxcar, 6042 black short gondola and a 6047 red SP caboose. The set also included an 1105-10 instruction sheet dated 8-59, a 1026 25-watt transformer, an 1103-11 envelope with wires, lubricant and CTC lockon and track. The set box was labelled "THE TEXAS SPECIAL/LIONEL/MADE BY THE LIONEL CORPORATION' with a drawing of a train, a cowboy on a horse, a mountain and cactus. On one side is a picture showing directions "to display, fold box top as shown."This box, which has a carrying handle built in, says "complete and ready to run,'although there is no apparent space in the box for the track! The items are not individually boxed, but there are inserts to separate them. In 1960, it was shown with an unnumbered 6042 black gondola with two canisters, a 6044 teal blue AIREX boxcar and unnumbered 6047 caboose. C. Rohlfing Collection. We hope that our readers will verify this information. The locomotive is an Alco A unit, O-27, red body with white lettering, sheet metal frame, opening where front coupler would be is closed off, dummy coupler on rear, no Magnetraction or rubber tires, no reverse, Type IIIA motor, no horn, light and weight. At this time, Lionel apparently felt that such "stripped-down units", because of their low quality, did not belong in their regular line and would reflect badly on the line. Yet, paradoxically, the mass marketers could readily sell these in quantity because of their obvious low price (probably $15 or less) while trading on the Lionel Line's quality reputation. Unfortunately, consumers got what they paid for and the Lionel Corporation's reputation for quality declined. Mr. Spence, however, reports that his example runs well, even though it is clearly a basic model. W. Spence comments. Alco A unit, O-27, red body with white lettering, sheet metal frame, opening where front coupler would be is closed off, dummy coupler on rear, no Magnetraction or rubber tires, no reverse, Type IIIA motor, no horn, light with weight. W. Spence Collection.  **15  25  40  75**

**1065 UNION PACIFIC** 1961, uncatalogued, Alco A unit, O-27, yellow body with red lettering and red stripe, sheet metal frame, opening where front coupler would be is closed off, dummy coupler on rear, no Magnetraction, no traction tires, no reverse, Type IIIA motor, Type III pickup, no horn, with weight.
(A) With light.  **15  25  40  75**
(B) No light. I.D. Smith observation.  **15  25  40  75**

**1066 UNION PACIFIC** 1964, uncatalogued, Alco A unit, O-27, yellow body with red stripe and lettering, sheet metal frame, opening where front coupler would be is closed off, dummy coupler on rear, no Magnetraction, no reverse, Type IVA motor, Type III pickup, no horn or weight.
**15  25  40  75**

**2023 UNION PACIFIC** 1950-51, Alco AA units, 0-27, die-cast frame, coil-operated couplers on cab ends, dummy middle couplers, Magnetraction, three-position E-unit, light in both units, Type I motor, Type I pickup, horn, excellent runner.
(A) 1950, yellow body with gray roof and frame, red stripes and lettering.
**50  75  120  200**
(B) 1950, same as (A), but black plastic body shell painted yellow, gray nose, gray-painted truck side frames. H. Powell Collection.
**300  650  900  1500**
(C) 1951, silver body and frame with black stripes and lettering, gray roof. Silver paint susceptible to mildew; mildew can be cleaned. Caution is recommended.  **65  95  150  250**
**NOTE:** The Anniversary Set from the year 1950 consisted of the 2023 Union Pacific Alco AA with the yellow and gray paint scheme and a gray

nose top, the 2481 Plainfield coach, the 2482 Westfield coach and the 2483 Livingston observation car. Other versions came with yellow-nosed locomotive. The gray-nosed 2023 represents the earliest stage of this locomotive's production and was supposedly included only with the Anniversary Set. However, some collectors maintain that a few gray-nosed 2023 Alcos were either sold separately or came with the freight set. In any case, this set is highly prized by collectors. C. Rohlfing and H. Powell comments.

**2024 CHESAPEAKE & OHIO** 1969, Alco A unit, O-27, blue body with yellow stripe and lettering, sheet metal frame, front and rear dummy couplers, one rubber traction tire, two-position E-unit, light, Type IVB motor, Type IV pickup, no horn or weight.  **15  25  35  60**

**2028 PENNSYLVANIA** 1955, GP-7 Road Switcher, O-27, tuscan body, light in cab end only. Rather Spartan design; no horn, no fuel tank below frame, no windshield, no number boards or headlight lenses, no ornamental horn. H. Powell and P. Ambrose comments.
**NOTE:** Some cabs have been relettered. Execellent and above must be original to bring prices noted.
(A) Yellow rubber-stamped lettering, riveted railing.  **90  150  250  350**
(B) Yellow rubber-stamped lettering, welded railing, rivet holes.
**90  150  250  350**
(C) Gold rubber-stamped lettering, welded rails, no rivet holes. H. Powell Collection.  **80  140  225  325**
(D) Welded rails, tan frame. P. Catalano, H. Powell and J. Algozzini Collections.  **125  200  300  450**

**2028 UNION PACIFIC** 1955 GP-7, shown in Advance Catalogue, but not manufactured.  **NRS**

**2031 ROCK ISLAND** 1952-54, Alco AA units, O-27, black body with white stripe and lettering, red middle stripe, die-cast frame, coil-operated couplers on cab ends, dummy middle couplers, Magnetraction, three-position E-unit, light in both units, Type I motor, Type I pickup, horn, excellent runner.
**75  120  200  300**

**2032 ERIE** 1952-54, Alco AA units, O-27, black body with yellow stripes and lettering, die-cast frame, coil-operated couplers on cab ends, dummy middle couplers, Magnetraction, three-position E-unit, light in both units, Type I motor, Type I pickup, horn, excellent runner.  **70  95  125  175**

**2033 UNION PACIFIC** 1952-54, Alco AA units, O-27, silver body and frame with black lettering, die-cast frame, coil-operated couplers on cab ends, dummy middle couplers, Magnetraction, three-position E-unit, light in both units, Type I motor, Type I pickup, horn, excellent runner. Very hard to obtain in excellent or better condition because the silver paint is highly susceptible to mildew. R. LaVoie comment.
(A) Smooth roof over motor.  **60  100  150  225**
(B) Dime-sized round bump over motor.  **60  100  150  225**

**2041 ROCK ISLAND** 1969, Alco AA units, O-27, black body with white stripe and lettering, red middle stripe, sheet metal frame, front and rear dummy couplers, light, Type IIB motor, Type IIIB pickup, two-position E-unit, no horn, with weight, catalogued with nose emblem but production pieces lack emblem.  **40  60  90  125**

See also Factory Errors.

**2240 WABASH** 1956, F-3 AB units, O-27, gray and blue body with white side panels and trim, yellow heat-stamped lettering (silk-screened on reproduction cabs), blue frame with black trucks, louvered roof vents, filled-in portholes, operating coupler on front of A unit, all other couplers are dummies, Magnetraction, three-position E-unit, light in A unit, single vertical motor, horn.  **200  250  325  425**

**2242 NEW HAVEN** 1958-59, F-3 AB units, checkerboard paint scheme, silver roof and frame, black nose, white, silver and orange sides, as shown in the 1958 catalogue; lettering heat-stamped on nose and sides (silk-screened lettering on sides and nose decal on reproduction cabs), silver frame with black pilot and trucks, louvered roof vent, filled-in portholes, operating coupler on front of A unit, all others are dummies, Magnetraction, three-position E-unit, light in A unit, single vertical motor, horn, often referred to as an O-27 engine because of its single motor, although it is shown only as a Super 0 engine in the catalogue. Reissued by Fundimensions as a twin-motored 8851-8852 AA pair in 1978. H. Powell and R. Hutchinson comments.  **175  250  350  475**

**GP-7S. Top shelf: 2028 Pennsylvania. Middle shelf: 2328 Burlington. Bottom shelf: 2337 Wabash. L. Nuzzaci Collection.**

**2243 SANTA FE** 1955-57, F-3 AB units, O-27 and 0, Santa Fe war bonnet passenger paint scheme, silver body with red cab, nose and stripe, yellow and black trim, black heat-stamped lettering, silver frame with black trucks, louvered roof vent, filled-in portholes, operating coupler on front of A unit, all other couplers are dummies, Magnetraction, three-position E-unit, light in A unit, single vertical motor, horn. This unit is often referred to as an 0-27 engine due to its single motor and its O-27 listing in 1955-56 but in 1957 it was catalogued in 0 Gauge only.         **75    125    175    250**

**2243C SANTA FE** 1955-57, F-3 B unit, came as part of 2243 and not catalogued separately; it matches 2383 AA units for which no B was made.

         **45    60    80    140**

**2245 TEXAS SPECIAL** 1954-55, F-3 AB units, O-27, red body and pilot with white lower panel and silver frame and trucks. This engine had the distinction of being the first O-27 version of the F-3. As such, it had only one motor. It was given a prominent location on page 10 of the 1954 catalogue, but in 1955 its image was sharply reduced compared to the 2243 Santa Fe. We know that this locomotive is mostly found with silver-painted trucks, but we also have several reports of this locomotive with black trucks. We also have reports of two different motors: the older horizontally-mounted unit and the later vertically-mounted unit. Finally, we note that the 1955 catalogue speaks of a "newly designed worm-geared motor..." It would appear that in 1955, Lionel put some Texas Special bodies on some black-truck Santa Fe chassis. The black-truck version is always found with

the later vertical motor. (P. Catalano comments). In addition, certain body shell changes may have occurred between 1954 and 1955, including the elimination of the portholes as separate pieces and the replacement of the two-piece ornamental horn by a one-piece die-cast unit. The B unit was produced both ways. Decor includes white star on A unit nose and combination Frisco/MKT decal on both sides of A unit near front door. The earlier version of this locomotive is the only O-27 F-3 ever made with open ports and ladders on the cab doors. C. Rohlfing, I.D. Smith, H. Powell and D. Orsello comments.

(A) 1954, cabs with portholes and two-piece ornamental horns; silver-painted frame and trucks, red pilot, horizontal motor.    **100    175    250    350**

(B) 1955, cabs without portholes and with one-piece die-cast ornamental horns; chassis with black-painted trucks, silver-painted pilots and vertically-mounted motor. M. Harrigan, D. Orsello and O'Brien Collections, P. Catalano, I.D. Smith and C. Rohlfing observations. (Orsello example missing star decal on nose; factory omission. More common in Midwestern states than in other areas, indicating that most of the 1955 production run was sent to that area.            **100    175    250    350**

**2321 LACKAWANNA** 1954-56, FM Trainmaster, gray body with yellow trim and maroon mid-stripe and lettering, side trim stripe and lettering are rubber-stamped, two operating couplers, Magnetraction, three-position E-unit, light both ends, twin vertical motors, horn, excellent runner. NOTE: Original cabs without screw cracks at the cab ends are hard to find and carry

Top shelf: 2321 Lackawanna FM Trainmaster with maroon top. Middle shelf: 2321 Lackawanna with gray top. Bottom shelf: 2341 Jersey Central. L. Nuzzaci Collection.

<table>
<tr><td></td><td>Gd</td><td>VG</td><td>Exc</td><td>Mt</td></tr>
</table>

a slight price premium. "Excellent" condition in our Fairbanks-Morse listings assumes crack-free cabs. C. Rohlfing and H. Powell comments. Battery cover plate has instructions stamped into plate. This continued to some early production black Virginian FMs. Then the instructions were printed on a sticker which was afixed to a blank battery cover plate.

(A) Factory prototype shown on cover of 1954 Lionel Advance Catalogue, screens on roof vent, very elaborate paint scheme. L. Shempp Collection.

$$\text{NRS}$$

(B) 1954, early: reddish-maroon roof and striping with interior lights mounted horizontally on a riveted bracket shaped like an inverted "L". M. Ocilka Collection.                    200  300  400  550

(C) 1954, later: dull maroon roof and striping, interior lights mounted vertically on riveted bracket which is just an upright piece. M. Ocilka Collection.                    200  275  375  500

(D) Same as (C), but roof ventilators are left unpainted, resulting in a maroon roof with gray ventilators. T. Budniak Collection.

200  275  375  500

(D) 1955-56, gray roof and body.                    175  225  300  425

**2322 VIRGINIAN** 1965-66, FM Trainmaster, operating couplers at both ends, Magnetraction, three-position E-unit, light at both ends, twin vertical motors, horn, excellent runner.

(A) Orange-yellow body with blue stripe and roof.    215  275  350  475

(B) Yellow body with black stripe. Question as to existence. Confirmation requested.                    **NRS**

(C) Same as (A), but decal number and logo on cab sides under windows rather than on both ends. P. Ambrose comment.    215  275  350  475

**2328 BURLINGTON** 1955-56, GP-7 Road Switcher, O-27, silver body with black lettering, red frame and handrails, lettering and emblem rubber-stamped, operating couplers both ends, Magnetraction, three-position E-unit, light at both ends, horn. Excellent condition assumes fresh-looking silver paint, which does not hold up very well on this engine.

80  125  200  300

**2329 VIRGINIAN** 1958-59, GE E33 or EL-C Rectifier electric, blue body with yellow stripe, lettering, handrail and frame, heat-stamped, single metal pantograph, operating couplers both ends, Magnetraction, three-position E-unit, light both ends, single vertical motor, pickup, horn, wiring easily adapted for overhead catenary operation, illustrated on page 69.

150  225  325  475

**2330 PENNSYLVANIA** 1950, GG-1 Electric, green with five gold stripes and red Keystone decal, five stripes rubber-stamped, twin metal pantographs, coil-operated couplers at both ends, Magnetraction, three-position E-unit, light at both ends, twin vertical motors, horn, wiring easily changed for overhead catenary operation, excellent runner.    225  325  450  650

**2331 VIRGINIAN** 1955-58, FM Trainmaster, rubber-stamped lettering and end crisscross (silk-screened on reproduction bodies), operating couplers at both ends, Magnetraction, three-position E-unit, light at both ends, twin vertical motors, horn, excellent runner.

(A) 1955, yellow-painted gray plastic body with black stripe and gold lettering. R. Shanfeld comment.    300  400  600  900

**Top shelf: 2331(A) Virginian FM Trainmaster, black/yellow. Middle shelf: 2322(A) Virginian, blue/yellow. Bottom shelf: 2331(B) Virginian, blue/yellow.**

(B) 1956-58, yellow-painted blue plastic body with blue stripe and yellow lettering. R. Shanfeld comment.                275 350 425 600

(C) 1957, yellow-painted gray plastic body with dull stripe and yellow lettering. R. Shanfeld comment.                300 375 450 700

**2332 PENNSYLVANIA** 1947-49, GG-1 Electric, five stripes rubber-stamped, twin metal pantographs, operating couplers both ends, no Magnetraction, three-position E-unit, light at both ends, single angle-mounted motor, harsh-sounding AC vibrator box horn, wiring easily adapted for overhead catenary operation, hard to find with stripes and lettering in good condition (silk-screened on reproduction bodies).

(A) Semi-gloss black body with "silver" stripes (see GG-1 article for discussion), Keystone is rubber-stamped very indistinctly on sides, red and gold 2332 Keystones at ends, rubber-stamped stripes typically smudged at ends of locomotive. Example observed came in box marked with 1947 dating and instruction sheet dated 12-47. Very hard to find. J. Bratspis Collection.                350 425 650 1000

(B) Same as (A), but flat black body paint.                350 425 650 1000

(C) Same as (A), but striping is regular gold variety instead of faded "silver". This may be the version previously listed as "very dark green, almost black".                250 350 600 900

(D) Semi-gloss dark green body with gold stripes, Keystone decal. This is the most common of the 2332 locomotives.                150 250 275 350

(E) Gloss Brunswick green body, gold rubber-stamped lettering and stripes, red and gold Keystone decals on ends but rubber-stamped Keystones on sides, red motor brushplates instead of the usual black. See photographs above. D and S. Erich Collections.                200 275 350 450

(F) Gloss Brunswick green body, no lettering or striping (or even evidence of it), large stick-on red and gold PRR Keystone with thin letters pasted to sides of cab. J. Whittam Collection.                **NRS**

**2333** F-3 AA units, 1948-49, screened roof vent, open portholes with lenses, grab-irons on nose, ladder on cab door, coil-operated couplers on cab ends, dummy middle couplers, no Magnetraction, three-position E-unit, light in both units, twin horizontal motors, horn.

(A) **SANTA FE** Santa Fe war bonnet passenger paint scheme, silver body with red cab, nose and stripe, yellow and black trim, black heat-stamped lettering (earliest production was rubber-stamped), celluloid porthole windows often missing, silver frame and trucks.                90 150 200 300

(B) **NEW YORK CENTRAL:** dark gray body with gray center stripe outlined with white trim, rubber-stamped trim, heat-stamped lettering, red and white GM decal on rear side door, gray frame and trucks. This item is catalogued as #2333 but it is referred to in the service manual as #2334; since the engine number-boards show 2333 we use that number.
                100 175 250 350

(C) 1948, same as (B), but rubber-stamped lettering larger in size than later production.                100 175 250 400

(D) Same as (B), but GM decal is black and white. E. Schwartzel and D. Embser Collections.                100 175 250 350

(E) **SANTA FE:** clear unpainted plastic body with Santa Fe nose decal and red and white GM decal. This very scarce variation was used for display purposes and may have come with a display track which would allow the locomotive to "run" without actually moving. Reader confirmation requested, especially concerning the special display track and mechanism involved. C. Weber Collection and comments.                **NRS**

The 2332 GG1 was first produced by Lionel in 1947 and usually came with a black brushplate. In 1946 Lionel manufactured some 726 steam locomotives with red, "LIONEL ATOMIC MOTOR" brushplates. Obviously some of these red brushplates were available for early 1947 GG1 production. We have located two of the red brushplate versions in Milwaukee. T. Rollo comments. D. and S. Erich Collections, B. Kojis photograph.

A closeup of the red brushplate on a GG1. D and S Erich Collections, B. Kojis photograph.

|  | Gd | VG | Exc | Mt |
|---|---|---|---|---|

(F) Same as (A), but black-painted body where silver color usually is present; shown this way in 1948 catalogue but not made. Since many 2333s had black plastic bodies, the prototype photographed for the catalogue was probably black unpainted plastic. M. Ocilka comment. **Not Manufactured**

(G) Same as (E), no striping on side, paste-on road name on side. Lower Collection.      —    —    —    750

(H) Same as (A), but red and white GM decals are above "BUILT BY LIONEL" at rear of cab, not on rear side doors, rubber-stamped Santa Fe lettering. We would appreciate reader ownership reports so we can evaluate how common or rare this version is. According to one report, only 500 examples were produced this way in early 1948. However, the number of reports we have gotten suggests that this variety is not as scarce as that, though it is certainly less common than (A). J. Breslin, B. Michel, Uptegraft, M.A. Brooks and J. Algozzini Collections.   100   175   250   350

**2333C** F-3B unit not made but a 2343C looks like it.    **Not Manufactured**

**2334** Number listed in Service Manual for 2333(B).

**2337 WABASH** 1958, GP-7 Road Switcher, O-27, blue and gray body with white stripes and lettering, black frame and handrails, heat-stamped lettering (silk-screened on reproduction bodies), Magnetraction, three-position E-unit, light at both ends, horn. A. Arpino comment.

(A) Dummy couplers at both ends.    90   140   225   300

(B) Operating couplers at both ends, purchased new in 1959. Probably late 1958 production. A. Arpino comment.    90   140   225   300

**2338 MILWAUKEE** 1955-56, GP-7 Road Switcher, catalogued as both 0 and 0-27, black and orange body with white and/or black lettering, black frame and handrails, operating couplers at both ends, Magnetraction, three-position E-unit, light at each end, horn.

(A) Orange translucent plastic shell that is painted black, unpainted orange band goes completely around shell, decal does not adhere well to orange shell, the orange plastic of the shell is very shiny, black lettering; believed to have been made for Sears. Only 100 examples reported to exist. C. Weber comment, O. Anderson Collection.   500   800   1100   1500

(B) Orange translucent plastic shell that is painted black both inside and out, orange band goes as far as cab and starts again after cab, black lettering on orange band, white lettering on black area.

      100   150   225   300

(C) Black plastic shell painted with dull orange band that goes as far as cab and starts again after cab, black lettering on orange band, white lettering on black area. Orange paint much more true to prototype's paint scheme than

unpainted orange examples. Black areas of shell also painted flat black. Somewhat hard to find. J. Bratspis Collection.   100   175   250   350

(D) Same as (C), but "BUILT BY LIONEL" missing from orange stripe and Milwaukee logo on cab is white on black background. W. Heid Collection.

                                   **NRS**

**2339 WABASH** 1957, GP-7 Road Switcher, blue and gray body with white stripes and lettering, black frame and handrails, heat-stamped lettering (silk-screened on reproduction cabs, operating couplers at both ends, Magnetraction, three-position E-unit, light at both ends.

      90   140   225   350

**2340 PENNSYLVANIA** 1955, GG-1, Electric, five gold stripes, red Keystone decal, stripe rubber-stamped, lettering heat-stamped, two metal pantographs, coil-operated couplers at both ends, Magnetraction, three-position E-unit, light at both ends, twin vertical motors, horn, wiring easily changed for overhead catenary operation, excellent runner. For the full

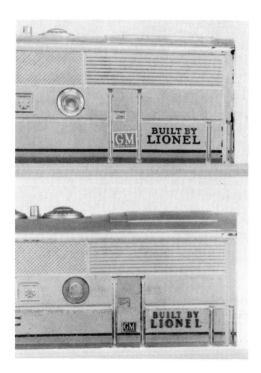

Two versions of the GM decal — large on top and small on bottom. R. Vagner Collection. G. Stern photograph.

Top shelf: 2338 Milwaukee Road GP-7 with intermittent orange stripe. Middle shelf: 2338 Milwaukee Road with orange stripe across cab. Bottom shelf: 2339 Wabash. L. Nuzzaci Collection.

story of the prototype, refer to **The Remarkable GG-1** by Karl Zimmermann (Quadrant Press, Inc.)

(A) Tuscan red, special Pennsylvania paint scheme used on a few GG-1s for the "Congressional" and the "Senator", shown in the 1955 catalogue as 2340-1. **250   400   600   900**

(B) Dark green, standard Pennsylvania paint scheme for freight and passenger service, shown in the 1955 catalogue as 2340-25.

**225   375   550   750**

**2341 JERSEY CENTRAL** 1956, FM Trainmaster, orange body with blue stripe and roof, white heat-stamped lettering, different spacing between "Jersey" and "Central" on each side, operating couplers at both ends, Magnetraction, three-position E-unit, light at both ends, twin vertical motors, horn, excellent runner, came with orange decal as well as white. P. Ambrose comment. The letter "J" is more deeply heat-stamped in the word Jersey and is readily visible to the eye to detect it from silk-screened copies.

(A) High gloss orange. Rubin observation. **500   750   900 1200**

(B) Dull orange. **400   500   750 1000**

**2343 SANTA FE** 1950-52, F-3 AA units, Santa Fe war bonnet passenger paint scheme, silver body with red cab, nose and stripe, yellow and black trim, black heat-stamped lettering, rubber-stamped top and side stripes (stripes and lettering silk-screened on reproduction bodies), silver frame and

trucks, screened roof vents, open portholes with lenses, grab-irons on nose, ladder on cab door, coil-operated couplers on cab ends, dummy middle couplers, Magnetraction, three-position E-unit, light in both units, twin horizontal motors, horn, excellent runner. **150   200   250   400**

**2343C SANTA FE** 1950-55, F-3 dummy B unit, silver body with red, yellow and black trim.

(A) 1950-52, screen roof vents, matches 2343. **40   75   125   175**

(B) 1953-55, louver roof vents, matches 2353. **40   75   100   150**

**2344 NEW YORK CENTRAL** 1950-52, F-3 AA units.

(A) Dark gray body with gray center stripe outlined with white trim, rubber-stamped trim with heat-stamped lettering (silk-screened on reproduction cabs), gray frame and trucks, screened roof vents, open portholes with lenses, grab-irons on nose, ladder on cab door, coil-operated couplers on cab ends, dummy middle couplers, Magnetraction, three-position E-unit, light in both units, twin horizontal motors, horn, excellent runner. Reissued by Fundimensions as an A-B-A trio, 8370-71-72, in 1983. **125   200   275   400**

(B) Same as (A), but decals for GM logo are orange and white, as pictured in 1952 catalogue, pp. 18-19. J. Algozzini Collection. **NRS**

**2344C NEW YORK CENTRAL** 1950-55, F-3 B unit, dummy B unit, dark gray body with gray center stripe and white trim.

(A) 1950-52, screen roof vents, matches 2344. **75   100   150   200**

(B) 1953-55, louver roof vents, matches 2354. **60   90   125   175**

Top shelf: 2346 Boston & Maine GP-9. Middle shelf: 2347 Chesapeake & Ohio GP-7. Bottom shelf: 2348 Minneapolis & St. Louis GP-9. L. Nuzzaci and R. Lord Collections.

**Gd  VG  Exc  Mt**

**2345 WESTERN PACIFIC**  1952, F-3 AA units, silver and orange body with black heat-stamped lettering (silk-screened on reproduction cabs), silver frame and trucks, screened roof vents, open portholes with lenses, grab-irons on nose, ladder on cab door, coil-operated couplers on cab ends, dummy middle couplers, Magnetraction, three-position E-unit, light in both units, twin horizontal motors, horn, excellent runner, no B unit made. Substantial premium for fresh and bright silver paint.  **200  300  500  800**

**2346 BOSTON & MAINE**  1965-67, GP-9 Road Switcher, heat-stamped lettering, operating couplers at both ends, Magnetraction, three-position E-unit, headlight, horn.
(A) Glossy blue body, black cab, white trim, lettering, frame and handrails.
**75  100  150  200**
(B) Black body, red ends, silver and red heat-stamped lettering, black MPC frame, without GP-9 roof blister, pre-production sample made after 1970. Listed here for user convenience. Eddins Collection.  **NRS**

**2347 CHESAPEAKE & OHIO**  1965, uncatalogued, GP-7 Road Switcher, made for Sears Roebuck and sold as part of set 79N 9836K (Sears number); see 1965 Set listings for details. This locomotive has a blue body with yellow heat-stamped lettering, frame and handrails, operating couplers at both ends, Magnetraction, three-position E-unit, headlight, horn, very hard to find. Even in mint condition, the paint on the handrails has usually flaked off. R. Lord and J. Algozzini comments.  **600  900  1500 2200**

See also Uncatalogued Sets.

**2348 MINNEAPOLIS & ST. LOUIS**  1958-59, GP-9 Road Switcher, red body with blue roof and white stripe, heat-stamped lettering, black frame and handrails, operating couplers at both ends, Magnetraction, three-position E-unit, headlight, horn.
(A) As described above.  **100  150  225  300**
(B) Same as (A), but black-painted rectifier base. (Factory original.) C. Rohlfing Collection.  **NRS**

**2349 NORTHERN PACIFIC**  1959-60, GP-9 Road Switcher, black body with gold and red striping, heat-stamped gold leaf lettering (silk-screened on reproduction bodies), gold frame and handrails, operating couplers at both ends, Magnetraction, three-position E-unit, headlight, horn.
(A) Gold heat-stamped lettering, as above.  **100  175  250  350**
(B) Gold heat-stamped "BUILT BY LIONEL", but gold rubber-stamped "NORTHERN PACIFIC" and "2349". D. Fleming Collection.
**150  200  275  375**

### GENERAL ELECTRIC EP-5 RECTIFIERS

**2350 NEW HAVEN**  1956-58, G.E. EP-5 Rectifier Electric, black plastic body with heat-stamped lettering (silk-screened on reproduction bodies), white and orange stripes, twin metal pantographs, operating couplers at both ends, Magnetraction, three-position E-unit, light at both ends, single vertical motor, horn, wiring easily changed for overhead catenary operation.

Top shelf:    2349 Northern Pacific GP-9.    Middle shelf:    2359 Boston & Maine GP-9.    Bottom shelf:    2365 Chesapeake & Ohio GP-7.    L. Nuzzaci Collection.

Many examples have been equipped with reproduction nose decals; originals in excellent condition are hard to find. The Lionel model of the EP-5 is considered accurate except for its trucks (the prototype had six-wheel trucks), but Lionel may have had another prototype in mind. Italian builders made a close copy of the EP-5 and sold it to the Chilean State Railways. This prototype had four-wheel trucks. R. Young comment.

(A) White "N", orange "H", painted nose trim, white New Haven lettering.                                                   **150    250    325    450**
(B) Orange "N", black "H", painted nose trim, orange New Haven lettering.                                               **250    400    600    900**
(C) Same as (A), but nose trim is decal.             **90    140    200    300**
(D) Same as (B), but nose trim is decal.             **200    300    400    600**
(E) Same as (C), but orange and white paint, stripes go completely through door.                                                       **100    150    250    350**
(F) Same as (C), but body is yellow plastic painted black. C. Rohlfing Collection.                                             **100    200    275    400**

**2351 MILWAUKEE ROAD**    1957-58, G.E. EP-5 Rectifier Electric, yellow unpainted plastic body with heat-stamped lettering (silk-screened on reproduction bodies), black roof and red stripe, twin metal pantographs, operating couplers at both ends, Magnetraction, three-position E-unit, light at both ends, single vertical motor, horn, wiring easily changed for overhead catenary operation.                              **150    225    300    450**

**2352 PENNSYLVANIA**    1958-59, G.E. EP-5 Rectifier Electric, tuscan red or brown body with single gold stripe, heat-stamped gold leaf lettering (silk-screened on reproduction bodies), gold-painted heat dissipator box atop cab shell, twin metal pantographs, operating couplers, Magnetraction, three-position E-unit, light both ends, single vertical motor, horn, wiring easily changed for overhead catenary operation.    **175    250    350    500**

**2353 SANTA FE**    1953-55, F-3 AA units, Santa Fe war bonnet passenger paint scheme, silver body with red cab, nose and stripe, yellow and black trim, black heat-stamped lettering, rubber-stamped top and side stripes (lettering and stripes silk-screened on reproduction bodies), silver frame and trucks, louvered roof vents, no front handrails, open portholes with lenses, ladder on cab door, coil-operated couplers on cab ends, dummy middle couplers, Magnetraction, three-position E-unit, light in both units, twin horizontal motors, horn, excellent runner, for B unit see 2343C.

(A) Notch cut out below coupler at bottom of pilot, 1953 production. R. LaVoie Collection.                                  **100    150    225    300**
(B) Smooth bottom on pilot, 1954-55 production.    **100    150    225    300**

**2353C SANTA FE**    F-3 B unit, not made; for B unit to match 2353 see 2343C (B).                                          **Not Manufactured**

**2354 NEW YORK CENTRAL**    1953-55, F-3 AA units, dark gray body, gray center stripe outlined with white trim, rubber-stamped trim with heat-stamped lettering (silk-screened on reproduction cabs), gray frame with

Top shelf: 2350 New Haven EP-5 with large orange N. Middle shelf: 2350 with large white N. Bottom shelf: 2351 Milwaukee Road. L. Nuzzaci and R. Lord Collections.

Gd  VG  Exc  Mt

gray trucks, louvered roof vents, open portholes with lenses, ladder on cab door, coil-operated couplers on cab ends, dummy middle couplers, Magnetraction, three-position E-unit, light in both units, twin horizontal motors, horn, excellent runner.    **110  175  250  350**

**2354C NEW YORK CENTRAL**  F-3 B unit not made; for B unit to match 2354 see 2344C (B).    **Not Manufactured**

**2355 WESTERN PACIFIC**  1953, F-3 AA units, silver and orange body with black heat-stamped lettering, silver frame and trucks, louvered roof vents, open portholes with lenses, ladder on cab door, coil-operated couplers on cab ends, dummy middle couplers, Magnetraction, three-position E-unit, light in both units, twin horizontal motors, horn, excellent runner, no B unit made. Substantial premium for fresh and bright silver paint.

(A) As described above.    **200  300  475  700**

(B) Nose decal on dummy unit. S. Blotner Collection.    **200  300  475  700**

See also Factory Errors.

**2356 SOUTHERN**  1954-56, F-3 AA units, green body with light gray lower stripe and yellow trim and lettering, lettering is rubber-stamped (silk-screened on reproduction cabs), louvered roof vents, open portholes with lenses, ladder on cab door, coil-operated couplers on cab ends, dummy middle couplers, Magnetraction, three-position E-unit, light in both units, twin horizontal motors, horn, excellent runner, black frame and trucks.    **175  250  400  550**

**2356C SOUTHERN**  1954-56, F-3 B unit, dummy B unit, green body with gray lower stripe and yellow trim, matches 2356.    **100  150  175  225**

**2358 GREAT NORTHERN**  1959-60, G.E. EP-5 Rectifier Electric, orange and green body with yellow stripes and lettering, lettering is heat-stamped (silk-screened on reproduction cabs), twin metal pantographs, operating couplers at both ends, Magnetraction, three-position E-unit, light at both ends, single vertical motor, horn, wiring easily changed for overhead catenary operation. Original GN end decals are almost always flaking.    **200  300  400  600**

**2359 BOSTON & MAINE**  1961-62, GP-9 Road Switcher, flat blue body, black cab and white trim, lettering, frame and handrails, lettering is heat-stamped, operating couplers at both ends, Magnetraction, three-position E-unit, headlight, horn.    **75  100  150  225**

**2360 PENNSYLVANIA**  1956-58, 1961-63, GG-1 Electric, twin metal pantographs, coil-operated couplers at both ends, Magnetraction, three-position E-unit, light at both ends, twin vertical motors, horn, wiring easily changed for overhead catenary operation, excellent runner. Numbers and lettering gold heat-stamped except for (F).

(A) 1956, tuscan body with five rubber-stamped gold stripes (silk-screened on reproduction or worn original cabs), catalogue No. 2360-1.    **250  450  650  900**

(B) 1956-58, same as (A), but dark green body, catalogue No. 2360-25.    **250  300  450  650**

(C) 1957-58, tuscan body with single, large, rubber-stamped gold stripe, decal with large PRR Keystone, graduated height ventilators. A. Tom collection.    **250  275  425  650**

(D) 1961, same as (C), but ventilators are same height.    **250  275  425  650**

| Engine Number | Color | Year Mfg. | Numbering and Lettering | Stripes | Side Keystone | End Keystone | Side Ventilator |
|---|---|---|---|---|---|---|---|
| 2332 | black | 1947 | rs: gold or silver | 5 rs: gold or silver | rs or gold and red decal | rs or gold and red decal with engine number in Keystone | graduated |
| 2332 | green | 47-49 | ↓ | ↓ | ↓ | ↓ | |
| 2330 | green | 1950 | Hs: gold | 5 rs: in gold | red and gold keystone | red and gold decal with engine number in Keystone | |
| 2340 | green | 1955 | | | | | |
| 2360(B) | green | 1956 | | | | | |
| 2360(A) | tuscan | 1956 | ↓ | ↓ | ↓ | ↓ | |
| 2360(C) | tuscan | 57-58 | hs: large gold numbers and letters | 1rs: large gold | large red and white decal | red and white decal with engine number in Keystone | ↓ |
| 2360(D) | tuscan | 1961 | | ↓ | | | same height |
| 2360(E) | tuscan | 61-62 | ↓ | painted stripe, much brighter | | | |
| 2360(F) | tuscan | 62-63 | decaled large numbers and letters in three sections | ↓ | ↓ | ↓ | ↓ |

(E) 1961-62, tuscan body with single, large, painted gold stripe, decal with large PRR Keystone, ventilators same height    **250  275  425  650**
(F) 1962-63, same as (E), but decaled large numbered letters on side.   **NRS**
(G) Same as (C), but rubber-stamped lettering and stripe, early production. A. Tom Collection.   **NRS**

**2363 ILLINOIS CENTRAL**  1955-56, F-3 AB units, brown body with orange stripe and yellow trim, rubber-stamped lettering and lines, black frame, trucks and lettering, louvered roof vents, filled-in portholes, operating coupler on front of A unit, all other couplers are dummys, Magnetraction, three-position E-unit, light in A unit, twin vertical motors, horn, excellent runner. "A" unit is gray shell "B" unit is orange shell.
(A) Black lettering.   **175  275  400  600**
(B) Brown lettering. H. Degano Collection.   **225  350  475  700**

**2365 CHESAPEAKE & OHIO**  1962-63, GP-7 Road Switcher, blue body, yellow handrails and lettering, heat-stamped lettering (silk-screened on reproduction cabs), dummy couplers at both ends, Magnetraction, three-position E-unit, light, no horn, no battery box fuel tank (though it was shown with a fuel tank insert in the catalogue). J. Algozzini comments.
(A) Yellow frame.   **80  125  175  250**
(B) Yellow-orange frame. J. Algozzini Collection.   **NRS**

**2367 WABASH**  1955, F-3 AB units, gray and blue body with white side panels and trim, yellow heat-stamped lettering (silk-screened on reproduction bodies), blue frame, black trucks, louvered roof vents, filled-in portholes, operating coupler on front of A unit, all other couplers are dummys, Magnetraction, three-position E-unit, light in A unit, twin vertical motors, horn, excellent runner.   **175  300  400  600**

**2368 BALTIMORE & OHIO**  1956, F-3 AB units, blue unpainted plastic body with white, black and yellow trim, rubber-stamped lines, heat-stamped numbers and lettering, black frame and trucks, louvered roof vents, filled in portholes, operating coupler on front of A unit, all other couplers are dummies, Magnetraction, three-position E-unit, light in A unit, twin vertical motors, horn, excellent runner. R. Lord comments. Also found with painted body. P. Ambrose comment.   **225  400  550  800**

**2373 CANADIAN PACIFIC**  1957, F-3 AA units, gray and maroon with yellow trim and lettering, heat-stamped top and sides (silk-screened on reproduction cabs), black frame and trucks, louvered roof vents, filled in portholes, operating couplers on cab ends, dummy middle couplers, Magnetraction, three-position E-unit, light in both units, twin vertical

motors, horn, no B unit made, excellent runner. Reissued by Fundimensions in 1973 as 8365-66 AA pair, part of Service Station Special set; that version is also very scarce. When these locomotives were sold as part of a set, they came in individual boxes marked 2373P and 2373T. (The "T" signifies a "tender", or non-powered unit.) When they were sold separately, the individual boxes above were packed inside a double-size corrugated carton. This packaging was typical of all F3 production. P. Ambrose comments.
(A) Black frame.   **400  600  700  950**
(B) Silver frame. We have received two independent reports of this version; both respondents acquired the examples from original purchasers. G. Brown reports that his example was acquired in boxes marked 2373P and 2373T, the normal routine, and that the trains were purchased new in East Paterson, N.J.  We are attempting to learn where and when other silver-framed units were sold. It would also be helpful to learn which inspection slips came with these pieces. Since silver frames could easily be substituted for black frames in a service station repair or other circumstances, very few buyers would be willing to pay a premium for this version. The Guide's consultants are divided in opinion about this version; some feel that the value of this piece should be the same as the usual version, while others feel that it should be valued at less than the black frame version. One commentator feels that this item belongs in the Factory Error section. We have valued it at the same rates as (A) and leave it to you to resolve the controversy. C. Weber and I.D. Smith comments, G. Brown and E. Trentacoste Collections. Additional reports requested.
   **400  600  700  950**

**2378 MILWAUKEE ROAD**  1956, F-3 AB units, gray plastic body with orange lower stripe trimmed in yellow, yellow heat-stamped trim and lettering, louvered roof vents, filled-in portholes, operating coupler on front of A unit, all other couplers are dummies, Magnetraction, three-position E-unit, light in A unit, twin vertical motors, horn, excellent runner.
(A) Yellow stripe along roof line.   **325  500  650  950**
(B) Without yellow stripe along roof line.   **300  475  550  800**
(C) A unit without stripe, B unit with yellow stripe along roof line. This is a legitimate pair.   **275  450  600  800**

**2379 RIO GRANDE**  1957-58, F-3 AB units, yellow body with silver roof and lower stripe, black trim and lettering, green panel in front of windshield, black frame and trucks, heat-stamped trim and lettering, decal nose,

Top shelf: 2352 Pennsylvania EP-5. Second shelf: 2358 Great Northern EP-5. Third shelf: 2329 Virginian rectifier electric. L. Nuzzaci Collection.

Gd VG Exc Mt

louvered roof vents, filled-in portholes, operating coupler on front of A unit, all other couplers are dummys, Magnetraction, three-position E-unit, light in A unit, twin vertical motors, horn, excellent runner. **200 275 375 500**
See also Factory Errors.

**2383 SANTA FE** 1958-66, F-3 AA units, Santa Fe war bonnet passenger paint scheme, silver body with red cab, nose and stripe, yellow and black trim, black heat-stamped lettering, rubber-stamped top and side stripes (stripes and lettering silk-screened on reproduction bodies), silver frame and black trucks, louvered roof vents, filled-in portholes, operating couplers on cab ends, dummy middle couplers, Magnetraction, three-position E-unit, light in both units, twin vertical motors, horn, excellent runner, for B unit see 2243C. This version reissued by Fundimensions in 1976 as a single-motored AA pair.
(A) Red cab, nose and stripe. **125 150 225 350**
(B) Orange red cab, nose and stripe. Lebo Collection. Additional reports requested. Probable early 1958 production. **NRS**

**2383C SANTA FE** F-3 B unit not made, for B unit to match 2383 see 2243C. **Not Manufactured**

**2550 BALTIMORE AND OHIO** 1957-58, Budd RDC baggage-mail car, dummy unit to match 400, silver body with blue lettering, operating couplers at both ends. Was sold separately and came with 400 and 2559 in 1958 set. R. Lord comment. **120 200 250 350**

**2559 BALTIMORE AND OHIO** 1957-58, Budd RDC passenger car, dummy unit to match 400, silver body with blue lettering, operating couplers at both ends. Was sold separately with second 2559 in 1957 set; R. Lord comment. **100 150 200 250**

**3360 BURRO** Crane, 1956-57, self-propelled operating crane, yellow body with red lettering, dummy couplers at both ends, reverse lever on side can be operated by hand or by a track trip, a very interesting operating unit. One track trip (not two) included in original box. S. Carlson comment.
(A) Yellow boom. **80 125 200 275**
(B) Yellow boom with small decal "danger". **100 175 275 375**
(C) Brown cab, possible factory prototype. Further comments requested. L. Bohn observation. **NRS**

**3927 LIONEL LINES** 1956-60, track cleaning car, orange body with blue lettering. Motor drives cleaning brush and does not drive wheels. Hence unit must be pulled by strong engine. A complete unit has two bottles, a brush and a wiper. Replacement brushes and wipers available. Original bottles marked "LIONEL". Not often found with all pieces original and intact.
(A) As described above. **50 75 100 125**
(B) With red running light. Kaim Collection. Additional sightings requested. **NRS**
(C) Unpainted dark green plastic body, white rubber-stamped lettering. The plastic pellets used in the injection mold machines are available in different colors. Lionel was consistent in using the same color pellets for its

production runs. This unusual car was likely produced by the factory before its major production run, to compare alternative color schemes. A. Otten Collection. **NRS**

**4810 SOUTHERN PACIFIC** 1954, FM Trainmaster, black body, red stripe, preproduction prototype, L. Shempp Collection, illustrated in this text; general design utilized by Fundimensions in 1979 for 8951. **NRS**

**5511** See 55.

**6220 SANTA FE** 1949-50, NW-2 diesel switcher, catalogued in three different ways in five Lionel catalogues. Despite this apparent variety, it was only made in 1949-50 with a 6220 number and the Santa Fe road name. The first version of the 1949 catalogue illustrates and lists an O-27 LIONEL diesel switcher numbered 622 for set 1457B, but this version was never made. Set 1457B actually included the 6220 Santa Fe in 1949. The second 1949 catalogue lists a 6220 diesel switcher but does not identify the road name. A parts list dated 1949 lists both the 622 and the 6220. The 1950 color-cover catalogue illustrates an O-27 NEW YORK CENTRAL NW-2 switcher numbered 622 for set 1457B, but the same catalogue lists "...No. 6220 Diesel Switcher loco with Automatic Bell..." on page 11. Finally, the 6220 ATSF was listed and illustrated correctly in the gold-cover 1950 catalogue and the red-cover "Sorry..." edition. A parts list dated 1950 refers to both locomotives and states that they differ from the 1949 versions. C. Rohlfing comments.

The 6220 is an O-27 version of the 622 and is identical to it except for the number; both numbers went through the changes made in 1950 to the axles, magnets and couplers. Like the 622, the 6220 was the first Magnetraction engine; black body with white lettering, die-cast frame, coil-operated couplers at both ends, three-position E-unit, light at both ends, Type I motor, Type I pickup, no horn, operating bell, excellent runner. Models made in 1949 will show little evidence of Magnetraction because of magnet mounting methods. The 1950 model has retained its Magnetraction much better. Not often found with bell truck intact and operating; most units need repair. R. LaVoie comments.

(A) SANTA FE 1949, with large GM decal on cab. D. Ely observation.
90 150 200 275

(B) SANTA FE 1950, with small GM decal on lower front side of motor hood, no weight in cab. D. Ely observation. Came in set 1457B in 1949. C. Rohlfing observation. 90 150 200 275

(C) Late 1950, same as (B), but weight cast in cab frame, D. Ely observation. 90 150 200 275

(D) LIONEL (1949) catalogued but not made. **Not Manufactured**

(E) NEW YORK CENTRAL (1950), catalogued but not made.
**Not Manufactured**

See also Factory Errors and Prototypes.

**6250 SEABOARD** 1954-55, NW-2 Switcher, O-27, blue and orange body with blue and white lettering, die-cast frame, coil-operated couplers at both ends, Magnetraction, three-position E-unit, light at both ends, Type I pickup, no horn, excellent runner.

(A) 1954, "SEABOARD" is a decal with closely spaced lettering. Foss comment. 100 150 250 350

(B) 1955, "SEABOARD" is rubber-stamped with widely spaced lettering. Foss comment. 90 125 200 300

# Chapter II

# STEAM LOCOMOTIVES

The Electronic Set came in two major versions, the 1946-1947 set which had a 4457 N-5 Pennsylvania metal caboose and the 1948-1949 set which came with the 4357 SP caboose. The 1948-1949 set is shown above. Although the engine was designated 671R by Lionel in its catalogue, with the "R" standing for remote, the locomotive was actually marked "671". H. Holden Collection, Bennett photograph.

## THE LIONEL ELECTRONIC SET: THE SECRETS REVEALED

### By Pat Scholes

**NOTE:** This article first appeared in the Rocky Mountain Division of the TCA's Newsletter, Volume 8, Number 2, Summer 1982. Used by permission of the author. Photographs by Marc Horovitz.

One of the most innovative aspects of Lionel's postwar production is the "Electronic Set". The new Pennsylvania S-2 Steam Turbine heads this special train. The set is equipped with two tiny radio receivers in the tender and one in each car. An additional "transformer" comes with each set; this "transformer" is actually a radio transmitter which is operated in conjunction with the regular transformer. The transmitter has ten buttons, each one a different color. The engine, tender

and cars each have a round colored decal whose color corresponds to a button color on the transmitter. Pressing one of the transmitter buttons sends a particular radio frequency along the track which is picked up by the corresponding receiver. This receiver then causes a specific action to occur, such as engine reversing, whistling, uncoupling, unloading, etc.

The greatest advantage of such an operating scheme is that any of these actions can take place at any point on the track, not just on a special track section. In fact, two trains can be run simultaneously on the same track because one can respond to the electronic commands while the other responds to normal transformer functions. Furthermore, since there are extra buttons on the transmitter which can control a second electronic set (which can easily be tuned to them), no fewer than **three** trains can be operated simultaneously and separately — on the same track! Lionel literature indicates that there are both high and low frequency receivers. Consequently, there is not complete flexibility to tune any receiver to any button on the transmitter. Despite this limitation, considerable flexibility exists within either the high or the low frequency range. This is very useful in running multiple trains on one track.

Potentially and actually, the Electronic Set is fun to operate. Considering the fact that these sets were introduced in the electronically primitive (by today's standards) year of 1946, they were quite a step towards the future. Unfortunately, there was a severe problem — cost. These sets were generally offered with a complement of accessories for $200, or singularly for $75. In the 1946 economy, that was quite a sum to spend on Junior for Christmas!

**The 4454 Baby Ruth boxcar from the electronic control set. Note the electronic set decal on the upper left corner.**

If you have an Electronic Set but are hesitant to run it because of its value, I might mention that you can run the complete set (tender and cars) by replacing the 671R engine with any 1946 2020, 671 or 726 locomotive. These engines have no E-unit lever protruding through the boiler. The reversing action is disabled by removing the E-unit wire from its connector on the motor brushplate. In other words, the electronic turbine has little difference from these other 1946 locomotives; only the black decal disc and the motor brushplate connectors. The big difference is the electronic tender — it has a radio receiver for reversing and operating the whistle.

The motor brushplate offers one of the quickest ways to determine whether or not the locomotive was originally part of the Electronic Set, since the black decal is often missing from these engines. After the 1946 production of Turbines and Berkshires, Lionel discontinued the use of the disconnect plug and socket to disable the E-unit. They began mounting the E-unit upright with the lever protruding from the boiler; this eliminated the need for the plug and jack connections — except on those engines which pulled the Electronic Sets. They needed the connection for the radio receiver wire from the tender. Therefore, in the "normal" mode, the E-unit could be disabled by either disconnecting the plug connector or by moving the E-unit lever. This redundancy in E-unit connections identifies the Electronic Set turbines made in 1947, 1948 or 1949. When the boiler has an E-unit lever and the brushplate has the plug and jack connector, the engine originally pulled an Electronic Set (if the brushplate has not been changed, of course). There was no difference in 1946 except for the black decal disc.

The Electronic Set is sometimes regarded as being rather mysterious. It really isn't too complicated in principle. The radio receiver is basically a tunable coil which can be adjusted to respond to a particular frequency by changing the position of a small threaded metal screw. This adjustment, by the way,

should only be done after actuating the corresponding button several times to allow the coil to "stabilize". The tuning can drift after years of inactivity, but return to its original state after attempted actuation. This is why the tuning adjustment should not be attempted until the button has been pushed several times.

When the coil is tuned correctly to a particular transmitter button, depressing the button will trigger the receiver relay. The relay then connects the track voltage to the E-unit, whistle or coupler, whichever is the case. Thus, nothing happens if the transmitter button is depressed but the track voltage is off. The only response is a barely audible click in the receiver.

Contrary to typical E-unit operation when the E-unit is activated by track voltage interruption, the Electronic Set E-unit is only activated when the transmitter button is pushed. This leads to noticeably quiet operation of the engine when in the electronic mode; no E-unit "buzz" is evident. This is because in the electronic mode the wire from the radio receiver relay in the tender is connected to the brushplate connector on the engine, and it is only "hot" when the tender receiver relay is activated.

The freight cars operate on the same principle. The radio receiver relay activates and then connects track voltage to the coil couplers via a center rail pickup roller on the truck, similar to normal tender truck rollers. In fact, this is why the Electronic Set couplers did not change from the coil type in 1948 when other units were changed to the mechanical type of coupler. There was not a simple way to trigger the pull-down mechanism for the uncoupling operation with the magnetically operated coupler.

The Dump Car is a special case. Its circuit is designed to uncouple at a quick touch of its corresponding button.

**The 5459 Dump Car has two electronically-controlled functions: uncoupling and dumping its loads.**

**The 1948 - 1949 electronic set came with the 4357 Caboose. This is a deluxe Lionel model with a light, plastic window insert, smokestack, railings and electronically-controlled couplers at both ends.**

However, if the button is depressed for a longer period, the car will dump. This car, therefore, uses one receiver for two operations.

The radio receivers, of course, are the main difference between the electronic freight cars and their regular counterparts. Secondary differences are the coupler connections and the presence of a center rail roller rather than the sliding shoe for normal coil couplers. The cars, including the tender, are numbered with four-digit numbers beginning with "4" or "5", rather than the familiar "2" or "3".

The electronic steam turbine is designated 671R; the "R" stands for "remote". However, the "R" suffix does not appear on the number under the cab. That remained 671. The electronic function is identified by the black decal disc on the engine.

Because of the uniqueness of the Electronic Sets, their operation is very enjoyable. Especially intriguing is the wide range of activities which are possible with multiple sets. If you have an operating layout, watch for an Electronic Set and (if you can afford it) add it to your railroad. I think you'll agree that there is something really special about reversing one train while blowing the whistle on the other, and having your 97 or 397 Coal Loader along a siding without a remote control track in sight!

**NOTE:** (from the editor) See **Greenberg's Operating and Repair Manual For Lionel Trains,** 1981 edition, pages 515-530, for diagrams, schematics and a complete service and operations analysis of the Electronic Control Set.

## THE REAL BEGINNING OF THE POSTWAR ERA:
## LIONEL'S SET 463W IN 1945

### By Robert Swanson

(Editor's Note: Bob Swanson is an avid Lionel train collector who specializes in the early Lionel postwar period from 1945 to 1950. His intense and, above all, complete powers of observation and logic can be found in both this article and in his study of the 9-1/4 inch Boxcars elsewhere in this book. These two articles represent his first writing efforts for the Greenberg Guides. Mr. Swanson resides in the town of Basking Ridge, New Jersey.)

In Ron Hollander's book **All Aboard!**, there are two tantalizing pictures of a Lionel train set which has so far been largely ignored by the collecting public. If you have the book, look for a moment at page 183. There you will find two publicity shots of the first postwar Lionel train set being delivered just in time for Christmas of 1945. Lionel's war contracts had ended on August 7, 1945, and the firm was feverishly assembling a train set in time for that year's

Plate 1: The 1945 Catalogue showed set 463W in fine detail. However, the actual components differed in several notable ways from the listings.

Christmas sales. Mr. Hollander's pictures show that set — a steam engine pulling four scale-detailed cars. This is Lionel's Set 463W, and it is time to bring it out of historical obscurity to give it the attention it deserves!

After all, if the sales of collector guides and other specialized books about train collecting are any indication, there is more interest in postwar Lionel trains than in all other eras of all other electric train manufacturers combined! Yet, for all that attention, many collectors associate the beginning of this popular era of electric trains with the introduction of smoke, the Pennsylvania S-2 Turbine and the Berkshire locomotive as shown in the 1946 catalogue. Most of us remember (and/or have heard many times) that oft-told story of the 1946 paper shortage which limited production of the 1946 Lionel catalogue and Lionel's clever response to the shortage by having **Liberty Magazine** print the entire catalogue as an advertising insert. But that was not the real beginning of the postwar Era at all. Production and sales of postwar Lionel trains began in the fall of 1945, a full year before the well-known **Liberty Magazine** escapade.

Plate 2: Each piece in the 1945 came in its own box. Two different types of boxes are known, the New York version and the Chicago version. Shown above are the New York version with component catalogue numbers correctly printed on each box.

Lionel's planning for postwar production did not begin in 1945, either. Internal Lionel memos dated as early as December 1942 and January 1943 were reprinted in the January 1983 issue of the **Train Collector's Quarterly**. These memos show clearly that early in the war, Lionel's executives were actively developing their postwar train designs and marketing strategies. With this small insight into Lionel's wartime train planning activities, it is not too surprising to find that Lionel was able to produce and distribute one train set, the 463W, in time for Christmas 1945. The set consisted primarily of prewar rolling stock mounted on the all-new die-cast trucks with knuckle couplers. It contained the old reliable 224 die-cast steam locomotive with a 2466W whistle tender, a 2458 all-metal double-door automobile car (marked with its prewar number, 2758), a 2555 single-dome tank car marked with the old 2755 number, a 2452 Pennsylvania black plastic gondola (the only all-new car) and a 2457 sheet metal Pennsylvania N5 illuminated caboose. Since individual items similar to these 1945 items, right down to the catalogue descriptions and numbers, were also produced in 1946 and 1947 (and some cars in 1948), the uniqueness and even the very existence of the 1945 set is largely unknown.

The limited awareness of the 1945 set in the train collecting community can usually be traced to the 4-page, 2-color 1945 Lionel catalogue. This catalogue itself is one of the rarest

Plate 3: Given both the shortages of paper and the limited time available for production in 1945, the Lionel 1945 catalogue is a remarkable publication.

pieces of postwar "paper", but excellent reproductions were printed in 1969 by Les Gordon and in 1975 by Bruce Greenberg. My own awareness of the 1945 set came about during a visit to Mr. Gordon's Indianapolis train store in 1974. I was looking at some old Lionel catalogues to complete my postwar collection when Les showed me his reprint of the 1945 catalogue. When I saw the 463W set pictured on pages 2 and 3, I was totally shocked because I had purchased this set five years earlier! I finally understood why I had not found this set in any regular postwar catalogue, since it had never occurred to me that there was any 1945 production. I also began to see that this set had unique features making it different from prewar or any subsequent postwar production.

This 1945 catalogue, like many Lionel catalogues, contains several inaccuracies and errors when it is compared to the items actually produced. For example, the tender is listed as a number 2224; however, it was marked and boxed as a 2466W tender. The caboose is correctly listed as number 2457, but the catalogue pictures it as the later 2472 caboose without illumination, window frames and inserts, steps and end windows in the cupola. The unlighted 2472 was not produced until 1946. Other discrepancies relating to the numbering of the tank and automobile cars will be discussed later.

The primary features which make the rolling stock in the 1945 set unique and identifiable are the trucks and couplers. The three-year interruption in electric train production during World War II created a tremendous demand for electric trains. The money to spend on them was there, thanks to a booming wartime economy. This pent-up demand made 1945 the ideal time to introduce a new coupler system incompatible with all the prewar couplers. (Lionel would compromise a little later by introducing coupler adapters.) Knuckle couplers and die-cast trucks were a major part of Lionel's strategy to manufacture more realistic toy trains. Improved realism would certainly benefit Lionel's sales over the long run, and the general demand for electric trains in late 1945 would minimize any temporary sales resistance caused by the incompatibility with previous coupler designs. So far, so good.

The only trouble with all this great timing was that Lionel had not been able to perfect and optimize the truck and coupler

Plate 5: The earliest 1945 trucks, Type IA, featured whirly wheels and thick axles.

Plate 4: The 1945 trucks all used a flying shoe design. The shoe made contact with the special uncoupling track rails to activate the coupler. Unfortunately the flying shoe design was not durable. Above is a Type IC truck with regular wheels and thick axles.

design during the war years in order to have it ready on such short notice for production in the fall of 1945. The result was the introduction of an unproven and imperfect truck and coupler which had many production and operational problems. The Lionel strategy apparently was to implement engineering and manufacturing "fixes" to these problems as quickly as they were discovered. The result was the production of at least eight different "flying shoe" truck and coupler variations during late 1945 and early 1946. Stated another way, Lionel apparently "fixed" the design of the early "flying shoe" truck about every three **weeks**, on the average!

These factory "fixes" were not the only repairs required, either. The owners of these early "flying shoe" trucks evidently experienced so many problems with them that they brought them back to Service Stations for repair in droves. To help the Service Stations resolve the myriad of repair problems, Lionel issued a series of seven "Authorized Service Station T.C. Truck Bulletins." These bulletins cover such subjects as couplers opening unexpectedly, burned-out coils, short-circuiting rollers, broken or loose coupler heads, broken fiber

Plate 6: Three different versions of the 224 locomotive. On the top shelf is the prewar version with long drawbars linking locomotive and tender. The tender has prewar trucks with stamped-steel side frames and a box coupler. On the second shelf is a 224 that came with the 1945 set. The locomotive and tender are coupled much more closely by a locomotive drawbar that fits into a slot into the tender floor. Note the black handrails along the boiler. On the bottom shelf is a 1946 model 224 with a rounded cab floor that projects beyond the cab side walls and clearly distinguishes this model. B. Greenberg photograph.

strips and cars jumping the track at switches. The latest of these bulletins is dated April, 1946. Ultimately, the "flying shoe" design was viewed by Lionel as so fragile that no amount of tinkering could save it from a well-deserved oblivion. By mid-1946, a completely new design (Type 3 in the truck and coupler article) was introduced. In 1948, the magnetic track-activated coupler solved the pickup shoe problem for good.

These early truck and coupler variations provide one important means of identifying items produced for the 1945 set. However, since trucks can be and often are changed, it is helpful to identify other unique features as well. To help the reader discern both the obvious and subtle uniqueness of the 1945 items, the photographs accompanying this article show, from top to bottom, prewar production, 1945 production and 1946 - 1947 production.

The obvious place to start is with the 224 locomotive. There are two features unique to the 1945 versions of this locomotive. First, the wire handrails are chemically blackened (or "blued"), rather than bright stainless steel, which is typical of both prewar and postwar production. Evidently stainless steel, which was in critical demand for military applications during the war, was not yet available for consumer products. Second, the drawbar is blackened steel with a very short vertical section at the end; this section with little "ears" is placed directly into an oval slot in the tender frame. (The 1945 224 is also the only postwar version of this locomotive with a squared-off cab end, like the prewar products.) The result of this arrangement is a much closer coupling of the engine and tender when compared with the prewar design, a change very consistent with Lionel's policy of producing "scale-like" realism in their popularly-priced toy trains. The other result of the 1945 drawbar

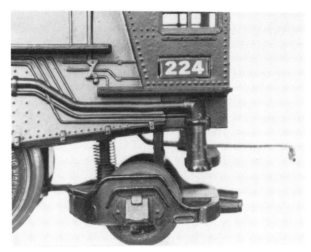

Plate 7: The 1945 224 came with a locomotive drawbar with a very small hooked end. This end fitted into a slot in the tender. It is difficult to disconnect the drawbar from the tender.

arrangement, however, is negative. It is very difficult to couple the engine and tender together without removing both from the track and replacing them on the track as a coupled unit — no easy procedure for a six or seven year-old boy, not to mention an older adult with "maturing" eyesight! The 1946 fix for this problem was the return of the tender drawbar, now redesigned with the engine drawbar to maintain close spacing between engine and tender. The close-coupling illusion was actually improved in 1946 by the addition of a rounded cab floor, bringing the locomotive even closer to the tender.

The 1945 version of the 2466W tender is unique to 1945 by not having a drawbar of any kind, either attached to the frame

Plate 8: The 224 set consisted of a locomotive, tender and four freight cars. On the center shelf is the X2758 boxcar and the 2755 tank car from the 1945 set. Note the pickup shoes on the trucks and the close coupling of the cars. The top shelf shows the prewar versions of the boxcar and tank car while the bottom shelf shows the 1946 X2458 boxcar and the 2555 Sunoco tank car. R. Swanson Collection.

or the truck pivot point. In fact, collectors unfamiliar with this tender often assume something is missing and add a drawbar. Instead of a drawbar, this tender has an oval hole in the metal frame approximately 3/8" x 3/16" to accept the drawbar directly from the engine. It also has blackened handrails made from wire similar in appearance to that used on the engine. The body is molded from the same injection-molded plastic used on the prewar 2666W tender. This leads us to the theory that the 1945 production was mostly the assembly of prewar parts which were then equipped with the new trucks and couplers. The fact that the 1945 2466W tender bodies are stamped "LIONEL LINES" in prewar white lettering, rather than the postwar silver, lends credence to this theory. Finally, the 1945 2466W tender is equipped with either Type 1A trucks ("whirly" wheels) or Type 1B trucks ("dished" wheels). Based upon many observations, I believe that production of the Type 1C truck (thick axle, regular wheels) did not begin until the early 1946 items were being assembled. By that time, virtually all of the Type 1A and 1B trucks had been used for the 1945 sets.

Production of the 2458 Automobile Car also represents the assembly of prewar parts with new trucks and couplers. The bodies for these cars were evidently painted and marked before the war, because cars with Type 1A or 1B trucks always carry the prewar number, 2758. (Perhaps, too, there was not time to change the heat stamp for 1945.) When these cars are found in their original boxes, the box number always agrees with the catalogue number — 2458. The only variations for the 2458 (marked 2758) Automobile Car relate to the trucks and couplers; several sub-variations of both Type 1A and Type 1B have been observed.

The 2555 tank car produced for the 1945 set presents a variation on the theme when it comes to assembling prewar parts. All of the parts except, of course, the trucks are from the prewar 2755 tank car, including the decals. However, the paint and the placement of the decals (number to the right, Sunoco decal to the left) are similar to the rare silver variation of the prewar 2755. Most prewar 2755 tank cars were gray. Surprisingly, the wire handrails on the 1945 version of the 2555 tank car were stainless steel in 1945, not black like the handrails on the engine and tender. Perhaps the handrails were cut and bent before the war — another use of leftover parts. Curiously, the cotter pins which attach the handrails to the tank are black, just like the cotter pins on the engine and tender! The 2555 tank car also provides something for the variation collector besides the usual Type 1A and 1B truck and coupler variations. There are at least two distinctly different 2755 number decals used on the 1945 tank cars. One decal has noticeably taller characters on the second line than the other. The taller lettered decal is also notched on both sides of the bottom line of printing, while the other is completely rectangular. Since both decals have been observed on cars with Type 1A and 1B trucks, it appears that the decals were used concurrently rather than consecutively.

The number discrepancies on both the tank car and the automobile car were corrected in early 1946. The accompanying photograph, bottom row, shows both cars with correct numbers, but with Type 2 trucks, indicating early 1946 production. The production of Type 3A trucks began in mid or late 1946.

The 2452 Pennsylvania gondola is the only all-new car contained in the 1945 set. (Editor's Note: For a discussion of the varieties of this car, see Richard Vagner's article on

Plate 9: In 1945 Lionel used different letter styles on its 2755 tank car. The decal on the top car has taller lettering on the second line compared to the decal on the lower car.

gondola production in this edition.) It has an injection molded plastic body, completely different from the 2812X prewar tinplate gondola it replaced. The only similarity between the 2812X and the 1945 version of the 2452 is that they were both supplied with four of the hollow two-piece barrels numbered 0209. In 1946 and later years, the 2452 gondola and its successors were equipped with solid one-piece wooden barrels or no barrels at all. The more plentiful 2452X gondola manufactured in 1946 and 1947, for O-27 sets, had neither barrels nor brakewheels.

Besides being the only "new" car in the 1945 set the 2452 gondola yields more variations than any other item manufactured in 1945 (it has a "new" date and "built" date of 12-45). The usual 1A and 1B truck variations can be found, along with different screws used to attach the body to the metal frame. Some screws are 6-32 machine screws which require the holes in the frame to be tapped. Other cars are found with thread-forming (or self-tapping) screws which do not require a separate tapping operation.

Another variation of the 2452 has to do with the finish of the large odd-shaped hole in the center of the plastic body. This large hole is shaped to match the profile of the electronic receiver unit — a clear indication that in 1945 Lionel was already preparing for the introduction of the Electronic Set. (Inter-office memos from Lionel show that the application of electronics was discussed as early as February of 1942.) What is not as obvious is that this large center hole also contains the "gates", or ports where the plastic was forced into the mold.

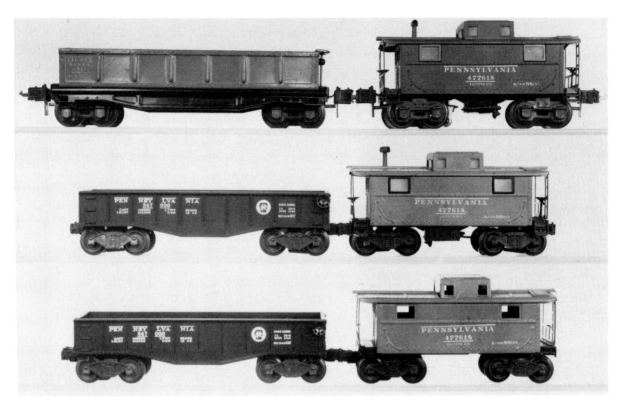

Plate 10:   The center shelf shows the 2452 gondola and a 2457 caboose from the 1945 set while the top shelf shows prewar equipment and the bottom shelf shows 1946 equipment.  The prewar 2757 caboose was continued in 1945 with a new color, new trucks and a new number 2457.  The prewar 2812 gondola was dropped and replaced with the 2452 gondola.  The bottom shelf shows the unlighted 2472 caboose first made in 1946.

Extra Hole          Gate Areas          Extra Hole

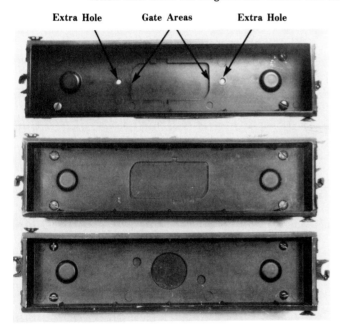

Plate 11:   The 1945 and 1946 gondolas had an irregular rectangular hole in the car floor for mounting the electronic set receiver.  In addition some 1945 gondolas had extra holes flanking the rectangular opening and were likely used for the electronic set wiring.  In 1947 Lionel modified the die to make a round hole.

These "gates" are about 3/4" wide and 1/32" high (about half the thickness of the car floor).  See photograph at left.  When the body was removed from the mold, the runners had to be broken off and the marked areas finished.  In very early 1945 production, the runners were evidently removed by hand, and

the areas were finished with either a knife or a file.  The hole edges in the gate areas appear very rough and uneven.  Very soon into the production run, Lionel probably produced a special tool to trim off the runner, because in most cars the marked areas are very even and uniform (as shown on the top car in Plate 11).   Close examination shows evidence of a shearing-type fracture, suggesting a special punch and die tool to trim the hole precisely.

The final variation is probably the most noticeable of all.  Some of the early gondola bodies have two extra holes molded into the body floor (see Plate 11).  These holes go through the exact center of the two locating posts on the bottom of the car body, which project through the matching holes in the metal car frame.  These holes were probably intended for wiring from a top-mounted electronic receiver to the trucks below.  When Lionel realized that the receiver could be mounted below the floor instead of on top, the holes were no longer needed.  The pins in the mold which caused these holes to be formed were simply removed, eliminating the holes.  The large irregular hole could not be removed as quickly, even though its original purpose was gone, because (as just mentioned) the large hole was involved with the entrance ports or gates.  It was not until 1947 that this area of the mold was reworked.

The 2457 caboose was another prewar carry-over, but it was painted a new color — red.  The prewar 2757 semi-detailed caboose was a very good model of the Pennsylvania N5 caboose, accurate in many details, including its dull brown or tuscan color.  However, Joshua Lionel Cowen knew that mothers bought lots of trains for their sons and that bright colors sold better than did dark ones.  After all, every mother knew that freight trains ended with the "little red caboose", and this idea was reinforced by the children's literature of the

Plate 12: The set carton for the 1945 set is very hard to find. Bob Swanson searched for several years before locating this carton.

time. Apparently, in 1945 the engineering department was persuaded to concede this point of realism for the sake of sales.

The prewar Pennsylvania Railroad markings were used on the postwar 1945 caboose. Since the Lionel number did not appear on the car body, there was no numbering error, as was the case with the automobile and tank cars. The correct postwar number, 2457, was rubber-stamped in silver on the underside of the frame.

The Type 1A and 1B trucks are the only confirmed variations among 1945 cabooses. However, it is not unusual to find a 2457 caboose with a Type 1A truck with "whirly" wheels on one end and a Type 1B truck with dished wheels on the other. This mix is rarely found on the other cars in the set. The mix can probably be explained by the fact that the caboose required one TCL-1 truck with a center-rail roller pickup for the light, while the other truck was a TC-1 without the roller. This meant two different supply bins for trucks on the caboose assembly line. Obviously, for some period of time the two bins had different vintages of trucks as "whirly" wheels were phased out and dished wheels were introduced.

The bottom row of Plate 10 shows late production of the 2452X gondola and the 2472 caboose. These cars are equipped with Type 3 trucks which space the cars about 1/4" further apart than the Type 1 trucks on the 1945 cars in the middle row. The close spacing was very realistic and operated reasonably well on O Gauge curved track, which is 31 inches in diameter. However, when the "flying shoe" design (Types 1 and 2) was applied to cars in O-27 sets, the spacing was a little too close for comfort, since this track has a 27-inch diameter. When backing around O-27 curves, two cars with these early couplers will sometimes touch and even derail. This problem was not apparent in 1945, since Set 463W always included O Gauge track.

Plate 10 also shows, on the third shelf, the 2472 caboose as shown in the 1945 catalogue, but not produced until 1946 for O-27 sets. The caboose pictured has Type 3A trucks, indicating late 1946 production. However, the earliest 2472 cabooses were equipped with Type 1C trucks (thick axles, regular wheels) or Type 2 trucks (regular axles and wheels). These early 2472 cabooses were probably included in the O-27 sets numbered 1405, 1409 and 1411, as shown in the Spring 1946 dealer catalogue, a seven-page catalogue which preceded the 1946 Advance Catalogue.

The boxes used with Set 463W also provide some insight into 1945 Lionel production. Although I have a number of engine and car boxes for 1945 items, I recently acquired a 463W set

box. Richard Stull of Lorain, Ohio had provided a first-hand description of this set box, so I knew what to look for. The part number on the set box is 463W-2. The tan corrugated box measures 14-1/4" long, 12-3/4" wide and 7" high. It has an orange, blue and white label pasted onto one of the 14-1/4" sides; the label reads "463W, 'O' Gauge Track, Freight Train Outfit With Built-In Whistle". The use of this label parallels late prewar practice. The box maker's seal shows that the box was made by the Gair-Bogota Corrugated and Fiber Box Corporation of Bogota, New Jersey. If any collector has information about another set box for the 463W set, we would like to hear about it.

Individual boxes for the 463W set components are not as hard to find as the set box itself. There are a number of interesting variations in the component boxes, as shown in Table 1. Some component boxes were apparently left over from prewar production. These boxes were overstamped in typical Lionel fashion to reflect the correct number of the item packaged inside. One set of rolling stock boxes from a 463W set found in the Chicago area came with the engine, tender, tank car and caboose boxes all overstamped. The cars in this set all had Type 1A trucks with "whirly" wheels, indicating early production. Since the new 2452 gondola had significantly different dimensions from the prewar 2812, it is not surprising that the gondola had a new box. However, the 2458 Automobile Car was so much a leftover that it still carried its prewar number, 2758, on its metal sides. Why was not it in a prewar 2758 box or a 2758 box overstamped with 2458? With all the 2758 bodies left over, why were not there any 2758 boxes left? Perhaps there were, and I just have not seen one yet. The reporting of a 2758 Automobile Car box overstamped with 2458 containing an automobile car marked 2758 but equipped with Type 1 postwar trucks is awaited.

The second set of rolling stock boxes exhibits no overstamping at all. The boxes were all printed with postwar numbers, even when the cars inside still carry the prewar number. The cars in this second set were all equipped with Type 1B trucks (dished wheels). This set was purchased from the original owner, who received it for Christmas of 1945 in Islip, Long Island, New York.

I believe that these two sets may represent the extremes of the 1945 production of the 463W set. The Chicago set with overstamped boxes, Type 1A trucks, "whirly" wheels and a 2452 gondola with extra holes in the body probably typifies the earliest 1945 production. On the other hand, the "New York" set with properly marked boxes, Type 1B trucks, dished wheels and a more refined 2452 gondola should be called the "New York" set; it probably represents the end of 1945 production of the 463W set. However, this is a somewhat risky generalization because most 463W sets probably contain a mixture of both types of wheels, not a homogeneous grouping as do these two sets.

There may be a plausible explanation for early 1945 production being found in Chicago or even further west, while the later production is concentrated more along the East Coast. It is a simple matter of time and transportation. In 1945, Lionel Trains were shipped, fittingly enough, by real trains. That meant time — days or even weeks, depending upon how far the sets had to be shipped. Electric trains destined for the Midwest and beyond probably had to leave the Lionel factory by early November to reach stores in time for Christmas of 1945. On the other hand, a truck full of electric trains could have left the Lionel factory in Irvington, New Jersey as late as

| ITEM | "CHICAGO" BOXES | "NEW YORK" BOXES |
|---|---|---|
| Engine | 224 over 1664;<br>11-1/2" x 3-7/8" x 3-1/4" | 224;<br>11-5/8" x 3-7/8" x 3-1/2" |
| Tender | 2466W over 0-2666W;<br>10-1/2" x 4" x 3-1/16" | 2466W;<br>9-1/8" x 3-11/16" x 2-15/16" |
| Automobile Car | 2458;<br>11-3/16" x 3-1/4" x 2-7/16" | 2458;<br>11-3/16" x 3-1/4" x 2-7/16" |
| Tank Car | 2555 over 2755;<br>11-3/4" x 4" x 3" | 2555;<br>11-3/4" x 4" x 2-15/16" |
| Gondola | 2452;<br>9-7/16" x 2-13/16" x 2-7/16" | 2452;<br>9-7/16" x 3-11/16" x 2-7/16" |
| Caboose | 2457 over 2757;<br>9 1/8" x 3 11/16" x 2 7/16" | 2457;<br>9-1/8" x 3-11/16" x 2-7/16" |

**TABLE 1: SET 463W COMPONENT BOXES**

December 20, 1945 and reached Macy's or any other New York City store on the same day, with several shopping days still remaining. Sounds like a reasonable theory, doesn't it?

But Jim Sattler of Honolulu, Hawaii relates the following story. Several years ago, he purchased a 1945 set from the original owner who received the set for Christmas in 1945. (Sounds familiar, I said.) But this set was received in Hawaii and in fact the original set box is stamped "The Hawaiian Electric Company, Ltd.", an approved Lionel Service Station and the main Lionel dealer in Hawaii at the time. If my plausible explanation (about early production being shipped west) had any validity this "Honolulu set" should have been about the first set off the line. (How much further west can you go than Hawaii? I do not think Lionel was sending electric trains to Japan in 1945.) Well, Jim reports that his "Honolulu set" is identical to my "New York set", all 1B trucks with dished wheels. So much for my plausible explanation. Any other ideas?

While I am doing this report on 1945 Lionel production, I should include one last subject: instruction manuals and sheets. My "New York" set came with an instruction manual "...copyrighted 1940, Form No. 926-5, Reprinted 1941". The original owner had only this one train set, so I conclude that this was the instruction manual included with this particular 1945 463W set. Other reports have confirmed this conclusion. Has anyone seen a "Form 926-5, Reprinted 1942" manual included with a 1945 set? Or an instruction manual actually dated 1945? If so, I would like to hear from you.

There is one instruction sheet dated in 1945: 11-45, to be exact. It is "Form No. RCS-8-140X-290M11-45 TT", titled "Instructions For Operating Lionel Electro-Magnetic Couplers". If the 1945 set contained a prewar instruction manual, the need for this sheet explaining the operation of the new knuckle couplers is obvious. What is not so obvious is why Lionel had at least three separate printings of this one instruction sheet, all dated 11-45! The only difference between the three sheets I have detected is minor lateral shifts in the second line of print under Figures 1 and 2 on the front page.

The words and figures are all the same. While I am on the subject of figures, let me point out that Figure 2 in the instruction sheet dated 11-45 contains very detailed line drawings of 9-1/4" boxcars (e.g., 2454 postwar molded plastic boxcars). I do not believe that these boxcars were available to the public in 1945, but their development was clearly well under way. The earliest 2454 boxcars came with Type 2 trucks (regular wheels and axles) and were probably produced starting in mid 1946. But...the 9-1/4" boxcars are another story, in fact a lengthy story told elsewhere in this edition.

The discussion of the 1945 items in this article is based upon direct observations of eight 463W sets by the author and on first-hand reports from about a half dozen experienced collectors from around the country who own 1945 items and/or complete 463W sets. The 1945 rolling stock features and variations discussed are all supported by independent observations of at least three identical examples. Single examples of other items containing some 1945 features have been reported; however, since these variations could have been "created" by combining components from two or more readily available prewar and postwar items, I feel that more examples must be documented to provide some confidence that the items represent true factory variations. It is likely that some of these unusual variations reflect Service Station repairs of the fragile "flying shoe" trucks and early postwar plastic parts.

Adequate and reliable data concerning factory variations during 1945 production have been very slow to surface. Do any readers have evidence that Lionel produced items, boxes or even complete sets besides those discussed in this article? If so, please let us know so we can improve the accuracy and competence of this article in future publications. I am sure that there is more evidence and information available which will ultimately come to light concerning this very interesting period of Lionel train production.

### ACKNOWLEDGMENTS

The author would like to acknowledge the tremendous encouragement and factual information provided by Bruce

221 New York Central

224

237

Balsley. When Bruce had only a "Chicago" set and I had only a "New York" set, we had many hard discussions about who had the "real" 1945 set. In the end, we realized that both sets were authentic 463W sets from 1945, and that there were combinations and variations of sets in between. I would also like to thank Cantey Johnson for his insight into the mold design for the 2452 gondola and Rich Stull for sharing his information about set and component boxes. Discussions and written material from Jim Sattler were also appreciated and very helpful. Continuing thanks are also extended to Ed Prendeville and Bob Morgan, whose vast inventory at the Train Collectors' Warehouse has yielded some important clues to understanding Lionel's early postwar production.

And a special note of thanks to Barbara Houtsma for typing and proofreading this manuscript. She converted my "scratch" into something that the publisher and editor could read!

### LOCOMOTIVE LISTINGS

Gd  VG  Exc  Mt

**Prices cited require locomotive with correct tender.**

**221** 1946-47, 2-6-4 die-cast boiler. This locomotive was based on one of two Henry Dreyfus stainless steel shrouding designs for the New York Central streamlined J-3 Hudson steamer. These locomotive shrouds were installed on the Hudsons in 1938, and since 10 of the J-3 Hudsons were fitted in this way, it is likely that several famous name trains were pulled by

This is the 221 (B) version with gray body and black-finished drivers without nickel tires. The striped decal on the tender is seldom found in this well preserved a condition; more often, the tender's lettering is badly chipped or restored with an after-market decal, which is readily available. R. Bartelt photograph.

this streamlined engine, whose boiler front looks for all the world like an ancient Roman gladiator's helmet. (R. Arcara and K. Wills comments.) The Lionel model is somewhat more modest, but internal memos dated as early as December 1, 1942 show that such a locomotive was planned for postwar O-27 production very early in the war years. (For these memos, which are fascinating insights into the thinking of the Lionel executives, see the **Train Collectors' Quarterly**, January 1983.) It has a handrail from the pilot to the cab, very shallow stamped bell and whistles, large lens with refracting qualities, drive and connecting rods, valve gear, crosshead integral to body casting, motor with brushplate on left side and forward, casting opened up to provide room for brush holders; motor held in by screw behind smokestack and rod in front of cab, right side has large, medium and

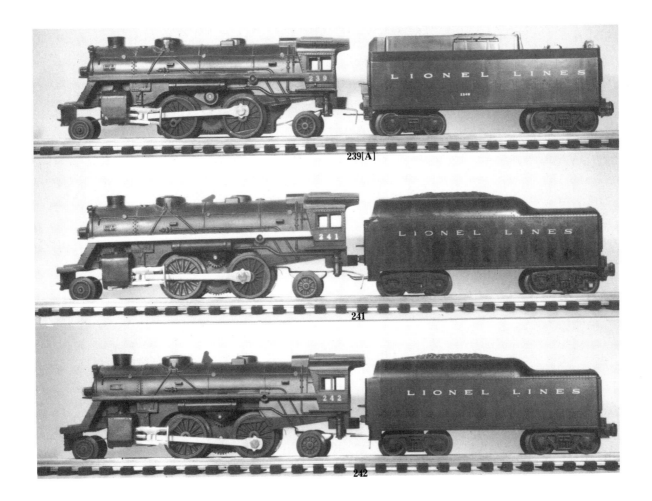

239[A]

241

242

small gears, readily visible sliding shoes, blind center driver, "221" rubber-stamped in silver or white/silver. 221T tender marked "New York Central" with decal in black and silver, staple-end trucks, coil coupler, also came with 221W whistle tender. The 1946 locomotives have a thinner pilot than the 1947 locomotives. J. Kotil comment.

(A) 1946, gray body, aluminum-finished drivers without tires.
                      **50   90  115  150**

(B) 1946, same as (A), but black-finished drivers. See illustration below.
                      **50   60   85  120**

(C) 1947, black body, black drivers with nickel tires.  **40   50   75  100**


**224** 1945-46, 2-6-2, black die-cast boiler; Baldwin nickel-rim disc drivers; O Gauge motor with gears on left and brushplate on right; drive, connecting and eccentric rods; die-cast front and rear trucks; cab detailed with two firebox doors; headlight; handrail rods run from cab to pilot on both sides; nickel-plated bell on bracket; motor held by screw at top rear of boiler and horizontal rod across boiler just above steam chest; tenders feature metal trim, including wire guard rail which goes around the back deck and is fastened by two steel cotter pins. This engine was also made prewar as 224 or 224E in either black or gunmetal. It has a squared-off cab floor and a longer drawbar with ears; its tender has the older box couplers. Priced for postwar version. The later tender is the 2466WX. The prewar version of this engine headed Lionel's first postwar set in late 1945; its tender was not equipped with a drawbar! See first listing below. R. Ervin and R. LaVoie comments.

(A) Late 1945 only, blackened metal handrails on engine, squared-off cab rear (as in prewar version) with blackened drawbar; 2466W tender with earliest open coil coupler and either whirly or dished wheels and blackened handrail around rear tender deck; white prewar "LIONEL LINES" lettering instead of postwar silver. This tender had no drawbar; instead, the ears on the locomotive drawbar fit into an oval hole punched into front of tender

frame. Came as part of first postwar set 463W only in late 1945. R. Swanson Collection and comments, P. Murray Collection.  **60   80  100  150**

(B) 1946, rounded cab floor end, chromed handrails, 2466W tender with chromed railing around back deck, tender drawbar, Type II trucks with brass roller pickups. R. Ervin and R. LaVoie comments.  **50   60   75  120**

(C) 1947, same as (B), but 2466WX tender with Type III trucks; (regular wheels, thin axles and closed coil couplers).  **50   60   75  120**

**233** 1961-62, 2-4-2, black plastic boiler, plastic side motor 233-100, two-position reverse, smoke, light, Magnetraction, 233W tender, which is the same as the 243W except that its coupler is non-operating. M. Denuty Collection.  **12   15   25   35**

**235** 1961, uncatalogued, 2-4-2, black plastic boiler, two-position reverse, smoke, light, Magnetraction, plastic side motor 236-100, 1130T tender with arch-bar trucks. M. Denuty comment.  **15   20   30   50**

**236** 1961-62, 2-4-2, black plastic boiler, white lettering, drive rod only, liquid smoke, light, plastic motor with ridged bottom, two gears visible on left side, brush holder on right side, rolled metal pickup, Magnetraction, fine cab interior detail.

(A) 1050T slope-back tender with arch-bar trucks and operating coupler, part of set 11222, the "Comanche", in 1962. M. Denuty comment.
                      **10   15   25   35**

(B) 1130T tender; offered for separate sale and as part of uncatalogued set X629, which included a 3519 satellite launching car, a 6650 rocket launching car, a 6470 explosives boxcar and a 6017 Lionel Lines caboose. See Uncatalogued Set chapter. S. Perlmutter Collection, M. Denuty comments.
                      **10   15   25   35**

**237** 1963-66, 2-4-2, black plastic boiler, drive rod only, liquid smoke unit, light, plastic motor 237-100 with ridged bottom, two gears visible on left side, brushplate holder on right side, middle rail pickups are rolled metal, rubber tire on right rear driver, fine detail inside cab, white stripe runs length of body, two-position reverse unit with fiber lever through boiler top;

243

244

245

see 1101 for discussion of boiler types. Unusual medium-width running board which makes its stripe narrower than the 241, 249 or 250; M. Denuty comment. Light has often been added as per repair book; H. Edmunds comment.

(A) 1130T streamlined tender lettered "LIONEL LINES", AAR trucks, ground pickup fingers on front truck, rear truck with fixed coupler, tender not numbered. W. Eddins Collection.          10  15  25  35

(B) Unnumbered, unlettered slope-back tender, AAR trucks, fixed coupler, galvanized frame. Came as part of uncatalogued set 19262, the "Apache", in 1963. P. Ambrose and M. Denuty comments.          10  15  25  35

**238** 1963-64, 2-4-2, black plastic body, plastic side motor, Scout-type two-position reverse, smoke, light, rubber tires, 234W or 242T tenders; see 1101 for discussion of body types.

(A) Tender lettered "LIONEL LINES".          10  20  35  50

(B) 1963, tender lettered "CANADIAN NATIONAL".          NRS

**239** 1965-66, 2-4-2, black die-cast body, step for bell, no bell.

(A) Plastic motor with ridged bottom, thick rubber-stamped number on cab, two gears showing, rubber tire on right rear wheel, liquid smoke unit, 16-spoke wheels, light, fiber lever on two-position reversing unit. C. Rohlfing Collection.          10  20  35  50

(B) Same as (A), but heat-stamped thin number on cab side. C. Rohlfing Collection.          10  20  35  50

(C) Better grade O-27 metal side motor with three-position reverse unit with control lever down, readily accessible brushes, locomotive retains slot in top for two-position reverse unit; 239(C) has a lighter stamping and a different type-face than do 239(A) and (B). The better motor was sometimes installed as a replacement for the fragile plastic motor; in fact, the Lionel Service Bulletin advised service stations to replace the entire motor rather than fool with the plastic-side motor. As a result, there are 239(A) and (B) versions with the better motor, and their type face will not be as described here.

However, all such motors were fitted after the factory production. This applies to many other small locomotives produced in these years; they are sometimes called "Complaint" locomotives because that is what put the better motor into them! R. LaVoie comments.          10  20  35  50

**240** Circa 1964, 2-4-2, uncatalogued by Lionel. Came as part of Sears space set 9820 only. Black plastic boiler, plastic side motor, two-position reverse, smoke, light, rubber tires (see 1101 for full discussion of locomotive types). This locomotive is particularly interesting because of its set, which included a 3666 cannon car, a 6470 exploding boxcar, an unnumbered flatcar with a green tank, a 6814 (C) rescue caboose, what appears to be a Marx-made transformer and a number of other pieces. This set, illustrated in color in the flatcar section, is described in more detail under the 3666 boxcar listing. Set value:          300  400  600  750

These observations are the result of the contributions of Vergonet, Bohn and Jarman. Some sets, possibly made in 1968 and numbered 11600, also came with an olive-colored range launching unit (add $100 to set values). Locomotive and tender value:          15  35  85  150

**241** 1958, uncatalogued, 2-4-2, die-cast body, wide white stripe along locomotive sides, fiber lever for reverse unit between domes, a motor with ridged bottom described as 239-100 in the parts manual, gears on left side, brushes on right side, liquid smoke unit, finely detailed cab interior, one rubber tire on right side driver. See 1101 for discussion of boiler types and comparisons with 237 and 242.

(A) One rubber tire on right rear driver; 234W tender with whistle and pickup rollers on each truck; fixed coupler; embossed "Built By Lionel" plate at lower front side of tender; shell fastened to frame by two-tabbed frame extension at rear and Phillips screw at front. L. Wyant Collection.          20  30  40  60

(B) 1965, two rubber tires, 234W tender with whistle, late AAR trucks with fixed coupler, came as part of uncatalogued JC Penney set 924-8287 in box dated Nov. 26, 1966. W. Eddins collection.          20  30  40  60

(C) 1130T streamlined tender without whistle.          15  20  30  40

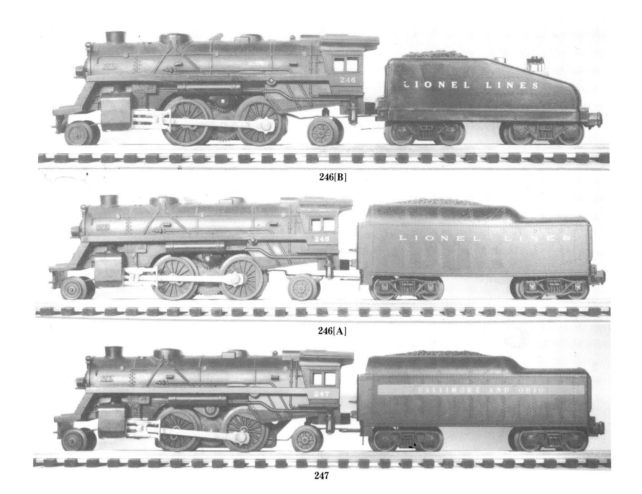

246[B]

246[A]

247

**242** 1962-66, 2-4-2, black plastic body, motor with grooved bottom, light, main rod each side, two gears visible on left side, brushes on right side, highly detailed cab interior, fiber lever for reverse unit through boiler top, stack has large hole because red gasket for smoke unit is not present. 1062T slope-back or 1060T streamlined tender with AAR trucks, one disc coupler, cab held to frame by two tabs in rear and Phillips screw in front; motor held in by slide on front and pin through cab on rear; see 1101 for a discussion of boiler types and comparisons with 237 and 241.

(A) With 1062T slope-back tender, extra copper ground strip. M. Denuty comments. **15    20    25    35**

(B) With 1060T streamlined tender and extra copper ground strip. M. Denuty comments. **20    25    30    40**

(C) 1964, with 1130T tender lettered "SOUTHERN PACIFIC", as part of set 19350; set also included 3409 helicopter car, unnumbered red flatcar with unknown load, red 6476 Lehigh Valley hopper and red 6059 M&St.L Caboose. M. Denuty Collection. **NRS**

**243** 1960, 2-4-2, black plastic body, two-position reverse unit with metal lever coming through boiler near cab, one drive rod on each side; O-27 metal-sided motor with two gears showing on left side and brushplate on right side; liquid smoke unit with bellows, highly detailed cab interior, motor held on by screw in front of reverse lever and plate in front of drivers, rubber tires, light. 243W tender, AAR trucks, disc coupler, one pickup roller for whistle and one wire for ground; see 1101 for a discussion of boiler types and comparison with 237, 241 and 242. **15    20    25    35**

**244** 1960-61, 2-4-2, black plastic body, bell ledge between stack and first dome, no bell, reverse lever between second dome and cab; liquid smoke with bellows, light, O-27 247-100 motor with metal sides, two gears on left side, brushes on right side, weight under cab. Tender lettered "LIONEL LINES", AAR truck in front, arch bar truck in rear with fixed coupler, tender cab mounted by two tabs in rear, screw in front, came with either 244T slopeback tender (1960) or 1130T streamlined tender (1961). M. Denuty comments. **15    20    25    35**

**245** 1961, 2-4-2, black plastic boiler, bell ledge between stack and first dome, no bell, small molded generator unit immediately in front of cab, motor mounted by pin through boiler and mounting plate in front, weight under cab, two gears visible on left, brush holder on right, smooth bottom 245-100 plastic motor, two-position reverse unit with fiber lever, detailed cab interior. Tender with arch bar trucks, fixed coupler, see 1101 for discussion of body type. **15    20    25    35**

**246** 1959-61, 2-4-2, black plastic boiler, bell ledge between stack and first dome, no bell, reverse lever slot between first and second domes; single main rod on each side, light, no smoke unit, Magnetraction. In late 1961, this locomotive came as part of set X-600, a special Quaker Oats promotion wherein the purchaser sent in two Quaker Oats box tops and $11.95 for the set, which included a 6406 gray unlettered flatcar with red automobile, a 6042 blue gondola with white lettering and four white "LIONEL"-embossed canisters, a 6076 red hopper car with white lettering, a red unlettered 6047 caboose, a 1016 35-watt transformer, eight pieces of 1013 curved track, two pieces of 1018 straight track and a lockon. Lionel informed its service stations about this set and reported that the buyers of this set "are asking where to buy more track and accessories to add to this set. Because of the many thousands of Quaker Oats sets being shipped across the country, you should be selling quite a bit of track and accessories to these new Lionel customers." Lionel went on to say that "if by chance any of the parts of the set have arrived damaged through the mail to these customers, we are giving them the choice of returning the damaged merchandise to us at the Factory or visiting you to have the parts repaired or replaced under our normal guarantee." Were a great number of these sets damaged in shipment? See also Uncatalogued Set chapter. L. Bohn comments, J. Divi Collection. Prices below for locomotive only; set price unknown. Also came as part of set 1111, which had a 6476 red Lehigh Valley hopper, a 6014 Chun King boxcar, a 3376 Operating Giraffe Car and a 6047 Lionel Lines caboose. T. Budniak Collection.

(A) No molded generator unit in front of cab, ridged bottom plastic motor

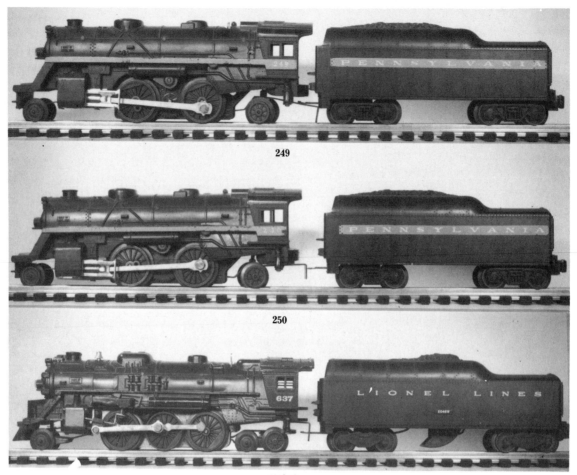

249

250

637[A]

**Gd VG Exc Mt**

246-100, Magnetraction, 246T or 1130T tender, tender not numbered. M. Denuty comments.　　15　25　30　35

(B) Molded generator unit in front of cab, smooth bottom plastic motor 246-200, no weight under cab, 244T slope-back tender, partially open in front pilot. M. Denuty comments.　　15　25　30　35

**247** 1959-61, 2-4-2, black plastic body, blue stripe with white lettering; tender lettered "BALTIMORE & OHIO", reversing unit, motor held by screw in rear and casting mounting front; light, liquid smoke unit with bellows. 247T tender with AAR trucks, disc coupler; cab fastened to frame by tab fasteners in rear, screw in front; no Magnetraction, weight or rubber traction tire and consequently a poor puller; see 1101 for discussion of body types. M. Denuty comments.　　20　30　40　55

**248** 1958, not catalogued, 2-4-2, black plastic boiler, O-27 motor with metal sides, two-position reverse unit, weight under cab floor, 1130T "LIONEL LINES" tender with AAR trucks and disc coupler; came with set X-610, retailer unknown. This set is unusual because although its components were inexpensive, it came with O Gauge track. See Uncatalogued Set chapter and listings for contents and further information. M. Denuty comments.　　15　20　40　60

**249** 1958, 2-4-2, black plastic body, bell ledge, no bell, black generator detail between reverse lever and cab, orange stripe with white lettering on both locomotive and tender. Tender lettered "PENNSYLVANIA", drive rod on each side, O-27 249 motor with metal sides, brushplate on right side, two-position reverse unit, metal weight underneath cab, no light in locomotive. 250T tender with AAR trucks, disc coupler, see 1101 for discussion of body types. Came with 1130T tender (written on tender box) as part of set 1609; T. Budniak observation.　　15　25　40　60

**250** 1957, 2-4-2, black plastic body, bell ledge, no bell, generator detail in front of cab, no reverse lever slot, orange stripes on locomotive and tender with white "PENNSYLVANIA" lettering; O-27 metal side motor, three-

position reverse unit, lever down, weight under cab floor, light in front of locomotive, no lens, two gears on left side, brushplate on right side, motor held in by Phillips screw behind second dome and slot in front of motor, cab interior highly detailed. 250T tender with AAR trucks, disc coupler; see 1101 for discussion of body types.　　15　25　40　60

**251** 1959 (date confirmation requested), 2-4-2, black die-cast boiler, light, two-position reverse with fiber reverse lever, brushes right side, white "251" on cab beneath window. Clark Collection.

(A) Slope-back tender with AAR trucks, fixed coupler.　15　20　30　40

(B) 250T-type tender, AAR trucks, fixed coupler.　15　20　30　40

**637** 1959-63, 2-6-4, catalogued as Super O but shares 2037 metal boiler casting, black with white lettering, smoke, Magnetraction.

(A) 2046W tender with whistle, lettered "LIONEL LINES", 1959, part of set 2531WS; G. Salamone Collection.　　40　60　85　150

(B) 736W tender lettered "PENNSYLVANIA", 1960, AAR trucks, disc coupler, part of set 2547 WS, but catalogue shows tender lettered "LIONEL LINES". Weisskopf Collection.　　40　60　85　150

(C) 736W tender lettered "PENNSYLVANIA"; part of set 2571 (1961), 13008 (1962) and 13098 (1963). M. Denuty Collection.　40　60　85　150

**646** 1954-58, 4-6-4, smoke, three-position reverse unit, shares boiler casting with 2046 and 2056, boiler casting evolved from 726 casting. 2046W tender with whistle, water scoop, bar-end metal trucks (1954-56) or AAR trucks with disc couplers (1957-58), two pickup rollers; with e ther heat-stamped or large or small rubber-stamped cab numbers. This boiler casting and all other New York Central "Alco" boiler castings (726, 736, 2046 and 2056) can be found with two types of cab windows. One type has a full cross-brace which divides the window into four equal-sized small windows. The other is missing one part of the cross-brace so that there are three windows instead of four. It is often mistakenly believed that the three-window casting has a broken window support brace. R. Griesbeck and R. Ervin observations.

646

665[A]

4671 Electronic control loco

(A) 1954, Die-cast trailing trucks, small rubber-stamped number. Foss Collection.                                    **75   125   175   250**

(B) 1954-58, trailing truck with plastic side frames, large rubber-stamped number. Foss Collection.                **75   125   175   250**

(C) Same as (B), but heat-stamped number. R. Ervin Collection.
                                                                    **75   125   175   250**

**665** 1954-59, 4-6-4, pill-type smoke unit, three-position reverse, Magnetraction, feedwater heater in front, plastic side frame on trailing trucks, shares Santa Fe Hudson boiler casting with 685, 2055 and 2065, with either rubber-stamped or heat-stamped cab numbers.

(A) 6026W tender with whistle, bar-end metal trucks, magnetic tab couplers.                                          **60   110   135   200**

(B) 2046W tender.                                                   **60    90   135   200**

(C) 1966, heat-stamped cab number, 736W tender lettered "PENNSYLVANIA", AAR trucks, disc coupler, two roller pickups. Purchased new in 1977. R. Hutchinson, P. Ambrose, R. Niedhammer Collections.
                                                                    **60    90   135   175**

**670** 1952, 6-8-6, Pennsylvania Steam Turbine shown in distributor's advance catalogue but not made. This was the number which was to be assigned to the Korean War non-Magnetraction version of this engine, but it was actually made as a 671RR with and without the RR markings. Other locomotives similarly affected were a 674 (produced as the 675) and a 725 (produced as the 726RR). Since these distributor catalogues were early versions, support is given to the idea that O-27 units (which are numbered correctly) were produced first in Lionel's manufacturing cycle and O Gauge units later. T. Rollo and R. LaVoie comments.        **Not Manufactured**

**671** 1946-49, 6-8-6 model of Pennsylvania S-2 Steam Turbine. Came with Instruction Sheet 926-25 showing lubricating instructions for locomotive and trucks. R. Hutchinson Collection. Also see 671RR.

(A) 1946, double worm-drive, horizontal reverse unit, smoke lamp with bulb with depressed area that used special 196 tablets, silver rubber-stamped number under cab window, no external E-unit lever, motor labeled "ATOMIC MOTOR", slotted brush holders, jack receptacles, red Keystone

on boiler front with gold lettering, shiny nickel rims on drivers, 671W tender with grab-rails front and back, railing on rear deck, white "LIONEL LINES" lettering, R. Ervin observation. One example observed has a 671W tender without grab-rails on the front. M. Goodwin Collection.   **50   100   150   250**

(B) Same as (A), but black Keystone with white heat-stamped or rubber-stamped "6200"; earliest production. R. Ervin observation, J. Bratspis and P. Rothenberg Collections.             **75   125   175   250**

(C) Same as (A), but red Keystone rubber-stamped "6200" in silver. R. Griesbeck and Taylor Collections. R. Niedhammer observation. Additional observations requested.                                              **NRS**

(D) 1947, single worm-drive motor, vertical reverse unit with E-unit lever projecting through boiler, new smoke unit with resistance coil and piston, white rubber-stamped number under cab window, motor stamped "LIONEL PRECISION MOTOR", non-slotted brush tubes, no jack receptacles, piping detail added to boiler immediately behind air pumps, bottom plate reads: "S-2   TURBO   LOCOMOTIVE   MADE   IN THE ...", red Keystone on boiler front, 671W tender with grab-rails front and back, railing on rear deck, "LIONEL LINES" lettering.
                                                                    **50   100   150   250**

(E) 1948, similar to (D), but thin blackened steel rims on flanged drives (first and fourth axles), bottom plate on middle rail collector reads "MADE IN THE ...", metal ballast, new streamlined, 12-wheel 2671W tender lettered "PENNSYLVANIA", tender has water scoop and plastic whistle case with whistle lying on side with opening through the water scoop, tender has backup lights, light bracket is similar to those found on prewar O Gauge cars; inside the tender is a piece of plastic painted red for the center red light and left as clear plastic for the two side lights, coil couplers. Many 2671W tenders have been retrofitted with reproduction parts for the backup lights. Original plastic piece projects into and slightly outside the three tender holes.                                     **100   175   250   400**

(F) 1948, same as (E), but tender does not have backup lights.
                                                                    **75   100   150   200**

(G) 1949, same as (F), but no rims on drivers. R. Ervin Collection.
                                                                    **75   100   150   200**

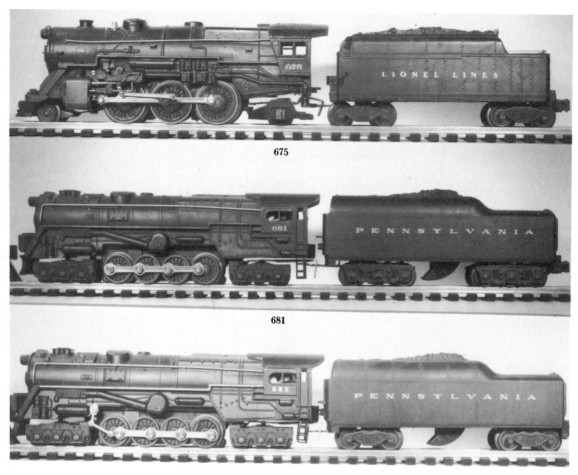

675

681

682

(H) Same as (F), but has 2671W tender with wide-spaced "LIONEL LINES" and backup lights; same tender as 736 produced in 1950-51. T. Klaassen Collection.                     100 150 225 300

**NOTE:** In 1972, the Train Collectors' Association produced a special boiler front designed to fit the 671, 681, 682 and 2020 S-2 turbines. This boiler front was made for the 1972 Pittsburgh convention and had special TCA stickers on the pumps and smoke box front. The casting differs from Lionel's original casting. Reader comments on the specific differences are requested. Although this is only a component, and not made by Lionel, it is closely associated with Lionel production and is located here for reader convenience.

**671R** 1946-49, 6-8-6, electronic control set, Lionel Precision motor with two jacks, decaled with black decal smaller than a dime and white-lettered "ELECTRONIC CONTROL" and "L" in center, boiler front has red Keystone with gold number "6200", smoke unit. Locomotive numbered "671" on cab. 4424W or 4671W tender with Type RU electronic control receiver affixed to frame underside, "LIONEL LINES" heat-stamped in silver, special electronic control decal, light gray with white-lettered "ELECTRONIC CONTROL", tender has handrails on rear deck and rear end and handrails on tender front, wire connects locomotive with tender, staple-end metal trucks, coil coupler operated by electronic control receiver; gray decal on tender matches gray button on control unit. The changes in this locomotive correspond to the changes in the regular 671 issue. In 1946-47, the Electronic Control Set included the 671R engine, a 4424W whistle tender, a 4452 gondola, a 4454 boxcar, a 5459 dump car and a 4457 caboose. It also included a special electronic control unit, ECU-1. In 1948, a 4357 SP-type caboose replaced the 4457. The set remained the same in 1949. See Pat Scholes article in this edition for further details. R. Lord and R. Ervin Collections.

(A) Locomotive and tender only.              100 150 250 350
(B) Price for set.                            200 400 700 875

**671RR** 1952, 6-8-6 Pennsylvania Turbine, see 671 for background. This locomotive is mechanically similar to 681 but does not have Magnetraction due to a shortage of Alnico magnetic material for axles caused by the Korean War. Locomotive may be marked either 671 or 671RR on cab beneath the window. Locomotive has one-piece wheels made from sintered iron. Although the illustration of this locomotive shows it with a 671W tender, the correct tender is a 2046W-50. This tender has 2046W-50 stamped on the frame in silver, though its box is labeled "2046W, PRR, WITH WHISTLE". It has four-wheel bar-end metal trucks, "PENNSYLVA-NIA" lettering in white, open holes at the tender rear and a marbled yellow plastic whistle housing. The locomotive number is rubber-stamped on the locomotive cab, and there is a hole in the chassis between the first and second pair of drive wheels where the magnets for Magnetraction would have been placed. R. LaVoie Collection.

(A) "671" on cab.                             75 100 150 200
(B) "671RR" on cab.                           75 100 150 200

**674 LIONEL LINES** 1952, 2-6-4, this number shown in distributor's advance catalogue, but actually made as non-Magnetraction 675.

**Not Manufactured**

**675** 1947, 2-6-2, die-cast boiler, essentially a modified 225 boiler with new boiler front and smoke units, Pennsylvania K-4s prototype, rubber-stamped cab numerals, drive, connecting and eccentric rods, smoke, light; label on cab roof underside reads "to remove the whitish smoke deposit from locomotive body, apply a little Lionel lubricant or vaseline and polish with a soft clean cloth", Baldwin disc wheels with nickel rims. 2466W or 2466WX tender with rear deck handrail, staple-end metal trucks, coil couplers, lettered "LIONEL LINES", whistle. Identical to 2025 except for number in 2-6-2 versions and to 2035 in 2-6-4 version. In 1947-49, the 675 and 2025 used a Type 675M-1 motor with Baldwin disc wheels featuring chromed tires. However, in 1950 Magnetraction required the use of a new motor with aluminum sides, the 2035-100, which used sintered-iron drivers listed as part 2035-178. In 1952, when Magnetraction was not used, Lionel reverted

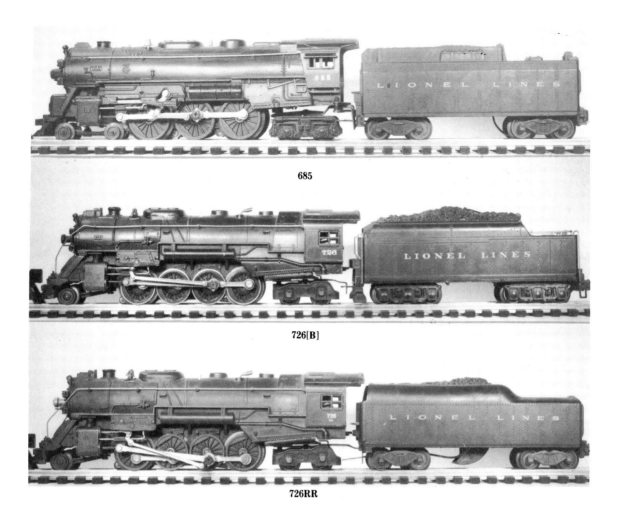

685

726[B]

726RR

to the steel frame, but the Baldwin disc drivers were not resurrected. Instead, drivers listed as part 2035-155 were used; these drivers were also used on the 1110/6110 steamers in the Scout line. In 1950, the 675 K4s was called a "Prairie"-type locomotive in Lionel's Model Railroading Book published by Bantam. That was correct for Lionel's 2-6-2 wheel designation, but the real K4 was a 4-6-2 Pacific — a wheel configuration never used by Lionel. R. Hutchinson comments.

(A) Early 1947, "675" rubber-stamped in silver on boiler front Keystone, unpainted aluminum wide-rim stack. Silver number on boiler front Keystone may also exist in heat-stamped version; confirmation requested. R. LaVoie Collection.    45    80    115    180
(B) 1948, "5690" in gold on red decal on boiler front. Kauzlarich Collection.    45    75    90    150
(C) 1948, "PRR" intertwined lettering in gold on red decal on boiler front. E. Zukowski Collection.    45    80    90    150
(D) 1948, similar to (B), but with new pilot with simulated knuckle coupler and lift pin; smokestack reduced in size.    45    75    90    150
(E) 1949, similar to (D), but with 6466WX tender with magnetic couplers    45    75    90    150
(F) 1952, 2-6-4, spoked drivers, Korean War issue without Magnetraction, four-wheel stamped sheet metal trailing truck, heat-stamped "675" on boiler front, 2046W tender with bar-end metal trucks, magnetic couplers, illustrated in Lionel Service Manual and 1952 catalogue as part of set 2177WS. W. Spence and R. Hutchinson comments, H. Powell, A. Arpino and R. Ervin Collections.    50    75    125    200
(G) Same as (F), but has pilot like (D) and came with 6466W tender. T. Budniak and T. Klaassen Collections.    50    75    125    200
(H) Same as (B), but came with 6466WX tender, coil couplers and staple-end metal trucks. In the 1948 production run, some tenders with this engine were numbered in the 6000 Series for magnetic trucks, but for O Gauge sets they kept the older coil couplers because the UCS remote track was not ready in time for 1948 O Gauge production. This is also true of the

rolling stock in these sets. See entries for 6456 hopper car and 6555 tank car. T. Rollo comments, T. Budniak Collection.    45    80    100    150
(I) Same as (F), but with "5690" in gold on red Keystone decal. D. Doyle and R. Niedhammer Collections.    50    75    125    200

**681** 1950-51, 1953, 6-8-6, smoke, three-position reverse unit, worm-drive motor, Magnetraction, 6200 on decal cab front. 2671W tender stamped "PENNSYLVANIA" in white or silver, six-wheel trucks with blind center wheels, water scoop, three holes in tender rear; O Gauge locomotive, rubber-stamped or heat-stamped cab numerals.
(A) 1950-51, "681" rubber-stamped on locomotive and "PENNSYLVANIA" rubber-stamped on 2671 or 2671 WX tender in silver or white letters. Came in box with outside flap lettered "681/LOCOMOTIVE/WITH SMOKE CHAMBER"; inside flap numbered 681-20, box had inside cardboard liner and locomotive was wrapped in Lionel paper. R. Griesbeck, R. Ervin and W. Schilling Collections.    75    145    170    250
(B) Same as (A), but 2671 W tender with heat-stamped "PENNSYLVANIA" in white, "681" heat-stamped on boiler cab. C. Rohlfing Collection.    75    145    170    250
(C) Late 1951 and 1953, "681" and "PENNSYLVANIA" in heat-stamped white lettering, 2046W-50 tender with four-wheel trucks, R. Griesbeck and R. Ervin Collections.    75    145    170    250

**NOTE:** An original 2671W tender shell for the 671, 681, 726RR and 736 locomotives can be faked by careful removal of the embossed number from the back nameplate of a Fundimensions tender shell.    I.D. Smith observation.

**682** 1954-55, 6-8-6, Pennsylvania S-2 Turbine prototype, similar to 681, but with lubricator linkage and white stripe on running board, 6200 on boiler front Keystone, heat-stamped "682". 2046W-50 tender with whistle, water scoop, bar-end metal trucks, magnetic couplers, three holes on tender rear filled in, tender lettered "PENNSYLVANIA", O Gauge locomotive.
   150    200    250    350

**685** 1953, 4-6-4, shares Santa Fe Hudson-type boiler with 665, 2055 and 2065; comments from those apply; 6026W tender, bar-end metal trucks with magnetic couplers, two pickup rollers and whistle, O Gauge locomotive.

(A) Early production: 2046W tender. Locomotive has embossed drive rod like 2046; later production lacks this embossing. Raised projections on crosshead guide plate where screws attach. D. Fleming Collection.
75  135  175  300

(B) Rubber-stamped 685 in silver below cab windows, 6026W tender with bar-end metal trucks. J. Wilson Collection.
85  145  195  350

(C) Same as (B), but 685 is heat-stamped in white below cab windows. W. Eddins Collection.
75  135  175  300

**686** Uncatalogued, c. 1953-54, 4-6-4.  Confirmation and additional information necessary. R. Hutchinson comment.
**NRS**

**703** 1946, 4-6-4, scale Hudson, postwar version of 763, catalogued but not made, prototype exists in MPC archives. L. Bohn comment.
**Not Manufactured**

**725** 1952, 2-8-4. Berkshire shown in distributor's advance catalogue, but actually made as non-Magnetraction 726RR.
**Not Manufactured**

**726(A)** 1946, 2-8-4, Berkshire, die-cast Baldwin disc drivers with pressed-on metal tires, Lionel atomic precision motor with double worm gear, boiler casting is modified prewar 226 boiler, turned handrail stanchions, two-plug receptacles on brushplate to disconnect E-unit or lock E-unit in place. One receptacle locks E-unit in forward, neutral or reverse and other plug activates E-unit so that it sequentially reverses, early smoke bulb unit, nickel-plated drive and connecting rods, valve gear, smoke box door swings open on hinges, flag holders, nickel-plated motor side not covered by cowling as on 726(B); plate that covered the bottom of the motor extends beyond ash pan and beyond beginning of last driver, in contrast to 726(B); the plate may be removed, allowing the drive wheel axle sets to be taken out. This is a revival of the prewar "BILD-A-LOCO" motor design. Ash pan integral part of motor base casting; motor on bottom says "726 O-Gauge Locomotive, Made in U.S. of America, the Lionel Corporation, New York", compare to lettering on 726(B). When bottom plate is removed worm driving and copper wheel bushings are visible, metal tires on Baldwin disc wheels, center drivers are blind, pilot truck guide plate is screwed on 726(A), and riveted on 726(B), solid wheel casting on trailing truck on 726(A) changed to have hollow area with bridge across casting in 726(B); same difference for pilot truck wheels. 2426W tender has metal top cab with six-wheel trucks, plastic side frames, coil coupler with sliding shoe, handrails and long rails on front, long rails and black deck railing with six stanchions; highly desirable tender, worth at least $150; same tender came with 773, 1950 version. 1946 tender has cast metal whistle soundbox, later tenders have plastic soundbox. Second version of 1946 has different frame and motor; early motor cannot be used on later frame because reinforcement was added to rear of chassis. Early locomotives which retain the original smoke bulb arrangement are considerably more scarce than the converted or later versions. D. Fleming comment. In addition, the casting of the early 1946 locomotive is open where the eccentric rod attaches to the boiler casting; in later production, this area is closed. J. Bratspis observation.
200  275  375  500

(B) 1947-49, generally similar to (A), but revised boiler casting with lengthened sand domes, cotter pin-type handrail stanchions, E-unit mounted vertically with lever penetrating top of boiler; plug receptacles on brushplate are eliminated; simulated coupler lift bar on front pilot, black flag holders, bottom plate reads "Made in U.S.A., the Lionel Corporation, New York, New York", riveted metal retaining plate for pilot truck, cowling added to side of motor to hide motor, simulated springs visible from side of locomotive, ash pan part of bottom frame butt-ends at rear set of drivers, resistance coil smoke unit. Large cab metal tender, 2426W; O Gauge locomotive.
200  225  325  425

(C) 1947 only, plain pilot without simulated front coupler, otherwise like (B), has 2426W metal tender, but with cast metal whistle soundbox, locomotive has 671M-1 motor. R. Griesbeck comment.
175  225  325  400

**726RR** 1952, 2-8-4, "RR" for Korean War issue without Magnetraction, cadmium-plated drive and connecting rods, valve gear, smoke unit, three-position reverse unit. Wedge added to boiler front casting to support headlight; present on all Berkshires from 1952-66. Tender has four-wheel

staple-end metal trucks, two pickup rollers, holes in tender rear filled in, whistle; less desirable tender than 2426W; O Gauge locomotive. G. Salamone comment. One example reported with 2046W tender chassis carrying 2671W tender shell (R. Brezak Collection). This points out that dealers often switched tender shells around to provide buyers with "PENNSYLVANIA" lettering on the tender shells — certainly creating problems for train scholars! Such post-factory shell swapping was common with the 726 and 736.

(A) Same as above.
100  170  225  300

(B) Similar to (A), but larger "726" and no "RR" on cab, nickel-plated rods, 2046W tender, holes in rear of shell, bar-end four-wheel trucks with magnetic couplers. R. Griesbeck and D. Fleming Collections.
100  170  225  300

(C) Same as (A), but six-wheel tender with "LIONEL LINES" in small white serif lettering widely spaced on the tender side. T. Klaassen Collection. **NRS**

(D) Same as (A), but came with 2046W-50 tender with bar-end trucks. C. Rohlfing Collection.
100  170  225  300

**736(A)** 1950-51, Berkshire, spoked-style drivers without tires, die-cast trailing truck, nickel-plated drive and connecting rods, valve gear, worm-drive motor, three-position reverse unit, Magnetraction, smoke, whistle, hinged smoke box door, grayish-silver rubber-stamped cab number, no bracket wedge on headlight casting, three-window boiler cab. Original box has Kraft-St. Joe Paper Co. logo, a 1950 date and a part number 736-20 with "736" stamped on both ends. All printing on the box is blue, not black. 2671W tender with six-wheel trucks, heat-stamped "PENNSYLVA-NIA" lettering, plastic truck side frames, water scoop, coil-operated couplers, holes in rear deck; O Gauge locomotive. R. Griesbeck comment. Also came with 2671WX tender having six-wheel trucks and "LIONEL LINES" markings in widely spaced letters, holes in rear deck, maroon plastic shell painted black, rubber-stamped "2671WX" in grayish-silver on underframe. In this stamping, the "X" appears larger than the other numbers and letters, as if it is a later addition. The tender box is orange and blue and is numbered 2671W-25 on the inside flap. The outer box flaps are marked "2671WX", and again the letter "X" appears to have been a later addition. The "X" denotes the "LIONEL LINES" lettering, but many purchasers wanted the more realistic Pennsylvania tender to follow their particular 736. Dealers thus substituted Pennsylvania tenders rather freely, accounting for the large number of 736 examples with the Pennsylvania tender. Since all sorts of boiler front, tender and shell combinations turn up, "purist" collectors should refer to the original catalogues for the "correct" engine and tender combinations. Because the rubber stamping did not wear well, and there were boiler front and marker light problems, the 1950-51 736 with the 2671WX "Lionel Lines" tender is the most desired of the 736 locomotives. T. Phelps and P. Ambrose comments.
175  225  300  450

(B) 1953-54, similar to (A), but heat-stamped lettering on cab, small bracket wedge on headlight casting, collector assembly attached with two screws, die-cast trailing truck, cadmium-plated rods; 2046W tender with four-wheel trucks, O Gauge locomotive. R. Griesbeck and R. Ervin comments.
175  225  275  400

(C) 1955-56: similar to (B), but sheet metal trailing truck with plastic side frames; 2046W tender with four-wheel trucks, O Gauge locomotive. R. Griesbeck and R. Ervin comments.
175  225  275  400

(D) 1957-60, same as (C), but collector assembly attached with one screw; 2046W tender. R. Griesbeck comment.
175  225  275  400

(E) 1961-66, same as (D), but 736W tender with plugged holes in the rear deck. R. Griesbeck comment and M. Goodwin Collection.
175  225  275  400

**746** 1957-60, 4-8-4, model of Norfolk and Western J, three-position reverse unit, Magnetraction, liquid smoke; 746W tender with whistle, bar-end metal trucks, magnetic coupler with tab, two roller pickups; engine and tender have red band outlined in yellow stripes, yellow lettering; "746" rubber-stamped on cab, tender lettered "NORFOLK AND WESTERN", O Gauge locomotive. Short stripe tender also lettered "746W".

(A) 1957 only, tender with long, full-length stripe and no 746W raised numbering, Rubin and Weiss observations. Also reported as part of 1958 set 2521WS. C. Weber Collection.
300  500  750  1000

(B) 1958-60, tender with short stripe and 746W raised numbering. Friedman observation.
250  400  650  800

736[A]

746[B] Long stripe tender

746[A] Short stripe tender

**773**(A) 1950, 4-6-4, scale model of New York Central J-3 Hudson. postwar version of prewar 763 and its more detailed brother, the 700E. The 773, unlike the 763 and 700E, will run on regular O Gauge tubular curve track and offers smoke and Magnetraction. Locomotive has plug jacks in cab for connecting three-position reverse unit. Label on underside of cab states: "To remove the whitish smoke...." Catalogued as O Gauge locomotive.
(A) Has lighter stamping of "773" on cab compared with (B). Comes with very desirable 2426W tender with six-wheel trucks. 1950 version has slide valve guides.                    **475  700  1100  1400**

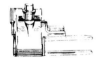

1950 Steam cylinder with slide valve guide

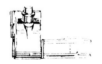

1961 cylinder without slide valve guide

(B) 1964, similar to 773(A), but with heavier heat-stamped number on cab, slide valve guides omitted from steam chest casting, steam chest not interchangeable with 773(A). "PENNSYLVANIA" tender with AAR trucks, disc coupler, two pickup rollers; "773" is more heavily stamped than on 773(A).                    **400  525  775  950**
(C) 1965-66, similar to (B), but with tender marked "NEW YORK CENTRAL".                    **400  550  800  1000**
(D) Similar to (B), but has 2426W tender with plastic whistle casing, 1964-style 773 stamp, no steam chest valve guides, white marker lights on boiler front and 1950-style roller pickups. Reportedly made for Macy's in 1956. Reader comments invited. T. Klaassen Collection.                    **NRS**
(E) Same as (C), but tender has larger "NEW YORK CENTRAL" lettering. Possibly represents the earliest 1965 production. S. Natoli Collection.                    **400  550  800  1000**

**1001** 1948, 2-4-2, first Scout locomotive, specially designed motor, 1001M-1 with two-position reverse unit integral to motor, motor has plastic sides and smooth bottom, with two pieces of copper rolled to form pickup rollers, awnings over windows. 1001T sheet metal Scout tender, Scout trucks and coupler, galvanized base, O-27 locomotive.  C. Rohlfing comment. The Lionel 1948 catalogue (page four) shows what appears to be the same locomotive (note horn atop boiler front and window sunshades!). The 1001 appears to be the first plastic boiler ever used by Lionel. This was also the first offering of the notoriously unreliable plastic case Scout motor, which used a highly unusual engineering design for its reverse unit involving movable brush holders. Although Lionel's obvious intent was to reduce costs, this motor proved so difficult to repair that if a customer complained loudly enough, the factory or the service station would replace this motor with the conventional metal-framed motor used in the 2034. The procedure is outlined in the Lionel service manual in section LOC-1110(1951), page 1, June 1953, and section LOC-2034, page 1, August 1953. Although the plastic boiler casting for this locomotive was highly detailed, it did not appear again until 1959, when in obvious financial distress, Lionel brought it back. There is a Marx plastic body which is almost identical to the 1001. This Marx copy of the 1001 was introduced in 1952. K. Wills and R. Bartelt comments.                    **12  15  25  35**

**1050** 1959, uncatalogued 0-4-0, plastic side motor, forward only, light, side rod, 1050 slope-back tender; O-27 locomotive.                    **12  15  25  35**

**1060** 1960-61, 2-4-2, same boiler as 1050, no reverse, main rod only, light. This engine was not shown in the consumer catalogue, since it was intended "to meet the needs of the low priced toy train market.... for pricing and delivery information, see your wholesaler or Lionel representative". The engine came with two different tenders with at least four different sets and is illustrated in the 1960, 1961 and 1962 Lionel Advance Catalogues. It has a plastic boiler with highly detailed cab interior and a curved metal piece for center rail pickup; we believe it was originally developed for the 1948 Scout locomotive. We describe this engine as an O-27 locomotive. We describe the larger tender as an 1130T which we think is patterned after the 2046 tender except for its smaller size. According to the Lionel Service Manual, the part number for this tender body is 1130-26 (I.D. Smith comment). We would

773[A] New York Central Hudson [1950]

773[C] New York Central Hudson [1965-66]

1001

Gd   VG   Exc   Mt

like to confirm this tender part number, which should appear on the interior of the tender shell. This 1130 tender is equipped with arch bar trucks. (C. Rohlfing observation.) The smaller tender is the 1050T slope-back type patterned after the 1615.

(A) 1130T tender, part of 1109 Huntsman Steamer set illustrated in 1961 Lionel Advance Catalogue. This set includes a 6404 flat with auto, a 3386 Bronx Zoo giraffe car and a 6047 caboose. All rolling stock has arch bar trucks and non-operating couplers. This set was also offered as a Green Stamps premium set in 1960. D. Fleming and C. Rohlfing comments.

                            12   15   25   35

(B) With 1050T slope-back tender, arch bar trucks and fixed coupler, part of 1123 Pacesetter set which appeared in the 1961 Lionel Advance Catalogue on page 14 and included a 6406 flat with auto, a 6042 gondola with canisters and an unlettered, unnumbered caboose. Reader assistance is asked in determining the original wholesale price and the numbers printed on the boxes. Rina comment. Locomotive and tender value:  12   15   25   35

(C) With 1130T tender, 3409 flat with helicopter, 6076 Lehigh Valley hopper and an unlettered, unnumbered caboose, the "Hawk" set, 1124, illustrated in the 1961 Lionel Advance Catalogue on page 14. Reader assistance is asked in determining the original wholesale price and the numbers printed on the boxes. Rina comment. Locomotive and tender value:

                            12   15   25   35

(D) With 1130T tender, 6402 flatcar with reels, 6042 gondola with two canisters and a 6067 caboose, eight sections of 1013 curved track, two sections of 1018 straight track and a 1026 transformer as set 11001, The Trailblazer, illustrated on page 2 of the 1962 Lionel Advance Catalogue. M. Rohlfing reports that his set has a brown unlettered flatcar with mold 1877-3 believed to be the 6402. He also reports that his caboose is unlettered, although the caboose illustrated in the catalogue was numbered. We suspect that most (if not all) of the Trailblazer sets actually produced are as Mr. Rohlfing describes, not as illustrated. Reader comments invited. Price for locomotive and tender only.        12   15   25   35

1061 1963-64, 0-4-0; also catalogued in 1969 as a 2-4-2, black highly detailed plastic boiler, similar to 1060 and 1062, plastic side motor, rolled metal pickups, drive rod without crosshead, no reverse, no light, slope-back tender with fixed coupler lettered "LIONEL LINES". This locomotive was part of set 11420, which sold for $11.95 in 1963-64 (the 1969 price was not included in the catalogue). This set possesses the dubious distinction of being Lionel's least expensive set since the 1930s. On the other hand, the set could be viewed as Lionel's very creative response to a difficult marketing situation. Lionel was buffeted by Marx production on one hand and race cars and space-related toys on the other. This set gave Lionel a chance to offer a competitive, inexpensive product. However, Lionel weakened its profit-making mechanism by such production — high quality toys at a premium price.

(A) With "LIONEL LINES" slope-back tender as described above.

                            12   15   25   35

(B) With 1130T tender lettered "SOUTHERN PACIFIC", AAR trucks, part of set 19328. P. Ambrose comment.     25   35   50   100

(C) Circa 1961-63: 0-4-0, drive rods, operating headlight with lens, no tires, "1061" decal over blackened heat-stamped "1060", unknown reverse unit, plastic side motor with rolled steel pickups, unlettered slope-back tender with arch-bar trucks and fixed coupler, tender was originally lettered "LIONEL LINES", but this was blackened out; came in set with unlettered mold 6511-2 blue flatcar with orange girder, unlettered red-painted black plastic SP-type caboose with black-tabbed frame and no end rails, also has one AAR truck with no coupler and one arch-bar truck with fixed coupler; 1025 transformer, four pieces of straight track and lockon. The train was mounted on a display board with screws to keep the train in place. This display board is 43-1/4" x 3-5/8" x 1-1/4". The set, 11415, came in a corrugated box lettered "MADE BY/THE LIONEL CORPORATION/NEW YORK N.Y." The box dimensions are 43-1/4" x 3-5/8" x 5". This set was recently sold by Madison Hardware in New York, which apparently had it in its warehouse for many years. P. Ambrose comments.     NRS

1060

1062[A]

1110

1062 1963-64, catalogued and made as 0-4-0, but also made as 2-4-2 for an uncatalogued set. Highly detailed plastic body similar to those used for 1050, 1060 and 1061. Body is apparently based on 1948 1001 Scout body. Plastic side motor, rolled metal pickups, drive rod without crosshead to reduce costs, two-position reverse with lever on boiler top, rubber tire on one driver, operating headlight, slope-back tender lettered "LIONEL LINES", but also came with unlettered tender in set 11311 from 1963. P. Ambrose comments. O-27 locomotive. This locomotive is included in the 11430 set listed in the 1964 catalogue. Priced at $14.95, the set came with a 6176 hopper, a 6142 gondola, a 6167-125 caboose, a 6149 remote control track, a 1026 25-watt transformer and track. Winton Collection. The locomotive was shown in the 1963 catalogue as an 0-4-0. C. Rohlfing Collection.

(A) 0-4-0, short headlight, drive rod without crosshead, slope-back tender, AAR trucks, fixed coupler, galvanized tender base, tender cab fastened by two tabs, contact on tender front truck provides locomotive ground. H. Holden Collection. Also came with unlettered slope-back tender as part of set 11311. P. Ambrose comment. 12 15 25 35
(B) 0-4-0, long headlight, no drive rod or crosshead, large unnumbered tender, probably 1130T, with AAR trucks, fixed coupler, contacts on tender front truck provide locomotive ground. H. Holden Collection.
12 15 25 35
(C) 2-4-2, short headlight, drive rod without crosshead, 1050T slope-back tender with galvanized base, AAR trucks, fixed coupler, tab fasteners for frame. Contact on front tender truck provides additional ground. Came with uncatalogued set 19500. C. Rohlfing Collection. 12 15 25 35
(D) Same as (A), but no extra contact on tender for additional ground. J. West Collection. 12 15 25 35

1101 1948, 2-4-2, Scout locomotive, die-cast boiler, sliding shoe pickups, drive rod with solid crosshead, three-position reverse unit, interior cab detail, 12 rib wheels, stripped down version of 1655 powered with regular 1655-2 motor; tender with metal bottom, top; Scout trucks and coupler.
12 15 25 35

The 1101 die-cast body has a small cast bell on a small step on the boiler's left side between the smokestack and its first dome. The 1101 body design was the basis for the later 230, 240 and 250 series locomotives. Some of the later locomotives retained the step even though the bell was no longer present, i.e., 241 and 243.

The 1101 has a straight slot for the E-unit lever since the lever moves in a straight line. When the 1101 design was adopted for the 243, the slot was changed to a curved design to accommodate the movement of the two-position reverse lever.

Other factors distinguish the 230, 240 and 250 series locomotives. Some have holes in the cab floor for weights (the 241 and 243), others do not. Some have thick running boards, others have thin ones. On some the reverse slot is between the first and second dome, on others between the second dome and cab.

1110 1948-52, 2-4-2, Scout with "LIONEL SCOUT" tender, die-cast boiler and cab similar to the 1101 but not interchangeable with it; Scout motor with plain plastic bottom, rounded copper pieces for pickups; drive rod with crosshead, fiber reverse lever, two-position reverse; tender with metal frame and top, Scout trucks, one Scout coupler. Lord comment.
(A) 1949, no hole on boiler front for smoke draft. 12 15 25 35
(B) 1951-52, hole in boiler front for smoke draft but no smoke unit.
12 15 25 35

1120 1950, 2-4-2, Scout with "LIONEL SCOUT" tender, die-cast boiler, headlight, no lens, fiber reverse lever, two-position reverse, plastic side motor with inaccessible brushes; rolled copper pieces for pickups; tender with metal frame and top, Scout trucks, one Scout coupler.
12 15 25 35

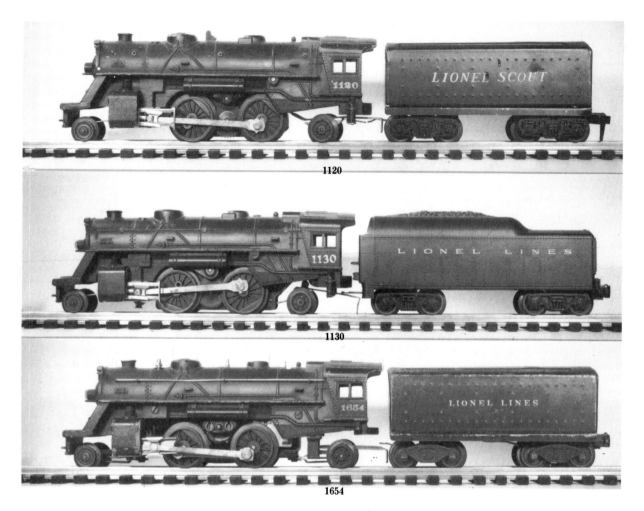

1120

1130

1654

**1130** 1953-54, 2-4-2, black plastic or die-cast body similar to die-cast 2034; early 1953 die-cast version is hard to find. 2034-100 motor with three-position reverse unit, short lever points down, headlight lens, main rods with guides, roller pickups which slide in and are held by a clip, large gear seen between drivers on left, brushplate on right. Came in set 1500 in 1953, which included 6066T tender, 6032 black short gondola, 6034 short Baby Ruth boxcar and 6037 tuscan caboose. All rolling stock in this set had Scout trucks with magnetic couplers. In 1954, this locomotive came with an 1130T tender with bar-end metal trucks and an operating coupler. O-27 locomotive. R. Lord, M. Denuty and R. LaVoie comments. We also have reports that the 1954 version of this engine had an 1130T tender with Scout trucks and magnetic couplers. Rohlfing and Powell comments.

(A) 1953: plastic body, 6066T tender.                    12    15    25    35

(B) Early 1953, die-cast body instead of plastic. Came as part of set 1500, as described above. There is a simple explanation for this locomotive, and it involves Lionel's economy with materials on hand. In 1952, Lionel made an identical locomotive except for the number, the 2034, and this locomotive did indeed have a die-cast body. For 1953, Lionel wanted to move production of the 2034 to its inexpensive Scout sets, so the firm changed the number to fit into the Scout series, the 1130, and decided to make the locomotive from a plastic casting, using the same dies. However, a few unstamped 2034 castings were left over from the 1952 runs, so Lionel rubber-stamped these 1130 and used them on the first sets made — probably not more than a few hundred. The irony is that the short screws used to attach the crosshead guides to the castings were not available, so Lionel solved that problem by using the longer screws designed for the new 1130 with the weight in the front — and to make up the difference in length, the firm included the weight with the die-cast chassis! This resulted in a little "track crusher" as heavy as a 2037! This die-cast version is very hard to find, but not many collectors know of its existence or, worse, care that it exists because it is a decidedly non-glamorous curio. There is no mention of

the die-cast 1130 in the Service Manual, either, perhaps because the low-budget items did not warrant the mention of manufacturing variations in this case. We have authenticated four examples from the collections of R. Niedhammer, R. Szabat, G. Halverson and R. LaVoie. I.D. Smith, R. LaVoie and C. Weber comments.                    20    35    45    70

1615

**1615** 1955-57, 0-4-0 Switcher, black die-cast body, "B6" on PRR oval builder's plate on boiler right side, red marker lights (sometimes omitted), O-27 motor with brushplate showing on left side and two gears showing on right, operating disc coupler in front, "L"-shaped locomotive drawbar has brass spring to insure good electrical ground with tender, detailed cab interior, small O-27 contact rollers, 1615T hollow plastic slope-back tender (too light for good operation when pushing cars), lettered "LIONEL LINES" in white, no bell in tender, metal trucks; O-27 locomotive, locomotive number either rubber-stamped or heat-stamped. D. Pickard reports that some of the common versions of the 1615 came with green marker lights or no marker lights. R. Niedhammer and P. Smith comments.

(A) 1955, number rubber-stamped in silver, blackened tender drawbar. R. Ervin Collection.                    55    100    140    225

(B) 1955-57, number heat-stamped in white, non-blackened drawbar. Ervin Collection.                    55    100    140    225

(C) 1957 only, same as (B), but AAR trucks on tender. P. Ambrose Collection. **40   75   125   200**

(D) Same as (B), but with grab-rails on front of steam chest and on the tender, as pictured in the 1955 catalogue and as found on the 1656. Probably represents the earliest 1955 production. R. Seghi and D. Pickard Collections. **175   250   400**

1625

1625 1958, 0-4-0, Switcher, black die-cast body, "B6" on PRR oval builder's plate on right side of smoke box, red marker lights (sometimes omitted), O-27 motor with brushplate showing on left side and two gears showing on right, dummy coupler in front, "L"-shaped locomotive drawbar has brass spring to insure good electrical ground with tender, detailed cab interior, small O-27 contact rollers, cadmium-plated rods, 1625T hollow plastic slope-back tender, no bell, O-27 locomotive. The Lionel Service Manual specifies a dummy front coupler, but an operating coupler is easily installed. The 1958 catalogue drawing shows the spring for the operating coupler. P. Smith comment. Came as part of set X-686X, which also had a 6014 Wix boxcar (this needs further confirmation), a 6111 cream flatcar with pipes, a 6151 cream Flatcar With Range Patrol Truck and a 6017 Lionel Lines tuscan caboose. This was purportedly a special premium set for Wix filter dealers. C. Weber observation.

(A) As described above. **65   125   200   300**

(B) Same as (A), but tender has AAR plastic trucks. P. Ambrose Collection. **65   125   200   300**

(C) Same as (B), but marker lights are omitted, dummy front coupler, gears show on right side instead of left, roller-type O-27 pickup, 1625T tender with AAR trucks. H. Powell Collection. **65   125   200   300**

1654 1946-47, 2-4-2, black die-cast boiler, nickel trim handrail on each boiler side, nickel bell and whistle, three-position reverse unit, metal reverse lever through boiler; sliding shoe motor 1654M-1 with brushplate on left side, motor fastened to boiler in part by long pin that goes through back of boiler casting, large gear between drivers on right side, drive and connecting rods attached to solid crosshead; O-27 locomotive, operates on O-27 track but not switches or crossovers.

(A) 1654W tender with whistle sheet metal base and top, staple-end trucks, coil coupler. **15   20   30   40**

(B) Same as (A), but 1654T tender without whistle. **15   20   30   40**

(C) With 221T tender lettered "NEW YORK CENTRAL" in stripes, staple-end trucks, whistle, coil coupler; came with 1947 Sears set 05961T. K. Wills comment. **NRS**

(D) Same as (C), but no whistle, set 05960T. K. Wills comment. **NRS**

1655 1948-49, 2-4-2, heavy black die-cast body with fine cab interior detail; light, drive and connecting rods, two sliding shoe pickups, improved 1655M-1 motor using double reduction gears (compare with 1654); brushplate left side, four visible gears, solid crosshead, 12-spoked wheels, nickel bell and whistle, three-position reverse, metal reverse lever through boiler near cab. 6654W sheet metal box tender with whistle, staple-end metal trucks. **15   20   35   50**

1656 1948-49, 0-4-0, Switcher, black die-cast body, B6 on right side, red marker lights; light, nickel bell on bracket; 1656M-1 motor identical to 1655-1 except equipped with contact rollers rather than sliding shoes; coil-operated front coupler; two plug/jack connections from locomotive to tender; left plug connects locomotive coupler to tender, rear truck pickup shoe; center plug provides extra ground for locomotive through tender wheels and body. 6403 slope-back tender, staple-end metal trucks, coil coupler (1948) and magnetic coupler (1949). Tender has bell, wire handrails and working backup light. I.D. Smith observation.

(A) "LIONEL LINES" closely spaced on tender, probably came with staple-end trucks with coil coupler. One version reported as rubber-stamped

1656

"6043B" on the tender underside, rather than the correct "6403B". We do not know if only a few were mis-stamped or whether most were mis-stamped. Reader reports requested. I.D. Smith comment. **125   175   225   300**

(B) "LIONEL LINES" spaced out on tender. Tender rubber-stamped "6403B" on underside, staple-end trucks with magnetic coupler, 1949 production. P. Ambrose comment. **125   175   225   300**

1665

1665 1946, 0-4-0, Switcher, black die-cast body, red marker lights, coil-operated front coupler and wire handrails, 1662M-2 motor shared with prewar 1662 with one gear showing on left side, brushplate on right, three-position reverse unit, two wires from tender plug into locomotive: left wire connects locomotive front coupler coil to tender sliding shoe, other wire provides better ground. 2403B slope-back tender with metal frame, body, bell and metal trucks; backup light on tender, "LIONEL LINES" heat-stamped on tender, staple-end metal trucks, coil coupler, wide-spaced lettering, separate Bakelite coal pile casting and wire handrail (although illustration does not show handrail). I.D. Smith comment.

**125   200   275   400**

1666 1946-47, 2-6-2, black die-cast locomotive, green marker lights, came with two different kinds of bells, three-position reverse unit mounted between the smokestack and the first dome, limited cab interior detail consists of two firebox doors, rounded rear cab floor, and either stamped-steel or die-cast pilot and trailing trucks. Came with several different tenders: 2666W (early), 2466W, 2466T and 2466WX with staple-end metal trucks with early or later coil coupler. The 1666 was also manufactured prior to World War II and differs most noticeably from the postwar versions in that it has a square rear cab floor, a long shank hook and a coffin-shaped tender with box couplers. Other, less noticeable differences are present as well. The postwar 1666 came with untapped holes through the lower front sides of the boiler. These holes may have been used to attach the boiler to the motor on some prewar 1666 locomotives. In these cases, a longitudinal rod passed through the hole at one end and threaded into a tapped hole at the other end. The postwar 1666 locomotives we have examined have their motors attached to the boiler by means of a screw inserted through a bar in the rear upper section of the motor. The bar helps support the motor side frames. This screw then fits into a tapped hole in the underside of the boiler casting; it is not accessible from atop the boiler shell, but must be unscrewed from underneath. Additionally, on the first dome behind the smokestack, the prewar 1666 has a pair of raised ovals which are not present on the postwar version. (The same change occurred to the 224 after 1938, during the prewar period). On the main casting of the prewar 1666 there is a drilled 3/32" hole immediately behind the top of the cylinders. The same hole on the postwar 1666 is larger, 3/16". The postwar version has a drilled hole exactly two inches in front of the 1666 number on the cab; there is no such hole on the prewar version. The handrails on the prewar 1666 were better made than the ones on the postwar version; handrails on this version corroded easily. P. Catalano comments.

1655

1666

2016

So far, we have not turned up any evidence that the 1666 was produced in late 1945. However, we have one report from J. Foss of a 1666 locomotive which came with a 2666WX tender, a 2454 PRR boxcar, a 2452 gondola and a 2457 caboose. All three of the cars and the tender have the early trucks with the open coil, whirly wheels and thick axles. There is a slim chance that this set may have been made in late 1945 rather than early 1946. Further comments requested.

The shells of the 2666W tenders differ considerably, though they have the same part number, 1666T-4. Apparently the shell die was reworked from its prewar configuration. The prewar version is lettered in white. It has a rounded-slot hole in the front of the shell, and the lower edge of the side is molded on a slant. On the rear, the ladder stampings are relatively shallow, the coal bulkhead wall is molded on a slant and the vent at the right on the bulkhead wall is large. The postwar 2666W shell is lettered in silver. It has a squared slot hole at the front of the shell, and its lower edge of its side is molded absolutely flat; there is no slant. At the rear, the ladder stampings are deeper, the coal bulkhead wall has a flat edge rather than a slanted edge and the bulkhead wall vent is smaller and shallower. R. Griesbeck comments.

(A) 1946, late, number plates with "1666" in silver on a black background. The bell mechanism consisted of two parts:  a cast bell with horizontal shaft mounted on stamped-steel bracket which in turn was fastened by a screw to the boiler. The pilot and steam chest were mounted by screws, which fitted in drilled and tapped holes in the boiler casting, the front truck was cast, the center drive wheel on each side had slots to receive the nibs of the cast eccentric crank, the eccentric crank was attached by a slot-headed screw, the rear truck mounting plate holes were drilled and tapped in the casting and the headlight socket had a screw base. The 2466WX tender had late coil couplers. C. Rohlfing Collection.     **25   50   70   85**

(B) 1947. The number "1666" was rubber-stamped in silver on the cab beneath the windows. The bell was a single-piece casting riveted to the boiler. The steam chest pilot casting was peened to studs in the boiler casting. The front truck was stamped-steel, the center drive wheel on each side had cast-in studs on which to attach the steel eccentric crank, the eccentric crank was attached by a hex-head screw. The boiler casting had undrilled depressions at both front and back that had been drilled and tapped on earlier engines. Blackmar Collection. This locomotive was not catalogued in 1947, but it was offered as part of a Sears set in 1947. Much harder to find than 1666 with separate plate, but collectors do not seem to be interested. K. Wills comment.     **25   50   70   85**

(C) 1946, early, same as (A), but came with 2666W tender with white heat-stamped "LIONEL LINES" lettering and early coil couplers, whirly wheels with thick axles. This tender, essentially the same as the 2466W, was probably an early postwar frame equipped with a leftover prewar cab. The prewar 1666 came with this tender, numbered 2666W, on a frame with prewar trucks in 1940-41. Additional confirmation requested. R. LaVoie Collection.     **25   50   70   85**

(D) Same as (A), but smooth sand dome and 3/8" high "X" on left firebox door; "X" designation does not appear on box. Lapan Collection.

**25   50   70   85**

**NOTE:** We have other reports of several 1666 locomotives with an "X" about 3/8" high stamped on the left firebox door inside the cab. We do not have further details aside from entry (D) above; reader comments requested. We also show a postwar 1666 with a sheet-metal 6654W tender in our photo section, but our respondents doubt that this engine was ever equipped with this tender as postwar production.

**1862** 1959-62, 4-4-0, modeled after Civil War "General", gray boiler, red cab, green 1862T tender, O-27 Gauge, without Magnetraction, two-position reverse, light; lacks some boiler banding and applied piping details found on

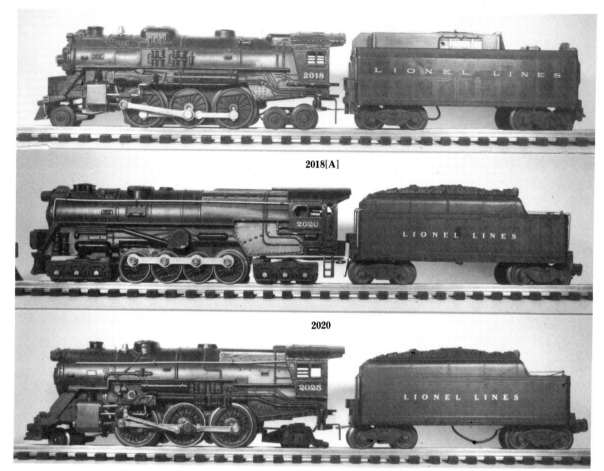

2018[A]

2020

2025[A]

1872, does not have smoke or whistle, price for locomotive and tender only. The 1959 production of this locomotive had a red headlight. In 1959-60, the screw on the cab rear was small and protruded beyond the cab. In 1960, this became a larger screw which was recessed. R. Vagner comment.

(A) Gray stack.                                    75   125   175   275
(B) Black stack.                                   75   125   175   275

**1872** 1959-62, 4-4-0, modeled after Civil War "General", gray chassis and boiler, red cab and pilot, black, red and green 1872T tender with gold lettering; O Gauge, Magnetraction, smoke unit, three-position reverse, came with coach 1875W with whistle in set. The 1960, and later production, of this locomotive had a black headlight. R. Vagner comment. Price for locomotive and tender only.                    100   150   250   400

1882

**1882** 1959-62, 4-4-0, modeled after Civil War "General", uncatalogued by Lionel, sold by Sears, black boiler and smokestack, orange pilot and cab with gold lettering, 1882T tender, does not have smoke unit or whistle. This engine was part of the Sears General set, which included the 1882, the 1866 mail car, a blue 1885 passenger car and the 1887 horse flatcar, 1959. The set also included an Allstate transformer which may have been made by Marx. Feldman Collection. Price for locomotive and tender only. Weiss Collection.                                   150   225   400   600

**2016** 1955-56, 2-6-4, light, does not have smoke or Magnetraction, similar to 2037 with box on pilot, three-position reverse unit, "LIONEL O-27" plate on bottom, cadmium-plated drive rod and connecting rod; 6026W tender, lettered "LIONEL LINES", with whistle, bar-end metal trucks, magnetic coupler with tab, O-27 locomotive.          20   35   60   90

**2018** 1956-59, 1961, 2-6-4, box on front pilot, cadmium-plated drive and connecting rods, smoke, three-position reverse unit. 6026W tender and whistle, bar-end trucks, magnetic coupler, "LIONEL LINES" on tender side; O-27 locomotive. Came in sets with 1130T tender. T. Budniak observation.

(A) Black.                                        25   40   65   100
(B) Blue, from Boy's Set, two known to exist.                    NRS

**2020** 1946-47, 6-8-6, model of Pennsylvania S-2 Steam Turbine. See discussion under 671. Catalogued as O-27 but identical to 671 which was catalogued as O Gauge.

(A) 1946, double worm-drive, horizontal reverse unit without external E-unit lever. Since lever does not penetrate boiler, locomotive cab interior includes two jacks on the brushplate holder. Plugs are inserted to disconnect the E-unit or lock the E-unit in one position. Motor labeled "ATOMIC MOTOR", slotted brush holders, shiny nickel drive rims. Locomotive has smoke bulb, part 671-62, with bulb marked GE797, 15 watts, 12 volts. The bulb has an indentation to hold "early" smoke tablets. The bulb did not produce sufficient smoke and bulb was replaced by the resistance coil (see B). However, Lionel furnished a kit to its service stations to convert the bulb unit to resistance coil units. Consequently, 2020(A)s will be found with resistance coil units. 2020W tender lettered "LIONEL LINES", staple-end trucks, coil coupler. Tender has trim on rear deck and rails on both rear and front ends. Tender stamped 2020W on bottom, Shewmake Collection and C. Rohlfing and M. Denuty comments.          75   100   140   200
(B) 1946, same as (A), but 2466WX tender, 1946. M. Walsh Collection.
                                                  75   100   140   200
(C) 1947, single worm-drive motor, vertical reverse unit with E-unit lever projecting through boiler, new resistance coil-type smoke unit with bellows, no plug jacks on motor brushplate, non-slotted brush tubes, added piping

2026[B]

2034

2035

Gd VG Exc Mt

detail on boiler casting. 2020W tender with staple-end trucks, handrails at four corners, magnetic coupler and plastic whistle box. R. Griesbeck Collection.                                                    **75 100 140 200**

(D) 1948, Same as (C), but flanged drivers have darkened rims, 6020W tender. This version also reported with 6466WX tender as original equipment; confirmation requested. R. Ervin and P. Mooney Collections.
                                                                         **75 100 140 200**

(E) 1949, same as (D), but no rims on drivers. R. Ervin Collection.
                                                                         **75 100 140 200**

(F) Same as (A) early unit, but has red Bakelite motor brushplate. This and similar examples were made during late 1946 and early 1947, when Lionel ran into a critical materials shortage and had to adapt to it. Red brushplates also show up on a few 2332 GG-1s, 726 Berkshires and 671 Turbines from this period. T. Rollo comments, J. Bratspis Collection.     **90 120 160 225**

**2025** 1947-49, 1952: 2-6-2, same as 675 (except number) but catalogued as O-27, 5690 on boiler front of (C) and (D). See comments under entry for 675. 2466WX tender with whistle, staple-end metal trucks, coil-operated coupler, railing on tender rear deck. Quite a few examples have been found with the bottom plate between the rollers stating "O Gauge Locomotive". Apparently Lionel did not bother to change these plates because the 675 and 2025 locomotives were, after all, identical except for their number. M. Goodwin comments.

(A) Early production, "2025" heat-stamped in silver on black Keystone, unpainted large aluminum smokestack, plain pilot without simulated lift pin and knuckle. Numbers on Keystones had a tendency to wear off easily; however, number indentations remain. Solid black Keystones may have once had decal, but solid unmarked Keystone of 1947 production may also have had rubber-stamped "2025" in silver which has worn off. See next entry. Comments here also apply to production of 675, 671 and 2020 locomotives. Number rubber-stamped below cab window; 2466WX tender with railings on rear deck only, staple-end trucks with late coil coupler. R. LaVoie, T. Klaassen and R. Niedhammer Collections.      **50 70 95 150**

(B) 1947, solid unmarked black Keystone on boiler front, no evidence of decal, large unpainted aluminum stack, plain pilot without simulated lift pin and knuckle, cab number rubber-stamped, 2466WX tender with handrails on rear deck only. This entry could be identical to (C) below with its boiler front number having worn away. However, R. Niedhammer reports that it is doubtful the factory produced the 2025 with rubber-stamped silver numbers on the boiler fronts. However, see next entry, which has been authenticated. (The 675 did have a rubber-stamped boiler front number.) C. Rohlfing Collection.                                         **50 70 85 125**

(C) 1947, same as (A), but number on Keystone rubber-stamped. May be identical to (B) above; see comments. R. Gallahan Collection.
                                                                         **50 70 95 150**

(D) 1948-49, same as 2025(A), but pilot with simulated knuckle and lift pin. 6466WX tender with magnetic coupler, 5690 in gold on red and gold Keystone on boiler front, black smokestack smaller than (A)-(C). R. Niedhammer Collection.                                              **50 70 85 125**

(E) 1952, 2-6-4, red and gold "5690" Keystone on boiler front, stack is a separate piece. Paint covers the seam and makes it appear a single piece; simulated knuckle and lift pin, black steel motor frame sides instead of non-magnetic aluminum, sintered-iron wheels, smoke, light, no Magnetraction, 6466W tender, staple-end trucks, magnetic coupler, whistle. R. Swanson comment. R. Hutchinson, R. Niedhammer and C. Rohlfing Collections.                                                      **50 70 85 125**

(F) 1948, same as (D), but 2466WX tender stamped "6466WX", coil coupler, staple-end trucks. This tender really belongs on a 675, since it was intended for the O Gauge sets of 1948 which could not be equipped with the magnetic couplers because the UCS remote track was not ready in time. It could well have been original with a 2025 as a separate sale item. R. Hutchinson Collection, R. LaVoie comments.                 **50 70 85 125**

(G) Same as (A), but 2466WX tender and "2025" on Keystone decal instead of "5690". The same number change occurred with 675; these examples are extremely scarce. R. Ervin Collection.                         **NRS**

**2026** 1948-49, 1951-53, 2-6-2, based on 1666, feedwater heater, box added to pilot, sand dome enlarged, smoke, light, sliding shoe pickups, drive rod, connecting rod, eccentric crank; die-cast trailing truck, steel-rimmed

98

2036

2037

2046

drivers. In 1948, the pickup wire was mounted erroneously on the front truck; it was soldered to the collector shoe, and it sometimes caused snags on the truck. In 1949, the error was corrected by soldering the wire to the power lug on the E-unit. T. McLaughlin and R. Ervin observations.

(A) 1948-49, 6466WX tender with staple-end trucks and whistle, old-style smoke lever, box marked "No. 2026 LOCOMOTIVE WITH SMOKE CHAMBER". Came as part of set 1429WS in 1948. T. McLaughlin Collection.                                             **40    50    70    90**

(B) 1951-53, 6466W or 6466T tender, rimless drivers, 2-6-4, no eccentric crank; roller pickups, stamped sheet metal trailing truck. I.D. Smith observation.                                             **40    50    70    90**

(C) 1952, spoked sintered-metal wheels, no tires, no Magnetraction because of Korean War Alnico magnetic metal shortage, 2-6-4 with four-wheel stamped sheet metal trailing truck, 2046-type tender, shown as a 2-6-2 in 1952 catalogue, also shown in the Lionel Service Manual, R. Hutchinson and R. Bartelt observations.                                             **40    50    70    90**

**2029** 1964-69, 2-6-4, light, smoke, rubber tires, main rod, side rod, 243W tender with whistle, available in 1967 although no catalogue was issued, O-27 locomotive.

(A) 243W tender heat-stamped "LIONEL LINES" in white.

**40    50    70    90**

(B) 1968 or 1969, 243W tender heat-stamped "PENNSYLVANIA" in white. This was reportedly a specially-commissioned tender stamping for a large New York train store. Very hard to find with this tender shell, which is worth at least $100. J. Bratspis Collection.        **125  150  175  200**

(C) 1968, 2-6-4, plate on bottom reads "THE LIONEL TOY CORPORA-TION, Hagerstown, Maryland 21740"; the trailing truck has "Japan" embossed on it; drive rod, connecting rods, brushplate on left side, blue insulating material covers E-unit and motor field coil; gears on right side, motor has both brass and dark-colored gears; motor attached by bar through back of firebox area and held in by grooves on front end; bracket holding the front truck is shiny metal, smoke unit bottom is also shiny metal;

three-position reverse unit, smoke. 234W Santa Fe-type tender with AAR trucks and center rail pickup on both trucks, fixed coupler, whistle, "LIONEL LINES" heat-stamped in white as is 234W; from the Hagerstown set which consisted of 6076 hopper, 6014 box, 6315 tank, 6560 crane and 6130 work caboose; price for locomotive and tender only.  **50    60    85  125**

(D) Locomotive with 1130T uncatalogued tender, "Southern Pacific", R. Hutchinson comment, LCCA magazine, Volume 5, No. 2. More information necessary.                                             **NRS**

**2034** 1952, 2-4-2, die-cast body, 2034-100 better grade motor with three-position reverse unit, light, succeeded by 1130 which has plastic body, weights in front and rear, came with 6066T tender which had Scout trucks with magnetic couplers. M. Denuty and R. LaVoie comments. O-27 locomotive.                                             **20    25    35    50**

**2035** 1950-51, 2-6-4, based on 2025 but with Magnetraction, drive rod, connecting rod, eccentric rod with new crank using half-moon fitting into wheel recess, trailing truck stamped-steel, sintered-iron drivers. 6466W tender with whistle but without handrails, O-27 locomotive.

(A) 1950, eccentric crank fastens to wheel recess by means of half-moon shaped fitting.                                             **50    60    75  125**

(B) 1951, same as (A), but crank fastened by two projecting pins, motor has armature cover plates (not on 2035 (A)), and has pickup rollers with fixed axles.                                             **50    60    75  125**

(C) 1950, 2-6-2, uncatalogued, illustrated in November, 1950 **Model Railroader,** apparently 675-212 trailing truck. Reported by Lower, Rapp and Jodon. We need additional confirmation of pieces that are known to be original with this truck arrangement.                                             **NRS**

**2036** 1950, 2-6-4, similar to 2026 (A), but with Magnetraction, rimless drive wheels, no smoke, sheet metal trailing truck, no handrails or eccentric rod. 6466W tender without handrails, O-27 locomotive.  **40    55    70  120**

**2037** 1954-55, 1957-58, 2-6-4, derived from 2026 and 2036, light, smoke, Magnetraction, "2037" usually heat-stamped under cab window in white,

2037-500[B] Girl's Set loco with square type tender

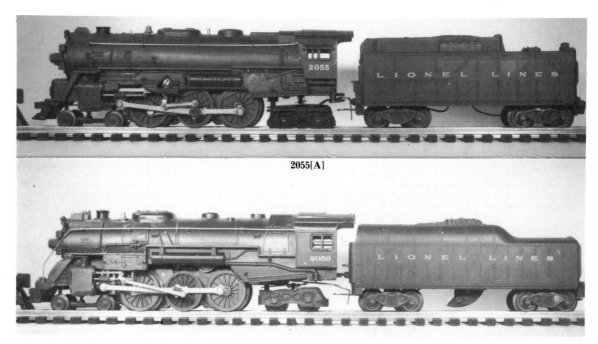

2055[A]

2056

| | Gd | VG | Exc | Mt |
|---|---|---|---|---|

but R. Niedhammer reports that some versions were rubber-stamped with two different type faces. We would like to learn which number stampings came with which sets so we may determine the manufacturing sequence. This locomotive identical to 637 except for number.

(A) 1957, 6026W tender.  50  60  85  125

(B) 1954-55, 1958-60, 6026T tender.  50  65  85  125

(C) 1961, came with 243W Lionel Lines square-back tender. M. Goodwin and G. Salamone Collections.  50  65  85  125

(D) Rubber-stamped cab number in silver, 6026T tender lettered "LIONEL LINES," rubber-stamped "6026T" on bottom of frame. M. Denuty Collection.  50  65  85  125

(E) Rubber-stamped cab number in regular serif-face "2037". This may be (A), (B) or another version. R. Niedhammer comment.  NRS

(F) Rubber-stamped cab number in small sans-serif "2037". This may be (A), (B) or another version. R. Niedhammer comment.  NRS

**2037-500** 1957, 2-6-4, pink body for "Girl's Set" with blue 2037 numbers beneath the cab window (2037-500 does not appear on cab), smoke, headlight lens, green marker lights, battery box on front pilot, nickeled simulated bell, three-position reverse unit, Magnetraction, drive rod and connecting rod only, brushplate on left side, gears on right side. Set includes hopper, gondola, two boxcars, caboose, 1130T tender and 1043-500 transformer. Reproduction locomotives have been made which are difficult to distinguish from originals, L. Bohn comment. Set:  800  1000  1300  1900

(A) 1130T streamline tender, trucks retained by push-in clips, tender came in box marked 1130-504. D. Doyle Collection.  300  400  500  600

(B) 6026 square-type tender, may be one of a kind. Formerly H. Degano Collection.  NRS

See also Factory Errors.

**2046** 1950-51, 1953, 4-6-4, die-cast New York Central-type boiler, gears on left side, brushes on right, drive rods, connecting rods, valve gear, three-position reverse unit, Magnetraction, shares casting with 646 and 2056, evolved from 726; 2046W tender with whistle, bar-end trucks, two pickups, magnetic coupler, with or without "2046W" lettering; O-27. Replaced temporarily in 1952 by 2056 version without Magnetraction. C. Rohlfing comment.

(A) 1950, metal trailing truck, number rubber-stamped in silver. R. Ervin and M. Ocilka Collections.  100  150  175  250

(B) 1951, same as (A), but number is heat-stamped in white. R. Ervin and M. Ocilka Collections.  100  150  175  250

(C) 1953, same as (B), but plastic trailing truck. R. Ervin and M. Ocilka Collections.  85  135  160  225

**A SPECIAL NOTE:** Lionel built a scale-detailed model of the New York Central Hudson in the late 1930s, the 700E, which was numbered 5344 on the cab. Lionel also built a less detailed 763E in those years. Another less detailed version of the 700E was made in 1950 and 1964; this was the postwar 773. In 1985, Charles Ro, the proprietor of a large Lionel distributorship, offered a replacement boiler numbered 5344 to convert Lionel locomotives 2046, 2056 and 646. This conversion boiler is, however, quite a bit smaller than the original 700E boiler marked 5344 and should not be confused with it.

**2055** 1953-55, 4-6-4, die-cast Santa Fe-type boiler, Magnetraction, drive rod, connecting rod, valve gear, smoke unit, light, boiler front pops out, shares boiler casting with 665, 685 and 2065, O-27.

(A) 1953, number rubber-stamped, 6026W square tender, bar-end metal trucks, magnetic coupler, whistle, "LIONEL LINES". R. Ervin Collection.  65  100  140  225

(B) 1954-55, same as (A), but heat-stamped number, 2046W tender. R. Ervin and D. Doyle Collections.  65  100  140  225

2065

6110

**2056** 1952, 4-6-4, die-cast NYC-type boiler, smoke, three-position reverse, gears on left, brushplate on right, black-finished motor side plates, reversing lever slot directly in front of cab. Rubber-stamped number on cab in silver. Came in brown corrugated box with "2056" stamped on both ends; 2046W tender has water scoop, whistle, bar-end trucks, magnetic coupler, tender lettered "LIONEL LINES" in larger type than that found on tender that came with 2046, catalogued as O-27, offered with two sets, Korean War issue of 2046 minus Magnetraction and with a few more subtle changes. Locomotive came in corrugated box marked "Densen Banner Co., Inc., Ridgefield Park, N.J." The locomotive box is stamped "2056" at both ends. The tender came in orange Lionel box marked "2046W Tender with whistle" on both ends and with part number 2046-59. R. Ervin and W. Schilling Collections.                                **90   150   190   275**

**2065** 1954-57, 4-6-4, die-cast Santa Fe-type boiler with feedwater heater above boiler front, smoke, Magnetraction, drive rod, connecting rod, valve gear, boiler casting on left is relatively plain. Trailer truck casting with plastic sides same as both 2065 and 2055, casting detail also shared with 665 and 685; 665 has a feedwater heater while 685 does not.
(A) 1954, rubber-stamped number on boiler, 2046W tender with whistle, bar-end trucks, magnetic coupler without tab. Came with Set 1516WS. R. Ervin Collection, P. Ambrose comment.                                **80   100   140   200**
(B) 1955-57, heat-stamped number on boiler, 6026W tender, bar-end trucks, magnetic coupler without tab. R. Ervin Collection, P. Ambrose comment.                                **80   100   140   200**
(C) 1954, heat-stamped number on cab, 2046W tender with whistle, bar-end trucks, magnetic coupler with two holes in activator plate (one is for plate rivet), came with set 1515WS. D. Doyle Collection.                                **80   100   140   200**

**2671** 1968, TCA Convention tender shell only, 2046-type shell with large "TCA" in white, TCA circular logo in white, "NATIONAL CONVENTION 1968 CLEVELAND, OHIO" in white, two lines overscored and underscored. Versions with gold and silver lettering also exist. Quantities produced: 1,146 white, 43 gold and 11 silver-lettered, J. Bratspis observation. Although this chapter is devoted to locomotives with tenders, we have listed this tender in this chapter since it is more easily located by our readers. Priced for white lettering.                                **—   —   —   75**

**4681** 1950, 6-8-6 electronic control locomotive and tender with set. Although catalogued, this locomotive was apparently never made for production purposes. This conclusion is based upon the absence of comments by readers about the omission over the last ten years. However, one prototype set is known to exist with this engine. R. Ervin and R. Lord observations.                                **Not Manufactured**

**6110** 1950-51, 2-4-2, black die-cast boiler, drive rod with crosshead, fiber reverse lever, two-position reverse, no light, Magnetraction, 6001T tender, O-27 locomotive. This Scout locomotive, similar to 1001, 1110 and 1120, does not use a conventional E-unit for reversing. Lionel created a very imaginative — and trouble-prone — motor design which made the reversing mechanism part of the motor itself and reduced costs. This motor has a two-part field. One part is pivoted to permit it to move when attracted by the energized winding on the stationary section of the field. As the movable field pivots downward, it moves a pawl engaging the geared drums of the brush holders, causing them to rotate. The rotation changes the connections to the armature windings with respect to the field windings, and thus reverses the motor direction. The movable field and pawl stay in the low position, locking the brush holder drums as long as the field winding is energized. When the current is interrupted, the pawl spring returns the movable field and pawl to their up positions. The Scout motor includes a fiber lever which protrudes through the boiler and locks the locomotive in either forward or reverse, as no neutral position is possible with this design. This locomotive has a smoke generator, but not the usual piston and cylinder arrangement found on more expensive locomotives. Rather, smoke is driven up the stack by air which enters through a hole on the boiler front. Consequently, forward motion is necessary for smoke! Its Magnetraction, like that of early Magnetraction diesels, uses a permanent magnet fixed transversely between the rear wheels, rather than having magnetic axles carry the magnetic flux through the wheels. The magnetic circuit is completed through the sintered-iron rear drivers. Sometimes this locomotive will be found as a "Complaint" locomotive, where the factory or Service Station has replaced the trouble-prone Scout motor with the 2034-type spur-gear motor. These repaired engines can be identified by a vacant slot atop the boiler where the fiber reverse lever once was. The tender came in a box marked 6001T and has "LIONEL LINES" in white lettering. The tender has no lettering on its bottom and Scout trucks. This engine came in set 1461S, which contained a 6002 black gondola, an X6004 boxcar in a box marked 6004 and a 6007 Die 3 caboose. The set sold for $19.95. These observations are compiled from the comments of R. Lord, J. Kotil, I.D. Smith and R. LaVoie. Locomotive and tender value.                                **12   15   25   35**

# Chapter III
# BOXCARS

## BOXCARS, REFRIGERATOR CARS AND STOCK CARS
### By Roland LaVoie

Like the real railroads, Lionel's railway operations used the boxcar and its variants as the most common rolling stock in its roster. These cars were made in so many variations that the only way to classify a Lionel boxcar is to define it as any car with a roof which is not a vat car, passenger car or caboose! These cars were made in all kinds of colors and featured a myriad of railroad markings. No Lionel railroad could be complete without at least a few of these cars obediently following their locomotives in freight trains.

The earliest "pure" boxcars were essentially all-metal prewar carry-overs equipped with postwar trucks and couplers. Soon after these first cars were produced, Lionel updated its lineup of boxcars with three basic body types. One type, used in Scout and other inexpensive sets, was the short type with non-opening doors. These boxcars are sometimes referred to as "plug-door" boxcars, but they are not really plug-door cars at all. (See the article by Norman Anderson, in the 5th edition of this Guide, for definitions and details.) Another type used a short body which had opening doors. The third type, easily the best of them, was the 6464-type boxcar, which was quite a bit longer than the other two types and had opening doors. These boxcars were highly realistic; they featured many different colors and road markings. So complex is the 6464 series that train scholars have identified several **hundred** variations!

All these cars were modified heavily as needed for different uses. Some had a bank slot added to the roof. Others had clear plastic inserts and circular grates added for the fanciful mint and aquarium cars. The 6464-type was changed into a double-door "automobile" car. Mechanisms of all descriptions were fitted, shoehorned or crammed into their interiors. One exotic type of boxcar had a pointed roof which parted to launch a missile, cannon shell or helicopter. Another type contained a big generator and had portholes on its sides. Workmen popped out of spring-loaded doors to survey the area or toss mail sacks out the door.

The stock cars followed a similar evolution. Three basic types were produced in the postwar years. The long, well-detailed 6356 two-level stock car made its debut in 1954. Several different road names followed in subsequent years. Lionel also produced a much shorter stock car with non-opening doors for operating purposes; this car was found in giraffe and sheriff-outlaw variations. Finally, Lionel made a short stock car which had opening doors; this car was used for the operating cattle car as well as several non-operating cars.

These cars varied in a similar fashion to their boxcar analogues. The 6356 was modified for the operating horse car and the poultry dispatch cars. One of the poultry cars featured a spring-operated "chicken sweeper" who swept the floor of the car when the door popped open. The horse and circus cars were changed to accommodate single doors and swing-down livestock ramps.

The refrigerator cars were not made in very many variations or numbers. The milk cars, of course, were the most numerous; they had opening hatches and sprung doors. A non-operating version of the short white milk car was also produced. A longer O Gauge milk car featured an entirely different method of construction; the car roof and ends were cast in one piece, while the base and sides were separate. It is a pity that the design of Lionel's 6672 refrigerator car was not produced earlier in the postwar years, because it was a rather handsome car. As it was, Lionel only made Railway Express and Santa Fe versions of this refrigerator car. It was made with plug doors and little metal mechanism plates, and was extremely well detailed. The roof and ends were one piece, while the base and sides were another piece.

It is no accident that the listings for the box, stock and reefer cars are so long. Lionel produced a large number of these cars because they offered an opportunity to use real railroad markings better than any other type of car. They were always popular with the train-buying public, but acquiring a complete collection of them is a task requiring extreme patience — not to mention extensive financial resources! With the exception of the flatcars, no other type of rolling stock served Lionel so well for so long.

638-2361 Van Camp's Pork & Beans Boxcar came with an uncatalogued set in 1962. The set was offered for $11.95 with a can label. H. Powell furnished a can label for our analysis, the critical piece of evidence.

**Gd VG Exc MT**

**638-2361 VAN CAMP'S PORK & BEANS** 1962, uncatalogued, Type II red body with white and yellow lettering, coin slot, 8-1/2" long, double non-opening door, body part 1004-3 (modified), one extra hole in car floor, arch bar trucks, fixed couplers, part of set 19142. Apparently some came with AAR trucks. In 1962, Lionel reported that "This year we will have a similar promotion to the Quaker Oats promotion set; (see steam locomotive 246 listing for details) under the sponsorship of Stokely-Van Camp." From the literature available, the locomotive from set 19142 appears to be a 1060, 1061 or 1062. The locomotive has an 1130T-type tender, this 638-2361 car, a 3309 Turbo Missile Launching Car, a 6402 gray 1877-mold flatcar with a brown automobile, a 6448 red and white exploding boxcar and an unlettered 6017 SP-type caboose. The set was offered on the label of a can of Stokely-Van Camp's Pork and Beans and cost $11.95. The offer expired on "March 31, 1963". One unanswered question: Why did Lionel choose such a strange number, completely foreign to its numbering system, for this car?

R. Loveless, C. Rohlfing, J. Breslin, H. Powell, L. Barrett and R. LaVoie Collections, L. Bohn and C. Rohlfing comments.          7    15    20    35

**X1004 PRR Baby Ruth** 1949-51, orange with blue lettering, 8" long, non-opening double doors on each side, Scout trucks and couplers. C. Rohlfing and J. Breslin comments.

(A) "Baby Ruth" in outline blue lettering, early Scout trucks without reinforcing ridge, gloss black underside. J. Breslin and J. Sattler Collections.          2    3    4    6

(B) "Baby Ruth" in solid blue lettering, late Scout trucks with reinforcing ridge, satin black underside. J. Sattler Collection.          2    3    4    6

(C) Similar to (B), but very heavily stamped blue lettering, late Scout trucks with reinforcing ridge and conversion magnetic couplers with extra hole in activator plate and round rivet. We do not know if the factory installed the conversion couplers or whether these were done by a Lionel Service Station. Reader comments invited. J. Sattler Collection.          2    3    4    6

**NOTE:** 2454 appears with two different road names.

**X2454 PENNSYLVANIA** 1945-46, orange with black lettering, numbered "65400", 9-1/4" long.

(A) Orange doors, Type 2 trucks. Foss and Clark Collections.          20    50    100    150

(B) Brown doors, Type 2 or 3A trucks. Foss and Arpino Collections.          20    40    80    120

**X2454 BABY RUTH** 1946, orange-painted orange plastic body, brown unpainted plastic doors, "Enjoy Curtiss Baby Ruth Candy" to left of door in black script; to right of door: PRR logo in black, "EW 9-11 / EH 13-0 / IL 40-6 / IW 9-2 / IH 10-4/ CU FT 3936 / X2454 / BUILT BY / LIONEL"; one large and one small hole in middle of frame, steps at corners, frame held to body by screws at corners, staple-end trucks, late coil couplers.          5    10    15    25

**2458X PENNSYLVANIA** 1946-47, double-door automobile car, brown with white lettering, compressor assembly on underframe, metal body, continuation of prewar 2758, lettered "CAPY. 100000 / LD. LMT. 117900 / LT. WT. 51100 NEW 3-41", with "right" and "left" metal doors.

(A) 1946, staple-end trucks with Type 3A early coil couplers, regular wheels, thin axles, brown fiber, rivet below "8" in "X2458". J. Sattler and R. LaVoie Collections.          10    15    30    60

(B) 1947, staple-end trucks with Type 3B late coil couplers, rivet below "8" in "X2458". J. Sattler Collection.          10    15    30    60

(C) 1947, same as (B), but no rivet below "8" in "X2458". J. Sattler and A. Arpino Collections.          10    15    30    60

**X2758 PENNSYLVANIA** 1945-46, double-door automobile car, brown metal body with white lettering, compressor assembly on underframe and steps and brakewheels. A similar car was produced in 1941-42 which had automatic box couplers. This car should have come as an X2458, but Lionel used a supply of leftover prewar bodies for its 1945 sets. R. Swanson comment. J. Kotil reports the following variations:

(A) Staple-end trucks, whirly wheels, early coil couplers.          10    15    30    50

(B) Staple-end trucks, early dish wheels. Came in box marked 2458. C. Rohlfing Collection.          10    15    30    40

(C) Staple-end trucks, regular wheels, late coil couplers.          10    15    30    50

**X2954 PENNSYLVANIA** Not catalogued, Bakelite painted tuscan, white lettering, metal trucks, coil-operated coupler, same body as 2954, made in 1941-42. It is unlikely that this car was produced by the factory with postwar trucks. In some cases service stations and individuals removed prewar trucks and replaced them with postwar trucks.          150    225    275    375

**3356 SANTA FE RAILWAY EXPRESS** 1956-60 and 1964-66, operating car from horse corral set, horses move by vibrator action from car to pen and back; green car, yellow lettering, brakewheel to right of operating doors, galvanized metal bottom. Price does not include corral. For corral add $15, $20, $30, $45.

(A) Lettered "BLT. 5-56", bar-end trucks, magnetic couplers with tabs.          30    30    40    60

(B) No built date, AAR trucks with disc-operating couplers.          20    35    45    70

**3357 HYDRAULIC PLATFORM MAINTENANCE CAR** Cop and hobo move between gray plastic car platform and black separate piece which straddles the track. Excellent condition requires original men and separate

trackside pice. Blue plastic Type II double-door body with non-opening doors with white lettering, early AAR trucks, disc-operating couplers, price includes platform. Sometimes referred to as "Cop And Hobo Car" by collectors. Reissued by Fundimensions in 1982 as 7901. Original figures have flesh-colored hands and faces; those on Fundimensions reissue are white. Original hobo was medium brown; reissue is dark brown. Original cop figure was medium blue; reissue is dark blue. I.D. Smith and R. LaVoie comments.

(A) Medium blue plastic. J. Sattler Collection.          15    25    35    60

(B) Darker blue plastic.          15    25    35    60

**3366 CIRCUS CAR** 1959-62, operating car with nine white rubber horses and 3356-150 corral. Vibrator coils under the car, corral vibrates and miniature rubber "fingers" on base of horse causes it to move forward. (Same mechanism as found on 3356.) Unpainted ivory plastic car, 10-3/8" long, metal trucks with bar-ends, magnetic couplers with tabs, one black sliding shoe, red roof and catwalk. White corral with white fence, gray walkway and red inner section. As operating car faces the viewer brakewheel is on left end and "BLT BY LIONEL" appears in red, heat-stamped lettering on lower right.

(A) Set.          80    100    120    170

(B) Car only.          45    50    70    110

**3370 Western and Atlantic Stockcar (1961-64)** has an outlaw and sheriff bobbing and shooting at each other. This same design was used in the 3376 Bronx Zoo car.

**3370 WESTERN & ATLANTIC** 1961-64, sheriff and outlaw bob and shoot at each other, green with yellow lettering.

(A) AAR trucks, disc-operating couplers.          15    25    35    60

(B) Arch bar trucks, disc-operating couplers. R. Hutchinson Collection.          15    25    35    60

**3376 Bronx Zoo stock car** features a giraffe bobbing through the roof. This imaginative but unrealistic design has proved very popular as it has been reissued in the 1980s!

**3376 BRONX ZOO** 1960-69, giraffe lowers head to pass under bridge unit, action caused by special rail unit with overhead section. (See accessory chapter, 3424-100, for discussion.) AAR plastic trucks with disc-operating couplers. We have also had reports of both blue and green cars with gold lettering instead of yellow; R. Niedhammer observation. Green car may have been part of a special set. We need to know which of the varieties listed below have this lettering. Reader comments are requested. Price for car only; for cam and telltale pole, add $8 to values.

| | Gd | VG | Exc | Mt |
|---|---|---|---|---|
| (A) Blue car, white lettering, brown-spotted giraffe. | 12 | 15 | 25 | 35 |
| (B) Blue car, white lettering, solid yellow giraffe. | 12 | 15 | 25 | 35 |
| (C) Green car, yellow lettering, solid yellow giraffe. | 20 | 35 | 50 | 75 |
| (D) Blue car, yellow lettering, brown-spotted giraffe. | 15 | 25 | 35 | 45 |
| (E) Blue car, yellow lettering, solid yellow giraffe. | 15 | 25 | 35 | 45 |

(F) Green car, yellow lettering, brown-spotted yellow giraffe. Lord and Weingart Collections. Came in box marked 3376-160. P. Ambrose comment. Also has dummy couplers and arch-bar trucks. I.D. Smith Collection.   20 30 50 75

(G) Same as (A), but no lettering. Breslin Collection.   **NRS**

**3386 BRONX ZOO** 1960, shown in the 1960 Advance Catalogue as part of set 1109 with 1060 locomotive (see 1060 locomotive for details). Also came with uncatalogued set X568NA, which included 220P and 220T in 1960. See Uncatalogued Set chapter for full contents. Shown in 1961 Advance Catalogue with 1065 Union Pacific Alco. P. Ambrose comment. Light blue body, white lettering. Price includes rail/overhead unit.

(A) Solid yellow giraffe, arch bar trucks, dummy couplers.   20 35 50 75

(B) Yellow giraffe with brown spots, AAR trucks, dummy couplers.   20 35 50 75

(C) Yellow giraffe with brown spots, arch bar trucks, dummy couplers, came with 1060 set cited above. D. Fleming and I.D. Smith Collections.   20 35 50 75

(D) Prototype: Bongo and Bobo car, "World's Only Performing Giraffes", illustrated on page 39 in LIONEL: A Collector's Guide and History, Volume IV. P. Catalano Collection.   — — 1300 —

(E) Same as (B), but teal blue body. G. Halverson Collection.   **NRS**

**3424 WABASH** 1956-58, operating brakeman, Type IIB blue plastic body with white lettering, white unpainted five-panel plastic door, "8-56", bar-end trucks with tab magnetic couplers, sliding shoe and roller pickup. Price includes two rail trip contacts and two overhead telltale pole units.

(A) White man, medium blue plastic body, blue sliding shoe.   20 30 40 60

(B) White man, lighter blue plastic body, white sliding shoe.   20 30 40 60

(C) White man, darker blue plastic body, blue sliding shoe.   25 35 50 75

(D) Dark blue man, flesh-colored face and hands, medium blue body, blue sliding shoe. J. Sattler Collection.   25 35 50 75

(E) White man, grayish-tinted medium blue body, blue sliding shoe. J. Sattler Collection.   25 35 50 75

**3428 UNITED STATES MAIL** 1959, operating door, usually Type III blue plastic body, red plastic five-panel door painted red, white and blue, usually early AAR trucks, disc-operating couplers.

(A) Gray plastic body painted red, white and blue, Type IIB body (see 6464 Boxcar discussion for body types), bar-end trucks, magnetic couplers, gray man carries gray mail bag. R. Vagner and A. Arpino Collections.   20 15 25 40

(B) Type III body, early AAR trucks, disc couplers, blue man carries gray mailbag.   10 15 25 40

(C) Same as (B), but gray man carries blue bag.   10 15 25 40

(D) Same as (B), but Type IIB body. J. Sattler Collection.   10 15 25 40

**3434 POULTRY DISPATCH** 1959-60, 1965-66, operating sweeper, activated by remote control track, illuminated. Reissued by Fundimensions in 1983 as 9221. We would like to learn when the bar-end truck versions were made and when the AAR truck versions were made.

(A) Gray plastic painted slightly darker brown, blue man with flesh-colored hands, face and broom; bar-end trucks with magnetic tab couplers.   30 60 90 120

(B) Same as (A), but gray man. J. Sattler Collection.   30 60 90 120

(C) Gray plastic body painted brown with white lettering, gray man, AAR trucks, disc-operating couplers.   30 60 90 120

**3435 TRAVELING AQUARIUM** 1959-62, lighted with "swimming" tropical fish; clear plastic car painted green with gold or yellow lettering; AAR trucks with disc-operating couplers and two pickup shoes. Aquarium windows appear wave-like; car interior painted silver to control light reflection; vibrator motor moves continuous belt creating illusion of swimming fish. This car, rather an exotic piece, was greeted with derision by collectors at its issue, but today it is considered a highly desirable item. Reissued by Fundimensions in 1981. M. Ocilka and P. Ambrose comments.

(A) Large "L" with gold circle and gold lettering: "Tank No. 1", "Tank No. 2".   60 80 200 300

(B) Same as (A), but no circle around large "L".   60 80 150 250

(C) Yellow lettering, no tank designations, no circle around large "L".   40 60 80 110

(D) Similar to (C), but heavier and brighter lettering.   40 60 80 110

(E) Same as (A), but no circle, no tank designation. H. Degano Collection.   50 70 140 240

**3454 PRR AUTOMATIC MERCHANDISE CAR** 1946-47, car throws out six plastic "Baby Ruth" cubes which resemble merchandise containers. Reproduction cubes do not read "Baby Ruth" and are medium brown. The car is 8-1/2" long measured from one end of the catwalk to the other along the top of the body, 3-1/8" high measured from the flange of the wheels sitting on a flat surface to the top of the catwalk and 2" wide. Lettering on the car is as follows: "AUTOMATIC / MERCHANDISE CAR / 3454 / CAPY 100000 / LDLMT 120800 / LTWT 48200 NEW 6-46" to left of door and "EW 9-11 / EH 13-0 / IL 40-6 / IW 9-2 / IH 10-4 / CUFT 3836 / x3454 / BUILT BY / LIONEL" to right of door. On the right above the lettering is a 1/2" diameter circle with a PRR Keystone logo in its center. Steps are at corners as part of stamped sheet metal frame; staple-end metal trucks, later coil couplers with sliding shoes, and brakewheel fastened to one end only by a rivet. The mechanism for this car can toss the cubes over a foot. On a prototype scale, that would mean a heavy carton thrown 50 feet, which certainly would qualify the prototype railroad worker for Olympic competition! See Robert Swanson's article on the 9-1/4" boxcar for a full discussion of this car's varieties.

(A) Flat silver paint on clear plastic shell, dark blue (almost black) lettering and logo, lettering is heat-stamped cleanly and evenly, body is fastened to frame by four 1/4" self-tapping black roundhead screws; operating mechanism wired to sliding shoes on trucks by flexible light blue wires; mechanism fastened to frame by two black roundhead screws, six dark brown plastic cubes. J. Sattler, Falter, W. Davis and R. LaVoie Collections.   30 50 80 100

(B) Same as (A), but medium blue lettering and logo, lettering and numbering not as crisply heat-stamped into body as (A); many numbers and some letters filled in with color. Body fastened to frame by four 5/8" self-tapping black roundhead screws. Operating mechanism wired to sliding shoes on trucks by one flexible black wire and one flexible blue wire. (C. Rohlfing reports an example with original blue and yellow wiring.) Came with six black plastic cubes. J. Sattler and W. Davis Collections.   30 50 80 100

(C) Same as (A), but red letters and numbers; heat-stamping not as crisp as (A); for example, the "8" in "120800" and the "8" in "48200" are filled in with color. Body fastened to frame by four 5/8" black self-tapping roundhead screws; operating mechanism wired to sliding shoes on truck by two black flexible wires; operating mechanism fastened to frame by two plated round-headed screws; came with six red plastic cubes. This car probably represents a limited production run or a very early production color sample, and it was most likely made shortly after the built date on the car (6-46). Extremely rare; possibly only six in existence. J. Sattler Collection.   500 750 1250 2000

(D) Same as (A), but method of mounting hatchway to roof differs, latch secured by same long pin used on early 3462 milk car, letters and numbers rubber-stamped instead of heat-stamped. W. Davis Collection.   30 50 80 100

(E) Tuscan-painted clear plastic body, white heat-stamped sharp and clear lettering, staple-end trucks with later coil couplers, metal doors painted tuscan, came with six red plastic cubes, blue wiring, gray roundhead screws fasten body to frame, earlier thin brass rod fastens hatch to roof. Extremely rare; courtesy of anonymous collector and P. Ambrose comments.   — 700 1000 1500

**3462 AUTOMATIC REFRIGERATED MILK CAR** 1947-48, operating car, man delivers milk cans, cream or white paint on clear plastic with black lettering including "RT3462", staple-end metal trucks with coil couplers,

**Top shelf:** X2458 and X2758 Pennsylvania double-door automobile boxcars. The 2758 was initially catalogued by Lionel in 1941 and 1942 and came with box couplers. It was used again in the 1945 with new staple-end trucks with knuckle couplers. The X2458 was catalogued in 1945 and 1946. **Bottom shelf:** X3854 Pennsylvania and X6454 Southern Pacific.

**Lionel produced two different versions of the X2454 boxcar. Both had a PRR Keystone on the upper right side. However, one was lettered "PENNSYLVANIA" on the left while the other was labeled "Baby Ruth" on the left. The former is shown above. L. Nuzzaci Collection.**

sliding shoes and metal doors. The car body is attached to the base by two metal springs; remove springs to access jammed cans. This is the most popular type of operating car made by Lionel. From 1947 through 1955, Lionel sold two and a half **million** of these cars! Price includes platform and seven cans.

(A) 1947, early brass-base mechanism with thinner metal stock and more folding than later mechanism. The base mechanism is attached to the car frame by three and, later, four brass tabs twisted 90 degrees. The 1947 base is one inch shorter than the 1948 base, as the earlier base does not include the pivot plate found on later models. A square sheet metal plate slides out under the milkman, carrying him with it. This plate is placed within a track in the brass base under the milkman's right foot. Considerably more scarce than later versions. D. Fleming Collection.

|  | 30 | 40 | 60 | 85 |

(B) Late 1947-48, more common mechanism with milkman attached to swinging can sweep arm.

|  | 15 | 20 | 30 | 40 |

**3464(A) AT&SF 63132** 1949-1953, operating car, man appears as door opens, orange with black lettering, early 1949 cars have brown doors, all other cars have black doors. See feature article for variations.

|  | 5 | 10 | 20 | 30 |

**3464(B) NYC 159000** 1949-1952, operating car, man appears as door opens, tan with white lettering, all cars have black doors. See feature article for variations.

|  | 5 | 10 | 20 | 30 |

**3472 AUTOMATIC REFRIGERATED MILK CAR** Man delivers milk cans, "RT 3472" on side. See 3462 entry for general description. Price includes platform and seven cans.

(A) Pink and gray-marbled plastic body painted cream white, black lettering, short metal roof hatch painted to match body, tin-plated door frame with aluminum doors, black underframe/floor with four steps; indentations on underframe for door frames; indentation visible from bottom; early operating mechanism, metal trucks with staple-ends, magnetic couplers, spring clips hold body and frame together.

|  | 15 | 25 | 35 | 45 |

(B) Same as (A), but white unpainted plastic.

|  | 15 | 25 | 35 | 45 |

(C) White unpainted plastic body, staple-end or bar-end trucks, magnetic couplers, long plastic loading hatch with two simulated ice hatches and portion of catwalk; no holes in body for door frame tabs; plastic doors, base now cut out for new door assembly, four steps.

|  | 15 | 25 | 35 | 45 |

(D) Same as (C), but pure white unpainted plastic body which contrasts with cream white hatch loading door and grayish-white plastic doors and frame.

|  | 15 | 25 | 35 | 45 |

(E) Same as (C), but grayish-white body, hatch and doors, whiter than (C).

|  | 15 | 25 | 35 | 45 |

**3474 WESTERN PACIFIC** 1952-53, operating car, man appears as door opens, silver body and doors with large yellow feather decal, black lettering.

|  | 10 | 25 | 40 | 65 |

**3482 AUTOMATIC REFRIGERATED MILK CAR** 1954-55, operating car, man delivers milk cans. This is the most popular type of operating car made by Lionel. White unpainted plastic, black lettering, body fastened to frame by Phillips-head screw at one end and sliding bar at other; frame base has two ridges, plastic doors, bar-end trucks with magnetic uncouplers, operating mechanism changed to pneumatic plunger. Price includes platform and seven cans.

(A) Large numerals "3482" on upper left and small "RT 3472" on lower right.

|  | 20 | 30 | 50 | 75 |

(B) Large numerals "3482" on upper left and small "RT 3482" on lower right.

|  | 15 | 25 | 40 | 60 |

**3484 PENNSYLVANIA** 1953, operating car with plunger mechanism, blue man appears as door opens, Type I clear plastic body painted tuscan, 1953-type black plastic door painted tuscan, bar-end trucks with magnetic couplers.

(A) Body and door painted tuscan-brown, gold lettering, J.Sattler Collection.

|  | 12 | 25 | 40 | 60 |

(B) Body and door painted tuscan-red, white lettering, J.Sattler and R. LaVoie Collections.

|  | 12 | 25 | 40 | 60 |

**3484-25 A.T.&S.F.** 1954, operating car with plunger mechanism, blue man with flesh-colored face and hands appears as door opens, found with Types I, IIA and IIB bodies (see Lionel 6464 Boxcar discussion for definitions of body types), bar-end trucks, magnetic tab couplers.

(A) 1954, Type I clear plastic body painted glossy or flat orange, white

**First shelf: 3356 Santa Fe REA, 3366 Circus Car. Second shelf: 6352-1 PFE, 6356-1 NYC Stock Car. Third shelf: 6376 Lionel Lines Circus Car, 6434 Poultry Dispatch. Fourth shelf: 6572 REA Refrigerator, 6556 MKT Stock Car. L. Nuzzaci Collection.**

**This photograph compares the 3484-25(B) (top) and the 3484-25(H) (bottom). Note the differences in the door styles and boxes. The faint ice hatch line is present on the roof of the 3484-25(H), though it is not visible in this photograph. The upper car came with the upper box without the -25 suffix. The lower car came with a box marked 3484-25. T. Rollo Collection, W. Kojis photograph.**

|  | Gd | VG | Exc | Mt |
|---|---|---|---|---|

rubber-stamped lettering, Santa Fe herald 1/2" diameter. J. Sattler Collection. **20 50 90 120**

(B) 1954, Type I clear plastic body painted flat orange, 1953-type black plastic doors painted shiny orange, heat-stamped white lettering, Santa Fe herald 7/16" diameter. **20 50 90 120**

(C) Type IIA clear plastic body painted shiny orange, 1953-type black plastic door painted shiny orange, heat-stamped white lettering, Santa Fe herald 7/16" diameter. **20 50 90 120**

(D) Same as (C), but heat-stamped black lettering, Santa Fe herald 7/16" diameter. Rare. **— 600 900 1200**

(E) 1954, Type IIB red plastic body painted flat orange, 1953-type black plastic door painted shiny orange, heat-stamped white lettering, 7/16" diameter, Santa Fe herald. **20 50 90 120**

(F) Same as (E), but door painted flat orange. **20 50 90 120**

(G) Type I clear plastic body painted shiny orange, 1953-type black plastic door painted shiny orange, heat-stamped black lettering, very rare. **NRS**

(H) Type IIB orange plastic body painted orange, 1956-type white door painted shiny orange, white lettering, bar-end trucks fastened by long pins, tabbed magnetic couplers, came in 1956 box without car number on all six sides and end flap marked only with car number but no road name; believed to be part of Sears Set, Sears Catalogue No. 79N 09606. T. Rollo Collection. **NRS**

First shelf: two different versions of the 3424 Wabash boxcar with operating brakeman. The left car has a medium blue body with all-white man. The car on the right has a darker blue body with man with dark pants and shirt. Second shelf: 3428 U.S. Mail with gray man and 3424 Poultry Dispatch with brown car and blue man. Third shelf: 3424 Poultry Dispatch with darker brown car and 3484 Pennsylvania operating boxcar. Fourth shelf: 3484-25 A.T.S.F. operating boxcar and 3494-1 N.Y.C. operating boxcar. L. Nuzzaci Collection.

**3494-1 N Y C PACEMAKER** 1955, operating car with plunger mechanism, man appears as door opens, bar-end trucks with magnetic couplers.
(A) Type IIA red plastic body with gray-painted areas, white rubber-stamped lettering, with a comma under the second "s" of "System".

20   50   90   120

(B) Type IIB dark blue plastic body painted pastel blue, 1956-type red plastic door painted buttercup yellow, black heat-stamped lettering, no comma under second "s" of "System". See picture in prototype section for this one-of-a-kind boxcar. **NRS**

**3494-150 M.P.** 1956, operating car with plunger mechanism, man appears as door opens, Type IIB gray plastic body with blue-painted areas, "Eagle" on left is 5/8 of an inch long, "XME" and "Merchandise Service" on lower right, no grooves, 1956-type yellow unpainted plastic door, bar-end metal trucks with magnetic tab couplers. **35  70  115  150**

**3494-275 STATE OF MAINE** 1956-58, operating car with plunger mechanism, man appears as door opens, Type IIB blue plastic body with painted white and red stripes and black heat-stamped lettering; bar-end metal trucks with magnetic couplers; letters "O", "F", "D" and "U" are placed on door sign boards. Lionel redesigned its boxcar door in 1956 to

accommodate these letters and the new door is known as the 1956-type door, blue plastic door painted white and red.
(A) "B.A.R." is underscored and overscored, dark red stripes. R. Brezak Collection. **30  40  55  75**
(B) Same as (A), but medium red stripes. **30  40  55  75**
(C) "B.A.R." is neither underscored nor overscored, "3494275" is omitted. **75  100  150  250**

See also Factory Errors.

**3494-550 MONON** 1957-58, operating car with plunger mechanism, blue man appears as door opens, Type IIB plastic body with white-painted stripe and heat-stamped white lettering (except (C), lettered "BLT 6-57", bar-end trucks with magnetic tab couplers 11" long, 1956-type maroon plastic door with white-painted stripe (except (C).
(A) Maroon plastic body and doors. **100  150  200  275**
(B) Same as (A), but missing "BLT 6-57" on one side. This is a collectible factory error. Numerous examples show the progressive fading of the "BLT 6-57" as the stamp deteriorated. **100  150  200  275**
(C) Blue plastic body and orange plastic doors painted maroon with decal lettering, prototype. **NRS**

First shelf: 3494-150 Missouri Pacific "Eagle" operating boxcar, 3494-275 State of Maine operating boxcar. Second shelf: 3494-550 Monon operating boxcar and 3494-625 Soo operating boxcar. Third shelf: 3435 Traveling Aquarium and 6445 Fort Knox Gold Reserve. Both cars use the same car body. Fourth shelf: 3530 EMD and 6530 Fire Fighting Instruction car. L. Nuzzaci Collection.

**Gd  VG  Exc  Mt**

**3494-625 SOO** 1957-58, operating car with plunger mechanism, blue man with flesh-colored face appears as door opens, Type IIB maroon plastic body painted tuscan-brown with white heat-stamped lettering, 1956-type maroon plastic door painted tuscan brown; bar-end trucks with magnetic tab couplers, car is 11" long.

(A) As described above.      **100 150 200 275**
(B) Gray body painted tuscan; maroon door painted tuscan. Hessler Collection.      **100 150 200 275**

**3530 ELECTRO MOBILE POWER** or "Operating GM Generator Car", 1956-58, operating car; opening the door completes the circuit for the accompanying floodlight through the lighting pole. The pole, 3530-30, has two leads which hook into the car roof and two leads that run from the pole to the 3530-12 searchlight. The searchlight has a magnet on the bottom. Inside the car is a large plastic generator, strictly for looks (the same generator is used on the searchlight car). Fuel tanks are found under the car and appear identical to the ones on the 1047 Switchman but not on the diesels. Blue plastic car body with white and blue lettering. Popovich reports two types of pole-transformer base units. One unit has a light blue base, the other a black base, but both utility poles are brown and the riser pipes are gray. We do not know which of the following car variations came with which pole types, except for (A) and (B).

(A) Orange generator, black base pole transformer, black fuel tank.
     **30 40 60 100**
(B) Gray generator, black fuel tank. Pole-transformer base unit comes with blue base. S. Blotner Collection, R. Hutchinson comment.
     **30 40 60 100**
(C) Same as (A), but white stripe extends through ladder to car end.
     **35 50 75 125**
(D) Orange generator, blue fuel tank, white stripe extends through ladder to car end.      **30 40 60 100**
(E) Orange generator, blue fuel tank, short white stripe. J. Kotil Collection.      **30 40 60 100**
(F) Same as (A), but bluish-green body. M. Ocilka Collection.
     **30 40 60 100**

**3619 HELICOPTER RECONNAISSANCE CAR** 1962-64, operating car with red HO-scaled helicopter, black propeller and black landing gear. The helicopter, stored inside, is launched by a spring-loaded device which is pressed to cock. The spring is released by a magnetic section of uncoupling track. Yellow or yellow-orange plastic car sides and ends with red and black lettering, AAR trucks with two disc-type couplers. Somewhat hard to find with intact helicopter and mechanism.

(A) Yellow.      **25 40 60 100**

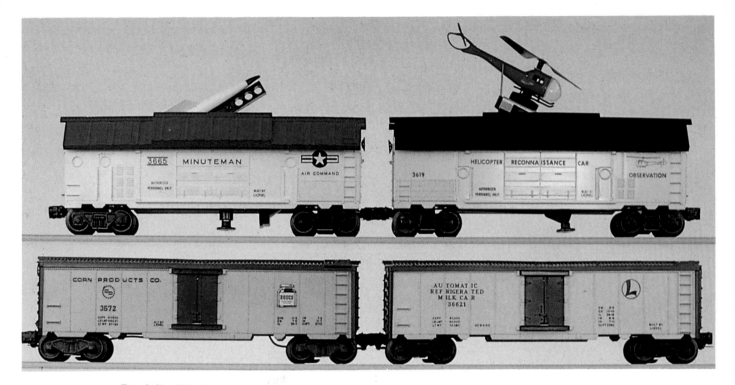

Top shelf: 3665 Minuteman with rocket, 1961 - 1964 and 3619 Helicopter Reconnaissance Car, 1962 - 1964. Bottom shelf: 3672 Corn Products Co. Car and 36621 Automatic Refrigerated Milk Car

3662-1 Automatic Refrigerater Milk Car and 3672 Corn Products Co. Car.

(B) Yellow-orange. H. Degano and J. Bratspis Collections.

              **35   50   100  150**

(C) Same as (A), but yellow helicopter. Shanfeld Collection.

              **25   45   70  125**

**3656 ARMOUR** 1949-55, operating cattle car with cattle and corral. Cattle sometimes need prodding but move more or less continuously from corral to car and back. Orange car with white or black lettering and brown paper decal on door on earliest versions. The presence of this Armour decal on this car and its non-operating version, the 6656, has aroused considerable controversy among collectors. Some feel that original Armour decals bring a substantial price premium; others feel that the decals make little (if any) difference. Until our readers help us to resolve this conflict, we have given the decal versions a slight price premium; reader comments are requested as to the worth of the decal versions. Car also has metal trucks, magnetic couplers, two sliding shoes. Price includes nine cattle and corral; original sets came with box of nine cattle. (A) and (B) are less common than other versions. (A) and (B) have early platform with orange gates, (C) and (D) have late platform with yellow gates.

(A) 1950 (possibly late 1949), ARMOUR sticker on door with white lettering on brown background, white car lettering including "LIONEL / LINES", staple-end trucks, magnetic couplers, activator flap without extra hole, rivet with flared end down. R. Lord and P. Bender comments. J. Sattler Collection.      **18   35   50   75**

(B) 1950 (possibly late 1949), same as (A), but black lettering on car, ARMOUR decal in black lettering, staple-end trucks, magnetic couplers. R.

Lord, P. Bender and M. Ocilka comments, B. Hudzik and D. Doyle Collections.      **18   45   60  100**

(C) No ARMOUR sticker, black lettering including "LIONEL / LINES", orange-painted clear plastic body, orange-painted blue plastic doors, staple-end metal trucks, magnetic couplers, extra hole in activator flap, round end rivet, dated late 1950-51 based on truck characteristics. J. Sattler Collection.      **20   25   40   60**

(D) 1951, LIONEL LINES in white lettering, orange-painted orange plastic runway doors, orange-painted die-cast sliding door, staple-end trucks with two activator flap holes, magnetic couplers. P. Bender, T. Budniak and Kaiser Collections.      **20   25   40   60**

(E) No ARMOUR sticker, white lettering including "LIONEL / LINES", orange-painted yellow-white opaque plastic, orange-painted orange plastic runway doors, orange-painted sliding door, bar-end trucks, magnetic couplers, holes in activator flaps, dated 1952-55 based on truck characteristics. J. Sattler, P. Bender, C. Rohlfing and Kaiser Collections.

              **20   25   40   60**

(F) Same as (E), but orange-painted clear plastic runway doors. C. Rohlfing Collection.      **20   25   40   60**

(G) Same as (E), but imperfection in sliding door casting on side with opening doors for cattle. J. Sattler Collection.      **20   25   40   60**

**3662-1 AUTOMATIC REFRIGERATED MILK CAR** 1955-60, 1964-66, operating car, man delivers late style milk cans without weighted magnets. White car with brown top and doors, "L" in circle, metal trucks with magnetic tab couplers. Price includes five cans and stand. Reissued by Fundimensions in 1985 as 9220 in Borden markings.

(A) Lettered "NEW 4-55", bright brown roof and ends.  **30  40  55  80**

(B) Same as (A), but dull, chalky brown roof and ends. Came with set 2523W in 1958. J. Merhard Collection.  **30  40  55  80**

(C) Same as (A), but later production, bright brown roof, AAR trucks, disc-operating couplers. R. LaVoie Collection.  **30  40  55  80**

(D) Same as (A), but without built date.  **40  50  70  100**

**3665 MINUTEMAN**  1961-64, operating car, fires either rocket or shells, white plastic sides, blue plastic roof that opens, AAR trucks.

(A) Red, white and blue rocket with blue tip on black firing unit, two disc-couplers, medium blue roof. C. Rohlfing Collection.  **20  30  45  70**

(B) Same as (A), but roof is dark blue (almost purple). C. Rohlfing Collection.  **20  30  45  75**

(C) Light blue roof. P. Ambrose comment.  **50  75  100  150**

(D) Green-olive drab marine cannon that fires silver-painted, 1-3/4" long wooden shells (shells came in plastic bag inside car), one disc coupler, one fixed coupler. W. Eddins Collection.  **25  40  55  95**

**NOTE:** It may seem incredible, but apparently there actually was a prototype for the 3665 and 3666 missile cars. According to a report by Steve Solomon in LCCA's **The Lion Roars** (December 1983, p. 2), the chassis and body for the real car were built by American Car and Foundry in Berwick, Pennsylvania, and the launching mechanism by American Machine and Foundry in Stamford, Connecticut. The car was 85-90 feet long and had launch control panels in the nose cone end of the car. Stability problems with the tie-down system apparently defeated the car's purpose because the track and the roadbed could not handle the strain of the launch. In addition, fixed tie-downs along the roadbed were not cost-effective. The car was built some time in 1960 or 1961.

**3666 MINUTEMAN**  Circa 1964, uncatalogued by Lionel, but offered by Sears as part of set 3-9820. Car has operating cannon which fires gray wooden shells 1-3/4" long. The car has white plastic sides with blue lettering and a blue plastic roof which opens. It came with the following set components: (1) a 240 locomotive; (2) an un-numbered gray flatcar with a green tank; (3) a 6470 "EXPLOSIVES" boxcar; (4) a 6814(C) Rescue caboose without stretchers; (5) a 1249 ALLSTATE TOY TRANSFORMER with a pink top, apparently made by Marx; and (6) 10 plastic soldiers. (A jeep has been mentioned in some reports.) The set box side reads as follows: SEARS SET 39820 ALLSTATE BY LIONEL/STEAM LOCOMOTIVE WITH LIGHT AND SMOKE/BOX CAR EXPLODES WHEN SHELL HITS/ROOF OF CANNON CAR OPENS AND SHELL IS FIRED AUTOMATICALLY/45 WATT TRANSFORMER WITH CIRCUIT BREAKER. Jarman, Vergonet and Bohn Collections. Price for 3666 car only.  **100  150  200  300**

**3672 BOSCO**  1959-60, operating milk car with yellow "BOSCO" milk cans; "Corn Products Co." on side, yellow sides, tuscan ends, roof door and lettering. Came with both painted and unpainted yellow plastic sides and with bar-end or AAR trucks; the version with unpainted sides has the AAR trucks and was the last run of the car. P. Ambrose comments. Price includes platform and seven yellow and brown-painted cans made especially for this car.

(A) 1959, with Bosco decal, painted yellow car sides, bar-end trucks with magnetic couplers.  **70  125  175  250**

(B) 1960, without Bosco decal, AAR trucks with disc couplers, unpainted yellow plastic sides.  **70  125  175  250**

(C) No lettering, Bosco decal on operating boxcar body and frame, prototype of an operating boxcar.  **—  —  —  750**

**3854 AUTOMATIC MERCHANDISE CAR**  1946-47, operating boxcar, tuscan with white lettering, 11" long and built to O Scale proportions. It is marked "3854" and "X3854", two sliding shoes on each truck (the only car so equipped; this was necessary to insure contact with the RCS remote track because of the car's length), circular hatch cover on roof, car throws out six brown plastic "Baby Ruth" containers resembling packing crates, detailed door latch and handle on non-operating side only. Same mechanism as used on smaller 3454 Merchandise Car. This is probably the rarest of all regular production postwar freight and passenger cars; it is basically a prewar car with modern trucks. R. Lord and H. Powell Collections and comments.  **150  220  320  450**

**4454 BABY RUTH (ELECTRONIC)**  1946-47, electronic receiver inside car, light orange with black lettering, brown doors, brown electronic control decal with white lettering.  **20  30  50  80**

**6004 BABY RUTH PRR**  1950, yellow unpainted plastic body with black lettering, Type I body, Scout trucks with magnetic couplers, part of set 1461S. This entry is not confirmed. Reader comments requested as to numbering on car sides.  **NRS**

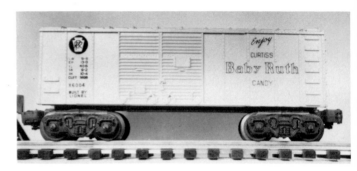

X6004 Baby Ruth Boxcar (1950) came with a low price Lionel set with Scout trucks but magnetic couplers.

**X6004 BABY RUTH PRR**  1950, non-operating double doors, 8-1/2" long, Scout trucks with magnetic couplers, part of set 1461S (see 6110 locomotive for details), orange unpainted Type I plastic body with blue lettering with "Baby Ruth" in outline. Though the car is numbered "X6004", it came in box numbered "6004" as part of set 1461S; I.D. Smith and C. Rohlfing comments.

(A) Heavily stamped blue lettering. J. Sattler Collection.  **2  3  5  10**

(B) Lightly stamped blue lettering. J. Sattler Collection.  **2  3  5  10**

(C) Same as (A), but black lettering, box marked "6004". D. Anderson Collection.  **NRS**

### 6014 INTRODUCTION

The 8-1/2" long 6014 boxcars came in numerous product or road names, colors and body types, although in the lean years of the late 1950s and 1960s, it is likely that only one body type was made. All 6014 boxcars have

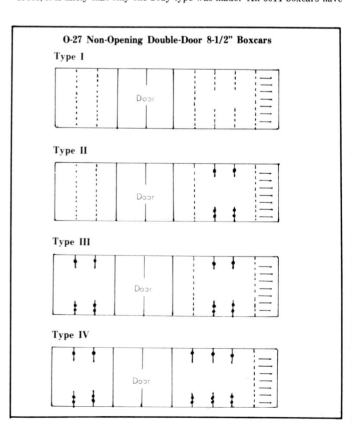

**O-27 Non-Opening Double-Door 8-1/2" Boxcars**

Type I

Type II

Type III

Type IV

non-opening double doors. The body shells are attached to the metal frames by means of a Phillips screw at one end and a large slot at the other end of the body which fits over a square metal projection in the frame. We have a report of a Type III body with a coin slot atop the roof; it is possible that other body types also have this slot. Lionel's habit of assigning suffixes to different production runs complicates the task of listing these cars. In the listings below, the cars are listed first by the known suffix numbers, then by an alphabetical listing of road or product names. The preceding diagrams illustrate the four basic body types of this series. Rivet rows are indicated by the light dashed lines on the car sides. The bold dots and lines indicate truncated rivet rows. Lionel removed these rivets to make car lettering easier and more attractive.

**6014 AIREX** Uncatalogued, red Type I body with white and yellow lettering. Early AAR trucks with disc couplers. J. Sattler and Roskoski Collections. We would like to learn what set this car came with. **NRS**

**6014 Bosco was made in red, orange and white. The red version is shown above. Lionel also applied the Bosco trade name to an operating milkcar.**

**6014 BOSCO PRR** 1958, Type 1 non-opening double door 8-1/2" boxcar, bar-end trucks, magnetic couplers, activator plate with extra hole and roundhead rivet.
(A) White with black lettering. R. LaVoie Collection.    15   20   30   50
(B) Orange body with brown lettering.    4   7   9   11
(C) Red body with white lettering, came with uncatalogued set 610 in 1958. J. Kotil and J. Sattler Collections.    4   7   9   11
(D) Orange body, black lettering. J. Kotil Collection.    4   7   9   11
(E) Same as (C), but AAR trucks. J. Kotil Collection.    4   7   9   11
(F) Same as (D), but has raised black lettering. S. Blotner Collection.    4   7   9   11
(G) Same as (D), but early AAR trucks, disc couplers. J. Sattler Collection.    4   7   9   11
(H) Same as (A), but early AAR trucks, disc couplers. J. Sattler Collection.    15   20   30   50

**6014 CAMPBELL SOUP** 1969, uncatalogued, red with white lettering, question as to existence. Was this a special promotional car issued in a way similar to the 6044-1X McCall's car? Confirmation requested. **NRS**

**6014 Chun King Boxcar came with an uncatalogued set headed by a 246, probably in the 1960s. We would like to learn the set contents and the details of the sales promotion.**

**6014 CHUN KING** Uncatalogued, non-opening double door car, 8-1/2" long, red Type I body with white lettering, bar-end trucks with tabs, magnetic couplers, activator plate with extra hole and roundhead rivet, came

with uncatalogued set with 246 steam locomotive; set number and contents unknown. Reader information requested. J. Sattler and T. Budniak Collections.    50   75   100   150

**6014 FRISCO** Non-operating double doors, 8-1/2" long, various type bodies and trucks; also see 6014-335.
(A) 1969, orange Type I body with blue lettering.    2   4   6   8
(B) 1964-66, 1968, white Type III body with black lettering, late AAR trucks, disc couplers. J. Sattler Collection.    2   4   6   8
(C) 1969, white Type III body with very heavy black lettering.    2   4   6   8
(D) White Type I body with black lettering, hole for bank, AAR trucks, one disc-operating coupler, one fixed coupler.    10   15   20   35
(E) Red Type I body with white lettering, bar-end trucks, magnetic couplers, activator plate with extra hole, round rivet. J. Sattler Collection.    2   4   6   8
(F) Cream unpainted Type I body with black lettering, early AAR trucks, two disc-operating couplers. J. Sattler Collection.    5   6   9   12
(G) Same as (A), but Type III body, very heavy lettering, late AAR trucks with disc couplers. J. Sattler and C. Rohlfing Collections.    2   4   6   8
(H) Same as (B), but Type II body.    2   4   6   8
(I) Same as (B), but has LCCA Meet overstamp. Came in box marked 6014-900 and was made by Fundimensions in 1975. Listed here for user convenience and identification. C. Rohlfing Collection.    3   5   7   10
(J) Same as (B), but bar-end trucks, magnetic couplers, activator plate with extra hole, round rivet. J. Sattler Collection.    2   4   6   8

**6014 PILLSBURY** Prototype, not manufactured. Elliott Smith Collection.    —   —   —   500

**X6014 BABY RUTH PRR** Type 1 non-opening double door 8-1/2" boxcar, bar-end trucks, magnetic couplers, activator plate with extra hole and round head rivet, black lettering, "Baby Ruth" in solid letters.
(A) 1957, flat, off white. J. Sattler Collection.    2   3   4   7
(B) 1957, shiny white. J. Sattler Collection.    2   3   4   7
(C) Red with white lettering, tabs on couplers. J. Sattler Collection, I. D. Smith comment.    4   8   12   25
(D) 1955-56, red Type I body with white lettering.    3   4   6   8
(E) Same as (B), but lighter red with metal trucks with bar-ends and magnetic tab couplers.    3   4   6   8
(F) 1951, white body, black lettering, bar-end metal trucks, magnetic couplers. Rohlfing Collection.    3   4   6   8

**NOTE:** Many of the 6014 cars were assigned suffixes by Lionel. The suffixes did not appear on the cars. We have organized our cars by numeric order including the suffix when known. We expect that some of the 6014 cars now listed without suffixes were also assigned suffixes by Lionel. This information often appears on the end of the box in which the car was packaged. We hope that our readers will assist us by providing this information.

**6014-1 FRISCO** Red Type I body with white lettering, body part number 6014-4. This car may be identical to 6014(E) Frisco listing above.    4   7   9   11

**This is the box end to the 6014-60 white Frisco with black lettering. G. Halverson Collection, G. Stern photograph.**

**6014-60 FRISCO** 1957-58, white Type IV body, black lettering, early AAR trucks, disc couplers, coin slot atop roof. G. Halverson Collection, P. Ambrose comments.    10   15   25   40

**6014-85 FRISCO** 1969, Type IV orange body, no bank slot, blue lettering, arch-bar trucks, one operating and one fixed coupler, may have come in box marked "6014-85", but this has not been confirmed. Came without individual box in sets 11730 and 11750. G. Halverson and P. Ambrose comments.

Gd VG Exc Mt

4   7   9   11

**6014-100 FRISCO** Type III white body, black lettering, late AAR trucks, one disc coupler, one fixed coupler, body part number 1004-3, has built date of 7-57 on side. Came in box marked "6014-100". J. Sattler and R. LaVoie Collections.

4   7   9   11

**6014-100 AIREX** Type III red body, 1960-61, part of uncatalogued set with 614 Alaska switcher, 6819 flatcar with helicopter, 6162 gondola, 6476 hopper and 6017 caboose. Further information about set and car numbers requested. R. Rupp Collection.

4   7   9   11

6014 Wix Boxcar was not catalogued by Lionel. However, we can date it as 1959 since it was found with uncatalogued set DX837.

**6014-150 WIX** Uncatalogued, Type I body with red lettering, early AAR trucks with disc couplers, came in box marked 6014-150. P. Ambrose comments. The "150" suffix does not appear on the car.

| | Gd | VG | Exc | Mt |
|---|---|---|---|---|
| (A) White. J. Sattler Collection. | 50 | 75 | 100 | 150 |
| (B) Cream-white. J. Sattler Collection. | 50 | 75 | 100 | 150 |
| (C) Cream. J. Sattler Collection. | 50 | 75 | 100 | 150 |

**6014-325 FRISCO** 1963-64, white body, heavy black lettering, body shell part number 6014-63, AAR trucks, one operating and one fixed coupler, may have come in box marked "6014-325", but this is unconfirmed. Car did come without individual box in sets 11341, 11460, 11480 and 11500. Body has no coin slot, but 1963 catalogue describes car as having one in its description of set 11341. P. Ambrose comments.

4   7   9   11

**6014-335 FRISCO** 1965-66, separate sale 1968, Type III snow-white body, first Service Manual part listing is 1964 (p. 53, V, of Greenberg reprint), coin slot on roof, black lettering, numbered "6014" but came in a box numbered "6014-335" in 1968. We believe that all the separate-sale items were likely numbered in this fashion. A 6014 boxcar resembling the 6014-335 came in a 1965-66 set (11530) and a 1968 set (11600). The set cars were not individually boxed. We assume that Lionel only made one style of 6014 boxcar in these lean years and that the sets actually contained what we call a 6014-335. G. Halverson and P. Ambrose comments. 

2   4   6   10

NO. 6014 - 335
LIONEL
BOX CAR

This is the end flap to the box containing the separate-sale 6014-335. G. Halverson Collection, G. Stern photograph.

**6014-410 FRISCO** 1969, Type IV body, no bank slot, arch-bar trucks, one operating and one fixed coupler, white body with black lettering, came in box marked "6014-410" in sets 11740 and 11760. Confirmation requested.

NRS

**6024 Nabisco Shredded Wheat Boxcar (1957)** with non-opening double doors. This car and the RCA Whirlpool were the first new product advertising cars since Baby Ruth.

**6024 NABISCO SHREDDED WHEAT** 1957, orange Type I body with black lettering, 8-1/2" long, non-opening doors, bar-end trucks with tabs, magnetic couplers, activator plate with extra hole, round rivet. J. Sattler Collection.

10   15   20   30

**6024 was assigned by Lionel to two different small boxcars, the RCA Whirlpool Boxcar and the Nabisco Shredded Wheat Car.**

**6024 RCA WHIRLPOOL** 1957, uncatalogued, red Type I body with white lettering, 8-1/2" long, non-opening doors, Type I body, early AAR trucks with disc couplers, one hole in floor. J. Sattler and C. Rohlfing Collections.

30   40   55   85

**X6034 Baby Ruth PRR** 1953, 8-1/2" long, non-opening doors.

| | Gd | VG | Exc | Mt |
|---|---|---|---|---|
| (A) Orange, Type I body with blue lettering, late Scout trucks with conversion magnetic couplers, activator plate with extra hole, round rivet. C. Rohlfing, J. Sattler and R. LaVoie Collections. | 5 | 8 | 12 | 20 |
| (B) Red with white lettering. | 5 | 8 | 12 | 20 |
| (C) Same as (A), but black lettering, confirmation requested. | 5 | 8 | 12 | 20 |

6044 Airex Boxcar

**6044 AIREX** Uncatalogued, 8-1/2" long, non-opening doors.
(A) Purple Type I body with white/bright yellow lettering.

|  |  |  |  |
|---|---|---|---|
| 15 | 25 | 35 | 50 |

(B) Medium blue Type I body with white and yellow lettering, arch-bar trucks, fixed couplers. J. Sattler Collection.

|  |  |  |  |
|---|---|---|---|
| 5 | 8 | 12 | 20 |

(C) Light blue Type I body with white and yellow lettering, arch-bar trucks, fixed couplers. J. Sattler Collection.

|  |  |  |  |
|---|---|---|---|
| 5 | 8 | 12 | 20 |

(D) Teal blue Type I body with white and orange lettering, arch-bar trucks, fixed couplers. J. Sattler Collection.

|  |  |  |  |
|---|---|---|---|
| 40 | 60 | 80 | 110 |

(E) Dark blue body, white and yellow lettering. J. Wilson and G. Halverson Collections. Very rare. **NRS**

In the 1960s Lionel produced a number of special boxcars for promotional use by other large companies. Little by little we have learned the backgrounds of these cars. From the lettering on the McCall car, we deduce that the advertising department of McCall's magazine was primarily responsible with participation by the advertising department of Nestle, the chocolate manufacturer. We know that the car was available through Chicago area Grocerlands. Hopefully a person who was involved with this car's design, production or distribution will be able to tell us more about it. C. Rohlfing comments.

**6044-1X No Lettering** Circa 1962-63, medium blue plastic 6014-type boxcar, Type I body, no lettering or numbering stamped on car, arch-bar trucks, dummy couplers, body part number 6044-3, paper decal on both sides, decal reads "McCall's Readers Buy Carloads Of Cocoa". Decal also pictures coffee cup and container of Nestle Sweet Milk Cocoa. AAR trucks, one disc and one dummy coupler. This car was reportedly distributed by Grocerland, a Chicago area supermarket chain; reader comments requested. Came in box overstamped "6044-1X". Eight known to exist. J. Algozzini, S. Mathis and C. Rohlfing Collections, P. Ambrose comments.

|  |  |  |  |
|---|---|---|---|
| — | — | — | 2500 |

6050 Libby's Tomato Juice Boxcar (1961) with green stems.

**6050 LIBBY'S TOMATO JUICE** 1961, special Libby's promotional car, Type III body with coin slot, 8-1/2" long, red and blue lettering, non-opening doors, AAR trucks.
(A) Green stems on vegetable image, deep blue diamond, early AAR trucks, disc couplers. J. Sattler Collection.

|  |  |  |  |
|---|---|---|---|
| 12 | 20 | 25 | 40 |

(B) Same as (A), but medium blue diamond, car labeled "PROD. / SAMPLE / 9-27-65 / 6050-175". J. Sattler Collection.

|  |  |  |  |
|---|---|---|---|
| 15 | 25 | 35 | 50 |

(C) Same as (A), but very dark blue diamond. J. Sattler Collection.

|  |  |  |  |
|---|---|---|---|
| 12 | 20 | 25 | 40 |

(D) Green stems missing from vegetable image.

|  |  |  |  |
|---|---|---|---|
| 50 | 75 | 100 | 150 |

(E) Green stems on vegetable decal, white outline separates bottom of tomatoes and glass from blue triangle. J. Algozzini Collection.

|  |  |  |  |
|---|---|---|---|
| 12 | 20 | 25 | 40 |

(F) Green stems on vegetable decal, white lines divide glass from tomatoes. J. Algozzini Collection.

|  |  |  |  |
|---|---|---|---|
| 12 | 20 | 25 | 40 |

(G) Green stems on vegetable decal, white outline around stems of both tomatoes. J. Algozzini Colection.

|  |  |  |  |
|---|---|---|---|
| 12 | 20 | 25 | 40 |

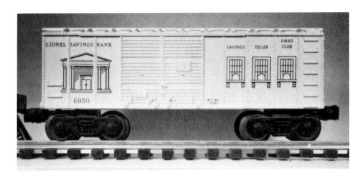

6050 Lionel Savings Bank Boxcar (1961) with coin slot.

**6050 LIONEL SAVINGS BANK** 1961, coin slot, white with green, 8-1/2" long, Type I body, non-opening double doors. C. Rohlfing Collection.
(A) White body, red lettering, green bank and windows, letters and logos all decals, AAR trucks, two operating couplers, large "BUILT BY LIONEL". B. Hudzik Collection.

|  |  |  |  |
|---|---|---|---|
| 9 | 13 | 18 | 25 |

(B) Same as (A), but letters and logos are heat-stamped, B. Hudzik Collection.

|  |  |  |  |
|---|---|---|---|
| 9 | 13 | 18 | 25 |

(C) Same as (B), but brighter white body, small "BUILT BY LIONEL", one operating and one dummy coupler. B. Hudzik Collection.

|  |  |  |  |
|---|---|---|---|
| 9 | 13 | 18 | 25 |

(D) Same as (B), but small "BUILT BY LIONEL", early AAR trucks, disc couplers. J. Sattler Collection.

|  |  |  |  |
|---|---|---|---|
| 9 | 13 | 18 | 25 |

(E) Same as (A), but dark cream body, early AAR trucks, disc couplers, prototype. J. Sattler Collection **NRS**
(F) Same as (A), but heat-stamped letters and logo, "6050" and "BLT BY LIONEL" not present, early AAR trucks, disc couplers. J. Sattler Collection.

|  |  |  |  |
|---|---|---|---|
| 9 | 13 | 18 | 25 |

6050 Swift Refrigerator (1962).

**6050 SWIFT REFRIGERATOR** 1962, red with white lettering unless specified.
(A) Type II body, coin slot, late AAR trucks, disc couplers. J. Sattler Collection.

|  |  |  |  |
|---|---|---|---|
| 10 | 15 | 20 | 30 |

(B) Type III body, coin slot, lettering high on car.

|  |  |  |  |
|---|---|---|---|
| 10 | 15 | 20 | 30 |

(C) Type III body, coin slot, white S in scroll between second and third step. S. Blotner Collection. **NRS**
(D) Type II body, no coin slot, AAR trucks, one disc and one fixed coupler. N. Oswald Collection.

|  |  |  |  |
|---|---|---|---|
| 10 | 20 | 30 | 40 |

**6352-1 PACIFIC FRUIT EXPRESS** 1955-57, Union Pacific logo, "63521" on car sides, operating ice car, Type IIB unpainted orange plastic body with unpainted light brown doors, bar-end trucks, magnetic couplers. Came with ice house and five ice cubes; original cubes have bubble found in middle, reproductions do not. Price for car only. Reissued by Fundimensions in 1982. For set, add $30, $55, $95 or $115.

|  | Gd | VG | Exc | Mt |
|---|---|---|---|---|

(A) Unpainted light brown doors, four lines of medium density lettering: "IL, IW, IH, CU.FT." on lower right ice house door side. **25 40 55 75**

(B) Same as (A), but heavier lettering. **25 40 55 75**

(C) Same as (A), but three lines of lettering: "IL, IW, IH" on lower right car door. **40 55 75 100**

(D) Same as (A), but peach tint to orange body. J. Algozzini Collection. **25 40 55 75**

**6356-1 N Y C** 1954-55: two-level stock car, 11-1/4" long, bar-end trucks, magnetic couplers, small or large lettering.

(A) Flat yellow-painted body with black lettering. **10 15 25 40**

(B) Medium yellow-painted body with black heat-stamped lettering. **10 15 25 40**

(C) White-painted body (reported as ivory, but probable color fade), unpainted black doors. Confirmation of authenticity requested. J. Algozzini Collection. **NRS**

(D) Gold-painted body, silver-painted roof, unpainted black doors, possible factory paint sample. J. Algozzini Collection. **NRS**

(E) Yellow-painted body, black rubber-stamped lettering. P. Ambrose comment. **20 30 50 80**

**6376 LIONEL LINES** 1956-57: "CIRCUS CAR", two-level stock car, white unpainted plastic body, red lettering and catwalk, "BLT 4-56", bar-end trucks, magnetic tab couplers. Similar car reissued by Fundimensions in 1978 as 9407, but with Standard O trucks. **20 30 50 70**

**6428 UNITED STATES MAIL** 1960-61, 1965-66: "RAILWAY POST OFFICE", Type IV gray plastic body painted red, white and blue, 1956-type deep red plastic door painted red, white and blue, heat-stamped black and white lettering, AAR trucks, disc couplers. We suspect that the later production differs from earlier production, very likely by early AAR and later AAR trucks. The early AAR trucks do not have the ends of the axles visible when viewed from the bottom, and the metal wheels are straight. The later trucks are open so that the axle ends can be seen, and the metal wheels have a dimple on their inner surface. Reader comments on other differences invited. P. Ambrose and R. LaVoie comments.

(A) Shiny red paint. **8 15 25 40**

(B) Flat red paint. **8 15 25 40**

(C) Flat red paint but no lettering on one side. Factory error, but common; examples are well known. **30 45 60 80**

**6434 POULTRY DISPATCH** 1958-59: illuminated car showing three rows of chickens on the way to market, but no "chicken sweeper" or mechanism as has 3434.

(A) Black plastic body painted red, white lettering, gray unpainted plastic doors with black lettering, bar-end trucks, magnetic tab couplers. R. LaVoie Collection. **30 40 55 75**

(B) Same as (A), but four levels of chickens instead of three on celluloid strips, even though the car is designed for three rows of chickens. S. Carlson Collection. **NRS**

**6445 FORT KNOX GOLD RESERVE** 1961-63, very unusual Lionel bank modeled on the aquarium car. Clear plastic car painted silver, but with unpainted windows for viewing gold bullion inside, black lettering. Differs from the 3435 aquarium car in that there are nickel-sized circular screens at car ends, (these were open areas on aquarium car), bank slot on top.

(A) Silver-painted plastic, gold bullion. **40 60 80 125**

(B) Gold-painted plastic with silver bullion, one of a kind. **NRS**

**6448 TARGET CAR** 1961-64, this car from the missile/space period has a spring-loaded swinging bar inside and separable sides and roof. When hit with a missile (or anything else), the swinging bar is released, causing the car to "explode". There is a "safety" rod which fits down through the roof into the frame, locking the swinging bar into place. (This rod is often missing when the car is found today, but a flat-headed long nail will also work.) Each part is different — one side is the "target" with two bulls' eyes, the other has "DANGER" warnings. It is quite an unusual Lionel car and is based on a modification of the Type II boxcar body, but rivet rows end to provide space for lettering "TARGET RANGE CAR". Ladder sections omitted on both sides to allow space for a red stripe that only appears on one side. The color of the sides and roof is unpainted plastic, with AAR trucks and two disc-operating couplers unless otherwise indicated. It comes with and without side slots and these slots differ in their locations — on one side

they are closer to the end than on the other side. Therefore, the car can only be reassembled in one way.

(A) Flat red sides, white roof and ends, white lettering, no slots in sides. **8 12 15 25**

(B) Same as (A), but slots on one side. **8 12 15 25**

(C) Same as (A), but shiny red sides, slots on one side. **8 12 15 25**

(D) Same as (A), but slots on both sides. C. Rohlfing Collection. **8 12 15 25**

(E) Same as (C), but no slots on sides. C. Rohlfing Collection. **8 12 15 25**

(F) Shiny red sides, ends, roof, white lettering, no side slots. **8 12 15 25**

(G) White sides, flat red ends and roof, red lettering. **8 12 15 25**

(H) White sides, shiny red roof and ends, red lettering, slots on both sides. **8 12 15 25**

(I) White sides, roof, ends, red lettering, slots on both sides. **8 12 15 25**

Lionel used the Baby Ruth advertisement on a number of its boxcars including X2454, X6004, X6014 and X6454. Lionel first adopted the Baby Ruth logo in the early 1930s with the 1514 boxcar and later with the 1679 Boxcar. The X6454 is shown above. R. Lord Collection.

The **6454 Boxcars** have been intensively studied by Robert Swanson. His comprehensive report is the feature article of this book and precedes the Diesel Chapter. The following listings summarize his findings.

**6454(A) BABY RUTH** 1948, orange with brown doors, black lettering, "Enjoy Curtiss Baby Ruth Candy" to left of door, PRR logo and dimensional data to right, either type 3B or type 4 trucks. **40 80 150 300**

**6454(B) NYC 159000** 1948, orange with black lettering, brown doors **20 40 60 100**

**6454(C) NYC 159000** 1948, brown with white lettering, brown doors **10 20 30 50**

**6454(D) NYC 159000** 1948, tan with white lettering, brown doors **10 20 30 50**

**6454(E) AT&SF** 63132, 1948, orange with black lettering, brown doors **10 20 30 50**

**6454(F) SOUTHERN PACIFIC 96743** 1949, light brown body and doors, white lettering, early SP herald: thin lines with break in outer circle between R and N. **15 25 40 60**

**6454(H) SOUTHERN PACIFIC 96743** 1951-52, red-brown body and doors, white lettering, late SP herald: thick lines with no break in outer circle **10 30 30 50**

**6454(J) ERIE 81000** 1949-52, brown body and doors, white lettering **10 20 30 50**

**6454(K) PENNSYLVANIA 65400** 1949-52, tuscan body and doors, white lettering **8 15 25 40**

## 6464 Boxcar Body Types
### By Dr. Charles Weber

Among postwar collectors, the study of the 6464 boxcars is the "granddaddy" of all postwar studies, with good reason. The manufacturing history of these cars is replete with variations of all kinds, and it has taken years of study to distinguish them. Because of the complexity of the body and

# LIONEL 6464 BOXCAR VARIATIONS

## By Dr. Charles Weber*

Dr. Charles Weber wrote the section on 6464 boxcars. His study, completed several years ago and recently updated, introduced a new level of sophistication to the study of Lionel variations. It should be noted, however, that Dr. Weber did not contribute the prices listed for the 6464 boxcars. It is his strongly held conviction, that the concern with prices detracts from the essential enjoyment of toy train collection. His willingness to contribute to this volume is most appreciated.

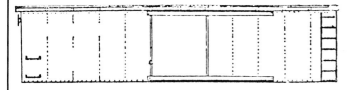

**Type I Side.** The car has three columns of rivets which are incomplete: columns 1, 2 and 3 counting from the left. All three columns are broken near the top, in addition column two is also broken near the bottom.

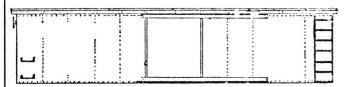

**Type II Side.** Columns 1, 2 and 3 plus Column 7 are incomplete. Columns 1 - 3 are broken near the top as with Type I. Column 2 has only three rivets left at the top and two left at the bottom. All the rivets in Column 7 are deleted. There are two versions of Type II cars which are distinguished by the absence or presence of a line on the roof on the brakewheel end which corresponds to the area of the ice hatch on the 6352-1 Operating Ice Car.

Type IIA cars do not have a line on the roof.

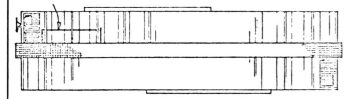

Type IIB cars have a line on the roof where the ice hatch was installed on the 6352.

**1953 Door** (two panels)  **1956 Door** (five panels)

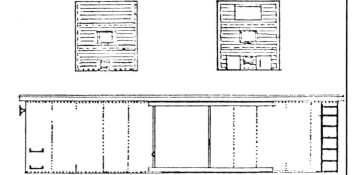

**Type III Side:** Column 1 has a break near the top (four rivets down), Column 2 has only three rivets at top and two at bottom. Column 7 has only two rivets at the top and two at the bottom. Type III has roof ribs.

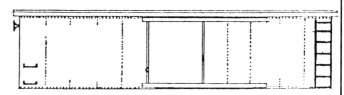

**Type IV:** Same as Type III, but Column 3 has only three rivets at top and two at the bottom. Type IV has roof ribs.

Drawings by Bob Fox

\* Dr. Weber gratefully acknowledges the assistance of the following people without whose assistance this research could not have been carried forth: Sid Brown, Ron Niedhammer, Allan Stewart, Ernie Davis, Dick Meerly, Joe Ryan, Lee Stuhl, Joe Ranker, Elliott Smith and Bill Fryberger.

frame types, not to mention the color and body mold differences, the known 6464 variations have multiplied geometrically since they were first studied in the late 1960s, when they were still being produced. Mastery of the 6464 Boxcars is one of the most challenging areas for the student of Lionel trains. Therefore, the purpose of this brief study is to familiarize the reader with the basic variations and to provide a tentative production history of these interesting cars, which succeeded the shorter 6454 Series in 1954.

This analysis of 6464 boxcar body types is, by necessity, speculative and is based on the assumptions that: (1) Lionel's production lines were run in an organized fashion; and (2) what was catalogued was produced at the appropriate time, except where noted.

We begin our analysis with a puzzle, appropriately enough. The usually accurate Lionel Service Manual indicates that the 6464 car bodies are mounted on the frame with a screw at each end rather than with one screw on one end and two tabs in slots on the other end. Twenty years ago, my many "sources" and I sought widely to find such a two-screw body, but to no avail. To my knowledge, no one has found such a body and I must conclude that this body does not exist except, possibly, as a mock-up "prototype" somewhere in the archives. We believe that all 6464 boxcars were produced with bodies having a screw hole at one end and two tab fastening slots at the other.

The normal Type I body was run in 1953 and 1954. In 1954 Lionel apparently used at least two separate molding machines. Alternatively, there may have been a changeover to Type II-A which occurred during the production season while Lionel made the items for Christmas, 1954. The fact that the -25, -50 and -75 cars have not been found to exist with other than Type I bodies implies that these three types of numbered cars were all made in 1953 and early 1954, and then subsequently sold until all stock was gone (except -50, which was catalogued through 1956.)

First shelf: 6464-1 Western Pacific, 6464-25 Great Northern. Second shelf: 6464-50 Minneapolis and St. Louis, 6464-75 Rock Island. Third shelf: 6464-100 Western Pacific in silver; 6464-100 Western Pacific in orange. Fourth shelf: 6464-125 New York Central and 6464-150 Missouri Pacific. L. Nuzzaci Collection.

In 1954, the -1 cars were still being produced along with the introduction of the -175 cars. It was then decided to make a new mold which eliminated the right second rivet row for ease of stamping larger heralds on the cars. This new mold was then used to make all of the rest of the new 1954 items namely the -100 (orange), -100 (silver), -125, -150, -200 and -225.

Virtually all of these 1954 cars are known to exist in more than one type of body mold. These cars can be classified into one of three categories: **Rare** (only one or a few examples is known to exist, probably due to leftover bodies run through the paint lines by "accident" or merely to clean out stock); **Scarce** (early runs as the changeover to the Type II-A body was being made); and **Prototype** (self explanatory).

The following is a list of how I categorize the unusual 1954 production of the 6464 cars:

| | |
|---|---|
| -1 (II-A) rare | -150 (I) prototype only |
| -100 (orange) (I) rare | -175 (II-A) rare |
| -100 (silver) (I) scarce | -200 (II-A) scarce |
| -125 (I) prototype only | -225 (I) scarce |

In 1955, Lionel continued to use the Type II-A body mold to produce the -100, -125, -150, -200 and -225 as well as the new -275 and -300 cars. The -50 and -175 cars were also catalogued, but not produced that year. Also in 1955, the boxcar mold was altered to produce the 6352 Ice Car and the door mold was changed to facilitate the -275 State of Maine lettering scheme.

For 1956, the Type II-A body mold was apparently repaired and again was used to produce the 6464 series boxcars. This change provided us with our third type of body mold which we have called the Type II-B. It should be noted that the II-B cars produced in 1956 run on magnetic "tab-type coupler" trucks (Type VII). The cars produced in 1956 with this body type include -275, -300, -325, -350, -375, -400, -425 and -450. The "factory closeouts" that year were the -50, -125 and -225.

The analysis of the Missouri Pacific 6464-150 car's production is a bit of a problem. It was not catalogued in 1956, but it has so many variations representing obvious production runs that it was very likely made sometime during 1956.

In 1957, Lionel re-used the car's Type II-B body mold. The -150 car is back in the catalogue along with the -275, -375, -400,

-425 and -450, the -300, -325 and -350 being dropped. As in 1956, these 1957 cars still have the Type VII truck and coupler mechanism. Cars new in the series in 1957 included the -475, -500, -510, -515, -525 and -650.

Close inspection of the 1957 Type II-B body shows that the mold was wearing out. Lionel rectified the problem in 1958 by producing a brand new mold which was also used in 1959 — the Type III. Externally, it is quite similar to the Type II-B except that the "mold repairs" are gone and the second row of rivets from the right was slightly replaced as "nibs" of two rivets each at the top and bottom of the car.

The big difference between the Type II and Type III molds is the reduction in weight due to thinner plastic. Strength is provided by molded ribs on the side of the roof. The fact that the Type III cars normally came with plastic AAR trucks also reduced the weight. (A typical body went from 104.4 grams to 94.6 grams, a reduction of 9.4 percent, while the entire car weight went from 310.6 grams to 240.6 grams, a reduction of 22.5 percent.) 1958 production included the -275, -425, -475, -500 and -525. Closeouts (not found in Type III cars) were the -510, -515 and -650. 1959 production included the -275, the new -825 and probably the -475.

In 1960, the mold was "corrected" by removing the two ribs on the right and much of the second row of ribs to the left of the door. This mold was then used on all subsequent Lionel production until MPC changed it in 1970. For completeness (and for the benefit of the neophyte collector), the cars found with this Type IV body mold are listed below:

-75 — 1969 metal trucks with tab
-200 — 1969 metal trucks with tab
-250 — 1966-67
-375 — 1966-67
-400 — 1969 metal trucks with tab
-450 — 1966-67
-475 — 1960, 1965-68 (See Repair Manual Truck Section to distinguish 1960 production.)
-500 — 1969 metal trucks with tab
-525 — 1964-67
-650 — 1966-67
-700 — 1961, 1966-67 (See Repair Manual cited above for -475 to distinguish 1961 production.)
-725 (orange) — 1962-68
-725 (black) — 1969 metal trucks with tab
-825 — 1960
-900 — 1960-63, 1965-67 (1960-61 production can be distinguished by referring to the manual cited above for -475 and -700.)
-TCA — cars from 1965 and 1967.

Some time during the mid 1960's, probably 1966, Lionel apparently found a small supply of Type III bodies and ran them through the production line with the current items to be painted and lettered. Cars occasionally found that fall into this category are the -250, -450, -700 and -900 cars.

It also appears that Lionel could not decide what to call the orange -725 New Haven. The Service Manual indicates this car was not catalogued until 1962, even though it was supposed to have been made in 1957 as a 6464-565. A dealer's parts list dated 8-59 advertises the body and doors for this car as being available, yet we have not been able to substantiate this. In the 1962 catalogue, the -725 car was described as a -735. In 1963, it shows up as a 6484 with an operating mechanism and a man. In 1964, we find the car shown as either a -735 or a -750 and a

-735 in 1965. Finally, Lionel got it right for 1966 and 1968! They also did allright in 1969, but the box was labeled 6464-735. Then they reverted back to the black scheme of the -425!

In the middle 1960s, Lionel was clearly in decline. The catalogues had become thinner, and innovation had vanished. Lionel merely reprinted the 1966 catalogue for 1967 and offered nothing new at all. At that time, many collectors felt that the Lionel Corporation was "dead" as a maker of trains. In 1968, collectors learned that the factory had been moved to Hagerstown, Maryland and that some items (such as the late 2029 locomotive) were being produced in Japan as well as Hagerstown.

In late 1968, rumors of the expansion of the Hagerstown operation gave Lionel enthusiasts hope that there was still a spark of life left in Lionel. More rumors in early 1969 gave hope that the 6464 Boxcars were about to be produced by a "new" company, but as 1968 ended, collectors wondered what was in store for them — real train production excellence, or just false hopes?

Collectors were delighted to see 6464 boxcars listed again in the 1969 catalogue. Even more enjoyable was the discovery that these cars were produced with the good old bar-end metal trucks. Next, the collectors found that Lionel was moving back to its plant in Hillside, New Jersey from which it had moved just a year before. (The recent move of Fundimensions from Mount Clemens, Michigan to Mexico and back again had a precedent, it would seem.) The production of Lionel Trains in Japan was abandoned. (The Orient has not been forgotten in recent years. The switches and bumpers produced by Fundimensions and Lionel, Inc. are made in Hong Kong.)

In 1969, the 6464 boxcar enthusiasts eagerly purchased and studied the reruns of the 6464 boxcars. Their subsequent study indicated that Lionel had used the old cars in the catalogue illustrations: 6464-75, Type 1; 6464-200, Type II A; 6464-400, Type II B; 6464-500, Type III; and 6464-425, Type III. My friends and I examined hundreds of new 1969-produced 6464 boxcars to see what had actually been made.

All of the 1969 production of the 6464 boxcars had been made with Type IV bodies with bar-end metal trucks and stamped metal frames. The truck frames were usually shinier than their predecessors. Colors of paint and lettering differed slightly from the original production runs. The lettering appeared to have been done with the original stamps, except that the built dates were left off the -75, -200 and the -500 cars. The -400 lost its 5-54 built date as well as two "H" letters next to it. The -425 stamp was not used at all, even though the catalogue showed it, and the New Haven cars were actually stamped 6464-725 but came in boxes stamped 6464-735.

Below is a chart showing the production of the 6464 boxcars from 1953 to 1969. The chart should be used in conjunction with the article above and with the specific discussion of frame and body types.

### A NOTE ABOUT THE 6464 LISTINGS

In previous editions, extensive work was done concerning many different variables which create collectible variations of 6464 boxcars. Most of these variables are significant and easily detectable; these involve body paint color (or, if the car is unpainted, the body color itself), trucks and couplers, frames and doors. However, one variable not so easy to detect is that of the body mold color. In the majority of cases, the 6464 boxcars are painted in a different color from the actual color of the plastic itself, and sometimes several different body mold colors are used, even though the paint stays the

## By Charles Weber
## YEARS - 1953 - 1969

| CAR | 53 | 54 | 55 | 56 | 57 | 58 | 59 | 60 | 61 | 62 | 63 | 64 | 65 | 66 | 67 | 68 | 69 |
|---|---|---|---|---|---|---|---|---|---|---|---|---|---|---|---|---|---|
| 6464-1 | X | X | | | | | | | | | | | | | | | |
| -25 | X | X | | | | | | | | | | | | | | | |
| -50 | X | X | X | X | | | | | | | | | | | | | |
| -75 | X | X | | | | | | | | | | | | | | | X |
| -100 Orange | | *7 X | *7 X | | | | | | | | | | | | | | |
| -100 Silver | | *7 X | *7 X | | | | | | | | | | | | | | |
| -125 | | X | X | X | | | | | | | | | | | | | |
| -150 | | X | X | *8 | X | | | | | | | | | | | | |
| -175 | | X | X | | | | | | | | | | | | | | |
| -200 | | X | X | X | | | | | | | | | | | | X | |
| -225 | | X | X | X | | | | | | | | | | | | | |
| -250 | | | | | | | | | | | | | | X | X | | |
| -275 | | | X | *7 | X | X | X | | | | | | | | | | |
| -300 | | | X | X | | | | | | | | | | | | | |
| -325 | | | | X | | | | | | | | | | | | | |
| -350 | | | | X | | | | | | | | | | | | | |
| -375 | | | | X | X | | | | | | | | | X | X | | |
| -400 | | | | X | X | | | | | | | | | | | | X |
| -425 | | | | X | X | X | | | | | | | | | | | |
| -450 | | | | X | X | | | | | | | | X | X | | | |
| -475 | | | | | X | X | X | X | | | | | X | X | X | X | |
| -500 | | | | | X | X | | | | | | | | | | | X |
| -510 | | | | | X | X | | | | | | | | | | | |
| -515 | | | | | X | X | | | | | | | | | | | |
| -525 | | | | | X | X | | | | | | X | X | X | X | | |
| -650 | | | | | X | X | | | | | | | | X | X | | |
| -700 | | | | | | | | | X | | | | | X | X | | |
| -725 | | | | | | | | | | *1 X | *2 X | *3 X | *4 X | *5 X | *5 X | *1 X | *6 X |
| -825 | | | | | | | X | X | | | | | | | | | |
| -900 | | | | | | | X | X | X | X | | | X | X | X | | |

*1 - shown in catalogue as -735
*2 - shown in catalogue as -6484 or -735
*3 - shown in catalogue as -750 or -735
*4 - shown in catalogue as -735 or -725
*5 - shown in catalogue as -725, listed as -735 and 6464
*6 - shown in catalogue as -425, but made as -725

*7 - 1954 catalogue shows car as orange with a white feather while the pulp catalogue shows a light colored car with a dark feather. 1955 regular catalogue shows an orange car with a blue feather while the pulp catalogue describes the car as "Silver with orange feather".
*8 - Not catalogued, but production characteristics imply that the car was produced.

## 6464 Body Types

Body type dates:
| | | |
|---|---|---|
| Type I | 1953 & 1954 |
| Type IIA | 1954 & 1955 |
| Type IIB | 1956 & 1957, possibly into 1958 |
| Type III | 1958, 1959 |
| Type IV | 1960 through 1969 |

## 6464 Door Types

Door types: 1953 - 1953 & 1954
1955 - 1955 - 1969

---

## 6464 Frames

**1953-54 - Two frame versions:** plain flat and flat. We suspect that the frame changed when changeover from body type I to IIA occured.

**PLAIN FLAT:** (except for truck indent, frame is flat and has 'Lionel etc.' stamped in bottom) - frame differs from 'flat', which follows, in truck indent area and mechanism of attaching truck.

Cross sections of frame indent areas:

**Plain flat found only with Type 1 trucks.**

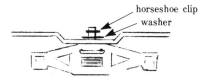

**Truck attached only with a horseshoe - no washers needed.**

**FLAT FRAME:** Used 1954 through 1956 and possibly 1957
1954 - flat frame - Type 6 trucks
1955 - (possibly) flat frame - Type 6 trucks
1955 - type 7 trucks, also, possibly Type 8 trucks
1956 (and maybe 1957) - Type 6 trucks

**TWO HOLE FRAME:** Same as flat frame except 2-1/4" diameter holes added. Observed examples believed to be from 1955 through 1958 although seems most prevalant on 1956-58 cars.

1955 - with type 2 trucks
1956,57 - with type 3 trucks
1958 - with type 4 trucks
(maybe 1959)

**TWO HOLE FRAME WITH SMALLER LETTERING:** Only three observed examples: a -525 believed to be 1957, an -825 believed to be 1960 and a -900 believed to be 1961, all with Type 9 trucks.

**TWO HOLE FRAME WITH DIMPLE:** same as two hole frame except: stamped lettering is gone and a unused depression has been added near the center of the frame.

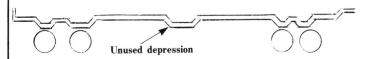

**Unused depression**

**One example from 1958 has been observed. However Type III -425 with Type 9 trucks was used from 1961 through 1969. This frame apparently is found on all boxcars from 1962-69, with Type 11 trucks through 1968, and Type 8 trucks in 1969.**

**Special note about 1969 production:**

The 1969 cars were produced with a mixture of old and new parts. Older frames used in 1969 usually have a flat finish or at best a semi-flat finish which usually appears to be produced by a chemical process. New frames made and used in 1969 are painted and tend to be glossier than earlier ones. Lionel also used both old and new trucks. The "new" trucks are very obvious because they are noticeably glossier and were painted with paint that was too thin. Therefore they show through plain metal at many places.

## 6464 Boxcar Trucks

TYPE 6
1952-54
Bar-end trucks
Magnetic couplers
Hole in armature assembly
Knuckle rivet round end up
Truck fastened by horseshoe
Flap rivet, head down

TYPE 7
1955 (??)
As Type 6, but with tab

TYPE 8
1955-1956-1957
Bar-end trucks
Magnetic couplers
Hole in armature assembly
Knuckle rivet up
Tab added to coupler
Fastened with mounting clip
Flap rivet, head down

TYPE 9
1957-61
Early AAR trucks
Metal knuckle
Axles not visible
Flush wheel hub

TYPE 10
Late 1961
Early AAR trucks
Delrin knuckle
Axles not visible
Flush wheel hubs

TYPE 11
1962-68
Early AAR trucks
Delrin knuckles
Visible axles
Raised wheel hub
Cam shape change

For truck illustrations, see Truck Chapter.

First shelf: two versions of the 6464-150 Missouri Pacific. Second shelf: 6464-225 Southern Pacific and 6464-200 Pennsylvania. Third shelf: 6464-175 Rock Island and 6464-2550 Western Pacific. Fourth shelf: two versions of the State of Maine boxcar.

same. In order to determine and study body mold colors, it is necessary to find chips or scratches which expose the underlying body mold color from both sides. If the car is mint or near mint, it is necessary to use destructive means to remove paint from both sides to clearly identify the body mold color.

While it is true that the body mold color can affect the finished color and shades of the paints, we do not believe that the majority of collectors and other persons interested in these boxcars really consider the body mold color as a factor creating a major variation in these cars. For the 6464 boxcars, the body mold colors is a subject which is important only to the most advanced collectors.

Keeping in mind that the purpose of **Greenberg's Guide to Lionel Trains, 1945-69**, is to serve the needs of our readers, the complexity of the 6464 listings has caused many problems for the majority of collectors. In fact, the listings are very difficult to use because of the mold color information. The extensive space devoted to these listings could be used for additional photographs or textual matter which most readers would find more helpful.

Therefore, for this edition we have made substantial revisions to the 6464 listings and have eliminated body mold color as a factor where such mold color is the only difference between the cars. We continue to report readily discernible variations in exterior body colors; note that these may or may not be caused by the underlying body molds themselves. In the process, we have simplified and reduced the number of entries greatly, in the hope that the listings will be more easy to use for the general train-collecting public.

Below, you will find what we consider to be a nearly complete listing of all major, easily detectable variations of these cars. Collectors who wish to continue their studies of the body mold variations should refer to our Fifth Edition, where a detailed listing is provided.

We will continue to receive reports and compile data concerning 6464 body mold colors. However, such information will not be reported in future editions of this book unless we determine that there is a significant interest in this variation element which warrants its complete documentation. If interest warrants, we will publish a 6464 newsletter. Please write to the Greenberg Publishing Company if you wish this newsletter.

**Gd VG Exc Mt**

**6464-1 WESTERN PACIFIC** 1953-54, usually silver with blue letters, Type I body painted silver, 1953-type door, black door mold painted silver, no decals, heat-stamped lettering, letter color varies.

| | Gd | VG | Exc | Mt |
|---|---|---|---|---|
| (A) Bright blue lettering. | 15 | 20 | 30 | 65 |
| (B) Medium blue lettering. | 15 | 20 | 30 | 65 |
| (C) Dark blue lettering. | 15 | 20 | 30 | 65 |

(D) Black lettering apparently applied by silk-screening. Lionel did not use this process in 1953-54. Further comments requested. **NRS**

(E) Red lettering, Type I frame, bar-end trucks with magnetic couplers, rare. J. Sattler Collection. 500 800 1200 2000

(F) Orange body and door, white lettering; one-of-a-kind. — — — 2000

(G) Dark orange body and doors, silver lettering; rare. R. M. Caplan Collection. 500 800 1200 2000

Top shelf: 6464-275 State of Maine with tri-color door, 6464-300 Rutland with outlined shield. Second shelf: 6464-325 B & O "Sentinel", 6464-350 MKT. Third shelf: 6464-375 Central of Georgia and 6464-400 B & O "Timesaver". Fourth shelf: 6464-425 New Haven with black body, 6464-450 Great Northern. L. Nuzzaci Collection.

(H) Same as (B), but car has orange, white and black square Western Pacific decal on third panel from right of door along car's lower edge. T. Klaassen Collection **NRS**

**6464-25 GREAT NORTHERN** Type I body painted glossy or flat orange, 1953-type door, black door mold painted glossy or flat orange, usually no decals, heat-stamped white lettering.

(A) Glossy orange body and door paint. T. Klaassen Collection.

|  |  |  |  |
|---|---|---|---|
| 15 | 20 | 30 | 50 |

(B) Flat orange body and door paint.

| 25 | 35 | 50 | 65 |

(C) Glossy orange body and flat orange door.

| 25 | 35 | 50 | 65 |

(D) Same as (B), except reddish-brown decals surrounded by white rim with black lettering. T. Klaassen Collection. **100 200 300 400**

(E) Tuscan painted body, reddish-brown decals surrounded by white rim with black lettering; one-of-a-kind. — — **1500** —

**6464-50 MINNEAPOLIS & ST. LOUIS** 1953-56, Type I body, painted flat or glossy tuscan, 1953-type door painted flat or glossy tuscan, no decals, white heat-stamped lettering.

(A) Flat tuscan body and door paint.

| 15 | 20 | 30 | 45 |

(B) Glossy tuscan body and door paint.

| 15 | 20 | 30 | 45 |

(C) Flat tuscan over copper-colored paint, glossy tuscan door; one of a kind. **NRS**

(D) Flat green with gold lettering, white plastic body. Rare. **NRS**

**6464-75 ROCK ISLAND** 1953-54, 1969, Type I body (except as noted) painted in shades of green or gray, 1953-type door (except as noted), door

painted glossy, flat or light green, no decals, heat-stamped gold lettering.

(A) Glossy green body and door paint.

| 15 | 25 | 35 | 55 |

(B) Flat green body and door paint.

| 15 | 25 | 35 | 55 |

(C) Light gray-painted body.

| 15 | 25 | 35 | 55 |

(D) Same as (B), except lighter green body paint (door is darker green).

| 15 | 25 | 35 | 55 |

(E) 1969, flat green body and door paint, Type IV body, 1956-type door, bright gold heat-stamped lettering, bar-end trucks with tab couplers, 6352-11 frame. I.D. Smith Collection.

| 15 | 20 | 30 | 50 |

(F) Same as (E), except light green door paint (lighter than car body).

| 15 | 20 | 30 | 50 |

(G) Silver-painted body and doors, black lettering. C. Grass Collection. **NRS**

**6464-100 WESTERN PACIFIC** 1954-55, Type II-A body except as noted, orange or silver body paint, 1953-type door painted orange or silver, white, gray-white or black rubber-stamped lettering, no decals.

(A) Type II-A body, silver body and door paint, black lettering, long yellow feather (18.7 cm).

| 30 | 50 | 75 | 125 |

(B) Same as (A), but short yellow feather (18.5 cm).

| 30 | 50 | 75 | 125 |

(C) Same as (A), but long yellow-orange feather.

| 30 | 50 | 75 | 125 |

(D) Same as (A), but short yellow-orange feather.

| 30 | 50 | 75 | 125 |

(E) Same as (C), but doors painted yellow instead of silver.

| 30 | 50 | 75 | 125 |

(F) Same as (E), but yellow-orange door paint. **30 50 75 125**

| | Gd | VG | Exc | Mt |
|---|---|---|---|---|

(G) Type I body, flat orange body and door paint, blue feather, numbered "1954" instead of usual 6464-100, three examples known. — — 2000 3000

(H) Same as (G), but lighter blue feather, numbered 6464-100. 100 200 300 450

(I) Same as (H), but darker orange body and door paint, blue feather, thicker and wider "WESTERN PACIFIC", larger "WP" and smaller "BUILT BY LIONEL" similar to 6464-250. T. Klaassen Collection. — — 1000 —

(J) Type II-A body, orange body and door paint, gray-white lettering, blue feather. 125 200 300 450

(K) Type I body, silver body and door paint, black lettering, short yellow feather. 45 75 90 125

**6464-125 NEW YORK CENTRAL** 1954-56, Type II-A body and 1953-type doors except as noted; no decals, white lettering except as noted; other characteristics vary as described.

(A) Type I light yellow-painted body, red-painted doors, black rubber-stamped lettering; one of a kind. **NRS**

(B) Glossy gray and flat red-painted body, unpainted red door, heat-stamped lettering, gray top row of rivets, no cedilia mark. 20 30 40 65

(C) Same as (B), but rubber-stamped lettering. 20 30 40 65

(D) Same as (B), but painted gray and unpainted red body. 20 30 40 65

(E) Same as (D), but red top row of rivets (half gray). 20 30 40 65

(F) Same as (B), but glossy red and glossy gray-painted body. 20 30 40 65

(G) Same as (D), but red top row of rivets. 20 30 40 65

(H) Same as (G), but flat red and gray-painted body. 20 30 40 65

(I) Red and glossy gray-painted body, red-painted door, rubber-stamped lettering, red top row of rivets, cedilia mark. 20 30 40 65

(J) Same as (I), but unpainted red 1956-type door. 20 30 40 65

(K) Same as (J), but unpainted red and flat gray-painted body. 20 30 40 65

(L) Flat red and flat gray-painted body, painted red 1953-type door, rubber-stamped lettering, red top row of rivets, half-width cedilia. 40 60 80 125

(M) Same as (K), but black rubber-stamped lettering. 20 30 40 65

(N) Same as (K), but unpainted red and glossy gray-painted body. 20 30 40 65

**6464-150 MISSOURI PACIFIC** Catalogued 1954-55 and 1957. This car has several interesting variations. First, the word "Eagle" comes in three sizes: large, 3/4" high, medium, 5/8" high and small, 1/2" high. Second, "Eagle" is found either to the left or right of the car. Third, the gray stripe on the car's side may be painted on a blue unpainted or blue-painted shell, or it may be the body color itself. In the latter case, blue paint creates the gray stripe effect. Fourth, the door may or may not have a painted gray stripe.

The following characteristics apply to all Missouri Pacifics except as noted: no decals (except (A)) and black and white rubber-stamped lettering.

(B) to (L) Have Type II-A bodies and 1953-type doors.

(A) Type I body painted blue and gray, 1953-type yellow unpainted door with gray-painted stripe, decal, right 3/4" Eagle, XME, preproduction sample, reportedly one-of-a-kind. **NRS**

(B) Navy blue body with painted gray stripe, yellow unpainted door with gray-painted stripe, right 3/4" Eagle, XME. 25 35 50 80

(C) Same as (B), except no XME. 25 35 50 80

(D) Same as (B), except body painted navy blue with painted gray stripe. 25 35 50 80

(E) Gray body painted royal blue to create the effect of a gray stripe, yellow door with painted gray stripe, right 3/4" Eagle, XME, "3-54" on left. 25 35 50 80

(F) Royal blue body with painted gray stripe, yellow door with painted gray stripe, right 3/4" Eagle, no XME. 25 35 50 80

(G) Violet body with painted gray stripe, light yellow door with gray stripe only, right 3/4" Eagle, XME. 25 35 50 80

(H) Same as (G), except no XME. 25 35 50 80

(I) Royal blue body with painted gray stripe, door painted plain dark yellow,

no door stripe, right 3/4" Eagle, no XME, seal on first panel. T. Klaassen Collection. 40 65 80 125

(J) Same as (I), but yellow door with painted gray stripe, right 3/4" Eagle. 25 35 80 80

(K) Same as (J), except navy body paint and no XME. 25 35 50 80

(L) Same as (K), except has XME. T. Klaassen Collection. 25 35 50 80

(M) Type II-A navy blue body with painted gray stripe, 1956-type dark yellow unpainted door, no door stripe, right 3/4" Eagle, no XME. 40 65 80 125

(N) Type II-A body painted royal blue and gray, 1956-type light yellow unpainted door, no stripe, right 5/8" Eagle, XME and grooves. 40 65 80 125

(O) Type II-A body painted royal blue and gray, 1953-type white door with stripe, right 5/8" Eagle, XME and grooves, left "3-54". 40 65 80 125

(P) Type II-A royal blue body painted gray, 1953-type light yellow unpainted door, right 5/8" Eagle, XME and grooves. 40 65 80 125

(Q) Type II-A navy blue body with painted gray stripe, 1953-type yellow unpainted door, right 5/8" Eagle, XME and grooves. 40 65 80 125

(R) Type II-A royal blue body with painted gray stripe, 1953-type yellow door with gray stripe, right 5/8" Eagle, XME and grooves. 25 35 50 80

(S) Same as (R), except violet body mold and MP Lines circular logo is in first panel to left of door. 300 500 750 1000

(T) Type II-A royal blue body with painted gray stripe, 1953-type yellow unpainted door, no stripe, right 5/8" Eagle, XME, grooves and seal on panel. 30 45 75 110

(U) Type II-B royal blue door with painted gray stripe, 1953-type dark yellow door with gray stripe, right 5/8" Eagle, XME and grooves. 30 45 75 110

(V) Same as (U), but door painted dark yellow, no stripe. 30 45 75 110

(W) Type II-A light gray body painted royal blue to produce gray stripe effect, 1956-type yellow unpainted door, no stripe, left 5/8" Eagle, XME. 30 45 75 110

(X) Type II-B body painted royal blue and gray, 1956-type yellow unpainted door, no stripe, left 1/2" Eagle, XME. 30 40 75 110

(Y) Same as (X), but dark yellow unpainted door. 30 45 75 110

(Z) Same as (W), but left 1/2" Eagle. 30 45 75 110

(AA) Same as (Z), but door has gray stripe no XME. 25 35 50 80

(BB) Same as (X), but unpainted 1956-type gray door. T. Klaassen Collection. **NRS**

**6464-175 ROCK ISLAND** Catalogued 1954-55, Type I body, except (D) (Type II-A), silver body and door paint, 1953-type black door, no decals, heat-stamped lettering in various colors.

(A) Light blue lettering. 25 35 60 85

(B) Medium blue lettering. 25 35 60 85

(C) Black lettering. 300 500 750 1000

(D) Type II-A gray body, medium blue lettering. **NRS**

**6464-200 PENNSYLVANIA** 1954-55, 1969. Most characteristics vary but, all are without decals and have white heat-stamped lettering. The 1969 production differs from the earlier production in several ways. The 1969 cars have Type IV bodies as opposed to Type I or II-A bodies in the earlier production. The 1969 cars also have 1956-type doors rather than the 1953-type, and bar-end trucks with tab couplers. The 1969 cars do not have built dates and have frames with a shinier finish, a dimple and two holes, rather than the earlier frames with a flat finish and embossed lettering. C. Weber and P. Ambrose comments.

(A) Type I body and 1953-type door painted tuscan brown. 30 45 75 105

(B) Same as (A), except body and door painted glossy tuscan red. 30 45 70 105

(C) Type II-A body and 1953-type black door painted tuscan red. 30 45 75 105

(D) 1969, Type IV body and 1956-type door painted tuscan brown, no "New 5-53" designation, bar-end trucks with tab couplers. I.D. Smith Collection. 20 30 45 75

(E) Same as (D), except door painted tuscan red. 20 30 45 75

(F) Same as (D), but has "New 5-53" designation. **NRS**

**6464-225 SOUTHERN PACIFIC** Catalogued 1954-56, Type II-A body except (A) (Type I), all with 1953-type black door molds, no decals, red, white and yellow rubber-stamped lettering.

(A) Type I body painted flat black, black-painted door, one of three. **NRS**
(B) Body and door painted flat black. 15 30 45 70
(C) Body painted glossy black, flat black-painted door, lighter stamping. 15 30 45 70
(D) Body painted glossy black, doors painted silver, then glossy black. 15 30 45 70
(E) Body painted black with silver roof, black-painted doors. **NRS**
(F) Same as (B), but white arrow, no red dot. T. Klaassen Collection. **NRS**

**6464-250 WESTERN PACIFIC** Catalogued 1966-67, Type IV body, 1956-type door, no decals, white rubber-stamped lettering.

(A) Light orange body paint, dark orange door paint, medium blue feather. 15 30 40 60
(B) Medium orange body and door paint, light blue feather. 15 30 40 60
(C) Same as (B), except medium blue feather. 15 30 40 60
(D) Same as (B), except dark blue (purple-blue) feather. 15 30 40 60
(E) Same as (A), but bar-end trucks, magnetic couplers. Available from Madison Hardware. We do not know if Lionel installed the trucks. T. Austern Collection. 15 30 40 60

**6464-275 STATE OF MAINE** Catalogued 1955, 1957-59, 1956-type door, no decals, white and black lettering, characteristics vary considerably, but are identified by groups when possible. The cars are arranged by body type.

**TYPE II-A BODIES:** With grooves and rubber-stamped.

(A) Body painted red and navy blue, red unpainted door. 30 60 90 150
(B) Same as (A), but red-painted door. 21 37 55 75
(C) Body painted red, white and royal blue, white door painted red and light royal blue. 21 37 55 75
(D) Body painted red and white, white door painted red and navy blue. 15 30 40 60
(E) Same as (E), except red and royal blue door paint. 15 30 40 60
(F) Body painted red, white and royal blue, door painted red and light royal blue. 15 30 40 60
(G) Same as (G), but red and dark royal blue door paint. 15 30 40 60
(H) Body painted red, white and navy blue, white door painted red and royal blue. 15 30 40 60

**TYPE II-B BODIES:**

(A) Royal blue body and door, red and white body and door paint, no grooves, white heat-stamped lettering and black rubber-stamped lettering. 15 30 40 60
(B) Same as (A), but lettered BAR only, no 6464. This body is known to exist with a 3494 frame, but such examples are most likely frame swaps. **NRS**
(C) Blue-violet body painted red and white, royal blue door painted red and white, no grooves, white heat-stamped lettering and black rubber-stamped lettering. 15 30 40 60

**TYPE III BODIES:** No grooves, heat-stamped white and rubber-stamped black lettering.

(A) Red, white and navy blue body paint, red and white door paint. 15 30 40 60
(B) Same as (A), but light blue body paint. 15 30 40 60
(C) Same as (A), but has royal blue door paint. 15 30 40 60
(D) Unpainted royal blue body with red and white body and door paint. 15 30 40 60
(E) Same as (A), but light blue body paint. 15 30 40 60

**6464-300 RUTLAND** Catalogued 1955-56; no decals; 1955 cars have rubber-stamped lettering; 1956 cars are heat-stamped.

**NOTE:** Some Rutlands have shown up with repainted doors because of the high Rutland prices. Three ways to distinguish a Rutland with a repainted door from one that has not been repainted are:
(1) Green paint on door bottom should match the body's paint perfectly.
(2) Where colors abut there should be some irregularity (i.e., beading, blurring or barely palpable ridge).
(3) On the bottom half of the back of the doors there should be a faint green, mist-like speckle caused by paint backspray.

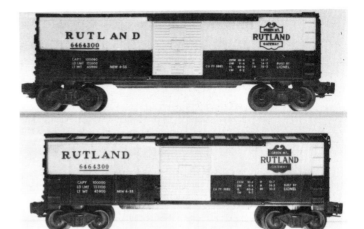

Two versions of the Rutland 6464-300. Outlined shield on top shelf, solid shield on bottom shelf.

(A) to (H) have Type II-A bodies; 1953-type doors except (F) (1956-type door).

(A) Dark green body paint; yellow unpainted door; dark green and yellow-orange rubber-stamped lettering; "R" on left. 15 35 55 75
(B) Very glossy dark green body paint; yellow unpainted door; dark green and yellow-orange rubber-stamped lettering; "R" on left. 15 30 40 60
(C) Dark green body paint; "split door" has yellow unpainted top and painted dark green bottom; dark green and yellow-orange rubber-stamped lettering; "R" on left. 300 500 750 1000
(D) Same as (A), but dark green and yellow rubber-stamped lettering; "R" on left. 15 30 40 60
(E) Same as (A), but light green and yellow rubber-stamped lettering; "R" on left. 15 30 40 60
(F) Dark green body paint; 1956-type unpainted yellow door; light green and yellow heat-stamped lettering; "R" on right. 12 25 35 70
(G) Super glossy dark green body paint; unpainted yellow door; dark green and yellow rubber-stamped lettering; "R" on left; solid shield herald. 500 700 1000 1500
(H) Same as (G), but dark green paint on body and bottom of "split door". — — 1750 2000

**TYPE II-B BODY:** Light green and yellow heat-stamped lettering; "R" on right.

(A) Dark green body paint; 1956-type unpainted door. 12 25 35 70
(B) Same as (A), but flat green body paint. 12 25 35 70
(C) Same as (B), but "split door" with dark green bottom. 300 500 750 1000
(D) 1953-type door; dark green and flat yellow body and door paint. 150 225 300 475
(E) Type II-A body, brown paint; 1953-type door with gold lettering; three known to exist. **NRS**

**6464-325 B&O SENTINEL** Catalogued in 1956 only; Type II-B body painted aqua-blue and silver; 1956-type door painted aqua-blue and silver; yellow, green and silver decals; navy blue and silver heat-stamped lettering. 80 130 200 275

**6464-350 MKT [KATY]** Catalogued in 1956 only; Type II-B body; 1956-type door; no decals; heat-stamped white lettering (except (E) black lettering).

(A) Tuscan red-painted body; dark cherry red unpainted doors. 60 90 150 225
(B) Tuscan brown-painted body and doors; paint on doors and sides very slightly mismatched. 60 90 150 225
(C) Same as (B), but maroon unpainted doors. 60 90 150 225
(D) Tuscan red unpainted body; dark cherry red unpainted doors. 60 90 150 225
(E) Girls set pink body, white door paint (?); black lettering; one-of-a-kind. **NRS**
(F) Maroon unpainted body; dark cherry red unpainted doors. 65 85 150 225

First shelf: 6464-475 Boston & Maine, 6464-500 Timken. Second shelf: 6464-510 New York Central from Girls' Set, 6464-515 MKT from Girls' Set. Third shelf: 6464-525 Minneapolis & St. Louis, 6464-650 Denver & Rio Grande. Fourth shelf: 6464-700 Santa Fe, 6464-725 New Haven. L. Nuzzaci Collection.

| | Gd | VG | Exc | Mt |
|---|---|---|---|---|
| (G) Shiny maroon unpainted body; maroon unpainted doors. | | | | |
| | 65 | 85 | 150 | 225 |
| (H) Maroon unpainted body, black unpainted doors. Confirmation requested. | | | | |
| | 65 | 85 | 150 | 225 |

**6464-375 CENTRAL OF GEORGIA** Catalogued 1956-57 and 1966-67; 1956-type silver-painted door; yellow and red decals except (D); heat-stamped lettering.

**TYPE II-B BODY MOLD:** Blt. 3-56 dates.

(A) Maroon body; silver-painted roof and oval; maroon and white lettering.

| | 20 | 35 | 55 | 85 |
|---|---|---|---|---|
| (B) Same as (A), except mottled oval. | 20 | 35 | 55 | 85 |

(C) Duller maroon body; silver-painted roof and gray oval; maroon and white lettering.

| | 20 | 35 | 55 | 85 |
|---|---|---|---|---|

(D) Maroon body; silver-painted roof and gray oval; red and white lettering.

| | 20 | 35 | 55 | 85 |
|---|---|---|---|---|
| (E) Same as (D), but bright maroon body. | 20 | 35 | 55 | 85 |
| (F) Same as (E), but maroon and white lettering. | 20 | 35 | 55 | 85 |

**TYPE IV BODY MOLD:** Silver roof and gray oval.

(A) Darker maroon body; red and white lettering; no built date.

| | 20 | 35 | 55 | 85 |
|---|---|---|---|---|
| (B) Same as (A), except maroon and white lettering. | 20 | 35 | 55 | 85 |

(C) Red-painted body; red and white lettering; with "BLT 3-56", late AAR trucks with disc couplers, box flap lettered "No. 6464-375 ..." where the 375 is rubber-stamped on a piece of paper that is glued over another number on the box, inside flap number is "6464-530", J. Sattler comment.

| | — | — | 2500 | 3000 |
|---|---|---|---|---|

(D) Maroon body; maroon and white lettering; no built date or decal.

| | 200 | 300 | 400 | 550 |
|---|---|---|---|---|
| (E) Same as (D), but has "BLT 3-56". | 200 | 300 | 400 | 550 |

**6464-400 B & O TIMESAVER** 1956-57, 1969; 1956-type door; heat-stamped lettering; other characteristics vary as described.

**TYPE II-B BODY MOLDS:** Orange, black and white decals; blue and white lettering (except (D) black and white lettering).

(A) Navy blue body painted orange and silver; orange-painted door stripe; "BLT 5-54".

| | 15 | 30 | 45 | 75 |
|---|---|---|---|---|

(B) Light navy blue body painted orange and silver; royal blue door with painted orange stripe, "BLT 5-54".

| | 15 | 30 | 45 | 75 |
|---|---|---|---|---|

(C) Royal blue body painted orange and silver; royal blue door with painted orange stripe; "BLT 5-54".

| | 15 | 30 | 45 | 75 |
|---|---|---|---|---|
| (D) Same as (C), but black and white lettering. | 15 | 30 | 45 | 75 |

(E) Dark blue body painted orange and silver; orange door stripe; "BLT 2-56".

| | 25 | 50 | 85 | 130 |
|---|---|---|---|---|

First shelf: 6464-725 New Haven, 6464-825 Alaska. Second shelf: 6464-900 New York Central. Third shelf: 6468 B & O Automobile car in blue, 6468 B & O Automobile car in tuscan. Fourth shelf: 6468-25 New Haven with large white N and 6468 New Haven with large black N. L. Nuzzaci Collection.

(F) Same as (E), except navy blue body painted orange and silver.

| | | | |
|---|---|---|---|
| 25 | 50 | 85 | 130 |

(G) Same as (E), except royal blue body painted orange and silver.

| | | | |
|---|---|---|---|
| 25 | 50 | 85 | 130 |

(H) Blue body with orange stripe; blue door with brown-orange stripe, "BLT2-54", unpainted roof. Confirmation requested. **NRS**

(I) Same as (H), except medium blue body and door molds; unknown door stripe, no mention of unpainted roof; black and white lettering. Confirmation requested.

| | | | |
|---|---|---|---|
| 25 | 50 | 85 | 130 |

(J) No body or door color or paint information; only "BLT 5-54" on one side and "BLT 2-56" on other. Further information requested. **NRS**

**TYPE IV BODY MOLDS:** 1969, medium bright blue body and doors and no built date.

(K) Body painted lighter blue, dull orange and silver; door painted lighter blue with bright orange; black and white lettering; dull point.

| | | | |
|---|---|---|---|
| 10 | 15 | 30 | 45 |

(L) Same as (K), except dull orange door paint and sharp point.

| | | | |
|---|---|---|---|
| 10 | 15 | 30 | 45 |

(M) Lighter blue, bright orange and silver body paint; lighter blue and dull orange door paint; black and white lettering; sharp point. **10 15 30 45**

(N) Same as (M), except dull point. **10 15 30 45**

(O) Dark blue; bright orange and silver body paint; lighter blue and bright orange door paint; blue and white lettering; sharp point. **10 15 30 45**

(P) Same as (O), except dull point, 6352-11 frame, bar-end trucks with tab couplers. I.D. Smith Collection. **10 15 30 45**

(Q) Yellow body painted light yellow and white; yellow door painted light yellow and white; blue or black and white lettering; no information as to decals or lettering application; no built date; 1969 "AAR" colored paint; one-of-a-kind. **— — 1200 —**

**6464-425 NEW HAVEN** Catalogued 1956-58 and manufactured. Catalogued in 1969 but not manufactured. The cars were made with Type II-A, Type II-B and Type III bodies.

**TYPE II-A BODIES:** Unpainted black plastic body, light orange unpainted door. T. Budniak Collection. **10 20 40 60**

**TYPE II-B BODIES:** All with unpainted black plastic bodies except (B).

(A) Light orange door; partial serif. **10 20 30 45**

(B) Glossy black body paint; light orange door; partial serif.

| | | | |
|---|---|---|---|
| 10 | 20 | 30 | 45 |

(C) Same as (A), but dark orange door and full serif. **8 15 25 37**

(D) Same as (C), but light orange door. **8 15 25 37**

(E) Same as (A), but orange painted door. **8 15 25 37**

(F) Same as (A), but black unpainted door. **8 15 25 37**

|  | Gd | VG | Exc | Mt |
|---|---|---|---|---|

**TYPE III BODIES:** Black-painted bodies, unpainted doors.

|  | Gd | VG | Exc | Mt |
|---|---|---|---|---|
| (A) Dark orange doors. | 8 | 15 | 25 | 37 |
| (B) Light orange doors. | 8 | 15 | 25 | 37 |

**TYPE IV:** Black-painted bodies and unpainted doors. These were catalogued in 1969 but were not produced. Rather, 6464-725 New Haven boxcars were produced and packaged in 6464-735 boxes. The evidence for this conclusion is based upon two kinds of observations. Charles Weber and his collector friends were actively engaged in the collection of 6464 boxcars from 1966-70 and carefully studied Lionel's contemporary production. They noted the 1969 catalogue listings and examined hundreds of the new 1969 cars, looking for the 1969 6464-425 cars as shown in the consumer catalogues. None of these cars were ever found. Furthermore, Dr. Weber's analysis of the 6464 development shows that all known 6464-425 cars have Type II-A, II-B or III bodies. The Type II bodies were last made in 1959, while the Type III bodies were last made in the early 1960s. A few leftover Type III bodies were used in the mid-1960s, but all known 1969 production used Type IV bodies.

**6464-450 GREAT NORTHERN** Catalogued 1956-57, 1966-67; 1956-type door; except (G) (1953-type); red, white and black decals, except (H) (without black); yellow and olive heat-stamped lettering.

(A) Type II-B dark olive body painted dark olive, orange and dark yellow; dark olive door painted dark olive, orange and light yellow; "BLT 1-56".

| 15 | 30 | 50 | 80 |
|---|---|---|---|

(B) Same as (A), except door painted dark olive and orange only, does not have yellow lines.

| 25 | 50 | 75 | 100 |
|---|---|---|---|

(C) Type III blue body painted dark olive, orange and dark yellow; light olive door painted light olive, orange and light yellow; "BLT 1-56".

| 30 | 55 | 85 | 125 |
|---|---|---|---|

(D) Type IV light olive body painted light olive, light orange and light yellow; light olive door painted light olive, light orange and light yellow; no built date.

| 15 | 30 | 42 | 70 |
|---|---|---|---|

(E) Same as (D), but dark orange body and door paint.

| 15 | 30 | 40 | 70 |
|---|---|---|---|

(F) Type IV light olive body painted light olive, orange and light yellow; light olive unpainted door, no built date.

| 15 | 30 | 40 | 70 |
|---|---|---|---|

(G) Type IV light olive body painted light olive and (?); 1953-type black door painted flat orange; no built date.

| 15 | 30 | 45 | 70 |
|---|---|---|---|

(H) Same as (F), but light olive door painted light olive, orange and light yellow; red decal only; no built date.

| 15 | 30 | 45 | 75 |
|---|---|---|---|

**6464-475 BOSTON & MAINE** Catalogued for separate sale and as part of sets for 1957-59, 1966 and 1968; offered as part of sets only in 1960. Also available in 1967. R. Ziska comments. 1956-type black unpainted door, except (N) and (O) (see text descriptions); no decals; black and white heat-stamped lettering.

(A) Type II-B medium blue unpainted body; "BLT2-57".

| 10 | 20 | 25 | 40 |
|---|---|---|---|

(B) Same as (A), but Type II-A body. T. Budniak Collection.

| 10 | 20 | 25 | 40 |
|---|---|---|---|

(C) Type III black body painted flat blue; "BLT 2-57".

| 10 | 20 | 25 | 40 |
|---|---|---|---|

(D) Type III unpainted light blue body; "BLT 2-57".

| 10 | 20 | 25 | 40 |
|---|---|---|---|

(E) Type III body painted medium blue; no built information.

| 10 | 20 | 25 | 40 |
|---|---|---|---|

(F) Same as (E), but has "BLT 2-57".

| 10 | 20 | 25 | 40 |
|---|---|---|---|

(G) Same as (F), except very light blue body paint.

| 10 | 20 | 25 | 40 |
|---|---|---|---|

(H) Type III body painted light blue; "2-57" date.

| 10 | 20 | 25 | 40 |
|---|---|---|---|

(I) Type IV body painted blue-purple, AAR trucks, "BLT 2-57".

| 8 | 15 | 20 | 32 |
|---|---|---|---|

(J) Type IV unpainted light blue body; "BLT 2-57".

| 8 | 15 | 20 | 32 |
|---|---|---|---|

(K) Same as (J), except no built date.

| 8 | 15 | 20 | 32 |
|---|---|---|---|

(L) Type IV unpainted medium blue body; "BLT 2-57".

| 8 | 15 | 20 | 32 |
|---|---|---|---|

(M) Type IV body painted darker blue; no built date.

| 8 | 15 | 20 | 32 |
|---|---|---|---|

(N) Same as (M), but "BLT 2-57".

| 8 | 15 | 20 | 22 |
|---|---|---|---|

(O) Same as (M), except white unpainted door mold; no built date; unblackened door runner rivets.

| 8 | 15 | 20 | 32 |
|---|---|---|---|

(P) Same as (M), but white door painted black; unblackened door runner rivets.

| 8 | 15 | 20 | 32 |
|---|---|---|---|

(Q) Same as (P), except light blue body paint.

| 8 | 15 | 20 | 32 |
|---|---|---|---|

(R) Type IV body painted blue-green; color similar to 2346 GP-9 diesel.

| 8 | 15 | 20 | 32 |
|---|---|---|---|

**6464-500 TIMKEN** Catalogued 1957-58 and 1969; 1956-type door; heat-stamped lettering, Type 2 frame, early AAR trucks (1957-58), bar-end trucks (1969).

(A) to (G) have Type II-B body; charcoal lettering; (except (G) shades of black); orange, black and white decal.

(A) Yellow unpainted body and door painted with white striping, 6352-11 frame, bar-end trucks with tab couplers. I.D. Smith Collection.

| 12 | 24 | 50 | 70 |
|---|---|---|---|

(B) Same as (A), except door painted golden yellow and white.

| 12 | 25 | 50 | 70 |
|---|---|---|---|

(C) Same as (A), except door painted yellow and white. | 12 | 25 | 50 | 70 |

(D) Yellow body and doors painted with both yellow and white.

| 12 | 25 | 50 | 70 |
|---|---|---|---|

(E) Yellow-orange body and doors painted with white striping.

| 20 | 35 | 50 | 70 |
|---|---|---|---|

(F) Orange-tinted body and yellow doors painted with white.

| 12 | 25 | 35 | 65 |
|---|---|---|---|

(G) Same as (D), but all decal lettering in shades of black; 6464-000.

| 12 | 25 | 35 | 65 |
|---|---|---|---|

(H) Type III yellow body and yellow door painted with white; orange, black and white decal; charcoal lettering. | 25 | 50 | 80 | 125 |

(I) to (P) have Type IV yellow body and doors; orange, black and white decals; charcoal lettering, except (K) and (M) to (P) (see text) and no built dates.

(I) Darker yellow and white body paint; lighter yellow and white door paint.

| 12 | 25 | 35 | 55 |
|---|---|---|---|

(J) Lighter yellow and white body paint; darker yellow and white door paint.

| 12 | 25 | 35 | 55 |
|---|---|---|---|

(K) Darker yellow and white body and door paint; glossy black lettering.

| 12 | 25 | 35 | 55 |
|---|---|---|---|

(L) Same as (K), but regular charcoal lettering. | 12 | 25 | 35 | 55 |

| (M) Yellow body paint; red heat-stamped lettering. | — | — | 1200 | — |
|---|---|---|---|---|
| (N) Green body paint; white heat-stamped lettering. | — | — | 750 | — |
| (O) Same as (N), but gold heat-stamped lettering. | — | — | 750 | — |
| (P) Same as (N), except red lettering. | — | — | 850 | — |

**NOTE:** Boxcars (Q) to (U) were made by MPC in 1970 for Glen Uhl. The cars carried a unique identification, "BLT 1-71 BY LIONEL MPC". These cars are listed here because of their 6464-500 numbers even though made after 1969. All yellow cars came with metal trucks as did 200 of the orange cars. It is reported that 500 yellow and 1,300 orange cars were manufactured.

(Q) Blank number-boards, yellow painted body and door; light orange, black and gray decals; glossy black lettering. Type V body as described in **Greenberg's Guide to Lionel Fundimensions Trains**. | 15 | 30 | 40 | 75 |

(R) Same as (Q), but light yellow body and door paint. Type V body as described in **Greenberg's Guide to Lionel Fundimensions Trains**.

| 15 | 30 | 40 | 76 |
|---|---|---|---|

(S) Blank number-boards, orange painted body and door; light orange, black and gray decals; glossy black lettering; AAR trucks. Type VI body as described in **Greenberg's Guide to Fundimensions Trains**.

| 15 | 30 | 40 | 80 |
|---|---|---|---|

(T) Same as (Q), except bar-end trucks. | 15 | 30 | 40 | 80 |

(U) "9200" number-boards; unpainted orange body; door painted orange; glossy black lettering; fifty made, AAR trucks. Type VII body as described in **Greenberg's Guide to Lionel Fundimensions Trains**. G. Halverson Collection. | 70 | 125 | 250 | 300 |

**6464-510 NEW YORK CENTRAL PACEMAKER** Catalogued 1957-58; light green-blue body paint; 1956-type door painted light flat yellow; no decals; black heat-stamped lettering, from Girls' Train, no cedilia or built date, from Girls' Train set. We have one report of this car acquired from an original owner with a light blue-green door. Further comments requested; T. Budniak Collection. See also next entry. Car has bar-end trucks with magnetic tab couplers.

(A) Type II-A body. | 100 | 150 | 325 | 450 |

(B) Type II-B body; support posts inside car body differently positioned than on Type II-A. J. Bratspis Collection. | 150 | 250 | 450 | 700 |

**6464-515 KATY** Catalogued 1957-58, from Girls' Train Set.

(A) Type II-B body painted light flat yellow; 1956-type door painted light green-blue, no decals; dark brown-charcoal heat-stamped lettering. We have one report of this car acquired from its original owner with a flat yellow painted door. Further reader comments requested; T. Budniak Collection. See previous entry; were these doors switched inadvertently in one set? Car has bar-end trucks with magnetic tab couplers. **100 200 350 425**

(B) Overstamped with 6464-150 lettering. **NRS**

(C) Tan body paint; sky blue door paint; beige lettering. **— — 1500 —**

(D) Light yellow body paint; sky blue door paint. **110 200 350 425**

**6464-525 MINNEAPOLIS & ST. LOUIS** 1956-type door, except (C) and (D) (1953-type); no decals; white heat-stamped lettering.

(A) Type II-B unpainted red body and doors. **10 20 25 40**

(B) Type II-B painted flat red body and doors. **10 20 25 40**

(C) Type II-B painted red body; 1953-type door painted red; doors and body paint match. **10 20 25 40**

(D) Same as (C), but 1953-type unpainted red door. **10 20 25 40**

(E) Type III body painted red; door painted red, AAR trucks. **10 20 25 40**

(F) Type IV body painted red; red unpainted doors. **10 20 25 40**

(G) Same as (F), except doors painted red on outside only. **10 20 25 40**

(H) Same as (F), but black unpainted door. **10 20 25 40**

(I) Type IV body painted maroon; unpainted white doors; color similar to 6464-375. **— — 750 —**

(J) Same as (A), but yellow lettering. J. Algozzini Collection. **NRS**

**6464-650 DENVER & RIO GRANDE WESTERN** Catalogued 1957-58 and 1966-67, usually found with silver-painted band on lower side and lower door and silver-painted roof. A black stripe usually separates the yellow and silver areas. The car has a yellow-painted body and doors with silver-painted bands across the body and doors and a silver-painted roof. The car also comes with an unpainted yellow body, but with silver-painted bands and a silver roof. Rare variations include cars without silver-painted roofs. The following items have 1956-type doors, no decals and black heat-stamped lettering.

(A) Type II-B light orange-tinted body, with silver-painted side band and roof; unpainted yellow door with silver-painted band; built date. **22 40 60 85**

(B) Same as (A), but Type II-B yellow body. **22 40 60 85**

(C) Type II-B body painted yellow with silver side band and roof; yellow unpainted door with silver-painted band. **22 40 60 80**

(D) Same as (C), but without black stripe on door separating yellow and silver areas. **25 50 75 100**

(E) Type II-B light yellow body with silver-painted side band and roof; unpainted yellow door with silver-painted door band; no black door stripe or built date. **NRS**

(F) Type II-B body painted light buttery yellow with silver-painted side band only; doors painted light buttery yellow with silver-painted door band; built date. T. Klaassen Collection. **NRS**

(G) Type II-B yellow unpainted body with silver-painted side bands only; yellow unpainted doors with silver bands; built date. **NRS**

(H) Type IV unpainted yellow body with silver-painted side bands and roof; yellow unpainted doors with silver-painted bands; no built date. **20 30 40 60**

(I) Type IV lighter yellow body with silver-painted side bands only, no silver paint on roof; yellow unpainted doors with silver-painted bands; no built date. **NRS**

(J) Type IV body with yellow-painted body including roof and with silver-painted side bands; door painted yellow with gray-painted band; built date. **300 500 750 1000**

**6464-700 A T & S F** Catalogued 1961 and 1966; also made in 1967; Type IV gray body, except (A) (Type III); 1956-type door, no decals; white heat-stamped lettering, except (E) (see text).

(A) Type III body with red paint; red unpainted door. Came in box marked with -700 suffix overstamped in black serif numbers on end. T. Klaassen Collection. **300 450 600 1000**

(B) Same as (A), but Type IV body painted red door. **18 40 75 115**

(C) Same as (B), except medium red body paint. **18 40 75 115**

(D) Same as (C), but silver door paint. **18 40 75 115**

(E) Same as (C), but red door paint; "FORD" lettering rubber-stamped on right. Lettering added outside of factory. **NRS**

(F) Lighter red body and door paint. **18 40 75 115**

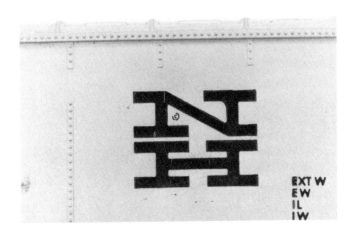

This unusual variation of the 6464-725 New Haven boxcar has a small copyright notice inside its logo. We wonder what prompted this addition, perhaps this change was suggested by the legal department of the railroad to protect its trademark. We do not know if this was put on by the factory.

**6464-725 NEW HAVEN** Catalogued 1962-66, 1968, and in 1969 as 6464-735; never made with this number; Type IV body, 1956-type unpainted door; no decals; heat-stamped lettering. Lionel did not issue a catalogue in 1967, but Lionel did use the 1966 catalogue as its guide to its 1967 sales program. Hence, we treat the 1966 catalogue as if it were the 1967, thereby creating a catalogue listing of 1962-68. In 1969 Lionel made black New Haven boxcars which were numbered 6464-725 on their sides. These cars came in boxes numbered either 6464-725 or 6464-425. The 1969 production had distinctive features discussed earlier in this chapter. However, the 1969 Lionel Catalogue showed black New Haven boxcars numbered 6464-425. It is our view that black New Haven cars numbered 6464-425 were not made in 1969. This view is based on the fact that Charles Weber and his friends were actively searching for these cars at that time and that the 6464-425 black New Haven cars that do exist do not have manufacturing characteristics consistent with 1969 production.

(A) Lighter orange body paint; black door, black shiny lettering. **20 35 75 125**

(B) Same as (A), except duller black lettering. **10 20 30 45**

(C) Medium orange body paint; high-gloss black lettering (shinier than A). **10 20 35 45**

(D) Same as (A), but medium orange body paint. **10 20 35 45**

(E) 1969, black body paint; orange-painted door; white lettering, bar-end trucks with tabs. **20 35 75 125**

(F) Same as (B), but has copyright circle with "C" in middle located within left inside crook of "N" in "NH" logo. Authenticity not confirmed. M. Pfahl Collection. **NRS**

**6464-735 NEW HAVEN** Not manufactured; see 6464-725 entry for explanation.

**6464-825 ALASKA** Catalogued 1959-60; 1956-type door; no decals; heat-stamped lettering.

(A) to (F) have Type III bodies.

(A) Body painted dark blue and yellow, doors painted blue; doors slightly lighter blue than body, yellow and orange lettering. **75 100 150 200**

(B) Same as (A), but dark yellow and orange lettering. **75 100 150 200**

(C) Dark blue unpainted body painted with yellow stripes; dark blue unpainted doors; yellow and orange lettering, doors and body match. **75 100 150 200**

(D) Dark blue body painted dark blue and yellow; doors painted dark blue; yellow and orange lettering. **75 100 150 200**

(E) Body painted dark flat blue and yellow; doors painted glossy dark blue; yellow and orange lettering. **75 100 150 200**

(F) Black unpainted door, other information unknown. **NRS**

(G) Type IV body, yellow unpainted door, other information unknown. **NRS**

(H) Type IV body painted dark blue and yellow; dark blue painted doors, light yellow and orange lettering; doors and body match. **90 130 180 225**

(I) Same as (H), except yellow and light orange lettering. **90 130 180 225**

|  | Gd | VG | Exc | Mt |
|---|---|---|---|---|

(J) Same as (H), except yellow and orange lettering.    **80  110  150  200**

(K) Same as (H), except white unpainted door; white lettering. The authenticity of this car has been questioned; reader comments are invited.

— — 1200 —

The 6464 Series boxcars were a successful Lionel product. In fact, so successful that an unknown Japanese company copied the cars! The Japanese version, a simple lithographed car, even had Lionel's New York Central number: 6464-900. C. Weber Collection and comment.

**6464-900 NEW YORK CENTRAL**  Catalogued 1960-67; Type IV body, except (A) (Type III black body); 1956-type door; no decals; red, black and white heat-stamped lettering.

(A) Type III body and doors painted light jade green; thinner red lettering.
**NRS**

(B) Light jade green-painted Type IV body and door; thinner red lettering.
**20  30  50  85**

(C) Dark jade green body and door paint; thicker red lettering.
**20  30  50  85**

(D) Same as (B), but black unpainted door, thicker red lettering.
**20  30  50  85**

**6464-1965 TCA SPECIALS**  (Pittsburgh) Uncatalogued but made in 1965 for TCA National Convention; Type IV body painted blue; 1956-type gray door, (except (C) black door); blue door paint, (except (C) unpainted); no decals; white heat-stamped lettering. 800 Produced.

(A) 6464-1965 on bottom.    **— — 250 300**

(B) 6464-1965X on bottom. Only 74 produced.    **— — 275 325**

(C) Unpainted black door; no number on bottom.    **NRS**

(D) On bottom, "Presented to Joe Ranker".    **NRS**

### 6464-TCA SPECIALS, 1967:

In 1967, as they had in other years, TCA asked Lionel to make their special convention car. Lionel was unable to do so, and therefore, TCA purchased a number of 6464 series boxcars and specially labeled them for the conventions. Each car was rubber-stamped "12th T.C.A. NATIONAL CONVENTION BALTIMORE MD. JUNE - 1967" on the bottom. They were also rubber-stamped with sequential numbers on the bottom. In addition, an extra brass door was supplied with each car. The brass doors were silk-screened in blue "TRAIN COLLECTORS ASSOCIATION ORGANIZED 1954 INCORPORATED 1957" and showed a railroad crossing signal lettered "NATIONAL CONVENTION BALT MD JUNE 67". It is believed that several hundred convention cars were distributed. It is reported, but not verified, that brass door reproductions have been made and that cars have been rubber-stamped to appear as if they were 1967 Convention cars. The following is a sampling of convention cars:

**6464-250 WESTERN PACIFIC**

(A) Type IV body painted dark orange, 1956-type door painted dark orange; no decals; white heat-stamped lettering, stamped 547.    **— — — 275**

(B) Similar to (A), but stamped "548"; dark blue feather.    **— — — 275**

(C) Similar to (A), but stamped "178"; unblackened rivets.
**— — — 275**

**6464-375 CENTRAL of GEORGIA**

(A) Type IV maroon body painted with silver oval, 1956-type door painted silver; yellow and red decals; white and red heat-stamped lettering; no built date, rubber-stamped "411".    **— — — 275**

**6464-450 GREAT NORTHERN**

(A) Type IV body painted light olive, 1956-type door painted light olive, orange and yellow, red, white and black decals; yellow heat-stamped lettering, rubber-stamped "228" or "254".    **— — — 275**

**6464-475 BOSTON & MAINE**

(A) Type IV dark blue unpainted body, 1956-type black unpainted door, no decals, black heat-stamped lettering, "BLT 2-57", rubber-stamped "580".
**NRS**

**6464-525 MINNEAPOLIS & ST. LOUIS**

(A) Type IV body painted red, 1956-type red unpainted doors, no decals, white heat-stamped lettering, "BLT 6-57", rubber-stamped "588".
**— — — 500**

**6464-650 DENVER & RIO GRANDE WESTERN**

(A) Type IV yellow unpainted body with silver-painted band and roof, 1956-type yellow unpainted door with silver-painted band, no decals, black heat-stamped lettering, rubber-stamped "387" or "483".    **— — — 275**

**6464-700 A T & S F**

(A) Type IV body painted red, 1956-type door painted red, no decals, white heat-stamped lettering, rubber-stamped "220" or "360".    **— — — 275**

**6464-735 NEW HAVEN**

(A) Type IV body, 1956-type door, no decals, black heat-stamped lettering, other details unknown.    **NRS**

**6464-900 NEW YORK CENTRAL**

(A) Type IV body, 1956-type door, no decals, white, black and red heat-stamped lettering, other details unknown.    **NRS**

**6464-000 BOSTON & MAINE**

(A) Type IV body, 1956-type door, black lettering, specially numbered "6464-000" rather than 6464-475, other details unknown, one-of-a-kind.    **NRS**

**6464-1970 TCA SPECIAL** (Chicago)  Uncatalogued but made in 1970, TCA National Convention car, Type V body painted darker yellow, 1956-type red door, no decals, white heat-stamped lettering, 1,100 produced. Type V body as described in **Greenberg's Guide to Lionel Fundimensions Trains.**

(A) Unpainted door.    **— — 90 110**

(B) Door painted red.    **— — 90 110**

**6464-1971 TCA SPECIAL** (Disneyland)  Uncatalogued but made in 1971, TCA National Convention car, 1,500 produced. NOTE: Other colors of this car have surfaced, but the white variety listed here is the only one known to be genuine factory production. See also Factory Errors and Prototypes.

(A) Type VII body painted white, 1956-type door painted yellow, no decals, red, black and blue heat-stamped lettering.    **— — 160 200**

**6468-1 BALTIMORE & OHIO**  1953-55, double-door automobile car, Type A body (does not have ice hatch line found on 6352-1), white heat-stamped lettering.

(A) Tuscan brown-painted black plastic body and doors, bar-end trucks, magnetic couplers with second hole in activator plate, round end rivet and off-center hole in base plate. J. Sattler Collection.    **75  110  150  250**

(B) Shiny blue-painted black plastic body and doors.    **9  12  18  30**

(C) Shiny blue-painted clear plastic body, shiny blue-painted black plastic door.    **9  12  18  30**

(D) Flat blue-painted clear plastic body, flat blue-painted black plastic door.    **9  12  18  30**

(E) Shiny blue-painted off-white opaque body. J. Kotil Collection.
**9  12  18  30**

(F) Flat blue-painted off-white opaque body. J. Kotil Collection.
**9  12  18  30**

**6468-25 NEW HAVEN**  Catalogued 1956-58, double-door automobile car, Type B* orange unpainted plastic body, (has faint ice hatch lines across roof near the brakewheel end, as on 6352-1:), four black plastic doors, bar-end trucks with magnetic tab couplers, unless noted, "BLT 3-56", single brakewheel. There are two frames: Type 1 has two non-functional holes while Type 2 has none.

(A) Large black N over large white H, black over white, with full serif, black "New Haven", white technical data, Type 1 frame. J. Sattler Collection.
**10  15  25  40**

(B) Same as (A), except with early AAR trucks with disc couplers. J. Sattler Collection.    **10  15  25  40**

(C) Same as (A), but four tuscan brown-painted doors (same as on 6468-1(A)), Type 2 frame. J. Sattler Collection.    **30  40  70  100**

(D) Same as (A), except with half serif and with lighter, semi-glossy orange body and Type 2 frame. J. Sattler Collection.    **10  15  25  40**

(E) Same as (D), but with completely reversed colors of lettering, white over Black. J. Sattler Collection. **40 70 125 190**

(F) Same as (E), except with lighter, flat orange body. J. Sattler Collection. **40 70 125 190**

(G) Same as (E), but half serif lettering. S. Blotner Collection. **70 110 140 190**

\* There are two types of automobile bodies:

**Type A** shows no evidence of the top of the body mold die being filled in after provision was made for an ice hatch for the 6352-1; and **Type B** has a faint line across the roof on the brakewheel end which evidences the top of the body mold die having been filled in after provision had been made for the ice hatch for the 6352-1.

**6470 EXPLOSIVES** 1959-60, Type III red plastic body with white lettering, AAR trucks with disc-operating couplers, spring-loaded car that explodes when hit by a missile. Body has been modified; rivet rows are short to leave "TARGET RANGE CAR" lettering on 6470.

(A) Red. **5 10 12 20**

(B) Orange-red. **5 10 12 20**

**6472 REFRIGERATOR** 1950, white unpainted plastic, black lettering, "4-50", "RT 6472", plastic doors, spring clips hold body to frame, magnetic couplers.

(A) Staple-end trucks. **5 7 10 18**

(B) Bar-end trucks. **5 7 10 18**

(C) Same as (B), but steps added. C. Rohlfing Collection. **5 7 10 18**

**6473 HORSE TRANSPORT** 1963-66, 1969: unpainted dark yellow body, heads bob as car rolls. With datable pieces from sets, or by an analysis of box types or purchase receipts, it is possible to date all the variations listed below. We hope that readers with datable pieces will write to us about them. P. Ambrose comments. Plastic beam which holds both horses' heads in place comes in either white or brown, as does center balance unit. We have verified white beam and white center balance units, brown beam with brown center balance units and white beam with brown center balance units. J. Algozzini Collection and comments. Sometimes the horses' head colors varied, too; we have one report of a car with one brown-headed horse and one white-headed horse. S. Carlson Collection. We need to know which of the cars below have which variations; reader comments requested.

(A) 1966, heavily stamped maroon-brown lettering, one operating and one dummy coupler, later AAR plastic trucks, from set 11560. P. Ambrose comments, R. Vagner and C. Rohlfing Collections. **5 7 10 18**

(B) Same as (A), but lightly stamped maroon-brown lettering. R. Vagner Collection. **5 7 10 18**

(C) Lightly stamped red lettering. **5 7 10 18**

(D) Lighter yellow body, red lettering, two operating couplers, late AAR plastic trucks. Popovich and R. Vagner Collections. **NRS**

(E) Same as (B), but pale yellow body and tuscan lettering. G. Halverson Collection. **NRS**

**6480 EXPLOSIVES** Type III body (see note in entry 6470), white lettering.

(A) Flat red roof, ends and sides, side grooves, AAR trucks. **8 15 20 35**

(B) Shiny red roof, ends and sides, side grooves, AAR trucks. **8 15 20 35**

(C) Flat red roof, ends and sides, no side grooves, arch-bar trucks. **8 15 20 35**

(D) Shiny red roof, ends and sides, side grooves on both sides, arch-bar trucks. **8 15 20 35**

**6482 REFRIGERATOR** 1957, white unpainted plastic car, non-operating versions of 3482, black "L" in double circle, "EW 9-11 EH 8-10 IL 29-6 IW 8-4 IH 7-5 CU.FT. 1834 RT 6482", opening doors with springs, body held to frame by tab at one end and Phillips-head screw at other, four non-operating ice hatches on roof, no brakewheels, sheet metal floor with two lengthwise ribs protruding outward for almost two-thirds of car length, but no holes for mechanism, AAR trucks, disc-operating couplers. Somewhat hard to find, but has not aroused much collector interest. Popovich and Jackson Collections. **15 30 50 75**

**6530 FIRE FIGHTING INSTRUCTION CAR** 1960-61, white lettering and doors, AAR trucks with disc-operating couplers. This car came without fire fighting instructions!

(A) Unpainted red plastic body. **20 30 45 65**

(B) Black plastic body. **— — 750 —**

**6556 KATY M-K-T** 1958 only, stock car, red plastic body painted red, white rubber-stamped lettering, white doors, two-level stock car, bar-end trucks, magnetic couplers. Came in only one set, 2513W, Super O, with 2329 Virginian. This is the most scarce stock car. R. Lord Collection. **60 100 150 200**

**6572 RAILWAY EXPRESS** 1958-59, 1963, refrigerator, red and white express decal, instrument panel on side with sliding cover, flat brown spring inside door guide shuts door. This car and its close match, 6672, come with plug-doors, as did their prototype. The plug-door fits into the car body side so that when it is shut, it fits flush with the side, unlike the overlapping doors found with most boxcars. The plug-door seals the interior more effectively. D. Griggs observation.

(A) 1958-59, blue plastic roof and green plastic sides painted dark green with dull gold lettering, bar-end trucks, magnetic tab couplers. **25 35 60 80**

(B) 1958-59, gray plastic painted light green, shiny gold lettering, bar-end trucks, magnetic tab couplers. **25 35 50 65**

(C) 1963, gray plastic body painted light green, dull gold lettering, AAR trucks, disc-operating couplers. **25 35 50 65**

(D) Green plastic roof and sides painted light green, dull gold lettering, AAR trucks, magnetic tab couplers. **25 35 50 65**

(E) Dark green plastic roof and green plastic sides painted flat dark green, dull gold lettering, 2400-series passenger trucks. This version was found in the 216 Burlington Alco set of 1958. P. Ambrose Collection. **35 50 75 90**

(F) Same as (D), but shiny gold lettering similar to that found on (B). D. Fleming Collection. **25 35 50 65**

**6646 LIONEL LINES** 1957, stock car, plastic body, black "L" in circle, 9" long.

(A) Orange-painted clear plastic body. **10 17 25 40**

(B) Orange unpainted plastic body. J. Kotil Collection. **10 17 25 40**

**6656 LIONEL LINES** 1949-55, stock car, black lettering, 9" long.

(A) Clear plastic body painted bright yellow, brown "ARMOUR" decal, large black "L" in circle above "6656", yellow decal lettering, red star, staple-end trucks, magnetic couplers, two oval holes on base steps, activator flap without extra hole and flared rivet. 1949 dating based on truck details and catalogue illustration. Collectors are sharply divided about the value of this piece. Some say that it should be valued far more highly than the non-decal version, while others maintain that it carries no value above the other versions. Until this conflict is resolved, we will continue to value it higher, as before, but the reader should be aware of the differences of opinion among experienced collectors. J. Sattler, R. Lord, R. LaVoie, S. Carlson, Warnick and Brooks Collections. **35 60 85 125**

(B) Bright yellow, large black "L" in circle above car number, "LIONEL / LINES / CAPY. 80000" in black, one brakewheel, metal door guides, staple-end trucks, magnetic couplers, activator flap with extra hole and flared rivet. Early 1950 dating based on truck characteristics. J. Sattler and Warnick Collections. **3 5 10 14**

(C) Same as (B), but activator flap with round end rivet, late 1950-51 dating based on truck characteristics. J. Sattler Collection. **3 5 10 14**

(D) Yellow-orange body, same lettering as (B), bar-end trucks, 1952-55. J. Sattler, D. Anderson, S. Carlson and Warnick Collections. **3 5 10 14**

**6672 SANTA FE** 1954-56, refrigerator car, white body with brown roof, instrument panel on side with sliding aluminum cover, brown spring inside door guide shuts doors, bar-end trucks, magnetic tab couplers. D. Griggs observations.

(A) 1955, black lettering with Lionel "L" in circle, chocolate brown roof. **15 25 35 55**

(B) 1956, same as (A), but without "L" and circle. **20 30 40 65**

(C) 1954, same as (A), but with blue lettering. **12 18 25 35**

(D) 1954, same as (C), but with three lines of data to right of door; much scarcer that other varieties. **30 40 50 70**

### UNNUMBERED AND UNLETTERED CARS:

Unnumbered 6014-style blue plastic double-door boxcar with non-opening doors, see 6044-1X reference using old listing.

We suspect that there are other unnumbered and unlettered boxcars. Reader comments invited.

**See prototype Boxcars in the Factory Errors Chapter.**

# Chapter IV
# CABOOSES

**By Roland LaVoie**

No freight train looks complete without one of those homes on wheels for the train crew, the caboose. Lionel made sure that its cabooses were among the most colorful of all its freight cars. Lighted or not, these cars have always been of interest to collectors and operators.

Prior to 1970 Lionel made five basic caboose body types: the Southern Pacific (SP), work caboose, Pennsylvania NC-5, Pennsylvania N5C and the bay window caboose. Each came with various add-ons, including lights, operating couplers at both ends, window inserts, smokestacks, toolboxes, etc. The Southern Pacific (SP) was by far the most popular style and the majority of Lionel's cabooses were based on the SP prototype.

Lionel began its caboose production in the postwar years with a prewar carry-over, the Pennsylvania all-metal N5. Both lighted and unlighted versions were produced, and this red caboose was extremely well detailed. It looks especially good when used with the 675/2025 Lionel K-4 Pacific steamer and since it is quite common, it is a favorite with operators.

By far, the most common of all the caboose styles was the Southern Pacific square cupola caboose with its cupola towards the rear of the car. It was produced with many different road names and levels of trim; some were lighted and elaborately detailed with metal battery boxes, smokestacks and ladders. Others had virtually no trim at all, and a few were even produced without lettering for the cheaper sets of the late postwar years. The most common of these cabooses are the ones lettered for Lionel Lines, carrying a 6257, 6357 or 6457 number. The better ones are easy to acquire and rather attractive in full trim. One unusual version of this caboose, highly prized today, was produced with a smoke unit. When the caboose was at rest and the current turned up, a thin wisp of smoke would come from the stack, as if the crew were cooking a meal.

In the early 1950s, Lionel began production of a beautifully detailed and handsome Pennsylvania Railroad N5C "Porthole" caboose. This caboose had a centered cupola, four round windows on each side and two round windows at each end. It was also produced in Lionel Lines, Virginian and Lehigh Valley markings, although the Pennsylvania was the only prototype railroad road to use this caboose.

Late in the postwar period, Lionel produced its most modern caboose in Lionel Lines and Erie markings, the bay window caboose. This long, slender-bodied caboose had no cupola. Instead, an alcove was built into each side of the car at the center, and the crew watched the train from the side rather than the top of the car. This caboose was outfitted with deluxe passenger trucks and couplers at both ends. All of the postwar bay window cabooses are desirable collector items, even though the type has become common during the MPC-Fundimensions-Lionel, Inc. era. The versions most in demand are the "C301" Erie (6517-75) and the 1966 TCA Convention Caboose (6517-1966).

Lionel also produced a fine series of work cabooses. Basically, these were flatcars outfitted with a caboose cab and toolboxes or bins. The earliest of these cabooses were extremely well detailed cars built onto a die-cast frame; they were always gray and had Delaware, Lackawanna and Western markings. Two of them even had a small searchlight mounted between the toolboxes, though Lionel finally discontinued its production probably because of the expense. Later versions were somewhat cheaper. The die-cast frame was replaced by a stamped-steel frame, and the toolboxes gave way to one large bin. None of the later work cabooses were lighted, but they were produced in many colors and road markings. Most of the later work cabooses are quite common, while some of the early ones are highly desirable and scarce.

Cabooses have always been interesting to operators and collectors alike. In fact, through a careful study of these cars, much information has been gathered concerning Lionel's construction practices. (See Joseph Kotil's analysis of caboose dies.) Many collectors specialize in the collection of cabooses. As is the case with most other types of Lionel freight cars, a collector can build a fine collection on a modest budget.

In this chapter, we list cabooses by catalogue number. Usually the catalogue number appears on the car's sides. The exceptions almost always involve a suffix. For example, one caboose is catalogued as a 6017-100; the 100 is the suffix, but it only has the number 6017 on its sides. In the text for this item, we explain that only 6017 is found on the car's sides. Any item whose catalogue number does not correspond to the number on the car's sides is identified.

In the first edition of the postwar Lionel Price Guide, two basic SP molds were identified: Type I and Type II. Since that time, further analysis by Joseph Kotil has uncovered significant new information about these cabooses. As a consequence, the information on caboose types has been expanded in the following manner. Type I is subdivided into Dies 1, 1A, 2, 2A, 3, 3A, 3B and 3C. Mold Type II is now called Die 4. Type I cabooses in this section have been reclassified as being Die 1 through Die 3C, whenever possible.

### SP CABOOSE DIES
#### By Joseph Kotil

The major elements of caboose construction as they relate to die identification are listed below, as are the definitions of Dies 1 through 4.

**A. Window Frames, Front and Rear Cupola Windows**
1. No window frames Dies 1, 1A, 2, 2A, 3, 3A, 3B and 3C
2. Window frames Die 4

**B. Step Construction**
1. Thin, early-type Dies 1, 1A, 2, 2A, 3, 3A, 3B and 3C
2. Thick, later-type Die 4

**C. Reinforced Stack Plug Opening**
1. Present Dies 1, 1A, 2, 2A, 3C and 4
2. Not present Dies 3, 3A, and 3B

**FIGURE 1: Three kinds of Stack Plugs**

**D. Stack Plug (where no stack)**
1. Above — plug raised parallel to roof slope Die 3
2. Rim — rim raised parallel to catwalk with recessed center Dies 1, 1A, 2 and 2A
3. Below — plug below roof line, parallel to catwalk Die 4

**E. Vertical Rivets Below Side Windows 3 and 4**
1. Eight rivets Dies 1, 2, 3, 3A and 3B
2. Four rivets Dies 1A, 2A, 3C and 4

**F. Ladder Slot**
1. Present Dies 1, 2 and 4
2. Not present Dies 3, 3A, 3B and 3C

**G. Wedges along Catwalk, Roof Panel 4**
1. Present Dies 3B and 3C
2. Not present Dies 1, 1A, 2, 2A, 3, 3A and 4

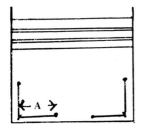

Low cupola roof railing
Long: "A" equals 11/32"
Short: "A" equals 3/16"

**FIGURE 2: Cupola Roof Railings**

**H. Cupola Roof Railings**
1. High roof railings Dies 1, 1A, 2 and 2a
2. Low, short roof railings (11/32") Die 3
3. Low, long roof railings (3/16") Dies 3A, 3B and 3C

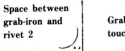 

Space between grab-iron and rivet 2

Grab-iron touches rivet 2

Grab-iron touches rivet 3

**FIGURE 3: Grab-Rail and Corner Rivets**

**I. Grab-iron at Corner**
1. Grab-iron touches rivet 2 Dies 1 and 1A
2. Grab-iron clears rivet 2 Dies 2 and 2A
3. Grab-iron touches rivet 3 Die 4

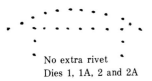 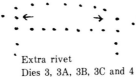

No extra rivet
Dies 1, 1A, 2 and 2A

Extra rivet
Dies 3, 3A, 3B, 3C and 4

**FIGURE 4: Rivet details at car end**

**J. Extra Rivet Between Door Rivet Row and Roof Rivet Row, at End**
1. No extra rivet Dies 1, 1A, 2 and 2A
2. Extra rivet Dies 3, 3A, 3B, 3C, 3D and 4

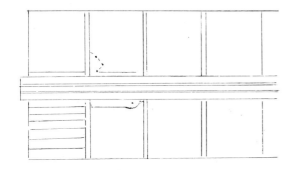

**FIGURE 5: Roof Details on Panel 2**

**K. Three Extra Rivets on Panel 2**
(Rivet and lines faintly seen reveal repair of damaged die on panels 1 and 2)
1. No damage and repair Dies 1, 1A, 2, 2A, 2B and 4
2. Damaged and repaired Dies 3, 3A, 3B and 3C

**L. Catwalk Overhang Supports**
1. No supports Dies 1, 1A, 2, 2A, 3, 3A, 3B and 3C
2. Supports Die 4

**A QUICK GUIDE TO DETERMINING CABOOSE TYPE:**

1. Does the caboose have a ladder slot through the roof?
Yes, then Type 1, 2 or 4. Go to paragraph 3.
No, then Type 3. Go to paragraph 2.

2. If Type 3, does it have a low long cupola railing or low short railing? (See characteristic H.) No, then plain Type 3. You have identified your car. Yes, does it have wedges along the catwalk? Yes, then it is Type 3B or 3C. Go to paragraph 7.
No, then it is Type 3A.

3. Does the caboose have window frames on the cupola windows facing front and rear?
Yes, then Type 4. You have identified your car. (Type 4 is the caboose with reinforcing ridges under the roof overhang at front and rear.)
No, then Type 1 or 2, go to paragraph 4.

4. Is there space between the rivet and grab-iron in lower right corner of the car? (See Figure 3.)
Yes, Type 2 car. Go to paragraph 5.
No, Type 1 car. Go to paragraph 6.

5. Are there eight rivets or four rivets below windows three and four?
Eight rivets is Die 2. You have identified your car.
Four rivets is Die 2A. You have identified your car.

6. Are there eight rivets or four rivets below windows three and four?
Eight rivets is Die 1. You have identified your car.
Four rivets is Die 1A. You have identified your car.

7. Are there eight rivets or four rivets below windows three and four?
Eight rivets is Die 3B. You have identified your car.
Four rivets is Die 3C. You have identified your car.

| | Gd | VG | Exc | Mt |
|---|---|---|---|---|

**C301** See 6517-75.

**1007 LIONEL LINES** SP Die 2 or 3, 1948-52, Scout caboose with Scout trucks, white lettering, "1007" behind "LIONEL LINES" on left side, "1007" in front of "LIONEL LINES" on right side. These locations imply that the same stamp was used on both sides. We have recently learned how to distinguish early from late Scout production. Early cars have trucks without ridges in bolsters while later cars have ridges. We would appreciate reader reports on trucks on the following cars.

| | | | | |
|---|---|---|---|---|
| (A) 1948, red trucks without ridges, came with 1101 uncatalogued set, two couplers. C. Rohlfing Collection.. | 1 | 1.50 | 2 | 3 |
| (B) 1948, lighter red, trucks without ridges, frame fastened to body by screw at each end, Die 2. J. Sattler Collection. | 1 | 1.50 | 2 | 3 |
| (C) 1949-52, same as (B), but trucks with ridges, one coupler. C. Rohlfing Collection. | 1 | 1.50 | 2 | 3 |
| (D) Orange-red. | 1 | 1.50 | 2 | 3 |

**2257 LIONEL** SP, 1948, staple-end trucks, usually with two late coil couplers, two brakewheels, white lettering, "2257" centered on side under cupola.

**DIE 1**

| | | | | |
|---|---|---|---|---|
| (A) Not illuminated, red, no stack, no toolboxes. | 2 | 3 | 4 | 6 |
| (B) Same as (A), but tuscan. J. Kotil Collection. | 2 | 3 | 4 | 6 |
| (C) Illuminated, tuscan, stack, toolboxes. | 5 | 7 | 12 | 18 |
| (D) Same as (C), but red. J. Kotil Collection. | 5 | 7 | 12 | 18 |

**DIE 2**

| | | | | |
|---|---|---|---|---|
| (A) Not illuminated, tuscan-painted clear plastic, brown stack, no toolboxes, only one coil coupler. J. Sattler Collection. | 2 | 3 | 4 | 6 |

**2357 LIONEL** SP Die 1 or 2, 1948, metal trucks with two operating coil couplers, white lettering, two ladders, brown stack, toolboxes, illuminated, window inserts, "2357" centered under cupola on both sides, two brakewheels mounted on outside of railing unless specified.

| | | | | |
|---|---|---|---|---|
| (A) Red. | 5 | 7 | 12 | 18 |

The Southern Pacific-type caboose (SP) was Lionel's most common version. It came in various models, some as "plain Janes" while others had more trim. The most deluxe versions had smokestacks, ladders, toolboxes, interior illumination and windows and couplers at both ends. The cabooses on the middle row have had stacks, ladders and toolboxes added.

### SP DIE CHARACTERISTICS

| | Die 1 | Die 2 | Die 3 | Die 4 |
|---|---|---|---|---|
| A. | No window frame on front and rear cupola windows | No window frame | No window frame | Window frame |
| B. | Thin steps | Thin steps | Thin steps | Thick steps |
| C. | Reinforced stack opening | Reinforced stack opening | Stack opening not reinforced | Reinforced stack opening |
| D. | Rim-type stack plug | Rim-type stack plug | Raised plug | Lower plug |
| E. | 8 rivets below windows 3 and 4 | 8 rivets below windows 3 and 4 | 8 rivets below window 3 and 4 | 4 rivets below windows 3 and 4 |
| F. | Ladder slots | Ladder slots | No ladder slots | Ladder slots |
| G. | No wedges by catwalk | No wedges by catwalk | No wedges by catwalk | No wedges by catwalk |
| H. | High cupola roof detail | High cupola roof detail | Low cupola roof detail | Curved cupola roof detail |
| I. | Side grab rail touches rivet 2 | Space between side grab rail and rivet 2 | Space between side grab rail and rivet 2 | Side grab rail touches rivet 3 |
| J. | No extra rivet on ends above door | No extra rivet on ends above door | Extra rivets on ends above door | Extra rivets on ends above door |
| K. | No die crack on roof | No die crack on roof | Die crack on roof | No die crack on roof |
| L. | No supports for catwalk overhang | No supports for catwalk overhang | No supports for catwalk overhang | Brackets support catwalk overhang |

| | Die 1A | Die 2A | Die 3A | Die 3C |
|---|---|---|---|---|
| | Same as above except | Same as above except | Same as above except | Same as 3 except |
| | (E.) 4 rivets below windows 3 and 4 | (E.) 4 rivets below windows 3 and 4 | (H.) low, long cupola roof railing | (C.) reinforced roof (plug for the 6557 Smoking Caboose and the 6017-100 B&M (1959) and possibly others); |
| | | | **Die 3B** | (E.) 4 rivets below windows 3 and 4 |
| | | | Same as 3 except | (G.) wedges present; |
| | | | (G.) wedges are present; | (H.) low, long cupola roof railing |
| | | | (H.) low, long cupola roof railing. | |

| | | | | Gd | VG | Exc | Mt |
|---|---|---|---|---|---|---|---|

(B) Tuscan painted clear plastic, Die 2. J. Sattler Collection.    5   7   12   18

(C) Same as (B), but brakewheels mounted towards car body, not towards outside. D. Fleming Collection.    5   7   12   18

(D) Same as (B), but black metal stack instead of brown. T. Budniak Collection.    4   7   12   18

**2419 DL&W** Work Caboose, 1946-47, gray with black lettering, die-cast frame; handrails, ladders, two toolboxes, brakewheels, die-cast smoke stack.

(A) 1946, staple-end trucks with early coil couplers. H. Holden Collection.    15   22   30   50

(B) 1946, staple-end trucks, late coil couplers, no stake marks. J. Sattler Collection.    15   22   30   50

(C) 1947, staple-end trucks, late coil couplers, stake marks.    15   22   30   50

Four examples of Lionel's N5C Porthole cabooses. Top left: catalogued as 6417-25 although numbered 64173 on side. Top right and bottom left: the renowned Lehigh Valley caboose. Lehigh Valley caboose is catalogued as 6417-50. The gray caboose is scarce but the tuscan one is one of the most highly priced postwar freight cars. Bottom right: 6417 Pennsylvania. L. Nuzzaci Collection.

**2420 DL&W** Work Caboose, 1946-48, gray with black lettering, die-cast frame; handrails, ladders, two toolboxes, searchlight, brakewheels, die-cast smokestack. An unusual brass contact finger was used to provide power to the light. The trucks were each mounted on a metal plate which in turn was secured to the frame. This is a very elaborate and handsome car. It must be handled with care, since the tall stack makes the roof susceptible to cracking if the car is packaged improperly.

(A) 1946, staple-end trucks with early coil couplers. H. Holden Collection.

           **20   30   55   85**

(B) 1946, darker gray cab and toolboxes on light gray frame, staple-end trucks, late coil couplers, no stake marks. J. Sattler and M. Ocilka Collections.

           **20   30   55   85**

(C) 1946, staple-end trucks, regular coil couplers, no stake marks, dark gray cab and toolboxes on dark gray die-cast frame, black serif lettering on frame.

           **20   30   55   85**

(D) 1947-48, staple-end trucks with regular coil couplers with stake marks. Gray body, black serif lettering on die-cast gray frame. J. Sattler, R. LaVoie and C. Rohlfing Collections.

           **20   30   55   85**

(E) Same as (B), but sans-serif rubber-stamped lettering on frame. T. Rollo Collection.

           **20   30   55   85**

**2457 PENNSYLVANIA** N5, 1945-47. Most versions have semi-gloss red-painted bodies with white heat-stamped lettering (but see note below about entries (A) and (B)) and black frames. Early models have steps at each corner and later models omit these steps. Car also has brakewheels at front and rear, black window frames, red or black smokestacks, plastic air compressor assembly attached to metal channel, illumination with glassine window inserts, staple-end trucks with one or two operating couplers and several different kinds of axles, wheels and couplers. (See our analysis of trucks, couplers and axles for chronological development.) Most have pierced cupola end windows, though some have been reported without them. Car has white lettering: "PENNSYLVANIA" underscored, "477618" underscored; earler production lettered "EASTERN DIV."; all lettering centered on car side. Car is also lettered "BLT 4.41 N5 P.R.R." towards one end. Earlier cars have rivet detail on catwalk; later cars lack this detailing. All cars are stamped "2457" in small silver numbers on the underside of the frame; they came in boxes marked "No. 2457 / 'O' GAUGE / ILLUMINATED / CABOOSE". The 1945 and early 1946 cars came with

The 2457 Pennsylvania N5 caboose was a carry-over from the prewar model.

brass barrel-shaped pickup rollers; late 1946 and 1947 cars came with cylindrical metal rollers. The earliest versions often came with a mix of whirly and dished wheels, sometimes even on the same trucks, as the whirly wheels were replaced by the dished wheels.

**NOTE:** The production history of this caboose is much more complex than we have reported it to be in the past.

(A) 1945, early, semi-gloss red body, red window frames, "EASTERN DIV.", front and rear cupola windows, thick axles, whirly or dished wheels, steps, earliest "flying shoe" coil couplers with black fiber strip, rivet detail on catwalk, "2457" stamped on bottom in silver, "BLT. 4.41 N5 P.R.R." on lower right of car side, battery box on frame, white rubber-stamped lettering (but see note above), plastic air compressor mounted on metal channel, came as part of 1945 set 463W.

           **10   15   25   35**

(B) Same as (A), but only one "flying shoe" coupler. Came with set 2101W in 1946. W. Schilling Collection.

           **10   15   25   35**

(C) 1946, slightly later, same as (A), but regular wheels, "flying shoe" couplers with red-brown fiber strips. I. D. Smith Collection.

           **10   15   25   35**

(D) 1946, later, regular wheels with thin axles, steps, no cupola end windows (unusual for this car; reader comments requested), no rivet detail on roof catwalk, two later coil couplers without stake marks. J. Foss observation; T. Budniak and P. Murray Collections.

           **10   15   25   35**

1007

2257

2357

4357

6017

6017-200

|  | Gd | VG | Exc | Mt |
|---|---|---|---|---|

(E) 1946, late, same as (D), but one later coil coupler without stake marks, pierced cupola windows. W. Schilling Collections. **10 15 25 35**

(F) 1947, early, semi-gloss red body, regular wheels with thin axles, four steps, staple-end trucks, one later coil coupler with stake marks, front and rear cupola windows, no "EASTERN DIV." lettering, has "BLT 4.41 N5 P.R.R." lettering, no rivet detail on roof catwalk, cylindrical metal pickup roller, battery box on frame, plastic air compressor assembly on metal channel, "2457" stamped in silver on bottom, red smokestack. C. Rohlfing Collection. **10 15 25 35**

(G) 1947, slightly later, same as (F), but no steps, has rivet detail on roof catwalk. I. D. Smith Collection. **10 15 25 35**

(H) 1947, same as (G), but black smokestack. I. D. Smith Collection.
**10 15 25 35**

(I) 1947, later, same as (G), but no rivet detail on catwalk and one late coil coupler with stake marks. R. LaVoie Collection. **10 15 25 35**

(J) 1947, same as (I), but two coil couplers with stake marks. Came as part of set 2125WS; box has early liner and logo as described in main entry description above. T. Rollo Collection. **10 15 25 35**

**2472 PENNSYLVANIA** N5, 1946-47, pictured in 1945 Christmas catalogue as part of set 463W, but catalogue lists 2457 lighted version; the 2472 version did not appear until the next year. Semi-gloss red-painted body with white heat-stamped lettering; "PENNSYLVANIA" overscored and "477618" underscored; "BLT 4.41 N5 P.R.R." on lower right; black frame, no window inserts or frames, rubber-stamped "2472" in silver on underside of frame, lacks battery box, air compressor and smokestack of 2457 version, several different kinds of staple-end trucks. This car originally came with only one coil coupler.

(A) 1946, early, no cupola end windows, lettered "EASTERN DIV." below "477618", early "flying shoe" coil coupler, regular wheels with thin axles,

red-brown fiber strip on coupler, "2472" on frame in silver. J. Kotil Collection. **4 7 10 18**

(B) 1946, later, same as (A), but later coil coupler without stake marks. J. Kotil Collection. **4 7 10 18**

(C) Same as (B), but later coil coupler with stake marks. C. Rohlfing Collection. **4 7 10 18**

(D) 1947, early, unpierced cupola end windows, no "EASTERN DIV." lettering, "2472" rubber-stamped in silver on frame, later coil coupler with stake marks. F. Atkins Collection. **4 7 10 18**

(E) 1947, later, pierced cupola end windows (possibly to use up leftover 2457 bodies as caboose was discontinued), no "EASTERN DIV." lettering, "2472" stamped on frame in silver, late coil coupler with stake marks. T. Lemieux Collection. **4 7 10 18**

The 2472 Pennsylvania N5 caboose, 1946-47.

**2857 N Y C** 1946, scale-detailed caboose, catalogued, but not manufactured. **Not Manufactured**

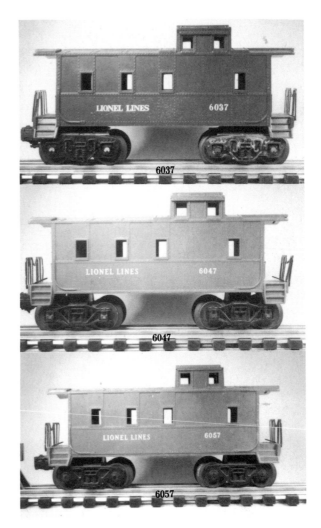

6017(L)

6017-50

6027

6037

6047

6057

**2957 N Y C** Circa 1946, originally manufactured 1940-42, refitted with postwar staple-end trucks with coil couplers by either Lionel service stations or owner. This caboose style, with considerable differences, was revived by Lionel, Inc. in 1986 in New York Central and Boston & Albany versions.

| | | | |
|---|---|---|---|
| 70 | 150 | 220 | 320 |

**4357 PENNSYLVANIA** SP Die 2, 1948-50, tuscan plastic body with white lettering, black frame, blue and white "ELECTRONIC CONTROL" decal, electronic control receiver, staple-end trucks, late taped coil couplers. J. Sattler Collection.

| | | | |
|---|---|---|---|
| 25 | 40 | 65 | 85 |

**4457 PENNSYLVANIA** 1946-47, N5, red metal body with white lettering, black frame, green and white "ELECTRONIC CONTROL" decal, electronic control receiver.

| | | | |
|---|---|---|---|
| 25 | 40 | 65 | 85 |

**6007 LIONEL LINES** 1950, SP Die 3, Scout trucks with magnetic coupler with extra hole in activator plate and round rivet down. Only trim is front and rear railings, screws fasten body and frame, came as part of set 1461S. Set 1461S was an inexpensive set and the rolling stock all used the combination of Scout trucks with magnetic couplers. J. Sattler and C. Rohlfing Collections.

| | | | |
|---|---|---|---|
| 1 | 1.50 | 2 | 3 |

**6017 LIONEL LINES** SP Dies, 1951-61, (for 6017 LIONEL see next entry) only trim is front and rear railings. This is one of Lionel's least expensive cabooses. All observed samples used the same stamp for both sides. Consequently "LIONEL LINES" is centered under window two on the left side and under windows three and four on the right side. Lionel used two different stamps for its more expensive cabooses to produce consistent lettering. All 6017 cabooses have frame tabs fastening body and frame unless otherwise specified. To facilitate reader use we have rearranged the varieties by die type for the Sixth Edition and changed the letter codes. Our goal for the next edition is to date these varieties. However, there is evidence that Dies 1 and 2, 1A and 2A were used simultaneously. Reader

reports on cars found with datable sets would be of great assistance in this project.

**DIE 1**

(A) Light tuscan-painted black plastic, white lettering, black frame, AAR trucks with one magnetic tab coupler.

| | | | |
|---|---|---|---|
| 1 | 1.50 | 2 | 3 |

(B) Tuscan-painted body, AAR trucks, one disc coupler. C. Rohlfing Collection.

| | | | |
|---|---|---|---|
| 1 | 1.50 | 2 | 3 |

**DIE 1A**

(A) Very light tuscan-painted orange plastic, AAR trucks, magnetic tab coupler. C. Rohlfing Collection.

| | | | |
|---|---|---|---|
| 1 | 1.50 | 2 | 3 |

(B) Flat tuscan-painted black plastic, AAR trucks, operating couplers, truck has small "4" embossed, rear coupler may have been added. H. Edmunds Collection.

| | | | |
|---|---|---|---|
| 1 | 1.50 | 2 | 3 |

(C) Brown-painted black plastic, AAR trucks, one disc-operating coupler. F. Stem Collection.

| | | | |
|---|---|---|---|
| 1 | 1.50 | 2 | 3 |

**DIE 2**

(A) Gray-painted black plastic with black lettering, black frame, plastic AAR trucks, one operating disc coupler. Came in box marked "6017-85". Came as part of Marine Corps set 1595 in 1958. P. Ambrose comments.

| | | | |
|---|---|---|---|
| 7 | 11 | 15 | 20 |

(B) Flat maroon-painted marbled gray plastic, plastic trucks, one disc coupler. NOTE: Marbled plastic is usually scrap material melted down and re-molded. Several colors produce the marbled look. This practice was common in the early postwar years and during the Korean War, when plastic was scarce. T. Budniak Collection.

| | | | |
|---|---|---|---|
| 1 | 1.50 | 2 | 3 |

(C) Dark brown-painted black plastic, early AAR trucks, disc coupler. J. Sattler Collection.

| | | | |
|---|---|---|---|
| 1 | 1.50 | 2 | 3 |

(D) Gray-painted orange-marbled plastic, early AAR trucks, disc coupler. J. Sattler Collection.

| | | | |
|---|---|---|---|
| 1 | 1.50 | 2 | 3 |

Four more examples of N5C Porthole cabooses. Top left: 6427-60 Virginian. Top right: catalogued as 6427 although numbered 64273 on side. Bottom left: 6437-25 Pennsylvania. Bottom right: catalougued as 6427-500 although numbered 576427 on side. L. Nuzzaci Collection.

|  | Gd | VG | Exc | Mt |
|---|---|---|---|---|

(E) Dull red with blue tint painted orange red plastic body, early AAR trucks, disc coupler. J. Sattler Collection. **1  1.50  2  3**

**DIE 2A**

(A) Red body painted dark flat tuscan-maroon, "LIONEL LINES" beneath third and fourth windows on one side and between first and second windows on other side, AAR trucks, disc coupler. C. Rohlfing Collection. **1  1.50  2  3**

**DIE 3A**

(A) Bright red with white lettering, black frame, staple-end trucks, activator flap with extra hole and roundhead rivet, body fastened to frame by two screws, 1950-51. C. Rohlfing Collection. **1  1.50  2  3**

(B) Shiny tuscan-maroon-painted tuscan body, bar-end trucks, magnetic coupler, black frame fastens with screws to body, Die 3A. Rohlfing Collection. **1  1.50  2  3**

(C) Same as (B), but magnetic coupler with tab. J. Sattler Collection. **1  1.50  2  3**

**DIE 3B**

(A) Unpainted shiny maroon plastic; screw fasteners, bar-end metal trucks, magnetic couplers at both ends (second coupler may have been added). H. Edmunds Collection. **1  1.50  2  3**

(B) Shiny tuscan-maroon paint, 6017 underscored, bar-end trucks, tab coupler, screws fasten body to frame. C. Rohlfing Collection. **1  1.50  2  3**

**DIE 4**

(A) Dark tuscan-painted black plastic, black frame with tab fasteners, early AAR trucks, one disc coupler. J. Sattler Collection. **1  1.50  2  3**

(B) Dark tuscan-painted red plastic, AAR trucks, one operating disc coupler, black frame with tab fasteners. **1  1.50  2  3**

(C) Brown-painted black plastic, AAR trucks, one operating disc coupler, black frame with tab fasteners. R. Ziegler Collection. **1  1.50  2  3**

**6017 LIONEL** Date not known, SP Die 3B. Note this is a different car from the 6017 LIONEL LINES noted above. "6017" underscored, bar-end metal trucks, black frame with screw body fastener, shiny maroon-tuscan unpainted body. Reader reports of this car with original datable sets are needed.

(A) One operating coupler. C. Rohlfing Collection. **2  3  4  6**

(B) Two operating couplers, one with tab and the other without. T. Budniak Collection. **1  1.50  2  3**

**6017-50 UNITED STATES MARINE CORPS** 1958, SP Die 1A, dark blue with white lettering, black frame with tab body fasteners, "601750" on front left side and rear right side, early AAR trucks, one disc coupler. J. Sattler Collection. Came in box marked 6017-60 when included with sets, but box marked 6017-50 when car was sold separately. G. Halverson comment. **12  17  25  50**

**6017-85** See 6017, Die 2, entry (A) above.

**6017-100 BOSTON AND MAINE** 1959, 1964-65, SP Dies 3C and 4, blue with white lettering, "6017" under cupola on both sides, black frame with tab body fasteners, AAR trucks, one operating coupler; catalogued as 6017-100 but only "6017" appears on car. H. Powell Collection. Came as part of uncatalogued Sears set; Beavin comment. Comes either with or without ladder slots in ends, K. Koehler comment and collection. Information needed about following variation types:

(A) Medium blue. **7  11  15  30**

(B) Lighter blue. R. Pauli Collection. **7  11  15  30**

(C) Purplish blue, rare. R. Pauli Collection. **40  65  200  350**

(D) Medium blue, high gloss. P. Ambrose comment. **8  13  19  35**

**6017-185 AT&SF** 1959, SP Die 4, light gray with red lettering, galvanized frame, tab body fasteners, no end rails, "6017" on rear left and front right sides, catalogued as "6017-185", but "6017" appears on car. J. Kotil comment.

(A) AAR trucks, one fixed coupler. **5  7  20  40**

(B) Front AAR truck with operating coupler, rear arch-bar truck with fixed coupler. **5  7  20  40**

(C) Late AAR trucks, one disc coupler, one fixed coupler. J. Sattler Collection. **5  7  20  40**

(D) Black frame, square end railings, stack plug flush with roof and reinforced from below, AAR trucks, one disc coupler. G. Cole and C. Rohlfing Collections. **5  7  20  40**

(E) Die 1A, bar-end metal trucks, one magnetic coupler, black frame, screw fastener, gray-painted black plastic, end rails. T. Budniak Collection. **7  12  20  40**

Top row:  Bay Window cabooses.  Lower rows:  Work cabooses

(F) Same as (E), but gray-painted red plastic body, unpainted red areas of body shell below frame level. R. LaVoie Collection.       7      12      20      40

(G) Same as (A), but maroon lettering. J. Algozzini Collection.       **NRS**

See also 6017-225 and 6017-235.

**6017-200 UNITED STATES NAVY**  1960, SP Die 4, light blue with white lettering, black frame with tab body fasteners, AAR trucks, one operating coupler; catalogued as "6017-200", but "6017" appears on car.

(A) As described above.       15      20      30      50

(B) Light blue body with aqua tint, blue platform and steps, tall stack, metal ladders and platform ends, battery boxes, clear plastic window inserts, bar-end metal trucks, two magnetic couplers. W. C. Hopper Collection.       **NRS**

**6017-225 AT&SF**  SP Die 4, red with white lettering, galvanized frame with tab body fasteners and no end rails, AAR trucks with operating front coupler and fixed rear coupler except (B), "6017" on left rear and right front sides. See 6017-235 and 6017-185 for other versions of A.T. & S.F.

(A) Red-painted black plastic. Foss Collection.       7      11      25      50

(B) Red-painted black plastic, late AAR truck with disc coupler, arch-bar truck with fixed coupler. J. Sattler Collection.       7      11      25      50

(C) Bright red with orange tint.       7      11      25      50

**6017-235 AT&SF**  SP Die 4, bright red-painted black plastic, white lettering, one "6017" (not 6017-235), boxes stamped "6017-235", black frame, with end rails, tab body fasteners, AAR trucks, one disc-operating coupler.  Shown with set 13018 in both the Advance and Consumer Catalogues of 1962. This is an uncommon car.  K. Armen, J. Kotil, P. Ambrose, T. Stucchio and R. LaVoie Collections.       15      25      35      50

**6027 ALASKA**  1959, SP Die 2A, blue with yellow lettering, black frame with tab body fasteners. Early AAR trucks with one operating disc coupler, "6027" on rear left and right sides. J. Sattler Collection.       15      22      30      50

**6037 LIONEL LINES**  1952-54, SP Die 3A, Scout trucks with magnetic couplers, white lettering, black frame with screw body fasteners, (these are unusual since Scout trucks usually have Scout couplers, but the 6037 has knuckle couplers. See the 6002 NYC Gondola for another example of this arrangement.)

(A) Brown, one magnetic coupler.       1  1.50      2      3

(B) Reddish-brown, one magnetic coupler.       1  1.50      2      3

(C) Lighter brown.       1  1.50      2      3

(D) Brown, two operating couplers. J. Sattler Collection.  1  1.50      2      3

(E) Orange-red, one magnetic coupler. G. Cole Collection.  1  1.50      2      3

**6047 LIONEL LINES**  1959, 1962, black frame with tab body fasteners, white lettering, Die 1A, 2A or 4. Entries have been rearranged for Sixth Edition.

(A) Die 1A, medium red unpainted plastic body, arch-bar trucks, one dummy coupler, tab-fastened frame, came as part of uncatalogued set 1105 in 1959 without a separate box. W. Spence Collection.       1  1.50      2      3

(B) Die 2A, medium red, arch-bar trucks, one fixed coupler. 1  1.50      2      3

(C) Die 2A, medium red, one arch-bar truck with fixed coupler, one AAR truck without coupler.       1  1.50      2      3

(D) Die 2A, dark red body, arch-bar trucks, one fixed coupler, from Sears set of 1959-60. Rohlfing Collection.       1  1.50      2      3

(E) Die 2A, light red, arch-bar trucks, fixed coupler. J. Sattler Collection.       1  1.50      2      3

(F) Die 2A, medium red, white lettering, AAR trucks, one disc coupler. D. Anderson Collection.       1  1.50      2      3

(G) Die 4, light red, arch-bar trucks, one fixed coupler.       1  1.50      2      3

(H) Die not known, tuscan unpainted body, tab-fastened frame, AAR trucks, one operating coupler. K. Koehler Collection.       **NRS**

**6057 LIONEL LINES**  1959-62, SP Type, black frame with tab body fasteners.

(A) Die 1A, medium red, AAR trucks, one coupler.       1  1.50      2      3

(B) Same as (A), red with pink tint.       1  1.50      2      3

(C) Die 4, red with slight orange tint, early AAR trucks, one operating coupler. J. Sattler Collection.       1  1.50      2      3

(D) Brown with white lettering.       1  1.50      2      3

(E) Die 4, red, AAR trucks.       1  1.50      2      3

(F) Orange.  See 6057-50

**6057-50 LIONEL LINES**  1962, SP Die 4, orange with black lettering, black frame with tab body fasteners, early AAR trucks, one operating coupler. J. Sattler Collection.       4      7      15      25

**6058 C & O**  1961, SP Die 4, tab body fasteners, early AAR trucks.

(A) Pale yellow body, one disc coupler, blue lettering, black frame. J. Sattler Collection.       9      12      17      30

(B) Medium yellow body, two disc couplers, black lettering, galvanized frame. J. Sattler Collection.       9      12      17      30

**6059-50 M St L**  1961-63, SP Die 4, AAR trucks, one disc coupler, one fixed coupler; white lettering, black frame with tab body fasteners.

(A) Dark maroon, very heavy lettering. J. Sattler Collection.       3      4      8      15

(B) Lighter maroon than (A).       3      4      8      15

**6059-60 M St L**  1963-69, SP Die 4, black frame with tab body fasteners, AAR trucks.

(A) Unpainted shiny red plastic, one disc-operating coupler, one fixed coupler. R. LaVoie Collection.       3      4      8      15

|  | Gd | VG | Exc | Mt |
|---|---|---|---|---|
| (B) Unpainted flat red plastic, one disc-operating coupler. | 3 | 4 | 8 | 15 |
| (C) Red-painted gray plastic, one disc coupler. | 3 | 4 | 8 | 15 |
| (D) Unpainted bright, red plastic, disc coupler. J. Sattler Collection. | 3 | 4 | 8 | 15 |

**6067** NO LETTERING 1962, SP Type, not illustrated, more information requested. ———   —   —

| | 1 | 1.50 | 2 | 3 |

**6119 DL&W** 1955-56, Work Caboose, low stack.
(A) Stamped, flat black frame, white "LIONEL" with serifs, red cab and tool bin; bar-end trucks, one tab-operating coupler. **10  15  25  35**
(B) Same as (A), but shiny black frame. J. Sattler Collection.

| | 10 | 15 | 25 | 35 |

(C) Stamped gray frame, black "LIONEL" without serifs, gray cab and tool bin, bar-end trucks, one tab-operating coupler. **10  15  25  35**
(D) Same as (C), but darker gray frame, cab and bin. **10  15  25  35**
(E) Stamped black frame, white "LIONEL" without serifs, red cab, short black stack, gray tool bin, bar-end trucks, tab-operating coupler. J. Sattler Collection. **10  15  25  35**
(F) Same as (E), but no frame lettering, smooth area on cab lettered "BUILT BY LIONEL", AAR trucks, orange and blue box numbered 6119. D. Anderson Collection. **10  15  25  35**
(G) Same as (F), but lettered "LIONEL" with serifs, AAR trucks, orange and blue box numbered 6119. (See 6119-100 below.) D. Anderson Collection. **10  15  25  35**
(H) Same as (G), but "LIONEL" without serifs, orange and blue box numbered 6119. (See 6119-100 below.) D. Anderson Collection. **10  15  25  35**

**NOTE:** The 6119 cabooses as a class show some predictable variations concerning their dates of manufacture, despite their basic similarity. This family of cabooses uses the same metal frame found on the 6111 flatcars,

but without one set of railings at one end. All these frames are embossed on the bottom in four lines: "MADE IN / U.S. OF AMERICA / THE LIONEL CORPORATION / NEW YORK, N.Y." The embossing stamp deteriorated with age; in the early examples, all four embossed lines are visible. In the later production, the top and bottom lines are almost impossible to discern; in between, there are progressive stages of visibility. Another set of changes involves the scribed wooden slats on the cabs. In the early examples, a relatively small smooth rectangular plate for lettering and logos interrupts the scribing, but the wooden slats start up again below the plate and continue to the bottom of the cab. In later models, this smooth surface is enlarged so that the wooden slats no longer are present at the bottom of the smooth surface. In addition, another smooth rectangular surface has been added to the immediate left of the logo rectangle. Other changes are more regular and involve the trucks and couplers.

**6119-25 DL&W** 1957-59, Work Caboose, orange unpainted cab and tool bin, orange-painted metal frame with serif "LIONEL" in black; over and underscored "D.L.&W. / 611925" on cab in black, short stack, bar-end trucks, frame painted darker orange than cab or bin.
(A) One tab coupler. R. LaVoie Collection. **10  15  20  30**
(B) One coupler without tab. J. Sattler Collection. **10  15  20  30**
(C) Circa 1960, stamped gray frame, black "LIONEL" without serifs, gray cab and tool bin, bar-end trucks, one tab-operating coupler, box marked "6119-25", car not numbered. D. Mitarotonda Collection. **NRS**

**6119-50 DL&W** Brown frame, white "LIONEL" with serifs, brown cab, tool bin, bar-end trucks, magnetic tab coupler, car numbered "6119" but box marked "6119-50". J. Sattler, C. Rohlfing and P. Ambrose Collections.

| | 10 | 15 | 25 | 35 |

**6119-75 DL&W** Gray frame, cab and tool bin, came in box marked "6119-75". P. Ambrose Collection. **6  12  20  35**

**6119-100 DL&W** 1963-66, Work Caboose, red cab, black stamped frame, gray tool bin, short stack, early AAR trucks, one disc coupler. Actually

138

2420 D.L. & W.

6119-25 D.L. & W.

6420 D.L. & W.

6429 D.L. & W.

6814 Lionel Rescue

6824 U.S.M.C. Rescue

numbered "6119" but came in orange box with blue lettering marked "6119-100". D. Anderson Observation.

(A) White rubber-stamped serif "LIONEL" on frame side. J. Sattler, C. Rohlfing and D. Anderson Collections.   **7  10  15  25**

(B) Same as (A), but lettering without serifs. D. Anderson Collection.   **7  10  15  25**

(C) Same as (A), but gray lettering on base instead of white. C. Rohlfing Collection.   **7  10  15  25**

**(6119-125)** NO LETTERING Circa 1960, Work Caboose, olive drab, AAR trucks, one disc-operating coupler, one fixed coupler.   **10  20  25  50**

**6120** NO LETTERING, work caboose, listed in Greenberg reprint of Lionel Service Manual on Page V-63 as 1961, Page V-57 as 1961; came with set 19142-502 in 1963. Car has unpainted yellow plastic cab and low-walled open bin. No part numbers are embossed on the yellow plastic pieces. Car has arch-bar trucks with one dummy coupler; black metal rear railing is integral to black-painted frame. We have one observation by R. Lord of this car with a black-painted plastic ladder on the cab, while others lack this painting.

(A) Flat black-painted stamped frame, cab with unpainted integral plastic ladder, smokestack hole on roof, but no stack; came with set 19142-502 in 1963. J. Sattler and Dodd Collections.   **4  6  8  12**

(B) Same as (A), but shiny black stamped frame, stack hole is plugged, unknown set number. Dodd Collection.   **4  6  8  12**

(C) Same as (B), but flat black frame. Dodd Collection.   **4  6  8  12**

(D) Same as (A), but bar-end trucks and stack. C. Rohlfing Collection.   **4  6  10  15**

**6130 SANTA FE** 1961, 1965-68, Work Caboose, stamped black frame, usually with unlettered frame sides, but "LIONEL" frame side lettering appeared in 1965 catalogue; ATSF herald in white on cab sides, small smokestack, unlettered builder's plate on cab, late AAR trucks, two couplers. With datable pieces, we should be able to identify the production

years of the variations listed below. Reader comments requested. P. Ambrose comments.

(A) Red cab and tool bin with pinkish cast, shiny frame, lettering on tool bin. J. Sattler Collection.   **10  12  18  25**

(B) 1965-68, red cab and tool bin, shiny frame, "6130 / ATSF / BUILT BY / LIONEL" lettering on tool bin, one disc coupler and one dummy coupler, ATSF herald on cab in white, sans-serif "LIONEL" in white on frame. C. Rohlfing Collection.   **10  12  18  25**

(C) Orange-red cab and tool bin, lettering on tool bin.   **10  12  18  25**

(D) Red cab, gray tool bin, no lettering on tool bin, illustrated as a separate sale item in 1969 catalogue. J. Sattler Collection.   **10  12  18  25**

(E) Orange-red cab and tool bin, lettering on tool bin, "LIONEL" on frame. R. Pauli Collection.   **10  12  18  25**

(F) Same as (B), but no "LIONEL" on frame. R. LaVoie Collection.   **10  12  18  25**

(G) Same as (B), but one late AAR truck, one early AAR truck. J. Sattler and L. Wyant Collections.   **10  12  18  25**

(H) Same as (B), but sans-serif lettering on frame and one operating coupler without dummy coupler on rear. D. Embser Collection.   **10  12  18  25**

**6157** Reported but not verified, more information needed.   **NRS**

## UNLETTERED AND UNNUMBERED CABOOSES

Lionel made a number of unlettered and unnumbered cabooses. These often came with inexpensive sets and the omission of letters and numbers probably can be explained by cost reduction. We have had difficulty in matching the catalogue numbers as they appear in the Service Manual with these unnumbered cabooses. Numbers do appear on their boxes. We would appreciate very much your assistance in matching cabooses with numbers. We have made some matches below. Known numbers are:

6167-25 red body, body mold number 6059-2; 6167-50 yellow body, body mold number 6167-52; 6167-100 body color unknown, body mold number

6167-102; 6167-125 red body, body mold number 6059-2 and 6167-150 (body color unknown), body mold number 6167-102.

**6167 LIONEL LINES** 1963, SP Die 4, galvanized frame with tab-fastened body, white lettering, AAR trucks.
(A) Red plastic body, one disc coupler, one fixed coupler, no end rails. T. Budniak Collection.                1    1.50    2    3
(B) Unpainted Type IV flat red plastic body, white lettering, early AAR trucks, galvanized frame, one disc coupler, one fixed coupler, no end rails; probably came with set 11311 from 1963. It seems very unusual for the very inexpensive set 11311 to have a 6167 caboose with couplers at both ends when the 1062 locomotive in the set does not have a front coupler. Since we have two reports of similarly equipped sets, it is very likely factory production. J. West Collection.                1    1.50    2    3
(C) Same as (A), but only one disc coupler. J. Kotil Collection.
                                        1    1.50    2    3

**6167-25 NO LETTERING**, SP Type 4 red unpainted plastic body, galvanized underframe, AAR trucks, frame with tab-fastened body, no end rails, came with set 11420 (1964) with 1061 locomotive and 6112 gondola in box probably numbered 6042-50, confirmation requested.
(A) Dummy coupler on one end. Light Collection.        1    2    3    5
(B) Dummy couplers both ends. J. Algozzini Collection.    1    2    3    5

**6167-50 NO LETTERING** 1964, SP Die 4, yellow unpainted plastic body, galvanized underframe, AAR trucks, fixed couplers, frame with tab-fastened body, no end rails.                1    1.50    4    8

**6167-85 UNION PACIFIC** 1964-69, SP Die 4, unpainted yellow plastic body, black lettering, AAR trucks, one disc coupler, one fixed coupler; frame with tab-fastened body, actually numbered "6167" on car.
(A) One disc-operating coupler, one fixed coupler.        6    9    15    35
(B) One disc-operating coupler, early AAR trucks. J. Kotil Collection.
                                        6    9    15    35

**6167-100 NO LETTERING**, 1964, SP Die 4, light red unpainted body, AAR trucks, one fixed coupler, galvanized frame with tab body fasteners and no end rail.                1    1.50    2    3

**6167-125 NO LETTERING** 1964, SP Die 4, arch-bar trucks, one fixed coupler, frame with tab body fasteners, with end rail.
(A) Dark brown unpainted plastic.            1    1.50    2    3
(B) Medium red unpainted plastic.            1    1.50    2    3
(C) "LIONEL LINES 6167" only on caboose, SP-4 die, AAR plastic trucks, one disc and one dummy coupler, part of set 11430. Winton Collection.
                                        1    1.50    2    3

**6167-150 NO LETTERING**, SP Die 4, unpainted yellow body, galvanized frame, tab fasteners, no end rails, arch-bar trucks with dummy couplers. We would like reader information about the set which included this car. E. Vieth Collection.                    2    3    5    7

**6219 C&O** 1960, Work Caboose, stamped flat black frame, blue cab with yellow lettering, blue tool bin.
(A) Early AAR trucks, one disc-operating coupler.    10    20    35    50
(B) Early AAR trucks, magnetic tab couplers. Highly unusual combination, confirmation requested, J. Sattler comment.            **NRS**

**6257 LIONEL** 1948-56, SP Dies, metal trucks, one operating coupler, frame fastened to body with screws. We have reclassified the 6257 cabooses for the Sixth Edition and have grouped them by the lettering on the side under the cupola.

**Type 1 Lettering**

**Type 1 Lettering**

**SP 6257:** white "SP" above underscored "6257" between third and fourth windows, "C-40-1 BUILT 9-47" below "LIONEL".

**Clear Plastic Bodies:**                    1    2    3    4
(A) Brownish-red.
(B) Flat red, Die 2, staple-end trucks, magnetic couplers, without extra hole in activator flap, flared rivet, 1949. J. Sattler Collection.

**Black Plastic Bodies:**                    1    2    3    4
(A) Flat red, Die 2, bar-end trucks, magnetic coupler, came in box with "6257" on outer flap and "6257-6" on inner flap as part of set 1479WS in 1952. W. Schilling, H. Edmunds and J. Sattler Collections.
(B) Brownish-red.
(C) Shiny brownish-red. H. Edmunds Collection.
(D) Light red, Die 2, one staple-end trucks, one bar-end truck. C. Rohlfing Collection.
(E) Light red, Die 1, staple-end trucks, magnetic couplers, C. Rohlfing Collection.
(F) Light red, Die 2, bar-end trucks, magnetic couplers. C. Rohlfing Collection.
(G) Die 1A, shiny light red, staple-end trucks, magnetic couplers. C. Rohlfing Collection.

**Gray Plastic Bodies:**                    1    2    3    4
(A) Brownish-red paint, Die 1, staple-end trucks. C. Rohlfing Collection.

**Type 2 Lettering**

**Type 2 Lettering**

**L in double circle, 6257 is underscored:**            1    2    3    4
We would like to learn the die and truck types of the following:
(A) Red-painted black plastic
(B) Dull red-painted black plastic
(C) Brownish-red-painted black plastic
(D) Unpainted bright red plastic, bar-end trucks, magnetic coupler, Die 3. J. Sattler Collection.

**Type 3 Lettering**

**Type 3 Lettering:**                        1    2    3    4
6257 without SP, "LIONEL" under windows 1 and 2.
(A) Bright red, bar-end trucks, magnetic coupler with tab, Die 3. J. Sattler Collection.

**6257-25 LIONEL** Die 3A, "L" in double circle, underscored "6257", unpainted bright red plastic body, bar-end trucks, one brakewheel,

"6257-25" on box end, car marked only "6257". J. Kotil and R. LaVoie Collections.                                                1 1.50   2   3

**6257-50 LIONEL**  Die 1 or 3A, box end marked "6257-50", car marked only "6257".

(A) "L" in double circle, "6257" underscored, unpainted bright red plastic body, no brakewheel, bar-end trucks, Die 1. J. Kotil Collection.
                                                1 1.50   2   3

(B) No "L" in circle, "6257" underscored, unpainted bright red plastic body, no brakewheel, bar-end trucks, Die 3A. J. Kotil Collection.
                                                1 1.50   2   3

(C) Same as (A), but Die 3A. C. Rohlfing Collection.   1 1.50   2   3

(D) Same as (B), but Die 3B. C. Rohlfing Collection.   1 1.50   2   3

**6257-100 LIONEL LINES**  1956-63, SP Die 4, red unpainted plastic, stack, AAR trucks, one disc-operating coupler, tabs fasten black frame and body, "6257-100" catalogue number, only "6257" on car.      1 1.50   2   3

**6257X LIONEL LINES**  1948 catalogue, page 5; came with two couplers instead of the usual one with the 6257 because it was part of the 1656 switcher outfit. However, only the existence of the box creates a premium value since the car is identical to the usual 6257 with the exception of the extra coupler. Hence the value depends on the box. J. Foss and R. Hutchinson observations.                   10  15  20  30

**6357 LIONEL**  1948-61, SP Dies, smokestack, "6357" underscored, "SP" above "6357" underscored, lighted, screws fasten black base to body, one magnetic coupler unless specified, "C-40-1" and "BUlLT 9-47", brakewheel, except as noted. The cars are organized by truck type for user convenience. We need to learn the die and truck types of many cars. Note that this caboose, like its 2257, 2357, 4357 and 6457 counterparts, was a "deluxe" model which came with a clear plastic insert molded to cover all the windows. G. Cole comment. This car was produced over an extraordinarily long time and has many variations. We hope that some of our readers may wish to make a special study of this caboose and its variations so we can provide dating for them. An article would be welcome.

**Staple-end trucks  1949-51:**                   4   8   12   20
(A) Die 1, brownish-red-painted black plastic, coil coupler, came in box re-marked from 2457 to 6357 as part of set 1445WS. R. Hutchinson and T. Rollo Collections.

(B) Flat red-painted black plastic body, no stack, magnetic coupler, Die 1, brakewheel, box overprinted from 2257. J. Sattler and P. Bender Collections.

(C) Bright red-painted, black plastic, Die 1, late coil coupler. R. Pauli Collection.

(D) Red-painted black plastic, Die 1, magnetic coupler, no stack. C. Rohlfing Collection.

(E) Pink marbled plastic painted flat red, Die 1, staple-end trucks, magnetic coupler, no stack, box overprinted from 2472, came as part of set 1429WS in 1948. T. McLaughlin Collection.

(F) Same as (D), but light red. C. Rohlfing Collection.

**Bar-end trucks, magnetic coupler, 1952-57:**       4   8   12   20
(A) Brownish-red-painted black plastic, two couplers, no stack.

(B) Brownish-red-painted black plastic, brakewheel, Die 2. J. Sattler Collection.

(C) Shiny maroon-painted black plastic, Die 2. J. Sattler Collection.

(D) Duller maroon-painted black plastic, Die 1. C. Rohlfing Collection.

(E) Maroon-painted black plastic, without "SP", coupler with tab, Die 3; J. Sattler Collection. This car was lettered using the same stamp for both sides with the result that the lettering on the left side is improperly located.

(F) Flat red-painted dark plastic, Die 2. G. Cole comment; J. Sattler Collection.

(G) Reddish-maroon-painted red plastic, die unknown. R. Ziegler Collection.

**NOTE:**  For car with L in double circle over 6357 see 6357-25.

**AAR trucks:**                                    4   8   12   20
(A) 1960, early AAR trucks, maroon-painted black plastic, Die 4, one disc coupler, no ladder, stack, no "SP". R. LaVoie Collection.

**6357-25 LIONEL**  SP Die 2, "L" in double circle over underscored "6357", ("6357-25" does not appear on car sides), lighted, stack, brakewheel, black base, screws fasten body to frame, bar-end metal trucks, one magnetic coupler.

(A) Reddish-maroon-painted black plastic body, came with 1954 set 1515WS and another 1955 set whose number we do not know yet. The -25 suffix does not appear on the car box, but the number 6357-8 appears on the inside flap of the box. D. Doyle Collection.           4   8   12   20

(B) Maroon-painted black plastic, tab coupler. J. Sattler Collection.
                                                4   8   12   20

(C) Brownish-maroon-painted black plastic.         4   8   12   20

(D) Gray with red lettering. (Do not know if gray-painted or gray plastic.)
                                                —  — 1000  —

(E) Same as (B), but description matches general heading of 6357; only the color differs. Box marked "6357-25"; came as part of set 2201WS. T. Budniak Collection.                                 NRS

(F) Same as (A), but two operating couplers. D. Anderson Collection.
                                                4   8   12   20

(G) Same as (A), but two operating couplers — one Type VI and one Type VII with tab. D. Anderson Collection.        4   8   12   20

**6357-50 1960, AT&SF,**  SP Die 4, "6357" not underscored, black plastic painted red, early AAR trucks, one disc coupler. Usually screw fasteners came only with tab frame body fasteners. Without "C-40-1", "BUILT 9-47" and "SP" found on the other 6357s. This caboose is probably as scarce as the tuscan Lehigh Valley, but until recently it had not received the publicity. Came in the Lionel combination HO and O Gauge set which is known as the "over and under" set only, in a box marked "6357-50". Very difficult to find. Stein, and Ambrose observations.   250  400  600  800

### N 5 C CABOOSE CATALOGUE NUMBERS

In the Fifth Edition we recatalogued the 6417-N5C cabooses. The following numbers come from **GREENBERG'S REPAIR AND OPERATING MANUAL FOR LIONEL TRAINS,** Third Edition, page 309, and represent a change from the Fourth Edition of this book. Further reclassifying was done for the Sixth Edition.

**6417 PENNSYLVANIA**  1953-57, N5C, "536417" on side, tuscan with white lettering, lights, bar-end trucks (PT-1 and 479-1), two magnetic couplers with tabs, lettered "BLT 2-53 N5c / LIONEL / L". (The part number for the caboose body is 6417-3. However, G. Cole reports an example with part number 6417-4, which is not reflected anywhere in the Service Manual. Reader comments requested.)
(A) With "NEW YORK ZONE".                         10  15  25  40
(B) Same as (A), but shiny red tuscan paint. T. Budniak Collection.
                                                10  15  25  40
(C) Without "NEW YORK ZONE".                      17  25  45  65
(D) Same as (A), but shiny reddish-tuscan-painted black plastic body. T. Budniak Collection.                              10  15  25  40
(E) Gray-painted black plastic shell, dark maroon lettering "NEW YORK ZONE" in sans-serif, "BLT 2-53 ...", "L" in circle, plug in light unit, bar-end trucks, magnetic tab couplers. Formerly H. Degano Collection.
                                                NRS
(F) Lime green-painted black plastic shell, dark maroon "NEW YORK ZONE" in sans-serif, "BLT 2-53 ...", one operating coupler, no tabs. Formerly H. Degano Collection.                         NRS
(G) Same as (E) but black lettering, two magnetic couplers. J. Sattler Collection.                                    —  — 1000
(H) Blue-painted opaque white shell, white lettering, "NEW YORK ZONE" in sans-serif, "BLT 2-53 ...", one magnetic coupler with tab. Two white labels on underside: "INSPECTION / DEP'T 82" AND "ORIGINAL / APPROVED / PAINTED SAMPLE / FROM VIN GREE". This sample was approved for color but does not have the correct number. According to the definitions in our chapter on prototypes, we classify this as a prototype. See chapter on Prototypes. J. Sattler Collection.

**64173**  See 6417-25.

**6417-25 LIONEL LINES**  1954, N5C, "64173" on side, tuscan with white lettering, lettered "BLT 11-53 ...". In the Fourth Edition and earlier editions, this car was numbered 6417-53. (The part number for the caboose body is 6417-26.)
(A) Magnetic couplers with tabs.                  10  15  25  35
(B) Magnetic couplers, no tabs. J. Kotil Collection.  10  15  25  35

**6417-50 LEHIGH VALLEY**  1954, N5C, numbered on side "641751", lettered "BLT 6-54 ...", Lionel "L" in circle on lower right car side, bar-end metal trucks (PT-1), magnetic couplers, apparently not lighted. (Listed as

**6417-25 LIONEL LINES**

6417-51 in Fourth Edition but changed in Fifth Edition to correspond to Service Manual entry which lists the body part number as 6417-50.)
(A) Tuscan with white lettering, tab couplers. Post-factory chemically-altered cars exist. Extreme caution required. **200 600 800 1000**
(B) Gray with red lettering. **20 30 65 100**
(C) Tuscan with gold lettering. Formerly H. Degano Collection. **— — 1200 —**
(D) Gray-painted clear plastic shell, blue heat-stamped lettering "BLT 6-54...", "L" in circle on lower right, plastic window inserts, press in light unit, bar-end trucks, magnetic couplers without tabs. Formerly H. Degano Collection. **— — 1000 —**
(E) Same as (D), but magnetic couplers with tabs. J. Sattler Collection. **— — 1000 —**
(F) Dark tan with red heat-stamped lettering, "BLT 6-54...", "L" in circle on lower right, plastic window inserts, press-in light unit, bar-end trucks, magnetic couplers without tabs. J. Sattler and formerly H. Degano Collections. **— — 1000 —**

**6417-51** See 6417-50.

**6419 DL & W** 1949-50, 1954-57, Work Caboose, staple-end trucks in 1949-50 and bar-end trucks in 1954-57, two magnetic couplers, die-cast frame originally from the 2419, "D L & W 6419" on cab side and black "LIONEL LINES" lettering on frame side, smokestack on roof, brakewheel at each end, steps at each corner. There are two major different versions of the 6419. The earlier cars have the cab fastened by four screws to the die-cast frame. The later cars have two cab tabs which fit into slots in the modified frame. However, in our data gathering we have not collected this information. We would be most appreciative if our readers would review their cars and report on colors, underlying plastic color, truck type and fastening method so that we can develop a complete report. We think the listings below are mostly accurate, but are missing several more variations. J. Sattler and R. LaVoie comments.
(A) 1948, light gray-painted black plastic cab, high stack, light gray-painted die-cast base, staple-end trucks, shiny fillister-head screws fasten truck plates to frame. Came with O-27 work set 1447WS as catalogued. The O Gauge 2143WS work set was catalogued with the 2420, the upgraded version of this caboose with a searchlight. P. Bender Collection. **10 15 25 35**
(B) 1949, light gray-painted clear plastic cab, light gray-painted die-cast base, staple-end trucks, high stack, magnetic couplers without hole in activator plate, came in 1949 set 1457B. C. Rohlfing and T. Budniak Collections. **10 15 25 35**
(C) 1950, same as (B), but hole in truck activator plates, blued screws fasten truck plates to frame, came with 1950 set 1457B. P. Bender Collection. **10 15 25 35**
(D) 1951, dark gray-painted black marble plastic, truck details not known. **10 15 25 35**
(E) 1951, light gray-painted pink plastic, truck details not known. **10 15 25 35**
(F) Orange plastic, catalogued but not manufactured. **Not Manufactured**
(G) 1952, light gray-painted marbled purple plastic, bar-end trucks, high stack, C. Rohlfing Collection. **10 15 25 35**
(H) 1953-55, light gray-painted clear plastic cab, light gray-painted die-cast frame, high stack, shiny fillister screws fasten truck plates to frame, black screws fasten cab and toolboxes to frame, came in box marked 6419 with cardboard inner liner stamped 2419, bar-end trucks, magnetic couplers, offset holes in activator plates. The work cabooses with high stacks kept

inner liners for their boxes long after the liners were discontinued on other cars. Our best guess is that the tall stack atop the cab made the cabs highly vulnerable to cracking and breakage without the liners. R. Hutchinson and R. LaVoie Collections. **10 15 25 35**

**NOTE:** The Lionel Service Manual (Greenberg reprint, pp. V-86-87), in sheets dated 9-56, describes the construction changes and the redesignation of the caboose numbers as follows: "...In 1955 a No. 6419-25 car with only one coupler was made for the O-27 line. In 1956 several changes were made in the frame casting and the cab to facilitate assembly, and the car numbers were changed to 6419-50 with two couplers and 6419-75 with one coupler. During this year also a number of 6419-50 cars were produced with trucks of the 478-479 type which are held to the truck brackets by means of clips instead of retaining washer..." We have renumbered our entries accordingly.

**6419-25 D L & W** 1955, Work Caboose, light gray-painted clear plastic cab, light gray-painted die-cast base, bar-end trucks with one magnetic coupler; came in box marked "for O-27 Track". "6419" only on cab. P. Bender Collection. **10 15 25 35**

**6419-50 D L & W** 1956-57, Work Caboose, light gray-painted clear plastic body, light gray-painted die-cast base, tabs molded into cab body and slots in base for new assembly method, "6419" only on cab, short plastic stack on cab, chromed pins. Box marked "6419-50". Came as part of Virginian Fairbanks-Morse freight set in 1956. R. Shanfeld comments.
(A) Trucks secured by horseshoe retaining washer, bar-end trucks with offset holes in activator flaps, two couplers. P. Bender Collection. **15 25 35 50**
(B) Same as (A), but trucks secured by spring clip, two couplers. **15 25 35 50**
(C) Same as (B), but light gray-painted clear purple plastic cab slightly darker base. C. Rohlfing Collection. **15 25 35 50**

**6419-57 N & W** 1957-58, Work Caboose, bar-end trucks, one magnetic tab coupler, cab fastened by tabs through frame slots, low stack, medium gray die-cast frame, "LIONEL LINES" in black letters, light gray boxes, light gray cab actually numbered "576419" in black, box stamped "6419-100" on end. P. Ambrose comments.
(A) One magnetic tab coupler. Formerly W. Eddins Collection. **35 45 65 90**
(B) Two magnetic tab couplers, two brakestands with wheels, black ladder on cab. P. Ambrose, J. Abraham and J. Alvatrain Collections. **35 45 65 90**
(C) Same as (B), but only one magnetic tab coupler. P. Ambrose Collection. **35 45 65 90**

**6419-75 D L & W** 1956-57, Work Caboose, light gray-painted clear plastic cab, light gray-painted die-cast base, cab secured to base by tabs and slots instead of screws, "6419" only on cab, bar-end trucks secured by horseshoe clips, activator plates with offset holes, short stack, one operating coupler, for O-27 sets. P. Bender Collection. **10 15 25 35**

**6420 D L & W** 1948-50, Work Caboose, staple-end trucks, magnetic couplers, dark gray die-cast frame with black "LIONEL LINES", dark gray cab, searchlight, tall stack, two brakewheels, dark gray toolboxes. Earliest production may have had coil couplers.
(A) 1948, late, coil couplers. H. Holden Collection. **30 50 75 100**
(B) 1949-early 1950, magnetic couplers, no holes in activator flaps. C. Rohlfing Collection. **30 50 75 100**
(C) 1950, later, same as (B), but extra hole in activator flap, round rivet end down. J. Sattler Collection **30 50 75 100**

**6427 LIONEL LINES** 1955-60, N5C, numbered "64273" on side, lights, tuscan with white lettering, "BLT 11-53", bar-end trucks, single tab magnetic coupler. "6427", the "official" Lionel number, is used in the Service Manual and 6427-3 is the part number for the body. Numbering in this edition now corresponds to Lionel's. **10 15 25 35**

**64273** See 6427.

**6427-60 VIRGINIAN** 1958, N5C, dark blue with yellow lettering, "6427" on side, "BLT 8-58", lighted, bar-end metal trucks, one magnetic tab coupler. (Body is part number 6427-63.)
(A) Yellow lettering. J. Sattler Collection. **50 85 160 225**
(B) White lettering, color sample. J. Sattler Collection. **— — 750 —**

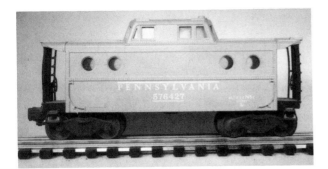

**6427-500 PENNSYLVANIA**

**6427-500 PENNSYLVANIA** 1957-58, N5C, from "Girls' Set", numbered "576427" on side, lighted, bar-end trucks, one coupler. Reproductions have been made and are reportedly marked.
(A) Sky blue with white lettering, production model.
50   75   125   250
(B) Flat yellow finish on black plastic body, extremely heavy white heat-stamped letters and numbers, one brakewheel, preproduction Lionel color sample not produced. Formerly H. Degano Collection.
—   —   1000   —
(C) Semi-gloss yellow paint on black plastic body and black heat-stamped lettering which is heavier nearer the "A" and lighter nearer the "P"; magnetic tab coupler, roller shows considerable wear; preproduction Lionel color sample not produced. Formerly H. Degano Collection.—   —   1000   —
(D) Same as (C) but even letter stamping, very little wear. J. Sattler Collection.
—   —   1000   —
(E) Pink-painted black plastic body, very heavily heat-stamped in white, bar-end trucks, one magnetic coupler, plastic window inserts, preproduction color sample for Girls' Set not produced. Formerly H. Degano Collection.
—   —   1000   —
(F) Same as (E), but two magnetic tab couplers. J. Sattler Collection.
—   —   1000   —

**6427 A T & S F** 1960, N5C, catalogued but not manufactured.
**Not Manufactured**

**6429 D L & W** 1963, Work Caboose, plastic cab, die-cast frame, toolboxes, two brakewheels, short stack, came in one set only, 13118, a premium freight set headed by a 736. However we have found two versions with different paint schemes and different trucks.
(A) Light gray cab, toolbox and frame, early AAR trucks, two disc operating couplers. J. Sattler Collection.   40   70   120   200
(B) Light gray cab, medium gray toolboxes, light gray die-cast frame, bar-end trucks, one magnetic tab coupler; P. Ambrose comment.
40   70   120   200

**6437-25 PENNSYLVANIA** 1961-68, N5C, tuscan with white lettering, "BLT 2-53", lighted, "6437" on side.
(A) Late AAR trucks, two couplers. R. Hutchinson comment. J. Sattler Collection.   10   15   25   35
(B) Same as (A), but only one coupler.   10   15   25   35
(C) Bar-end trucks, one magnetic coupler.   10   15   25   35

**6447**

**6447 PENNSYLVANIA** 1963, N5C, tuscan with white lettering, "BLT 2-53", non-illuminated, used in one Super O set, AAR trucks, one coupler. P. Ambrose comment. J. Sattler Collection.   40   60   120   200

**6457 LIONEL** 1949-52, SP type, "L" in double circle over underscored "6457", "LIONEL" under first two windows, "C-40-1" and "BUILT 9-47" centered in two lines under "LIONEL", lighted, smokestack, ladders, battery box, two brakewheels, two operating couplers, black box fastens with screws to body, "BUILT 9-47". Schmaus observation.

**STAPLE-END TRUCKS**
(A) Gloss brown-painted black plastic; black stack, ladders, brakewheels and battery boxes, Die 1, came in box marked on end "6457 / CABOOSE / LIONEL" with inside flap "6457-7" as part of set 2167WS in 1950. C. Rohlfing and W. Schilling Collections.   8   12   18   25
(B) Same as (A), but red plastic mold. C. Rohlfing Collection.
8   12   18   25
(C) Brown-painted black plastic, brown stack, Die 1.   8   12   18   25
(D) Same as (C), but Die 2. J. Kotil Collection.   8   12   18   25
(E) Same as (A), but flat brown-painted black plastic. C. Rohlfing Collection.   8   12   18   25

**BAR-END TRUCKS**
(A) Brownish-maroon-painted black plastic, black stack.   8   12   18   25
(B) Flat maroon-painted black plastic, two magnetic couplers, black trim, Die 2. C. Rohlfing Collection.   8   12   18   25
(C) Same as (F), but brown-painted black plastic. C. Rohlfing Collection.
8   12   18   25

**6517 LIONEL LINES** 1955-59, Bay Window, red with white lettering, lighted, stack, die-cast O-27 passenger trucks, two magnetic couplers.
(A) "BLT 12-55" and "LIONEL" underscored.   25   35   60   90
(B) "BLT 12-55" and "LIONEL" not underscored, red.   J. Sattler Collection.   20   30   50   75
(C) Same as (B), but darker red. J. Sattler Collection.   20   30   50   75
See also Factory Errors.

**6517-75 ERIE** 1966, Bay Window, with white lettering, stack, lighted, die-cast O-27 passenger trucks, two operating couplers.
(A) Flat medium red-painted body.   135   190   275   350
(B) Dull brick red-painted body, clearly different from (A).   T. Budniak Collection.   135   190   275   350
(C) Orange-painted black plastic, one of three Lionel preproduction color samples; car base rubber-stamped "6517-75" and "LIONEL" in silver. Formerly H. Degano Collection.   —   —   1500   —

**6517-1966 T.C.A.**

**6517-1966 TCA** Convention bay window caboose, 1966, dull orange-painted body with white "TCA" on caboose bay, white TCA logo at left of bay, octagonal convention data lettering to right of bay in white, AAR four-wheel passenger die-cast trucks, two magnetic couplers. 700 produced for convention in Santa Monica. It has been reported that Lionel mistakenly produced the first 500 cars in red and had to repaint them orange.
—   —   220   275

**6527 LIONEL** Bay Window Caboose, not illuminated. Listed in Lionel Service Manual, Greenberg reprint, V-112 (8-56) and V-119 (6-60) as available with parts listing. No samples of this caboose have ever been found. R. Hutchinson comment.   **Not Manufactured**

**6557 LIONEL** 1958-59, SP Die 3C, with smoke unit, black plastic painted brown, white lettering, "BUILT 9-47", bar-end metal trucks, magnetic tab coupler, one brakewheel at rear, included small 1/2 ounce bottle of 909 Smoke Fluid in box. Only the 7-volt 55 lamp should be used in this caboose; use of any other lamp could burn out the smoke unit. S. Carlson, T. Rollo and R. LaVoie comments.
(A) Regular catwalk. S. Carlson Collection.   50   75   150   200

|  | Gd | VG | Exc | Mt |
|---|---|---|---|---|

(B) Slightly raised hump on catwalk.                          **50  75  150  200**

(C) Black plastic body painted dark tuscan, white lettering, bar-end trucks, magnetic tab couplers at both ends, regular catwalk, black plastic smoke deflector, lettering and numbering reversed so that "6557" is under cupola and "LIONEL" is at front of caboose, brown smoke unit, no brakewheel, open slots on bottom plate which fastens smoke unit to frame (closed on regular production), possible prototype or very limited run, extremely rare. T. Klaassen Collection.                          **—  —  —  800**

(D) Same as (C), except white smoke unit with brown smoke deflector on stack instead of usual black. Same comments as (C). H. Powell Collection.
                          **—  —  —  800**

**6657 Rio Grande** 1957-58, SP Die 1 or 2, yellow body with silver lower band, black lettering, bar-end metal trucks, tab magnetic coupler, smokestack, lighted.

(A) Without smoke unit, Die 1. J. Sattler Collection.   **50  75  100  125**

(B) With brown smoke unit.                       **350  450  550  750**

**6814-1 LIONEL** 1959-61, Work Caboose, "RESCUE UNIT", short stack, white cab and tool bin, red lettering, light gray base, man, two stretchers, oxygen tank unit, AAR trucks, two couplers, "6814" appears on car.

(A) As described above.                          **20  40  60  90**

(B) Same as (A), but with Red Cross emblem on plastic yard-type stand.
                          **50  75  100  130**

(C) Black frame, no stretchers, man or oxygen tanks, "LIONEL" in white sans-serif lettering on frame side, no brakewheels, AAR trucks, one disc-operating coupler, one fixed coupler, made by Lionel for Sears set 9820, circa 1964. Also see 3666 boxcar and 240 locomotive and tender, made by Lionel for Sears circa 1968. Lebo and Powell Collections. **30  50  70  125**

(D) Same as (A), but only one disc coupler. C. Rohlfing Collection.
                          **20  40  60  90**

**6824 U.S.M.C.** 1960, Work Caboose, "RESCUE UNIT", short stack, olive drab cab, toolbox tray unit with insert with lettering "AIR / OXYGEN / PUMP", frame with white sans serif lettering "U.S.M.C.", blue man, two stretchers, oxygen tank unit, early AAR trucks, one disc coupler. J. Sattler Collection.                          **30  50  70  125**

**6824 RESCUE UNIT** Circa 1960, Work Caboose, no number on car, short stack, olive drab cab and toolboxes, white cross, black frame with white serif "LIONEL", AAR trucks, tab front coupler, no rear coupler; Catalano observation. Probably came in box with suffix mark after number; reader comments requested.                          **30  60  70  125**

**NO NUMBERS**

(A) SP Die 4, olive drab unpainted plastic, galvanized base, tabs fasten base to body, one fixed coupler, open on top, AAR trucks, no lettering, no back railing, resembles olive drab hopper, gondola and turbo missile cars. J. Wilson Collection. We need to learn this car's catalogue number and set number.                          **NRS**

(B) SP Die 4, yellow unpainted body, black-painted frame, tab fasteners, end handrails only, one dummy coupler, arch-bar trucks. Could be 6067, 6167-25, 6167-125(C) or 6167-150; reader comments invited. T. Budniak Collection.                          **NRS**

(C) SP Die 4, brown unpainted body, black-painted frame, tab fasteners, end handrails only, one dummy coupler, arch-bar trucks. Came with set 19262 in 1963, but set did not contain any information identifying the car's number. P. Ambrose comment. J. Sattler Collection.                          **NRS**

(D) SP Die 4, bright orange-red unpainted body, black-painted frame, tab fasteners, end handrails only, one dummy coupler open on top, early AAR trucks. Catalogue and set number not known, year not known. J. Sattler Collection.                          **NRS**

(E) SP Die 4, bright orange-red unpainted body, black-painted frame, tab fasteners, end handrails only, one dummy coupler open on top, arch-bar trucks. Catalogue and set number not known, year not known. J. Sattler Collection.                          **NRS**

SP Types: See 6067, 6167-50, 6167-100 and 6167-125.

Work Caboose: See 6119-25, 6120, 6824.

# Chapter V

# CRANES AND SEARCHLIGHTS

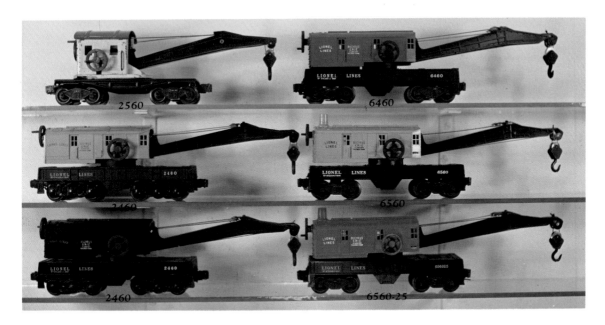

The 2460s and 6460s do not have a smokestack. The 6560 and 6560-25 do have smokestacks. Note that "Lionel Lines" is on one line on the 2460s but on two lines on the 6460s, 6560s and 6560-25s.

## By Roland LaVoie

Real railroads called them "Big Hooks" — those huge steam-powered cranes kept on hand for the inevitable derailment or more serious emergency. They could lift the heaviest locomotives and put them back on the tracks. If an emergency were to occur at night, these big machines could be sent out in a work train with powerful searchlights mounted on flatcars.

Lionel made excellent models of both of these cars in the postwar years. Many an operator's layout had a train composed of a searchlight car, crane and work caboose on a siding, just in case. Some operators carried things to extremes. It is reported that playwright Ben Hecht, a big Lionel fan, liked to stage wrecks on his main lines and untangle them with the crane car.

Lionel began its postwar cranes by carrying the metal prewar crane into 1946 and 1947. This rather small crane operated well, but lacked realism. It was dwarfed by some of Lionel's newer rolling stock, so Lionel soon began to produce a very attractive model of the big Bucyrus-Erie cranes used for many years by prototype railroads. The first of these cranes had die-cast frames and six-wheel trucks; they were indeed impressive! Early models were gray with black lettering and black with white lettering, but as production went on Lionel also made red-bodied cranes.

The Bucyrus-Erie crane operated by means of two wheels. The wheel at the rear of the cab raised or lowered the boom, while the wheel at the side raised and lowered the hook. The crane was strong enough to lift any freight car, but it could not lift a heavy die-cast locomotive. It was not equipped with

outrigger booms to keep from turning over, unlike American Flyer's excellent Industrial Brownhoist crane car, or a track clip such as came with Lionel's 219 Standard Gauge crane.

Lionel reduced the production costs of its Bucyrus-Erie models by changing from six-wheel to four-wheel trucks and by replacing the die-cast frame with a plastic frame. On the other hand, later models were improved with a smokestack towards the rear of the crane cab.

Lionel also produced a flatcar with a derrick in the later postwar years. This car was made with a red flatcar body and a yellow boom. There is a small crank which allowed the operator to lift loads with the derrick's hook. It is not a bad car to have in one's collection, but it lacks the massive quality which is so appealing in the Bucyrus-Erie crane car.

The last postwar run of the 6560 Bucyrus-Erie figured in a toy train mystery which still has not been totally resolved. The crane was made in Hagerstown, Maryland, as part of a freight set with a 2029 steam engine in 1969, the last year of postwar production before the takeover of Lionel train manufacture by General Mills. Apparently General Mills found themselves with a considerable quantity of leftover 6560 cranes from the Hagerstown facility, so they had boxes made for them and catalogued them as their own production. It is still not clear whether or not Fundimensions actually produced any of these cars in 1970 or 1971, though the firm was certainly distributing them. As it turns out, the Fundimensions cranes are almost identical to the Hagerstown ones, but the red color of their cabs is a little darker and the rivet fastening the wires to the top of the boom is blackened or bronzed, not chromed.

Lionel's searchlight cars were extremely well made; all but one model had gray die-cast depressed-center bases. The depression in the base usually held a plastic generator, strictly for appearance, while the searchlight was mounted on one end of the car. Production began with the 6520 car in 1949. On this car, the operator could turn the searchlight on and off by means of a remote control track. A metal strip was connected to a slender pawl hidden inside the plastic generator. Each time the metal strip beneath the car was pulled down by a magnet in a remote track, the contact was either broken or restored.

Two variations of this car used a searchlight housing mounted on a vibrator motor so that the light would rotate. The earliest version retained the on-off pawl switch of the 6520, while the later version lacked this feature. A third conversion of the 6520 became the Extension Searchlight Car, first made in 1956. The searchlight was attached to the car base by a magnet instead of a rivet. Wires led from the light housing to a reel of wire mounted at the center depression of the flatcar, while a small generator was attached to the other end. The operator could unreel the light, unwind the cord and place the searchlight quite some distance from the car itself.

The final version of the searchlight car, sometimes referred to as the "Night Crew" car, was made from 1961 to the end of the postwar period. This searchlight was mounted on a superstructure attached to a standard Lionel plastic flatcar. A blue rubber man stood guard over the assembly. Although reasonably well made, it lacked a great deal of the massiveness of the earlier searchlight cars, and thus was not as appealing.

The crane and searchlight cars were a colorful and important part of Lionel's postwar rolling stock. It was a badge of honor for a young boy to own one of the Bucyrus-Erie cranes and re-rail a freight car in the bright light of a searchlight car. Of such elements was the great play value of Lionel Trains composed.

**Gd VG Exc Mt**

### THE SIX-WHEEL TRUCKS ON THE 2460 CRANE

The deluxe six-wheel trucks with plastic side frames used on the 2460 cranes were similar to, but not quite identical with the six-wheel trucks used on the 2625, 2627 and 2628 Irvington, Madison and Manhattan passenger cars (1946-50) and the large 2426W tenders which came with the 726 Berkshire locomotive (1946-49) and the 773 Hudson (1950). We have observed two different types of these trucks, which Lionel numbered "6TC-1", used on the 2460 crane cars in 1946-50, as follows in chronological order:

**TYPE 1:** Untaped copper wire coil, double-ended fiber plate behind coil with provision for connecting wire on one side of electromagnetic coupler and square hole on other side; rivet through bottom plate with round end down as viewed from underside.

**TYPE 2:** Black-taped copper wire coil, double-ended fiber plate behind coil with provision for connecting wire on one side for electromagnetic coupler and square hole on other side; different top bolster with two 1/8" bent tabs on each end of bolster; rivet through bottom plate with flared end down as viewed from underside.

A third type of this truck was used on the 2625, 2627 and 2628 passenger cars; it is described as follows:

**TYPE 3:** Black-taped copper wire coil, single-ended fiber plate behind coil with provision for electromagnetic coupler; rivet through bottom plate with flared end down as viewed from underside.

See Tom Rollo's article on the "Madison" passenger cars in the passenger car chapter for a full discussion of the trucks used on those cars.

**2460 BUCYRUS ERIE** Crane, catalogued 1946-50, always depicted in catalogues with a black cab with white lettering, no smokestack, "LIONEL LINES" in serif lettering in a single arch on side of cab, hook turned ninety

degrees from line of cab, six-wheel passenger-style trucks with electromagnetic coil couplers, die-cast metal frame. However, a very few 2460 cabs were made with a two-line cab lettering. This crane is described as (F). Note that all 2460 cranes have cabs with six bolsters to fasten six screws from the cab floor.

(A) "LIONEL LINES" in black serif letters in single arch on left side of semi-glossy gray cab, "WT-375,000 2 18NH" without hyphens heat-stamped on right sides of frame under "LIONEL", "2460" heat-stamped on right sides of frame in thin, narrow numbers identical to (BA), Type 1 trucks, handle on rear handwheel on the boom elevating screw assembly is 1/4" long. This is the most sought-after of all the regular production postwar cranes. J. Sattler Collection.    50    70    100    180

(B) "LIONEL LINES" in white serif letters in single arch on left side of black cab, "WT-375,000 2 18NH" without hyphens heat-stamped on left sides of frame under "LIONEL", "2460" heat-stamped on right sides of frame in thin, narrow numbers, Type 1 trucks, handle on rear handwheel on the boom elevating screw assembly is 1/4" long. S. Carlson and J. Merhar Collections.    25    35    50    85

(C) "LIONEL LINES" in white serif letters in single arch on left side of black cab, "WT-375,000 2 18NH" without hyphens heat-stamped on left sides of frame under "LIONEL", "2460" heat-stamped on right sides of frame in thick, wide numbers, Type (1) trucks, handle on rear handwheel on the boom elevating screw assembly is 3/8" long. S. Carlson and J. Merhar Collections.    25    35    50    85

(D) "LIONEL LINES" in black serif letters in single arch on left side of highly glossy gray cab, "WT-375,000 2 18NH" with hyphens heat-stamped on left sides of frame under "LIONEL", "2460" heat-stamped on right sides of frame in thin, narrow numbers identical to (A), Type 1 trucks, handle on rear handwheel on the boom elevating screw assembly is 3/8" long.    50    70    100    180

(E) "LIONEL LINES" in white serif letters in single arch on left side of black cab, "WT-375,000 2 18NH" with hyphens heat-stamped on left sides of frame under "LIONEL", "2460" heat-stamped on right sides of frame in thick, wide numbers identical to (B), Type 2 trucks, handle on rear control wheel 3/8" long.    25    35    50    85

(F) circa 1949-50, "LIONEL LINES" in white serif lettering in two lines on the left side of the dull black cab, "WT-375,000 2 18NH" without hyphens heat-stamped on the side of the frame. Type 2 trucks, handle on rear control wheel 3/8" long, circa 1949-50. J. Kotil Collection.    25    35    50    85

**NOTE:** No crane cars were catalogued in 1951. In 1952, the 6460 Crane Car was catalogued and made and was supplied with both black and red cabs. The cabs on the 6460 Crane Cars differed from the 2460 cabs in the following two significant ways:
1. The words "LIONEL LINES" were in white sans-serif letters in two lines on the left side of the cab with the top line arched and the bottom line straight for 6460. However, 2460 (C) also has this lettering.
2. The bolsters inside the cabs which accepted the two center cab mounting screws on the 2460 cabs were removed so that the 6460 cabs were mounted with only four cab mounting screws rather than six as on the 2460.

Although another variation of the 2460 was reported in previous editions with a red cab with the words "LIONEL LINES" in white sans-serif letters in two lines on the left side of the cab with the top line arched and the bottom line straight, it now appears certain that such observations were of 2460 Crane Cars which had replacement 6460 cabs. Such interchangeability was suggested in the Lionel Service Manual, and by disregarding the two center cab mounting screws, the 6460 black and red cabs can easily be mounted to the 2460 Crane Cars.

**2560 LIONEL LINES** Crane, 1946-47, continuation of prewar 2660 design with modifications, light yellow metal cab with red roof, "L" in circle, "LIONEL / LINES" and "2560" rubber-stamped on cab, black stamped metal frame, staple-end metal trucks, coil-operated couplers.

(A) Black boom with words "LIONEL CRANE" on sides and with pin in end of boom which holds a pulley for hook cable. (**NOTE:** Examples of the prewar 2660 Crane Car and the prewar 165 Triple-Action Magnet-Crane have been observed with green booms with the same pin and pulley arrangement as on this car.) Flat black frame, 1946 production without staking marks on underside of each coupler knuckle.    15    20    35    60

(B) Brown boom with words "LIONEL CRANE" on sides and with large nickel rivet in end of boom which serves as a pulley for hook cable, gloss black frame, 1946 production without staking marks on underside of each coupler knuckle.                15    20    35    60

(C) Green boom with words "LIONEL CRANE" on sides and with large nickel rivet in end of boom which serves as a pulley for hook cable, flat black frame, 1947 production with four staking marks on underside of each coupler knuckle.                15    20    35    60

(D) catalogued 1946-47, but not made, maroon cab with red roof.
**Not Manufactured**

**3360 BURRO CRANE**   See Chapter I.

**4460 BUCYRUS ERIE**   Crane car, shown in 1950 Advance Catalogue for Electronic Set, but never made.                **Not Manufactured**

A comparison of the bold, expanded serif lettering on 6460(A) on top, and the thin, condensed serif lettering on 6460(B). R. Griesbeck Collection and photograph.

**6460 BUCYRUS ERIE**   Crane, catalogued 1952-54, "LIONEL LINES" in white sans-serif letters in two lines on left side of cab with top line arched and bottom line straight, no smokestack, "6460" heat-stamped on right sides of frame, hook turned ninety degrees from line of cab, four-wheel bar-end trucks, die-cast metal frame, handle on rear handwheel on the boom elevator screw assembly in 1/4" long.

(A) Black cab, "LIONEL LINES" heat-stamped on left sides of frame in bold, serif expanded letters, "Wt-375,000-2-18NH" heat-stamped on left sides of frame under "LIONEL'" with hyphens. R. Griesbeck Collection.
15    25    35    50

(B) Same as (A), but "LIONEL LINES" heat-stamped on left sides of frame in thin, serif, condensed letters, "WT-375,000 2 18NH" without hyphens. R. Griesbeck, J. Sattler and R. LaVoie Collections.    15    25    35    50

(C) Same as (B), but gray plastic cab painted red. See also 6460-25 entry below, which may be identical to this entry.    25    35    50    75

(D) Same as (B), but black plastic cab painted red. T. Budniak, J. Sattler and R. LaVoie Collections.    25    40    60    100

(E) Orange-red cab with black lettering depicted on page 29 of 1952 Catalogue, but not made.                **Not Manufactured**

(F) Same as (A), but green molded plastic cab painted black. M. Nicholas Collection.                15    25    35    50

**6460-25 BUCYRUS ERIE**   Crane, 1954. Although catalogued as 6460-25, this crane is actually numbered 6460. Red-painted gray plastic cab, white sans-serif "LIONEL LINES" lettering in two lines, bar-end trucks, round rivet head faces down, hole in coupler activator plate, die-cast base. Came in box marked "No. 6460 / OPERATING WORK CRANE / 25 LIONEL 25" with box part number 6460-30; part of set 1523. This is the first time we have been able to link the 6460-25 catalogue number to a specific set piece. J. Kotil suggests that the -25 suffix was Lionel's indicator for the red cab. Note that this may be the same car described in entry 6460(C) above. P. Iurilli and J. Merhar Collections.    25    35    50    75

**6560 BUCYRUS ERIE**   Crane, catalogued 1955-58, 1968-69, large smokestack in same color as cab, "LIONEL LINES" in sans-serif letters in two lines on left side of cab with top line arched and bottom line straight, cab fastened to metal cab plate assembly (part 6560-17) with three tabs which protrude from cab plate assembly and pass through three slots in cab (one at

the bottom of back of cab under handwheel and one each at the bottom of each side at the front of cab), handle on rear handwheel on the boom elevator screw assembly is 1/4" long, molded plastic frame, smaller hook than on earlier cars with hook in line with cab, four-wheel, bar-end metal trucks with extra hole in activator plate and with roundhead rivet visible from underside, magnetic couplers.

(A) Reddish-orange cab, strikingly different from usual red, white lettering on cab only, no lettering or numbers on frame sides, trucks attached by 4-32 x 7/32 Binder Head truck mounting screws (the Lionel Service Manual indicated that "The first several thousand of the 6560 Crane Cars were built with No. 484-1 truck mounted by means of a 4-32 x 7/32 binding head screw." See page V-115 of Lionel Service Manual. The Manual also states that the "first 10,000 6560 crane cars were made with trucks attached with" such screws. See page V-264 of Lionel Service Manual) instead of 1002-6 truck mounting clips as on other 6560 crane cars. No tabs on couplers, came in 1955 set 2245WS and in box numbered "6560X OPERATING WORK CRANE 25 LIONEL 25" (the "X" is rubber-stamped on box end), "6560-26" on box flap and the number "6560-25" on all four long sides of the box. R. Griesbeck, P. Ambrose and J. Sattler Collections.
50    75    125    200

(B) Gray cab, black lettering, "LIONEL LINES" heat-stamped on left sides of frame in bold, serif, expanded letters, "WT-375,000-2-18NH" heat-stamped on left sides of frame under "LIONEL" with hyphens same as 6460 (A), "6560" heat-stamped on right sides of frame, trucks attached by truck mounting clips (part 100 2-6), tab couplers, open-style crank wheels, came with 1955 set 1527 with 1615 steam switcher and also a 1955 610 Erie set. P. Ambrose comment. J. Sattler and R. LaVoie Collections.    30    40    50    75

(C) Same as (B), but red cab, white lettering. Box end flaps marked: "No. 6560 OPERATING WORK CRANE LIONEL 25", but this car is clearly a different unit than 6560-25 shown below. That car is marked "656025" on its frame, while this car is marked "6560" only. Yeckel Collection.
15    25    35    50

(D) Same as (B), but red cab, white lettering, no lettering or numbering on frames, box marked "No. 6560X / OPERATING / WORK CRANE / 25 LIONEL 25" on outside flap; box part number 6560-26. W. Eisenhauer Collection.                22    30    50    100

This is the 6560(D) crane. Note the complete absence of lettering on the frame.

(E) Red cab, white bold serif lettering, both handwheels are solid rather than open and have short crank handles, twin-pulley screw mounting, no part number on frame inside. J. Sattler, R. LaVoie and I. D. Smith Collections.                15    25    35    50

(F) Same as (C), but without 6560 number on frame, frame mold 2460-5. Further clarification of this mold number is requested; the truck mounting holes were in different places between the 2460 and 6460-6560 frames to allow for the earlier six-wheel trucks. See next entry. R. Griesbeck, R. Grossano, D. Doyle and R. Lord Collections.    20    30    45    65

(G) Same as (F), but frame mold number is 6560-5. S. Perlmutter Collection.                20    30    45    65

(H) Same as (C), but black cab with stack, early screw-fastened trucks. P. Ambrose Collection.                50    75    125    200

(I) Same as (E), but closed AAR plastic trucks with disc couplers. C. Rohlfing Collection.                15    25    35    50

(J) Same as (E), but darker red cab. C. Rohlfing Collection.
15    25    35    50

### THE HAGERSTOWN SET AND THE 6560 CRANE

Among collectors, there has been much confusion and contention about the 6560 Crane cars which were made in Hagerstown, Maryland as part of set 11600 in 1968-69 (see 2029 locomotive for details).

The problems have come about because collectors could not distinguish the postwar 6560 Crane Cars with the 11600 Hagerstown set from the other 6560 Crane Car marketed by Fundimensions in 1971. That is easy to understand, because the 6560 Crane Cars with the dark blue frame found in Fundimensions boxes are almost — but not quite — identical to the cars included in the Hagerstown set. The 6560 Hagerstown crane (at least in its most common version) and the 6560 Fundimensions crane share the same very dark blue boom and cab base, the same AAR trucks and even the same wheel sets — the only known use of the postwar flat-surfaced wheel on a Fundimensions car except for the use of some leftover postwar bar-end trucks on a few tank cars. There are only two differences between the cars (aside from the all-important boxes), and these two differences are very subtle. First of all, the Fundimensions and Hagerstown cranes both have translucent red plastic cabs, but the Fundimensions shade of red is just a little darker. Both cabs have a red color which looks like the shade of red found on a stale cherry-flavored Life-Saver candy piece. The most sure way to tell these two cranes apart (and, incidentally, a sure way to differentiate them from the older Hillside production) is to look at the top of the boom where the wires are fastened near the two aluminum reels. On the common Hillside production cranes, this piece is fastened by a small black slotted-head screw. On the Hagerstown crane, this screw is replaced by a chromed rivet. On the Fundimensions crane, this rivet is either blackened, unplated or bronzed. To complicate matters, earlier production runs of the 6560 Crane Cars have also been found in the 11600 Hagerstown set.

The boxes used for the Hagerstown and Fundimensions cranes help to distinguish the pieces, too, if they are available. The Fundimensions crane comes in a Type I red, white and blue Fundimensions box with red descriptive lettering and a cellophane window. The Hagerstown crane comes in an orange and white checkered box differing from the other Hagerstown boxes because its number is printed on the end flap in orange rather than rubber-stamped in black. The box part number is 12-247 and the printing reads "NO. 6560-25 / OPERATING / CRANE CAR".

The following is a list of all varieties known to be part of the 11600 Hagerstown set. Regardless of variations in boom and base color, lettering or its absence or color configurations, we are fairly certain that the 6560 cranes made in Hagerstown all used the translucent red plastic cab instead of the solid red plastic cab of the earlier Hillside production. Reader confirmation on thse varieties is requested.

**6560 BUCYRUS ERIE** Crane, catalogued 1968 in special promotion sheet and in 1969; large smokestack in same color as cab, "LIONEL LINES" in sans-serif letters in two lines on left side of cab with top line arched and bottom line straight, cab fastened to metal cab plate assembly (part 6560-17) with three tabs which protrude from cab plate assembly and which pass through three slots in cab (one at the bottom of back of cab under handwheel and one each at the bottom of each side at the front of cab), solid rather than open handwheels, handle on rear handwheel on the boom elevator screw assembly is 1/4" long, molded plastic frame, smaller hook than on earlier cars with hook in line with cab, four-wheel, late AAR plastic trucks, disc couplers.

(A) Translucent red cab, white lettering, very dark blue frame and boom, "LIONEL LINES" heat-stamped on left sides of frame in bold, serif, expanded letters, "WT 275,000-2-18 NH" heat-stamped on left sides of frame under "LIONEL" with hyphens same as 6460 (A), "6560" heat-stamped on right sides of frame, trucks attached by rivets with roundhead visible when looking down from top of base. P. Catalano observation, R. LaVoie Collection. | 20 | 30 | 45 | 60
(B) Same as (A), but dull black frame. | 20 | 30 | 45 | 60
(C) Same as (B), but no lettering on frame. | | | | NRS
(D) Same as (A), but one operating and one dummy disc coupler. | 20 | 30 | 45 | 60
(E) Same as (A), but both couplers are non-operating. | 20 | 30 | 45 | 60
(F) Same as (A), but orange-red cab. | 20 | 30 | 45 | 60

**NOTE:** The above observations were made by James Sattler, Philip Catalano, I.D. Smith, Ron Griesbeck, Roland LaVoie and Glenn Halverson.
**6560-25 BUCYRUS ERIE** Crane, catalogued 1956, red cab, large smokestack in same color as cab, "LIONEL LINES" in sans-serif letters in two lines on left side of cab with top line arched and bottom line straight, cab fastened to metal cab plate assembly (part 6560-17) with three tabs which

protrude from cab plate assembly and which pass through three slots in cab (one at the bottom of back of cab under handwheel and one each at the bottom of each side at the front of cab), molded plastic frame, "656025" heat-stamped on right sides of frame, handle of rear handwheel on the boom elevator screw assembly is 1/4" long, smaller hook than on earlier cars with hook in line with cab, four-wheel, bar-end metal trucks, magnetic tab couplers.
(A) Red cab. | 30 | 45 | 65 | 100
(B) Same as (A), but red-orange cab. S. Carlson observation. Confirmation requested. | | | | NRS

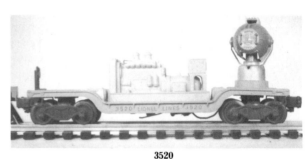

3520

## SEARCHLIGHTS

**3520 SEARCHLIGHT** 1952-53, "LIONEL LINES" on gray die-cast frame, orange diesel generator unit, steps, bar-end trucks, one brakewheel, die-cast searchlight revolves by vibrator mechanism, remote control on-off switch for searchlight concealed within plastic generator casting.

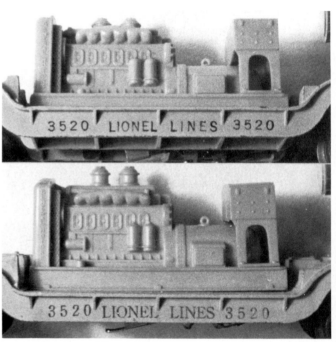

A comparison of the 3520(A) with sans-serif lettering and numbering (top) with 3520(B) with serif lettering and numbering. R. Griesbeck Collection and photograph.

(A) "3520 LIONEL LINES 3520" on frame in plain sans-serif numbering and lettering. R. Griesbeck and R. LaVoie Collections. | 15 | 22 | 30 | 50
(B) Same as (A), but lettered in larger serif letters and numbers. See photo for comparison. R. Griesbeck Collection. | | | | NRS
See also 3620X entry below.

**3530 GENERATOR** See Boxcars.

**3620 SEARCHLIGHT** 1954-56, "LIONEL LINES" in sans serif lettering on gray die-cast frame (lettering is found in both light and heavy faces), orange diesel generator, steps, bar-end trucks, one brakewheel, searchlight revolves by vibrator mechanism, no remote control on-off switch. Parvin observation.

3620

(A) Thin lettering, bright orange plastic generator, gray searchlight housing. B. Stekoll Collection.　　　　**12　17　25　40**
(B) Same as (A), but thicker lettering, later production. B. Stekoll Collection.　　　　**12　17　25　40**
(C) Same as (A), but dull orange plastic generator. B. Stekoll, M. Ocilka and R. LaVoie Collections.　　　　**12　17　25　40**
(D) Same as (A), but metal part of searchlight housing is chemically blackened rather than aluminum finished. J. Bratspis Collection.
　　　　**12　17　25　40**
(E) Thin lettering, dull orange plastic generator, orange plastic searchlight hood painted gray. Hood is same shade of orange as generator; however, gray paint does not match gray paint on flatcar or the gray shade of the normal gray plastic searchlight hood. Possibly, the factory ran out of gray plastic and molded the searchlight hoods out of the same plastic used for the generator for a time. They then painted the hood gray. This may explain entry (F). Extremely hard to find. B. Stekoll Collection.
　　　　**50　100　150　225**
(F) Gray die-cast flatcar base, "3620 LIONEL LINES 3620" rubber-stamped in black sans-serif letters, bright red-orange generator and bright red-orange searchlight housing. **NOTE:** A detachable variation such as the searchlight housing raises the inevitable question of substitution. That is why we had not listed this variation. In this case, however, the color of the housing and the generator are perfectly matched. Note that the car is actually shown with an orange searchlight housing on page 20 of the 1954 catalogue, and see entry (E) above for further corroboration of this car. In terms of value, this car should not be priced higher than (E) above because the piece would be easy to fake by removal of the gray paint. Other examples have slightly different shades of orange plastic in their searchlight hoods. In any case, both entries are extremely hard to find. A. Tom, M. Ocilka and D. Schwab Collections.　　　**50　100　150　225**
(G) Same as (F), but medium orange plastic generator and searchlight housing. M. Ocilka Collection.　　　**50　100　150　225**
(H) Thick lettering, dull orange plastic generator, bright red-orange searchlight housing, as illustrated on page 20 of 1954 catalogue. Reader confirmation requested. P. Ambrose comment.　　**50　100　150　225**
**3620X LIONEL LINES** Searchlight, 1955, sans-serif light-faced "3520 LIONEL LINES 3520" lettering on gray die-cast frame, orange diesel generator, one brakewheel, bar-end trucks fastened by horseshoe clip, no remote control on-off switch. Came with set 1539 in 1955 in box marked 3620X. A. Staebler Collection.　　**25　30　40　65**

3650

**3650 EXTENSION SEARCHLIGHT** 1956-59, gray die-cast base, black lettering, "LIONEL LINES" without serif, gray plastic searchlight unit on red base held by magnet to steel plate in die-cast frame, gray generator, red reel with green cord and crank (often missing) supported on black frame, bar-end trucks, magnetic tab couplers.

(A) Light gray die-cast frame, two brakewheels. R. LaVoie Collection.
　　　　**15　25　40　60**
(B) Dark gray die-cast frame, one brakewheel. Somewhat hard to find. P. Ambrose comment.　　　　**30　50　90　150**
(C) Same as (A), but olive tint to paint on gray frame. S. Blotner Collection.　　　　**NRS**

6520

**6520 SEARCHLIGHT** 1949-51, gray die-cast base, die-cast searchlight, staple-end trucks, magnetic couplers, on-off switch, manual rotation of light, one brakewheel, steps. We would like to have more detailed truck and fiber switch information so that we can more precisely date the varieties listed below.
(A) Green diesel generator, shiny smooth gray light housing.
　　　　**50　100　150　200**
(B) 1949, green diesel generator, crinkle gray light housing, black fiber switch unit, activator flap without extra hole, rivet with flared end down. J. Sattler Collection.　　　　**50　100　150　200**
(C) Green diesel generator, glossy smooth black light housing. J. Breslin Collection.　　　　**50　100　150　200**
(D) 1951, orange diesel generator, gray crinkle light housing, brown fiber switch unit, no extra hole in activator flap, rivet with flared end down. R. LaVoie Collection.　　　　**15　22　30　50**
(E) 1950, maroon diesel generator, gray crinkle light housing, brown fiber switch unit, extra hole in activator flap, rivet with flared end down. R. LaVoie Collection.　　　　**15　22　30　50**
(F) Early 1950, maroon diesel generator, smooth gray light housing, brown fiber switch unit, activator flap with extra hole, rivet with flared end down. J. Sattler Collection.　　　　**15　22　30　50**
(G) Tan diesel generator, gray metallic enameled light. Very hard to find.　　　　**100　200　300　400**
(H) early 1950, orange diesel generator, gray smooth light housing, brown fiber switch unit, activator flap with extra hole, rivet with flared end down. J. Sattler Collection.　　　　**15　22　30　50**

6822

**6822 SEARCHLIGHT** 1961-69, red frame with white lettering, blue man, lighting unit lettered "TRACK / MAINTENANCE" and has simulated shovels, wire rolls, oxygen tanks, AAR trucks, disc-operating coupler(s). Same design used for Fundimensions searchlight cars, but blue man not included.
(A) Black lighting unit base, gray searchlight housing, mold 6511-21, early AAR trucks, disc couplers. C. Rohlfing Collection.　**10　20　30　40**
(B) Gray lighting unit base, black searchlight housing, mold 6511-2, one disk coupler, one fixed coupler, late AAR trucks. J. Sattler Collection.
　　　　**7　10　15　30**

# Chapter VI

# FLATCARS

In prototype railroading, the lowly flatcar has a rich and varied history. In fact, during the early days of railroading, nearly every car was essentially a flatcar with a structure built onto it. For example, early tank and vat cars were really wooden decks with the tank or vat superstructures attached to them in some way. (An excellent example of this construction can be found at the Strasburg Railroad near Lancaster, Pennsylvania, where a tank car made in 1906 features a wooden deck with a steel tank atop it.) However, as the needs of railroads changed, so did the flatcars. Bulkheads were mounted onto the flatcar ends to hold loads in place. Modern flatcars often have facilities for mounting highway trailers. Truly, the flatcar has been an all-purpose car for America's railroads.

It should come as no surprise, then, that Lionel's postwar flatcars reflected the same changes and the same functions. These cars carried everything from transformers to Christmas trees for Lionel. Since the flatcar was very inexpensive for Lionel to make, it made economic sense to promote these cars, especially within train sets. It is no accident that this chapter is as long as it is.

The earliest postwar flatcars were well detailed, with scribing to suggest wooden decks — except that they were die cast. All of them were painted gray, as the real ones often were, and if they were not merely decks with railings, they were adapted to other purposes. With a cab and two toolboxes, they became work cabooses. A variant of this casting had a depressed center. This flatcar then became the carrier for transformers, cable reels and other loads; in modified form, it was the base for the die-cast searchlight cars. An extra-long variant of this car had four trucks and carried a transformer or two plastic bridge girders.

Lionel's first plastic flatcars were made from four dies, one of which had at least four variations. The flatcar listing of molds and dies by Michael Ocilka, contained in this chapter, provides a breakdown of these construction variations. These cars proved to be most versatile for Lionel Corporation. In the early postwar years, there was not a bulk load which could not be found carried in miniature on these cars. Later on, the Lionel flatcars became the carriers of the structures for the Military and Space loads. Some carried atomic waste canisters; others carried rocket, cannon, helicopter and satellite launching mechanisms. Automobiles, trucks and cranes were frequent travelers upon Lionel's flatcars, not to mention numerous pieces of construction equipment.

In the late 1950s, a shorter plastic flatcar was made. Originally intended as a base for the horse car of the "General" set, this car, most often unmarked, was found in many an inexpensive set in Lionel's last years. A stamped metal short flatcar was also made and adapted readily to loads with stakes such as pipes and logs. Finally, a plastic flatcar with an upward arch in its center became the base for the Allis-Chalmers condenser car, the Mercury Space Capsule car and a missile firing car.

In spite of the fact that Lionel's chief reason for making so many flatcars may have been economic, it must be remembered that these cars also had considerable play value. If a child did not like Lionel's load, he could substitute his own very readily. Many a "foreign" toy car, tank or truck has made circuits around a Lionel layout. Collectors are just beginning to realize the variability and interest of these cars, and one might expect that values for some of the scarcer varieties will change accordingly. It is still quite possible to acquire a large collection of flatcars at very nominal prices.

### 6424 FLATCAR MOLDS
### By Michael J. Ocilka

The 2424 car is marked with the numbers 6424-11 molded on the underside.

DIE 1: Two stake holes on the sides of the car at diagonally opposing ends, two small circular holes on the center line of the car.

DIE 2: 13 stake holes instead of two; circular holes on center line are plugged, but detectable.

DIE 3: 13 stake holes, plugged center holes and four rectangular holes added.

DIE 4: Two stake holes, open circular holes and four added rectangular holes.

Lionel did not put numbers on the sides of some of its flatcars. We list these by catalogue number when known and put the catalogue number in parantheses. See our listing of unnumbered cars at the end of the regular listings.

**1877 FLAT WITH FENCE AND HORSES** 1959-62, brown unpainted plastic body, brown fence with six interior dividers, white lettering, six horses: two white, two tan and two black, horses marked with B B logo on underside, arch-bar trucks, disc couplers. J. Sattler Collection.

|  | 20 | 30 | 40 | 60 |

**One version of the 1877 came with a load consisting of a jeep, guntrailer and 10 soldiers. T. Groves Collection.**

**(1877) NO NUMBER** circa 1960-65, 1877 Type. Car catalogue number does not appear on car, hence it appears in parentheses. However, the car is embossed with 1877-3 at one end on underside. T. Groves comment.
(A) Flatcar with logs, unpainted gray plastic, three logs, no stakes, AAR trucks, one disc coupler, one fixed coupler. 

|  | 1 | 2 | 3 | 5 |

(B) Flat without stakes or load, unpainted brown plastic, arch-bar trucks, fixed couplers.

|  | 1 | 1.50 | 2 | 4 |

(C) Flat without stakes or load, unpainted gray plastic, arch-bar trucks, fixed couplers. H. Edmunds Collection. Used for Sears military tank car flat; L. Bohn comment.

|  | 1 | 1.50 | 2 | 4 |

(D) Unpainted tuscan flat with yellow auto, part of set 19142-100. See also 6406 entry. Dupstet Collection, P. Ambrose comment. **NRS**
(E) Flat without stakes, unpainted gray plastic, arch-bar trucks, dummy couplers; moss-green-colored flexible plastic load consisting of jeep embossed with "M" on underside, separate gun trailer and 10 soldier figures. The load components are made from the same kind of plastic used for the green tank which came with the 1964 Sears set 3-9820. This flatcar came with an uncatalogued set headed by a 221 Alco locomotive, a 6112(B) gondola, a 3349(B) olive drab turbo missile launching car, a 6651 USMC Cannon car and a 6824 work caboose. Although this set is different from the J.C. Penney uncatalogued set 19334, its number is not currently known. T. Groves Collection. **NRS**
(F) Same as (E), but one operating coupler. E. Heid Collection. **NRS**
(G) Same as (E), but tank is tan G. Wilson Collection. **NRS**

**NOTE:** See also Entries 6401, 6401-50, 6402 and 6402-50.

**1887 FLAT WITH FENCE AND HORSES** 1959, tuscan with yellow lettering, yellow fence with six interior dividers, horses marked with B B logo on underside, arch-bar trucks, disc couplers, part of uncatalogued Sears O-27 set.
(A) Six horses: two white, two tan and two black. J. Sattler Collection.

|  | 60 | 85 | 125 | 170 |

(B) Same as (A), but came with one extra tan horse. T. Klaassen Collection.

|  | 60 | 85 | 125 | 170 |

**2411 FLAT WITH BIG INCH PIPES** 1946-48, same gray die-cast frame as 2419 Work Caboose, three black metal pipes with grooves at end, or three wood logs; staple-end trucks, late coil couplers, brakewheels, black serif-lettered "LIONEL LINES" on side and "2411" on underside, six black stakes, four steps, two sets of end rails. J. Sattler comments.
(A) 1946, three black metal pipes, late closed coil couplers without staking marks underside of casting lacks six small squares. C. Rohlfing Collection.

|  | 7 | 15 | 22 | 40 |

(B) 1947-48, three large unstained or five small stained wood logs, couplers have staking marks, thinner rubber-stamped number on base, six small squares on underside of casting. R. Swanson and J. Foss comments, C. Rohlfing and R. LaVoie Collections.

|  | 5 | 10 | 15 | 25 |

**2461 TRANSFORMER CAR** 1947-48, gray die-cast depressed-center belly frame with black serif-lettered "LIONEL LINES", staple-end trucks, late coil couplers with sliding shoes, two brakewheels. Insulators sometimes broken, prices quoted in excellent and mint categories are for cars with unbroken insulators, which are very hard to find. Broken or glued insulators reduce this car's condition to Very Good, regardless of condition of rest of car. Original replacement transformers are available, but so are reproductions. The original transformer pieces have rigid, fragile, shiny white plastic insulators; the reproductions have semi-translucent flexible plastic insulators which are far less fragile. The prototype railroad car for this Lionel model was pictured in the 1940 printing of Lionel's **Handbook For Model Builders**, as were the prototypes for the 3359 twin-bin dump car, the 3459-69 coal dump cars, the 6315-25 triple-dome tank cars and — incredibly — the 3434-6434 Poultry Dispatch cars. R. LaVoie and T. Rollo comments.
(A) Black transformer, small white decal on one side with "Transformer" and "L" in circle.

|  | 15 | 20 | 35 | 50 |

(B) Red transformer, same decal as (A).

|  | 15 | 20 | 35 | 50 |

(C) Red transformer, same decal as (A), no lettering on frame.

|  | 20 | 30 | 50 | 65 |

(D) Red transformer, no decals or lettering, center insulators same length as side insulators (usually they are longer possibly replacement insulators). C. Rohlfing Collection.

|  | 20 | 30 | 50 | 65 |

(E) Red transformer, decal on both sides with "Transformer" and "L" in circle. J. Algozzini Collection.

|  | 20 | 30 | 50 | 65 |

**(3309) TURBO MISSILE LAUNCHING CAR**, 1963-64. Also see 3349. The description "turbo missile" refers to a wheel-shaped flying disc launched by a spring mechanism. This version does not have lettering or numbering on the flatcar base. See the Greenberg reprint of the Lionel Service Manual, V-37.
(A) Light red plastic car, no number or lettering, blue launch mechanism, all-red missile, blue missile holder, arch-bar trucks, fixed couplers; R. Royer comment. Note that 3309 does not have an extra missile rack while 3349 does; additionally, most of the 3349 versions have operating couplers, while this version has two dummy couplers. This car came with set 11321 in 1963 and most likely with several other sets. P. Ambrose comments.

|  | 10 | 20 | 35 | 50 |

(B) Same as (A), but cherry red flatcar body. R. Royer comment.

|  | 10 | 20 | 35 | 50 |

(C) Same as (A), but light blue launcher, AAR trucks, one operating and one dummy coupler. R. Royer and J. Breslin comments.

|  | 10 | 20 | 35 | 50 |

(D) Same as (A), except gray "General"-type flatcar. S. Blotner Collection.

|  | 10 | 20 | 35 | 50 |

(E) Same as (B), but has extra missile rack like 3349; came with 3309 instruction sheet which showed extra missile rack. T. Budniak Collection.

|  | 10 | 20 | 35 | 50 |

(F) Same as (B), but AAR trucks with operating disc couplers. C. Rohlfing Collection.

|  | 10 | 20 | 35 | 50 |

**3330 FLAT WITH OPERATING SUBMARINE KIT** 1960-61, flat (6511-2 mold) with disassembled rubberband-powered submarine requiring assembly, parts came in plastic bag, also included assembly instructions, blue car, white-lettered "LIONEL" with serifs, early AAR trucks, disc couplers, gray submarine lettered "U.S. NAVY 3830". J. Sattler Collection.

|  | 20 | 35 | 50 | 125 |

**(3349) TURBO MISSILE LAUNCHING CAR** 1962-65 and 3349-100, 1963. (Also see 3309.) Reportedly, 3349 usually has one missile storage rack in addition to the launch mechanism while 3309 does not have a missile storage

Four TOFC (Trailers on Flatcars) from Lionel's postwar production. Top left: 6430 with gray vans and sign slots but no signs. Top right: 3460 from 1955 with green "LIONEL TRAINS" vans. Bottom left and right: two 6430s with COPPER-JARRETT vans. L. Nuzzaci Collection.

**Gd VG Exc Mt**

rack in addition to its launch mechanism. Although 3349 was repeatedly illustrated in the catalogue with a number on the side, samples have only been found without numbering or lettering except for (B). The car does not have a mold number on the underside. I.D. Smith comments that the 3650 and the 3349 appear to share the same mold and neither has a part number. Although 3650 has a die-cast body, Lionel was apparently able to use the die-cast mold to make the 3349 body. The 3349 has AAR trucks with two disc couplers except (C) and (D). Blue launch mechanism, white and red "missiles" which actually resemble a wheel, blue missile rack. The missile storage rack fits into slots in the car frame. There is an extra set of slots for a second missile rack.

(A) Light red body; P. Catalano comment. **10 20 35 50**
(B) Olive drab body, no lettering or numbering, no mold number on underside of base, one operating and one dummy coupler, came with uncatalogued set 19334 made for J. C. Penney and headed by a 221 USMC Alco, 1963-64. Set also included 6076(M) hopper, 6112(B) gondola and 6824 Rescue Unit caboose. Components came in flat outfit box; no separate boxes. P. Catalano, P. Ambrose, H. Powell and G. Wilson comments.

**30 50 75 125**
(C) Red body, no lettering, aqua blue launcher and missile rack (blue with a slight green tinge), one fixed and one disc coupler. G. Halverson Collection. **10 20 35 50**
(D) Same as (A), but has dummy couplers. S. Lapan Collection.

**15 25 45 65**

**3361-55 LOG DUMP** 1955-58, unpainted gray plastic with black lettering, four stained wooden dowels 4-9/16" long, bar-end trucks, magnetic tab couplers, metal channel runs car length and holds operating mechanism. Some cars came in larger boxes when the car was offered for separate sale; these were marked 3361 only. P. Ambrose comment.

(A) "LIONEL LINES" with heavy 7/32" serif letters, "336155" on right in large serif numbers, car dimensions to left in sans-serif lettering, drive gear for operating mechanism is white plastic. L. Backus and M. Ocilka Collections. **8 15 20 30**
(B) Same as (A) but black plastic drive mechanism, magnetic couplers without tabs. J. Sattler Collection. **8 15 20 30**
(C) "LIONEL LINES" with lighter serif letters than (A), "336155" on left, dimensions data to right, drive gear is solid black plastic. K. Koehler, L. Backus and M. Ocilka Collections. **8 15 20 30**
(D) "LIONEL LINES" in 1/8" sans-serif letters, darker gray plastic body,

car number to right and dimensions data to left, drive gear is medium orange plastic. J. Sattler and L. Backus Collections. **8 15 20 30**
(E) Same as (A), but original box marked "3361X", box part number 3361-28. This usually signified that the car was made to be included in sets. Since there was room in the set box for the dumping bin, Lionel was able to pack this car in a smaller box and designate it as a set car with the "X" marking on the box. (R. Brezak example had black drive gear instead of white.) T. Rollo and R. Hutchinson comments, T. Budniak and R. Brezak Collections. **8 15 20 30**

This is the 3362/3364 Hagerstown box which contained an unmarked 3362 dump car. G. Halverson Collection, G. Stern photograph.

**3362/64 FLAT WITH HELIUM TANKS or LOGS** 1961-63, 1965-69, dumps three silver-painted wooden tanks or three large dark-stained logs, unpainted dark green plastic body, mold 2, with "LIONEL LINES" serif lettering, "LD LMT 128800, LT WT 40200, CAPY 100000" in white sans-serif lettering, metal channel runs length of car, magnetic operation, AAR plastic trucks, one disc and one dummy coupler. Some reports say that although all of these cars were stamped 3362, this car was referred to as 3364 when it was equipped with logs instead of helium tanks; C. Rohlfing, P. Ambrose and I.D. Smith comments. However, the nomenclature of this car may not be so simple; see Entry (C) below.

(A) With helium tanks, early 1960s box marked "No. 3362 / LIONEL / HELIUM TANK / UNLOADING CAR". P. Ambrose Collection.

**8 15 25 40**
(B) With logs, early 1960s box marked "No. 3364 / LIONEL / LOG UNLOADING / CAR". Car, however, retains its 3362 number; in this box, it

is much harder to find than (A). P. Ambrose and Popp Collections.

|  | 15 | 25 | 35 | 55 |

(C) No lettering on car; box (1969-type) has "3362 / 3364" and "OPERATING / UNLOADING CAR". Came with two helium tanks and instruction sheet for "3362-15 Lionel Helium Tank Unloading Car". Most likely, no cars were ever stamped 3364. Instead, the unlettered and unnumbered car was packed in this Hagerstown box in 1968 and 1969 and designated as "3364," even though the 3362 number was retained to coincide with the instruction sheets. We need to know which car came in the boxes made from 1965-66, when it should have been packed in the late boxes with either a white and blue locomotive picture on the long side or a cellophane display window. J. Algozzini, G. Halverson, P. Ambrose and G. Wilson Collections. **10  20  30  50**

**3364 LOG DUMP**  Catalogued in 1965-69, but probably not made with 3364 number on its side. See box photo above 3362 / 64 entry. Also see entries 3362 / 64(B) and (C).

**3409 HELICOPTER LAUNCHING CAR**  1961-62, helicopter with black plastic spring-wound launch mechanism, manually cocked and released; light blue unpainted flatcar, white lettering; Type B helicopter (see 3419), arch-bar trucks, fixed couplers, mold 3419-30. R. Pauli Collection.

|  | 14 | 25 | 35 | 60 |

**3409 SATELLITE CAR**  Circa 1961, uncatalogued, light blue flat, white lettering, manual release, black and silver satellite, yellow microwave disc on gray superstructure, AAR trucks, operating disc couplers. G. Wilson Collection. **25  40  65  100**

**3410 HELICOPTER LAUNCHING CAR**  1961-62, light blue flat, white lettering, black launch mechanism and black support for rear of helicopter, Type B helicopter (see 3419) early AAR trucks, disc couplers. J. Sattler Collection. **13  25  40  65**

**3413 MERCURY CAPSULE CAR**  1962-64, car launches rocket into air, Mercury capsule separates and returns via parachute. Red plastic frame,

white-lettered "LIONEL" only without numbers, gray superstructure with red spring-loaded rocket launcher; gray Mercury capsule nose with parachute inside of rocket, red rocket base; early AAR trucks, one disc coupler, one fixed coupler, mold 6511-2. J. Sattler Collection.

|  | 25 | 45 | 65 | 95 |

**3419 REMOTE CONTROLLED HELICOPTER LAUNCHING CAR**  1959-65, similar to 3409 in function, but usually with two slots with levers on top and large 2" black winder designed to be released (after manually cocked) by UCS, 6019 or 6029 magnet track; with alternate manual lever and lock lever on car top near black plastic piece which holds copter tail assembly rigid prior to flight, flatcar mold 3419-30, early AAR trucks, disc couplers. Also came with one slot, one lever and 1-1/4" winder. C. Rohlfing comment. This car preceded the 3409. C. Lang comment.

**HELICOPTER TYPES:**
(A) Gray "NAVY" with two rotors and four tip pods, yellow tail assembly.
(B) Gray "NAVY" with one rotor, no tip pods, yellow tail assembly.
(C) All-yellow unmarked helicoper, one rotor, no tip pods.
(D) Red with single rotor, no tip pods, came with 3619.
**NOTE:** Helicopters are easily interchanged. We assume that the reports that we received as to which helicopter came with which version are accurate.

**TWO LEVERS, 2" WINDER:**
**NOTE:**  The colors are arranged from lightest to darkest.
(A) Aqua-blue body, Type A helicopter. This helicopter with two rotors is more desirable than the single-rotored version. P. Ambrose comment.

|  | 20 | 35 | 50 | 75 |

(B) Light blue body, Type B or C helicopter. J. Sattler and F. Salvatore Collections. **13  25  35  50**

(C) Royal blue body, Type A helicopter. J. Sattler and H. Powell Collections. **20  35  50  75**

(D) Dark blue, almost purple, Type C helicopter. **13  25  40  65**

3451

3460

3461

3470

3509

3510(B)

3519

|  | Gd | VG | Exc | Mt |
|---|---|---|---|---|

(E) Same as (C), but Type A helicopter has white rotors and tips. H. Powell Collection. **20 35 50 75**

**ONE LEVER, 1-1/4" WINDER:**

(A) Medium blue body, Type A helicopter. J. Sattler Collection
**20 35 50 75**

(B) Same as (A), but Type B helicopter. J. Sattler Collection.
**15 25 35 50**

(C) Purple body, Type B helicopter. C. Rohlfing Collection.
**13 25 35 50**

**3429 U.S.M.C.** 1960, U.S. MARINE CORPS operating helicopter car, olive drab paint over blue plastic car, white lettering, same mechanism as 3419, Type B helicopter, but with USMC markings instead of Navy lettering. (See 3419 for helicopter types.) One control lever on car's top surface, other on car's side; winder could be remotely released. Came as part of set 1805: Land, Sea and Air Gift-Pack, 1960 catalogue, p. 17. We have had reports of Type A and C helicopters and Navy-marked Type B helicopters with this car, but the Type B helicopter with USMC markings is the only correct one for this car. The panel agrees that only Type B helicopters came with this car. The panel disagrees as to whether only USMC Type B or both Navy and USMC Type Bs are correct. P. Ambrose and P. Catalano comments.
**30 50 80 125**

**3451 LOG DUMP** 1946-47, black die-cast base, white lettering, staple-end trucks, coil couplers, five stained wood dowels 5-1/16" long, one brakewheel.

(A) 1946, shaft retainers for the swivel movement are riveted with round-head rivets from the top and swaged from the bottom; nickel-sized hole between second and third set of stakes; heat-stamped lettering, no staking marks on coupler heads. **10 15 25 40**

(B) 1947, shaft retainer rivets are integral to casting and swaged from top, hole about size of half dollar on frame, heat-stamped lettering, staking marks on coupler heads. T. McLaughlin Collection. **10 15 25 40**

(C) Same as (B), but rubber-stamped lettering, late coil couplers. J. Sattler and Latina Collections. **10 15 25 40**

(D) Same as (A), but rubber-stamped lettering. Typically, this version's lettering is very blurred. C. Rohlfing Collection. **10 15 25 40**

(E) Same as (B), but larger than normal box marked "No. 3451 / AUTOMATIC / LUMBER CAR / 25 LIONEL 25"; probable separate sale car which had to include dumping bin. P. Ambrose comment. **10 15 25 40**

**3460 FLAT WITH TRAILERS** 1955, red unpainted plastic flatcar, mold 6511-2, white lettering, metal strip holds trailers, bar-end trucks, magnetic tab couplers, trucks fastened to frame by metal plate; metal plate slides into two slots at each end of car; trailers are dark green with aluminum sign reading "LIONEL TRAINS", end decal reads "FRUEHAUF DURAVAN", lower right-hand decal reads "FRUEHAUF", van with single axle, four wheels. Harder to find than nearly-identical 6430 version. R. LaVoie Collection. **15 25 35 50**

**3461 LOG DUMP** 1949-55, five logs stained dark brown, white heat-stamped lettering, "LIONEL LINES", one brakewheel.

(A) 1949-53, black die-cast frame and dump unit; staple-end trucks, magnetic couplers. **10 20 25 40**

(B) 1954-55, green die-cast frame, black dump unit, bar-end trucks, magnetic couplers, box marked either 3461-25 or 3461X. We believe that the "X" box indicated that this car was part of a set and was packed without a bin, since there would be room inside the set box itself for the bin. Version (A) is also found this way. T. Rollo and R. Hutchinson comments, T. Budniak and R. LaVoie Collections. **14 20 35 50**

(C) 1952-55, black die-cast frame and dump unit, bar-end trucks, magnetic couplers. Kaiser Collection. **10 20 25 40**

**3470 TARGET LAUNCHER** 1962-64, dark blue unpainted flatcar, mold 6511-2, no lettering; white superstructure with red letters, red lever on top activates motor; blue balloon carriage on top; car came with white Lionel balloons, which when inflated by operator and motor was turned on would raise the balloon approximately 1" above the balloon carrier; the balloon would then follow the moving car; the white superstructure is easily

removed by pressing the tab on the underside at the brakewheel end of the car, two dry cell batteries are placed in the white superstructure for operation; early AAR trucks, disc couplers, plastic blower nozzle, mold 6511-2. J. Diggle comment.

(A) Clear plastic blower nozzle. J. Sattler Collection.    **12  25  40  60**
(B) Same as (A), but light blue unpainted flatcar. S. Blotner Collection.
    **12  25  40  60**
(C) Red plastic blower nozzle. J. Diggle Collection.    **12  25  40  60**
(D) Light gray blower nozzle. J. Diggle Collection.    **12  25  40  60**

**3509 MANUALLY OPERATED SATELLITE CAR** 1961-62, green flatcar body, white lettering, black and silver satellite, gray superstructure holds yellow microwave disc; manually-operated by side lever, AAR trucks, disc couplers, mold 3419-30. Shown with green flatcar body in 1962 catalogue, but see entry in Factory Errors for exception.    **15  25  40  60**

**See also Factory Errors and Prototypes.**

**3510 RED SATELLITE CAR** 1961-62, white "LIONEL" lettering on side, but no number; black and silver satellite, arch-bar trucks, fixed couplers. P. Catalano comments.

(A) Darker red car, gray superstructure, yellow microwave disc.
    **25  40  60  90**
(B) Red car, no superstructure. Verification requested.  **9  20  30  40**
(C) Red body, mold 3419-30, flatcar bottom has molded solid "box" between "NEW YORK" and "N.Y." of corporate identification, gray superstructure, yellow microwave dish, small black winder manually operated by lever that extends under the car side. J. Sattler and G. Halverson Collections.    **25  40  60  90**

**3512 LADDER CO.** 1959-61, red unpainted plastic body, 6424-11 mold, Die 4, white lettering, truck mechanism causes light shield to rotate causing light rotation, man rotates at other car end; mechanism uses rubber belt which almost always deteriorates; early AAR trucks, disc couplers, three small metal nozzles, two ladders in addition to main ladder. Nozzles and other parts often missing. M. Ocilka comment.

(A) Black ladder. J. Sattler Collection.    **22  40  70  100**
(B) Silver ladder. J. Sattler Collection.    **32  55  90  150**

**3519 REMOTE CONTROL SATELLITE CAR** 1961-64, green base, white letters, gray superstructure with yellow microwave disc, black and silver satellite, early AAR trucks, disc couplers; car activated manually by lever under side or by remote control track, mold 3419-30. J. Sattler and R. LaVoie Collections.    **15  25  35  50**

**3535 AEC SECURITY** 1960-61, black base, mold 6511-2, red building, white letters, gray gun on roof, gray rotating-type searchlight with vibrator motor, early AAR trucks, disc couplers, one pickup roller. Slight modification of this body used for 520 Box Cab Electric. J. Sattler Collection, J. Hubbard comment.    **20  30  50  80**

**3540 OPERATING RADAR CAR** 1959-60, red car base, mold 6511-2, white letters, gray superstructure with yellow microwave disc; black and silver radar antenna; blue seated man with flesh-colored hands and face; radar unit panel same as that used for 44 Rocket Launcher with dials and gauges; lighted green radar screen with black lines and white dots; one roller pickup for radar screen light; rotating radar tower powered by rubber band drive attached to disc and axle; rubber band usually deteriorates; early AAR trucks. Same body used by Fundimensions in Laser Train set of 1981. J. Sattler and G. Wilson Collections.    **25  55  90  125**

**3545 LIONEL TV CAR** 1961-62, black base, white letters, blue superstructure with yellow TV camera and base; 6511-2 mold, blue man with flesh-colored face and hands in seated position looking into TV projection screen mounted within yellow frame; screen shows a Santa Fe diesel coming and an open railroad track in the direction the car is moving; to the rear of seated figure is a movable light structure that "illuminates" the cameraman's subject; TV cameraman rotates by rubber band attached to disc and axle; rubber band usually deteriorates, early AAR trucks, disc couplers; M. Ocilka, I.D. Smith and M. Harrigan comments. We have had a report of one car with a TV camera whose base and camera body are a different color, but details are lacking. Reader comments requested.    **25  50  90  125**

**3820 Flat with operating submarine.**

**3820 FLAT WITH OPERATING SUBMARINE** 1960-62, olive drab car, mold 6511-2, white-lettered "USMC", gray submarine marked "U.S. NAVY 3830", AAR trucks, disc couplers. **17 25 45 75**

**3830 FLAT WITH OPERATING SUBMARINE** 1960-63; blue car, mold 6511-2, white-lettered "LIONEL", gray submarine with black-lettered "U.S. NAVY 3830", AAR trucks, disc couplers. **12 25 35 60**

**NOTE:** There are three different 6111 flatcars.

**6111(A) LIONEL flatcar. Note sans-serif lettering. Pro Custom Hobbies Collection.**

**6111 FLAT WITH LOGS** 1955, stamped-steel car, black serif lettered "LIONEL".
(A) Yellow-painted, three logs, bar-end trucks. **1 2 4 10**
(B) Yellow-painted, six stained wood dowels, AAR trucks, disc couplers. J. Sattler Collection. **1 2 4 10**
(C) Red-painted, six stained wood dowels, early AAR trucks, disc couplers. J. Sattler Collection. **1 2 4 10**

**6111 FLAT WITH PIPES OR LOGS** Circa 1955-56, painted stamped-steel frame; frame similar to preceding 6111, probably held pipes or logs, pipe or log holders.
(A) Gray-painted frame, "LIONEL" in white sans-serif lettering, AAR trucks, disc couplers. Schreiner and Light Collections. **2 3 6 12**
(B) Light gray-painted frame, aluminum-finished pipes, "LIONEL" in white serif lettering, bar-end trucks, tab couplers. White and J. Kotil Collections. **2 3 6 12**
(C) Light gray-painted frame, six stained wooden dowels for load, "LIONEL" in white serif letters, early AAR trucks, disc couplers. J. Sattler Collection. **2 3 6 12**
(D) Dark gray-painted frame, "LIONEL" in serif lettering, AAR trucks, came with log load. C. Rohlfing and J. Kotil Collections. **2 3 6 12**
(E) Same as (D), but "LIONEL" in sans-serif lettering. J. Kotil Collection. **2 3 6 12**
(F) Dark gray-painted frame, "LIONEL" in serif lettering, early AAR trucks, disc couplers, six plastic pipes. J. Sattler Collection. **2 3 6 12**
(G) Dark blue-gray-painted frame, "LIONEL" in serif lettering, AAR trucks. J. Kotil Collection. **2 3 6 12**

**6111 FLAT WITH PIPES** 1957, red or maroon-painted stamped-steel car, white-lettered "LIONEL", pipes.
(A) Red body, lettering with serifs. H. Holden Collection. **2 3 5 10**
(B) Red body, lettering without serifs, bar-end trucks, magnetic tab couplers. T. Budniak and R. LaVoie Collections. **2 3 5 10**
(C) Same as (A), but cherry red body, AAR trucks, two disc couplers. T. Budniak Collection. **2 3 5 10**
(D) Maroon-painted body, serif lettering, AAR trucks, two disc couplers. C.

Rohlfing and G. Wilson Collections. **5 8 15 25**
(E) Same as (B), but AAR trucks. L. Steuer Collection. **2 3 5 10**

**6111-75 FLAT WITH LOGS,** 1955 and 1958.
(A) 1955, yellow-painted stamped-steel frame, black serif lettering, three large wooden logs, bar-end trucks with magnetic tab couplers, orange and blue box marked 6111-75. D. Anderson Collection. **3 5 10 15**
(B) 1958, uncatalogued; dark red-painted sheet metal body, white serif lettering, six small stained brown logs, early AAR trucks, two couplers, number appears only on box end flap, part of uncatalogued set X-610. D. Doyle Collection. **3 5 10 15**
(C) Cream-painted body, black sans-serif lettering, four black stakes, three plastic pipes. C. Weber observation. **3 5 10 15**

**6121 FLAT WITH PIPES** 1955, yellow-painted stamped-steel frame, black-lettered "LIONEL", came with four pipes, according to page V-65 of Greenberg reprint of Lionel Service Manual. R. LaVoie comment. See next two entries.
(A) Lettering with serifs. **2 3 5 10**
(B) Lettering without serifs. **2 3 5 10**

**6121-25 FLAT WITH LOGS** 1955, yellow-painted stamped-steel frame, black lettering, came with set of six small logs, according to Greenberg reprint of Lionel Service Manual, p. V-68. Bar-end trucks with magnetic couplers, extra hole in armature and off-center hole in coupler base plate; came in box marked 6121-25. R. LaVoie, P. Ambrose and I.D. Smith comments. **2 3 5 10**

**6121-60 FLAT WITH PIPES** 1955, yellow-painted stamped-steel frame, black lettering, came with set of five pipes, according to Greenberg reprint of Lionel Service Manual, p. V-69. No numbering on car; early AAR trucks, two disc couplers, came in box marked 6121-60 as part of uncatalogued set X-610. Also reported with six plastic pipes. R. LaVoie comments, D. Doyle Collection. **2 3 5 10**

**6151 FLATCAR WITH PATROL TRUCK** 1958, stamped-steel car, black serif lettering, steps, white plastic patrol truck cab lettered "LIONEL RANCH", in black, with longhorns insignia; black plastic body lettered "RANGE PATROL", truck made by Pyro.
(A) Yellow-painted flatcar, bar-end trucks, magnetic couplers. **12 25 40 75**
(B) Orange-painted flatcar, early AAR trucks, disc couplers. J. Sattler and H. Degano Collections. **17 25 40 50**
(C) Light yellow-painted flatcar, early AAR trucks, disc couplers; shown on page 2 of 1958 catalogue. T. Budniak and J. Bratspis Collections. **12 25 40 60**
(D) Same as (A), but cream-painted flatcar body. C. Weber observation. **12 25 40 60**

**6175 FLATCAR WITH ROCKET** 1958-60, red and white rocket with blue letters, gray rocket rack, elastic cord holds rocket to rack, early AAR trucks, disc couplers. Illustration erroneously shows a rocket from 6407.
(A) Black plastic car, die 2, 6424-11 mold, white lettering. M. Ocilka Collection. **20 35 50 75**
(B) Same as (A), but die 3, 6424-11 mold. M. Ocilka Collection. **20 35 50 75**
(C) Red plastic car, mold 6511-2, white lettering. J. Sattler Collection. **20 35 50 75**
(D) Same as (A), but red flatcar. M. Ocilka comment. **20 35 50 75**

**6262 FLAT WITH WHEELS** 1956-57, white lettering, gray superstructure with slots to hold eight sets of Lionel wheels and axles; magnetic tab couplers.
(A) 1956, black flatcar, mold 6424-11, die 1, bar-end trucks. M. Ocilka Collection. **15 20 35 50**
(B) 1957, black flatcar, mold 6424-11, die 2, AAR trucks, operating disc couplers. M. Ocilka comment, G. Wilson Collection. **15 20 35 50**
(C) 19566, red flatcar instead of black. Very hard to find. P. Ambrose comment, H. Powell and T. Rollo Collections. **20 50 85 120**
(D) No lettering on black flatcar, mold 6424-11, die 4. G. Wilson Collection. **NRS**

**6264 FLAT WITH LOG LOAD** 1957, lumber for fork lift car, red plastic car, mold 6511-2, white lettering, brown lumber rack, black stakes, one brakewheel, truck mounting plates that fit into car grooves. Very hard to find with original box.

Three depressed-center flatcars and two flatcars with construction equipment loads. First shelf: 6518 Transformer car. Second shelf: 6418(E) with black girder. Third shelf: 6418(B) with pinkish-orange girder. Fourth shelf: 6816 with bulldozer (left) and 6817 with scraper (right).

(A) Bar-end trucks, magnetic tab couplers. J. Sattler and P. Ambrose Collections.     **12   25   35   50**

(B) AAR trucks, disc couplers. G. Wilson Collection.    **12   25   35   50**

(C) Same as (B), but 6264 to left of "LIONEL". F. S. Davis Collection.
           **12   25   35   50**

**6311 FLAT** 1955, reddish-brown plastic body with metal pipes, mold 6511-2; bar-end trucks, magnetic tab couplers, truck mounting plates that fasten with screws. R. Pauli Collection. Came with 2028 PRR GP-7 set and was also available as a separate item. Included seven stakes and three pipes. Much harder to find than 6511. P. Ambrose comments.
           **12   20   30   40**

**6343 BARREL RAMP CAR** 1961-62, red with white lettering, 6424-11 mold, die 4, early AAR trucks, disc couplers with six stained brown barrels, part of set 11222. J. Sattler Collection.    **8   15   25   40**

**6361 FLAT WITH TIMBER** 1960-61, 1964-69; green plastic, three real wooden sticks with bark, always with one larger and two slightly smaller sticks, held by chains with spring on underside; metal channel provides support for car; early AAR trucks, disc couplers. This car is a commendable attempt at realism, and a train headed by a switch engine pulling a string of these cars looks quite attractive on an operating layout. The editor has had to resist the temptation to classify these cars by the type of wood — pine, birch, cherry or maple — used for the sticks! Excellent or mint examples of these cars are prized. Came with small instruction sheet showing how chains were to hold the logs.

(A) Dull white rubber-stamped lettering, black timber chains. J. Sattler and R. LaVoie Collections.    **20   30   45   65**

(B) 1968-69, no lettering, gold chains, came in Hagerstown box marked "6361 / TIMBER CAR". R. Shanfeld Collection.   **30   50   70   100**

(C) Lighter green flatcar, no lettering, black timber chains. This car came in a late Hagerstown box in 1968-69. R. LaVoie comments, G. Halverson Collection.    **30   50   65   90**

(D) Same as (C), but dull white rubber-stamped lettering is present. J. Algozzini Collection.    **30   50   65   90**

(E) Darker green, dull white rubber-stamped lettering, gold-finished chains. J. Algozzini Collection.    **30   50   70   100**

(F) Same as (B), but black chains, AAR trucks, one operating and one dummy coupler. N. Ritschel Collection.    **30   50   65   90**

**6362-55 TRUCK CAR** 1956, carries three Lionel bar-end trucks without couplers, car itself also has bar-end trucks. D. Mitarotonda comment.

(A) Clear plastic painted orange, magnetic tab couplers, serif lettering.
           **7   14   30   45**

(B) Orange unpainted plastic, magnetic couplers, sans-serif lettering. J. Kotil and D. Mitarotonda Collections.    **7   14   30   45**

(C) Same as (B), but magnetic tab couplers. J. Sattler and R. LaVoie Collections.    **7   14   30   45**

(D) Orange unpainted plastic, magnetic couplers, serif lettering. J. Kotil Collection.    **8   15   25   40**

(E) Same as (D), but magnetic tab couplers. J. Sattler Collection.
           **7   14   30   45**

**6401 NO LETTERING** Flatcar; "General"-type with mold 1877-3, AAR trucks, one operating and one dummy coupler.

(A) Gray unlettered plastic body, no truss rods, came in small box without

load. G. Halverson, R. LaVoie and W. Triezenberg Collections.

3  5  8  12

(B) Light gray car with gray two-wheel van, mold 1877-3, AAR trucks, one disc coupler, one fixed coupler. Box type unknown. R. Pauli Collection.

3  7  15  25

**6401-50 FLATCAR**  Circa 1960?, gray plastic car, probably mold 1877-3 although Service Manual cites part number 6401-51 as frame. Probably has no number or lettering, AAR trucks, one operating coupler, one fixed coupler. Confirmation requested as to box; car number probably appears on box end. P. Ambrose comment. **NRS**

**6402 FLAT WITH REELS OR BOAT**  Medium gray plastic car, mold 1877-3.

(A) 1962, part of set 11001; color of flatcar body and reels unknown. Reader comments requested. **NRS**

(B) 1964, orange reels marked "LIONEL", two elastic bands hold reels in place, unlettered car, late AAR trucks, disc couplers. J. Sattler Collection.

3  6  9  15

(C) 1969, blue boat.

4  8  12  20

(D) Same as (B), but brown flatcar. Possibly identical to (A) above; further comments requested. A. Arpino Collection. 3  6  9  15

**6402-50 FLATCAR WITH CABLE REELS**  1964, medium gray plastic car, mold 1877-3 "General" flatcar, although Service Manual calls for part number 6402-51. "6402" on car side. 6402-50 is the catalogue number. Orange reels marked "LIONEL", elastic bands hold reels in place, AAR trucks, one operating coupler, one fixed coupler. 2  3  5  11

**6404 FLATCAR**  Not catalogued in 1960 Consumer catalogue, but shown in 1960 Advance Catalogue.

(A) Black body with struts, mold 1877-3, arch-bar trucks, two dummy couplers. Came with brown auto with gray bumpers. Part of special low-priced set 1109, "The Huntsman Steamer ... designed for the toy market and ... not ... included in the Lionel consumer catalogue". For more information about this set, see the entry for 1060 in the steam locomotive

section. Car was possibly also offered as a Merchants' Green Stamp premium car, and possibly by other mass merchandisers as a low-priced "leader". We would like information from the 1960 Merchants' Green Stamp catalogue. This car is also reported with dark red or green automobiles with gray bumpers. J. Algozzini comment, D. Fleming Collection and observation, Vaughn Collection. **14  22  35  60**

(B) Black body without struts, mold 1877-3, late AAR trucks, disc couplers, mauve-colored premium Lionel automobile with gray bumpers, reportedly from Merchants' Green Stamp set, but no evidence specifically linking it to this set. Reader comments invited. J. Sattler comment. **NRS**

**6405 FLAT WITH TRAILER**  1961, brown plastic flat, mold 1877-3 with struts; early AAR trucks, disc couplers; yellow trailer marked "MADE IN THE U.S. OF AMERICA / THE LIONEL CORPORATION / NEW YORK N.Y.", trailer has single axle with two rubber wheels and a thin axle with small plastic wheels that is snapped down to support trailer. The trailer has corrugated sides and slots for plates, but no plates; the Piggyback outfit trailer has a large axle with four rubber wheels. J. Sattler Collection.

10  15  30  50

## COMMENTS ON THE STUDY OF THE 6406
### By Bruce Greenberg

The study of 6406 goes back to our original 1977 publication where we observed a brown unpainted, unlettered, unnumbered flatcar in the Eddins Collection and tentatively identified the car as 1877(B). We described the car and indicated that the car base originated in the "General" set. We had no listing for 6406 and no set listings. Our focus in 1977 was to describe Lionel items individually and to note the visual differences. We had very limited information about the dating of the technical changes that we observed.

In the 1979 edition we separately listed the 1877 No Number cars, recognizing them as a specific category for study. However our 1979 book continued the focus of our 1977 book on individual items.

In 1982, we made a thorough analysis of the Lionel Service Manual to attempt to identify the uncatalogued and unnumbered cars. For the first time we listed 6406 based on the Service Manual. We surmised that it was unlettered and unnumbered since we had not received any reader reports. (We assumed that by 1982 our readers had reported all known Lionel rolling stock numbers that appeared on the cars.) This assumption was correct. However we expected that our readers would identify it based on the box end numbering.

I was disappointed by the lack of reports on the 6406 following the publication of the 1982 edition. Consequently when I prepared the 1983 edition I retained the 1982 discussion but added the following comment: "This request for confirmation was also printed in the (sic) 1981 edition of this book. The car probably does not exist."

The 1985 edition of Lionel Postwar marked a significant departure from our previous editions in a number of ways. We explicitly changed our focus from reporting on individual items to looking at how items changed over time and dating those changes. We also looked at items as parts of sets and tied the item characteristics to set dating. Richard Vagner played a critical role in this rethinking with his ground breaking article on gondolas in the 1983 edition. In the 1985 edition we reported on a number of uncatalogued sets with detailed analyses of their contents. This led in turn to more reports being filed by other collectors. During this time, Harold Powell reported on a 6406 based on linking his car with set 1123 which only appeared in the 1961 Advance catalogue. With additional reports received over the last few months we now can identify and date the 6406 Flat With Auto!

**6406 FLAT WITH AUTO** 1961, mold 1877-3, tuscan unpainted plastic "General"-style flatcar, AAR trucks, two dummy couplers, no struts, no lettering or numbering.
(A) Came in set 1123, the "Pacemaker", in 1961 with 1060 locomotive. No lettering or numbering; no load on sample observed. H. Powell Collection.
                                          **3  5  8  10**
(B) Came with Set X-600, a Quaker Oats promotion set. (See entry for 246 steam locomotive for set details.) Has yellow auto with clear windows and gray plastic bumpers as load. We had listed this car in the 1982 and 1983 editions based upon the Lionel Service Manual and asked for its confirmation. We were planning to delete it from future editions when reports from A. LaRue and H. Powell confirmed the car. From Mr. LaRue's report, we have tentatively concluded that this 6406 is the same car we list under 1877(D) from the Dupstet Collection. Also sold as part of uncatalogued set 19142-502 in 1963; car did not have separate box. A. LaRue, H. Powell, J. Divi and R. Dupstet Collections; P. Ambrose comment.        **7  10  12  15**
(C) Gray plastic flatcar body, no struts, no letters or numbers, arch-bar trucks, two dummy couplers, dark brown premium car with gray bumpers; came with set headed by a 242 locomotive; set also included a 638-2361 Van Camp's boxcar, a 3349(A) turbo missile launching car with extra missile rack, a 6448(A) target range boxcar and a 6167-125 caboose. R. Loveless Collection.                    **NRS**
(D) Same as (C), but flatcar has plastic struts and AAR trucks, from uncatalogued set 19262 of 1963. P. Ambrose comment, G. Wilson Collection.      **NRS**

**(6407) FLAT WITH ROCKET** 1963, red flatcar, no numbers, white letters, gray superstructure holds large white and red rocket (Mercury Capsule). The rocket is erroneously shown on the 6175. The pencil sharpener nose pieces were reportedly made by Sterling, Inc., a major manufacturer of school supplies during the time. R. Shanfeld comment.

(A) Blue rocket nose piece which is a pencil sharpener that can be removed and used; rocket does not launch. J. Sattler Collection.  **60 150 225 300**
(B) Same as (A), but blue rocket nose piece is not a pencil sharpener. P. Catalano comment.                         **60 100 175 275**
(C) Red rocket nose piece, pencil sharpener. E. Trentacoste Collection.
                                              **NRS**
(D) Same as (A), but black rocket nose piece. Reader confirmation requested as to source; reportedly made on special order of supply house. R. Shanfeld Collection.             **NRS**
(E) Same as (A), but rocket is lettered "ASTRONAUT" in large red vertical letters, gold rocket nose piece which is not a pencil sharpener. R. Shanfeld Collection.             **NRS**

**6409-25 FLAT WITH PIPES** Reader comments needed: Which of the following entries is the proper car for set 11311?
(A) Red body, mold number 6511-2, no number, no brakewheel, white-lettered "LIONEL", AAR trucks, fixed couplers, three gray plastic pipes. Reported as part of set 11311. G. Halverson and Schreiner Collections.
                                        **3  5  8  12**
(B) Gray unpainted plastic body, mold 1877-3, no lettering or numbering, no brakewheels, AAR trucks, one operating and one dummy coupler, probably part of set 11311 from 1963. However, the car illustrated on pages 2 and 3 of the 1963 catalogue has a "fishbelly" undercarriage rather than the flat undercarriage of this car. Further reader reports requested. J. West Collection.            **3  5  8  12**

**6411 FLAT WITH LOGS** 1948-50, gray die-cast frame rubber-stamped "6411" on underside, black "LIONEL LINES" serif lettering, two brakewheels, end railings, came with three logs stained medium brown and measuring 5/8" thick and 3-15/16" long. Not illustrated, but identical to 2411 except for number and load.
(A) 1948, staple-end trucks, coil couplers. I.D. Smith and S. Carlson Collections.                       **5  10  15  20**
(B) 1949-50, same as (A), but magnetic couplers. I.D. Smith and Schmaus Collections.                   **5  10  15  20**

**6413 MERCURY PROJECT CAPE CANAVERAL** 1962-63, blue plastic car, does not have mold number, white letters, two gray plastic unlettered Mercury capsules held by bands with cloth coating; metal plates hold capsules, early AAR trucks, disc couplers. Very hard to find in intact condition; capsules are usually missing. M. Ocilka comment.
(A) Powder blue car, has brakewheels. G. Wilson Collection.
                                    **15  35  50  70**
(B) Aquamarine car, one operating and one dummy coupler, no brakewheels. G. Wilson Collection.          **15  35  50  70**

## THE 6414 AND ITS AUTOMOBILES: ORIGINAL OR REPRODUCTION?

The 6414 Evans Auto Loader Car was a very popular item in the mid-1950s, and for the collector one of its stranger aspects is that the value of the car lies in the little automobiles supplied with it much more than the auto carrier itself. From 1955 through the early 1960s, these little automobiles were everywhere in Lionel Land. They were apparently modeled after the 1955 Ford or Mercury Club Coupe, judging by the body style. They were used on the 6424 Auto Flatcar as well as many types of 1877-style flatcars included in inexpensive sets. Sometimes the cars came in premium versions with clear plastic window glass and chromed bumpers. At other times, the bumpers were gray rather than chromed, and at still other times the cars came in greatly cheapened versions with no clear plastic windows. The rarest of these cars are the dark brown, dark red and bright green versions with clear plastic windows and gray bumpers; these are highly prized by knowledgeable collectors.

Unfortunately, as with many Lionel freight cars with detachable parts, the 6414 Auto Carriers are often found with the cars missing. It is only natural that collectors would want to find the little autos, so a thriving reproduction market has sprung up to meet the demand. However, the reproduction autos are not marked as such, so it would be easy to pass them off as the genuine article. At present, these reproduction autos sell for $5.00 apiece, while the more common original ones usually sell for a bit more. How can the collector tell the reproduction auto from the original ones if there are no markings?

Although the reproduction autos are very good copies of the original Lionel autos, there are a few subtle differences which set them apart from the genuine article. These differences are as follows:

1. LENGTH: Strange as it may seem, the reproduction autos are 1/16" shorter than the original ones. The difference can be seen by standing the cars upon their ends; the extra 1/16" in the original car appears to be in the door areas.

2. BODY PLASTIC: The plastic used on the original cars has a semi-gloss, very smooth finish to it. When the car is held up to the light, the viewer can see four translucent areas at each corner of the hood. The plastic used on the reproduction is somewhat duller in finish and a bit grainier; the translucent areas are far less apparent.

3. BODY TRIM: Minute bits of plastic flashing are sometimes left at the edges of the windows on the reproduction autos; this flashing is seldom seen on the genuine cars. The body and door rub strip which runs the entire length of the car's side is a little ragged on the reproduction cars, and the strip runs almost all the way to the headlights with just a barely discernible gap. On the genuine cars, the rub strip is smoothly executed, and there is a small but distinct gap between the end of the strip and the headlights.

4. WHEEL HOUSINGS: On the reproduction cars, the rubber wheels are larger and they fill up the entire space of the wheel wells. On the original cars, the rubber tires are made of a harder rubber compound, and they are smaller; they leave a distinct gap in the wheel well. In many cases, the original cars' rubber tires have a distinct patina of aging as well; this is absent from the reproduction cars' tires, for obvious reasons.

5. BASES: The underside of the original car is gloss black with a distinct shine; the lettering is sharply executed. On the reproduction cars, the base is a dull black, and the lettering is somewhat heavier than on the genuine cars.

6. LAP MARKS: In the plastics trade, a lap mark is a place where the liquid plastic knits together in the injection molding machine, sometimes leaving a faint but detectable line in the plastic. On the original cars, there is sometimes such a mark on the car's hood which runs from the rear of the hood just left of center and curves to hit the hood ornament, where it ends. No such mark is present on the reproduction cars, but these cars sometimes show a faint lap mark running down the center of the roof.

These remarks were compiled from the editor's observations and those of Richard Shanfeld and Joseph Bratspis, and several other knowledgeable collectors. We thank these gentlemen for their assistance.

Gd VG Exc Mt

6414 AUTO LOADER 1955-57, red base, 6511-2 mold, white letters, black metal superstructure. Cars are marked on underside "THE LIONEL CORPORATION / NEW YORK NEW YORK" at the rear and "MADE IN / U.S. OF AMERICA" at the front. See the preceding comments for a full discussion of the original and reproduction automobiles. Prices for excellent and mint entries below assume the presence of four genuine Lionel automobiles in more common varieties; subtract about $7.00 for each missing automobile.

(A) Premium cars with windshields, bumpers, rubber tires; car colors vary; most are yellow, red, blue and white. "6414" on right side of car, bar-end trucks, magnetic tab couplers.　　10　20　40　60
(B) Same as (A), but "6414" on left side, AAR trucks, two disc couplers. R. LaVoie and C. Rohlfing Collections.　　10　20　40　60
(C) Four red premium cars with gray non-chrome bumpers, bar-end trucks, magnetic tab couplers, "6414" on right.　　10　20　55　75
(D) Four cheap cars without bumpers, wheels or windshields, two red cars and two yellow cars; simulated wheels on the exterior with an interior space where the axle would have been attached; a red and a yellow car each have an attachment for axle, the other red and yellow cars do not, "6414" on left side; early AAR trucks, disc couplers, box marked "6414-85", cars with axle attachment stamped "4" under roof, while cars without axles attached are stamped "1" under roof. "PT. NO. 6068-3" stamped under cars with axle attachment. J. Sattler and J. Algozzini Collections.　　8　15　20　40
(E) Decal version made for Glen Uhl by Lionel; 200 reportedly made with black decals with yellow letters "6414 AUTO LOADER EVANS / EVANS", red autos with gray plastic bumpers and black wheels, late AAR trucks, one disc coupler, one fixed coupler; frame only lettered "LIONEL".
　　40　70　140　240
(F) 1966, four red premium cars with gray non-chrome bumpers, AAR trucks with disc operating couplers, "6414" on left. R. Hutchinson Collection.　　10　20　55　75
(G) Four dark brown premium cars with chrome bumpers, "6414" to right, bar-end trucks, magnetic couplers, mold 6511-2. These automobiles are very hard to find. A. Tom Collection.　　10　20　115　175
(H) Four medium green premium cars with chrome bumpers, "6414" to left, AAR plastic trucks, one disc and one fixed coupler. These green autos are possibly the hardest ones to find of all. A. Tom Collection.
　　10　20　155　225
(I) Four yellow premium cars with gray bumpers, "6414" on left, two operating couplers. L. Savage Collection.　　12　20　50　75
(J) Four brown premium autos with gray bumpers, "6414" on right. These autos are very hard to find. J. Sattler and J. Algozzini Collections, B. Stekoll comment.　　12　20　115　175
(K) Four green premium cars with gray bumpers, "6414" on left, early AAR trucks, disc couplers. These autos are very difficult to find. Another example of this combination has turned up in the collection of A. Arpino, but other details are lacking. J. Sattler Collection.　　—　—　—　400
(L) Same as (A), but autos are found in dark cream, gold, ivory (not white) and purple (not blue or aqua). J. Algozzini Collection.　　NRS
(M) Same as (B), but mold 6511-2, black plastic flatcar base instead of usual red. J. Algozzini Collection.　　NRS

6416 BOAT LOADER CAR 1961-63, red base, 6511-2 mold, white letters, black metal superstructure with white letters, four boats, early AAR trucks, disc couplers. CAUTION: The blue boats were made for Lionel by Athearn and have no lettering. Currently Athearn is making boats with red hull, brown interior piece and white top. These are readily available at $5.00 each. It is believed by some authorities that only boats with blue tops, brown interior pieces and white hulls are original. If this view becomes widely accepted, it will substantially affect the values noted below. However, see notes for individual entries. Reader comments invited.
(A) Boats with white hull, blue top, brown interior piece. J. Sattler Collection. This is the most common variety; P. Ambrose comment.
　　25　40　60　125
(B) Boats with red hull, top and interior piece. G. Wilson Collection.
　　40　70　100　150
(C) Boats with white hull, blue top, red inner piece. S. Blotner Collection.
　　25　40　60　125
(D) Boats with red hull, white top, white inner piece. This boat may have been more properly included with an HO piece instead of the 6416. H. Powell comment. However, P. Ambrose believes that some cars did come with red-hulled boats, especially if Lionel ran short of the normal white-hulled boats. Note that since red-hulled boats are currently being made by Athearn, they may have been placed with cars which did not originally have them. Hence, there should be no difference in value between this version and (B) above. M. Ocilka Collection.
　　40　70　100　150
(E) Boats with white hull, red top and black inner shells. M. Ocilka comment.　　25　40　60　125

Four depressed-center flatcars. Top shelf: two cars with transformer loads. Bottom shelf: two cars with cable reel loads.

(F) Two boats with white hulls, blue tops and brown interiors and two boats with blue hulls, white tops and brown interiors. R. Lord Collection.

                   **25   40   60   125**

**NOTE:** Boats with red hull, white deck and brown inner shell are apparently being reproduced and are indistinguishable from the originals. H. Powell, P. Catalano and P. Ambrose comments.

**6418 FLAT WITH U.S. STEEL GIRDERS** 1955-57, depressed-center, die-cast gray body, four trucks with bar-ends, magnetic tab couplers, two brakewheels. For O Gauge only, will not pass through O-27 switches. With datable pieces, we should be able to determine the production years of the variations below. F. Knight and P. Ambrose comments.

(A) Two all orange "LIONEL" girders. P. Catalano comment.

                   **17   30   40   75**

(B) Pinkish-orange girders with black "U.S. STEEL" lettering. P. Catalano comment.

                   **17   30   40   75**

(C) Black girders with white "U.S. STEEL" lettering, and "6418" on lower right. H. Degano comment.

                   **25   37   50   85**

(D) Red girders with white "U.S. STEEL" lettering. S. Blotner Collection.

                   **25   37   50   85**

(E) Black girders, black "LIONEL" lettering outlined in white, small box containing "BUILT BY LIONEL" to the left of the large "L" in "LIONEL". The same girders were commonly used on the 214 Plate Girder Bridge. R. Hutchinson comment, B. McLeavy Collection.   **25   37   50   85**

**6424 FLAT WITH TWO AUTOS** 1956-59, black plastic flatcar with white lettering, black metal superstructure to keep autos from falling off; bar-end trucks, magnetic tab couplers. Comments on automobiles and values found in 6414 entry apply here as well. This car is usually found with two of the more common premium autos — white, yellow, turquoise or red.

(A) 1956, mold 6424-11, Die 1, bar-end trucks, magnetic tab couplers, number on right. J. Kotil and R. LaVoie Collections.   **8   15   30   50**

(B) 1957, mold 6424-11, Die 2, AAR trucks, disc couplers, number on right. J. Kotil Collection.   **8   15   30   50**

(C) Mold 6511-2, AAR trucks, disc couplers, number on left. J. Kotil and R. Gluckman Collections.   **8   15   30   50**

(D) Same as (A), but red flatcar.   **12   25   65   100**

(E) Same as (C), but red flatcar. J. Algozzini Collection.

                   **12   25   65   100**

(F) Same as (C), but mold 6424-11, Die 1. M. Ocilka Collection.

                   **8   15   30   50**

**6430 FLATCAR WITH COOPER-JARRETT VANS** 1955-58, red plastic base, mold 6511-2, white lettering; trucks are fastened to plate, plate slides into car.

(A) "6430" appears on right side of car, trailer mounting unit is screwed onto car; Cooper-Jarrett Van is gray plastic with an aluminum sign with an orange arrow and black lettering. J. Sattler Collection.   **7   15   30   45**

(B) "6430" appears on the left side of car, mold 6424-11; see next entry, 6431.   **7   15   30   45**

(C) Cooper-Jarrett Van in white plastic.   **7   15   30   45**

(D) 1955-58, two dark green plastic trailers, metal signs on sides lettered "Lionel Trains", small decal on right front of each trailer lettered "Fruehauf", also decal center top front of each trailer lettered "FRUE-HAUF Dura-Van", trailers with four rubber tires, bar-end metal trucks, magnetic tab couplers, one brakewheel. See 3460 entry for nearly identical car. H. Powell Collection.   **7   15   30   45**

(E) Same as (A), except Cooper-Jarrett signs are copper-colored, not aluminum. S. Blotner Collection.   **7   15   30   45**

This is the Midge Toy tractor included with the 6431 flatcar set. Note the plain box with its markings and the attachment of the tractor to the trailer. G. Halverson Collection, G. Stern photograph.

**6431 FLAT WITH VANS** 1966 only, red plastic flat with white lettering and numbers; "6430" appears on left side; 6431 is a special set with a Midge Toy tractor and two white unlettered trailers; the red die-cast tractor is marked: "Midge Toy, Rockford, Illinois, U.S.A., Patent 2775847", tractor

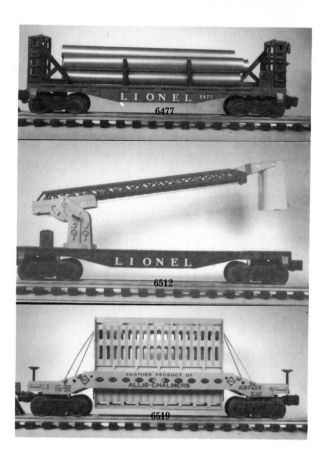

This is a view of the underside of the Midge Toy Tractor with the 6431 set. Note the embossed identification markings on the underside of the cab behind the front axle. G. Halverson Collection, G. Stern Photograph.

has fifth wheel, a plug that fits into an enlarged hole in the trailer; the trailer mounting bracket and the flatcar trucks are riveted to the car; AAR trucks, disc couplers, one brakewheel. The white vans used on this car were also used with the 461 loading platform accessory. The 6431 set came in two kinds of packaging. One version came in a 1966-style showing the flatcar and the two trailers through a plastic window and the tractor was located in the same box in a special area made from the box end flaps. The box was rubber-stamped 6431 on its end. It was also marked with part number 12-247. The (A) variation came with this packaging. R. Hutchinson and P. Ambrose comments.

The other version came in an enlarged box marked 6431 on its end with room for the Midge tractor and van in a separate white cardboard box marked "No. 1261". See photographs below. G. Halverson comments.

|  | Gd | VG | Exc | Mt |
|---|---|---|---|---|

(A) White vans, no slots for signs, flatcar mold 6424-11, die 3. G. Halverson and E. Heid Collections. 20 40 50 75

(B) Same as (A), but mold 6511-2. J. Algozzini Collection.

20 40 50 75

(C) Same as (B), but mold 6511-2, vans are bright yellow instead of white; they have slots for signs, but no signs. H. Powell, E. Heid and J. Algozzini Collections. 30 40 65 90

**6440 FLAT WITH VANS** Red unpainted plastic flatcar, mold 6511-2, white LIONEL lettering and "6440" to left, AAR plastic trucks.

(A) 1960, no van mounting units, two gray unpainted plastic vans with side slots for nameplates, but nameplates are absent, bottom of vans embossed "MADE IN U.S. OF AMERICA / THE LIONEL CORPORATION / NEW YORK, N.Y." in three lines, trailers have one two-wheel axle each, two disc couplers, box marked "No. 6440 FLATCAR WITH PIGGY BACK VANS". Blotner, Landry, Marshall, Shewmake, Surratt and Toone Collections.

15 30 60 75

(B) 1961, same as (A), except vans have "COOPER-JARRETT" nameplates and car has one disc-operating and one dummy coupler. M. Ocilka and E. Heid Collections. 15 30 60 75

(C) Same as (B), except two disc couplers. W. Sykes Collection.

15 30 60 75

**6461 TRANSFORMER CAR** 1949-50, gray die-cast depressed-center base, black lettering, black plastic transformer with decal with white lettering "Transformer" and L in circle, two brakewheels, steps, insulators sometimes broken, price quoted is for unbroken insulators, staple-end metal trucks, magnetic couplers, see color illustration. Lionel also made an earlier version with coil couplers numbered 2461. Like its earlier version, this car is very difficult to find with intact insulators on the transformer case. Broken, missing or glued insulators reduce the car's condition to Very Good, regardless of rest of car's condition. Replacement transformer pieces are available, but they have flexible plastic insulator poles, while the originals had brittle, shiny white insulator poles. R. Lord, T. Rollo and R. LaVoie observations.

(A) 1949, activator flap without extra hole and with round end rivet. J. Sattler Collection. 12 22 40 55

162

(B) 1950, activator flap with extra hole and flared end rivet. R. LaVoie Collection.                              **12  22  40  55**

**6467 BULKHEAD CAR**  1956, red flat with black bulkheads with stakes and white lettering, mold 6511-2, called "Miscellaneous Car", bar-end trucks, magnetic tab couplers. Did not come with Liquified Gases tank. See next entry.                              **13  25  35  50**

**6469 LIONEL LIQUIFIED GASES**  1963, red flatcar, white letters, no numbers, large liquified gas cylinder lettered "Lionel", "ERIE" and "6469". 6467 is often found with this liquified gas cylinder but it did not come with it; AAR trucks, disc couplers, see color illustration.
(A) Mold 6424-11, Die 4. M. Ocilka Collection.  **25  40  65  100**
(B) Mold 6511-2, four holes as used on 6805 are plugged. A. Arpino Collection.                           **25  40  65  100**

**6475**  Vat Cars. See Chapter XII, Tank And Vat Cars.

**6477 BULKHEAD CAR WITH PLASTIC PIPES**  1957-58, red base, black bulkheads, white letters, stakes, came with five plastic pipes as load, R. Cretelle and C. Rohlfing comments. Despite our name for it, the box end is labeled "NO. 6477 / MISCELLANEOUS / CAR", mold 6511-2.
(A) Bar-end trucks, magnetic tab couplers. J. Sattler and R. LaVoie Collections.                          **15  25  40  60**
(B) AAR trucks, disc couplers. R. Pauli Collection.  **15  25  40  60**
(C) One bar-end truck and one AAR truck; identical original riveting. K. Koehler Collection.                             **NRS**

**6500 FLAT WITH BONANZA PLANE**  1962, 1965, black flatcar, white lettering, no number on car, 6511-2 mold, AAR trucks, disc couplers, red and white plane, one wing lettered "N2742B", see color illustration. Very hard to find with intact plane.
(A) Plane has red top and white bottom. P. Catalano comment.
                                         **40  85  140  200**
(B) Plane has white top, red bottom. P. Catalano comment.
                                      **50  100  210  325**
(C) Same as (B), but gray "General" flatcar. S. Blotner Collection.
                                      **50  100  250  400**

**6501 FLAT WITH JET BOAT**  1963, red base, white-lettered "LIONEL", no numbers on side of frame, mold 6511-2, AAR trucks, disc couplers, boat with white hull, brown top, brown deck, no lettering, boat uses baking soda mixed with water to create a gas given off at nozzle. J. Sattler Collection.
                                         **17  30  40  70**

**6502-50 FLAT WITH BRIDGE GIRDER**  1962, also illustrated in 1963 Advance catalogue with set 11415. No number, blue unpainted plastic car, mold 6511-2, orange unpainted Lionel 214 bridge side, AAR trucks, fixed couplers.
(A) Blue unpainted plastic. J. Sattler Collection.  **10  15  20  35**
(B) Deeper blue unpainted plastic.                **10  15  20  35**
(C) Same as (A), but one disc coupler, one fixed coupler.  **10  15  20  35**

**6502-75 FLAT WITH BRIDGE GIRDER**  1962.
(A) Black flatcar with orange girder, mold 6511-2, no number on car, car has "LIONEL" in white serif lettering, arch-bar trucks with two non-operating couplers. Possibly part of Sears set. J. Bratspis Collection.
                                         **10  25  40  60**
(B) Blue car with white lettering and orange girder, mold 6511-2, Morse observation.                             **NRS**

**6511 FLAT WITH PIPES**  1953-56, 6511-2 mold, white lettering, black stakes, three aluminum-colored plastic pipes, bar-end trucks, stamped-steel truck mounting plate.
(A) Brown flatcar, white lettering, magnetic tab couplers. J. Sattler Collection.                             **6  12  20  30**
(B) Dark red flatcar, white lettering, magnetic couplers.
                                         **6  12  20  30**
(C) 1953, same as (B), but die-cast truck mounting bracket. C. Rohlfing and R. LaVoie Collections.              **6  12  20  30**

**6512 CHERRY PICKER CAR**  1962-63, black or blue base, mold 6511-2, white letters, no number on car, orange structure at end of ladder with gray man inside, structure swivels to outside, black metal ladder extends twice the length of unextended ladder, gray superstructure holds ladder, AAR trucks, disc couplers.
(A) Black base. J. Sattler Collection.             **19  35  50  85**
(B) Blue base.                                   **NRS**

**6518 TRANSFORMER CAR**  1956-58, gray-painted die-cast depressed-center car, black transformer with white lettering "LIONEL / TRANSFOR-MER / CAR", white plastic insulators which are easily broken (but more flexible than those of the 2461 or 6461), four bar-end trucks, magnetic couplers with tabs, two brakewheels, for O Gauge only, will not pass through O-27 switches. W. Knight comment.  **18  35  55  85**

**6519 ALLIS-CHALMERS**  1958-61, condenser car, orange base, blue letters, gray condenser held by metal wires, two brakewheels; wires and brakewheels often broken or missing, AAR trucks, disc couplers.
(A) Orange base, light blue lettering. R. Gluckman Collection.
                                         **25  35  50  75**
(B) Darker orange base, darker blue lettering. R. Gluckman Collection.
                                         **25  35  50  75**
(C) With metal trucks, not known if variation (A) or (B).  **NRS**

**6544 MISSILE FIRING CAR**  1960-64, blue frame, gray launcher, red firing knob, four white small rockets, AAR trucks, disc couplers, two brakewheels.
(A) White-lettered console. H. Degano comment.    **14  23  33  55**
(B) Black-lettered console. H. Degano comment.    **20  35  70  110**

**6561 REEL CAR WITH DEPRESSED CENTER**  1953-56, die-cast gray or brown frame, usually black lettering "6561 LIONEL LINES 6561", two plastic reels marked "LIONEL", wound with aluminum coil, same base as searchlight car with modification to hold reels, steps, two brakewheels, bar-end trucks, elasticized cord with clips holds reels in place. See color illustration. We have had reports of reels for this car in several different configurations, but this car originally only came with the wide aluminum wire. Lionel also sold these reels with wire for layouts; that is why some cars show up with insulated wire on these reels, or even reels which are empty. Cars from original sets apparently always came with the wide aluminum wire. The gray plastic reels with this wire are somewhat more difficult to find with the car than are the orange reels. G. Wilson and P. Ambrose comments.
(A) Gray plastic reels, gray frame. J. Sattler Collection.  **15  25  35  55**
(B) Gray plastic reels, brown frame, silver lettering. J. Sattler Collection.
                                         **13  30  50  80**
(C) Deep orange plastic reels, gray frame. J. Sattler Collection.
                                         **10  20  30  40**
(D) Light orange plastic reels, gray frame. J. Sattler and R. LaVoie Collections.                            **10  20  30  40**
(E) Same as (D), but light glossy frame finish. J. Algozzini Collection.
                                         **10  20  30  40**
(F) Same as (D), but darker glossy frame finish. J. Algozzini Collection.
                                         **10  20  30  40**

**6630 IRBM LAUNCHER**  1960-64, black car, white letters, mold 6511-2, blue superstructure with black missile firing ramp, pushing levers cock launching unit, ramp rises to a 30 to 45 degree angle prior to takeoff due to air pressure generated by bellows at front end, arch-bar trucks with fixed couplers; made for Sears set. G. Wilson, J. Keen and C. Rohlfing comments.
(A) Red rocket tail section, white top, blue tip. J. Keen Collection.
                                         **17  35  45  65**
(B) All-red rocket with blue tip. G. Wilson Collection.  **17  35  45  65**

**6640 USMC LAUNCHER**  1960, olive drab car and superstructure, black firing ramp, see 6630 for explanation of mechanism, white rocket with blue tip, AAR trucks, disc couplers, mold 6511-2. J. Sattler Collection.
                                         **25  40  65  100**

**6650 IRBM LAUNCHER**  1959-63, red car base, blue superstructure, white letters, black firing ramp, white and red missile with blue nose, same mechanism used for 6630, see 6630 for explanation, early AAR trucks, disc couplers.
(A) Mold 6424-11, Die 2. M. Ocilka Collection     **13  25  35  60**
(B) Mold 6511-2, came as part of set 2549W in 1960. J. Sattler and J. Algozzini Collections.               **13  25  35  60**
(C) Mold 6424-11, Die 3, C. Rohlfing Collection.  **12  25  35  60**

**6651 U S M C CANNON**  Circa 1960-61, not catalogued, olive drab car, gun and superstructure, mold 6511-2, white lettering "BUILT BY / LIONEL / U.S.M.C. / 6651", fires three or four projectiles, silver-painted wooden projectiles 1-7/8" long, early AAR trucks, disc-operating couplers, came with uncatalogued set headed by 221 USMC Alco diesel. D. McCarthy and J. Sattler Collections.                        **17  35  50  75**

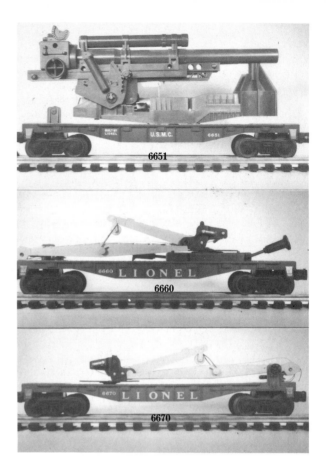

**6660 FLATCAR WITH CRANE**  1958, dark red flat, mold 6424-11, white lettering with "6660" to left of serif "LIONEL", black sub base, black rotating base, outriggers, ochre boom, early AAR trucks, disc couplers.
(A) Silver crank handles, hook on cable end. P. Catalano comment.

|    |    |    |    |
|----|----|----|----|
| 17 | 35 | 55 | 70 |

(B) Black crank handles, round bar magnet inside of red plastic housing on cable end. P. Catalano comment.  **17  35  55  70**
(C) Same as (A), but mold 6511-2. R. Gluckman Collection.

**17  35  55  70**

**6670 FLATCAR WITH BOOM**  1959-60, red unpainted body, yellow boom, no outriggers, AAR trucks, disc-operating couplers.  Note that three varieties follow.  We would like to learn which of these types came with which sets.
(A) Darker red body, mold 6511-2, "6670" to right of "LIONEL". D. Fleming Collection.  **13  25  35  50**
(B) Brighter red body, mold 6424-11, Die 2, "6670" to left of "LIONEL". D. Fleming Collection.  **13  25  35  50**
(C) Same as (B), but mold 6511-2. L. Savage and J. Algozzini Collections.

**13  25  35  50**
(D) Same as (A), but number to left of "LIONEL". F. S. Davis Collection.

**13  25  35  50**

**6800 FLAT WITH AIRPLANE**  1957-60, red car, black and yellow Beechcraft Bonanza airplane with retractable landing gear and folding wings; plane is marked on bottom "No. 6800-60 AIRPLANE / THE LIONEL CORPORATION / NEW YORK N Y / MADE IN U. S. OF AMERICA". I.D. Smith comments.
(A) Plane with black upper and yellow lower fuselage, 6424-11 mold, Dies 2 or 3, AAR trucks, disc couplers, "6800" to left of "LIONEL". J. Sattler Collection.  Also came in box marked "NO. 6800 / FLATCAR / WITH / AIRPLANE" as part of Sears set 79N09657. I.D. Smith observation.

**20  35  60  80**
(B) Plane with yellow upper and black lower fuselage, 6424-11 mold, Die 1B, metal trucks attach via metal plates attached by slot-head screws, "6800" to right of "LIONEL".  **20  35  60  80**

(C) Same as (A), but lighter red flatcar body, mold 6424-11, Die 2. M. Ocilka Collection.  **20  35  60  80**
(D) Same as (A), but plane is labeled "BONANZA" in rubber-stamped lettering on fuselage. "Triple T" Collection.  **NRS**
(E) Plane with yellow upper and black lower fuselage, mold 6511-2, late AAR trucks, disc couplers; this is the most common of the four major airplane variations. P. Catalano comment, J. Letterese Collection.

**20  35  60  80**
(F) Same as (A), but bar-end trucks with tab couplers, mold 6424-11, Die 1. C. Rohlfing Collection.  **20  35  60  80**

**6801 FLAT WITH BOAT**  1957-60, red plastic body, white lettering, boat usually with cream deck and clear windshield, boat numbered 6801-60 and available separately in box marked in that way (see Accessory chapter), AAR trucks, disc couplers, "6801" usually left of "LIONEL".
(A) Turquoise boat hull, flatcar mold 6511-2.  **12  22  40  55**
(B) Same as (A), but mold 6424-11, Die 2. Warswick Collection.

**12  22  40  55**
(C) Medium blue hull, flatcar mold 6511-2. R. LaVoie Collection.

**12  22  40  55**
(D) Brownish-yellow hull, flatcar mold not known.  **12  22  40  55**
(E) White hull, brown deck, no number in boat, bar-end trucks, metal plates fasten trucks to base, "6801" to right of "LIONEL", flatcar mold 6511-2. R. Gluckman Collection.  **12  22  40  55**

**6802 FLAT WITH BRIDGE**  1958-59, red flat, white lettering, black plastic bridge sides lettered in white "U.S. STEEL", one brakewheel, "6802" to left of "LIONEL", early AAR trucks, disc couplers.
(A) Flatcar mold 6424-11, Die 2. J. Sattler Collection.  **5  10  15  25**
(B) Flatcar mold 6511-2. R. Pauli Collection.  **5  10  15  25**

**6803 FLATCAR WITH TANK AND TRUCK**  1958-59, two gray U.S.M.C. vehicles, tank and truck with microwave disc, early AAR trucks, disc couplers.
(A) Mold 6424-11, Die 2. J. Sattler Collection.  **25  50  85  125**
(B) Mold 6511-2. J. Algozzini Collection.  **25  50  85  125**

6804 **FLAT WITH U S M C TRUCKS** 1958-59, red plastic flat, white lettering, "6804" to left of "LIONEL", gray U.S.M.C. trucks, one with microwave disc, one with two guns.

| | | | | |
|---|---|---|---|---|
| (A) Mold 6424-11, Die 2. J. Sattler Collection. | 25 | 50 | 85 | 125 |
| (B) Mold 6511-2. J. Algozzini Collection. | 25 | 50 | 85 | 125 |

6805 **ATOMIC DISPOSAL FLATCAR** 1958-59, red plastic car, mold 6424-11, Die 3, white letters, "6805" on left side, two Super O rails run car length, two removable grayish-tan or gray disposal containers with "RADIOACTIVE WASTE" in black and "DANGER" in red, each letter of "DANGER" is underlined, containers have red flashing lights, bar-end metal trucks, magnetic tab couplers. The Fundimensions reissue comes with gray canisters. However, they can be differentiated from the Lionel canisters rather easily. The Lionel canisters are black plastic painted gray; the mold number inside is 6805-6 with either a 1 or a 2 opposite the mold stamping. (The mold made two canisters at a time, and these numbers showed which side of the mold made the individual canister. The same process is used with gondola cars.) The words "RADIOACTIVE WASTE" are slightly larger than those found on Fundimensions reproductions. In addition, the Fundimensions canisters are unpainted gray plastic, rather than black plastic painted gray. I.D. Smith, J. Lebo and R. LaVoie Comments.

| | | | | |
|---|---|---|---|---|
| (A) Gray canisters. | 13 | 25 | 45 | 65 |
| (B) Grayish-tan canisters. | 13 | 25 | 45 | 65 |
| (C) Unpainted bright red plastic body, mold 6424-11, "LIONEL" in white serif lettering, no number on car, black plastic canisters painted light gray, black and red lettering on containers, arch-bar trucks, one operating and one dummy coupler. R. Shanfeld Collection. | 13 | 25 | 45 | 65 |

6806 **FLAT WITH U S M C TRUCKS** 1958-59, red plastic flat, mold 6424-11, Die 2, white lettering, "6806" on left side, AAR trucks, disc couplers.

(A) Two gray plastic U.S.M.C. trucks: one with radar disc truck, other a hospital truck with U.S. Navy insignia on van rear. The U.S.M.C. trucks on this and other similar cars are lettered "PYRO / MADE IN / U.S.A" on underside. P. Ambrose comment.     25     50     85     125

(B) Gray U.S.M.C. radar disc truck, and gray plastic open-windowed snack bar truck with lettering "MOBILE USO CANTEEN" with small chimney, door with white anchor. Lionel Train & Seashell Museum comment.     **NRS**

| | | | | |
|---|---|---|---|---|
| (C) Same as (A), but mold 6511-2. J. Algozzini Collection. | 25 | 50 | 85 | 125 |
| (D) Same as (A), but one gray truck with loudspeakers instead of hospital truck. G. Wilson Collection. | 25 | 50 | 85 | 125 |

6807 **LIONEL FLAT WITH BOAT** 1958-59, red plastic flat.

| | | | | |
|---|---|---|---|---|
| (A) Mold 6511-2, white lettering, "6807" on left, large gray amphibious-type boat, known as DKW, made by Pyro, early AAR trucks, disc couplers. G. Wilson Collection. | 21 | 35 | 50 | 80 |
| (B) Same as (A), but 6424-11 mold, Die 2. L. Savage Collection. | 21 | 35 | 50 | 80 |

6808 **LIONEL FLAT WITH U S M C TRUCKS** 1958-59, red plastic flat, "6808" on left, early AAR trucks, disc couplers, one U.S.M.C. gray mobile searchlight truck, one gray two-gun tank.

| | | | | |
|---|---|---|---|---|
| (A) Mold 6424-11, Die 2. | 25 | 50 | 85 | 125 |
| (B) Mold 6511-2. J. Algozzini Collection. | 25 | 50 | 85 | 125 |

6809 **LIONEL FLAT WITH U.S.M.C. TRUCKS** 1958-59, red plastic flat, mold 6424-11, Die 2, white lettering, "6809" on left, early AAR trucks, disc couplers, gray U.S.M.C. trucks: one with cannon, other hospital van with U.S. Navy insignia.

| | | | | |
|---|---|---|---|---|
| (A) Hospital van with Navy insignia on one side. | 25 | 50 | 85 | 125 |
| (B) Hospital van with Navy insignia on both sides. | 25 | 50 | 85 | 125 |
| (C) Same as (B), but mold 6511-2. J. Algozzini and F. Cordone Collections. | 25 | 50 | 85 | 125 |

6810 **LIONEL FLAT WITH TRAILER** 1958, red plastic flat, mold 6424-11, white lettering, "6810" on left, AAR trucks, disc couplers, white trailer, black-painted plate with copper-colored arrow, black and white-lettered "COOPER JARRETT INC".     9     15     20     30

6812 **TRACK MAINTENANCE CAR** 1959, red plastic flat, white lettering "6812" on left of "LIONEL" on frame, 6511-2 mold, early AAR trucks, disc couplers, superstructure with two blue men, platform cranks up and if cranked up far enough will come out.

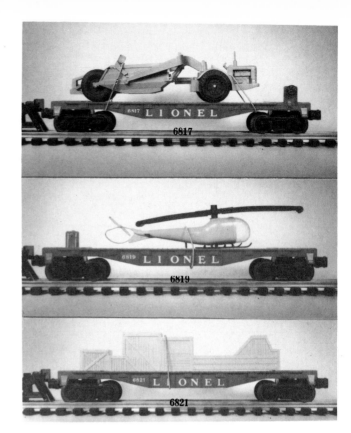

| | Gd | VG | Exc | Mt |
|---|---|---|---|---|
| (A) All-dark yellow-gold superstructure. J. Algozzini Collection. | 9 | 17 | 30 | 45 |
| (B) Black base and gray top, flatcar mold 6511-2. J. Algozzini Collection. | 9 | 17 | 30 | 45 |
| (C) Gray base, black top. J. Sattler Collection. | 9 | 17 | 30 | 45 |
| (D) All-cream base and top. J. Sattler Collection. | 25 | 40 | 75 | 115 |
| (E) Dark yellow base, gray top. Askenas comment. | | | | NRS |
| (F) Black base, black top. Askenas comment. | | | | NRS |
| (G) Black base, dark yellow top. Askenas comment. | | | | NRS |
| (H) Light yellow base and top. P. Iurilli Collection, Askenas comment. | | | | NRS |
| (I) All-gold superstructure. J. Algozzini Collection. | | | | NRS |
| (J) Same as (A), but mold 6424-11, Die 3. F. S. Davis Collection. | 9 | 17 | 30 | 45 |
| (K) Same as (H), but mold 6424-11, Die 3. F. S. Davis Collection. | | | | NRS |

**6816 FLAT WITH ALLIS-CHALMERS BULLDOZER** 1959-60, red or black plastic flat, white letters, "6816" on left, early AAR trucks, disc couplers, orange plastic Allis-Chalmers bulldozer, black rubber treads, lettered "HD 16 Diesel" and "Torque Converter".

| | Gd | VG | Exc | Mt |
|---|---|---|---|---|
| (A) Red plastic car, mold 6511-2. | 20 | 50 | 80 | 120 |
| (B) Black plastic car, mold 6424-11, die 4. Wirtz and M. Ocilka Collections. | 20 | 50 | 80 | 120 |
| (C) Red plastic car, mold 6424-11 Die 2. M. Ocilka Collection. | 20 | 50 | 80 | 120 |
| (D) Same as (A), but lighter orange bulldozer. J. Algozzini Collection. | 20 | 50 | 80 | 120 |
| (E) Same as (C), but lighter orange bulldozer. J. Sattler Collection. | 20 | 50 | 80 | 120 |
| (F) Red plastic flatcar, mold 6424-11, Die 4, bulldozer lettered in black only "TORQUE CONVERTER", does not include "HD 16 DIESEL", the words "TORQUE CONVERTER" are centered on the bulldozer side, "ALLIS CHALMERS" is in white behind the bulldozer seat. D. Fleming and E. Heid Collections. | 20 | 50 | 80 | 120 |

See also Factory Errors.

**6817 FLAT WITH ALLIS-CHALMERS SCRAPER** 1959-60, red plastic flat, white letters, "6817" on left, early AAR trucks, disc couplers, orange plastic scraper with black rubber tires.

| | Gd | VG | Exc | Mt |
|---|---|---|---|---|
| (A) 6424-11, Die 2. J. Sattler Collection. | 20 | 50 | 80 | 120 |
| (B) 6511-2 mold. M. Ocilka observation. | 20 | 50 | 80 | 120 |

**6818 TRANSFORMER CAR** 1958, red plastic base, white lettering on frame: "6818 LIONEL", one brakewheel, black plastic transformer with white heat-stamped lettering "LIONEL / TRANSFORMER / CAR" on one side on some cars and both sides on others, early AAR trucks, disc couplers.

| | Gd | VG | Exc | Mt |
|---|---|---|---|---|
| (A) Base mold 6424-11, Die 2. R. LaVoie Collection. | 5 | 10 | 25 | 35 |
| (B) Base mold 6511-2, transformer lettering on both sides in white lettering: "LIONEL / TRANSFORMER / CAR" with "6818" to left of "LIONEL". Came in box marked "No. 6818 / FLATCAR / WITH / TRANSFORMER / LIONEL"; box flap has 6818-11, came with Sears set 79N09657. I.D. Smith observation, J. Sattler Collection. | 5 | 10 | 25 | 35 |

**6819 FLAT WITH HELICOPTER** 1959-60, red plastic car, mold 6424-11, Die 3, white lettering, "6819" on left, early AAR trucks, disc couplers, gray Type B helicopter with separate yellow plastic tail section, single black rotor, clear plastic nose, operating-type helicopter without launching mechanism. See 3419 for helicopter typology. M. Ocilka Collection.

    15   25   40   60

6820 Flat with Helicopter — does not have launching mechanism.

**6820 FLAT WITH HELICOPTER** 1960-61, light blue-painted black plastic flatcar, white letters, "6820" on left, mold 6424-11, Die 4, early AAR trucks, disc couplers, gray Type B "NAVY" helicopter, separate yellow plastic tail

section, single black rotor, clear plastic nose, with white and red "Little John" missiles fastened by red piece to helicopter, operating-type helicopter without launching mechanism. J. Sattler comments.

(A) As described above. J. Bratspis Collection.  25  50  85  150
(B) Same as (A), except darker blue flatcar. S. Blotner Collection.
25  50  85  150

**6821 FLAT WITH CRATES**  1959-60, red unpainted plastic flatcar, white lettering "6821" on left side. The same crate structure had been used on the 3444 Animated Gondola, except that here there is no slot for the operating lever, and the two screw holes in the crate structure are plugged. Additionally, these crates have no lettering. G. Wilson and P. Ambrose comments.

(A) Mold 6424-11, Die 3 or 4. M. Ocilka Collection.  10  15  20  30
(B) Mold 6511-2. C. Rohlfing Collection.  10  15  20  30

**6822 SEARCHLIGHT CAR**  See "Cranes and Searchlights".

**6823 FLAT WITH IRBM MISSILES**  1959-60, red plastic car, white lettering, "6823" on left, AAR trucks, disc couplers, two red and white missiles with blue tips, front of one missile fits into rear of other missile, same missiles as on 6630 and 6640 missile launching cars.

(A) Mold 6424-11, Die 3.  15  25  35  50
(B) Mold 6511-2. K. Koehler Collection.  15  25  35  50
(C) Same as (A), but all-white rockets. (See photo below.) 15  25  35  50

This is the 6823 flatcar with Nike IRBM missiles in their cradles. Note the all-white rockets on the lower car and the "nesting" of the missiles in their racks.

**6825 FLAT WITH TRESTLE BRIDGE**  1959-62, red plastic car, mold 6511-2, white lettering, "6825" on left side, early AAR trucks, disc couplers, with bridge designed for HO rolling stock. G. Wilson and P. Ambrose comments.

(A) Black bridge.  12  18  25  40
(B) Gray bridge.  8  15  20  30
(C) Same as (A), but mold 6424-11, Die 3, "6825" on right side of "LIONEL" lettering. G. Halverson, R. Gluckman and F. Cieri Collections.
15  20  30  50
(D) Same as (A), but mold 6511-2, black lettering, pink-orange flatcar body. R. Gluckman Collection.  NRS
(E) Same as (A), but mold 6424-11, Die 4. F. Cordone Collection.
12  18  25  40

**6826 FLAT WITH CHRISTMAS TREES**  1959-60, red plastic base, mold 6511-2, "6826" on left, early AAR trucks, disc couplers, several scrawny trees. Hard to find with original trees. J. Sattler Collection.
15  25  40  75

**6827 FLAT WITH P & H STEAM SHOVEL**  1960-63, black plastic car, mold 6424-11, Die 4, white lettering, "6827" on left side followed by "LIONEL", AAR trucks, disc couplers, came as kit, shown assembled. M. Ocilka comments. Originally came with small booklet, "P & H: The Story of a Trademark", and an unusual 6827-113 instruction sheet which had a large yellow image of the steam shovel overprinted on the usual black and white instruction sheet. I.D. Smith and P. Catalano comments. Reader comments needed:  Did this steam shovel come with both black and gray rubber treads?

(A) Light yellow unpainted plastic steam shovel lettered in black in front of side door:  "QUALITY / P & H / SERVICE" inside of an oval; not illustrated. R. Davis Collection.  14  30  45  70
(B) Dark yellow unpainted plastic steam shovel lettered in black behind door:  "MAGNE TORQUE" inside of rectangle with double circle over rectangle, illustrated in text. R. Davis Collection.  14  30  45  70

**6828 FLAT WITH P & H CRANE**  1960-63, 1968, black or red plastic flatcar, mold 6424-11, Die 4, "6828" on left, AAR trucks, disc couplers, crane with black chassis, yellow or yellow-orange cab, lettered "HARNISCHFEGER MILWAUKEE WISCONSIN" and "P & H" embossed on cab and on boom near top. Originally came with same booklet as 6827, above, and 6828-149 instruction sheet pictured and lettered like that of the 6827.

Gd VG Exc Mt

Equipped with metal hook, part 6560-13. I.D. Smith and P. Catalano comments, A. Arpino Collection. Reader comments invited: Did this crane come with both black and gray treads?

(A) Yellow cab, black flatcar.      16   25   45   80

(B) Yellow-orange cab, red flatcar. Mold number for this car needed.
     16   25   45   80

**6830 FLAT WITH NON-OPERATING SUBMARINE** 1960-61, blue plastic car, mold 6511-2, white letters, "6830" on left, AAR trucks, disc couplers. Came with factory-assembled "U.S. NAVY SUBMARINE 6830", gray with black letters. The winding nose on this sub did not turn, and the submarine does not have the drive mechanism parts: 3, 5, 6, 8, 11 and 21, which came with the 3330 submarine kit or the factory assembled 3830. See Greenberg reprint of Lionel Service Manual, pp. V-157-58. P. Ambrose and I.D. Smith comments.      16   25   40   60

**6844 FLAT WITH MISSILES** 1959-60, black plastic flatcar, mold 6424-11, Die 1, also Die 4, white lettering, "6844" to left, early AAR trucks, disc couplers, gray superstructure holds six white Lionel missiles.

(A) As described above. M. Ocilka and I.D. Smith Collections.
     16   25   35   60

(B) Same as (A), but red unpainted plastic flatcar, light gray missile superstructure. A. Tom and G. Halverson Collections.   20   50   90   150

**NO NUMBER** See also 1877, 3309, 3349, 6401, 6401-50 and 6406.

One of the areas for future research is determining the catalogue numbers and loads of the no-number flatcars, gondolas, cabooses and hoppers produced by Lionel. The following is a listing of reported cars. One method of identification is from original boxes and / or original set components. If you have "no number" cars in original boxes or with original sets, we would appreciate very much your assistance.

**Short Flatcars:**

(A) Olive drab flatcar. See 6401-50.      1   1.50   2   3

(B) Gray flatcar with green tank. The flatcar is embossed with mold 1877-3 and also embossed "MADE IN U.S. OF AMERICA / THE LIONEL CORPORATION / NEW YORK, N.Y." on its underside. No other lettering or numbering is present on the car. Car has late AAR plastic trucks with one disc and one dummy coupler. The moss-green tank has a swivel turret and two molded green plastic wheel / axle sets. The tank is lettered "Q" inside the turret and "5" or "S" on underside. The turret can be removed with care. This car came in a military set made for Sears with a 240 locomotive. For details of this set, see the entries for the 240 steam locomotive and the 3666 cannon-firing boxcar. J. Sattler, Vergonet, Bohn and Jarman Collections.      50   100   150   200

(C) Gray plastic car with two orange LIONEL reels. See 6402.

(D) Yellow-painted, stamped-steel flatcar, black-lettered "LIONEL". See 6121-25.

**10" Flatcars:**

(A) Red plastic flatcar, mold 6511-2, white-lettered "LIONEL" (serif or sans-serif?), AAR trucks, one disc coupler, one fixed coupler. Pauli Collection.      1   1.50   2   3

(B) Same as (A), but two fixed couplers.      1   1.50   2   3

(C) Unpainted tuscan flatcar with yellow autos. See 6406.

(D) Red plastic flatcar, mold 6511-2, serif white-lettered "LIONEL", arch-bar trucks, two fixed couplers, no brakewheel. J. Kotil Collection.
     1   1.50   2   3

(E) Same as (D), but no lettering, AAR trucks.   1   1.50   2   3

(F) Black plastic flatcar, mold 6511-2, serif white-lettered "LIONEL" arch-bar trucks, two fixed couplers, no brakewheel. J. Kotil Collection.
     1   1.50   2   3

(G) Blue plastic flatcar, mold 6511-2, no lettering, arch-bar trucks, two fixed couplers, no brakewheel. J. Kotil Collection.   1   1.50   2   3

(H) Same as (G), but AAR trucks. J. Kotil Collection.   1   1.50   2   3

(I) Red 10" flatcar, white "LIONEL", no number, arch-bar trucks, fixed couplers, no brakewheel, no load, 6511-2 mold. R. Schreiner Collection.
     **NRS**

(J) Red 10" flatcar lettered "LIONEL" with large red, white and blue rocket. Blue nose of rocket is Mercury capsule, mold 6511-2, AAR trucks, fixed couplers. See 6407.

# Chapter VII

# GONDOLAS

Top shelf: 6462 with "N" in second panel and 1002 scout gondola. Middle shelf: 6462 and 1002. Bottom shelf: 6562 and 1002.

## DATING LIONEL'S GONDOLAS:  1945 - 1969

### By Richard Vagner

### 2452 / 6462 / 6452 CARS

In 1945, at the end of the Second World War, Lionel produced a single train set which consisted of reruns of prewar cars except for one new car, the black 2452 Pennsylvania gondola. (Editor's Note: See Robert Swanson's article on the 1945 Lionel Set in this edition.) There were not many of these train sets made during the limited time period following the end of hostilities and the first Christmas season that followed. There is an interesting question about when the die for this car was made. According to the 1945 annual report of The Lionel Corporation on May 7, 1945, the War Production Board rescinded order L-81 which had restricted the use of metal to the toy industry. The Corporation reported that its plans for reconversion and "several new items are well advanced". Hence it is likely that sufficient time existed for creation of the new gondola die. There is also another possibility — that the die was made during the war period when Lionel realized the potential of using this type of plastic for trains. Lionel was an acknowledged leader in this field, and it is logical that the firm had some wartime experience in molding this plastic. The fact that none of these gondolas have been found from the prewar period seems significant in light of the fact that the same type

of detailing was used on many of the "semi-scale" cars Lionel made in the late 1930s, and the lack of any examples from this period.

Another question along the same lines concerns when the dies for the postwar coupler were created. An answer may lie in something A. C. Gilbert did at American Flyer. The changeover from O Gauge to S Gauge meant that the new American Flyer trains were not compatible with previous trains. The wartime break gave American Flyer the opportunity to make the change at a time when they did not have to worry about demand and the lack of compatibility. Did Lionel follow the same line of reasoning with the new coupler since it was not compatible with the old type? Since the coupler uses a similar type of uncoupling mechanism to the prewar type, Lionel may have been on the verge of changing and the wartime break gave them the needed chance to make the change without the compatibility problems that would have been involved.

The Lionel 2452 gondola is a fascinating piece to study, since it shows how complex the design and manufacturing process is on a relatively simple item. It also shows vividly the continuing concern with manufacturing and assembly costs as they relate to the changes over the years. This gondola is abundant and relatively inexpensive and makes a good research candidate. The changes allow dating to each year between 1945 and 1949.

Lionel made the 2452 with and without brakewheels. The top gondola, 2452 has brakewheels (see lower right corner). The lower gondola 2452X does not have brakewheels. Note that both cars have the earliest version of the coil coupler with the flying pickup shoe. This assembly was easily broken. Notice that the upper gondola has lost its shoe on the right truck. R. Vagner Collection.

With its new coupling system, Lionel also introduced new trucks, new wheels and new axles. As with the innovations of the late 1930s, problems arose with the new products which led to a series of rapid changes in the problem areas. The early coil coupler mounting bracket was made from cloth impregnated with rosin. This material is called phenolic fiberboard. The phenolic board proved to be very fragile and was probably difficult to assemble. The prewar style pickup shoe was riveted to a small metal brace which in turn was fastened to the marcarta board by two small tabs. The marcarta board was mounted to the truck by a pin and slot arrangement, and the entire assembly has proved to be nearly impossible to repair successfully. The small coil that activated the coupler must have been a source of problems, since many of them when found today are inoperable.

This earliest unit was soon replaced by a much sturdier and simpler unit which fits over the axles; this unit can be replaced by simply popping the wheels and axles out of the trucks and changing the entire coupler assembly. The late coil coupler still utilizes the pickup shoe and the coil to activate the coupler, but the coil is almost twice the size of the earlier one. The coil has a plunger which pushes against the coupler knuckle to keep the knuckle closed. The coil is actually a solenoid in which the plunger is pulled against a spring which returns the plunger to the original position following the uncoupling. An easy way to check the operation of the coupler itself is to rap the end of the car sharply against your palm. If the plunger is operable, the coupler will open when the plunger moves. This, however, does not prove the solenoid is operable; one would still have to check the solenoid electrically to determine if the coil itself will move the plunger.

In 1948, this coupler type was changed to a mechanically operated coupler which operates by a movable plate being attracted to a track mounted magnet which opens the coupler as the plate moves. This design proved successful and was used for a number of years, although there were changes which occurred frequently enough to allow dating to definite time spans.

The axles and wheels follow a similar pattern of rapid changes, although they soon arrive at an acceptable type which was used until the era of plastic took over and dominated Lionel trains. These changes are discussed in detail in the Truck Chapter as well as in the 9-1/4" boxcar article.

The black plastic body of the 2452 is well detailed with cast-on rivets, ladders and braces. There is one peculiarity

about the new design. In spite of the wealth of cast-on detail, Lionel left out one feature which was on the railroad cars of that time. If one looks at the end of most freight cars, one will see two round depressions at the lower edges on both sides. These are called poling pockets, and in the early days of railroading they had a definite function. The engines of those days carried a large wooden pole hung on the side of the tender. This was used when the engine was on one track and a car was on another parallel track where it was desired to move the car without switching the engine to the other track. The pole was placed in the poling pockets of the engine and car respectively, and the engine could then push the car. It was necessary for the switchman to hold the pole in place while the engine was being moved into position to push the car. Needless to say, this was a dangerous process, and more than a few switchmen were injured when the pole shattered. In 1945, when the Pennsylvania gondola was introduced, this detail was left off the gondola. However, in 1949, when the larger 6462 gondola was introduced, the poling pockets were included. Then, about 1960, Lionel introduced a short gondola with a detailed undercarriage which used the part number 6112-86. This gondola body has the poling pockets and uses an end identical to that of the 6462 gondola. Thus, at the point in time when the poling pockets were being phased out by the real railroads, Lionel was putting them onto their newer models!

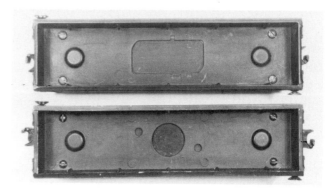

This photograph shows the Type I-A body mold (bottom) and the Type I-B body mold (top). Note the two extra holes added to the Type I-B mold and the different sizes of the screws fastening the body to the frame. Also note the distance by which the couplers extend from the ends of the car close coupling was indicative of early 1945 product.

The lettering on the Pennsylvania gondola is rubber-stamped in white and only minor stamping changes occur over the years this car was run. Actually, the designation of 2452 in this report also includes the 4452 electronic unit, the 1948 6462/6452 and the 6452 of 1949. There is one feature about this car which has caused some confusion. This is the rectangular hole in the floor where the electronic unit on the 4452 was placed. This rectangular hole is in all the earliest gondolas, whether they had the electronic unit or not. When the electronic unit was installed, the car number 4452 was stamped on the side of the car. There are number changes over the years and some minor stamping variations which will be described under each variation. The road name PENNSYLVANIA is stamped across the second to fifth panel. The number 347000, which remains the same over the entire series of this car, is under the road name. There are two lines of informational data under this on the left and additional data on the right side under the Lionel car number. The Lionel car number changes over the years and is the primary means of identifying the different cars in the series. The PRR logo is in the eighth panel. The car comes with applied metal brakewheels and a load of six wooden barrels. Initially, the car for the 1945 set was supplied with four 0209 wooden barrels which were hollow and could be opened, but by 1946 the barrels had become solid pieces.

Shown above are two 2452 gondolas. Look carefully at the lettering to the right of the PRR Keystone and logo. On the last data line, the top example has a small "G27" mark, while the lower car has a larger "G27".

Truck and coupler changes discussed elsewhere in this book can be used to date and order 1945 - 1946 production. the listings which follow this section show the truck coupler progression. During the production run of 1947, Lionel changed the hole in the floor of the 2452 from the previous rectangular hole to a round hole. The screws fastening the car body to the metal frame were also changed from large pan-headed ones to smaller round-headed ones. One other variation also shows up in this and the following year; some cars come with a rubber stamped 2452X on the bottom of the frame. This indicates a special car, probably meant for O-27 sets, which did not come equipped with brakewheels and did not have the normal load of six wooden barrels. (Editor's note: Recent information has turned up a few 1946 cars marked 2452X as well.)

In 1948, Lionel changed the number on this car to 6452 and dropped the use of the applied brakewheels. The number change was not implemented correctly, and as a result this car has 6462 on the side and 6452 stamped on the bottom. This car is quite common. The number change has been thought to signify the change to the new mechanical coupler, but many of these cars are found with the late coil couplers.

As discussed elsewhere in this book, the 1948 Lionel catalogue implied that the O Gauge line came with the coil couplers and the O-27 line came with the new magnetic couplers. We assume that the catalogue accurately represented Lionel's intent. The simpliest explanation for the O-27 cars with O Gauge coil couplers is that Lionel had not completed either the new special track section or the new couplers in time for 1948 O-27 production and therefore continued the older couplers with the O-27 equipment.

### 6452

Previously it was pointed out that Lionel used the number 6462 on the 6452 Gondola and stamped the bottom of the frame

with the correct number. (Actually, the number 6462 was applied a year later in 1949 to the new longer gondola.) Lionel's method of correcting this mistake was to stamp the correct number under the car. It is probable that at the time the number was changed the new longer gondola was in the planning stage and the number confusion was not caught until the cars were already produced. Since previously the number was generally stamped on the bottom, the addition of the number was nothing new.

### 1002

In 1948 Lionel introduced a new number to the gondola series, the 1002 Scout gondola. This gondola used the same basic body previously used on the Pennsylvania gondolas, but the seven holes in the bottom were filled in with plugs in the die. Also, additional holes were added to the die to allow the trucks to be riveted to the body, since the steel frame was no longer used.

In 1949 the Pennsylvania gondola was made with the correct number, 6452, on the side and the new mechanical coupler. There is no number stamped on the bottom. This is an uncommon car, but it is by no means rare. This car represents Lionel's using up previously made bodies until they were exhausted. This is verified by examining the 6452 gondola from this year. There is no evidence of the holes for the rivets used to hold the trucks on the Scout gondola. The Scout gondola, as pointed out above, shows where the die was plugged, as do the later cars in this series, the 6032 with Scout trucks, the 6012 with bar-end trucks and the 6112 with bar-end trucks and plastic AAR trucks from about 1956 forward. The 6452 Pennsylvania gondola is always found with the earliest mechanical coupler as factory production.

Thus, in a period of five years there are at least 19 separate datable variations of this one Pennsylvania gondola. Finding all of them is relatively easy. There are only three which can be described as difficult to find, the earliest whirly or dished wheel version and the electronic gondola. The remainder are common and relatively inexpensive.

This is the 6452/6462 gondola, Version (B) above. This car shows the third version of the G27 lettering. R. Vagner Collection.

There are several small changes which do not themselves provide any extra information for the collector. In early 1946, the phenolic board used for the early coil coupler changes color, and the regular wheel versions can come with either the earlier black or the later brown phenolic board. This seems to apply to the thick and thin axle versions utilizing the regular wheels. In 1947, before the number changes to 6462 and 6452, the size of the G27 marking in the informational data on the right side of the car changes to a larger size. A third version of the 627 is found on the 6452 gondolas. See accompanying photograph.

Examining this series of cars shows how Lionel made changes over the years that seem to represent responses to cost factors as well as operating and repair problems. Although at this point in time it is difficult to ascertain exactly the reason for all the changes, some are apparently cost related, such as the changes in the couplers. Others are more difficult to understand, such as the change from whirly wheels. This was prototypical of actual railroad wheels, but the whirly-wheel design may have been difficult to manufacture and most likely few people noticed this extra detail. The use of the X designator to indicate the cars without brakewheels and barrels probably represents the effort to utilize the same car for both the top of the line and the lower-priced sets.

### LONG 6462 CARS

In 1949, the Lionel Corporation introduced a new longer gondola which was to carry the New York Central markings in every year it was produced until the demise of Lionel trains. The new car was 10-3/8 inches long and was well detailed with a very realistic appearance. The detailing included rivets, steps, brakewheels, brakewheel chains and interior detailing. This car was included in most of the better freight sets produced during the remaining 21 years of Lionel's history. During the production run of this car 13 different number/color combinations were produced which are all relatively easy to find. In addition a large number of visual variations were produced including herald position, number of lines of weight data, presence or absence of the built date, brakewheels and steps. There were also variations in truck types and couplers. Other changes include die modifications, truck connectors, color differences, frame changes and various combinations of the above. Using only the visual variations which can be seen with the car sitting on the shelf, about 30 different combinations can be found and if the other manufacturing changes are included, over 50 different variations of the basic 13 number/color combinations can be found.

A matrix can be constructed which uses the changes from year to year on one axis and each number/color combination produced on the other axis. By utilizing the changes found on any car it can be dated to specific time frames within the matrix. The matrix can be used to insure the correct gondola is in a set for a given year and it can tell the year a set was manufactured and if the car has been altered. When the changes apply to other Lionel cars it can date them within appropriate time frames.

Previously most of the information as to when certain rolling stock was produced has come from the Lionel consumer catalogues. However, by using other sources such as the advance catalogues, the service manuals and study of known datable sets, it has become possible to add to the catalogue information and in some cases show that the catalogue did not depict accurately some individual cars. There are gondolas shown in the catalogue in years in which they were not produced and, conversely, gondolas have been identified from years in which the catalogue does not indicate production. In a few cases it appears that Lionel used up surplus stock the following year and did not indicate the item as being available in the catalogue. There are also gondolas shown in the catalogue in colors in which they have never been found and units that can be shown to be from that year in other colors.

Any gondola can be classified from the matrix and placed into a time frame regardless of the inaccuracies of the catalogue.

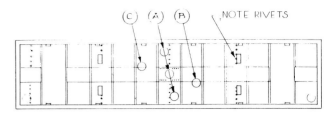

Type I molds.
Ia: center only (three a's only)
Ib: center plus right (three a's plus b)
Ic: all (three a's, b, c)                    **Drawing by Trip Riley**

The NYC gondolas introduced in 1949 are 10-3/8 inches from coupler centers or 9-5/8 inches outside body length. (In prototype practice, railroad cars are measured from coupler center to coupler center, rather than coupler ends, as the former measurement will actually provide accurate information on the length of a train because it compensates for the overlap within the couplers.) The NYC gondolas come in five different mold variations which separate the cars into distinct time frames. The first mold was what is called body mold Type Ia. This mold is only found on the black 6462 gondola from 1949, the first year of its production. To identify the Type Ia and later Type I molds look inside the gondola on the floor in the center panel. There are three round mold marks on a diagonal in this panel. The center mark is the point at which the plastic was injected into the mold and may be either raised or depressed. The other two marks are from plugs in the mold and are on the diagonal in the same panel. Mold Types Ib and Ic are variations of the Type Ia and are the result of adding extra round plug marks to the die. Type Ib is identified by the addition of another round plug in the panel to the right of the center panel. To determine the right-hand side of the gondola, examine the four rectangular holes into which the metal tabs that secure the body to the frame are fastened. On the floor inside the car on the left side of one pair of these holes will be found three rivets on the edge of the hole. This goes to the right. To identify a Type Ib body mold look in the panel to the right of the center panel for the round plug mark. This body mold is only found in the tuscan red and black 6462 gondolas produced in early 1950.

The next body mold type is the Type Ic which first appeared in mid-1950. Type Ic is identified by the addition of another round plug in the panel to the left of the center panel. The Type Ic is found on the tuscan red and black 6462s and the 6002 black gondola with the Scout trucks and mechanical couplers. This Type Ic continues into 1953 on the tuscan red and black 6462s.

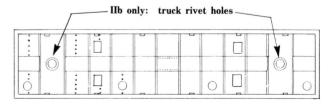

Type IIa: plastic molded clips hold metal frame, no holes for trucks
Type IIb: metal frame not used, trucks riveted directly to body, holes for truck rivet.

**Drawing by Trip Riley**

Next is body mold Type IIa beginning in 1954. This was a completely new mold, and the machine with its dual dies produced two cars at a time. On the floor of the car were now four round plug marks in panels one, five, nine and thirteen. Under the body, hidden by the metal frame is a part identification number. It is 6462-2 and underneath it is a "1" or "2" indicating which of the two molds it was formed in. This body mold was used on the light red-painted, red plastic, black, green and pink 6462s, the red gray and black 6562s, the first black 6062s in 1959 and the red 6342 Culvert gondolas. This mold was used from 1954 to 1958, and cars using this mold were produced into 1959 to use up the remaining 6342s and to make the 6062 with the metal underframe.

The final mold Type IIb was introduced in 1959. This mold was changed to eliminate the metal underframe and allow the trucks to be riveted directly to the gondola floor. There were a very few of the yellow 6162-60 Alaska gondolas made using metal trucks held to the plastic body by the use of the sheet metal clip introduced in 1957. However this was soon changed to the use of the plastic AAR trucks held on by the rivet that was used for the remainder of Lionel's production of these gondolas.

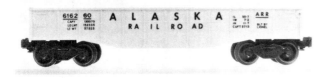

This is the 6162-60 Alaska gondola with bar-end trucks, as found in set 1611. R. Vagner Collection.

The production of the 6162-60 Alaska gondola used an exploded rivet to fasten its bar-end trucks. Although bar-end truck examples are probably much more scarce than those with AAR trucks, they cannot be valued more highly, since trucks are easily switched. R. Vagner Collection.

## 6062 CARS

The earliest 6062s used the metal underframe with plastic trucks riveted to the metal frame. It is possible that the 1959 production or a major portion of it used the metal underframe. This car is uncommon but shows up fairly frequently if it is looked for diligently. Lionel was a creative company and used all available materials when possible. It is probable that other rolling stock during this transition year have features that would show this same sort of creativity. The majority of early type 6062s are found without the metal underframe and it is

apparent that the metal underframe cars were only produced until the stock of black plastic bodies was exhausted.

The Type IIb body mold was used on the black 6062, the blue and red 6162, the yellow 6162 Alaska gondola and the red 6342 culvert gondola produced from 1966 to 1969. This mold was used from 1959 to 1969. The mold numbers 6462-2/1 or 6462-2/2 are readily visible with the elimination of the frame. It appears that equal numbers of both mold "1" and "2" are found.

## 6462 CARS

The black 6462 is the only gondola found in the first four mold types: Types Ia, Ib, Ic and IIa. The tuscan red 6462 gondola is found in only mold Types Ib and Ic. The painted red and unpainted red plastic 6462 is only found in mold Type IIa. The green and pink 6462s and the gray, black and red 6562s are only found in mold Type IIa. The red 6342 and black 6062 are found in both mold Types IIa and IIb. The yellow, blue and red 6162s are found only in mold Type IIb.

The next major visible distinguishing feature is the position of the N in the NYC and the style of lettering used for the herald. From 1949 to 1955 the N is found in the second panel and from 1956 to 1969 the N is in the third panel. The lettering style changes from the early serif to the later block type lettering.

The black 6462 and 6002 are only found with the N in the second panel. The tuscan red 6462 is only found with the N in the second panel while the painted red ones can be found with the N in the second or third panel. The red plastic 6462 is only found with the N in the third panel. The green 6462s are found with the N in the second or third panel. The pink 6462, the gray, red and black 6562s, the red 6342, the black 6062 and the blue and red 6162s are all found with the N in the third panel. The yellow 6162 does not have the NYC herald and therefore does not fit into any of the above classes.

The third major distinguishing feature of these cars is the type of trucks. There are two major types of trucks with two variations of each type. From 1949 to 1959 the 10-3/8 inch gondolas had metal trucks with die-cast sides. From 1949 to 1951 these were the staple-end variation and from 1952 to 1958 they were the bar-end variation. From 1959 on all of these gondolas, except the few yellow Alaska 6162s that the factory equipped with metal trucks and the 6342 red culvert gondolas that remained from stock made prior to the changeover from the metal frame, came with plastic trucks. The earliest of these plastic trucks had a metal pin holding the coupler knuckle, while after 1962 until 1969 the pin was part of the coupler knuckle which was cast of plastic.

With the above information it is possible to examine the bar graph and see that certain variations are now falling into datable time frames. It can be seen that the black 6462 is the only car that was made in the first four body mold types. The 1949 variation is the only car found in mold Type Ia and also the only long gondola made in 1949. In 1950 the black and tuscan red 6462s are found in body mold Types Ib and Ic. The 6002 was only made in 1950 and is only found in body mold Type Ic. Thus it is easy to see that the progression in manufacturing dates is from the black 6462 to the black and tuscan red 6462s and then the black 6002.

However there are still more possibilities to be explored in this time frame. The earliest 6462s in both black and tuscan red are found with three lines of weight data. The black is found in both mold Types Ia and Ib while the tuscan red is

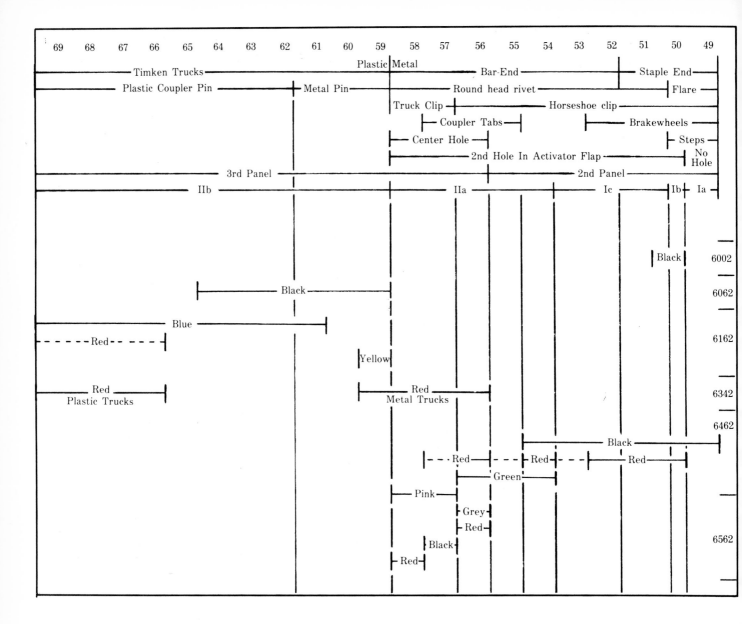

found only in mold Ib. Then if the black 6002 is examined it will be found that on the floor at both ends of the car is the beginning of a die break that follows through until the change to body mold Type IIa. However the tuscan red 6462s do not have any evidence of this die break in either body mold Type Ib or Ic. Thus it is possible to say that the black 6462 in body mold Type Ib probably predates the tuscan red 6462 and that all the bodies for all the tuscan red 6462s in both molds Ib and Ic were made prior to the production of the black 6002 gondolas. The unusually high color consistency of the tuscan red gondolas is thus explained by the fact that they were all made and painted at one time and assembled as needed into at least 1952. An unanswered question is what happened to the mold requiring the addition of the plug that differentiates Type Ib from Type Ic?

A further change occurs in 1950 that probably dates further the black and tuscan red 6462s. When Lionel created the 6002 they removed the steps from the frame that are found on the 1950 black and tuscan red 6462s. If we assume that all black and tuscan red gondolas without steps were made after the 6002 was produced, we can effectively date them to 1951. Then in 1952 Lionel introduced the bar-end truck and consequently

all bar-end truck equipped cars must date 1952 and later. The 1951 black and tuscan red gondolas can be further dated to 1951 by one other change that occurred in 1950. On the bottom of the coupler plate on the earlier 6462s there is a rivet holding the movable portion of the plate to the plate itself. On the gondolas with steps this rivet is usually found with a flared end showing. On the 6002 the end of the rivet that is showing is rounded. This change continues for the remainder of the use of the mechanical coupler. Thus the cars without steps and with the rounded rivet obviously were produced following the production of the 6002.

Lionel was a systematic company that followed a program throughout the year to manufacture their toy trains. It seems logical that they produced one type of car and then when enough were made to fill anticipated orders they started to produce the next series and so forth. Since the 6002 represented the lower end of the line and it is obvious that it was produced after the 6462s in 1950, it seems to follow that the next series in the black and tuscan red 6462s would have been 1951 production. Thus with the help of the manufacturing changes it is possible to date presumptively the first four years production of these gondolas.

174

When we examine the 1952-1953 production it is found that there are no changes to differentiate these two years. However in 1954 Lionel introduced a new color and a different color on the red 6462s. They also changed from body mold Type Ic to body mold Type IIa. The new color was the green 6462 and it is only found in body mold Type IIa. They apparently ran out of the tuscan red bodies that were painted in 1950 and started painting the red gondolas a light red. The black 6462 is also found in this body mold in the last year it is to be produced. In 1955 Lionel introduced the tab coupler which is the mechanical coupler with a tab sticking out to allow easier uncoupling by hand. It is probable that the green and red 6462s from this year came with this tab coupler although they are not commonly found. It is possible that the tab was a late 1955 introduction and most of the 6462s of that year did not have them installed.

In 1956 Lionel changed the lettering of the herald and moved the N to the third panel. Thus the painted red and green gondolas are found with the N in either panel and again are datable by this change. Probably during 1956 Lionel changed the red 6462 to a self-colored plastic, and when the green bodies ran out they discontinued the color. The red plastic 6462 continues probably into 1958, but empirical evidence is lacking to verify this.

Thus by examining the changes it is possible to date within narrow time frames the entire production of 6462 gondolas. Some of these changes apply to other Lionel rolling stock and they can also be dated. There are some other variations in the 6462 gondolas over the 1950-1956 time period that do not change the accuracy of the dating, but tend to confirm that the changes occurred within the predicted years. The steps have already been mentioned. In 1950 the die used to cut out the frames was modified to eliminate the steps. This was done on the 6002, but once the die was changed the following gondolas did not come with steps. The rationale for dropping the steps was probably based on cost. The steps protruded out from the basic frame and it was necessary to use a larger piece of metal, to make a frame with the steps. Assuming that Lionel made 500,000 of these gondolas each year and each gondola frame required an extra half inch of metal it required almost four extra miles of metal to include steps on these gondolas. There was a considerable amount of money involved. One other reason has been advanced for the elimination of the steps. In 1950 Lionel changed from a ten inch box to a shorter box. By removing the steps it was possible to easily swivel the trucks to place the coupler under the car frame, thus allowing the use of a much shorter box. As previously pointed out Lionel was always willing to change to lower the cost of production. If the above rationale is correct then Lionel achieved a double savings. They eliminated the wastage of several miles of steel, they lowered the amount of material necessary to make boxes for the gondolas, and they further lowered the size of the shipping box that was necessary to ship the gondolas which, in turn, lowered the amount of warehouse space necessary to store the shipping boxes prior to shipping after they manufactured the cars. In 1949 Lionel priced the 6462 gondola at $4.50, the 6456 hopper at $4.25 and the 6465 tank car at $4.00. In 1950, the gondola was priced at $3.95, the hopper at $3.95 and the tank car at $3.75. These price reductions were likely made possible by the change in frame design.

Thus the early 1950 production of the 6462 gondolas had steps and also brakewheels. In 1951 the brakewheels were eliminated from the black 6462. Later that year the built date was

eliminated from the black 6462. The tuscan red 6462 retained its brakewheels and built date throughout its production run. This might indicate either of two possibilities. One was that the black car was used in the lower-priced sets while the tuscan red car was part of the higher-priced sets. The other possibility was that the tuscan red cars were painted, stamped and had the brakewheels installed in 1950. If the latter is true then they had to have been stored without frames because in 1952 they came with bar-end trucks. Since the trucks were installed on the frame before the frame was fastened to the body, this would have to be true. Thus in the first five years of production there were eight recognizable versions of the black 6462. The tuscan red 6462 has seven variations over the four years it was produced.

If one were to consider mold colors that these cars came in, the number of possible variations increases dramatically. At this time the mold colors that are known include clear, blue, gray, green, brown, pink and black. The black cars were painted in 1949 and 1950 and then made in black plastic until 1954 when some were painted over pink molds. Since this was three years before the Girls' Train they were not painted over as was the case with some of the Girls' Train engines.

The coupler variations have been mentioned in passing but they constitute a valid method of dating the cars provided the coupler has not been changed.

**Gd    VG    Exc    Mt**

**1002 LIONEL** 1948-52, white lettering, from the Scout set, with Scout couplers, 8" long. In 1950, Lionel produced a special train for dealers to allow them to demonstrate the pulling power of Magnetraction. This train had an engine with Magnetraction (either a 2035 or a 2036) and either 12 or 14 gondolas and a caboose. The gondolas came in red, black and probably silver and yellow. These gondolas had Scout trucks fastened with hollow rivets and knuckle couplers rather than Scout couplers. After the holiday season, many stores sold off their gondolas from this train separately. The train came with a special layout in which the entire train disappeared into a two-foot tunnel! (This effect is possible with a loop concealed by the tunnel below the platform surface; the train goes into the tunnel and around the loop, and just as the caboose disappears, the engine emerges from the other end of the tunnel, giving the impression of a train compressed like an accordion!) These special demonstration layouts may also be the source for the 154 Highway Flashers with red or orange-painted bases instead of the usual black ones. T. Rollo and C. Rohlfing comments.

(A) 1950, blue unpainted plastic, white lettering. H. Holden Collection.

|  | 1 | 1.50 | 2 | 3 |
|---|---|---|---|---|
| (B) 1948, black unpainted plastic, white lettering. | 1 | 1.50 | 2 | 3 |
| (C) Silver with black lettering. | 40 | 70 | 150 | 200 |
| (D) Yellow with black lettering. | 30 | 70 | 150 | 200 |
| (E) Red with white lettering. N. Oswald Collection. | 30 | 70 | 150 | 200 |
| (F) Light blue with black lettering. H. Holden and R. Lord Collections. | | | | |

**NRS**

**2452 PENNSYLVANIA** 1945-47. This is a fascinating piece to study, since it shows how complex the actual design and manufacturing process can be for a relatively simple car. It also indicates Lionel's continued concern with reducing manufacturing and assembly costs.

Black body, white lettering, black metal underframe held to body by four fillister-head screws in corners of body floor, steps at corners, built date "NEW 12-45", usually brakewheels; always found with staple-end trucks. The 1945 and 1946 production models have couplers without staking marks; the 1947 models have four staking marks on the couplers. The body mold Type Ia is found on 1945 and 1946 models; body mold Type Ib is found on 1947 models. The earliest models came with small opening barrels; most of these cars had no barrels included.

Body Mold Type Ia: rectangular opening approximately 2" x 1" in center of floor in body does not go through metal frame, body fastened to frame by large flat-headed slotted screws. The opening was designed to fit a frame supporting the electronic control unit found in 4452.

Five different versions of A.T. & S.F. operating barrel cars. Top shelf: 3562-1. Middle shelf: 3562-25(E) and 3562-25(A). Bottom shelf: 3562-50 and 3562-75.

| | Gd | VG | Exc | Mt |
|---|---|---|---|---|

(A) 1945, rough edges on rectangular center hole, extra holes, Type 1A trucks (whirly wheels), "2452" stamped on frame, Type Ia body, small G-27.

| | 2 | 4 | 6 | 10 |
|---|---|---|---|---|

(B) 1945, same as (A), but smooth edges. **2 3 5 8**

(C) 1945, same as (A), but smooth edges, Type 1B trucks. 2 3 5 8

(D) 1945, same as (A), but smooth edges, no extra holes, Type 1B trucks.

**2 3 5 8**

(E) 1945, same as (D), except "2452" is underlined. **2 3 5 8**

(F) 1946, Type 1C trucks, Type Ia body, small G-27, no number on frame.

**2 3 5 8**

(G) 1946, same as (F), but Type 2 trucks. **2 3 5 8**

(H) 1946, same as (F), but Type 3A trucks. **2 3 5 8**

(I) 1947, Type 3B trucks, Type Ib body, small G-27, no number on frame.

**2 3 5 8**

(J) 1947, same as (I), but large G-27. **2 3 5 8**

Our chronology of the 2452 is primarily based on our understanding of Lionel truck development as supplemented by reports on original boxed sets which can be dated by set number and content. We would appreciate very much additional reader reports on original boxed sets that contain 2452s or 2452Xs.

**2452X PENNSYLVANIA** See 2452 for background. 2452X does not have brakewheels while 2452 does. "2452X" is stamped on the frame.

(A) 1946, Type 2 trucks, Type Ia body, small G-27. **2 3 5 8**

(B) 1946, Type 3A trucks, Type Ia body, small G-27. **2 3 5 8**

(C) 1947, Type 3B trucks, Type Ib body, large G-27. **2 3 5 8**

Body mold Type Ib, round opening approximately 1" in diameter in center of floor in body does not go through metal frame, body fastened to frame by smaller round-headed slotted screws.

**3444 ERIE** 1957-59, cop chases hobo, vibrator motor, unpainted red plastic body with white lettering, on-off switch, "BLT 2-57". This ingenious car showed Lionel's engineering skill. The cop and hobo figures were attached to a continuous loop of 16 mm film by U-shaped metal brackets attached at the feet and on the lower edge of the film. The film looped around two spools with sprockets powered by the vibrator motor; the crates concealed the spools and the film. Reissued with the same mechanism by Fundimensions in 1980 as 9307.

(A) Tan-colored crates. **25 35 45 60**

(B) Clear unpainted plastic crates. Piker Collection. **NRS**

(C) Same as (A), but crates are darker tan. J. Algozzini Collection.

**25 35 45 60**

**3562-1 A T & S F** 1954, operating barrel car, man "unloads" barrels, black with white lettering, actually numbered "35621", "NEW 5-54", bar-end trucks, magnetic couplers, six wooden barrels, plastic unloading bin. This car was reissued in 1983 by Fundimensions as the 9290 black Union Pacific barrel car with yellow lettering and the next year as the 9225 Conrail in tuscan. R. Hutchinson comments.

(A) Black-painted body with black central barrel trough, earliest production. P. Catalano observation. **45 65 100 150**

(B) Same as (A), but yellow lettering. J. Sattler Collection. (One sample observed with chemically-altered lettering, C. Weber observation.) **NRS**

(C) Black body with yellow trough. J. Sattler and T. Rollo Collections.

**50 70 125 175**

(D) Gray with red letters. **200 300 400 500**

**3562-25 A.T.&.S.F.** 1954, operating barrel car, man "unloads" barrels, actually numbered "356225", "NEW 5-54", six wooden barrels, plastic unloading bin, bar-end trucks, magnetic couplers.

(A) Gray-painted plastic body with dark blue lettering, bar-end trucks, magnetic couplers, body has molded plastic tab along edge to hold base upon which a man is attached so that barrels are not dumped in transit. A metal tab fits into the gap between the plastic tab and the side edge to lock the man into place. T. Lemieux Collection. **15 20 30 50**

(B) Same as (A), but does not have molded plastic tab. T. Lemieux Collection. **15 20 30 50**

(C) Same as (A), but royal blue lettering, considerably brighter color than dark blue version. G. Halverson and R. LaVoie Collections.

**15 25 35 55**

(D) Same as (A), but royal blue lettering, no tab. C. Switzer Collection

**15 25 35 55**

(E) Gray with red lettering, no tab. J. Sattler Collection. **60 100 150 200**

**3562-50 A T & S F** 1955-57, operating barrel car, man "unloads" barrels, actually numbered "356250", "NEW 5-54", six stained wooden barrels, plastic unloading bin, plastic tab along edge of car locks metal base holding man into place, bar-end trucks, magnetic couplers with one truck with a tab and the other without.

(A) Bright yellow unpainted plastic, black lettering. J. Sattler and R. LaVoie Collections. **15 25 40 55**

(B) Darker yellow-painted gray plastic body, black lettering, box stamped 3562-25Y. Probably first run using 3562-25 body shells and boxes. Easier to

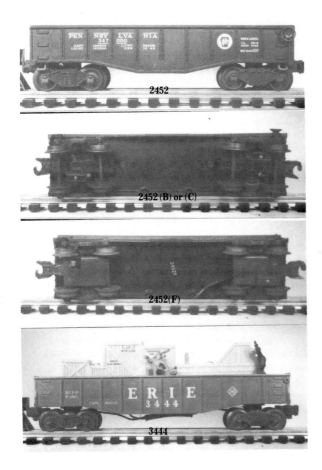

2452

2452 (B) or (C)

2452(F)

3444

4452

6002

6012

6032

find in the Midwest than on the East Coast, lending credence to the theory that Lionel's earliest production of any given item was shipped to the West for the holiday selling season. R. LaVoie and R. Shanfeld Collections, T. Rollo and P. Ambrose comments.　　　　　　　**25　40　55　75**

(C) Same as (B), but two tab couplers, man cast in very dark rubber, box number unknown, came with 1955 set. D. Doyle Collection.

　　　　　　　　　　　　　　　　　　　　**25　40　55　75**

**WARNING:** Most authorities have established a white 3562-50 with black lettering as a chemically-altered fake.

**3562-75 A T & S F** 1958, operating barrel car, man "unloads" barrels, "NEW 5-54", six wooden barrels, plastic unloading bin, bright unpainted orange with black lettering, plastic tab along rear edge to fasten base of man, bar-end trucks, magnetic couplers with tabs. J. Sattler Collection.

　　　　　　　　　　　　　　　　　　　　**20　35　50　75**

**4452 PENNSYLVANIA** 1946-48, special black gondola with white lettering for electronic control set with electronic control unit.

(A) 1946, Type Ia body, Type 3A trucks.　　　　**30　45　60　80**
(B) 1947, Type Ia body, Type 3B trucks.　　　　**30　45　60　80**
(C) 1947-48, Type Ib body, Type 3B trucks.　　　**30　45　60　80**

**6002 N Y C** 1949, black unpainted plastic body with white lettering, "BLT 2-49", 9-9/16" long, Scout trucks with magnetic couplers. Somewhat difficult to find, but not in any significant collector demand. R. LaVoie and T. Rollo Collections.　　　　　　　　　　**4　6　10　15**

**6012 LIONEL** 1951-56, black unpainted plastic with white lettering, 8" long, no brakewheel.

(A) 1951, staple-end trucks, magnetic couplers; from set 1477S. C. Rohlfing Collection.　　　　　　　　　　　　　**1　1.50　2　3**

(B) 1956, bar-end trucks, magnetic tab couplers; came in set with 520 boxcab electric. G. Cole, R. Kruelle and C. Rohlfing Collections.

　　　　　　　　　　　　　　　　　　　　**1　1.50　2　3**

(C) Same as (B), except no tabs on couplers. T. Budniak Collection.

　　　　　　　　　　　　　　　　　　　　**1　1.50　2　3**

**6032 LIONEL** 1952-53, black unpainted plastic, Scout trucks, operating magnetic couplers, 8" long, no brakewheel, white lettering. Came in set

headed by 1130 Scout steam locomotive in 1953. M. Denuty and R. LaVoie Collections.　　　　　　　　　　　　　**1　1.50　2　3**

**6042 LIONEL** Uncatalogued, 8-1/8" long, detailed undercarriage and box interior, unpainted plastic, white lettering, fixed couplers open at top, brakewheel embossed in plastic car sides, red or white canisters.

(A) Black unpainted plastic, arch-bar trucks, dummy couplers, came in set X-600. J. Kotil and J. Divi Collections. This car has also been found in uncatalogued set 1105; see next entry. M. Rini Collection.

　　　　　　　　　　　　　　　　　　　　**1　1.50　2　3**

(B) Blue unpainted plastic, early AAR trucks, detailed undercarriage and interior, no mold number, dummy couplers, came in uncatalogued set 1105 in 1959. J. Kotil and W. Spence Collections.　　　**1　1.50　2　3**

**6042-125 LIONEL** Same as 6042, but blue unpainted plastic, numbered "6042".

(A) Blue unpainted plastic, detailed undercarriage, arch-bar trucks with dummy couplers, came as part of uncatalogued set X-716. F. Davis Collection.　　　　　　　　　　　　　　　**1　1.50　2　3**
(B) Same as (A), but shinier blue unpainted plastic.　**1　1.50　2　3**

**6062 N Y C** 1959-64, glossy black plastic body, white lettering, "N.Y.C." overscored, "6062" underscored, "NEW 2-49", 6462-2 mold, early AAR trucks, disc couplers. T. Budniak, C. Rohlfing and R. LaVoie Collections.

(A) No detail on undercarriage, no load present with car. T. Budniak and C. Rohlfing Collections.　　　　　　　　　　**3　7　10　15**

(B) Same as (A), except three empty dark orange Lionel cable reels, came with uncatalogued set 19110. D. Anderson Collection, P. Ambrose comment.　　　　　　　　　　　　　　　**3　7　10　15**

(C) Stamped metal undercarriage similar to 6462, came in box marked 6062-4 on outside flap. Note that the metal undercarriage was eliminated with the introduction of the 6062; it would seem that this car is an exception. T. Budniak and R. Schreiner Collections.　　　**3　7　10　15**

**6062-50 N Y C** Circa 1968-69, glossy black unpainted plastic, "N.Y.C." overscored, "6062" underscored (not 6062-50), no "NEW 2-49", (compare with 6062 previously), 9-9/16" long, detailed plastic undercarriage, no brakewheels molded on side, body mold "6462-2" on base underside,

6042

6062

6112

6142

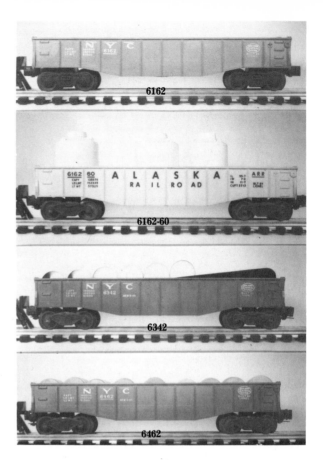

6162

6162-60

6342

6462

6062-50 appears only on the box end. Car has AAR plastic trucks, one disc-operating coupler and one fixed coupler, two red unpainted plastic canisters with "LIONEL" molded on top. This car came in an orange and white box lettered "LIONEL" in large white letters and then "LIONEL TOY CORPORATION / HAGERSTOWN, MARYLAND". Talley and Falter Collections.                    **2    4    8    14**

**6112 LIONEL**  Circa 1956-58, 8" long, plain undercarriage and box interior, disc-operating couplers. Truck undersides come with many different numbers, for example, 5 and 3, 7 and 2, 2 and 0, 4 and 8 etc., appear on blue cars. R. Griesbeck comment. The following markings pertain to the following cars, according to an analysis by P. Ambrose: Box marking 6112-1 came with either a painted black car or an unpainted white car; box marking 6112-85 came with an unpainted blue car; and box marking 6112-135 came with an unpainted black car.

(A) 1956: black body, white lettering, four red canisters rubber-stamped "LIONEL AIR ACTIVATED CONTAINER / CAPY. 20000 / Lt.Wt.4400 / 61125", bar-end trucks fastened by sheet metal clip, listed in Service Manual (Greenberg reprint, V-47) as 6112-50, but box was probably not marked that way. P. Ambrose comment, J. Kotil and R. Vagner Collections.                    **1    2    3    4**

(B) Same as (A), but unpainted blue body. Reader comments requested concerning box end numbering. I.D. Smith Collection.    **1    2    3    4**

(C) 1958, black body, white lettering, early AAR trucks, disc couplers, listed as 6112 in Service Manual (Greenberg reprint, V-48). Four red canisters stamped as in entry (A).                    **1    2    3    4**

(D) White unpainted plastic body, black lettering, four red canisters, early AAR trucks. Somewhat hard to find. R. Vagner Collection.

**4    7    11    15**

(E) Blue unpainted plastic body, white lettering. Early AAR trucks, three black-lettered white canisters. L. Bohn and R. Vagner comments.

**1    1.50    3    6**

(F) Teal blue unpainted body, AAR trucks, disc couplers, white lettering, came with three white canisters. C. Rohlfing Collection.    **4    7    12    20**

**(6112) LIONEL**  1963-64, olive drab or blue, 8" long, plain undercarriage and box interior, brakewheels molded on side, body mold number

"6112-86" molded into base underside, AAR trucks, catalogue number uncertain, parentheses indicate number does not appear on car, original box will probably provide catalogue number.

(A) Unpainted blue plastic, AAR trucks, one tab and one fixed coupler. Part of uncatalogued set 19334 made for J. C. Penney. P. Ambrose and R. Schreiner Collections.                    **1    2    3    4**

(B) Unpainted olive drab plastic, disc-operating couplers, came with olive drab flat (3349) and olive drab work caboose (6824), part of set 19334 sold by J.C. Penney, 1963-64; P. Catalano, G. Wilson and P. Ambrose comments.

**10    20    30    50**

(C) Same as (A), but two non-operating couplers. This car was apparently sold in set 11420 (1964) with a 1061 locomotive and 6167-25 caboose. The gondola was probably not separately boxed as the set likely came in a box with dividers. Light Collection.                    **1    2    3    4**

**6112-1 LIONEL**  Blue unpainted body, 8" long, white lettering, came in box marked 6112-1 with four red canisters; AAR trucks, part of set X-610.

**1    1.50    2    4**

**6112-135 LIONEL**  1958, black plastic body, 8" long, three white canisters lettered "LIONEL AIR ACTIVATED CONTAINER", numbered "6112" on car although box numbered "6112-135".

(A) Bar-end trucks with tab couplers, box lettered "No. 6112-135 / CANISTER CAR / LIONEL", box part number 6112-137, box date coding BC-583 / 11", "BERLES CARTON CO. INC. / PATERSON, N.J." P. Catalano observation.                    **1    2    3    4**

(B) Early AAR trucks, disc couplers, box part number 6112-137; box date coding "BC-586/4" (note different code from (A)) and "BERLES CARTON CO. INC. / PATERSON, N.J.", part of Sears set 79N09657. I.D. Smith observation.                    **1    2    3    4**

**6142 LIONEL**  1961-66, 8-1/8" long, detailed undercarriage, box interior and sides, unpainted plastic, white lettering, AAR trucks, one disc-operating coupler, one fixed coupler.

(A) Black unpainted plastic.                    **1    1.50    2    3**

(B) 1970, black unpainted plastic, with Symington-Wayne trucks (introduced by MPC in 1970), one manual-operating coupler with plastic tab, one fixed coupler with open top, with "old" Lionel number, probably from leftover bodies. This is more properly early Fundimensions production, but it is

6462 "N" in second panel from left, "NYC" in serif letters, line under "6462" two lines of weights, no brakewheel, no steps, no "new" date, magnetic tab couplers, bar-end trucks.

6562 "N" in third panel "NYC" in sans-serif lettering, no line under or over "6562", three lines of weights, no brakewheels, no steps, "NEW 2-49", magnetic tab couplers, bar-end trucks.

listed here for convenience. (Similar combinations are also seen with hoppers.) **1   1.50   2   3**

**6142-50 LIONEL** 1961-63, 1966, unpainted shiny green plastic, white lettering "LIONEL" and "6142", AAR plastic trucks with one disc and one dummy coupler, one molded brakewheel each side, body mold 6112-86, no built date, two red canisters. Possibly included in 1065 diesel set in 1961. Additional information requested. Came in set 11560 in 1966. I.D. Smith and C. Rohlfing observations. **1   1.50   2   3**

**6142-75 LIONEL** 1961-63, same as 6142 but unpainted blue plastic, numbered "6142", with white canisters, 6112-88, mold 6112-86, AAR trucks, disc couplers. C. Rohlfing Collection. **1   1.50   2   3**

**6142-100 LIONEL**
(A) 1964, light green unpainted plastic body, no lettering, mold 6112-86. Molded brakewheels, late AAR trucks, one disc and one dummy coupler, two white 6112-88 canisters, part of set 11430. Further confirmation requested. Winton Collection. Also came as part of J.C. Penney set 924-8287, 1965. L. Wyant collection. **1   1.50   2   3**
(B) Green body, 6142 only on car, AAR trucks, two disc couplers, mold 6112-86, came with four white canisters with "61125" printed on canister. T. Budniak Collection. **1   1.50   2   3**

**6142-150 LIONEL** Circa 1961-63?, same as 6142 above but unpainted blue plastic, with "6142" numbered cable reels. Need information as to whether 6142-150 has a body mold number. **1   1.50   2   3**

**6142-175 LIONEL** Circa 1961-63?, probably similar to 6142 above although body's part number differs from previous entries numbered "6142". Need information as to whether 6142-175 has a body mold number.
**1   1.50   2   3**

**6162 N Y C** 1961-69, unpainted plastic body, white lettering, 9-9/16" long, "N" in third panel from left, "N.Y.C." overscored, "6162" underscored.
(A) 1961, blue, "NEW 2-49", early AAR trucks, two disc couplers. Came in set 1609; box imprinted "6162-1 GONDOLA CAR WITH CANISTERS", three unlettered white canisters. T. Budniak Collection. **2   5   7   10**
(B) 1962, blue, no "new" date, later AAR trucks, disc couplers, three unlettered white canisters, box originally labeled "6112-1 CANISTER CAR" but has white paper sticker numbered "6162" over original lettering. R. Griesbeck and K. Koehler Collections. **3   5   7   10**
(C) 1969, red, no "new" date, late AAR trucks or one AAR truck and one arch-bar truck, one disc coupler, one fixed coupler, heavy heat-stamped letters. One example observed came with one AAR truck and one arch-bar truck. R. Vagner and K. Koehler Collections. **2   5   7   10**

**6162-60 ALASKA** 1959, yellow unpainted body, dark blue lettering, three white canisters as part of set 1611, which came with a suitcase-style box with an interliner cardboard cutout to hold three white or red canisters. H. Powell comments.
(A) Bar-end trucks, magnetic couplers, came as part of set 1611 above. H. Powell, R. Vagner and M. Ocilka Collections. **20   25   35   50**
(B) Same as (A), but AAR plastic trucks, two disc couplers, came with four plain red canisters. R. Vagner and M. Canzoneri Collections.
**20   25   35   50**

**6162-110 N Y C** 1966, blue unpainted body, no "new" date, late AAR trucks. Came in box marked 6162-110.
(A) One disc and one dummy coupler, came with two red canisters, orange box with blue lettering, box end covered with white tape 1-1/2" wide stamped "6162-110". R. Hutchinson, T. Budniak, R. Griesbeck and D. Anderson Collections. **3   5   7   10**

(B) Two disc couplers, three white canisters, orange box with blue lettering and regular orange ends marked "6162-110" with part number 6162-111 on interior box flap. R. Hutchinson, D. Anderson and R. LaVoie Collections.
**3   5   7   10**

**6342 N Y C** 1956-58, 1966-69, special gondola for culvert loader with black metal channel, culverts roll down channel, 9-9/16" long, red unpainted plastic, white lettering, "N.Y.C." overscored, three lines of weights, "6342" not overscored.
(A) 1956-57, "NEW 2-49", Type 7 trucks (bar-end, magnetic couplers with tabs), trucks secured with horseshoe clip, Type IIa body. **7   10   15   25**
(B) 1957-58, same as (A), but trucks secured with sheet metal clip.
**7   10   15   25**
(C) 1966-69, no "new" date, late AAR trucks, Type IIb body, came with 348 manual culvert unloader. R. Hutchinson and P. Ambrose comments.
**7   10   15   25**

**6452 PENNSYLVANIA** 1948-49, short gondola, 8", black-painted plastic body, white lettering, quarter-sized hole in bottom of body, holes and embossings in base, staple-end trucks, "PENNSYLVANIA" overscored by line on top, numbered "347000", reporting marks on left in two lines: "CAPY 140000 LT WT 56500 / LD LMT 153500 NEW 12-45". Reporting marks on right in four lines: "6452 LIONEL / IL 56-2 / CU FT 1745 / BLT 12-45 G27". This car, like the 2452, was designed to accept the electronic control unit. Some trucks have pickup shoes, and some were reportedly manufactured with ECUs for the 1950 electronic control set. R. Lord comments. **1   1.50   2   5**

This car has two versions: the 1948 version with "6462" on its side and "6452" on its underside, and the 1949 version with "6452" on the side and no stamping on the frame bottom. Metal underframe, brakewheel disc with center hole but without brakewheel.
(A) 1948, numbered "6462" on the side and rubber-stamped "6452" on the underside; steps at corners, Type 3 staple-end trucks with late coil couplers and sliding shoes, Type Ib frame (see 2452 listings). R. Vagner Collection.
**4   7   10   20**
(B) 1949, numbered "6452" on side but no rubber-stamped number on frame, Type 4 staple-end trucks with magnetic couplers and no extra hole in activator flap. R. Vagner Collection. **2   5   7   10**

**Note:** The 6462 listings have been substantially revised for the 6th edition of this work. We no longer report whether NYC is overscored and whether 6462 is underscored. We made this change since our data indicate that all 6462s with N in the second panel have 6462 underscored and do not have NYC overscored. Our data also indicate that all 6462s with N in the third panel have NYC overscored and 6462 underscored. Finally a 6462s with N in the second panel have NYC with serifs while 6462s with N in the third panel have NYC without serifs. If readers have 6462s that do not fit these patterns, we would appreciate hearing from them. Color shades have also been deleted from this edition. These differences were deleted because a user could not identify his car without having other cars of other shades for comparison.

**6462 N.Y.C.:** 1949-1956, 9-9/16" long. Cars are arranged by color with additional varieties listed under 6464-25, 6462-75 and 6462-125. Black cars come with six unstained solid wood drums with two hoops and bottom and top rims, while other cars came with six, brown-stained barrels with hoops. For more information about these cars, please consult the article by Richard Vagner earlier in this chapter.

**BLACK GONDOLAS 1949-1954:** The following cars all have "N" in second panel from left. Four different kinds of bodies: Ia, Ib, Ic and IIa. Drawings showing the body types are found earlier in this chapter. There are two versions of weight data: three lines (1949-51) and two lines (1950-54). Earlier cars have three lines of weight data and later cars have two lines of weight data. Reader reports on weight data would be appreciated.

(A) 1949, Type 4 trucks (staple-end, magnetic coupler, activator flap with one hole), steps, brakewheels, Type Ib body.   2   4   8   10

(B) 1950, same as (A), but Type Ib body.   2   4   8   10

(C) 1950-51, Type 5A trucks (staple-end, magnetic coupler, activator flap with two holes, rivet in activator flap with flared end down), no steps, brakewheel, Type Ic body.   2   4   8   10

(D) 1951-52, Type 5B trucks (staple-end, magnetic coupler, activator flap with two holes, rivet in activator flap with round end down), no steps, brakewheel, Type Ic body.   2   4   8   10

(E) 1952-53, same as (D), but Type 6 trucks (bar-end, magnetic coupler, activator flap with two holes, rivet in activator flap with round end down).   2   4   8   10

(F) 1953, same as (D), but Type 6 trucks, no brakewheel.   2   4   8   10

(G) 1954, Type 6 trucks, no steps, no brakewheel, Type IIa body.   2   4   8   10

**RED GONDOLAS: 1950-52, 1954, 1956-57:** There are three major color variations: tuscan red, light red, unpainted red plastic. There are many fine shadings of these three primary color types. We reported these shadings in previous editions but it was extremely difficult for readers to use this information without cars to reference. The color information needs to be more fully integrated with the chronology that follows. Truck types are defined under the black gondolas listings which preceed this section as well as in the truck chapter.

**1950-54:** "N" in second panel from left

(A) 1950, Type 4 trucks, Type Ib body, tuscan red, steps, brakewheel.   2   4   8   10

(B) 1950-51, Type 5A trucks, no steps, brakewheel, Type Ic body, tuscan red.   2   4   8   10

(C) 1951-52, Type 5B trucks, no steps, brakewheel, Type Ic body, tuscan red.   2   4   8   10

(D) 1952, Type 6 trucks, no steps, brakewheel, Type Ic body, tuscan red.   2   4   8   10

(E) 1954, Type 6 trucks, no steps, no brakewheel, Type IIa body, light red.   2   4   8   10

**1956-57:** "N" in third panel from left. The following cars are reported as either light red painted plastic or unpainted red plastic.

(F) 1956, Type 7 trucks (bar-end, magnetic couplers, tab), horseshoe clips mount trucks, no steps, no brakewheel.   2   4   8   10

(G) 1957, Type 7 trucks, truck clips mount trucks, no steps, no brakewheel.   2   4   8   10

**GREEN GONDOLAS: 1954-56:** All are made with Type IIa bodies, no steps and no brakewheels, metal underframe.

(A) 1954, Type 6 trucks, "N" is in second panel from left.   3   5   9   14

(B) 1955, Type 7 trucks, "N" is in the second panel from the left, two lines of weights.   3   5   9   14

(C) 1956, Type 7 trucks, "N" is in the third panel from the left, three lines of weights.   3   5   9   14

**6462-25** Green-painted black plastic body, very white lettering, metal underframe, "N" in second panel from left, line under "6462", no "new", two lines of weights, no hole in underframe, no steps, no brakewheels, Type 6 trucks (bar-end, magnetic couplers without tabs), numbered "6462" only, "6462-25" is catalogue number that appears on box. The car comes in several shades of green. J. Kotil and R. Pauli Collections.   3   5   9   12

**6462-75** Red-painted black plastic body, white lettering, "N" in third panel from left, "NEW 2-49", three lines of weights, Type 6 trucks, (bar-end, magnetic couplers), numbered "6462", "6462-75" is catalogue number that appears on box.

(A) Bright red paint. R. Pauli Collection.   3   5   9   14

(B) Shiny darker red. J. Kotil Collection.   3   5   9   14

(C) Dull red. J. Kotil Collection.   3   5   12   20

Catalogue number no known.  Note molded brakewheel.

**6462-100 N Y C  1951-54**

(A) Red unpainted plastic body, metal trucks, no brakewheels, reader confirmation requested. P. Ambrose comment.   **NRS**

(B) Red-painted black plastic body, white lettering, metal underframe, NYC overscored, "N" in third panel from left, "NEW 2-49", bar-end trucks, magnetic couplers, no brakewheels, older orange and blue box marked 6462-100, 1954, part of set 2223W. R. Shanfeld and D. Anderson Collections.   3   5   10   14

(C) Same as (B), but unpainted red body, two brakewheels. E. Heid Collection.   3   5   10   14

**6462-125 N Y C  1954-57**, red unpainted plastic body, white lettering, metal underframe, lines over "N.Y.C.", "N" in third panel, "NEW 2-49", three lines of weights, no brakewheel, no steps, Type 7 trucks (bar-end trucks, magnetic tab couplers), only "6462" appears on car, "6462-125" is catalogue number that appears on box. Came with 1615 steam switcher in 1955 as part of set 1527 with six brown barrels; this set also included the 6560 crane car with gray cab. P. Ambrose and R. Vagner comments. Came with 1956 set 1553W as well. C. Rohlfing comment. Also see 6562. J. Kotil Collection.

(A) Dull red. J. Kotil Collection.   3   5   9   14

(B) Shiny red, no line under 6462. R. Griesbeck Collection.   3   5   9   14

(C) Same as (B), but "6462" is underscored. C. Rohlfing Collection.   3   5   9   14

**6462-500 N Y C  1957-58**, pink-painted body, black lettering, from Girls' Set, lines over "N.Y.C.", "N" in third panel from left, line under "6462", "NEW 2-49", Type 7 trucks (bar-end metal trucks, magnetic tab couplers), three lines of weights, no brakewheel, no steps, note that 6462, not 6462-500, appears on car. R. Vagner comment.   40   75   125   175

**6562 N Y C  1956-58**, metal underframe, lines over "N.Y.C.", "N" in third panel from left, no line under "6562", "NEW 2-49", bar-end metal trucks, magnetic tab couplers, three lines of weights, no brakewheels, no steps, 9-9/16" long, 3/16" hole in center of metal base. H. Degano observation.

(A) 1956, unpainted gray plastic, maroon lettering, gray plastic is lighter and less shiny than (D), magnetic couplers with tabs, no mold number, metal base. Came in box marked 6562-1. D. Fleming Collection.   7   13   25   40

(B) 1956, 1958, red unpainted plastic body, white lettering. Came in box marked 6562-25.   7   13   25   40

(C) 1957, black unpainted plastic body, white lettering. Came in box marked 6562-50. P. Ambrose Collection.   7   13   25   40

(D) Unpainted gray plastic, red lettering, gray plastic is darker and more shiny than (A), magnetic couplers without tabs, no mold number, metal base. Came in box marked 6562-1. D. Fleming Collection.   7   12   25   40

**NOTE:** Cars marked 6462 coming in boxes marked 6562-1 may be the result of packaging errors. Before we list any of the 6562-1 cars above as separate entries, we will need more detailed descriptions of each of these cars from readers. Sorting out these cars may be an intricate puzzle.

**NO NUMBER** 8-1/8" long, detailed undercarriage and box interior, blue unpainted plastic, no lettering, AAR trucks, fixed couplers, "61 12-86" mold number embossed in bottom, catalogue number not known. R. Schreiner Collection.   1   1.50   2   3

**NO NUMBER** Green unpainted plastic, short gondola, length unknown, interior detail unknown, AAR trucks, one fixed coupler, one disc-operating coupler, mold number and catalogue number not known. R. Schreiner Collection.   1   1.50   2   3

**NOTE:** On those 9-9/16" cars with a metal underframe, the mold number (part number) is under the metal under frame.

# Chapter VIII

# HOPPERS AND DUMP CARS

**Lionel made three basic dump cars: the intermediate size car had two different catalogue numbers, 3459 and 3469.**

For the transportation of loose loads in bulk quantities, nothing is quite so handy as the hopper car, either in its open or closed versions. In the coal mining regions of the country, long trains of black hopper cars carrying "black diamonds" to power plants are a familiar sight. In the Midwest, equally long trains of covered hopper cars carry grain to market with ease. The Lionel Corporation's freight consists would have been incomplete without at least a few of these handy freight carriers.

In 1946 Lionel offered a new operating dump car, the 3459 to complement the 3559, a carry-over from a prewar model. The first of Lionel's new hopper cars appeared in late 1947 or (more likely) early 1948. This was the car marked "LEHIGH VALLEY 25000", which was a familiar sight throughout all of postwar production. The first versions of this car had metal plates holding the trucks, but later versions were all plastic - the same developmental history as the gondola cars. They came with Lehigh Valley markings in black, maroon, red, gray and yellow colors. The short hopper car carried other railroad markings such as the 6076 Santa Fe in gray.

The short hopper car was adapted into an operating version in Norfolk and Western markings for use with an overhead coal ramp. The operator would fill the car with coal (preferably from a coal loader). Then, the train would back up a ramp until the hopper car at the end would hook onto a coupler mounted at the rear of the ramp. At the touch of a button, the car's hatches would open and dump the coal into a waiting trough below the ramp. Then, the operator would press another

button, and the car would uncouple and roll down the ramp to await pickup by the train.

In 1954, Lionel began its production of a large covered hopper; the first version of this "Cement Car", as Lionel called it, was made in Norfolk and Western markings. The roof cover had 12 hatches which could open, but operators had to be very careful of their fragility. Later cars were produced in other road markings, and some were made without covers. In the uncovered versions, Lionel usually included a center spreader bar which fit into two holes high up on the car sides. Real railroads had this bar attached to the car sides to keep the sides from bulging outwards with a heavy load. Lionel put it there to keep the thin plastic sides from cracking when squeezed by an over-enthusiastic child. These big cars were extremely well-detailed and handsome additions to a layout.

Lionel produced several varieties of coal dumping cars throughout the postwar years. The firm kept making its Marx-like 3659 prewar dump car (renumbered 3559); this car was very short, with a V-shaped red bin and black ends. The bin tilted when the car was activated by the uncoupling-unloading track. This dump car was only made in 1946. In that year, Lionel began production of another all-metal dump car, the 3459/3469. This car had a rectangular bin which tilted so that the side of the bin opened and dumped the car's load. Most of these cars were made in black, but green versions are also found, and early aluminum and yellow versions are rare and highly prized.

The last coal dumping hopper made by Lionel was the strange 3359-55 Twin Bin dumping car of 1955-1957. This car featured two gray plastic bins which operated in sequence instead of simultaneously. The action was accomplished by means of a rotating cam beneath the bins which advanced in steps. About 10 pushes of the operating button would dump both bins. Lionel claimed that this car had a prototype which was used by the City of New York for gravel-dumping purposes, and this prototype does appear in the 1940 edition of **Model Builder**.

Considering the quantities produced, it is rather surprising that Lionel did not make its hopper cars in more road names. The small hoppers are almost always found in Lehigh Valley markings, and there are only six road markings for the 50-ton "quad" hopper (though there are more varieties than that). Probably Lionel did not feel the need to change the road markings to sell the cars, since the short hoppers especially

were mostly included in sets rather than sold separately. Whatever the case, most of the hopper and dump cars are quite easy to obtain today, although it is difficult to build a collection of all the varieties. A full study of the Lehigh Valley hopper cars is needed to match the ones done for the New York Central gondolas and the 9-1/4" boxcars.

## HOPPER BODY TYPES

At first glance hopper body Type I and Type III appear to have similar side views. However, a close inspection of the Type I body's lower center section indicates a row of rivets forming an inverted V. In the Type III body types the additional rivets were added to form a triangle.

With Type III body types, the inverted V of Type I is closed off by a line of rivets along the bottom edge of the car.

Type I and Type III bodies also differ in their interior details as shown below.

# Hopper Body Types

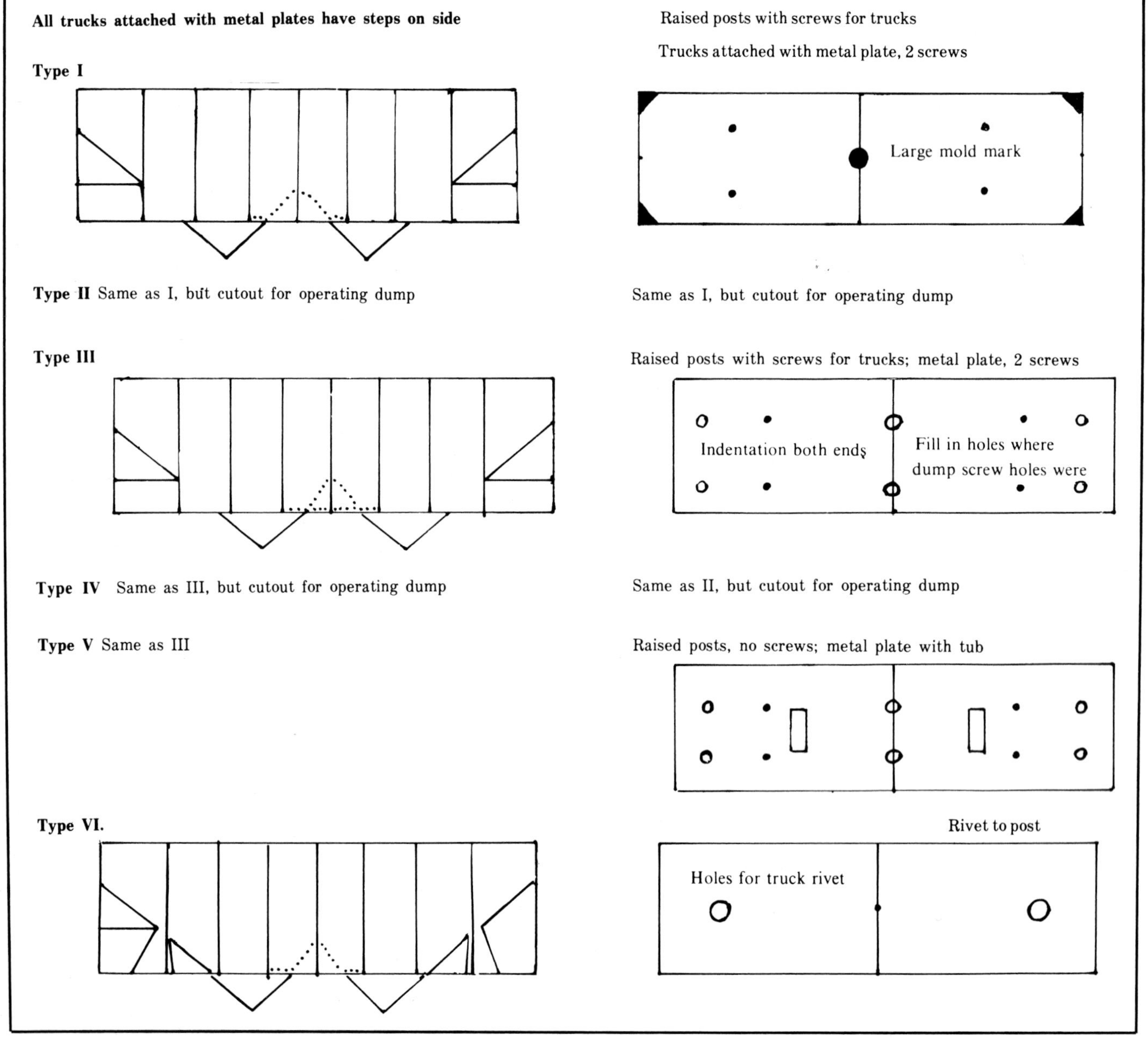

**All trucks attached with metal plates have steps on side**

**Type I**

Raised posts with screws for trucks

Trucks attached with metal plate, 2 screws

Large mold mark

**Type II** Same as I, but cutout for operating dump

Same as I, but cutout for operating dump

**Type III**

Raised posts with screws for trucks; metal plate, 2 screws

Indentation both ends

Fill in holes where dump screw holes were

**Type IV** Same as III, but cutout for operating dump

Same as II, but cutout for operating dump

**Type V** Same as III

Raised posts, no screws; metal plate with tub

Rivet to post

**Type VI.**

Holes for truck rivet

**2456 LEHIGH VALLEY** 1948 only, Type IA body, white lettering, "NEW 1-48", "BLT-1-48" and "LIONEL 2456", one brakewheel, (Type 3B) staple-end trucks, with late coil couplers, with knuckle staked at four points, steps, 8-9/16" long, slotted screws hold truck plates to body (later cars have Phillips-head screws).

(A) Flat black. T. Budniak and J. Sattler Collections. **5  10  15  25**

(B) Shiny black paint over marbled plastic. H. Holden and R. LaVoie Collections. **5  10  15  25**

**2856 B & O** 1946-47, scale-detailed hopper car; catalogued in black in 1946 and in gray in 1947. This car has the dubious distinction of being the only Lionel car catalogued for one year in one color and a second year in another color but not manufactured in either color; J. Sattler comment. As an ironic sidelight, Tom RRollo has pointed out that Lionel pictures this car in its 1948 instruction booklet on page 4 in the lower right-hand corner. It would appear that Lionel may have made at least one of these hoppers, in that case! When Lionel catalogued this car in 1947, it would have been the most expensive non-operating car available, with a price of $8.00. Compare that with the $7.50 price of the 2855 tank car or even the 2625 Pullman!

**Not Manufactured**

**2956 B & O** 1940-42, scale-detailed hopper car; black die-cast body, white lettering, "BLT 3-27", "532000", "2956", working die-cast bottom hatches, staple-end trucks, coil couplers, apparently not manufactured after 1942; car most likely converted from tinplate trucks to staple-end trucks by service station or owner. Illustrated in 1946 catalogue but listed as 2856. See entry above. Listed here for reader convenience. **100  175  250  350**

**3359-55 LIONEL LINES** 1955-58, twin gray bins which tilt, red simulated power unit mounted on black frame, bar-end trucks, magnetic couplers with or without tabs, came with two OTC contactors, cam rotates and dumps bins in alternation, also came with 160 long receiving bin and 96C controller. The prototype for this car is shown in the 1940 issues of **Model Builder**. P. Ambrose and T. Rollo comments; J. Sattler Collection. **9  15  25  35**

**3449 LIONEL LINES** 1946, ore dump car, silver bin, blue Lionel Lines lettering; same as 3459(A), but different number. Came as part of 1946 freight set headed by a smoke-bulb 671 turbine. This number could be a factory prototype or error; we need more information. M. Gesualdi Collection. **NRS**

**3456 N & W** 1950-55, black with white lettering, "BLT 8-50", "NEW 8-50", operating bottom hatches, steps, brakewheel, 8-9/16" long. Offered for separate sale and sold as part of 456 Coal Ramp. This is still the only operating hopper fully compatible with that ramp. Some Fundimensions operating hoppers work with the ramp, some do not. The problem is that the pull-down activator on some cars does not line up with the magnet on the ramp. R. LaVoie and C. Switzer comments.

(A) 1950-51, black-painted, Type II body, Type 5B staple-end trucks, with magnetic couplers with two holes in the activator flap, activator flap rivet with roundhead down and large off-center hole in base plate. J. Sattler Collection. **12  20  25  40**

(B) Black paint on brown plastic, Type IV body, bar-end Type VI trucks. C. Rohlfing Collection. **12  20  25  40**

(C) Black paint on blue plastic, Type IV body, bar-end Type VI trucks. C. Switzer Collection. **12  20  25  40**

(D) Black paint on white plastic, Type IV body. J. Kotil Collection. Information as to truck type requested. **12  20  25  40**

**3459 LIONEL LINES** 1946-48, "AUTOMATIC DUMP CAR", bin dumps, all with black frame and simulated dump mechanism, two brakewheels, staple-end trucks, coil couplers. The bins on all observed cars are aluminum, and in most cases the bins are painted black. We currently do not have a means of distinguishing 1947 from 1948 production other than from set consist information. Unfortunately truck and box characteristics do not distinguish these years. The magnetic couplers are found with the 3469. See next entry for 3469.

(A) 1946, aluminum-finished bin with blue lettering, black mechanisms and ends, coil couplers. The knuckle is fastened to the metal support only by the rivet and there are no stake marks. In 1947, the knuckle casting is bent or staked into the steel support bracket. J. Sattler Collection. **40  75  125  175**

(B) 1946, same as (A), but black-painted bin. **15  25  40  60**

(C) 1947-8, all-black car, white lettering. The knuckle casting is bent into the steel support bracket. J. Sattler Collection. **9  15  25  40**

(D) 1948, green-painted bin, black frame and mechanism, white lettering. Came in 1948 set 2137WS. C. Rohlfing Collection. **20  30  40  60**

(E) Yellow-painted body with black heat-stamped lettering, rare. We would like to observe this car for further study. **NRS**

(F) 1946, same as (B), but receiving bin which came with car is made of a black dump car body bin fabricated of steel instead of aluminum. Came in set 1415WS. However, the bin was catalogued in 1947. C. Rohlfing Collection. **20  30  40  60**

**3469 LIONEL LINES** 1949-55, "AUTOMATIC DUMP CAR", bin dumps, black frame and simulated dump mechanism, bin is made from aluminum, two brakewheels. One example has been found in an original box marked 3469X; T. Budniak comment. Since this car was available for six years, there are likely a number of yet undiscovered variations. Clearly the boxes differed in this time period. Most likely, the smaller boxes marked "3469X" did not include a 160 dumping bin and were meant for sets. Also the trucks varied: staple-end with different activator flaps as well as bar-end trucks. We look forward to reader comments.

(A) 1949-51, staple-end trucks. C. Rohlfing comment. **9  12  25  35**

(B) 1952-55, bar-end trucks. C. Rohlfing comment. **9  12  25  35**

(C) Same as (B), but came in box marked 3469X, part number 3469X-2, two brakewheels. T. Budniak Collection. **9  12  25  35**

**3559 COAL DUMP CAR** 1946-48, rerun of 3659 prewar car with new staple-end trucks, black frame and usually a black plastic end unit, red bin, silver or white "3559" rubber-stamped on underside.

(A) Early 1946, Type 2 trucks with early coil couplers. **7  10  15  25**

(B) Late 1946, Type 3A trucks with late coil couplers and knuckle attached to supporting plate only by integral stud, no stake marks. Not confirmed. **NRS**

(C) 1947-48, Type 3B trucks with late coil couplers, knuckle attached to supporting plate by stud and by staking at four points. J. Sattler Collection. **7  10  15  25**

(D) Same as (C), but dark brown plastic mechanism housing, inspection tag "T-4768 M.R. / V-4758 M.B. / 51148". J. Sattler Collection. **15  20  30  50**

**5459 LIONEL LINES** 1946-49, "AUTOMATIC DUMP CAR" with green and white "ELECTRONIC CONTROL" decal, black car with white lettering, electronic control receiver hidden inside frame of car; staple-end trucks, coil-operated couplers, inspection tag "T-4768 M.R. / V-4758 M.B. / 51148". J. Sattler Collection. **22  35  60  80**

**546446** See 6446-1 or 6446-25.

**6076 (A-C) A T S F** 1963, Type VI gray plastic body, black lettering, "BUILT BY LIONEL", no date, no brakewheels, special promotional set for Libby (19263) with 1062 locomotive with Southern Pacific tender, 8-9/16" long. Variation lettering changed in !Sixth Edition.

(A) AAR trucks, one disc coupler, one fixed coupler. R. Shanfeld Collection. **9  15  20  30**

(B) Arch-bar trucks, fixed couplers. J. Sattler Collection. **9  15  20  30**

(C) One AAR truck with disc coupler; one arch-bar truck with fixed coupler. **9  15  20  30**

**6076 LEHIGH VALLEY** 1963, Type VI body, 8-9/16" long, no brakewheels. Variation lettering changed in Sixth Edition.

(A) Gray body, black lettering, "BUILT 1-48", no "new" date, AAR trucks, one disc coupler, one fixed coupler. Formerly W. Eddins Collection. **4  6  8  12**

(B) Black body, white lettering, "BUILT 1-48", "NEW 1-48", early AAR truck with disc coupler, late AAR truck with fixed coupler. J. Sattler Collection. **4  6  8  12**

(C) Same as (B), but arch-bar trucks, fixed couplers. J. Sattler and R. LaVoie Collections. **4  6  8  10**

(D) Same as (B), but without "new" dates. **4  6  8  10**

(E) Same as (B), but without "built" and "new" dates. R. Pauli Collection. **4  6  8  10**

(F) Same as (B), but fixed couplers. J. Kotil Collection. **4  6  8  10**

(G) Red with white lettering, "BUILT 1-48", "NEW 1-48", arch-bar trucks fixed couplers, came with set X-600. J. Divi Collection. **4  6  8  10**

(H) Dull yellow-painted gray body, black lettering, "NEW 1-48", "BUILT

Top shelf:  6456 and 6456.  Second shelf:  6456 and 6456.  Third shelf:  3456 operating hopper and 2956 scale-detailed prewar hopper with postwar trucks.

Gd VG Exc Mt

1-48", "CAPY 100000; LO LMT 128300; CU. FT. 1860". AAR trucks, one disc-operating and one dummy coupler, no brakewheel. Sekely Collection.

**2   3   5   6**

(I) No number, black body, white-lettered "CAPY 100000 LD LMT 128300 CU FT 1860", no "BLT" date, no "NEW" number, AAR trucks. R. Schreiner Collection. (We need assistance in identifying Lionel's number for this car. The original box probably bears the Lionel catalogue number.)

**NRS**

**6076: NO LETTERING** Type VI body.

(A) Unpainted olive drab body, early AAR truck with disc coupler, late AAR truck with one fixed coupler, with open top. J. Sattler, D. McCarthy and G. Wilson Collections. Part of uncatalogued set headed by 221 Alco and an uncatalogued J.C. Penney set; hard to find. **10   20   35   50**

(B) Unpainted gray plastic body, early AAR trucks, fixed couplers, came as part of uncatalogued set 19262 (1963) and with set 11311 (1963). P. Ambrose comment; R. Griesbeck and J. Kotil Collections. **2   4   6   10**

**6076-75 LEHIGH VALLEY** 1963. Illustrated as part of set 11321 with 211 locomotive. We believe that the car is actually numbered 6076. We would like to have a description of this car. **NRS**

**6076-100 NO LETTERING** 1963, bright yellow unpainted plastic, Type VI body, AAR trucks, one disc and one dummy coupler, embossed lettering on underside: "MADE IN THE U.S. OF AMERICA / BY THE LIONEL CORPORATION NEW YORK"; came as part of set 11311 with 1062 locomotive. See 1062 steam locomotive entry, Chapter II, for details. We think that this car is identical to the one we report as 6176 (No Lettering) reported from set 11430; reader comments invited. J. West Collection.

**2   4   7   10**

**6176 LEHIGH VALLEY** 1964-66, Type VI body, no brakewheel. All observed cars come with AAR trucks; most have one operating and one dummy coupler, but some have two dummy couplers.

Greenberg's Lionel Service Manual, pp. V-70, 71 and 73, reports four different 6176 models: 6176-25 with body part 6176-2; 6176-50 with body part 6076-88; 6176-75 with body part 6176-76; and 6176-100 with olive drab body part 6176-101; this latter car came as part of uncatalogued set 19334 made for J. C. Penney (P. Ambrose comment). All four are reported with AAR trucks having one operating and one dummy coupler. The first catalogue appearance of the car occurs in 1964 on page 3, where a light-colored, unlettered and unnumbered 6176 is shown as part of set 11430 and a dark-colored Lehigh Valley lettered and numbered car is shown with set 11440 and catalogued as 6176-50.

On pages 4 and 5 of the 1964 catalogue, several more 6176 hoppers are listed. A dark-colored Lehigh Valley example is catalogued as 6176-50 with set 11450, while a light-colored Lehigh Valley is catalogued as 6176-75 with set 11460. Set 11480 came with a dark-colored Lehigh Valley catalogued as 6176-50, while set 11510 came with a light-colored Lehigh Valley car catalogued as 6176-75.

In 1965, the 6176 is again catalogued in both dark-colored and light-colored lettered versions, but this time the catalogue does not provide the suffix. In 1966, the 6176 is catalogued in yellow with sets 11500 and 11520 and in black with sets 11540, 11550 and 11560. We ask that readers with these sets contact us and report the color, trucks, body type, built dates and new dates of their cars so that we can establish years of production and understand the Lionel suffix code.

### 6176 YELLOW CARS

(A) Dark yellow, blue lettering, "NEW 1-48", "BUILT 1-48", "LIONEL 6176", AAR trucks, one disc coupler, one fixed coupler. **3   5   7   10**

(B) Same as (A), but without "new" date, late AAR trucks. J. Sattler Collection. **3   5   7   10**

(C) Same as (A), but medium yellow. J. Sattler Collection. **3   5   7   10**

(D) Light yellow, black lettering, "new" not present, "BUILT 1-48" and "LIONEL 6176" both present, AAR trucks, disc couplers, set 12730 (1966). J. Kohl Collection. **3   5   7   10**

(E) Same as (D), but one disc coupler, one fixed coupler. **3   5   7   10**

(F) Light yellow, black lettering, "NEW 1-48", "BUILT 1-48" and "LIONEL 6176" all missing. R. Pauli Collection. **3   5   7   10**

(G) Same as (A), but black lettering. Part of set 11430. J. Kotil and Winton Collections. **3   5   7   10**

(H) Dark yellow, no built date, no new date, no car number, one late AAR truck with disc coupler and small protruding semi-circle next to L in circle on underside of truck and one late AAR truck with fixed coupler. J. Sattler Collection. **3   5   7   10**

(I) Same as (D), but has "NEW 1-48". R. LaVoie Collection. **3   5   7   10**

### 6176 GRAY CARS

(A) Gray with black lettering, "NEW 1-48" not present, "BUILT 1-48" present, late AAR trucks, one disc coupler, one fixed coupler. J. Sattler Collection. **3   5   7   10**

(B) Same as (A), but with "NEW 1-48". Set 19350-500, J. Kotil Collection. **3   5   7   10**

Top Shelf: 6446-1 N & W quad hopper which is numbered 546446 on the side, 6536 M St L quad hopper. Second shelf: 6436 and 6636. Third shelf: 6346 and 6736.

### 6176 BLACK CARS

(A) 1966, black body, white lettering, AAR trucks, one disc and one fixed coupler, no number, built date or new date on car, came in set 11560 with 211 locomotive in 1966. C. Rohlfing Collection.       3       5       7      10

(B) Black body, white lettering, no number, AAR trucks, dummy couplers, no new date, came in uncatalogued set 19500. C. Rohlfing Collection.
                                                                    3       5       7      10

**6176(N)  NO LETTERING**, 1964, deep bright yellow, Type VI body, late AAR trucks, one disc coupler, one fixed coupler, from set 11430, 1964. J. Sattler and Edwards Collections.       2       4       7      10

**6346-56 ALCOA**  1956, 50-ton quad hopper, silver paint with blue lettering, "NEW 6-56", hatch covers, Alcoa labels, no center brace hole, brakewheel, bar-end trucks, magnetic couplers. See also Factory Errors.

(A) With tab couplers. J. Sattler Collection.       12      25      30      45

(B) Without tab couplers. J. Sattler Collection.       12      25      30      45

**6436**  See 6436-110.

**6436-1 LEHIGH VALLEY**  1955, uncatalogued, 50-ton quad hopper, gray plastic painted black, white lettering, "NEW 3-55", no covers, bar-end trucks, magnetic tab couplers, one brakewheel. Cummings comment.

(A) Center spreader bar holes without spreader, came as part of 1955 catalogued set.       10      15      25      40

(B) Without center spreader bar holes.       15      30      45      60

(C) Center spreader bar holes with spreader. J. Sattler Collection.
                                                                   10      15      25      40

(D) Center spreader bar holes without spreader, yellow lettering, no brakewheel. J. Sattler Collection.       10      15      25      40

**6436-25 LEHIGH VALLEY**  1955-57, 50-ton quad hopper, no covers, maroon with white lettering, "NEW 3-55", brakewheels, bar-end trucks, magnetic couplers, box end reads "No. 6436 / HOPPER CAR / 25 LIONEL 25", box part number 6436-30.

(A) No tabs, confirmation requested       10      15      25      40

(B) Tab couplers, spreader bar, no brakewheel. J. Sattler Collection.
                                                                   10      15      25      40

(C) Same as (B), but has brakewheel. R. LaVoie Collection.
                                                                   10      15      25      40

(D) Gray plastic painted maroon, no cover, white lettering. A. Arpino Collection.       10      15      25      40

**6436-100**  See 6436-110.

**6436-110 LEHIGH VALLEY**  1963-68, 50-ton quad hopper, red-painted gray plastic with white lettering, spreader, no covers, AAR trucks, magnetic

couplers, brakewheel. Car may be numbered 6436 or 6436-100. See variations below. Car may or may not have lettering "NEW 3-55". All cars have "BLT BY / LIONEL", but we do not know if all varieties have built dates.

(A) Numbered only "6436", no new or built dates, came in box numbered 6436-110, late AAR trucks. J. Sattler and D. Fleming Collections.
                                                                   10      22      30      55

(B) Numbered "6436-100", has "NEW 3-55", no built date, came in box numbered 6436-110. J. Kotil Collection.       40      60      90      125

(C) Numbered "6436-100" without new or built date, came in box numbered 6436-110. J. Kotil Collection.       10      22      30      55

(D) Numbered only "6436", "NEW 3-55", no brakewheel, has covers, box marked "6446-60", brighter red than (A). J. Algozzini, P. Ambrose, R. Shanfeld and D. Fleming Collections.       40      60      90      125

(E) Same as (D), but black body and covers instead of bright red. P. Ambrose Collection.       40      60      90      125

**6436-1969 TCA**  1969, uncatalogued, 50-ton quad hopper, special run of 1,000 for 1969 TCA Convention, "BLT BY LIONEL 4-69", spreader bar, no cover, red-painted body with white convention data and lettering, white palm tree and white TCA logos; late AAR trucks, disc couplers. J. Sattler Collection.       —       —      100      135

**6436-500 LEHIGH VALLEY**  1957-58, 50-ton quad hopper from Girls' Set, numbered "643657" and "NEW 3-55".

(A) Lilac car with maroon lettering.       75      100      175      250

(B) Burgundy-painted black plastic shell, white heat-stamped lettering, "NEW 3-55", one metal spreader bar; Lionel preproduction paint sample. H. Degano Collection.       —       —      1000      —

(C) Same as (A), but no center spreader bar holes. C. Darasko Collection.
                                                                   75      100      175      250

**6446-1 N & W**  1954-55, 50-ton quad hopper, "NEW 6-54", "546446" on side, bar-end trucks, roof with 12 covers held on by three metal clips, brakewheel. (In earlier editions this item was catalogued as a 54-6446 and variations had different letter designations.)

(A) Gray plastic body painted gray, black lettering, covers, "BLT BY LIONEL", spreader bar, confirmation requested.       13      25      35      60

(B) Light gray, black lettering, confirmation requested.       13      25      35      60

(C) Gray plastic body painted gray, black lettering, without center brace hole, magnetic couplers, "BLT BY / LIONEL", inspection tag "4551 / R.A. 511".       13      25      35      60

(D) Gray body, brace holes and brace, no roof, plastic trucks, 1963 couplers, more details requested.       13      25      35      60

6076

6076(N)

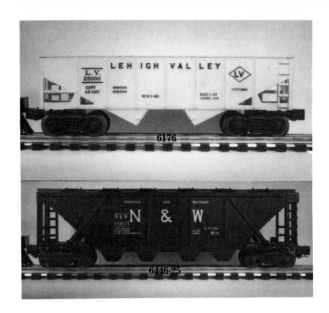

6176

6446-25

| | Gd | VG | Exc | Mt |
|---|---|---|---|---|

**6446-25 N & W** 1955-57, 50-ton quad hopper, numbered "546446", and "NEW 6-54", roof with 12 covers. (Note: We have changed hopper classifications from previous editions so that our numbers correspond to Lionel's cataloguing system.)

(A) Black-painted gray plastic, white lettering, 6446-25 on car sides, no center brace hole, bar-end trucks, magnetic couplers, brakewheel "BLT BY LIONEL NEW 6-54"; box end lettered "6446 CEMENT CAR 25 LIONEL 25". J. Kotil and P. Ambrose Collections. **10 20 30 45**

(B) Same as (A), but center brace hole with brace, tab magnetic couplers. **10 20 30 45**

(C) 1963, gray unpainted plastic, black lettering, center brace hole, no brace, AAR trucks, disc couplers, box end marked "6446 CEMENT CAR", part of set 13098. H. Powell, P. Ambrose and J. Kotil Collections. **10 20 40 60**

(D) Gray plastic painted gray, no cover, no center brace hole, bar-end trucks, car sides stamped 6446-25. P. Ambrose Collection. **10 20 40 60**

(E) 1970-71, royal blue, white lettering, produced by MPC; only 400 produced, MPC's smallest regular production run. These cars are characterized by an unusual number of plastic lap marks caused by irregular flow of the plastic into the car dies. These were reportedly trial stampings to test the die, but Glen Uhl, a noted Ohio Lionel dealer at the time, purchased these shells and sold them. Listed here for your convenience, although an MPC product with a postwar number. **50 75 125 200**

(F) Same as (A), but no brakewheel. T. Budniak Collection.
**9 15 25 45**

(M-Q) Specials made for N & W that are rare and very desirable, but are not catalogued.

(M) Gold with white lettering. **— — 1000 —**

(N) Pink with black lettering. **— — 1000 —**

(O) Light blue plastic painted light blue, white lettering.
**— — 1000 —**

(P) Same as (G), but with covers and center brace holes.
**— — 1000 —**

(Q) Silver with white lettering. **— — 1000 —**

**6446-60 LEHIGH VALLEY** 1963 only, see entries 6436-110 (D) and (E) above. The catalogue used this number to differentiate this car from the 6436-110, which was an open hopper.

**6456 LEHIGH VALLEY 25000** 1948-55, "NEW 1-48", "BUILT 1-48", steps, brakewheel, except as noted. There were major changes in these listings between the Fifth and Sixth Editions of this work. With the Sixth Edition the listings are reclasssified by body type and truck type. J. Sattler made major contributions to the redrafting of this section. Our goal for the next edition is to provide more dating information.

**6456 Type I Bodies: Staple-end Trucks**

(A) 1948, black with white lettering, late coil couplers, Phillips-head screws hold truck plates to body, identical to 2456 except for "LIONEL 6456" on side and Phillips screws. This factory-assembled version was used in some 1948 sets. We would like to identify the set(s) in which this car came. The car comes in a box marked New York, Chicago, San Francisco and no interior box flap number. See also the 6555 tank car listings. T. Rollo, R. LaVoie and T. Taylor Collections. **8 12 25 35**

(B-1) 1948-1949, black with white lettering, Type 4 trucks with magnetic couplers with one hole in activator flap with a rivet with its flared end down, centered hole on base plate, no inspection tags, box marked "NEW YORK CHICAGO", no interior box flap number. J. Sattler Collection.
**5 7 9 20**

(B-2) Same as (B-1), but inspection tag "T-5004 M.C. / V-4551 R.M. / 51148". J. Sattler Collection. **5 7 9 20**

(B-3) Same as (B-1), but inspection tag "T-5004 M.C./ V-4551 R.M. / 51148", interior box flap number "6456-10", box marked "NEW YORK CHICAGO". J. Sattler Collection. **5 7 9 20**

(C) Black with white lettering, Type 5 trucks with magnetic couplers with second hole in activator flap, rivet with flared end down on activator flap, centered hole on base plate, inspection tags "V-6235 B.L.M. / 51148" and "8210 / 511", no interior box flap number, box marked "NEW YORK, CHICAGO SAN FRANCISCO". J. Sattler Collection. **5 7 9 20**

(D) 1950, black with white lettering, Type 5 trucks with magnetic couplers with second hole in activator flap, off-center hole on base plate on one truck and centered hole on large plate on other truck, rivet with flared end down on activator flap, inspection tag T-5004 M.C. / 511", interior box flap number "6456-10", box marked "NEW YORK CHICAGO". J. Sattler and C. Rohlfing Collections. **5 7 9 20**

(E) 1950-51 black with white lettering, Type 5B trucks: magnetic couplers with second hole in activator flap, rivet with round end down on activator flap. C. Rohlfing Collection. **5 7 9 20**

(F) Maroon with white lettering, staple-end trucks, Type 5B trucks, second hole, rivet with round end down. J. Sattler and C. Rohlfing Collections.
**5 7 9 12**

(G) Maroon with cream lettering, further truck details not available. R. Griesbeck Collection. **5 7 9 20**

**6456 Type I Bodies: Bar-end Trucks**

(A) Black with white lettering. J. Sattler Collection. **5 7 9 12**

(B) Shiny red-painted opaque white body, yellow lettering.
**30 50 100 200**

(C) Same as (B), but white lettering. K. Koehler Collection.
**30 75 200 300**

**6456 Type III Bodies: Staple-end Trucks**

(A) Maroon with white lettering, more truck information needed, box end marked "No. 6456 / RED / HOPPER CAR" with interior flap number

"6456-55", inspection sticker "4928 M.H. / 511". J. Sattler Collection.

|  | 5 | 7 | 9 | 20 |

(B) Dark maroon with white lettering, box lettering not known.

|  | 5 | 7 | 9 | 20 |

### 6456 Type III Bodies: Bar-end Trucks

(A) Maroon with white lettering, bar-end trucks, box end marked "No. 6456 / RED / HOPPER CAR" with interior flap number "6456-55", no inspection sticker, part of set 1479WS in 1952. J. Sattler and W. Schilling Collections.

|  | 5 | 7 | 9 | 20 |

(B) 1954, gray-painted clear plastic with maroon lettering, bar-end trucks, magnetic couplers with second hole in activator flap, round end rivet in activator flap and large off-center hole in base plate, box end marked "No. 6456 / RED / HOPPER CAR" with interior flap number "6456-55", came as part of set 1515WS in 1954. J. Sattler Collection.

|  | 5 | 7 | 9 | 20 |

(C) Shiny red paint over opaque body, yellow lettering, box end flap reads "6456-75", box part number 6456-79, further truck details needed. C. Rohlfing Collection.

|  | 15 | 22 | 40 | 70 |

(D) Black with white lettering,

|  | 5 | 7 | 9 | 20 |

(E) Reddish-maroon with white lettering, bar-end trucks, round-headed rivet, extra hole in activator plate and large hole centered in coupler base plate, came with set 1479WS in 1952.

|  | 5 | 7 | 9 | 20 |

(F) Same as (B), but box is marked "No. 6456 / HOPPER CAR / 25 LIONEL 25", box part number 6456-29, part of set 1523. J. Merhar Collection.

|  | 5 | 7 | 9 | 20 |

### 6456 Type V Bodies

(A) Shiny black unpainted plastic, white lettering, bar-end trucks, no brakewheel.

|  | 5 | 7 | 9 | 20 |

(B) Shiny black unpainted plastic, white lettering, AAR trucks, disc couplers.

|  | 5 | 7 | 9 | 20 |

(C) Flat black unpainted plastic, white lettering, AAR trucks, disc couplers.

|  | 5 | 7 | 9 | 20 |

### 6456 Type VI Bodies

(A) Shiny black unpainted plastic, white lettering, AAR trucks, disc couplers, no brakewheels.

|  | 5 | 7 | 9 | 20 |

**6476 LEHIGH VALLEY 25000** 1957-58, 1960-62, 1964, 1968-69 "NEW 1-48", "BUILT 1-48". The 1964 catalogue lists a 6476-125 Lehigh Valley Hopper Car as part of either Set 12700 with the 736 locomotive or set 12720 with the 2383 locomotive. We believe that the car is actually numbered 6476. We would appreciate hearing from a reader who has either set and this car so that we can positively identify it. We would also like to identify the 6476 that came with the 1968 Hagerstown 11600 set.

### 6476 Type V Bodies

(A) Red plastic body, white lettering, bar-end trucks, magnetic tab couplers, brakewheels, steps.

|  | 5 | 7 | 9 | 20 |

(B) Gray plastic body, black lettering, AAR trucks, disc couplers, steps.

|  | 5 | 7 | 9 | 16 |

(C) Red plastic body, white lettering, AAR trucks, disc couplers, steps, no brakewheels. R. LaVoie Collection.

|  | 5 | 7 | 9 | 16 |

(D) Darker red plastic body, white lettering, AAR trucks, disc couplers.

|  | 5 | 7 | 9 | 16 |

### 6476 Type VI Bodies

(A) Red plastic body, white lettering, AAR trucks, disc couplers.

|  | 5 | 7 | 9 | 16 |

(B) Pale red plastic body, white lettering, early AAR trucks, disc couplers, no brakewheel, metal coupler knuckle springs instead of usual plastic. Box marked "No. 6476 / LIONEL / HOPPER CAR", part number 6476-9. J. Sattler and R. LaVoie Collections.

|  | 5 | 7 | 9 | 16 |

(C) Black unpainted plastic body, white lettering, early AAR trucks, disc couplers, no brakewheel. J. Sattler Collection.

|  | 5 | 7 | 9 | 16 |

### 6476 Unknown Body Type

(A) Red body, yellow lettering, AAR trucks, disc couplers. K. Koehler Collection.

|  |  |  |  | NRS |

**6476-85 LEHIGH VALLEY** Type V black unpainted plastic body, white lettering, steps, AAR trucks, disc couplers, reported in box marked 6476-85, box part number 6476-89, came with Sears set 79N09657. I.D. Smith comment; J. Kotil Collection.

|  | 5 | 7 | 9 | 16 |

**6476-125 LEHIGH VALLEY** Catalogued in 1964 as part of set 12700 with the 736 or set 12720 with the 2383. It is also listed in Service Manual, probably with "6476" on side and "6476-125" on original box; more information requested.

|  |  |  |  | NRS |

**6476-135 LEHIGH VALLEY** 1964-66, 1968-69; actually numbered 6476. Light yellow, black lettering, "new" not present, "BUILT 1-48" and "LIONEL 6176" both present, AAR trucks, disc couplers. Came in box marked 6476-135. (See photo.) We would like to learn the body type. One reported example actually had Fundimensions Symington-Wayne trucks from late 1970 which appeared to be original.

(A) 1964-66, late Lionel box marked "NO. 6476-135 / LIONEL / HOPPER CAR". P. Ambrose, R. Shanfeld and G. Halverson Collections.

|  | 3 | 5 | 10 | 18 |

(B) 1968-69, same as (A), but came in Hagerstown box marked on only one end in black rubber-stamped ink: "NO. 6476-135 / HOPPER CAR". R. LaVoie Collection.

|  | 3 | 5 | 10 | 18 |

**6476-160 LEHIGH VALLEY** 1969. Illustrated as part of set 11750 with 2029 locomotive and also listed as available for separate sale. Described as a black car. Although catalogued with the suffix -160 it was actually numbered 6476. We would like to identify this piece. Reader assistance requested.

|  |  |  |  | NRS |

**6476-185 LEHIGH VALLEY** 1969. Illustrated as part of set 11740 with 2041 locomotive and also listed as available for separate sale. Described as a yellow car. Actually numbered 6476. We would like to identify this piece. Reader assistance requested.

|  |  |  |  | NRS |

**6536 M St L** 1958-59, 1963, 50-ton quad hopper, red-painted black plastic, white lettering, center brace, no covers, "BLT 6-58". P. Ambrose comment.

(A) 1958, bar-end trucks, magnetic tab couplers. H. Powell Collection.

|  | 12 | 20 | 35 | 50 |

(B) 1959, early AAR trucks, two operating couplers. J. Sattler and H. Powell Collections.

|  | 12 | 17 | 25 | 40 |

(C) 1963, AAR plastic trucks, one operating and one dummy coupler, no brakewheel, unpainted red plastic. H. Powell Collection.

|  | 12 | 17 | 25 | 40 |

**6636 ALASKA** 1959-60, 50-ton quad hopper, black plastic body with orange-yellow lettering, does not have Eskimo shown in catalogue, no covers, center brace, early AAR trucks, disc couplers.

(A) No brakewheel

|  | 17 | 25 | 35 | 60 |

(B) Brakewheel. Patton Collection.

|  | 17 | 25 | 35 | 60 |

(C) White lettering, brakewheel. A question has been raised as to whether this car originally had yellow lettering which was subsequently changed to white lettering by an owner. Reader comments invited. J. Sattler comment.

|  |  |  |  | NRS |

**6736 DETROIT & MACKINAC** 1960-62, 50-ton quad hopper.

(A) Red plastic, white lettering, no covers, center brace, early AAR trucks, disc couplers. J. Sattler Collection.

|  | 17 | 25 | 35 | 60 |

(B) Same as (A), but face of figure on Mackinac Mac logo obliterated by white blotch caused by die flaw; a common variation and thus not listed in Factory Error section, even though technically it is a factory error. It is estimated that slightly less than half of the production came with the imperfection; it is even shown with the blotch in the 1958 catalogue! R. LaVoie and J. Algozzini Collections.

|  | 20 | 30 | 40 | 70 |

**546446** See 6446-1 or 6446-25.

**NO LETTERING** See 6076, 6076-100 and 6176.

# Chapter IX
# PASSENGER CARS

Top shelf: 2400 Maplewood and 2409 Santa Fe. Second shelf: 2414 Santa Fe and 2422 Chatham. Third shelf: 2429 Livingston and 2436 Mooseheart. Fourth shelf: 2445 Elizabeth and 2481 Plainfield. L. Nuzzaci Collection.

|  | Gd | VG | Exc | Mt |
|---|---|---|---|---|

**1865 WESTERN & ATLANTIC** 1959-62, 1860-type coach, yellow with brown roof and lettering, unlighted, fixed couplers.
(A) As described above. **13 20 30 40**
(B) Same as (A), except has interior illumination. T. Klaassen Collection. **NRS**

**1866 WESTERN & ATLANTIC** 1959-62, 1860-type mail-baggage.
(A) Yellow with brown roof and lettering. **17 20 30 40**
(B) Unpainted lemon yellow, no lettering. **NRS**
(C) Same as (A), except has interior illumination. T. Klaassen Collection. **NRS**

1866 Western & Atlantic

1875 Western Atlantic from the General set. W. Eddins Collection, Bennett photograph.

188

Top shelf: 2442 and 2430 Pullmans.  Bottom shelf:  6440 Pullman and 6441 observation.  L. Nuzzaci Collection.

**1875 WESTERN & ATLANTIC**  1959-62, coach, yellow with tuscan roof and lettering, offered separately, similar to 1865.

|  |  |  |  |
|---|---|---|---|
| 40 | 60 | 100 | 150 |

**1875W WESTERN & ATLANTIC**  1959-62, coach with whistle; yellow with tuscan roof and lettering, lights, came with Five Star General Set, lighted, operating couplers.

|  |  |  |  |
|---|---|---|---|
| 40 | 60 | 80 | 100 |

**1876 WESTERN & ATLANTIC**  1959-62, mail-baggage, lights, came with Five Star General Set; similar to 1866.

|  |  |  |  |
|---|---|---|---|
| 25 | 40 | 60 | 90 |

**1885 WESTERN & ATLANTIC**  1959, blue with white lettering, brown top, lighted, uncatalogued by Lionel. Offered by Sears as part of set 79 N 0966 with 1875 W coach car, 1887 flatcar with horses and 1882 engine. B. Weiss Collection.

|  |  |  |  |
|---|---|---|---|
| 75 | 150 | 250 | 350 |

**EDITOR'S NOTE:**  The 2400-Series passenger cars produced in 1950 and 1953 pose a special problem for collectors.  These include numbers 2421, 2422, 2429, 2481 and 2482.  The factory produced cars in which the holes for the roof mounting screws did not quite line up with the brackets in the car's body.  As a result, many roofs cracked the end bulkheads of the cars when they were installed in the correct position.  Lionel often assembled the roofs backwards, with the rain shields at the wrong end of the car, to avoid this problem.  Collectors should not try to re-mount the roofs of these cars in the correct alignment to avoid cracking the car ends.  Cars with these numbers should be carefully examined before purchase.  This data comes to us courtesy of Tom Rollo, who has experienced the problem.

**2400 MAPLEWOOD**  1948-49, Pullman, "LIONEL LINES", green sides, yellow window outlines, white lettering, gray roof, lights.

|  |  |  |  |
|---|---|---|---|
| 15 | 20 | 45 | 65 |

**2401 Hillside**

| **2401 HILLSIDE** | 1948-49, observation, matches 2400. | 15 | 20 | 45 | 65 |
|---|---|---|---|---|---|
| **2402 CHATHAM** | 1948-49, Pullman, matches 2400. | 15 | 20 | 45 | 65 |

**2404 SANTA FE**  1964-65, Vista Dome, aluminum paint on plastic with blue lettering, not illuminated.

|  |  |  |  |
|---|---|---|---|
| 12 | 18 | 22 | 30 |

| **2405 SANTA FE** | 1964-65, Pullman, matches 2404. | 12 | 18 | 22 | 30 |
|---|---|---|---|---|---|
| **2406 SANTA FE** | 1964-65, observation, matches 2404. | 12 | 18 | 22 | 30 |

**2408 SANTA FE**  1966, Vista Dome, aluminum paint on plastic, blue lettering, window inserts, lighting. Came with only one set, 11590, with 212 Santa Fe Alco AA, 2409 and 2410. P. Ambrose Collection.

|  |  |  |  |
|---|---|---|---|
| 12 | 18 | 25 | 35 |

**2409 SANTA FE**  1966, Pullman, matches 2408. P. Ambrose Collection.

|  |  |  |  |
|---|---|---|---|
| 12 | 18 | 25 | 35 |

**2410 SANTA FE**  1966, observation, matches 2408.  P. Ambrose Collection.

|  |  |  |  |
|---|---|---|---|
| 12 | 18 | 25 | 35 |

**2412 SANTA FE**  1959-63, Vista Dome, silver with blue stripe through windows, lights.

|  |  |  |  |
|---|---|---|---|
| 12 | 20 | 30 | 40 |

| **2414 SANTA FE** | 1959-63, Pullman, matches 2412. | 12 | 20 | 30 | 40 |
|---|---|---|---|---|---|
| **2416 SANTA FE** | 1959-63, observation, matches 2412. | 12 | 20 | 30 | 40 |

**2421 MAPLEWOOD**  1950-53, Pullman, "LIONEL LINES", aluminum-painted sides.

(A) 1950-51, gray roof, black stripe. P. Ambrose comment.

|  |  |  |  |
|---|---|---|---|
| 20 | 25 | 40 | 65 |

(B) 1952-53, aluminum-painted roof and no stripes. P. Ambrose comment.

|  |  |  |  |
|---|---|---|---|
| 20 | 25 | 35 | 50 |

(C) Black roof with orange stripe. R. Lord Collection.  Further sightings requested.  **NRS**

**2422 CHATHAM**  1950-53, Pullman, "LIONEL LINES".

| (A) Matches 2421 (A). | 20 | 25 | 40 | 65 |
|---|---|---|---|---|
| (B) Matches 2421 (B). | 20 | 25 | 35 | 50 |

**2423 HILLSIDE**  1950-53, observation.

| (A) Matches 2421 (A). | 20 | 25 | 40 | 65 |
|---|---|---|---|---|
| (B) Matches 2421 (B). | 20 | 25 | 35 | 50 |

**2429 LIVINGSTON**  1952-53, Pullman.

(A) Matches 2421(A). A. Arpino Collection.  Further comments requested.  **NRS**

| (B) Matches 2421 (B). | 20 | 30 | 45 | 65 |
|---|---|---|---|---|

**2430 PULLMAN**  1946-47, sheet metal, blue with silver roof, silver door / window inserts.

| (A) Silver letters, staple-end trucks, early coil couplers. | 12 | 15 | 25 | 45 |
|---|---|---|---|---|
| (B) White letters, staple-end trucks, later coil couplers. | 12 | 15 | 25 | 45 |

**2431 OBSERVATION**  1946-47, sheet metal, blue and silver roof, silver door / window inserts.

| (A) Silver letters, staple-end trucks, early coil couplers. | 12 | 15 | 25 | 45 |
|---|---|---|---|---|
| (B) White letters, staple-end trucks, later coil couplers. | 12 | 15 | 25 | 45 |

**2432 CLIFTON**  1954-58, Vista Dome, "LIONEL LINES", aluminum paint with red lettering, lights.

|  |  |  |  |
|---|---|---|---|
| 12 | 20 | 30 | 40 |

| **2434 NEWARK** | 1954-58, Pullman, matches 2432. | 12 | 22 | 30 | 40 |
|---|---|---|---|---|---|
| **2435 ELIZABETH** | 1954-58, Pullman, matches 2432. | 12 | 22 | 30 | 40 |

**NOTE:**  There are two different passenger cars numbered 2436.

**2436 SUMMIT** 1954-58, observation, "LIONEL LINES", silver with red lettering, lights, matches 2432.
12 20 30 50

**2436 MOOSEHEART** 1957-58, observation, "LIONEL LINES", aluminum-painted plastic, red-lettered "Mooseheart", came as part of a conventional passenger set, 1608W in 1958, as well as part of an unusual set with a Railway Express refrigeration car REX6572 in green with gold lettering and 2400-series passenger trucks and a 216 Burlington Alco A unit in red trim. Price for Mooseheart only.
20 35 45 65

**2440 PULLMAN** 1946-47, sheet metal body, staple-end trucks, coil couplers. R. Ervin observation.
(A) 1946, blue with silver roof and lettering, early coil trucks.
15 22 30 45
(B) 1947, green with dark green roof, yellow door / window inserts, white lettering.
15 22 30 45

**2441 OBSERVATION** 1946-47, matches 2440.
(A) Matches 2440 (A). 15 22 30 45
(B) Matches 2440 (B). 15 22 30 45

**NOTE:** Lionel used "2442" for two different passenger cars.

**2442 PULLMAN** 1946-47, brown sheet metal, gray door / windows inserts, lights, staple-end trucks, coil couplers. R. Ervin observation.
(A) 1946, silver letters. 15 25 40 55
(B) 1947, white letters. 15 25 40 55

**2442 CLIFTON** 1956, Vista Dome, "LIONEL LINES", aluminum paint, red window stripe, lights. P. Ambrose Collection.
15 25 40 60

**2443 OBSERVATION** 1946-47, matches 2442 PULLMAN.
(A) 1946, silver letters. 15 25 40 55
(B) 1947, white letters. 15 25 40 55

**2444 NEWARK** 1956, matches 2442 CLIFTON. 15 25 40 60

**2445 ELIZABETH** 1956, matches 2442 CLIFTON. 20 30 50 75

**2446 SUMMIT** 1956, matches 2442 CLIFTON. 15 25 40 60

**2481 PLAINFIELD** 1950, Pullman, "LIONEL LINES", yellow with red stripes, part of 1950 Anniversary set with 2482, 2483 and 2023(A) diesel. Price for 2481 only.
40 60 130 175

**2482 WESTFIELD** 1950, Pullman, matches 2481. 40 60 130 175

**2483 LIVINGSTON** 1950, observation, matches 2481. 40 60 130 175

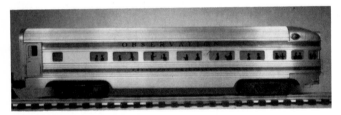

2521 President McKinley observation

**2521 PRESIDENT McKINLEY** 1962-66, "OBSERVATION", extruded aluminum with black lettering and gold stripe, lights. 40 60 75 100

**2522 PRESIDENT HARRISON** 1962-66, "VISTA DOME", matches 2521.
(A) Regular production match for 2521. 40 60 75 100
(B) Top gold strip marked "GRILLE" in black serif lettering at both ends of cars. T. Klaassen Collection. NRS
(C) Top gold strip marked "PARLOR" in black serif lettering at both ends of car and number "2345" is present in door window in large serif numbers. T. Klaassen Collection. NRS

**2523 PRESIDENT GARFIELD** 1962-66, "PULLMAN", matches 2521.
40 60 75 100

**2530 RAILWAY EXPRESS AGENCY** 1954-1960, large-door versions 1954 only; came in set 2222 WS in 1954 catalogue, small-door versions 1954-60. B. Weiss and J. Algozzini comments. Large-door version is not known to have been produced with hex-head rivets; this version produced only with glued-on side plates. P. Catalano comment.

(A) Small doors, nameplate between doors, "LIONEL LINES" not present.
50 70 85 125

2530 REA with small doors

(B) Small doors, nameplate partially below doors, no dots before or after "LIONEL LINES".
50 70 85 125
(C) Small doors, nameplate partially below doors, with dots before and after "LIONEL LINES".
50 70 85 125

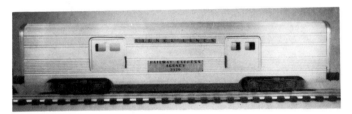

2530 REA with large doors

(D) 1953-54 only, large doors, nameplate partially below doors, no dots before or after "LIONEL LINES". Hard to find and highly desirable. Construction change was made so that door cut-outs did not have to go through reinforcing strut on inside of aluminum extrusion. B. Weiss and R. LaVoie comments.
120 175 250 325

**2531 SILVER DAWN** 1952-60, observation, extruded aluminum, lights. This car went through at least six distinct variations involving changes in the light pickup assembly and plates. Changes were also made in the shape of the coupler drawbar and in the truck mounting channel. See the Greenberg reprint of the Lionel Service Manual, pp. V-25-28. We have not resolved the dating of the two kinds of roundhead rivets, although one commentator, P. Ambrose, believes that roundhead rivet sizes were randomly installed and cannot be chronologically distinguished. We have not distinguished the use of glued-on plates on flat channels with and without dots, since at the present we have insufficient data. Reader comments are requested. These cars were reissued by Fundimensions in 1980 with 9500-Series numbers as part of a Burlington Zephyr set.

(A) 1952, small roundhead rivets, ribbed channels, light socket wired to truck; H. Powell comments.
25 40 55 70
(B) 1952, same as (A), but light socket extension contacts truck; confirmation requested.
25 40 55 70
(C) 1952-53, glued-on plates, ribbed channels, light socket wired to truck; part of set 2190W in 1953. P. Ambrose comment.
25 40 55 70
(D) 1953, same as (C), but light socket extension contacts truck. Also found as part of set 2190W in 1953. P. Ambrose comment.
25 40 55 70
(E) 1953, roundhead rivets, ribbed channels, light socket extension contacts truck. Also found as part of set 2190W in 1953. P. Ambrose comment.
25 40 55 70
(F) 1953, large black roundhead rivets, ribbed channels, light socket extension contacts truck. M. Ocilka comment.
25 40 55 70
(G) 1954-55, hex-head rivets, ribbed channels, light socket extension contacts truck; part of set 2224W in 1955. P. Ambrose comment.
25 40 55 70
(H) 1956, small roundhead rivets, ribbed channels, light socket extension contacts truck; part of set 2270W in 1956. P. Ambrose comment.
25 40 55 70
(I) 1958-60, glued-on plates, wide flat channels, light socket extension contacts truck, without dots on nameplates. C. Rohlfing comment, B. Chin Collection. Part of set 2518W in 1958. P. Ambrose comment.
40 60 80 100
(J) 1958-60, same as (I), but dots on nameplates.
40 60 80 100

**2532 SILVER RANGE** 1952-60, Vista Dome, extruded aluminum, "LIONEL LINES", lights. This car has to be analyzed in the same fashion as the 2531 entry above. It probably has the same variations, but these need confirmation.

(A) Glued plates.                                25  40  55  75
(B) Plates with roundhead rivets.                25  40  55  75
(C) Plates with hex-head rivets.                 25  40  55  75
(D) 1955-60, glued-on plates, wide flat channels, no dots on plates. C. Rohlfing comment, B. Chin Collection.            40  60  80  100
(E) Same as (D), but dots on nameplates.         40  60  80  100
(F) Same as (D), but has plate lettered "ASTRA DOME" instead of "SILVER RANGE". Reader comments requested. B. Pearce Collection.
                                                            NRS

**2533 SILVER CLOUD** 1952-60, Pullman, extruded aluminum, "LIONEL LINES", lights.
(A) 1952, small roundhead rivets, light socket wired to truck. M. Ocilka Collection.                                    25  40  55  75
(B) 1952, same as (A), but light socket extension contacts truck roller assembly. M. Ocilka Collection.                25  40  55  75
(C) 1953, large black roundhead rivets, light socket extension contacts truck roller assembly. M. Ocilka comment; confirmation requested.
                                                 25  40  55  75
(D) 1953-54, hex-head rivets, light socket extension contacts roller assembly.                                          25  40  55  75
(E) 1955-60. glued-on plates, wide flat channels, dots before and after "LIONEL LINES" and "SILVER CLOUD", light socket extension contacts roller assembly.                                     40  60  80  100
(F) Same as (E), but no dots on plates. C. Rohlfing comment, B. Chin Collection.                                        40  60  80  100

**2534 SILVER BLUFF** 1952-60, Pullman, extruded aluminum, "LIONEL LINES", lights.
(A) 1952, small roundhead rivets, light socket wired to truck. M. Ocilka Collection.                                    25  40  55  75
(B) 1952, same as (A), but light socket extension contacts truck roller assembly.                                       25  40  55  75
(C) 1953, large black roundhead rivets, light socket extension contacts truck roller assembly. M. Ocilka comment; confirmation requested.
                                                 25  40  55  75
(D) 1953-54, hex-head rivets, light socket extension contacts truck roller assembly.                                    25  40  55  75
(E) 1955-60, glued-on plates, wide flat channels, dots before and after "LIONEL LINES" and "SILVER BLUFF", light socket extension contacts truck roller assembly.                                   40  60  80  100
(F) Same as (E), but no dots on plates. C. Rohlfing comment, B. Chin Collection.                                        40  60  80  100

**THE CONGRESSIONAL SET:** 2340 or 2360 GG-1, 2541, 2542, 2543 and 2544.

**2541 Alexander Hamilton observation**

**2541 ALEXANDER HAMILTON*** 1955-56, extruded aluminum observation, "PENNSYLVANIA", lights, maroon stripe with gold lettering; this and all the aluminum passenger cars are designed for O Gauge track only. H. Powell Collection. These cars were reissued by Fundimensions in 1979 with 9500-Series numbers and a brighter aluminum finish.     50  75  110  160

**2542 BETSY ROSS*** 1955-56, Vista Dome, Pullman, matches 2541.
                                                 50  75  110  160

**2543 WILLIAM PENN*** 1955-56, Pullman, matches 2541.
                                                 50  75  110  160

**2544 MOLLY PITCHER*** 1955-56, Pullman, matches 2541.
                                                 50  75  110  160

**THE CANADIAN PACIFIC SET** As catalogued, this set consisted of a 2373 AA F-3 diesel, three 2552 Vista Domes and one 2551 observation. Lionel

dealers encountered sales resistance to this combination and so the 2553 and 2554 were often substituted for two 2552 Vista Domes.

**2551 Banff Park observation**

**2551 BANFF PARK** 1957, extruded aluminum observation, " CANADIAN PACIFIC", lights, maroon-brown stripe with gold lettering. H. Powell Collection.                                     75  110  150  185

**Canadian Pacific Skyline 500 Vista Dome**

**2552 SKYLINE 500*** 1957, Vista Dome, matches 2551.
                                                 75  110  140  185
**2553 BLAIR MANOR*** 1957, Pullman, matches 2551.
                                                 100  135  175  250
**2554 CRAIG MANOR*** 1957, Pullman, matches 2551.
                                                 100  135  175  250
**2561 VISTA VALLEY*** 1959-61, extruded aluminum observation, "SANTA FE", lights, metallic red stripe with silver lettering. This car and its mates, the next two entries, are at least as hard to find as the cars in the Canadian Pacific set, perhaps even more scarce. R. Shanfeld and H. Powell comments.
(A) "SANTA FE" in small letters.                 50  100  175  250
(B) "SANTA FE" in large letters.                 50  100  175  250

**2562 Regal Pass Vista Dome**

**2562 REGAL PASS*** 1959-61, Vista Dome, matches 2561.
(A) "SANTA FE" in small letters.                 50  100  175  250
(B) "SANTA FE" in large letters.                 50  100  175  250
**2563 INDIAN FALLS*** 1959-61, Pullman, matches 2561.
(A) "SANTA FE" in small letters.                 50  100  175  250
(B) "SANTA FE" in large letters.                 50  100  175  250

---

\* Excellent reproductions have been made by Williams Electric Trains. In 1979, Fundimensions reissued the Congressional Set with 9500-Series numbers.

2625 Irvington from the Madison Series

**Note:** Lionel used 2625 for three passenger cars with different names.

**2625 IRVINGTON\*\*** 1946-50, Pullman, "LIONEL LINES", Bakelite body painted tuscan, white lettering, six-wheel metal trucks with plastic side frames, lights.

(A) Plain window inserts.                                    50  80  150  250
(B) 1950, window inserts with silhouetted people.    50  80  150  250
(C) Same as (B), but "LIONEL LINES" painted over in matching tuscan, yellow decal "PENNSYLVANIA" road markings above roof, yellow decal numbers over tuscan-painted heat-stamped numbers. We would like reader comments as to whether these cars were converted outside the factory or actual factory production as part of a special set. See similar entries under 2627 Madison and 2628 Manhattan below. J.J. Frank, Jr. Collection.    **NRS**

**2625 MANHATTAN\*\*** 1946-47, Pullman, matches 2625(A) IRVINGTON.
                                                             60  90  150  250

**2625 MADISON\*\*** 1946-47, Pullman, matches 2625(A) IRVINGTON.
                                                             60  90  150  250

---

\*\* Williams Electric Trains and Edward Kraemer have made excellent reproductions of the 2625-2628 series passenger coaches. The Williams examples have been made in many different colors and road names.

**2626 SAGER PLACE** Observation, 1946, shown in advance catalogue but not made. There are two pieces of evidence which show that a prototype may have been produced. In the second version of the 1946 Instruction Manual (green cover with orange lettering), the lamp replacement chart gives a replacement lamp for the 2626. In the 1950 edition of the Bantam book **Model Railroading**, there is a picture of an observation car crossing a trestle bridge on page 159. Although the picture is heavily retouched, the car strongly resembles a Madison-style car. T. Rollo comments.
                                                        **Not Manufactured**

**2627 MADISON** 1948-50, Pullman, matches 2625 IRVINGTON.
(A) Plain window inserts.                              50  90  150  250
(B) 1950, window inserts with silhouetted people.    50  90  150  250
(C) Yellow decal "PENNSYLVANIA" overlays, matches 2625(C) IRVINGTON above. J.J. Frank, Jr. Collection.    **NRS**

**2628 MANHATTAN** 1948-50, Pullman, matches 2625 IRVINGTON.
(A) Plain window inserts.                              50  90  150  250
(B) 1950, window inserts with silhouetted people.    50  90  150  250
(C) Yellow decal "PENNSYLVANIA" overlays, matches 2625(C) IRVINGTON above. J. J. Frank, Jr. Collection.    **NRS**

**2630 PULLMAN** 1938-42, light blue sheet metal body, gray roof, gray window inserts. This car and its matching observation 2631, were catalogued by Lionel from 1938-42. We have an unconfirmed report that these cars were also made my Lionel in 1946 with staple-end trucks. Reader comments invited. C. Switzer comment.    **NRS**

**2631 OBSERVATION** 1946, matches 2630.    **NRS**

**6440 PULLMAN** 1948-49, green sheet metal body, dark green roof, white lettering, yellow door / window inserts, lights, staple-end trucks and magnetic couplers. R. Ervin observation.    15  22  30  50

**6441 OBSERVATION** 1948-49, matches 6440.    15  22  30  50

**6442 PULLMAN** 1949, brown sheet metal body and roof, gray windows / door inserts, lights, staple-end trucks and magnetic couplers.
                                                     18  30  45  65

**6443 OBSERVATION** 1949, matches 6442.    18  30  45  65

# Chapter X

# TANK AND VAT CARS

A variety of tank cars including three single-dome cars, two three-dome cars and a single-dome chemical tank car (with platform around dome).

## TANK CARS
### By William Schilling

Lionel's tank car line had three basic types by 1948. An inexpensive single-dome car, an intermediate two-dome car and a premium price single-dome car. The single-dome, inexpensive car, the 1005, was made without applied trim and utilized inexpensive Scout couplers and trucks. The Scout trucks were a simple design with plastic side frames instead of the die-cast sides found on the more expensive cars. Metal tabs formed as part of the frame fastened the body to the frame. The inexpensive cars' frames were usually finished by chemical blackening rather than enamel painting. The body consisted of a tank with an integrally cast dome with the separate tank ends cemented in place.

The second type, the 6465, was a two-dome car with railings on each side, and the new magnetically-activated trucks were activated by a magnet in the track. The tank was fastened by screws to the sheet metal frame. The two-dome car had a tank with the domes and ends cemented in place. If you examine a tank body interior, you will see that the dome cavities are closed off by the tank shell itself. We assume that the tank shell was cast with the dome cavities closed off and walls protruding upward to make the cavities. A cap was then glued in place.

The most expensive car in 1948 was the single-dome 2555 car with a metal tank, plastic dome, separate metal ends and a die-cast frame. This car also used the deluxe trucks. The

trucks had wound coil couplers and consisted of many small pieces which were probably tediously hand-assembled. A single screw fastened the tank to the frame. The car was decorated with a handrail along each side, a ladder on each side, a brakewheel and a diamond warning placard. The car had an air tank on the bottom.

The 1005 Sunoco was sold as part of the Scout set, Lionel's least expensive set in the late 1940s. Note the Scout couplers.

The first series of inexpensive tank cars, the 1005 Scout cars, was introduced in 1948 and offered until 1950. In 1952, Lionel introduced the 6035. This car continued the Scout frame, Scout truck side frames and single-dome simple tank without trim. The lettering and diamond design were silk-screened. The lettering was blue and the diamond was yellow with red arrow and blue "SUNOCO" extending beyond the diamond.

The next inexpensive single-dome car was the 6015 Sunoco catalogued from 1954 through 1955. The car was shown in the 1954 catalogue with the plastic side frame trucks that were used with the 6035. The illustrated car also had a black ladder extended to the frame. We assume that Lionel painted a 6035 in yellow for the catalogue illustration and that the production models came with the bar-end trucks. We can not explain the ladder shown in the catalogue.

The 6015 continued the double indented frame of the 6035 which is 7-3/4 inches (19.7 cm) long. All four observed examples were painted with black enamel. All four cars had the small roundhead rivet. All have the large offset hole which is 13/32 inches (10 mm) from one side and 7/32 inches (5 mm) from the other.

In 1956 Lionel apparently dropped the SUNOCO logos from most if not all of its tank cars and utilized the GULF logo in its place. We assume that Lionel had a licensing agreement with Sunoco for Lionel use of the Sunoco trademark. We wonder why this relationship ended. Consequently Lionel produced an inexpensive GULF single-dome tank car in black and numbered this car as 6025. This car was offered again in 1957 and 1958. We hope to be able to identify the year by year differences in this car.

The first deluxe postwar tank car was the 2755 offered in 1945 as part of Set 463W. Lionel started off its premium postwar tank cars listings with confusion. The prewar gray 2755 was illustrated with the "GAS / SUNOCO / OILS" all within the diamond on the right. However the set listing was for a 2555 Oil Car. Lionel actually delivered a 2755 with the diamond on the left and the car number on the right. The 1945 cars can be identified by their distinctive trucks.

The deluxe line of postwar tank cars consisted of two catalogued cars in 1946, the 2555 with silver finish and the 2855 with either gray or black finish. Both cars used the prewar 2955 frame which is labeled "PART NO. 955-6" and "NO. 2955 MADE IN U.S. OF AMERICA". The cars are constructed with a sheet metal tank and separate sheet metal ends. The dome assembly is a one-piece plastic unit. The entire car is fastened together by a long screw that starts on the underside of the frame, goes through the tank and threads into the dome. In the price sheet which accompanied the 1946 catalogue, the 2555 is listed at $5.50 while the 2855 is listed for $7.50. However there are major discrepancies between the listings in the Lionel catalogue and their illustrations. In fact the illustrations are apparently wrong! For example, although the 2555 is listed with three sets on page 9, it is illustrated each time with the 2755 that came with the 1945 set. At the top of page 11, Lionel lists a 2855 but illustrates a 2755 and at the bottom of page 11 lists a 2855 and Lionel illustrates a black prewar 2955 with railing running around the end. On page 13, Lionel describes a 2855 and illustrates a black prewar 2955 and lists a 2555 and illustrates an aluminum-finished 2755. Since we have found both gray-finished and black-finished 2855s we do not know if these were both available in 1946 or if only one was available.

In contrast to 1946, the 1947 catalogue is apparently an accurate report on the tank car line. In 1947 Lionel lists a 2555 and illustrates a correctly numbered car with sets 2121WS and 2123WS on page 13. The tank car is illustrated with "SUNOCO" inside the diamond. We would like to learn from our readers if these sets contain this car version. A black 2855 is listed and illustrated with the correct number on page 17 as part of set 2129WS with a 726 locomotive. The black car has a diamond with "GAS / SUNOCO / OILS" all inside the

diamond. On the separate sale pages, the 2555 and 2855 are again illustrated as described above and listed. The 2555 is priced at $5.50 while the very similar 2855 is priced at $7.50. The routing card holders which are found on the 2855 and not on the 2555 cost the prospective owner $2.00. We assume, until other information is presented, that only black 2855s were available in 1947.

In 1948 Lionel dropped the 2855 from its line and listed and illustrated the 2555 with "SUNOCO" completely inside the diamond with the Santa Fe and New York Central F3 sets. We would like reader verification of this detail. Although much of the Lionel line changed from 2000-series numbers to 6000-series numbers in 1948, the 2555 did not change as it retained its coil couplers and was not fitted with magnetic couplers.

The large single dome car was again offered in 1949. Its number changed to 6555 reflecting the change from coil couplers to magnetic couplers. The car was illustrated with "SUNOCO" completely inside the diamond and without the routing card holders. These details need to be confirmed by observation. The car was last catalogued in 1950 and the illustration showed the routing card holders.

**NOTE:** The listings and variation definitions in this chapter were substantially changed in both the 1984 and 1987 editions of this book.

Gd  VG  Exc  Mt

**1005 SUNOCO** 1948-50, single-dome, gray unpainted plastic tank, tank fastened to frame by metal tabs on frame bent over tank, from Scout set with Scout couplers. We have three different versions of this car. We would appreciate reader assistance in dating these, possibly from sets with known dates or other cars with differences in frame finish.
(A) Chemically-blackened frame with steps (chemically-blackened frame will not produce paint chips when scraped). W. Schilling Collection.

1    2    3    6

(B) Same as (A), but without steps. W. Schilling Collection.

1    2    3    6

(C) Black enamel-painted frame with steps (enameled frame will produce paint chips when scraped), early Scout trucks. W. Schilling and J. Sattler Collections.

1    2    3    6

The 2465(A) Sunoco was illustrated, as shown above, in the 1946 Lionel catalogue on pages 2 and 12. This car is also shown in the 1950 edition of the Bantam book Model Railroading. Note the unusual decal placement. I is a scarce car. P. Struhltrager Collection.

The intermediate series of tank cars began with the two-dome 2465 Sunoco tank cars. We have identifed six major steps in the development of the 2465 during the three years it was catalogued. We believe that the cars had the following chronological order.

**2465 SUNOCO** 1946-48, two domes, silver-painted plastic tank with black or blue decal lettering or blue rubber-stamped lettering. The car had either one of two different diamond decals or silk-screened diamond, staple-end trucks, coil couplers, steps, two wire handrails and "2465" rubber-stamped in silver on the underside of the frame. All known 2465 cars have frames with similar hole patterns and four steps. There are two versions of the frame, however. One has a plain side and the other has an indent centered on each side. The indents are 15/16" long (24 mm).

The 2465 tank cars had a single large plastic tank casting (usually clear plastic) to which was added two end pieces and two domes. The four additional pieces were glued in place; the dome pieces were glued with the valves either in an inner or outer position. The tank in turn was fastened to the metal frame by two screws. The type of screws varied over the years. Either the body shell or the frame was put in a jig and the other piece fastened to it. (Most likely, the frame was fastened, since it is much more sturdy than the body shell.) In comparison, the 1005 Scout tank included lineup plugs in the frame for the tank. Screw fasteners were more expensive than folded metal tabs.

**2465(A)** 1946, early; Type 1 trucks with early "Flying Shoe" coil couplers, no lettering and a "GAS SUNOCO OILS" decal with all three words within the diamond centered on the tank side. The car is illustrated in the 20-page version of the 1946 catalogue on pages 2 and 12. This car was first reported by David Dunn and confirmed by Phillip Struhltrager, who graciously supplied the photograph.          **10    20    40    80**

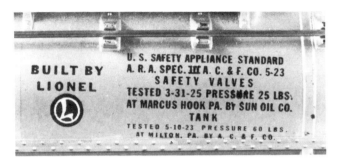

The 2465(B) has **eight lines** of technical information.     **W. Schilling Collection.  R. Bartelt photograph.**

**2465(B)** 1946, later; Type 2 trucks with early coil couplers with thin axles and regular wheels, black decal lettering; "SUNOCO" is within the diamond. There are eight lines of technical information on the right side of the car: "U.S. SAFETY APPLIANCE STANDARD / A.R.A SPEC. III A. C. & F. CO. 5-23 / SAFETY VALVES / TESTED 3-31-25 PRESSURE 25 LBS. / AT MARCUS HOOK PA. BY SUN OIL CO. / TANK / TESTED 5-10-23 PRESSURE 60 LBS. / AT MILTON, PA BY A.C. & F.CO." The last two lines are in much smaller type.          **4    6    10    16**

The 2465(B) has "SUNOCO" within the diamond.

**2465(C)** 1946, late; Type 3A trucks with late coil couplers, no stake marks on couplers, one sample had black plastic body, dome caps and end caps painted silver, and the same decal lettering and diamond as (B), rubber-stamped "2465" on the frame underside. J. Sattler Collection.
          **4    6    10    16**

The 2465(D) has only **six lines** of technical information.     **W. Schilling Collection.  R. Bartelt photograph.**

**2465(D)** 1946, late; Type III trucks with late coil couplers and blue decal lettering. "SUNOCO" extends beyond the diamond. The technical data on the right side was changed by eliminating the last two lines of data which were in much smaller type, rubber-stamped "2465" on the frame underside. J. Sattler Collection.          **4    6    10    16**

**2465(D) and later cars have "SUNOCO" extending beyond the diamond. W. Schilling Collection.**

**2465(E)** 1947, early; Type 3B trucks with late coil couplers, stake marks, with silk-screened lettering and diamond. "SUNOCO" extends beyond the diamond.          **4    6    10    16**

**2465(F)** 1947-48; same as the 2465(E), but has an indent on the frame sides. This indent was put into the frame so that the frame could be used for the 3462 Automatic Milk Car, new in 1947. R. LaVoie Collection.
          **4    6    10    16**

In addition to the six major varieties that we have observed, there is also variation in the screws that fasten the tank to the frame. We would expect that with enough data we can date the changes in screw fasteners. We do not know the type of screw that came with the 2465(A). 2465(B) came with a white slotted-roundhead screw. 2465(C) came with either white slotted-roundhead screws or black slotted-roundhead screws. 2465(D) came with white pan-head-slotted screws or black roundhead-slotted screws. 2465(E) came with black Phillips screws. 2465(F) came with black roundhead-slotted screws. This car breaks the pattern of change from slotted to Phillips screws.

2555 Sunoco, P. Bennett photograph.

**EDITOR'S NOTE:** The 2555, 2755, 2855 and 2955 single-dome tank cars sometimes cause problems for collectors because prewar and postwar production can be mixed-up. Many 2755 gray tank cars are found converted to postwar trucks and couplers by Service Stations, although the 2755 in silver is the only true postwar production. Technically, the 2755 should be called a 2555, since Lionel merely used up leftover 2755 decals in its 1945 production of the 463W set before beginning the use of the correct decals in early 1946. As far as we know, all postwar 2755 tank cars are found in boxes marked 2555! Most frames are embossed with a 2955 part number. The 2555 and 2855 are true postwar tank cars; the 2955 may have been made after the War, but most likely prewar cars were equipped with postwar trucks and sold in very small quantities. All of these cars are hard to find with fully intact decals. On prewar cars, the Sunoco arrow decal was on the right of the car and the rail marking and number decal was on the left. This pattern was reversed for all known postwar tank cars; see photos.

**2555 SUNOCO** 1945-48, single-dome, silver-painted metal tank, yellow diamond, staple-end trucks, coil couplers, one brakewheel, single screw fastens frame to tank, plastic air compressor unit attached to frame, one brakewheel. The decal backgrounds are often dirty in appearance.
(A) Early 1946, staple-end Type 1C trucks, early coil couplers, thick axles, black decal lettering: "GAS / SUNOCO / OILS" all within diamond, technical data decal on left has rectangular corners, "S.U.N.X. 2555 / CAP'Y-100,000 LBS. LT.WT 42,000 / LIONEL LINES". W. Schilling Collection.          **12    17    30    45**

|  | Gd | VG | Exc | Mt |
|---|---|---|---|---|

(B) Early 1946, same as (A), but Type 2 trucks. W. Schilling Collection.

| | 12 | 17 | 30 | 45 |

(C) 1947, Type 3B trucks, otherwise same as (A). J. Sattler Collection.

| | 12 | 17 | 30 | 45 |

(D) 1947, Type 3B trucks, rubber-stamped on frame "2555", otherwise same as (A). W. Schilling Collection. **12 17 30 45**

(E) 1948, staple-end trucks, late coil couplers, black decal lettering: "SUNOCO" extends beyond diamond, technical data decal on left has rounded corners. (6555(C) also has rounded decal corners.) Lettering on right matches right lettering on (A). W. Schilling and R. LaVoie Collections. **12 17 30 45**

(F) 1948, late; staple-end trucks, late coil couplers, black decal lettering: "GAS / SUNOCO / OILS" all within diamond, does not have bold lettering found on right of earlier models, only technical data with L logo on right. Data reads: "U.S. SAFETY APPLIANCE STANDARD / A.R.A. SPEC. III A. C. & F. CO.5-23 / SAFETY VALVES / TESTED 3-31-25 PRESSURE 25 LBS. / AT MARCUS HOOK PA. BY SUN OIL CO. / TANK". Silver rubber-stamped "2555" on underside of frame. W. Schilling, J. Bratspis and T. Rollo Collections. **12 17 30 45**

(G) Staple-end trucks, magnetic couplers, with flared rivet and no extra hole on activator plate, diamond markers at each end, otherwise same as (E). Car is not marked 2555 at any place on the car. At least one sample came in a box marked "6555" obliterating original "2555" box marking, came with set 2151 from 1949. This is probably better classified as an early 6555 transitional piece. W. Schilling and Donangelo Collections.

| | 12 | 17 | 30 | 45 |

(H) 1948, "GAS / OILS" omitted from diamond decal on left, "SUNOCO" goes beyond diamond, technical data on right is the same as (A), no rubber-stamped lettering on underside of frame, staple-end trucks with late coil couplers. J. Sattler Collection. **12 17 30 45**

(I) Same decal on left as (H) and same data as (F) on right. Data on right has blue lettering while data on left is black data. Rubber-stamped "2555" on underside of frame. Since this tank - frame combination was unexpected, we tested for originality. If the screw holding the frame to the tank has not been previously unloosened, it will emit a "snap" sound when turned counterclockwise. The screw did not snap when turned. We would appreciate reader confirmation of the originality of this combination of tank and frame. J. Sattler Collection **12 17 30 45**

(J) Same as (D), but no rubber-stamped "2555" on frame. J. Sattler Collection. **12 17 30 45**

(K) Same as (E), but "SUNOCO" decal is blue. J. Sattler Collection.

| | 12 | 17 | 30 | 45 |

(L) Same as (D), but "SUNOCO" in left decal extends beyond diamond, technical decal data on left has dark blue (almost black) lettering and rounded corners. Right decal same as (E), but light blue instead of black. J. Sattler Collection. **12 17 30 45**

**2755 Sunoco with "GAS / SUNOCO / OILS" all within the diamond, P. Bennett photograph.**

**2755 S U N X** 1945, single-dome, silver tank, black decal lettering, "GAS / SUNOCO / OILS" all within diamond on the left, staple-end metal trucks, early coil couplers without bottom plate, black brakewheel, two diamond-shaped routing card holders with one on each side, one screw fastens frame and tank, four steps pressed into die-cast frame. Frame lettering indicates its original source: "PART NO. 955-6" and "NO. 2955 MADE IN U. S. OF

AMERICA". This was the premium Lionel tank car. This car was illustrated in the 1946 catalogue and described as 2555 but probably not made in 1946. We would like reader confirmation of a 2755 tank car known to be of postwar origin because of its silver tank, but in a box marked "2755" instead of "2555". We suspect that all postwar 2755 tank cars came in boxes marked "2555". Many collectors also believe that the postwar 2755 was only found with the 1945 463W set.

**NOTE:** The 2755 was made before World War II and is found with a gray-painted tank and box couplers with the diamond decal on the right. The gray-painted tank was not made in the postwar period but is often found converted to postwar trucks.

(A) Whirly wheels. J. Sattler Collection. **20 30 70 100**

(B) Dish wheels, thick axles, black fiber. J. Sattler, T. Rollo and J.Kotil Collections. **20 30 70 100**

**2855 S.U.N.X.**

**2855 S U N X** 1946-47, single-dome, usually black-painted sheet metal tank, white decal lettering, staple-end metal trucks, coil couplers, black brakewheel, four steps, a screw fastens tank to frame, usually four routing card holders.

(A) "GAS / SUNOCO / OILS" within diamond on left, also lettered "CAP'Y 10,000 GALS." on left. On right decal with white lettering: "S.U.N.X. 2855 / CAPY. 100,000 LBS. LT. WT. 42,000 SHARON 5-29", no diamond sign holders; see top shelf of color illustration. J. Sattler Collection. **40 60 100 175**

(B) "GAS / OILS" omitted from diamond, "SUNOCO" goes beyond diamond, reader comments requested about technical data as compared to (A). J. Sattler comment. **40 60 125 200**

(C) Same decal as (B) on left, right decal with "BUILT BY / LIONEL" and L logo and data: "U.S. SAFETY APPLIANCE STANDARD / A.R.A. SPEC. III A. C. & F. CO.5-23 / SAFETY VALVES / TESTED 3-31-25 PRESSURE 25 LBS. / AT MARCUS HOOK PA. BY SUN OIL CO. / TANK", gray-painted tank, diamond-shaped routing card holders on frame, rubber-stamped "2855" in silver on underside of frame. The car was rubber-stamped since the number was no longer included in the decal as with (A). This permitted the technical decal to be used on other models. However, the frame stamping is the only way by which this car can be identified as a 2855. See second shelf of color illustration. J. Sattler Collection. **45 70 100 150**

**2955 S U N X** 1940-42, 1946, single-dome, black die-cast tank and frame. This car primarily differs from the 2555, 2755 and 2855 in its use of a die-cast tank since the other three cars have stamped-steel tanks. Although made with both "SHELL" and "SUNOCO" markings in the prewar period, only the "SUNOCO" name is found in the postwar examples.

(A) 1940-42, stamped-steel tinplate trucks, box coupler. prewar product, but placed here as a reference. **110 175 300 460**

(B) Circa 1946, staple-end metal trucks, coil couplers. We need additional confirmation that this car was made after World War II and is not a prewar car mounted with postwar trucks. **110 175 275 375**

**6015 SUNOCO** 1954-55, single-dome, 8" long, "LIONEL LINES", bar-end trucks, body fastened to frame by tabs, frame has two indentations on each side.

(A) Yellow-painted gray plastic, magnetic couplers with small roundhead rivet and offset hole. W. Schilling and J. Kotil Collections. **2 4 6 8**

(B) Dark yellow tank, black lettering, magnetic tab couplers. W. Schilling Collection.    **2   4   6   8**

(C) Yellow unpainted plastic tank, black lettering, magnetic tab couplers. W. Schilling and J. Kotil Collections.    **2   4   6   8**

**6025 GULF** 1956-57, single-dome, 8" long, "LIONEL LINES", body fastened to black frame with tabs.

(A) Black shiny tank, white lettering, orange Gulf emblem, bar-end trucks with off-center holes in bottom plate, magnetic tab couplers. R. Gluckman Collection.    **2   5   7   10**

(B) Gray tank, blue lettering, bar-end trucks with off-center holes in bottom plate, magnetic tab couplers. W. Schilling Collection.    **2   4   7   10**

(C) Gray tank, blue lettering, AAR trucks with disc couplers, orange Gulf emblem. W. Schilling Collection.    **2   4   6   8**

(D) 1957, orange tank, thin blue lettering, AAR trucks with disc couplers. W. Schilling Collection.    **2   4   6   8**

(E) Same as (C), but thick lettering. W. Schilling and J. Sattler Collections.    **2   4   6   8**

(F) Black unpainted shiny tank, white lettering, orange Gulf emblem surrounded by blue and white circle, frame with side indent, AAR trucks. B. Werley Collection. Further confirmation requested.    **NRS**

(G) Same as (A), but black "GULF" lettering. Reader comments requested. R. Gluckman Collection.    **NRS**

**6035 Sunoco, P. Bennett photograph.**

**6035 SUNOCO** 1952-53, single-dome, unpainted gray plastic dome, continuation of Scout 1005 with Scout truck side frames but magnetic couplers, very dark blue silk-screened lettering and yellow, dark blue and red silk-screened diamond. The body was fastened to the frame with metal tabs which are part of the frame. The frame has two indents each, 7/32 inches (5 mm) wide on each side, and has no steps. All observed samples have chemically-blackened frames.

Two different kinds of plastic side frame trucks were used. Both trucks have the small roundhead rivet. One truck, however has the large hole centered on the truck bottom plate while the other has the hole 3/8 inches (10 mm ) from one side and 3/16 inches (5 mm) from the other.

(A) Centered hole. W. Schilling and R. LaVoie Collections.    **1   2   3   5**

(B) Off-center hole. W. Schilling Collection.    **1   2   3   5**

**NOTE:** There are two different 6045 tanks.

**6045 CITIES SERVICE** 1959-60, not catalogued, two domes, green tank, white lettering "CSOX 6045", body fastened to blackened frame with tabs. We would like to learn the set(s) that the 6045 CITIES SERVICE came with.

(A) Arch-bar trucks, fixed couplers. Came as part of uncatalogued set 1105 in 1959. W.F. Spence and W. Eddins Collections.    **6   9   12   20**

(B) AAR trucks, one fixed and one disc coupler. W. Schilling and J. Sattler Collections.    **6   9   12   20**

**6045 LIONEL LINES** 1958, 1963, two domes, "L" in circle, body fastened to frame with tabs. Plastic knobs line up casting and frame.

(A) 1958, light gray tank, blue lettering, AAR trucks with disc couplers, "BLT 1-58".    **2   4   6   8**

(B) Same as (A), but fixed couplers. W. Schilling Collection.    **2   4   6   8**

(C) Same as (A), but arch-bar trucks, fixed couplers. Strong and J. Sattler Collections.    **2   4   6   8**

**6045 Lionel Lines, P. Bennett photograph.**

(D) 1963, orange tank, black lettering, AAR trucks with AAR bearings, disc couplers, no built date.    **2   5   7   10**

(E) Similar to (D), but black tank ends, "BLT BY LIONEL" in two lines, fixed couplers. W. Schilling Collection.    **2   5   7   10**

(F) Same as (C), but unpainted greenish-beige plastic tank. J. Sattler Collection.    **NRS**

**NOTE:** There are three different 6315 tank heralds.

**6315 GULF** 1956-59, 1968-69, chemical single-dome, metal catwalk around dome; screw fastens tank and frame, "BLT 1-56"; see color illustration.

(A) Glossy burnt-orange and black tank, bar-end trucks, magnetic tab couplers.    **15   22   40   60**

(B) Same as (A), but flat-painted redder-orange tank.    **15   22   35   55**

(C) All-orange unpainted tank, AAR trucks with disc couplers; no built date. L. Steuer and T. Budniak Collections.    **8   12   20   35**

(D) 1968-69, same as (C), but no built date. Came in 1968 Hagerstown box labeled "6315 / CHEMICAL / TANK CAR" on both ends. Car has two later AAR trucks with disc couplers. R. Shanfeld and J. Sattler Collections.    **8   12   20   35**

**6315 LIONEL LINES** 1963-66, chemical single-dome, metal catwalk around dome, ladder, a single screw fastens tank and frame, orange tank, black lettering, AAR trucks with disc couplers. J. Sattler Collection. See also next entry.    **7   12   25   40**

**6315-50 LIONEL LINES** 1963-66, same description as 6315-60 entry below, except came in box marked "6315-50" which had a tight fit. P. Ambrose comment.    **7   12   25   40**

**6315-60 LIONEL LINES** 1966, single-dome tank car, unpainted orange tank, black lettering and "L" circular logo, handrails may differ from earlier versions in shape at tank ends, late open-axle AAR trucks with two disc couplers (earlier versions may have closed-axle trucks). Came in box marked "NO. 6315-60 / LIONEL / CHEMICAL / TANK CAR", later Sixties-style box with rectangular picture of locomotives and "LIONEL TOY CORPORATION / HILLSIDE, N.J." lettering, box had much looser fit than 6315-50 box above. P. Ambrose and R. LaVoie observations; J. Sattler, R. Hutchinson and J. Bratspis Collections.    **7   12   25   40**

**Lionel has made special cars for TCA National Conventions. Above is a 1972 Chemical Tank Car 6315 — 1972. P. Bennett photograph.**

**6315-1972 TCA 18th NATIONAL CONVENTION** 1972, chemical single-dome, special for TCA, limited run of 2,000, bar-end trucks, magnetic tab couplers; manufactured by Fundimensions, but listed here because of number. J. Sattler Collection.    **—   —   50   80**

**6415 SUNOCO** 1953-55, three domes, silver tank, body fastened to black frame with one screw; black plastic frame with steps and four warning panels, one brakewheel, plastic air tank, wire railing around tank, metal channels join trucks to plastic frame except for (J). This was the premium tank car in the Lionel line for 1953-55. Since many variations were produced, we would like reader assistance in dating these variations based upon known production dates. P. Ambrose comment. D. Doyle reports that some, possibly all, 6315 examples came with wire railings slightly rounded at the ends; these ends differ from the squared-off ends of the 6425 Gulf three-dome tank cars. See color illustration, top row.

(A) Black lettering, "6600 GALS", "6415" to right, bar-end trucks, magnetic tab couplers, activator plate with extra hole, round end rivet, silver brakewheel, "L" in circle with extra line. W. Schilling Collection.

5 10 15 20

(B) Same as (A), but no tabs, 3-1/2" long metal strip to center, off-center hole on truck pickup plate, inspection tag "V-6235 B.L.M. / 51148". W. Schilling Collection 5 10 15 20

(C) Same as (A), but "6415" not on tank. 5 10 15 25

(D) Same as (A), but "6415" not on tank, no tabs. W. Schilling Collection.

5 10 15 20

(E) Same as (A), but blue lettering, early AAR trucks, disc couplers, black brakewheel. W. Schilling Collection. 6 12 20 30

(F) Black lettering, "8000 GALS", "6415" to right, bar-end trucks, magnetic tab couplers, silver brakewheel. "L" in circle, no extra line. J. Kotil Collection. 5 10 15 20

(G) Same as (F), but no tabs. W. Schilling Collection. 5 10 15 20

(H) Same as (F), but "TANK", instead of "6415". R. Schreiner and R. LaVoie Collections. 5 10 15 20

(I) Same as (H), but no tabs. W. Schilling Collection. 5 10 15 20

(J) Same as (F), but no brakewheel, one-piece plastic frame without metal strip from trucks, arch-bar trucks, disc couplers with tabs, numbered "6415-T-10A" on the bottom of the frame. W. Schilling Collection. **NRS**

(K) Same as (E), but blue lettering, "TANK" appears on right, one silver brakewheel. I.D. Smith Collection. 5 10 15 25

(L) Blue-black lettering "8000 GALS" under diamond, last line of six line technical block on right reads "TANK", black brakewheel, trucks not known, reader comments invited. J. Sattler Collection. 5 10 15 25

**6425 GULF** 1956-58, three domes, silver tank, orange GULF circle, blue lettering, "BLT 2-56", black frame, bar-end trucks, magnetic tab couplers; see color illustration. In 1956 Gulf replaced Sunoco in the Lionel tank car fleet. Consequently the three-dome car number was changed from 6415 to 6425. 10 15 25 45

**6426 SUNOCO** Circa 1967, blue-painted tank with yellow lettering: "6426 / BLT 10 67" and "CAPACITY 100000 LBS. / 10194 GALS." Has Lionel two-dome body, frame and trucks, but is likely not a factory produced item. Listed here for reader reference. J. Algozzini comments. 5 8 12 20

**6427 ESSO** Circa 1967, red-painted two-dome tank, "ESSO" oval emblem decal, white lettering "6427" and "BLT 10 67 / CAPACITY 100000 LBS. / 10194 GALS." Although this car has a Lionel tank, trucks and frame, it is most likely not a factory product item. We do not know at this time who painted and decaled this and the 6426 tank car listed above. Listed here for reader reference. W. Schilling Collection; J. Algozzini and C. Weber comments. 5 8 12 20

6463 Rocket Fuel. P. Bennett photograph.

**6463 ROCKET FUEL** 1962-63, two domes, body fastened to black frame with tabs, AAR trucks with disc couplers.

(A) Blue tank, white lettering. W. Eddins Collection. We would like to learn if other blue tanks exist. **NRS**

(B) White tank, red lettering. 6 8 15 25

**NOTE:** There are four different road names found on 6465s: SUNOCO, LIONEL LINES, CITIES SERVICE and GULF. The catalogues show the following progression of manufacture: 1948-55: "SUNOCO"; 1956: no name; 1957: not catalogued; 1958-59: "LIONEL LINES"; 1960-62: "CITIES SERVICE"; 1963: "LIONEL LINES" listed as 6465-150, no color shown in catalogue; 1964: "LIONEL LINES" listed as 6465-150, no color shown in catalogue; 1965: "LIONEL LINES" listed as 6465; 1966: "LIONEL LINES" in orange with black ends; 1968-69: uncatalogued. P. Ambrose comment.

**6465 Sunoco tank without steps. Step removal resulted in substantial production savings.**

**6465 SUNOCO** 1948-56, two domes, silver-painted plastic tanks with blue or black silk-screened or rubber-stamped lettering. Staple-end or bar-end trucks, coil couplers or magnetic couplers, several different frames, different colors of plastic. The 1956 production is of special interest since the catalogue illustrations show the car without the "SUNOCO" lettering. We would like to learn what 1956 production actually looked like.

All observed 6465 tank cars have a stud riveted to the truck and are fastened to the frame by a horseshoe clip.

See Robert Swanson's discussion of boxcar frames in our feature article for this edition for more details about these frames. We have provided the boxcar frame numbers for reference purposes.

### 6465 PRODUCTION LISTING

**Type 1 Frame:** same as boxcar frame 1a (straight sides) or 1b (indented sides); (1948).

(A) Type 1 frame, black roundhead slotted screws, silver rubber-stamped "6465" on underside of frame, aluminum-painted clear plastic, staple-end trucks mounted by a steel stud with a ring for a horseshoe clip. The stud is fastened to the truck by a rounded flared end which sometimes splits, late coil couplers (Type 3b), silk-screened lettering and logo, "SUNOCO" extends beyond diamond, "CAPACITY 8000 GALS." On the right "U.S. SAFETY APPLIANCE STANDARD / .R.A. SPEC. III A.C & F. CO. 5-23 / SAFETY VALVES / TESTED 3 / 31 / 25 PRESSURE 25 LBS. / AT MARCUS HOOK PA. BY SUN OIL CO. / TANK." W. Schilling Collection. 2 4 6 10

**Type 2 Frame:** same as boxcar frame 3 (1948)

(B) Type 2 frame, silver or black roundhead slotted screws, same lettering on frame and tank as (A), staple-end trucks (Type 4) mounted by a brass stud with a ring for a horseshoe clip. The stud is fastened to the the truck by a flared star end. This change in stud material and flaring design from (A) probably was due to breakage problems with the steel stud. Brass has considerably more flexibility. Magnetic couplers, silver-painted pink translucent body, blue plastic dome caps and clear plastic end caps, part of set 1429WS in 1948. R. Gluckman and T. McLaughlin Collections.

                                       **2    4    6   10**

**Type 3 Frame:** same as boxcar frame 4 (1949)

(C) Type 3 frame with steps, silver or black roundhead slotted screws, same lettering on frame and tank as (A), staple-end trucks mounted by a brass stud with a ring for a horseshoe clip. The stud is fastened to the truck by a flared star end. The dome caps are made from red, white, blue or yellow plastic which is painted to match the tank. The domes on most other tank varieties are consistently clear plastic. The tanks on this variation are found with clear plastic painted silver and multicolored plastic painted silver. W. Schilling Collection.     **2    4    6   10**

**Type 4 Frame:** same as boxcar frame 5a (1950)

(D) Type 4 frame, same as Type 3 but without steps. In the 1950 Lionel Advance Catalogue on page 5 the 6465 is shown without steps as part of set 1463W. It is also shown without steps on page 6. Black roundhead slotted screws, same lettering on frame and tank as (A), staple-end trucks mounted by a brass stud with a ring for a horseshoe clip. The stud is fastened to the truck by a flared star end. The activator flap is fastened by a flared rivet. There is a second hole in the activator flap as well as a hole in the truck bottom plate. The dome caps are made from clear plastic which is painted to match the tank. The tanks on this variation are found with clear plastic painted silver and multicolored plastic painted silver. W. Schilling Collection.     **2    4    6   10**

(E) Same as (D), but with dark gray tank instead of silver. When the tank car is held to the light, many pin holes are evident. One of the samples had a paint run. It is possible that this variety represents a batch with a substandard silver paint. W. Schilling Collection.     **2    4    6   10**

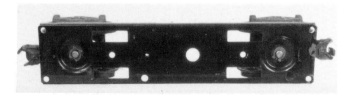

**Type 5 Frame:** same as boxcar frame 5b (1950)

(F) Type 5 frame, black roundhead slotted screws, same lettering on frame tank as (A), staple-end trucks mounted by a brass stud with a ring for a horseshoe clip. The stud is fastened to the truck by a rivet without flared star end down (Type 5A truck). The activator flap was fastened by a flared rivet. There is a hole in the activator flap as well as a hole in the truck bottom plate. The dome caps are made from clear plastic which is painted to match the tank. The tanks on this variation are found with clear plastic painted silver. W. Schilling Collection.     **2    4    6   10**

**Type 6 Frame:** same as boxcar frame 6 (1950)

(G) Same as (F), but Type 6 frame. W. Schilling Collection.

                                         **2    4    6   10**

**Type 7 Frame:** same as boxcar frame 7 (1954-53)

(H) Type 7 frame, four different kinds of screws: black roundhead slotted, silver roundhead slotted, black roundhead Phillips, silver roundhead Phillips. Same lettering as (A). Bar-end trucks mounted by a brass stud with a ring for a horseshoe clip (Type 6 truck). The stud was fastened to the truck by a flared star end. The activator flap was fastened by a roundhead down rivet and had a hole in it. There is also a hole in the truck bottom plate. D. Doyle reports that the activator plate holes on this version can be found either centered or offset. This version also came with silver-painted black dome caps in a box marked "6465" on the outer flaps and "6465-7" on the inside flap as part of set 1479WS in 1952. W. Schilling Collection.

                                         **2    4    6   10**

(I) Same as (H), but with last line of data on right side of tank changed to "6465" from "TANK". Lionel omitted the silver rubber-stamped "6465" which had previously been stamped on the underside of each car. We presume that this was a cost reduction measure. We do not know the date of this change. However, readers who have original sets with this tank car may be able to assist us. We may be able to precisely date their sets and consequently date the change from TANK to 6465 lettering on the side. W. Schilling Collection.     **2    4    6   10**

(J) Same as (I), but with tab magnetic couplers. W. Schilling and D. Doyle Collections. We would appreciate reader reports on original sets containing this variation.     **2    4    6   10**

**Type 8 Frame:** not used in boxcars.

(K) Same as (H), but Type 8 frame. W. Schilling and R. LaVoie Collections.     **2    4    6   10**

(L) Same as (H), but Type V trucks, rubber-stamped 6455 on frame (note different number), tank fastened by black roundhead Phillips screw. F. Pendley Collection.     **NRS**

(M) Same as (H), but staple-end trucks, hole in activator plate, roundhead rivet, 1951. J. Sattler Collection.     **2    4    6   10**

(N) Same as (H), but die repair at right end of one tank side. J. Sattler Collection.     **2    4    6   10**

(O) Same as (K), but tank fastened by silver roundhead Phillips screw and die repair at right end of one tank side. J. Sattler Collection.

                                         **2    4    6   10**

(P) Same as (O), but tank fastened by black roundhead Phillips screw, smaller and sharper rubber-stamped "6465" on underside of frame. J. Sattler Collection.     **2    4    6   10**

The year 1956 marked the end of Sunoco tank cars in the Lionel line. Thereafter Lionel produced Gulf, Cities Service, Rocket Fuel and Lionel

Lines. We wonder why this change occurred. It could be that Lionel terminated its licensing agreement with Sun Oil - or the other way around. The small Sunoco signs on the accessories (256 and 356 stations) also end at this point. They are replaced by Gulf signs in 1957 and later.

In 1958 Lionel introduced a new model of the two-dome tank car. The car was redesigned to substantially reduce manufacturing and assembly costs. First the applied hand railing was replaced by a cast-in plastic railing. Second, the tank was mounted by two tabs to the newly designed Type 9 frame. This reduced the need to fasten two screws. The redesigned frame had substantially more visible openings which was an improvement.

Note the new Type 9 frame with its six rectangular openings. However only one of the two original tabs remain. The other tab broke in the disassembly of the car. We do not recommend disassembling the car from its frame! W. Schilling Collection.

### Type 9 Frame

The new Type 9 frame had six rectangular openings, 1/4" x 1" with round corners, two tab hole openings about 1/2" x 1/2" and triangular openings at each corner. To securely fasten the tank to the frame, tabs from the tank fitted into new aligning slots in the frame. This method had been used earlier with the inexpensive Scout tank car. Lionel also provided a 1/8" diameter screw hole in the frame center which was not used for this car.

The car continued the cemented ends and domes of the previous models but with revamping of the dies for the end pieces. The tank proper was substantially redesigned with underside openings centered under each dome. Internally, there is a plastic support beam which is located at the mid-point of the tank and is mounted vertically. It can be seen by removing one of the tank ends. Ends are stamped "Part No. 2455-6". They are not glued, they are merely inserted into car ends.

Plastic trucks which are properly known as AAR trucks replaced the bar-end die-cast trucks of the earlier tank cars. The magnetic couplers were replaced by the much simpler disc coupler. The trucks were fastened by rivets rather than horseshoe clips and are nearly impossible to remove.

The changes reflected sophisticated engineering efforts and produced a very attractive car for substantially lower cost.

**6465 GULF** 1958, two domes, black plastic tank, dark gun-metal frame, plastic simulated handrails around the tank, tank fastened to frame by two tabs, no frame indentation, Type 9 frame with six rectangular slots, white lettering: "BLT 1-58 / BY LIONEL" centered on the side and "LIONEL LINES / 6465" to the right. Orange, blue and white "GULF" logo on the left, no rubber-stamping on bottom, AAR trucks with disc couplers.
(A) Black-painted plastic tank. J. Foss and W. Schilling Collections.

23  35  65  100

(B) Unpainted black plastic tank. Mueller and W. Schilling Collections.

23  35  65  100

**(6465-60) GULF** 1958, two domes, gray-painted black plastic tank, dark gun-metal frame, plastic simulated handrails around the tank, tank fastened to frame by two tabs, no frame indentation, frame with six rectangular slots, blue lettering: "BLT 1-58 / BY LIONEL" centered on the side and "LIONEL LINES / 6465" to the right. Orange, blue and white "GULF" logo on the left, no rubber-stamping on bottom, AAR trucks with AAR bearings, disc couplers, "6465-60" appears on box ends while "6465" appears on car. W. Schilling and C. Rohlfing Collections. 6  9  12  20

**6465 LIONEL LINES** 1958-59, two domes, "L" in circle, plastic simulated handrails around the tank, Type 9 frame with six rectangular openings and no steps and no indentations, AAR trucks with Timken bearings.

**6465(C) LIONEL LINES** has an unpainted orange tank with black ends. W. Schilling Collection.

(A) Black unpainted plastic tank, white lettering, "BLT 1-58", disc couplers. W. Schilling Collection.  4  7  10  15
(B) Orange unpainted plastic tank, black lettering, no built date, one disc coupler, one fixed coupler, confirmation requested.  NRS
(C) Orange unpainted plastic tank, black ends, "BLT / BY LIONEL" varies in height, centered on car, one fixed coupler, one disc coupler. I.D. Smith, W. Schilling and R. LaVoie Collections. Also sets 11540 and 11560, 1966, C. Rohlfing Collection.  4  7  10  15
(D) Same as (C), but two disc couplers. W. Schilling Collection.
4  7  10  15

The 6465 CITIES SERVICE comes in various shades of green. W. Schilling Collection.

**6465 CITIES SERVICE** 1960-62, two domes, various shades of green, plastic simulated handrails around the tank, Type 9 frame with six rectangular openings and no steps and no indentations, AAR trucks, white lettering "CSOX / 6465 / CAPY 80000 / P. I. WT. 50000" on the left, "CITIES SERVICE" in the center and "A.R.A. / SPEC III / BLT BY / LIONEL" on the right.
(A) Green-painted black plastic, disc couplers. W. Schilling and R. LaVoie Collections.  6  10  15  25
(B) Green-painted gray plastic, disc couplers. W. Schilling Collection.
6  10  15  25
(C) Same as (B), but one disc coupler, one fixed coupler. W. Schilling Collection.  6  10  15  25

6555 Sunoco from late 1948-50. The basic design for this car can be traced to 1940 and the 715 and 2955 tank cars. R. Bartelt photograph.

**6555 SUNOCO** 1949, single-dome, silver tank, staple-end trucks, magnetic couplers, brakewheel, ladders, handrails, diamond-shaped routing card holders on each end. The frame is embossed "NO. 2955 MADE IN U.S. OF AMERICA" and "PART NO. 955-6" representing the prewar origins of the frame die. This was the updated version of the premium single-dome 2555. Lionel changed the number when it changed from coil couplers to magnetic couplers. These cars differ from their predecessors in that the corner steps are gone. Lionel dropped steps from much of its line in 1950, but the process started in 1947 with the 2555 tank cars, 2458 automobile car and the 2457 caboose. This resulted in a very substantial cost saving as detailed by Robert Swanson in his article in this book. We have observed two cars, noted below, without steps. We have not observed 6555 cars with steps. We would like to confirm which of the following variations is from 1949 and which is 1950. Reports on original 1949 and 1950 sets with these cars would be most helpful. We already have some information based on the truck activator flap information. The 1949 production was made with activator flaps with only one hole which was for the rivet which was flared end down (Type 4 truck). Early 1950 production had a second hole added to the activator flap (Type 5A truck). Late 1950 production included the second hole, but the rivet was now round end down (Type 5B truck).

(A) Late 1948 or early 1949, late coil couplers with stake marks (Type 3b), 6555 decals but rubber-stamped "2555" on frame bottom. This car is identical to one version of the 2555 except for its use of the 6555 decals. It is most likely a transitional car meant to be included in the O Gauge sets of 1948, which retained their coil couplers. **10 15 30 45**

(B) "GAS / SUNOCO / OILS" all within diamond, hold black lettering, truck details and step details not known. J. Kotil Collection.
**10 15 30 45**

(C) "SUNOCO" goes beyond diamond, black lettering, round corner decal on left and decal with right angle corners on right, activator flap with second hole and flared rivet end down (Type 5A trucks), no steps, circa early 1950. J. Sattler Collection. **10 15 30 45**

(D) "SUNOCO" beyond diamond, less bold lettering, blue-black ink, round corner decal on left and decal with concave rounded bottom corners on right, activator flap with second hole and flared rivet end down, inspection tag lettered "V-4921 E.M. / 511", no steps, circa early 1950. J. Sattler and J. Kotil Collections. **10 15 30 45**

## VAT CARS

6475 Libby's vat car. P. Bennett photograph.

**NOTE:** There are three different vat cars numbered 6475.

**6475 LIBBY'S CRUSHED PINEAPPLE** Light blue or aqua car; vats have white and silver labels and red and blue letters.
(A) AAR trucks, disc couplers. **20 30 40 65**
(B) Arch bar trucks, fixed couplers. **20 30 40 65**
(C) Aqua car, early AAR trucks, fixed couplers. J. Sattler and J. Kotil Collections. **20 30 40 65**
(D) Light blue, AAR trucks, fixed couplers. J. Kotil Collection.
**20 30 40 65**

6475 Heinz 57 vat car. P. Bennett photograph.

**6475 HEINZ 57** 1965-66, tan car with brown roof, green lettering, different shades of tan and brown from 6475 PICKLES (see below), green vat labels with red lettering, late AAR trucks, one operating and one dummy coupler. For quite some time, we had stated that a reliable informant suggested that the HEINZ 57 cars were "the product of a lark and not genuine Lionel". Opinion is still sharply divided about this car. J. Algozzini feels that the car is not factory production. However, C. Weber points out that collectors were seeking out this car in the late 1960s, prior to the time when many fakes were produced; there was no price premium on this car at that time which would justify the effort required to fake them. In addition, P. Ambrose reports a specific description of this car (above) which would seem to establish it as a genuine factory product. This car may have been a special promotional car; it is very hard to find. We would like further reader input about this car; there may be an interesting story here!
**60 100 150 250**

6475 Pickles vat car. P. Bennett photograph.

**6475 PICKLES** Tan car body, brown roof, metal frame, AAR trucks, disc couplers, dark green lettering on frame: "TLCX / CAPY 135575 / LD LMT 115225 / BLT BY LIONEL / 6475".
(A) Four yellow vats with black slats, red-lettered "PICKLES", early AAR trucks. J. Sattler Collection. **15 25 35 60**
(B) Four dark yellow vats with brown barrel staves and hoops both vertically and horizontally; vats are labeled "PICKLES" in red serif lettering. J. Breslin Collection. **10 18 25 40**
(C) Same as (A), but light brown vats. S. Blotner Collection. **NRS**
(D) Same as (A), but red vat lettering is missing. S. Blotner Collection.
**NRS**

(E) Four yellow vats, no staves or hoops, red-lettered "PICKELS" (note misspelling), collectible factory error, one late AAR truck with disc coupler, one early AAR truck with fixed coupler. J. Sattler Collection.
**20 30 45 70**

6475(B), no staves (vertical strips) or hoops (horizontal strips).

# Chapter XI

# ACCESSORIES

**By Roland LaVoie**

The battle for the toy train market was a ferocious struggle in the postwar years. Lionel, American Flyer and Marx all tried to carve out their own particular niches within the industry, and when one of these companies felt feisty enough, it would try to muscle in on the other's territory. In the highly competitive toy train industry, the advantage always went to the most innovative producer. All of these trains had their particular advantages and disadvantages, but when the smoke of battle had cleared, the Lionel Corporation reigned supreme.

It is well recognized that Lionel achieved this supremacy through superior marketing techniques, fine quality control (at least most of the time) and great engineering. However, it is not generally recognized that Lionel's three-rail track put the company in a much better position than American Flyer to exploit its strengths. American Flyer's two-rail track meant that both rails had to supply power and be insulated. This meant that any wiring for switches and accessories had to be somewhat complex. On the other hand, Lionel's three-rail track meant that the company had two ground rails to work with. Therefore, the Lionel Corporation was in a far better position, electrically speaking, to design special operating tracks, cars and accessories. The company also possessed brilliant engineers to take advantage of this electrical flexibility.

The result of Lionel's exploitation of its electrical abilities was an array of operating cars and accessories which has never been equaled. These amazingly diverse operating devices added big profits to the company and, perhaps more importantly, strengthened the illusion for children that they were creating their own little world which they could control. In the postwar years, busy little workmen swarmed all over Lionel Land, tossing milk cans, dumping barrels or coal, dispatching train orders or flipping mail sacks out of doors. Lionel Land later became a little more sinister as missiles, satellites and rockets arched above plywood boards everywhere, but that was only a reflection of the times, for the late 1950s and early 1960s saw an ominous escalation of the arms race.

The first operating cars continued some of the principles perfected in the late prewar years. Die-cast coal and log dump cars dumped their commodities into trackside trays, while a little silver boxcar tossed packing crates haphazardly out of its doors. They were only preludes for some incredibly clever cars to follow. In 1947, the most popular of all these accessories, the "Automatic Refrigerated Milk Car", began a long run. Children (and adults) never tired of seeing a little man, dressed in immaculate white, fling the doors of the car open to heave a little metal can of milk onto a platform. This car was soon accompanied by the popular cattle car, which featured little rubber cows tramping along runways of a stock pen and moving (somewhat reluctantly) into and out of a short orange stock car.

As the years went by, Lionel refined its engineering techniques to produce other clever operating cars. A brakeman standing atop the Automatic Brakeman Car ducked when he hit a telltale and stood up again after he cleared the tunnel or bridge. Did it matter that this was 19th Century railroading applied to a 20th Century car? Not at all! In another amusing car, a giraffe sticking his head out of the roof of a boxcar ducked his head when he approached a telltale. A little blue workman standing atop a gondola kicked wooden barrels off the car and (perhaps) onto another ramp, where another workman sent them up an incline to a second car. In a funny re-creation of railroad melodrama, a policeman chased a hobo around and around the packing crates of a gondola, never catching him. A spring-loaded boxcar "blew up" quite harmlessly when hit by a missile. Helicopters flew somewhat erratically either from a flatcar or a launching tower, as did satellites or rockets.

The trackside accessories were, if possible, even more clever than the operating cars. All kinds of action took place on the Lionel layout equipped with many accessories. Beacons revolved, searchlights shone, towers blinked and oil wells bubbled. Little baggage carts scurried into and out of a freight station. A busy worker pushed plastic ice cubes into a refrigerator car, while coal towers and loaders clanked and whirred under the burden of their plastic loads (only Lionel No. 206 Coal, if you please). Turntables and engine transfer tables were available for the truly ambitious railroaders, and crossing signals of all kinds flashed miniature red warnings to avoid mock disasters at grade crossings. Semaphores moved and signals winked; water tower spouts descended and, at a little newsstand, a puppy ran around a fire hydrant while his paperboy master turned to offer a newspaper. It was all calculated to create the illusion of a busy, innocent and idealized world — and it succeeded beyond anyone's expectations!

Among train collectors and operators, these accessories retain their charm even today. Although many accessories bring high prices, a good number of them were made in such quantities that they will always be reasonably priced. For example, it is quite possible to buy an original Lionel milk car, complete with stand and milk cans, in excellent condition for forty dollars or less. When one considers that the car sold new for $11.95 in 1952, that is a real bargain in today's toy train marketplace.

There is much more to these accessories than price, however. Today's world of video games and computers are dynamic and clever beyond anything Lionel ever invented, but the user of these devices is always utilizing somebody else's creativity. With Lionel's accessories, one could create a whole world in miniature — a world infinitely more certain than the real one, and a world which is ruled by the operator as a benevolent dictator. Perhaps the wish to create those worlds, however unrealistic, is responsible for the phenomenal growth in popularity of toy train collecting. Such creativity may not be very "practical", but it tends to bring out the artist and idealist in each of us. In an age of technology, that is a truly welcome endeavor.

|  | Gd | VG | Exc | Mt |
|---|---|---|---|---|

**011-11 INSULATING PINS** 1940-60, for O Gauge, white or black, each.

.03 .05 .05 .05

**011-43 INSULATING PINS** 1961, for O Gauge, per dozen.

.40 .75 1 1.50

**T011-43 INSULATING PINS** 1962-66, for O Gauge, per dozen.

.50 .75 1 1.50

**020X 45 DEGREE CROSSOVER** 1946-59, for O Gauge.
(A) Black base, brown Bakelite center stamped "LIONEL CORP. / 020X / CROSSING / NEW YORK", red center insulation. R. LaVoie Collection.

1.50 2 4 10

(B) Same as (A), but black Bakelite center and black insulation. R. LaVoie Collection.

1.50 2 4 10

**020 90 DEGREE CROSSOVER** 1945-61, for O Gauge.
(A) Black base, indented center with cross-shaped projection, solid metal rail connector under base, center held with visible rivet, red insulators, aluminum and black plate reads "MADE IN U.S. AMERICA / No. 020 / CROSSING / THE LIONEL CORP. / N.Y." R. LaVoie Collection.

1.50 2 4 8

(B) Same as (A), but later version, rail connector under base has punched circular hole, black insulators, no plate, larger center with square projection heat-stamped "No. 020 / CROSSING / MADE IN / U.S. OF AMERICA / LIONEL CORP. / N.Y." R. LaVoie Collection. 1.50 2 4 8

**T020 90 DEGREE CROSSOVER** 1962, 1966, 1969, for O Gauge.

1.50 2 4 8

Reader comments requested as to differences between this and regular 020 production.

**022 REMOTE CONTROL SWITCHES** 1945-69, new curved control rails, new long curved rails, new auxiliary rails, new long straight rail, new location for screw holes holding bottom. For more information see Lionel Service Manual. When sold in pairs, came with two 022 controllers, two lens hoods and two constant voltage plugs. These switches were also made during prewar period of 1937-42; prewar identification plates carry legend "AUTOMATICALLY CONTROLLED / 1-1/4" GAUGE SWITCH", while postwar issues have legend "LIONEL / REMOTE CONTROL / NO. 022 / O GAUGE SWITCH". R. Gluckman comment. 25 40 55 75

**022LH REMOTE CONTROL SWITCH** 1950-61, left-hand switch for O Gauge, with controller. 10 15 30 40

**022RH REMOTE CONTROL SWITCH** 1950-61, right-hand switch for O Gauge, with controller. 10 15 30 40

**022-500 O GAUGE ADAPTER SET** 1957-61, combines Super O with O track. 1 1.50 2 3

**T022-5000 O GAUGE ADAPTER SET** 1962-66, combines Super O with O track. 1 1.50 2 3

**022A REMOTE CONTROL SWITCH**, 1947, modified 022 switch issued during period of critical materials shortages. As manufactured, the 022A excluded the following parts: terminal plate assembly 711-129; contact plate 711-217; fitted contact plate 711-37. Large metal bottom plate was never installed. Identification plate was changed to read "022A". The switches were still non-derailing, but due to a shortfall of 022 controllers during an extremely busy period of production, they came with an 1121-100 double switch controller normally issued with the 1121 O-27 switches. The box was marked "No. 022A / SUPERSEDES NO. 022 / NON-DERAILING REMOTE CONTROL / O GAUGE SWITCHES" on its end. When the factory resumed installation of the bottom plates and renumbered the switches as 022, the first plates were made of brushed lightweight aluminum instead of black-painted stamped steel. Hard to find complete and boxed in original condition. Priced for intact pairs in boxes. T. Rollo and D. Cole Collections and comments. — — 100 125

**025 BUMPER** 1946-47, O Gauge illuminated black bumper with a piece of track, late prewar carry-over. L. Bohn comment. 3 5 8 14

**026 BUMPER** 1948-50, die-cast bumper with spring-loaded gray metal energy absorber, bayonet bulb socket, four wide feet, center rail pickup with notch.
(A) 1948, gray only. Somewhat hard to find. C. Rohlfing comment.

10 15 25 40

(B) 1949-50, red. 3 5 8 14

025          026

**027C-1 TRACK CLIPS** 1947, 1949, for O track, per dozen.

.50 .75 1 2

**19G 14 VOLT LAMP** Green, packaged two to a box. B. Stiles Collection.

— — — 10

**30 WATER TOWER** 1947-50, with operating spout.
(A) Single-walled plastic tank, solenoid makes spout move; gray die-cast base, brown plastic frame, translucent amber tank with two binding nuts on gray roof. Number on die-cast base changed in unusual way; base was carried over from 38 water tower, which had number embossed into base. On the 30, this number is blanked over and the number "30" is rubber-stamped in black serif numbers atop the blank. 6-1/8" wide x 10-1/8" high. R. LaVoie and T. Rollo Collections. 25 50 80 125
(B) Double-walled plastic tank without place for hose connections, gray die-cast base, black metal frame, apparently a transition piece between the water-equipped 38 and the new 30 using leftover parts. 40 75 150 220

30(A)                    30(B)

30(B)

**31 CURVED TRACK** 1957-66, Super O, 36" diameter.

.30 .50 .60 .80

**31-7 POWER BLADE CONNECTOR** 1957-61, Super O.

— — — .25

**31-15 GROUND RAIL PIN** 1957-66, Super O, per dozen.

— — — .75

**31-45 POWER BLADE CONNECTION** 1961-66, Super O, per dozen.

— — — .75

| | Gd | VG | Exc | Mt |
|---|---|---|---|---|

**32 STRAIGHT TRACK**  1957, Super O.  .35 .50 .75  1

**32-10 INSULATING PIN**  1957-60, Super O, per dozen.
— — —  .50

**32-20 POWER BLADE INSULATOR**  1957-60, Super O.
— — —  .10

**32-25 INSULATING PIN**  Part of 1122-500, O-27 adapter set.
— — —  .10

**32-30 GROUND PIN**  Part of 922-500 O Gauge adapter set.
— — —  .10

**32-31 POWER PIN**  Part of 022-500 O Gauge adapter set.
— — —  .10

**32-32 INSULATING PIN**  Part of 022-500 O Gauge adapter set.
— — —  .10

**32-33 GROUND PIN**  Part of 1122-500 O-27 adapter set.
— — —  .10

**32-34 POWER PIN**  Part of 1122-500 O-27 adapter set.  — — — .10

**32-45 POWER BLADE INSULATION**  1961-66, per dozen, for Super O.
— — —  .75

**32-55 INSULATING PIN**  1961-66, for Super O, per dozen.
— — —  .75

**33 HALF CURVED TRACK**  1957-66, Super O, 4-1/2".
.25 .50 .85  1

**34 HALF STRAIGHT TRACK**  1957-66, Super O, 5-3/4".
.25 .50 .75  1

**35 BOULEVARD LAMP**  1945-49, 6-1/8" high, finial top, "crown of thorns" cap often broken and hard to find in intact condition, opalescent shade. Found in both aluminum and gray versions; also made prewar from 1940-42. Individually boxed; used 1447 screw-base bulb. A. Arpino comments and Collection; R. Hutchinson Collection.  8  15  20  35

36                    37

**36 OPERATING CAR REMOTE CONTROL SET**  1957-66, for Super O. Includes 90 Controller. S. Carlson comment.  1  2  4  8

**37 UNCOUPLING TRACK SET**  1957-66, for Super O.  Includes 90 Controller. S. Carlson comment.  1  2  4  7

38                    38

**38 WATER TOWER**  1946-47, water put in outside chamber of amber double-walled tank; then, by gravity, water flows to base of outer chamber, after which it is pumped by motor back up into inside chamber out of sight;

when action stops, water returns to outside chamber by gravity. Accessory also has solenoid-operated spout. The pump motor may be the same motor used for the "OO" Gauge locomotives produced in the prewar years; reader confirmation requested. Fortunately for train layouts, water does not come out of the spout. Tan die-cast tank base "No. 38", brown die-cast frame, amber-tinted plastic double-walled tank with two rubber hoses subject to deterioration. Roof with metal center post for water plug in center, two binding posts for roof with rubber gaskets and speed nuts. Came with little clear plastic funnel. Also came with envelope of water tank coloring tablets, 38-70; when these tablets were used, the water showed much better within the tank walls. Excellent examples are hard to find because the exposure to water and leakage sometimes corroded the plastic and metal parts. See Ron Hollander's **All Aboard!** for an amusing story about the design and production of this piece. H. Powell Collection.

(A) Brown roof.  60  175  275  400
(B) Red roof.  50  150  250  350

**38 ACCESSORY ADAPTER TRACKS**  1957-61, pair, for adapting 55, 154, 497, 3360 and 3414 to Super O.  1  2  4  8

**39 SUPER O OPERATING SET**  1957.  1  2  4  8

**39-25 OPERATING SET**  1961-66, Super O, uncoupling and operating units.  1  2  4  8

**40 HOOK UP WIRE**  1950-51, 1953-63, with orange cable reel, insulated 18 Gauge wire.  1  2  3  4

**40-25 CONDUCTOR WIRE**  1956-59, 15" of four conductor wire.
1  3  4  5

**40-50 CABLE REEL**  1960-61, 15" of three conductor wire.
1  2  3  4

**41, 153C, 145C**

**41 CONTACTOR**  Double-pole weight-activated contactor first introduced in prewar years in 1936. Two large adjustment wheels.  .40 .60 .80  1

**042 MANUAL SWITCHES**  1946-69, pair for O Gauge, change in 1950 from screw-type lamp socket to bayonet-type lamp socket. Red die-cast lever, sometimes broken off but easily replaced.  Price per pair.
10  20  35  50

**43 POWER TRACK**  1959-66, 1-1/2" track section with ground and power terminals.  1.50  2  3  4

**44-80 MISSILES**  1959-60, set of four for 44, 45, 6544 and 6844.
3  5  7  10

**POSTWAR VARIETIES**

**45/45N AUTOMATIC GATEMAN**  1945-49, except as noted, all have red roofs, the later gateman figure, no chimneys, no red acetate inserts in light well, die-cast crossbuck warning signs and 1449 R screw-base red light bulbs in recess under base.  All except 1948 and 1949 production have yellow-green-painted bases.

(A) 1946, silver-painted pole, chrome finial cap, crossbuck in high position, rubber-stamped identification rectangle on bottom of base, white-painted shack, red-painted door. J. Bratspis Collection.  15  20  30  45

(B) 1947, silver-painted pole, chrome finial cap, crossbuck in middle position, black rubber-stamped identification rectangle on bottom of base, white-painted shack, red-painted door. C. Weber and J. Kotil Collections.
15  20  30  45

(C) 1948, silver-painted pole, chrome finial cap, crossbuck in mid-pole position, rubber-stamped "45N" in black on underside of base in sans-serif lettering where depression holding pole is, base painted darker green than previous examples (less yellow cast), white-painted shack, red-painted door. J. Kotil, L. Bohn, R. Mancus, J. Algozzini and P. Catalano Collections.

|  | 15 | 20 | 30 | 45 |

(D) 1949, same as (C), but pole is thinner and crossbuck is at low position. T. Rollo Collection.

|  | 15 | 20 | 30 | 45 |

(E) 1949, same as (D), but shack is painted cream color; came in orange and blue Lionel box in this year only. T. Rollo and R. LaVoie Collections.

|  | 15 | 20 | 30 | 45 |

**48 INSULATED STRAIGHT TRACK** 1957-66, Super O.

|  | .75 | 1 | 1.50 | 2 |

**55-150 TIES** 1957-60, 24 ties for 55 Tie Jector.

|  | 1.50 | 2 | 3 | 7 |

56

**56 LAMP POST** 1946-49, 7-3/4" high.
(A) 1946-47: One-piece die-cast base and pole, 45N green, translucent plastic lens, matching green top cap.   **10  20  35  50**
(B) 1948-49: Same as (A), but darker green, unpainted metal cap.
**10  20  35  50**

**58 GOOSE NECK LAMP POST** 1946-50, ivory, 7-3/8" high. Die-cast postwar base without cutouts; "THE LIONEL CORPORATION / NEW YORK" on base. Two binding posts on base; used bulb L1441W. Also made prewar as early as 1922 in peacock and maroon colors. R. Hutchinson and H. Powell Collections.   **8  12  25  40**

**61 GROUND LOCK ON** 1957-66, Super O.   **.25  .40  .50  1**

**62 POWER LOCK ON** 1957-66, Super O.   **.25  .40  .50  1**

**64 HIGHWAY LAMP POST**, 1945-49, die-cast and extremely fragile. Wires like those on 35 Lamp Post; used special white globe bulb with subminiature base, L452W, which came in its own box and is worth $10 by itself. Box is marked "No. 64-15 14V OPAL", but bulb itself marked 452. Excellent and Mint conditions below assume presence of working bulb. Lamp post is 6-3/4" high and is painted 45N Green. B. Stiles and T. Rollo Collections.

|  | 10 | 15 | 35 | 50 |

70            71            75

**70 YARD LIGHT** 1949-50, black, 4-1/2" high, has swiveling die-cast head, two thumb-nut binding posts, chromed pole, black Bakelite round base, individually boxed, used 363 bulb. This light was also used as part of the earliest version of the 397 Coal Loader. R. Hutchinson Collection.

|  | 10 | 20 | 35 | 50 |

**71 LAMP POST** 1949-59, gray, die-cast, 6" high, with hexagonal globe and base; came individually boxed and pre-wired, used 53 bulb. Earlier versions had construction problems, and die was changed. R. Hutchinson and T. Rollo Collections.   **2  5  10  20**

**75 GOOSE NECK LAMPS** 1961-63, set of two black lamps, each 6-1/2" high, base 1-1/2" x 7/8". Came in box with cellophane window and had clear plastic-coated mini-wires — an unusual practice for Lionel. R. Hutchinson and R. Young Collections. Reissued by Fundimensions in 1980 as 2171. Price per pair.   **5  10  15  25**

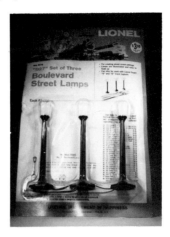

76

**76 BOULEVARD STREET LAMPS** 1955-66, 1968-69, set of three plastic light poles with two-pin base bulbs. Earlier versions came packed three to a set in cellophane window box; later versions came in sets of three on shrink-wrapped cardboard. Dark green unpainted plastic with white hexagonal globes. Essentially a plastic version of the 71. Price per unit. R. Hutchinson Collection.   **2  3  4  6**

**88 CONTROLLER** 1946-50, normally "on" button used for direction reversing. Also made prewar from 1938-42. Meant for use as reversing control for transformers such as R, V and Z.
(A) Binding posts on 1" centers, rivet between posts. I.D. Smith Collection.   **.50  .75  1  2**
(B) Binding posts on 1/2" centers, later production. I.D. Smith Collection.
**.50  .75  1  2**

89

**89 FLAGPOLE** 1956-58, fabric American flag in red, white and blue with purple or blue Lionel pennant with white lettering, white shaft, tan plastic base with four green corner plots made from sponge, 11" high, reissued by Fundimensions in 1983, original hard to find. L. Bohn comments.
(A) Dark blue Lionel pennant. M. Rubin Collection.   **10  15  30  45**
(B) Purple Lionel pennant.   **10  15  30  45**

**90 CONTROLLER**, large red button embossed with "L".
(A) Plain black plastic case without notches.   **.25  .50  .75  1.00**
(B) Same as (A), but flat surface above button is covered by a thin aluminum plate over cardboard for labeling the accessory to be operated. The plate folds over and attaches to the bottom of the plastic casing by two indentations which fit into cutouts in the casing. Earlier models lack these

| | Gd | VG | Exc | Mt |
|---|---|---|---|---|

cutouts, and this version is easy to find without the aluminum plate. R. LaVoie Collection.    .50  1.50  2  3

(C) Same as (A), but raised plastic letters, "No. 90 CONTROL" overscored and underscored on top surface. I.D. Smith Collection.    .50  1.50  2  3

**91 CIRCUIT BREAKER** 1957-60, electro-magnetic action, adjustable from 1 to 6 amps, 4-3/4" x 1-3/8", light tan case, large aluminum thumb nut connectors, lighted red push button. R. LaVoie Collection.
1  2  3  5

92

93

**92 CIRCUIT BREAKER CONTROLLER** 1959-66, 1968-69, fixed load breaker.    .50  .75  1  2

**93 WATER TOWER** 1946-49, aluminum-finished, black spout, red base, "LIONEL TRAINS" decal with red letters outlined in black and a black line around decal edge. R. Lord comments, R. LaVoie Collection.
7  12  25  40

**96C CONTROLLER** All metal, two binding posts, red push button. Binding posts are closer together than on early versions of 88 controller, which looks similar. This is a normally off switch, while the 88 is a normally on switch. I.D. Smith and C. Rohlfing observations.    .25  .50  .75  1.00

97

**97 COAL ELEVATOR** 1946-50, coal carried from tray to bunker by continuous chain with buckets; switch controls bunker exit chute; yellow bunker with red metal roof, black Bakelite base (some versions have been reported with dark mottled plastic bases and chutes), aluminum-colored metal frame; two binding posts on one side; three posts other side, with controller. A version made in 1948 came in a box marked 97-74. Reader comments requested on other box markings and dates. D. Doyle Collection.
50  75  135  185

**100 MULTIVOLT - DC / AC** Power Pack, 1958-66.    NRS

**109 TRESTLE SET** Sold with set 2574 in 1961 catalogue, pages 40 and 41, additional sightings requested. Apparently this trestle set was made of heavy cardboard instead of the usual plastic, and it came packed in a plain paper bag inside the set. C. Weber Collection, R. Hutchinson comment.    NRS

**110 TRESTLE SET** 1955-69, set of 22 or 24 graduated piers. Piers are gray or black; black are more desirable. Came with both O Gauge and O-27 Gauge fishplates and screws for attaching track to trestle; fittings packed in

brown envelope. Packing boxes varied in size and color over the years.

(A) Plain brown box labeled on one of the long sides, "110-23" which is Lionel's part number for the box. Note that 110-22 parts envelope comes with variation (A). The box was manufactured by Densen Banner. The box is 23" long by 5" wide x 4-1/4" high. Came with 110-22 parts envelope. Came with gray trestles. G. Halverson Collection. Note that values for Excellent and Mint require the complete packaging.    3  8  15  25

(B) Plain brown box labeled on one of long sides "110-35" which is Lionel's part number for the box. Box was manufactured by Express Container Corp. Plain brown box with red and blue lettering. A manila parts envelope marked "110-35" came inside box; G. Halverson Collection.
3  8  15  25

(C) Same as (B), but black trestles and yellow box labeled "110-35" manufactured by Star Corrugated Box Company Inc. Came with parts envelope "110-26". Black trestles. G. Halverson Collection.
3  8  15  25

(D) Box labeled "Lionel No. 110 22-piece Graduated Trestle Set". Came in orange and blue box 11" long, 8" wide and 4" high. Gray trestles. Box labeled "110-38 Manufactured by United Container Co." Hillside box. Later production. G. Halverson Collection.    5  10  15  25

(E) Same as (C), but gray trestles and orange box with black lettering.
3  8  15  25

Note that the first three variations come with 24 piers while the last one has only 22. Variation (D) has a 1061 Scout set illustrated on the box cover. The set is on a trestle moving to the right of the box.

**111 TRESTLE SET** 1956-69, set of 10 large piers.    3  5  8  10

**111-100 TRESTLE PIERS** 1960-63, two 4-3/4" piers.    1  2  3  5

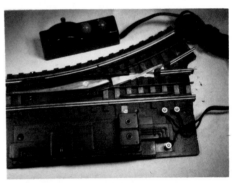

112

**112 SUPER O SWITCHES** 1957-66, remote control, pair with controllers. The 112 was produced only during 1957. In this version, the contact springs above the track bed are pushed down by passing wheel flanges. Apparently, this arrangement was not entirely satisfactory, because Lionel redesigned the switch in 1958, designating it the 112R. (That number and letter are found stamped on the switch's base.) In the redesigned version, the contact springs are brushed by the backs of wheel flanges, the swivel rails and springs are improved and the motors have slightly larger and extended motor housings. Both versions came with 022 controllers. S. Carlson Collection and commments.    20  40  75  95

**112LH SUPER O SWITCH** 1962-66, left-hand with controller.
10  20  35  45

**112RH SUPER O SWITCH** 1962-66, right-hand with controller.
10  20  35  45

**112-125 SUPER O SWITCH** 1957-61, left-hand, with controller, remote control.    10  20  35  45

**112-150 SUPER O SWITCH** 1957-61, right-hand, with controller, remote control.    10  20  35  45

**114 NEWSSTAND WITH HORN** 1957-59, brown plastic base with bench on right side, yellow plastic building, silver roof, diesel horn operated by battery, battery circuit completed through controller, four connecting clips on base, bayonet-type lamp socket.    20  35  75  125

**115 LIONEL CITY STATION** 1946-49, with automatic train control stop, red metal base, cream side with red window and door trim, red roof, two aluminum-finished die-cast external lights and one interior light, three binding posts, 13-5/8" long, 9-1/4" wide, 8-1/2" high, carry-over from

114            115

125

prewar production. Reader comments requested concerning version with vermilion roof and base instead of red; this would have been prewar color, but some may have been made in the early postwar period. C. Rohlfing, M. Ocilka and I.D. Smith comments.            **100   150   250   350**

118

**118 NEWSSTAND WITH WHISTLE**   1958, brown plastic base with three mounting plates, building is yellow-sided with silver plastic roof, whistle unit and light inside, bench is flanked on left side by two green "sponge" bushes.            **20   35   75   125**

**119 LANDSCAPED TUNNEL**   1957, 14" long, 10" wide, 8" high.

            **2   3   5   7**

120

**120 90 DEGREE CROSSING**   1957-66, Super O.            **1   2   3   7**

**121 LANDSCAPED TUNNEL**   1959-66, 14" long, 12" wide, 12" high.

            **2   3   5   7**

**122 LAMP ASSORTMENT SET**   Orange box containing 66 bulbs with chart. For full details and photos, see Tom Rollo's light bulb discussion in Volume 2. B. Stiles Collection.            **NRS**

**123 LAMP ASSORTMENT**   1955-59, orange box with 48 assorted bulbs, 13-3/4" x 7-3/4" x 1-3/4", with white simulated steam locomotive headlight beam and five oversized pictures of lamps on box cover. Box lid has "LIONEL" in white on blue field, "REPLACEMENT LAMP ASSORT-MENT" in orange, and "No. 123" and "FOR MODEL TRAINS & ACCESSORIES" in blue. G. Salamone and B. Stiles Collections.            **NRS**

**123-60 LAMP ASSORTMENT**   1960-63, same configuration as 123, but larger box with 120 assorted lamps. Curiously, these lamps show less variation by type than did those in the earlier set. G. Salamone and B. Stiles Collections. For full discussion, see T. Rollo's light bulb article in Volume 2.            **NRS**

**125 WHISTLE SHACK**   1950-55, similar to 145 Gateman, but contains whistle, not lighted (but see comments below), medium red or maroon roof, medium red or maroon toolbox top, roof and toolbox lid easily interchanged with other units, white building, red windows and door, red sticker with

gold-lettered "LIONELVILLE" over door, frosted plastic window in door; other windows without plastic. C. Rohlfing and G. Halverson comments.

### SOME COMMENTS ABOUT THE 125 WHISTLE SHACK
#### By Thomas S. Rollo

The 125 Whistle Shack was a very popular accessory during its run from 1950 to 1955. With its powerful motor derived from those used in the whistle tenders, it was a good solution for whistleless outfits, and its operation was very reliable. Even today, it serves as a good whistle source for operators whose transformers have whistle controls which are just about worn out. The only real problem is that the double-stick sponge pads holding the whistle mechanism to the shack base decay. When this happens, the whistle unit falls out of its shack and no longer operates. Fortunately, this is easy to fix by the application of new double-stick sponge pads.

Since the 125 uses the same house body as the 145 Gateman, this accessory must have been very efficiently produced. The 125 was not lighted, so only two large Fahnstock clips were needed under the roof. Every once in a while, a whistle shack would show up with a house structure meant for the 145 Gateman; this would mean that there were three clips and a lamp mounted to the third clip on a piece of spring steel. This is more of a curio than a rarity.

The red and maroon roofs are easily intermixed, so with the passage of so many years it is difficult to assign specific roof colors to specific years. It is thought that most of the red roofs and toolbox lids were produced during 1950 and some of 1952, but hard evidence for this is lacking. Most of the dating for this accessory comes from boxes which are known to be the originals for the stations enclosed. Instruction sheets have also been of some help, but the operation of the accessory changed so little that new sheets were not frequent.

The base colors and whistle casing colors show an interesting pattern of development. The first whistle casings of 1950 were solid black plastic, but they soon gave way to examples made from marbled plastic. Like many other accessories, the 125 Whistle Shack used remanufactured scrap plastic during the Korean War years, which accounts for the mottled appearance of the plastic. The base colors reflect a preoccupation with accuracy. The dark gray bases of 1950 and most of 1951, when at least a third of the total were produced, gave way to two kinds of green bases in late 1951 and all of 1952. The first green base was a bright apple green translucent plastic, while the second one has a rather unattractive shade of solid green which is exactly the color of Crest toothpaste! The green bases were superseded in 1953 by the light gray base, which ran until the end of production in 1955.

Thus, the following four versions of the 125 Whistle Shack can be dated with some accuracy:

(A) 1950-early 1951, dark gray base, red or maroon toolbox and lid (sometimes mixed), solid black plastic whistle casing, long oil wick on motor, box with all-blue lettering, instruction sheet dated 8-50. T. Rollo and R. LaVoie Collections.            **7   10   30   50**

(B) Late 1951-52, bright apple green translucent base, mottled plastic whistle casing, long oil wick on motor, red or maroon roof and toolbox lid, box with OPS price on white sticker, instruction sheet dated 8-50. P. Ambrose comment, T. Rollo, S. Carlson and R. LaVoie Collections.

            **10   15   35   60**

(C) 1952-early 1953, same as (B), but dull green solid-color base, box with OPS pricing printed directly onto box. One example found with factory-installed light bulb and third Fahnstock clip; more may exist. T. Rollo and R. LaVoie Collections.            **10   15   35   60**

(D) Late 1953-55, same as (A), but light gray base, maroon roof and toolbox lid, no long oil wick on motor, solid black plastic whistle casing, box with either red and blue printing or orange square with blue printing, instruction sheet dated 4-53. This version seems to be more common in the Midwest. T. Rollo Collection.                7    10    30    50

**128 ANIMATED NEWSSTAND** 1957-60, newsdealer moves, newsboy turns, pup runs around hydrant, 8-1/2" long, 6-1/4" wide, 4-1/4" high. Green building, red roof, tan base, red hydrant. Hard to find with original newspaper, which is inserted into boy's hand and easily lost. Revived by Fundimensions in 1982 as 2308.        20    60    100    150

130

**130 60 DEGREE CROSSING** 1957-61, Super O.        1    2    4    8

**131 CURVED TUNNEL** 1959-66, 28" long, 14" wide, 12" high.
                2    3    5    10

**132 PASSENGER STATION** 1949-55, maroon plastic base, white building, green trim and roof, red-brown chimney, illuminated, with thermostatically-controlled stop feature, 6-1/2" high, 12-1/8" long, 8-1/4" wide, three binding clips, train stop control lever controls length of pause, base plastic is shinier than 133 base plastic. C. Rohlfing Collection.        11    20    30    50

132

133

**133 PASSENGER STATION** 1957, 1961-62, 1966, illuminated, maroon base, white building with green doors and windows, green roof with matching green chimney (unlike red-brown chimney of 132), two binding clips on bottom. Similar to 132 but without train stop control. The version produced only in 1966 has a smaller Lionelville sign (part 145-25) than that used on previous editions (part 132-31). The older sign completely filled the space provided and was framed in gold, while the sign used in 1966 was identical to that used on the 125 and 145 accessories. This 1966 version came in an all-white box lettered in orange "No. 133 / ILLUMINATED / PASSENGER STATION" in two lines above the sealing tape. "LIONEL TOY CORPORATION / HILLSIDE, NEW JERSEY" is below the sealing tape. C. Rohlfing and T. Rollo Collections.        11    15    25    35

**137 PASSENGER STATION** Catalogued in 1946, but only made prewar.
                **Not Manufactured**

138

140

**138 WATER TOWER** 1953-57, brown plastic single-walled tank with operating spout, plastic roof without screw posts and without holes, differs from roofs on 30 and 38, gray plastic base, brown plastic frame, 10-1/8" high, base 6-1/8" x 6-1/8".
(A) 1953 only, gray plastic roof. T. Rollo Collection.        35    45    70    100
(B) 1954-57, bright orange plastic roof. T. Rollo Collection.
                30    40    60    85

**140 AUTOMATIC BANJO SIGNAL** 1954-66, warning sign with moving arm, flashing moving arm causes light flashing, contactor 7-1/2" high, shown in original box. Reissued by Fundimensions with original postwar markings, but catalogued as 2140 and found in Fundimensions Type II box.
                5    10    25    35

**142 MANUAL SWITCHES** 1957-66, Super O, pair.        10    15    20    30

142-125

**142-125 LEFT-HAND SWITCH** 1957-61, Super O, manual.
                5    7    10    15

**142-150 RIGHT-HAND SWITCH** 1957-61, Super O, manual.
                5    7    10    15

**142LH MANUAL SWITCH** 1962-66, Super O, left-hand.
                5    7    10    15

**142RH MANUAL SWITCH** 1962-66, Super O, right-hand.
                5    7    10    15

145

**145 AUTOMATIC GATEMAN** 1950-66, white plastic clapboard-sided house on medium green-painted metal base, red and gold "LIONELVILLE" sticker atop door, small white plastic crossbuck warning sign with black lettering attached to main base with die-cast rectangular base secured by two small screws, red door, two windows with red plastic inserts, glassine

208

window and door pieces, three Fahnstock clips for wiring hidden by detachable roof, lamp socket secured by spring steel strip, takes 431 large-globe bayonet-based clear lamp.

(A) 1950, galvanized base bottom, red roof and toolbox lid, blue-suited gateman figure with flesh-painted face and hands. J. Algozzini and L. Bohn Collections. 15 20 30 45

(B) 1951, same as (A), but maroon roof with red toolbox lid. G. Wilson, J. Algozzini, B. Greenberg and G. Cole Collections. 15 20 30 45

(C) 1952-57, same as (B), but spacer washer added to door post at bottom, "ears" added to toolbox lid to prevent its falling out of shack structure, maroon or red toolbox lid. G. Wilson Collection. 15 20 30 45

(D) 1957-66, same as (C), but all-blue unpainted gateman figure. J. Kotil and G. Wilson Collections. 15 20 30 45

**145C CONTACTOR** 1950-60. .50 .75 1.50 2

**147 WHISTLE CONTROLLER** 1961-66, also known as horn controller. Uses one "D" size battery. Delivered DC current for horn or whistle by means of "snap" switch which created pickup, then holding voltage. This switch was finicky and broke easily. When Lionel used this type of controller for its HO production, the firm changed it to a brass rotating wheel which made and broke momentary contact. This was the 0147 Controller; though it looked like the 147, it was not the same at all. V. Rosa, B. Stekoll, R. LaVoie and I.D. Smith Collections and comments.
.50 .75 1 1.50

**148 DWARF TRACKSIDE LIGHT** 1957-60, buff-colored plastic body, black lens unit, red and green pin-type bulbs, three binding clips on bottom, requires 148C DPDT switch for operation, hard to find, especially with original 148C controller. Reissued by Fundimensions in 1984 as 2115, but included a regular 153C contactor. Many operators do not realize that the 148 was meant to be manually operated. Add at least $10 for presence of 148C switch. L. Bohn and R. LaVoie comments. 15 35 50 80

148                    150

**150 TELEGRAPH POLE SET** 1947-50, set of six brown plastic poles with metal base clips. Came in dark blue cardboard display box. T. Rollo Collection. 5 10 25 40

151                    151

**151 SEMAPHORE** 1947-69, moving plastic blade with yellow-painted tip with red and green translucent plastic inserts, black die-cast base, silver-painted metal shaft, red ladder, metal bulb assembly, three binding posts on base top, with contactor.

(A) As described above. 10 15 25 40

(B) 1957 only, same as (A), but unpainted aluminum pole. This version came in a red box (not the usual orange) known to be produced only in late 1956 and 1957; its instruction sheet was also dated 1957. See color photo above. T. Rollo Collection. 15 20 30 50

(C) Same as (A), but red-painted semaphore blade instead of usual yellow. S. Carlson Collection. NRS

(D) 1947 only, green-painted base, center post grounded to base, base embossed "MADE IN U.S. OF AMERICA / THE LIONEL CORPORATION / NEW YORK". N. Oswald, Sr., T. Rollo and G. Halverson Collections.
25 30 45 60

152

**152 AUTOMATIC CROSSING GATE** 1945-49, red-painted die-cast base, large metal gate with black paper strip, small pedestrian gate, bayonet base bulb, two screw posts on base top, with contactor. This gate was made with a small pedestrian gate on the opposite side of the base. Many examples are found without this gate. This has led to the assumption that some examples were produced without the pedestrian gate. Recent research has shown that all examples of the 152 did indeed come with the pedestrian gate. In the first place, all boxed examples are long enough, be they prewar or postwar, to include the pedestrian gate. That pedestrian gate was always very temperamental. The 152 main gate returned to its upright position by means of a spring in the base, rather than by a counterweight as did the later 252. The spring is adjusted for correct tension by means of a screw in the base. If the spring tension is too little, the gate will not rise all the way. The pedestrian gate operates through a small tab on its right side which fits under a corresponding tab on the main gate. Since the pedestrian gate falls by gravity, the entire mechanism freezes if the pedestrian gate is ever so slightly bent or the spring tension is not just right. The 152 gates missing their pedestrian gates usually show missing paint on the two pedestrian gate pivot studs. It is very likely that many frustrated owners removed the pedestrian gates to avoid the freeze-up problem. Since some pedestrian gates were inevitably lost, examples turn up without these gates. However, as produced by the factory, the 152 was probably always equipped with the pedestrian gate. The instruction booklets from 1946-49 always showed the 152 with its pedestrian gate, as did the 153C instruction sheet dated 3-48. T. Rollo Collection and comments, G. Wilson and R. LaVoie Collections, C. Weber comments. 10 15 20 35

**153 AUTOMATIC BLOCK CONTROL** 1946-59, two position with contactor for controlling two trains on single track, green die-cast base, aluminum shaft, orange ladder, black metal ladder holder, black die-cast lamp shell; common ground post is center post, 9" high. Also made in prewar period from 1940-42.

(A) 1946-49, base contains resistor in series with ground for using 6-8 volt screw-base bulbs. I.D. Smith and C. Rohlfing comments.
10 15 20 30

(B) 1950-59, no resistor, uses 12-14 volt bayonet-base bulbs. I.D. Smith and C. Rohlfing comments. 10 15 20 30

(C) Same as (B), but unpainted aluminum pole, considerably lighter in

153                154(A)                154(B)

155

156

weight than other versions, 1957 only, came in red box with 1957 instruction sheet. T. Rollo Collection.                                    10    15    20    30

**153C CONTACTOR**   single pole, double throw.      .50  1.00    2     4

**153-24 8 VOLT LAMP**  Green, in box. B. Stiles Collection.    —    —    —3

154

154C, OTC

**154 AUTOMATIC HIGHWAY SIGNAL** 1945-69, crossbuck with two alternately flashing red bulbs, operating by 154C contactor, 8-3/4" high, three screw posts, black base. Researchers have turned up black and white photos of dealer displays showing 154 crossing signals with light painted bases which contrast with the very dark accessory posts. We have verified that 154 pieces with red and orange bases were made in 1950. We hypothesize that these pieces were meant for use on accessory displays and were sold off after the holiday season. Furthermore, examples exist of these signals painted orange or red on the outside only. Thus, some pieces may have been repainted by Lionel for use on displays in other years as well. T. Rollo comments.

(A) White-painted die-cast X-shaped sign with black raised lettering, "STOP" in white lettering on black die-cast part; screw socket bulbs.
                                                    7    10    20    30
(B) White plastic X-shaped sign with black raised lettering, "STOP" in raised white lettering on black plastic; bayonet socket bulbs. L. Steuer, Jr. Collection.                                          7    10    20    30
(C) 1950, same as (A), but orange-painted metal base, rare. Came with instruction sheet dated August 1950. H. Brandt Collection, L. Bohn comment.                                        25    50    75    100
(D) 1950, same as (A), but metal base painted red on interior and exterior, rare. L. Bohn comment.                          25    50    75    100
(E) 1957, same as (B), but unpainted aluminum post, much lighter in weight than other versions. T. Rollo Collection.        7    10    20    30
(F) Same as (A), but flat lettering on die-cast crossbuck. C. Rohlfing Collection.                                        7    10    20    30

**155 BLINKING LIGHT SIGNAL WITH BELL** 1955-57, similar to 154, but with large base containing bell. Black and white plastic base, black shaft, black plastic railroad crossing sign with white lettering, "STOP" raised white lettering, bayonet-type bulbs.
(A) 1955, early mechanism with copper blade contacts, small screw holes in metal fastening tabs on base. R. LaVoie Collection.   10    15    25    40
(B) 1956-57, later mechanism with spring contacts and rubber grommets on metal fastening tabs on base; works better than early version. R. LaVoie comment.                                      10    15    25    40
(C) Same as (A), but no black stripes on base. G. Salamone Collection.
                                                              **NRS**

**NOTE:** 155 was also used by Lionel to refer to the prewar Station Platform.

**156 STATION PLATFORM** 1946-51, two screw-base No. 50 6-8 volt lights, miniature billboards, green-painted Bakelite plastic base, unpainted die-cast metal uprights, red-painted Bakelite plastic roof, 12" long, 3-1/4" wide, 5-1/8" high, includes four signs. Also made in prewar period from 1938-42. For the background of the signs used on postwar versions of this, the 157, the 256 and 356 stations, refer to Barry Keener, "Lionel Lithograph Signs", **Train Collectors' Quarterly**, Vol. 29, No. 1 (January 1983), p. 33, where they are illustrated. A future edition of this Guide will contain an article on the chronological development of these signs.        15    25    40    65

157(A)

157(B)

**157 STATION PLATFORM** 1952-59, lighted, with miniature billboards, maroon (common) or red (unusual) plastic base, black metal post, green plastic roof, 12" long, 5-1/8" high, 3-1/4" wide. At least 11 different signs exist for this particular station. Some of the more common combinations are listed below. L. Bohn comment.
(A) Campbell Soup, Switch to Rival Dog Food, Baby Ruth and Sunoco; signs can be interchanged, some are less common.        6    10    20    30
(B) Same as (A), but with different signs:  Dogs Prefer Rival, Airex, Baby Ruth and Sunoco.                                  6    10    20    30
(C) Red plastic base, darker green roof, Airex, Gulf, Rival and Baby Ruth signs. Roof is made from thinner plastic and requires paper mask to shield light. M. Ocilka and F. S. Davis Collections.   15    25    40    60
(D) Same as (C), but two Gulf signs and no Baby Ruth sign. M. Rubin and T. Rollo Collections.                                15    25    40    60

**160 UNLOADING BIN** 1952-57.
(A) Short.                                          .25   .50    1     2
(B) Long (for 3359-55 twin-bin dump car).          .25   .50    1     2

**160**

**161**

175

**161 MAIL PICKUP SET** 1961-63, the mail bag transfers from stand to car, tan plastic base contains coil, red shaft with red and white semaphore, red plastic bag holder, red plastic bag painted gray, hollowed out, contains a magnet. The accessory came with a second magnet which is meant to be glued to the car. Excellent and Mint values assume the presence of the second magnet in unused condition.   **20   50   75   100**

**163 SINGLE TARGET BLOCK SIGNAL** 1961-69, as train approaches, signal light changes from green to red automatically, can be wired to control a second train in a two-train operation; contactor and wires. Version produced in 1969 came in plain white box with accessory data stamped in black ink on one end only.   **7   15   20   30**

**163**

**164**

**164 LOG LOADER** 1946-50, logs unloaded from car to bin and carried to top by chain, then fall into stake-ended platform. Upon command the stakes move from a vertical to horizontal position; the logs then roll into a waiting car on another track. Accessory comes with two-button controller, on/off black button on left side. Orange "Unload" button on right side, 9" high, 11-1/4" wide, 10-3/4" long, with controller and logs, base and roof painted black, molded phenolic plastic. Very noisy but effective operation.
(A) Green metal base, yellow die-cast frame, red plastic roof.
**65   85   150   200**
(B) Same as (A), but green roof.   **NRS**

**167 WHISTLE CONTROLLER** 1945-46, with two buttons: one for whistle, one for direction. (Several different types have been made.) Most do not work when found now, but those that are still functional are used for the older R, V and Z transformers. They use 5 volts in operation.
**1   2   3   5**

**175 ROCKET LAUNCHER** 1958-60, tan metal base track, boxes cover part of motor unit, white and red rocket, black plastic superstructure on gray plastic base, gray crane with gray plastic base, gray top and yellow boom, crane lowers satellite onto missile; countdown apparatus, firing button. Tower crane approximately 17" tall; crane with boom, cable and magnet; magnet meets metal band at end of rocket, crane lifts rocket from car or other location and locates it on missile launching platform, rocket controller launches missile; crane track fits 282R Gantry Crane. Hard to find in intact condition.   **50   85   150   225**

**175-50 EXTRA ROCKET** 1959-60, for 175.   **1.50   2   3   8**

**182 MAGNET CRANE** 1946-49, winch raises and lowers block and tackle, spoked-wheel control knob, differs from solid wheel of 282R, derrick revolves 360 degrees, includes one 165C controller that came with earlier prewar crane; plastic base, aluminum-painted crane, 2460(A) crane car, black plastic cab. "LIONEL LINES" (two lines), "Lionel" in arched line, higher gray stack than on 282R; Electro-magnet has black plastic case with ridges; 282R has simple sheet metal "hat" containing magnet; "Cutler Hammer" on magnet case on 182, red metal ladder. A. Arpino comments.
(A) As described above.   **70   90   150   200**
(B) Same as (A), but black stack instead of gray. C. Rohlfing Collection.
**70   90   150   200**

**182**

**L191 12 VOLT LAMPS**, box of ten, clear globes, midget cartridge bases, one box end labeled "TEN No. L191 / MINIATURE LAMPS / 12 V. CLEAR MIG. CART. BASE". I.D. Smith Collection.   **NRS**

**192 OPERATING CONTROL TOWER** 1959-60, illuminated control room, rotating anemometer, vibrator-powered. Does not come with radar antenna. Gray plastic base, green frame, yellow tower room, green roof, orange ladders, two binding clips on bottom. Reissued by Fundimensions in 1984

**192**   **193**   **195**

as 2316 in different colors. This version very hard to find in intact condition; bulb heat usually has melted the roof.  **60  100  150  225**

**193 INDUSTRIAL WATER TOWER**  1953-55, gray plastic base, dark green shed, painted metal frame, black cardboard pipe, gray plastic top painted silver with red flashing light, two binding clips on bottom, 14-3/4" high. This accessory came with two sizes of top tank pieces; one is 3/16" larger in diameter than the other. F.J. Cordone and S. Carlson comments and Collections.

(A) Red metal frame.  **25  40  60  90**
(B) Black-painted metal frame. G. Salamone, E. Trentacoste and B. Weiss Collections.  **35  50  90  150**

**195 FLOODLIGHT TOWER**  1957-69, eight lights on one side; optional second eight lights may be affixed to other side using 195-75 extension, tan plastic base, gray and silver plastic tower with red "LIONEL", metal and plastic eight-light unit; two clips on bottom, tan top piece without projection and with two round and two half-moon holes, two Fahnstock clips on base bottom, J. Breslin and I.D. Smith comments. 12-1/2" high.

(A) As described above.  **10  15  25  40**
(B) Medium tan base embossed "199 MICROWAVE TOWER" in capitals and red rubber-stamped "195 FLOOD LIGHT". J. Breslin and J. Bratspis Collections.  **15  25  45  60**

**195-75 EIGHT BULB EXTENSION**  1958-60, for 195, not illustrated.
**3  4  8  20**

**196 SMOKE PELLETS**  1946-47, 100 pellets in a sealed plastic container for bulb-type smoke unit only. We believe the catalogue illustrations to be wrong. These pellets were highly vulnerable to moisture. As a result, Lionel packaged them in a small clear plastic container resembling a miniature lunch pail with a black bail wire to keep the lid tightly shut. This container had no identification except the legend "KEEP TIGHTLY CLOSED". It may have been enclosed within a cardboard box as depicted in the catalogue, but evidence for this is lacking. Value quoted does not depend upon the presence of the smoke pellets themselves. I.D. Smith and R. LaVoie comments, V. Rosa, R. LaVoie and J. Gordon Collections.
**—  —  20  30**

**197 ROTATING RADAR ANTENNA**  1958-59, plastic base; black plastic frame with orange letters, "LIONEL", orange platform, vibrator mechanism rotates radar screen. 12" high, base 3" x 4-1/2". Antenna is missing from sample illustrated. Somewhat hard to find in intact condition. M. Rubin comment.

(A) Gray base.  **12  25  50  75**
(B) Orange base.  **12  35  65  100**

197                         199

**199 MICROWAVE RELAY TOWER**  1958-59, two parabolic antennae, three blinking lights, two binding clips on bottom; gray plastic tower, white antenna, "199 MICROWAVE TOWER" embossed on underside, top piece of plastic on gray tower is tan with small projection, as opposed to top piece of 195, which is flat; this top piece has two round holes for rods and two rectangular holes (as opposed to half-moon holes of flat 195 top piece). J. Breslin and I.D. Smith observations.

(A) Very dark gray plastic base.  **18  40  65  95**
(B) Tan plastic base; this base usually came with 195, but some examples

were in fact marked for the 199. See 195 (B) above. M. Rubin Collection.
**18  40  65  95**

(C) Same as (A), but black top piece on tower. G. Wilson Collection, P. Ambrose comment. Some collectors believe this was the authentic tower top piece, not the tan piece. However, tan pieces are found with the projection appropriate to the 199.  **18  40  65  95**

**206 ARTIFICIAL COAL**  1946-68, half-pound burlap bag with red-lettered "No. 206", "ARTIFICIAL COAL", "The Lionel Corporation, New York". "Made in U.S. of America".  **—  —  6  8**

206, 207

**207 ARTIFICIAL COAL**  Considerably smaller bag than 206, same lettering, except "Corp." rather than "Corporation".  **—  —  4  7**

**209 BARRELS**  1946-50, set of four.  **—  1.50  3  5**

**213 RAILROAD LIFT BRIDGE**  Shown in 1950 catalogue only; prototype made, MPC archives has crude mock-up, collector owns engineering sample. L. Bohn comment.  **Not Manufactured**

214

**214 PLATE GIRDER BRIDGE**  1953-69, 10" x 4-1/2"; center sheet metal base thinner than 314, black plastic sides.

(A) "LIONEL" on both sides, "BUILT BY LIONEL" in small letters in rectangular box. R. LaVoie Collection.  **2  3  5  10**
(B) "U S STEEL" on both sides instead of "LIONEL", "BUILT BY LIONEL" in small letters in rectangular box, "USS" within white-edged circle on both sides, "6418" at bottom right of girders. This appears to be a use of surplus girders for the 6418 flatcar. C. Spitzer, M. Rubin and C. Weber Collections.  **8  15  25  40**

252(A)                         252(B)

**252 CROSSING GATE**  1950-62, black plastic base with two binding posts on underside, clip-in bulb assembly with bayonet base; plastic gate with black metal counterweights; metal support rod at gate end, clear plastic strip with two red markers; gate 9-3/4" long, with contactor. Lionel Service Manual details change in construction concerning fastening of gate to pivot rod inserted into base. Earlier versions show hole for rod as square when gate is down; later versions show hole as diamond-shaped.

(A) White plastic boom.  **7  10  20  30**
(B) Cream-colored boom. This variety may be due to aging.
**7  10  20  30**

256

262

264

253

**253 BLOCK CONTROL SIGNAL** 1956-59, 7" high, signal halts train automatically; tan plastic base 4" x 2" with black signal control box, white plastic lamp shell, pin-type bulbs, variable duration stop, level controls length of stop, three binding posts on bottom, hard to find intact with original lamp shell. L. Bohn comment.     **10  20  30  45**

**256 FREIGHT STATION** 1950-53, maroon platform, white house with green windows, green door and roof; picket fence with billboards; lighted, two clips on bottom, 15" long, 5" wide, 5-1/2" high. According to 1950-51 catalogues, this accessory did not come with adhesive posters; the catalogues read ..."Insert bulletin boards where you can post your own schedules". The 1952-53 versions came with adhesive signs for station sides: 256-35 Airex, 256-36 U. S. Savings Bonds, 256-37 Airex, 256-38 Red Cross, 256-39 Be A Scout and 256-40 Community Chest. The posters came in a brown envelope, 256-42, with two 81-32 connecting wires. Billboards were Baby Ruth, Rival Dog Food and Sunoco. T. Rollo comments, C. Weber Collection. See 156 reference for billboard signs.     **6  12  20  30**

257

**257 FREIGHT STATION WITH DIESEL HORN** 1956-57, matches 256 but with battery-powered horn and control button.
(A) Maroon base, green roof, as on 256 Station.    **20  35  65  90**
(B) Brown base instead of maroon, burnt-orange Rival billboard with thin black lettering. F.S. Davis Collection.    **30  45  70  100**

**260 BUMPER** 1951-69, red die-cast body with spring-loaded black plastic energy absorber, illuminated with bayonet bulb, spring-loaded clips for outside rails.
(A) 1951-57, four wide feet, center rail pickup with notch, will not fit Super O track. S. Carlson comment.    **3  6  10  15**
(B) 1958-66: Four narrow feet, center rail pickup without notch. This change was made to accommodate Super O track beginning in 1958, since the wide-footed version would not fit that track. Probably first made in 1958, though not shown in catalogues until 1960. S. Carlson comments.     **3  6  10  15**
(C) 1968-69, black plastic bumper with black plastic energy absorber, center rail pickup without notch, came with Hagerstown set 11600. Also available for separate sale in Hagerstown orange and white box. E. Trentacoste and I.D. Smith Collections and observations. This version also fits Super O track; earlier red metal varieties do not fit Super O; very difficult to find. Earliest Fundimensions bumper in 1971-72 designed the same way. M. Ocilka Collection and comment.    **10  15  20  25**

**262 HIGHWAY CROSSING GATE** 1962-69, combination flashing light and gate, black plastic base, shaft and light unit, black plastic railroad crossing sign with metal counterweight, does not have clear plastic strip or red lenses as does 252, lights have pin base and shine together when accessory is activated, but they do not flash in alternation as do those of the 154.

**264 OPERATING FORK LIFT PLATFORM** 1957-60, lift truck goes to loaded lumber car 6264, brings lumber back to platform. Includes platform with black metal base, brown deck area, white crane, orange lift truck with

blue man, red flatcar 6264 with timbers, platform 10" long, 10-5/8" wide, 5-1/2" high.    **50  85  140  225**

**270 O GAUGE METAL BRIDGE**, possibly late 1945 or early 1946, vermilion-painted framework, no aluminum signs or slots for them on side girders as have the prewar versions, yellow and green "LIONEL" decal replaces aluminum signs. Usually considered a prewar product in deep cherry red with aluminum signs, but this unusual version may have been an early postwar product and so is listed here. Reader comments requested. R. LaVoie Collection.    **15  20  30  40**

282

**282 GANTRY CRANE** 1954, gray plastic crane with metal base, black cab with white lettering, "LIONEL" arched, "LINES" straight across, glued-on gray smokestack on cab, magnet on end of hook, cab turns clockwise or counter-clockwise, "cable" raises or lowers, magnet turns on and off, three-lever controller 282C, cab sits on maroon plastic base with simulated metal plate, cab turns on maroon plastic drum. No boom detailing, no cab number, screw-fastened cab. Does not come with track that fits wheels on base, however rocket launcher track is right size. Cab from this accessory is sometimes found mounted on a 6460 Crane Car, but it is not factory production.
(A) 1954, black electromagnet, gray stack. S. Carlson Collection.
    **60  90  150  225**
(B) 1955, silver-plated electromagnet, glued black stack on cab. S. Carlson Collection.    **60  90  150  225**
(C) Same as (A), but red crane cab, T. Klaassen Collection.    **NRS**
(D) Same as (A), but earliest production came with two special rails with ties. Further reader comments requested.    **NRS**

**282R GANTRY CRANE** 1956, similar to 282 in appearance and function but with changes in the mounting and gearing of the motor and a modified platform casting and platform assembly. Cab is numbered "282R", has molded stack integral to cab instead of glued-on, and is clip-fastened to base instead of screw-fastened. S. Carlson Collection. Operates more smoothly than its predecessor.    **60  90  150  225**

**299 CODE TRANSMITTER BEACON SET** 1961-63, black transmitting kit with three binding clips and silver-printed decal showing Morse Code Tower, black plastic base, gray recording unit, black top, elongated flashing bulb with unusual filament. Top is gray plastic searchlight with white scored plastic lens, metal bracket.    **20  40  55  85**

**308 RAILROAD SIGN SET** 1945-49, five die-cast white-enameled metal signs with black lettering.    **10  15  25  35**

299

308

309

**309 YARD SIGN SET** 1950-59, nine plastic signs with die-cast metal bases, orange box with blue lettering, blue cardboard interior box liner with silver lettering. Color of orange and lettering on box varies.    **3  6  12  20**

310

**310 BILLBOARD** 1950-68, unpainted green plastic frame with cardboard Campbell Soup advertisement, Campbell boy in red, with yellow background, red lettering; red, yellow and black soup can. This is one of probably 50 different billboard designs that Lionel made over the years; set of five frames; 1957-only frames with yellow base squares are hard to find and worth at least three times as much as the usual variety. L. Bohn comment.    **1.00 1.50 2.00 5.00**

## SOME COMMENTS ABOUT THE LIONEL BILLBOARDS
### By I.D. Smith

Beginning in 1949, Lionel offered a billboard assortment, the 310. The assortment usually consisted of five green unpainted plastic frames with an uncut sheet of eight different billboards. The billboards made through 1956 included the word "STANDARD" in black letters. Thereafter "STANDARD" was dropped from the sign. Over 50 different billboard advertisements were offered. See Volume 2 of this Guide for a listing of billboards.

It is important to note that these postwar billboards were not the first time Lionel mentioned billboards. Larger ones had been produced for Standard Gauge, and Lionel's magazine **Model Builder** featured many articles about billboards. The billboard story begins as early as 1935 with an article entitled "Model Billboards" in the August 7, 1935 issue of **Model Builder**. In the May-June issue of 1937, a very small ad from one A. Henderson of Laurelton, New York, appeared in the same magazine. This ad offered "7 colorful ads" for 25 cents and a "kit" for $1.00. In the November-December issue of 1937, Mr. Henderson's ad had grown to a full page and featured railroad billboard reproductions of such American favorites as Ex-Lax, Lucky

Strike, Shell, Ford and RKO. In the June 1939 issue of **Model Builder**, a model railroad photograph shows a Jell-O billboard. In the April 1940 issue, Lionel featured an article about building model billboards and offered "...a prize of $10 for the best reproduction of the 24-sheet billboard of the Curtis Candy Company." In October 1940, **Model Builder** announced the winner of that contest, and in November of 1945, **Model Builder** ran another article about "Billboards Along Your Right-Of-Way" showing a model railroad station platform billboard decorated with matchbook covers for copy.

313

**313 BASCULE BRIDGE** 1946-49, green Bakelite bridge base, die-cast metal base underneath motor, sheet metal superstructure on bridge, red light on bridge top, pale yellow bridge tender building with orange windows and red roof, five binding posts, black metal alignment frame with permanently affixed lockon, 21-1/2" long, 9-1/4" high when bridge is level. Prewar version has silver-painted or gray-painted superstructure, while postwar version has unpainted aluminum superstructure. M. Ocilka observation. C. Weber has examined two bridges from the collections of R. Nikolai and J. Eastman and has come up with another way of determining prewar from postwar production. Apparently the prewar examples had a motor which raised the bridge by means of gears, while the postwar motor raised the bridge by a modified spring drive. To accommodate the postwar spring drive, structural changes were made in the bridge. The postwar gear housing tops are larger than the prewar ones, and the postwar house has a narrow vertical cut-out to allow for the spring. The gear shaft of the prewar motor attaches at the end of the gear housing, while the spring shaft of the postwar version attaches at the center of the gear housing.
(A) 1946-47, lens cap for light atop bridge is a small plug-in unit identical to those used on the R, V and Z transformers. (Part R-68.) R. Hutchinson, C. Rohlfing and M. Ocilka comments.    **150 200 300 425**
(B) 1948-49, lens cap for light atop bridge is threaded and ribbed; larger cap does not interchange with earlier cap. (Part RW-27.)    **150 200 300 425**
**313-82 FIBER PINS** 1946-60, each.    **.05 .05 .05 .08**
**313-121 FIBER PINS** 1961, per dozen.    **— — — 1.50**

314

**314 SCALE MODEL GIRDER BRIDGE** 1945-50, single span, 10" long, heavy sheet metal plate for base, die-cast sides fastened by rivets, "LIONEL" rubber-stamped in black on both sides; also lettered in small box with rounded corners "BUILT BY LIONEL". Carry-over from prewar version made in 1940-41 with silver finish and 9/32" high lettering and in 1942 with same gray as used on 92 Floodlight tower.
(A) 1945-46, gray as used on prewar 92 Floodlight tower, 5/16" high lettering which is slightly above an imaginary line drawn through the center of the bridge. C. Rohlfing and J. Algozzini Collection.    **2  5  10  15**
(B) 1947-50, different shade of gray from (A), 3/8" high centered lettering, lettering centered on bridge side. C. Rohlfing and J. Algozzini Collection.    **2  5  10  15**

**315 TRESTLE BRIDGE** 1946-47, silver-painted sheet metal, illuminated with binding posts in center of span on top, 24-1/2" long.    **15  30  45  70**

315

**316 TRESTLE BRIDGE** 1949, 24" x 6-1/8", unlighted.
(A) Painted gray, rubber-stamped "316 TRESTLE BRIDGE" on bottom. C. Rohlfing Collection.                    **10   15   30   45**
(B) Unpainted aluminum, no rubber-stamping. C. Rohlfing Collection.
                                              **10   15   30   45**

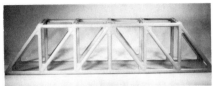

317

**317 TRESTLE BRIDGE** 1950-56, gray-painted sheet metal, 24" by 6-1/8" wide.                    **5   10   15   20**

321

**321 TRESTLE BRIDGE** 1958-64, sheet metal base, gray plastic sides and top, 24" long, 7" high, 4-1/2" wide. Labeled "BUILT BY LIONEL" in lower right corner of both sides. S. Carlson Collection.     **5   7   10   15**

**332 ARCH UNDER BRIDGE** 1959-66, came unassembled, gray plastic sides and black metal deck.                    **10   20   30   40**

332

334

**334 OPERATING DISPATCHING BOARD** 1957-60, blue attendant with white face and hands hurries across catwalk and appears to change information in illuminated slots, green board, white lines, plastic lettered material inside unit changes "information". Tan plastic base with three binding clips, clock on top and two speaker units, reverse side shows large billboard "AIREX", "REEL ROD REELS", color picture of man fishing, lower section has Lionel Travel Center, 9-7/8" long, 4-1/8" wide, 7-1/2" high.                    **50   100   125   175**

**342 CULVERT LOADER** 1956-58, culvert pipes stored on sloping ramp, picked up by pincher unit and transferred to car, loaded into special gondola car 6342, length of unit is 11-1/2" x 10" x 6", includes loading station with black metal base and tan plastic box-like unit; red building, dark gray roof; 6342 controller, connecting wires and culvert section; illustration shows 342 and 345 arranged for operation. Price includes car, which was packed inside a section of the accessory box but did not have its own box; accessory is very difficult to keep in proper adjustment. L. Bohn comment.
                                              **50   75   125   175**

342                                           345

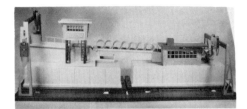

342,345

**345 CULVERT UNLOADING STATION** 1958-59, traveling crane controlled by remote control, lowers magnet to gondola car, magnet picks up culvert section and transports it onto station, unit has black metal base, gray ramp, red tower building with gray roof, orange post on crane, black horizontal piece; 12-1/2" long, 9-1/2" wide and 7" high; includes gondola designed for use with 342; this 6342 was packed inside the accessory box but did not have its own box. Culverts roll from 345 across special bridge onto 342; accessory is very difficult to keep in proper adjustment. L. Bohn comment.                    **70   150   200   325**

**346 CULVERT UNLOADER** 1965, hand-operated. Made for Sears, same as 345, except lacks motor mechanism; hand crank extends through platform top, R. Hutchinson observation. This accessory was included as part of Sears No. 9836 set, which also included the extremely rare 2347 C & O GP-7 Diesel locomotive. This manual version of the regular issue 345 culvert unloader has a base which is lettered as such. A large metal crank protrudes from the base of the unloader. Black metal base and tower ladders; gray superstructure; tuscan tower and mechanism stanchions; gray roof. "LIONELVILLE / CULVERT PIPE / CO." in gold sans-serif letters on tower side surrounded by gold rectangle. Embossing on side of superstructure reads "No. 345 CULVERT UNLOADER / THE LIONEL CORPORATION, NEW YORK / MADE IN THE U.S. OF AMERICA". (Note number.) Came in box labeled "No. 346 / OPERATING CULVERT UNLOADER". Lionel later issued this unloader outside of the Sears set. In doing so, the company pasted a "No. 348" label on the box over the 346 number, despite the fact that the unloader itself was identical to the one included in the Sears set. This accessory included a 6342 gondola with AAR trucks and dummy couplers. The gondola was not issued its own box, but was packed inside the accessory box. R. Lord comments, P. Beavin Collection.                    **50   80   125   175**

**347 CANNON FIRING RANGE SET,** Circa 1962-64. Olive drab plastic battery with four cannon barrels and four silver shells. Each barrel has a firing pin which is set prior to use. A silver shell is placed in each cannon. The firing wheel is then rotated slowly, firing the shells in sequence. Came with uncatalogued Sears set. Instructions 347-10 (8/64) came with unit. (We need to learn the Sears set number and its contents.) Jarman Collection.                    **75   100   150   225**

348

**348 CULVERT UNLOADER**  1966-69, manual loader, with car. See entry for 346. P. Beavin Collection.          **50   80   125   175**

350

356

**350 ENGINE TRANSFER TABLE**  1957-60, motorized table moves train from one track to another, 17-1/2" long and 10-3/8" wide, black sheet metal with plastic tie, fastened through bottom by rails fastened through holder, control unit with three yellow buttons and one red button; yellow building with red light on top; building lifts off motor underneath; illustration shows motorized table in the center flanked by two extension units, one on each side. Packaged in brown cardboard box 17-3/4" x 12" x 5", blue printing, two packing inserts. Also contained parts envelope 350-89 which contained rail brackets, a lockon and an instruction sheet. P. Catalano, S. Carlson and R. Hutchinson comments.          **65   130   175   250**

**350-50 TRANSFER TABLE EXTENSION**  1957-60, metal base with plastic ties, metal rails. Came in lightweight orange and blue box 17-1/2' x 12-1/2' x 1-3/4' with cardboard inserts and parts envelope 350-898 which contained additional rail brackets and grounding strips but no instruction sheet. R. Hutchinson Collection.          **25   40   90   150**

**352 ICE DEPOT**  1955-57, white shed, red roof, blue man with orange arms and paddle, cubes put in end with chute that raises; chute has a cube permanently fastened at end. Another version had five cubes fastened at end, operating mechanism moves, opens car hatch, cubes come out at end with man; came with 6352-1 car, depot, cubes, station 11-3/4" long, 4" wide, 8-1/2" high, two binding posts. Reissued by Fundimensions in 1982 as 2306 with car numbered 6700. Reportedly, some units came without the metal base; reader comments requested. M. Rubin observations.
(A) Brown plastic base.          **50   75   125   200**
(B) Red plastic base.          **50   75   125   200**

352(A)                                         353

**353 TRACK SIDE CONTROL SIGNAL**  1960-61, signal changes from green to red as train passes, can be wired to control two trains; 9" high, tan plastic base and control box; white plastic shaft, black plastic lamp housing, black metal ladder, three control posts, three binding posts on top of base
          **5   10   20   30**

**356 OPERATING FREIGHT STATION**  1952-57, maroon plastic base, white shed with green windows, door and roof, picket fence without billboard signs at least in some years (although C. Rohlfing believes that the accessory did come with billboards in most years). Station comes with six adhesive signs or posters to be mounted on station walls; see 256 entry for description. Two baggage men with carts run out onto platform and back into station. These carts have rubber pads with fingers on their bases; they are powered by a vibrator motor mounted beneath the metal station base.

Usually, one cart is dark or medium green and the other is orange, but red carts have also been found. Both men on the carts are dark blue. The 1952 catalogue showed the carts with baggage loads, the fence with billboards and no posters on the side walls; however, the Greenberg reprint of the Lionel Service Manual (VI-201) reports that early production had one cart with baggage and the other without. The Service Manual also notes that the baggage loads were discontinued because one cart would run faster than the other. This information is confusing and contradictory. At this time, we have evidence that at least some 1953 examples came with lithographed metal loads for both carts. We expect (but cannot confirm) that the loads also came with the 1952 examples and that the 1954 examples omitted the baggage loads but added the station posters. The lithographed baggage loads have been available for many years as a repair part. Some reporters believe these to be original loads which were probably sold off by the factory when they were discontinued from the station. However, others feel that these baggage loads are reproductions. Reader reports concerning datable original stations and their configurations would be of considerable assistance in resolving these questions. This station was reissued by Fundimensions in 1984 as 2323 with different colors. Our report is substantially changed from our last edition. Comments by L. Bohn, P. Ambrose, G. Wilson, C. Weber, B. Weiss and R. LaVoie.
(A) 1952, both carts with lithographed metal baggage loads, billboards, no posters. Not confirmed.          **NRS**
(B) 1953, carts have lithographed baggage loads, no billboards, no posters. P. Ambrose comment.          **20   35   60   85**
(C) 1953, later, carts do not have loads, no billboards, no posters. Not confirmed.          **NRS**
(D) 1954-57, carts do not have loads, no billboards, posters.
          **20   35   60   85**
(E) Same as (D), but light green plastic roof, approximately Penn Central green. Probable 1957 production. S. Lapan Collection.          **30   45   70   120**

362

**362 BARREL LOADER**  1952-57, barrels move up the ramp by vibrator action, gray plastic base, yellow ramp, brown plastic fence, 19" long, 4-1/8" wide, 4" high.  Car not included in price, came with six brown-stained wooden barrels, 364C controller, rubber track spacers, metal platform extension and metal track spacing guides.
(A) 1952-54, cream-colored man. Came with instruction sheet dated 8-54. T. Rollo Collection.          **30   45   60   100**
(B) 1955-57, blue-colored man; this version came with 4-55 instruction sheet. G. Salamone and R. LaVoie Collections.          **30   45   60   100**

**362-78 SIX WOODEN BARRELS**, box of six small wooden barrels for barrel car or platform. Came with 362 Barrel Loader where box liner had cutouts to hold small box, 3562 Barrel Car, and was available for separate sale. They also came with some examples of Lionel's gondolas (e.g. 6462-125 of 1955 in set 1527), but were not boxed. They also came unboxed with the 6343 Barrel ramp car. P. Ambrose comments, G. Halverson Collection.
          **2   4   6   9**

**364 CONVEYOR LUMBER LOADER**  1948-57, gray crackle finish, red belt conveys logs; red ladder; two green, one red spotlight lens; three blue binding posts. "LIONEL ATOMIC MOTOR", 27-7/8" long, 3-3/16" wide, 4-1/8" high, came with logs, controller switch.

**364**

(A) As described above.                                    30  45  60  100

(B) Shiny gray paint with later Lionel motor similar to that used on 397 Coal Loader. M. Ocilka Collection.                30  45  60  100

### 364C ON-OFF SWITCH
1948-64. Some samples have a red slide instead of a black one; these are somewhat scarcer than the all-black variety. I.D. Smith comment. This control was also made as a single-pole, double-throw switch. S. Carlson comment.                    1  1.50  2.00  3.00

### 365 DISPATCHING STATION
1958-59, elevated control room shows dispatchers at work, simulated radio antenna, loud speakers; 11" long, 5" wide, 6-1/2" high; not illustrated.          35  50  75  100

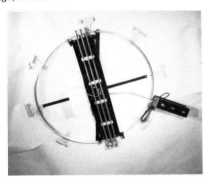

**375**

### 375 TURNTABLE
1962-64, rotates track, powered by two D cells, black metal table rotates on O Gauge curve rail, friction drive.

50  100  145  225

### 390C SWITCH
1960-64, double pole, double-throw switch, for HO reversing loop layouts, hard to find. L. Bohn comment. As with the 364C switch, some samples came with a red slider instead of a black one. I.D. Smith comment.                  .50  1.00  2.00  3.00

**394**              **394**

### 394 ROTARY BEACON
1949-53, light bulb heat drives beacon, bulb has dimple 11-3/4" high, base 5" x 5". Painted versions much harder to find than unpainted aluminum version.

(A) 1949, red-painted stamped-steel framework painted with one corner down; came in late 1949 box (no San Francisco markings or part number) and an instruction sheet dated 8-49. T. Rollo Collection.
15  30  40  60

(B) 1949-50, dark green-painted steel framework, rare. M. Rubin Collection.                                          25  40  60  80

(C) 1950-53, unpainted aluminum tower with black lettering on plate, box has part number. T. Rollo Collection.      8  12  20  30

(D) Same as (C), but aluminized sticker instead of aluminum plate. Additional sightings requested. C. Weber Collection.      NRS

(E) Same as (C), but red-painted base and black ladder. Appears to be a hybrid of (A) and (C). H. Powell Collection.      NRS

            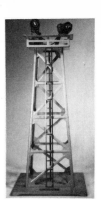

**395(E)**        **395(B)**        **395(A)**

### 395 FLOODLIGHT TOWER
1949-50, 1952-56, tower with four black die-cast floodlight units, ladders, two binding clips on bottom.

(A) 1949-50, yellow-painted tower, hardest of all versions to find.
35  60  90  125

(B) 1952, silver-painted stamped-steel tower, as opposed to unpainted aluminum tower. Much heavier than unpainted version. Box has preprinted OPS stamping which dates accessory. T. Rollo Collection.
15  25  40  65

(C) 1953-54, all-red-painted tower with black ladder and lights. Lahti and R. LaVoie Collections.                        15  25  40  65

(D) 1954-55, unpainted aluminum tower. Keith, T. Budniak and J. Cusumano Collections. The easiest way to distinguish this version from the silver-painted tower is to note the lighter weight of this version. R. LaVoie comment.                                        10  15  25  35

(E) 1955-56, green-painted tower. This is a common variety of the tower. However, one example has been reported by Michael Ocilka which has been rubber-stamped "APR 20, 1955" on the underside of the base. A second stamped version with the same date has been sighted by R. LaVoie. We wish to know if other towers have been similarly stamped with dates and what those dates might be.                    8  15  30  40

**NOTE** The production sequence of the 395 Floodlight Tower is apparently quite complex. Despite the apparent solidity of the dating above, it is not absolutely known when Lionel switched colors because the Service Manual states that "... the color available at the time will be shipped" whenever a replacement tower structure is ordered. However, we now have good information about the relative scarcity of these towers. The yellow tower is extremely hard to find and is the most scarce of the versions. Next in scarcity is the painted silver tower, followed closely by the red tower. The unpainted aluminum tower appears to be a very common version, and the green one may be the most common variety of all. We have also had reports of factory conglomerations of these varieties. The 394 and 494 Rotating Beacons have similar construction variations, although nowhere near as complex as this tower. We would appreciate comments from our readers about the relative dates and scarcity of each of these versions.

**397(A)**            **397(B)**

### 397 DIESEL OPERATING COAL LOADER
1948-57, car dumps coal into large tray, tray vibrations (more or less!) move coal to conveyor, conveyor carries coal up and fills car; 10-1/2" long, 7-7/16" wide, 6" high.

(A) Early model with yellow diesel cover, 70 Yard Light mounted on gray die-cast metal base, red coal holding unit, two motor binding posts, wires hooked directly to lamp post. We have had some reports of a mottled plastic coal tray rather that a red-painted one. Reader comments invited. This version desirable and hard to find.          100  150  225  350

410

413

(B)  Same as (A), but no yard light.  **90  140  200  325**

(C)  Later model with blue-painted white plastic diesel motor cover, red and white "GM DIESEL POWER" decal, came with 364C Controller but without yard light.  R. LaVoie and S. Carlson Collections.

**30  40  75  125**

(D)  Similar to (C), but has shiny red plastic tray, later-type motor and rubber coupling.  M. Ocilka Collection.  **30  40  75  125**

**410 BILLBOARD BLINKER**  1956-58, designed to attach to the 310 Billboard.  Black sheet metal base; black metal back with two binding clips; die-cast metal light unit for 51 6-8 volt bayonet-base bulbs, timing via metallic strip.  Reissued by Fundimensions in 1982 as 2307.  Original very hard to find.  L. Bohn and N. Cretelle comments.  **10  20  30  40**

**413 COUNTDOWN CONTROL PANEL**  1962, controls rocket launching, gray plastic with black lettering; red dial, countdown set lever, and start and fire buttons; on the underside are two mounting posts, through which the circuit (between the two posts) is completed by depressing the "fire" button.  **6  9  12  20**

**415 DIESEL FUELING STATION**  1955-67, man comes out of building; fuel pipe moves to fueling position; gray metal base, white building with red trim and roof and gray metal base, yellow base on fueling pipe and on diesel sand tank, blue tank with white lettering, three binding posts on top side of base; 9" wide, 9" long, and almost 10" high.  **30  50  100  150**

415

419

**419 HELIPORT CONTROL TOWER**  1962, helicopter launched by spring mechanism, red control tower with gray roof, clear windows, with spring mechanism visible inside, pull ring for spring release protrudes from base of tower.  Yellow radar disc, yellow helicopter with black blades, white lettering on tower "LIONEL HELIPORT", not lighted, terminal base 11" x 5" x 5-1/2" high.  Very hard to find in intact condition.  **75  125  200  275**

**443 MISSILE LAUNCHING PLATFORM**  1960-62, includes platform, missile and exploding ammo dump, 11" x 12".  **10  15  20  30**

**445 SWITCH TOWER**  1952-57, blue tower man runs up and down stairs with red lantern, other blue tower man comes in and out of building; white building, green windows, balcony and roof; maroon plastic base; three binding clips on bottom.  Reissued by Fundimensions in 1984 as 2324.

**20  30  50  70**

**448 MISSILE FIRING RANGE SET**  1961-63, with camouflage and exploding target range car, tan plastic base; 9" x 5-1/2", gray plastic launching unit 6544-5, (launching unit also came on flatcar).  Small white rockets, 6448

445

448

Target Range Car with AAR trucks, two disc-operating couplers, black metal frame, white and red side, white side with red lettering, ends and roof

**25  35  50  75**

450

**450 SIGNAL BRIDGE**  1952-58, spans two tracks, gray plastic base, black metal frame, two sets of red and green lights, inside width 7-1/2", inside height 6", three binding posts on each side.  **15  25  35  50**

**450L SIGNAL BRIDGE HEAD**, black replacement hood for this and other signal accessories; fastens to accessory by spring clips.  C. Rohlfing comment.  **3  5  10  15**

452

455

**452 SIGNAL BRIDGE**  1961-63, also known as "Overhead Gantry Signal", signal changes from green to red as train approaches, bridge 7-3/4" high, gray plastic base with metal grip for fastening unit, black-painted metal frame ladder, black plastic light unit, direction of light unit can be reversed.

**40  60  80  150**

**454 CONSTRUCTION SET**, listed on page 35 of 1948 catalogue.  Came in large oak box with elaborate cardboard display partitions to hold the different pieces.  The large number of miniscule pieces would have been intimidating to anyone, youth or adult, who wanted to complete a project.  B. McLeavy comments and collection.  **NRS**

**455 OIL DERRICK**  1950-54, pumping motion, bulb heat causes bubbling action in tube, four aluminum oil barrels, 9-1/4" long, 5-1/2" wide and 14-1/2" high, orange diesel unit.  Reissued by Fundimensions in 1981 as 2305 with Getty Oil signs instead of Sunoco.

(A)  Red metal base, apple green metal tower, red tower top.

**50  80  140  200**

(B)  Dark green metal base and tower.  Further confirmation requested.

**NRS**

(C) Same as (A), but green tower top; slightly more common than (A). Juenemann Collection.      **50   75   125   175**

**456**

**456 COAL RAMP** 1950-55, with 3456 N & W operating hopper 9-1/2" long, not shown, gray metal ramp with red light, 35" long, 3-3/16" wide and 6-3/16" high, shown with 397 Operating Coal Loader for continuous action, price for 456 with special hopper car, red coal receiving tray, steel support rods to hold tray over 397 coal loader, special 456C controller. L. Bohn and S. Carlson comments.
(A) 1950-52, dark blue-gray ramp; service manual denotes darker color with "X" after part numbers, fine stranded wire used for handrails. C. Rohlfing and R. Hutchinson comments. For at least one year, the 3456 Operating Hopper Car came packed in its own box with an end flap marked 3456-26. R. Hutchinson Collection.      **48   60   90   150**
(B) 1952-55, light gray ramp, cloth "fishing line" handrails. C. Rohlfing and R. Hutchinson comments.      **48   60   90   150**

**460**

**460 PIGGYBACK TRANSPORTATION** 1955-57, hand crank and lever on platform (visible in illustration) cause lift truck to move 360 degrees and cause truck platform to raise and lower, flatcar and two trailers not illustrated. Since this platform was also used for the 462 made after the 460 but before the 461, perhaps indentations for wheels found in the 460 were removed for the 462 production run, when the frame was modified, and not put back in when the 461 was produced in 1966. D. Anderson comments.      **20   30   50   75**

**460P PIGGYBACK PLATFORM** Carton lettered "PLATFORM", made for those already having a piggyback flatcar with vans; red lift truck, white rubber-stamped lettering "ROSS TRAILOADER". P. Catalano observation.      **20   30   40   65**

**460-150 TWO TRAILERS FOR FLATCARS.**
(A) Box label has "No.460-150 / TWO TRAILERS". Two white Cooper-Jarrett vans with copper signs, four rubber tires on one axle for each van. G. Halverson Collection.      **—   —   —   35**
(B) Same as (A), but pre-1958 box, two green Fruehauf vans. P. Ambrose Collection.      **—   —   —   40**
(C) Same as (A), but vans are gray instead of white. Pre-1958 box. H. Powell Collection.      **—   —   —   35**

**461**

**461 PLATFORM WITH TRUCK AND TRAILER** Circa 1966, uncatalogued; gray plastic base, white trailer with single axle and two wheels, tractor marked "MIDGE TOY, ROCKFORD, ILL. U.S.A. PATENT 2775847". We would like to learn more about the 460P and the 461. How do these accessories differ mechanically and cosmetically? Who sold them?

H. Powell comments. Designed to be used with 6431 car which has identical tractor and trailer components; see that entry in flatcar chapter. R. Hutchinson comment. We also have reports of two types of platforms, one with indentations for trailer wheels and one without. Which platform goes with which of the varieties listed below? B. Stekoll comment.
(A) Red lift truck with four wheels in front and one in rear; white rubber-stamped "ROSS / TRAILOADER" inside of white-outlined rectangle, separate cast metal steering column. See P. Catalano's report on 460P above. B. Stekoll and H. Powell Collections.      **25   50   70   100**
(B) Red lift truck with black press-on decal with white lettering "ROSS / TRAILOADER", separate cast metal steering column. B. Stekoll Collection.      **25   50   70   100**
(C) Red lift truck without lettering or decal, plastic steering column part of body. B. Stekoll Collection.      **25   50   70   100**
(D) Came with red 6430 flatcar, 6511-2 mold, AAR trucks, yellow Cooper-Jarrett vans with copper and black signs, vans have enlarged hole to hook up to truck. H. Powell Collection.      **60   90   125   175**

**L461 14 VOLT BULBS** Ten to a box; box labeled on one end "TEN NO. L461 / MINIATURE LAMPS / 14V. CLEAR INDENTED SCR. BASE." I.D. Smith Collection.      **NRS**

**462 DERRICK PLATFORM SET** 1961-62, derrick handles "radioactive" waste containers, lifts containers from car to platform, platform has three black cranks similar to those on the 6560 Crane, one crank rotates crane unit, one moves lifts, raises and lowers boom, a third raises and lowers table, plastic radioactive containers similar to those found on flatcars but without lighting assembly, 8-1/2" long, 11" wide, 1-3/4" high, buff plastic base, yellow crane boom. Somewhat hard to find.      **50   90   150   200**

**462**

**464**

**464 LUMBER MILL** 1956-60, simulates the transformation of logs into dressed lumber, vibrator mechanism inside moves finished lumber, gray plastic base; white mill building with red door, gray shed, length 10-1/2", width 6", height 6", logs, lumber, controller and mill. Some bases are slightly darker gray than others; D. Doyle comment. Reissued by Fundimensions in 1980 as 2301, the first of the major postwar accessories issued in the most recent production period of Lionel. This reissue is virtually identical to the older version except for the mill window, which lacks the 464 number.      **30   60   90   140**

**465 SOUND DISPATCHING STATION** 1956-57, operator speaks into microphone, voice comes out of 4" loudspeaker in station; battery-powered, buff-colored plastic base, red room, gray roof, yellow microwave tower on roof, gray microphone with left red button for train, right red button for talk, gray plastic ladder into station, also includes lockon insulating pins, wires and four batteries, length 11", width 5", height 5", antenna 3".      **30   45   60   100**

**470 MISSILE LAUNCHING PLATFORM** 1959-62, missile tilts and flies, tan plastic base, blue missile launching unit base, black cradle, white, red

465

470

and blue missile, includes target car; 6470 in set; note Quonset hut-type building on platform.                     **12   17   25   35**

**480-25 CONVERSION COUPLER** 1950-60, converts Scout coupler to remote control operation.                     **.50  1.00  1.50  2.00**

**480-32 CONVERSION MAGNETIC COUPLER** 1961-69, converts Scout coupler to remote control operation, has finger tab which is not present on 480-25. I.D. Smith observation.                     **.50  1.00  1.50  2.00**

**494 ROTARY BEACON** 1954-66, vibrator-driven rotating red and green light, 11-3/4" high, base 5" x 5", bayonet-type bulb; two binding clips on bottom.

(A) Red-painted tower with silver-lettered black metal plate on base. R. LaVoie and S. Carlson Collections.                     **10   15   30   45**

(B) Unpainted aluminum tower, tabbed metal nameplate on base as in (A). C. Switzer Collection.                     **10   15   30   45**

(C) Silver-painted metal tower and top. Cummings and C. Rohlfing Collections. This version considerably heavier in weight than (B).
                                                                  **10   15   30   45**

    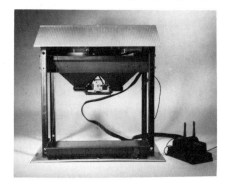

494                                    497

**497 COALING STATION** 1953-58, red plastic bin carries coal to top of structure, coal empties into overhead storage area, released from storage into waiting car, gray metal base, black metal posts, red metal bin, translucent green plastic roof, with controller with one lever for up and down, other lever dumps load, 10" high, 6" x 9-1/2" base. Reissued by Fundimensions in 1984 as 2315, but with gray roof.

(A) 1954-58, medium translucent green roof, same as above.
                                                          **50   75   125   200**

(B) 1953, very dark green roof.  E. Trentacoste Collection, T. Rollo comment.                     **60   85   140   225**

**565 CONSTRUCTION SET**, listed on page 36 of 1948 catalogue. Further details needed; reader comments invited.                     **NRS**

**671-75 SMOKE BULB** See entry for 703-10 below.

703-10

**703-10 SPECIAL SMOKE BULB** 1946, box shows 671-75. This number originally scheduled for a scale Hudson steam engine which was never made. Original bulbs are very scarce; reproduction bulbs have been made by the North American Philips Electric Company and packaged in original Lionel boxes.  Price for original bulb.

(A) Box marked "No. 703-10 / SMOKE LAMP / 16-18 VOLTS" on end flap. D. Doyle Collection.                     **—   —   —   20**

(B) Box marked "No. 671-75 / SMOKE LAMP / 12 VOLTS" on end flap. D. Doyle Collection.                     **—   —   —   20**

(C) Same as (B), but box overstamped to read "18 VOLTS" on end flap. R. LaVoie observation, D. Doyle Collection.                     **—   —   —   20**

**711 REMOTE CONTROL 072 SWITCHES**, pair, 1935-42, wide radius. Prewar product, but listed here because of heavy use by postwar operators. See also 721 entry.                     **50   75   100   150**

**721 MANUAL 072 SWITCHES**, pair, 1935-42, wide radius. Prewar product, but listed here because of heavy use by postwar operators.
                                                          **25   50   75   100**

**760 072 TRACK** 1954-57, 16 sections of O curved track with 72" diameter, each section 14" long.  (Note that reproduction track is available).
                                                          **15   20   35   45**

**868 ACCESSORY PROMOTION** 1958; Lionel offered an unusual boxed set of accessories to Service Stations.  The cost to these stations was substantially below wholesale.  This set included a 494 rotary beacon in a pre-1959 box, a 128 animated newsstand, a 252 crossing gate with cellophane see-through packaging, 310 billboards with 1958 billboards, a set of three 76 Boulevard Lamps in cellophane packaging, a 260 bumper, a folded 950 Railroad Map and a sheet of 12 railroad trading cards, each of which showed a locomotive from a different railroad with a quiz question. P. Ambrose comment.                     **NRS**

**902 ELEVATED TRESTLE SET**, 1960, came as part of uncatalogued set X568NA (see also Uncatalogued Sets).  Came packed in paper bag which was factory stamped "902 ELEVATED TRESTLE SET" in large letters with pictures for assembly.  The trestles themselves had to be punched out from heavy cardboard sheets. P. Ambrose and C. Weber Collections. Another version of this accessory came in a cardboard container which reads "MADE 1959 THE LIONEL CORPORATION".  The container held 10 cardboard punch-out trestles, 10 railroad signs, a girder bridge and a tunnel. J. Algozzini Collection.                     **NRS**

909                                    919

**909 SMOKE FLUID**  1957-68, two ounces for 746, 1872, 243, etc.

— — — 2

**919 ARTIFICIAL GRASS**  1946-64, half-pound bag of artificial grass, red lettering on bag.

— — 3 5

920

**920 SCENIC DISPLAY SET**  1957-58, includes four feet of mountain paper with two tunnel portals, black and gray plastic portals with "HILLSIDE" embossqd on top, "L" in circle, and "1957" in lower right, came as set of two. Also includes paints, gravels and bags of yellow and green grass. Very hard to find in original condition. P. Ambrose and S. Carlson comments.

15 30 60 90

**920-2 TUNNEL PORTALS**  1957, pair of realistically molded cut stone tunnel portals. Part of 920 Scenic Display Set of 1957; also sold separately. Portals have "1957" molded on them. L. Bohn Collection. Reissued by Fundimensions in 1984 as 2113, but with "LIONEL" instead of "HILLSI-DE" molded into them. L. Bohn and R. Hutchinson comments.

8 15 20 35

**920-3 GREEN GRASS**, 1957; bag is printed "GREEN GRASS / FOR / MODEL TRAIN LAYOUTS / L / THE LIONEL CORPORATION / NEW YORK / N.Y. / Made In U.S. of America 920-17". Bag is 11" high by 5" wide. Part of 920 Scenic Display Kit. LaRue Collection.

.50 1 3 5

**920-4 YELLOW GRASS**, 1957; bag is printed "Yellow Grass for Model Train Layouts / L / The Lionel Corporation / New York, N.Y. / Made In U.S. of America 920-18". Bag is 7" high and 5" wide. Came with 920 Scenic Display Kit with 920-2, 920-3, 920-5 and 920-8. LaRue Collection.

.50 1 5 9

**920-5 ARTIFICIAL ROCK**  1958, expanded mica-type mineral.

50 1 2 3

**920-8 LICHEN**  1958, treated and colored for realistic shrubbery.

50 1 2 3

**925 LIONEL LUBRICANT**  1946-69, large tube.  .50 1 2 3

**926 LIONEL LUBRICANT**  1955, smaller tube.  .25 .50 1 2

927

**927 LUBRICATING AND MAINTENANCE KIT**  1950-53, metal tube of lubricant, glass vial of lubricating oil, can of track-cleaning solvent, cleaning sticks, small brush, emery boards, small rag, smoke pellet bottle and wooden smoke pellet tamper. Seldom found in intact condition. Versions have been found with 1952 and 1953 instruction booklets, part 927-14. R. Hutchinson, I.D. Smith and C. Weber Collections and comments.

2 4 7 15

**928 MAINTENANCE AND LUBRICANT KIT**  1960-63, includes oil, lubricant, "Track Clean", packaged originally in shrink-wrap. Not easily found in mint condition.

2 3 5 15

943

**943 AMMO DUMP**  1959-61, target "explodes" on impact, spring-loaded mechanism inside, gray metal base, green plastic body, 3" long, 5" wide, 4" high, four plastic parts; one each labeled "B" "A", two unlabeled ends.

4 6 8 15

950

**950 U.S. RAILROAD MAP**  1958-66, by Rand McNally, full color 52" x 37".

3 8 12 20

Items 951 to 969 and 980 to 988 were produced for Lionel by Bachmann Bros., Inc. of Philadelphia, Pa., manufacturers of Plasticville buildings. The sets contain regular Plasticville items, although sometimes in different quantities or combinations than Bachmann Plasticville sets.

According to Dick Reddles, Bachmann Vice President, Lionel shipped its traditional orange and blue boxes to Bachmann in Philadelphia and Bachmann packed the boxes with Plasticville and shipped them back to Lionel.

To be "Mint" or "Excellent" the following items must include the Lionel box with the Lionel number.

**951 FARM SET**  1958, 13 pieces, truck, tractor, jeep, horses, cows, harrow, plow, wagon and footbridge.  3 7 20 30

**952 FIGURE SET**  1958, 30 pieces, people, fire plug, fire alarm box and metal boxes.  3 7 15 25

**953 FIGURE SET**  1960-62, 32 pieces including paint brush, not illustrated.  2 7 15 25

**954 SWIMMING POOL AND PLAYGROUND SET**  1959, 30 pieces; 12 fence pieces, six trees, slide, swing, teeter-totter, round-riding, bench, table with umbrella, two chairs, two chaise lounges, pool. Hemmert Collection.

3 7 15 30

**955 HIGHWAY SET**  1958, 22 pieces; two buses, auto, seven telegraph poles, 10 yellow street signs, seven green street indicators.

3 7 15 30

**956 STOCKYARD SET**  1959, 18 pieces; corral, cows, railroad signs.

3 7 15 30

**957 FARM BUILDING AND ANIMAL SET**  1958, 35 pieces; four farm structures, fence, gate, pump, horse, fowl and domestic animals.

3 7 15 30

**958 VEHICLE SET**  1958, 24 pieces; three autos, two fire trucks, ambulance, bus, street signs, fire alarm box, mailbox, fire plug, traffic light.  3 7 15 30

**959 BARN SET**  1958, 23 pieces; dairy barn, horses, fowl and domestic animals; orange and blue traditional box, not illustrated.  3 7 15 30

**960 BARNYARD SET**  1959-61, 29 pieces; three farm buildings, dog house, tractor, truck, wagon, hoe, fowl, domestic and farm animals.

3 7 15 30

**961 SCHOOL SET** 1959, 36 pieces; school, flagpole, two buses, street signs, fence pieces, shrubs and benches. 3 7 15 30

**962 TURNPIKE SET** 1958, 24 pieces; interchange, stanchions, five telegraph poles, four autos, ambulance, bus and street signs.
3 7 18 35

**963 FRONTIER SET** 1959-60, 18 pieces; cabin, windmill, fences, cows and pump. 3 7 15 30

**964 FACTORY SITE SET** 1959, 18 pieces; factory with water tower, auto, four telegraph poles, railroad signs. 3 7 18 35

**965 FARM SET** 1959, 36 pieces, dairy barn, three farm buildings, farm equipment, fowl, domestic and farm animals. 3 7 15 30

**966 FIRE HOUSE SET** 1958, 45 pieces; firehouse, fire engines, alarm box, hydrant, ambulance, bus, autos, traffic light, street signs, street post, bench, mailbox, people, telegraph poles and pine trees. 3 7 15 30

**967 POST OFFICE SET** 1958, 25 pieces; post office, mailbox, people, benches, street lights, street post, traffic lights, truck and autos .
3 7 15 30

**968 TV TRANSMITTER SET** 1958, 28 pieces; TV station, fence, gate, people, mailbox, fire plug, jeep, two autos and trees. 7 10 20 35

**969 CONSTRUCTION SET** 1960, 23 pieces; house construction materials, workers and autos. 10 18 30 45

**Lionel Plasticville continues at 980**

970

971

**970 TICKET BOOTH** 1958-60, 46" high, 22" wide, 11" deep, simulated blackboard on front, green roof with "LIONELVILLE" sign, trimmed in red, clock on roof reads "7:07"; trimmed in green and red, came packed flat in carton; carton has label with "3592-1" and manufactured by United Container Corporation, Philadelphia, PA., "United for Strength".
25 37 50 75

**971 LICHEN** 1960-64, box with green, yellow and brown lichen, 4-1/2 ounces. 2 3 4 6

**972 LANDSCAPE TREE ASSORTMENT** 1961-64, four evergreens, three flowering shrubs, lichen. 2 3 4 6

**973 COMPLETE LANDSCAPING SET** 1960-64, includes 4" x 8" roll of grass mat, one 16" x 48" roll of earth, ballast and road mats . 3 4 6 8

**974 SCENERY SET** 1962-63, 4" x 8" grass mat, two 3-D background mountains, bag of lichen, nine assorted trees. 4 6 8 10

**Lionel Plasticville continues**

**980 RANCH SET** 1960, 14 pieces; loading pen, cattle, pigs, sheep and farm implements. 3 7 15 30

**981 FREIGHT YARD SET** 1960, 10 pieces; loading platform with carts, switch tower, telephone poles and railroad men. 3 7 15 30

982

**982 SUBURBAN SPLIT LEVEL SET** 1960, 18 pieces; split level house, pine trees, auto, ranch and fence. 3 7 15 30

**983 FARM SET** 1960-61, seven pieces; dairy barn, windmill, Colonial house, horse, cows and auto. 10 20 35 50

**984 RAILROAD SET** 1961-62, 22 pieces; switch tower, telegraph poles, loading platform, figures, R.R. signs and accessories. 3 7 15 30

**985 FREIGHT AREA SET** 1961, 32 pieces; water tower, work car, loading platform, switch tower, watchman's shanty, telegraph poles, autos, R.R. signs and accessories. 7 11 18 35

**986 FARM SET** 1962, 20 pieces; farm house, barn and 18 domestic animals. 5 11 15 32

**987 TOWN SET** 1962, 24 pieces; church, gas station, auto, street signs, bank and store. 10 18 35 50

**988 RAILROAD STRUCTURE SET** 1962, 16 pieces; railroad station with freight platform, water tank, work car, hobo shacks, bench, figures, crossing gate and shanty. 6 11 15 32

**1008 UNCOUPLING UNIT** 1957, plastic clip-on uncoupler which works by spring-loaded tangs which grab disc on AAR-equipped trucks. Does not, as a rule, work very well. .50 1 1 2

**1008-50 UNCOUPLING TRACK SECTION** 1948, Scout-type, manual uncoupler unit is permanently fastened to track piece. .25 .50 1 1.50

**1013 CURVED TRACK** 1958-69, O-27, 9-1/2" long. .10 .15 .20 .40

**1013-17 STEEL PINS** 1946-60, O-27, each. — .05 .05 .05

**1013-42 STEEL PINS** 1961-68, per dozen. — — .60 .80

**1018-1/2 STRAIGHT TRACK** 1955-69, O-27 Gauge, 1/2 section.
.10 .15 .30 .50

**1018 STRAIGHT TRACK** 1945-69, O-27, 8-7/8" long.
.10 .15 .30 .40

**1019 REMOTE CONTROL TRACK SET** 1946-48, for O-27 Gauge, with controller. 1.50 2 5 8

**1020 90 DEGREE CROSSING** 1955-69, O-27 track. 1.50 2 3 6

**1021 90 DEGREE CROSSING** 1945-54, O-27 track, 7-3/8" square.
1.50 2 3 6

**1022 MANUAL SWITCH** 1953-69, pair, for O-27 track.
2 4 10 15

**1023 45 DEGREE CROSSING** 1956-69, for O-27. 1.50 2 3 6

**1024 MANUAL SWITCHES** 1946-52, pair O-27, directional wiring, same moving rails as 1121 Remote Switches, circular metal red and green-painted direction markers, wide keystone-shaped aluminum and black plate reads "No. 1024 / THE LIONEL CORPORATION / MADE IN U.S. / OF AMERICA". 5 7 10 15

**1025 ILLUMINATED BUMPER** 1946-47, black with lamp and one section of O-27 track. 3 7 10 15

**1045 OPERATING WATCHMAN** 1946-50, large blue Bakelite man with flesh-colored hands and face, white flag, aluminum-colored post, two binding posts on bottom, red base. A very popular accessory in its time despite being ludicrously out of scale (the man is much taller than the trains). Also made during prewar period, 1938-42.

(A) Nickel warning sign with black letters. 8 12 20 40

(B) Brass sign with black lettering. 8 12 20 40

1045(A)          1045(B)

1047

**1047 OPERATING SWITCHMAN** 1959-61, switchman waves flag as train approaches, green metal case, blue switchman with red flag, flesh-colored face and hands, five railroad ties with clip holding three, blue diesel fuel tank unit on base, two binding posts, black die-cast base on rail crossing sign, white plastic sign with black letters, 4-1/2" high. Reissued by Fundimensions in 1983 as 2128 in different colors. This accessory was probably made only in 1959, since it sold very poorly and it took several years to clear out the existing stock. The reissued Fundimensions version did not sell well, either, probably because the 145 and 2145 Gatemen perform the same action more colorfully. The postwar version is very hard to find. R. LaVoie comments.                     **30   50   100   175**

**1121 REMOTE CONTROL SWITCHES** 1946-51, pair of O-27 switches, each with two indicator lenses and rounded motor cover, single controller 1121-C-60 with two levers and four indicator light lenses, switches are 9-3/8" x 6-7/8" and came with either bright or satin rail finish. Units used screw-type bulbs to 1950; bayonet-type bulbs thereafter. Also produced in prewar period from 1937-42 with metal switch cover box and metal controller cover with red-painted levers. Reliable operation, especially when directional feature is not as necessary as it would be on a reversing loop or a larger layout. R. LaVoie comments.
(A) Flat plastic direction indicator lenses on switches.     **7   15   25   40**
(B) Protruding rubber direction indicator lenses on switches, rivet location on bottom differs from (A).                              **7   15   25   40**

**1122 REMOTE CONTROL SWITCHES** 1952, early production, pair of O-27 switches, each with rotating direction indicator and a single controller 1122-100 with two levers and four indicator light lenses, non-derailing design. Five notches on switch box cover, insulated rails on outside with insulating break in rail itself so that no insulated pins were needed. The moving rails were fastened to the drive rod with a large circular rivet. A light was mounted on a separate socket which plugs into a notch accessible through an arch-shaped hole in cover. Came at first with swiveling directional lenses with exposed surfaces which broke easily; later versions have recessed lenses. Flat frog point and wide frog rail. Operational problems and "teething" troubles led to a substantial redesign in 1953; see 1122E entry. R. LaVoie comments.
(A) 1952, direction indicator with exposed lenses.     **10   20   30   40**
(B) 1953, direction indicator with recessed lenses.     **10   20   30   40**

**1122E REMOTE CONTROL SWITCHES** 1953-69, pair of O-27 switches, each with rotating direction indicator and a single controller, 1122-100, with two levers and four indicator light lenses.
(A) Three notches on redesigned rounded switch cover which allowed clearance for larger locomotives. (Note that Lionel also sold this rounded cover to retrofit the older switches; this version had the arched cutout for the light socket.) Light clip redesigned to be completely internal, thus eliminating the arched cut-out and separate light socket. The insulated rails

were moved to the two inside short rails which branch from a rounded frog point; insulating pins now required. The long curved and straight rails were made solid without any breaks, and a metal track insert was placed on the frog to prevent premature wear of the plastic base by wheel flanges. This switch had its moving rails fastened to the drive rod by a large clover-shaped rivet. The rack in the mechanism was redesigned and the frog rail made much narrower. The bracket for the directional indicator was reinforced. Stamped "MODEL 1122 (E)" on galvanized base bottom; reliable operation compared to predecessor. R. LaVoie comments.
                                                   **10   20   35   45**
(B) Same as (A), but later production, small circular rivet fastens moving rails to drive rod instead of clover-shaped rivet.     **10   20   35   45**

**1122LH SWITCH** 1955-69, O-27, remote control, left-hand with controller.
                                                   **5   12   18   23**
**1122RH SWITCH** 1955-69, O-27, remote control, right-hand with controller.
                                                   **5   12   18   23**
**1122-234 FIBER PINS** 1958-60, O-27 each.     **.03   .05   .05   .05**
**1122-500 O-27 GAUGE ADAPTER** 1957-66, for combining O-27 and Super O, four ground rail pins, two insulating pins, three power rail pins.
                                                   **.25   .50   1   2**
**L1445 18 VOLT LAMPS** Box of ten, one box end labeled "TEN No. L1445 / MINIATURE LAMPS / 18V. CLEAR BAY. BASE". I.D. Smith Collection.
                                                   **NRS**

**1640-100 PRESIDENTIAL KIT** 1960, car decals, whistle stop audience, Presidential candidate. One decal labeled for Republicans and one for Democrats; designed to be attached to O-27-style 2400-Series passenger cars. J. Bratspis Collection.     **10   15   25   35**

**2003 TRACK "MAKE-UP" KIT FOR "O-27 TRACK"** 1963, box has black over print "MAKE THIS EXCITING 'LOOP-TO-LOOP' LAYOUT!" Contains eight 1013 curved track, two 1018 straight track and one 1023 45-degree crossover. R. Griesbeck Collection.     **NRS**

**3330-100 OPERATING SUBMARINE KIT** 1960-61, kit that after assembly operates under water.     **10   15   25   40**

3356-150(B)

**3356-150 HORSE CAR CORRAL** Horse moves by vibrating action, galvanized metal base; white plastic frame.
(A) Green and brown interior plastic liners, black horses, came with matching car; price for corral only.     **10   15   25   40**
(B) Same as (A), but with gray and red interior liners and white horses, price for corral only.     **15   30   50   75**
(C) Red watering trough instead of gray. E. Trentacoste Collection.     **NRS**

3366-100, 362-78          3356-100, 3656-9

**3366-100 NINE WHITE HORSES** 1959-60, extra horses for 3356.
                                                   **5   7   10   20**

**3424-75**  See next entry.

**3424-100 LOW BRIDGE SIGNAL SET**  Track clip, grounding clip (Brakeman Car) or long outside cam plate (Giraffe Car), orange pole, white tell-tale strands. Two required for 3424 Operating Brakeman Car; one for 3376-86 Giraffe Car. See note below.          8    12    18    25

**NOTE**  Every box for the above accessory is marked "3424-100 Low Bridge Signal Set". However, there were two distinct combinations for this accessory, one for the 3424 Wabash Brakeman Car and one for the 3376-86 Giraffe Car. The Lionel Service Manual refers to the giraffe car version as 3424-75, although no box is known to be marked that way. The differences are as follows: the 3424 Brakeman Car came with two boxed 3424-100 telltale poles. Each box included the telltale and a base with spring-mounted track clips. Four two-rail grounding rails came with the brakeman car, two for O and two for O-27 track. This ground rail was fastened to the base by twisting its metal tangs into holes in the bottom of the base. The 3376-86 Giraffe Cars also came with the telltale pole and track base, but the ground rails were replaced by a long, spring-loaded bar which fastened outside the rails to a small indentation in the track clip and pressed against the outside rail sides at its ends. We need to hear from a reader who has a 3376 Bronx Zoo Giraffe Car in its original packing box to be sure of the designation of this accessory for the giraffe car; reader comments are requested. J. Roskoski and R. LaVoie comments.

3462(A)                    3462(B)

**3462P MILK CAR PLATFORM**  All metal unit.
(A) Green base, white platform frame, gray steps, unpainted platform, came with milk car, price for platform only.          2    3    5    10
(B) Brown base, gray steps, unpainted platform, yellow railing, came with Bosco car, price for platform only.          20    28    35    50

**NOTE**  Research of several 3462P platforms shows that this number was stamped on the bottom base of all milk car platforms. All samples observed were from original 3472 and 3482 boxes. It is safe to conclude that 3462P is the only existing number for this platform. R. LaVoie comment.

3530

**3530 SEARCHLIGHT WITH POLE AND BASE**  Came with blue generator car marked 3530, searchlight has red base with magnet, gray plastic housing, plastic lens, green wire and bayonet-type bulb, telegraph pole is brown unpainted plastic; black unpainted plastic base is marked "SERVICE TRANSFORMER THE LIONEL CORPORATION NEW YORK, N.Y." with aluminum metal tube, two green wires emerge from the aluminum tube, hook into the female receptacles on the boxcar. Price with car. S. Blotner Collection and comments.          25    50    75    100

**3656 STOCKYARD WITH CATTLE**  Cattle powered by vibrator motor march through pen into car and out, stockyard is a metal unit with plastic gates, loading ramp, came with 3656 operating cattle car, price for pen only.
(A) Early version with two rubber grommets at each end, chain on right-hand side (as unit faces camera), does not have decal in center, operates better than later unit.          7    10    15    25

3656(A)

3656(B)

(B) Later model with metal plate on center of unit visible in illustration, binding post right side, rubber supporting pads underneath platform, platform lifts out, not permanently fastened, yellow metal frame and gate, shiny metal platform, green base with ramp for cows.          5    7    12    20
(C) No chain or holes for chains, but base has nameplate. Appears to be a factory conglomeration of versions (A) and (B). Cummings Collection.          **NRS**

**3672-79 SEVEN BOSCO CANS**  1960, for 3672 car.          15    20    30    40
**3927-50 COTTON TRACK CLEANING PADS**  1957-60, round cardboard container.          .50    1    2    6
**3927-75 TRACK CLEAN FLUID**  1957-69, non-flammable detergent.          .50    1    2    3
**5159 MAINTENANCE AND LUBRICANT KIT**  1964-68.          1    2    3    4
**5159-50 MAINTENANCE AND LUBRICANT KIT**  1969.          1    2    3    4
**5160 OFFICIAL VIEWING STAND**  1963, included with Lionel auto racing sets; while not strictly a train accessory, we note this unit because of growing collector interest. The accessory was based on the 419 Heliport and / or the 456 Dispatching Station. It had a buff unnumbered base, a red room labeled "LIONEL SPEEDWAY" in white, gray roof, gray ladder to base, yellow microwave tower on roof, two white flagpoles on roof, two yellow speaker horns on roof, unlighted; cardboard window insert with scene of nine men broadcasting a June 1963 auto race with a 1963 Corvette Sting Ray (the first model of this car) in first place. Accessory is 11" long x 5" deep by 6" high. V. Rosa and S. Carlson Collections.          50    75    100    125
**6019 REMOTE CONTROL TRACK**  1948-66, for O-27 track, unloading and uncoupling. Wiring often deteriorates.
(A) 1948, chrome finish; came with set 1445 WS and very likely with other sets as well. R. Hutchinson Collection.          1    2    3    4
(B) 1949-69, same as (A), but black finish.          1    2    3    4
**6029 UNCOUPLING TRACK SET**  1955-63, O-27, uncoupling only.          .25    .50    1    2
**6112-25 CANISTER SET**  Four dark red canisters with white "LIONEL / AIR ACTIVATED / CONTAINER" lettering in box marked "No. 6112-25 / CANISTER SET". G. Halverson Collection.          4    8    15    25
**6149 REMOTE CONTROL UNCOUPLING TRACK**  1964-69.          .25    .50    1    2
**6414-25 FOUR AUTOMOBILES**  Boxed set of four cars includes four premium autos for 6414 Evans Auto Loader car in red, white, yellow and blue versions. J. Algozzini Collection.          —    —    25    35

6418

**6418 BRIDGE**  See entry for 214(C) in this chapter.
**6650-80 MISSILE**  1960, for 6650, 6823, 443 and 470.          1    2    4    6

**6801-60 BOAT** White-hulled boat for 6801 flatcar; has brown top piece with white interior. Came in separate box marked "6801-60". J. Bratspis Collection, R. LaVoie observation.  — — 18 25

**6816-100 ALLIS CHALMERS TRACTOR DOZER** 1956-60. Very hard to find.  25 50 75 100

**6817-100 ALLIS CHALMERS MOTOR SCRAPER** 1959-60. Very hard to find.  25 50 75 100

**6827-100 HARNISCHFEGER TRACTOR SHOVEL** 1960.  5 10 25 45

**6828-100 HARNISCHFEGER MOBILE CONSTRUCTION CRANE** 1960.  15 25 45 65

**OC CURVED TRACK** 1945-61, 10-7/8", O Gauge. .15 .25 .40 .70

**TOC CURVED TRACK** 1962-66, 1968-69, 10-7/8", O Gauge. .15 .25 40 .70

**OS STRAIGHT TRACK** 1945-61, O Gauge. .20 .30 .40 .70

**TOS STRAIGHT TRACK** 1962-69, O Gauge. .20 .30 .40 .70

**OC1/2 HALF SECTION CURVED TRACK** 1945-66, O Gauge. .20 .30 .40 .70

**TOC1/2 HALF SECTION STRAIGHT TRACK** 1962-66, O Gauge. .20 .30 .40 .70

**OTC LOCKON** See illustration of 154 contactor. Includes O Gauge extension pins. 1 2 3 5

**OC18 STEEL PINS** 1945-59, each. .02 .03 .05 .05

**OC51 STEEL PINS** 1961, dozen. .20 .30 .50 .75

**TOC51 STEEL PINS** 1962-69, dozen. .20 .30 .50 .75

**011-11 FIBER PINS** 1946-50, each. .03 .03 .05 .05

**T011-43 FIBER PINS** 1962-66, dozen. .20 .30 .40 .60

**UTC LOCKON** 1945, fits O-27, O and standard Gauge track. .25 .50 .75 1.25

**RCS REMOTE CONTROL TRACK** 1945-48, for O Gauge, five rails, does not have electromagnet. 1 2 3 4

**ECU-1 ELECTRONIC CONTROL UNIT** 1946. 10 20 40 60

CTC Lockon          SP Smoke Pellets

**CTC LOCKON** 1947-69, for O and O-27 track. .20 .50 .75 1

**UCS REMOTE CONTROL TRACK** 1949-69, for O Gauge. Reissued by Fundimensions as no. 5149. 3 5 8 15

**LTC LOCKON** 1950-69, with light, for O and O-27 track. 3 4 5 7

**SP SMOKE PELLETS** 1948-69, 50 tablets per bottle. — — — 5

## TRANSFORMERS

Transformers are usually bought to operate trains and related items. Hence if a transformer is not operating it has little if any value. (If a transformer is repairable, after it is repaired, it will yield the values indicated.) Several of the larger models such as the KW, V, VW, Z or ZW have some minimal value - even if completely burned out — for knobs, plates and nuts. In the listing that follows, we report only Good, Excellent and Mint conditions and the value assigned assumes that the transformer is in operating condition. In recent years, the more popular transformers have jumped sharply in value, reflecting more people entering the tinplate collecting hobby and Lionel's inability to manufacture transformers of more than 100 watts due to Federal safety guidelines for electric toys. The result is more people chasing fewer transformers, which is bound to affect prices very heavily. For example, in some metropolitan areas the big ZW transformer is selling for over $200, even though we list it well below that. Lionel, Inc. is working on a solid-state transformer, reputedly the MW, to remedy this scarcity. R. LaVoie comments.

**1010** 1961-66, 35 watts, circuit breaker. 1 1.50 3
**1011** 1948-49, 25 watts. 1 1.50 3
**1012** 1950-54, 40 watts. 1 1.50 3
**1014** 40 watts, handle colors either red, black or silver. Rohlfing observation. 1 1.50 3
**1015** 1956-60, 45 watts. 1 1.50 3
**1016** 1959-60, 35 watts. 1 1.50 3
**1025** 1961-69, 45 watts, circuit breaker. 1 1.50 3
**1026** 1961-64, 25 watts, made as early as 1961; came with set 1123 made in that year. C. Rohlfing comment. 1 1.50 3
**1032** 1948, 75 watts, reverse and whistle controls. 9 14 18
**1033** 1948-56, 90 watts, whistle control. Very good reputation for reliability. R. LaVoie comment. 20 30 35
**1034** 1948-54, 75 watts. 15 20 25
**1037** 1946-47, 5-17 volts, 40 watts. 1 1.50 3
**1041** 1945-46, 60 watts, whistle control, circuit breaker. 5 7 11
**1042** 1947-48, 75 watts, whistle control, circuit breaker. 9 14 18
**1043**
(A) 1953-57, 50 watts, black case. 2 3 5
(B) 60 watts, ivory case with gold-plated speed control and binding post for Girls' Set. Black base, embossed in stylized letters "SA". 40 50 60
**1044** 1957-69, 90 watts, whistle control, direction control. 20 30 35
**1053** 1956-60, 60 watts, whistle control. 5 8 11
**1063** 1960-64, 75 watts, whistle control, circuit breaker. 9 14 18
**1073** 1962-66, 60 watts, circuit breaker. 3 5 17
**1101** 1948, 25 watts. 1 1.50 3
**A** 1947-48, 90 watts, circuit breaker, 14-24 volts. 8 10 18

**KW** 190 watts, operates two trains with whistle control, circuit breaker. Favored by many operators due to separate 14 volt fixed circuit. After many years of operation, the carbon rollers on this, the V, the Z, the VW and the ZW must be replaced. Roller and rivets are readily available. I.D. Smith comments.
(A) 1950-56, coil and lamination assembly not riveted, no stamping on base underside. 60 75 100
(B) 1957-65, same as (A), but riveted coil assembly, stamping "KW (R)" on bottom plate. (I.D. Smith reports one example stamped "MODEL TW (R)", probably a minor factory error.) 60 75 100

**LW** 1955-66, 125 watts, green "power on" light, buttons for direction and horn, circuit breaker. 30 35 45

**Q** 1946, 75 watts, 6-24 volts, whistle control. 8 12 18

**R** 1946-47, two independent circuits, two voltage ranges, 6-24 volts.
(A) 100 watt version. 15 20 30
(B) Same, but faceplate says "110 watts". C. Rohlfing Collection. Reader comments requested. 15 20 30

**RW** 1948-54, 110 watts, circuit breaker, whistle control. 20 30 35

This photo of an original box for the S Transformer shows that the catalogue was in error when it described this transformer as a 75-watt unit. T. Rollo Collection, W. Kojis Photograph.

**Gd VG Exc Mt**

**S** 1947 only; catalogued as 75 watt but produced as 80 watt; dial-type rheostat, whistle and reversing controls. C. Rohlfing and T. Rollo Collections. **10 15 20**

**SW** 1961-66, 130 watts, two-train operation, whistle on one throttle only, no reverse buttons, pilot light. **30 40 50**

**TW** 1953-60, 175 watts, whistle control. Unique among all Lionel transformers in that it has a separate power source for constant voltage to accessories which is completely independent of the main coil — in effect, a "transformer within a transformer"!

(A) 1953, has Terminal Post B. See Greenberg reproduction of Lionel Service Manual, VII-46. C. Rohlfing Collection. **40 50 70**

(B) Same as (A), but does not have Terminal Post B. C. Rohlfing Collection. **40 50 70**

**V** 1946-47, 150 watts, four independent circuits, no whistle or direction controls. Many operators use two 167C Controllers for this purpose when they use this, the R and the Z transformers. **30 40 50**

**VW** 1948-49, 150 watts, four independent circuits, whistle and direction controls for two throttles. **60 80 100**

**Z** 1945-47, 250 watts, four independent circuits, 6-25 volts each. See comment under V transformer, above. **50 65 75**

**ZW** 1948-49, 250 watts, four independent circuits, whistle and direction controls. **65 100 145**

**ZW** 275 watts, four independent circuits. Excellent examples in great demand. Earlier examples with Bakelite circuit breakers which hold up much better than later wafer-type; replacement Bakelite circuit breakers are available for about $10. Original box brings $5.00 premium. **100 125 175**

# Chapter XII

# TRUCKS AND COUPLERS

Lionel produced at least seven major types of metal freight car trucks, each of which is described below: (Several of these trucks were used for passenger cars.)

The earliest 1945 trucks, Type 1A, came with whirly wheels. Note that the axle end has been turned down, creating a collar to control wheel gauging.

**The two photos show side and bottom views of staple-end trucks. The left photos are the side and bottom views of a Type 2 truck with early coil coupler, regular axles and regular wheels. The right photos show the side and bottom views of a Type 1 truck with early coil coupler and thick axles. The wheel types are not visible.**

**TYPE 1** Staple-end Metal Trucks with Early Coil Couplers, Thick Axles. The first postwar trucks have a remotely-operated knuckle coupler that is controlled by a coil mounted behind the knuckle. A sliding shoe contacts the special remote control uncoupling track section and is mounted on a jury-rigged bracket which in turn is mounted on a phenolic board. The bracket is readily visible on the underside of the truck. The truck side frames are fastened by a rivet swaged over resembling a "staple end". The trucks came with three major different kinds of wheels. First, the wheels were made with a whirl pattern on the inside back surface; second, the wheels were made with a depression giving a dish appearance; third, regular wheels were used which ride on thickened axles.

Type 1A: Whirly wheels, thick axles, 1945.

Type 1B: Deep dish wheels, thick axles, 1945.

Type 1C: Regular wheels, thick axles, very early 1946.

Each of the subtypes is in turn subdivided into more varieties. See Volume 2 of this book for details.

**TYPE 2** Staple-end Metal Trucks with Early Coil Coupler, Regular Axles, Regular Wheels: early 1946. This is similar to Type 1 but has wheels with regular back inside surfaces and axles of usual thickness of one diameter for their entire length. The axles have staked points .41" from each end of the axle to control wheel gauging.

**Side and bottom views of the Type 3 and Type 5 versions of the staple-end truck. On the left are side and bottom views of a Type 3A truck with late coil coupler. On the right are side and bottom views of a Type 5 truck with magnetic coupler. The activator plate has one hole through which a rivet passes and a second hole which is open. The rivet is swaged and the swaged end is down. Since the swaged end of the rivet is down, this is classified as a Type 5A. There is also a large off-center hole in the baseplate of this truck.**

**TYPE 3** Staple-end Metal Trucks with Late Coil Coupler: 1946-47. This coupler also uses an opening knuckle activated by a coil and plunger and the truck side frames have the "staple-end" fastening. The mounting bracket for the sliding shoe is integral with the metal plate that covers the bottom of the truck.

Type 3A: without stake marks on coupler knuckle underside, 1946.

Type 3B: with four stake marks on coupler knuckle underside, 1947.

**TYPE 4** Staple-end Metal Trucks with Magnetic Coupler and Without Extra Hole on Activator Flap: 1948-49. Lionel found that it could produce a highly reliable coupling action without the expense and complication of a coil plunger unit. Rather than having a wound coil on each truck, as required by the earlier trucks, the new system placed the coil in the special uncoupling track. Lionel designed a coupler that opens by pulling down a flap on the underside of the truck. The coil pulls the flap which is connected to the coupler by a lever arrangement so that the knuckle opens. The flap has one hole through which a rivet passes. The rivet is swaged on the underside. Type 4 was the beginning of a highly successful design.

**TYPE 5** Staple-end Metal Trucks with Magnetic Coupler, and Extra Hole on Activator Flap: 1950-51. The truck is mounted by a brass stud with recessed ring for a horseshoe washer. This type is the same as Type 4 but another hole has been added to the activator flap behind the rivet. Lionel made this truck in two versions: 5A with the rivet swaged on the underside of the activator flap and 5B with the round end of the rivet down and the rivet swaged on the top side of the activator flap.

Type 5A: rivet with swaged end down, early 1950.
Type 5B: rivet with round end down, late 1950-51.

**Two versions of the bar-end truck are shown. On the right are side and bottom views of a Type 6 truck. Note that the rivet which passes through the activator plate has its round end down. On the left are side and bottom views of the Type 7B truck with tab. This truck is fastened to the car frame by means of a truck mounting clip. In contrast, Type 7A was mounted using a stud and horseshoe washer. See the photograph showing the side views of Type 3 and 5 trucks for examples of the stud used with Type 7A.**

**TYPE 6** Bar-end Metal Trucks with Magnetic Coupler, and Extra Hole on Activator Flap: 1952-54. Lionel modified Type 5 by changing the method of fastening the side frames to the bolster with a bar fitting into the side frames. The top of the bolster is embossed. The rivet through the activator flap is mounted with round end down as with Type 5B trucks. See article by Mr. Pehringer in Volume 2 for details.

**TYPE 7** Bar-end Metal Trucks with Magnetic Coupler, Extra Hole on Activator Flap and Tab: 1955-57. Lionel modified Truck Type 6 by adding a tab to facilitate hand uncoupling. This design change made the trains easier for children to play with at some slight sacrifice of realism.
Type 7A: truck fastens to car frame by horseshoe washer fitting to recessed slot on pivot stud, 1955
Type 7B: truck fastens to car frame by truck mounting clip, 1955-57, 1969.

Although the majority of bar-end trucks were produced between 1952 and 1957, some use continued through 1969. In 1969 Lionel issued boxcars with Type 7B trucks.

**TYPE 8:** Plastic AAR trucks with disc couplers, 1957-1969.

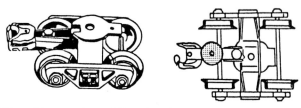

**Side and bottom views of Type 8 AAR trucks.**

**TYPE 8A:** Plastic AAR side frames with "TIMKEN" emblem on bearing surfaces; the outer wheel hub is flush with outer wheel edge compared with Type 8D. The axle ends are not visible when viewed from beneath the car, leaf spring from metal disc and rod to coupler pinion has small attachment hole and is lanced, plastic coupler head with metal coupler knuckle, disc pulls leaf spring down when attracted by magnet in uncoupling track or pulled down manually, regular trucks attached to cars by metal rivet, trucks requiring electrical ground have metal ground washer inserted between truck bolster and car frame and are attached by mounting clip, 1957-early 1961.

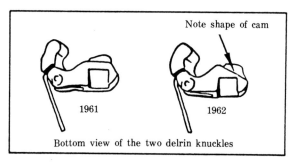

**Left: delrin knuckle used with Type 8B trucks. Right: knuckle used with Type 8C. Type 8A used a metal knuckle.**

**TYPE 8B:** Later 1961, same as Type 8A, except coupler has first version of plastic Delrin knuckle with integral and visible copper metal spring, leaf spring has larger attachment hole and lancing is eliminated.

**TYPE 8C:** Same as Type 8B, except has second version of plastic Delrin knuckle with integral plastic spring and different shape, late 1961.

**TYPE 8D:** Same as Type 8-C, but wheel hubs project above wheel surfaces, axle ends visible when viewed from bottom of truck, 1962-69.

**Side and bottom views of the Type 9 truck.**

**TYPE 9:** Plastic arch-bar trucks with disc couplers, 1957-69, essentially the same as Type 8 trucks, except truck sides modeled after arch-bar trucks of Civil War period. These trucks are somewhat fragile, since they are of an open design.

**NOTE:** Both Type 8 and 9 trucks were also issued with dummy couplers lacking the operating mechanism. Both types accepted a snap-in roller carriage for illumination of certain cars.

TRUCK SIDE

**The Scout truck consisted of a stamped metal frame into which plastic side frames were pressed.**

**TYPE 10A:** Stamped sheet metal truck frames, plastic truck sides which snap onto frame sides, large coupler head with plastic swing-out knuckle which is not compatible with other Lionel couplers, 1948-50. Lionel sold coupler conversion kits to convert these trucks into regular magnetic couplers.

**TYPE 10B:** Same as Type 10A, but trucks are equipped with magnetic couplers. These Scout trucks were used in several inexpensive sets from 1949-53. Activator plate is same as those found on regular staple-end or bar-end issues of the period, but sides remain Scout-type plastic inserts.

**The side view of the Type 11 truck.**

**TYPE 11:** Four-wheel passenger-type trucks, O-27 Gauge, 1948-64.

**TYPE 11A:** Shorter die-cast side frame with two simulated springs, light collector pickup, sliding shoe, articulated coupler arm, solenoid operated coil coupler assembly, 1948-52.

**TYPE 11B:** Same as Type 11A, but sliding shoe assembly replaced by magnetically-activated plate which operates spring attached to coupler head when pulled down, 1953-64.

**NOTE:** Both Type 11 trucks came with or without the pickup roller for lighting, and they were also made without a coupler assembly for the rears of the observation cars. This truck was also used for the bay window cabooses.

**Left: Type 12 die-cast four-wheel O Gauge passenger truck. Right: Type 11B die-cast four-wheel O-27 Gauge passenger truck.**

**The side view of the Type 12 truck.**

**TYPE 12:** Die-cast four-wheel passenger trucks, O Gauge, 1952-66. Long truck side plates with four simulated springs, magnetically-activated plate triggers spring attached to coupler knuckle when pulled down; also made plain and with illumination pickup roller for O Gauge aluminum passenger cars.

**TYPE 13:** Six-wheel trucks.

**TYPE 13A:** Stamped metal truck frame, plastic truck side pieces inserted into frames, flanged wheel sets on ends and blind middle wheel sets, metal plate with sliding shoe and coil coupler assembly mounted on fixed short drawbar, 1946-50, used only on 2460 Crane Car.

**TYPE 13B:** Same as Type 13A, but has pickup roller assembly, sliding shoe, longer articulated drawbar and coil couplers without tape, 1946-48, used for 2625, 2627 and 2628 "Madison" passenger type cars.

**TYPE 13C:** Same as Type 13B, but black tape added to cover coil surfaces, 1949-50

**TYPE 13D:** Same as Type 13C, but has shorter articulated drawbar; used on rear of 2671W and 2426W tenders, 1946-51. (Version without coupler used at front of tender.)

# INDEX

*By Dallas Mallerich III*

| ITEM | PAGE | ITEM | PAGE | ITEM | PAGE | ITEM | PAGE | ITEM | PAGE | ITEM | PAGE | ITEM | PAGE | ITEM | PAGE |
|---|---|---|---|---|---|---|---|---|---|---|---|---|---|---|---|
| 1032 | 225 | 2023 | 60 | 2340-C | 41 | 2379-C | 36 | 2461-C | 161 | 3357 | 103 | 3494-150 | 107 | 4810 | 71 |
| 1033 | 225 | 2023-C | 57 | 2341 | 64 | 2383 | 70 | 2465 | 195 | 3359 | 183 | 3494-150-C | 108 | 5159 | 224 |
| 1034 | 225 | 2024 | 60 | 2341-C | 62 | 2383-C | 39 | 2465-C | 194 | 3359-C | 181 | 3494-275 | 107 | 5159-50 | 224 |
| 1037 | 225 | 2024-C | 59 | 2343 | 64 | 2383C | 70 | 2472 | 134 | 3360 | 147 | 3494-275-C | 108 | 5160 | 224 |
| 1041 | 225 | 2025 | 98 | 2343-C | 39 | 2400 | 189 | 2481 | 190 | 3360-C | 48 | 3494-550 | 107 | 5459 | 183 |
| 1042 | 225 | 2026 | 98 | 2343C | 64 | 2400-C | 188 | 2481-C | 188 | 3360 | 70 | 3494-550-C | 108 | 5511 | 71 |
| 1043 | 225 | 2028 | 60 | 2344 | 64 | 2401 | 189 | 2482 | 190 | 3361-55 | 152 | 3494-625 | 108 | 6002 | 177 |
| 1044 | 225 | 2028-C | 61 | 2344-C | 33 | 2402 | 189 | 2483 | 190 | 3362 | 152 | 3494-625-C | 108 | 6004 | 110 |
| 1045 | 222 | 2029 | 98 | 2344-C | 39 | 2404 | 189 | 2521 | 190 | 3364 | 152 | 3509 | 155 | X6004 | 110 |
| 1047 | 223 | 2031 | 60 | 2344 | 64 | 2405 | 189 | 2522 | 190 | 3364 | 153 | 3510 | 155 | 6007 | 135 |
| 1050 | 91 | 2032 | 60 | 2345 | 66 | 2406 | 189 | 2523 | 190 | 3366 | 103 | 3511 | 155 | 6012 | 177 |
| 1053 | 225 | 2033 | 60 | 2345-C | 33 | 2408 | 189 | 2530 | 190 | 3366-C | 106 | 3519 | 155 | 6014 | 110 |
| 1055 | 56 | 2033-C | 57 | 2346 | 66 | 2409 | 189 | 2531 | 190 | 3370 | 103 | 3520 | 148 | X6014 | 111 |
| 1055 | 60 | 2034 | 98 | 2346-C | 66 | 2409-C | 188 | 2532 | 190 | 3376 | 103 | 3530 | 148 | 6014-1 | 111 |
| 1060 | 91 | 2035 | 98 | 2347 | 66 | 2410 | 189 | 2533 | 191 | 3386 | 104 | 3530 | 108 | 6014-60 | 111 |
| 1061 | 91 | 2036 | 98 | 2347-C | 66 | 2411 | 151 | 2534 | 191 | 3409 | 153 | 3530 | 224 | 6014-85 | 112 |
| 1062 | 91 | 2037 | 98 | 2348 | 66 | 2412 | 189 | 2541 | 191 | 3410 | 153 | 3530-C | 108 | 6014-100 | 112 |
| 1063 | 225 | 2037-500 | 98 | 2348-C | 66 | 2414 | 189 | 2542 | 191 | 3413 | 153 | 3535 | 155 | 6014-150 | 112 |
| 1065 | 56 | 2040 | 60 | 2349 | 66 | 2414-C | 188 | 2543 | 191 | 3419 | 153 | 3540 | 155 | 6014-325 | 112 |
| 1065 | 60 | 2046 | 98 | 2349-C | 67 | 2416 | 189 | 2544 | 191 | 3424 | 104 | 3545 | 155 | 6014-410 | 112 |
| 1066 | 60 | 2055 | 100 | 2350 | 66 | 2419 | 132 | 2550 | 70 | 3424-C | 107 | 3559 | 183 | 6015 | 196 |
| 1073 | 225 | 2056 | 101 | 2350-C | 68 | 2420 | 133 | 2551 | 191 | 3424-75 | 224 | 3559-C | 181 | 6017 | 135 |
| 1101 | 93 | 2065 | 101 | 2351 | 67 | 2421 | 189 | 2552 | 191 | 3424-100 | 224 | 3559-C | 181 | 6017 | 136 |
| 1101 | 225 | 2240 | 60 | 2351-C | 68 | 2422 | 189 | 2553 | 191 | 3428 | 104 | 3562-1 | 176 | 6017-C | 132 |
| 1110 | 93 | 2240-C | 31 | 2352 | 67 | 2422-C | 188 | 2554 | 191 | 3428-C | 107 | 3562-1-C | 176 | 6017-50 | 136 |
| 1120 | 93 | 2242 | 60 | 2353 | 67 | 2423 | 189 | 2555 | 195 | 3429 | 154 | 3562-25 | 176 | 6017-85 | 136 |
| 1130 | 94 | 2242-C | 31 | 2353-C | 33 | 2429 | 189 | 2559 | 70 | 3434 | 104 | 3562-25-C | 176 | 6017-100 | 136 |
| 1121 | 223 | 2243 | 61 | 2353C | 67 | 2429-C | 188 | 2560 | 146 | 3435 | 104 | 3562-50 | 176 | 6017-185 | 136 |
| 1122 | 223 | 2243-C | 31 | 2354 | 67 | 2430 | 189 | 2561 | 191 | 3444 | 176 | 3562-50-C | 176 | 6017-200 | 137 |
| 1122E | 223 | 2243C | 61 | 2354-C | 34 | 2430-C | 189 | 2562 | 191 | 3449 | 183 | 3562-75 | 177 | 6017-225 | 137 |
| 1122LH | 223 | 2245 | 61 | 2354C | 68 | 2431 | 189 | 2563 | 191 | 3451 | 154 | 3562-75-C | 176 | 6017-235 | 137 |
| 1122RH | 223 | 2245-C | 31 | 2355 | 68 | 2432 | 189 | 2625 | 191 | 3454 | 104 | 3619 | 108 | 6019 | 224 |
| 1122-234 | 223 | 2257 | 131 | 2355-C | 34 | 2434 | 189 | 2626 | 191 | 3454-C | 9 | 3619-C | 109 | 6024 | 112 |
| 1122-500 | 223 | 2321 | 61 | 2356 | 58 | 2435 | 189 | 2627 | 191 | 3456 | 183 | 3620 | 148 | 6025 | 112 |
| L1445 | 223 | 2321-C | 62 | 2356-C | 34 | 2436 | 190 | 2628 | 191 | 3456-C | 184 | 3620X | 149 | 6025 | 197 |
| 1615 | 94 | 2322 | 62 | 2356-C | 39 | 2436-C | 188 | 2630 | 191 | 3459 | 183 | 3650 | 149 | 6027 | 137 |
| 1625 | 95 | 2322 | 63 | 2356C | 68 | 2440 | 190 | 2631 | 191 | 3459-C | 181 | 3656 | 109 | 6029 | 224 |
| 1640-100 | 223 | 2328 | 62 | 2357 | 131 | 2441 | 190 | 2671 | 101 | 3460 | 154 | 3656 | 224 | 6032 | 177 |
| 1654 | 95 | 2328-C | 61 | 2358 | 68 | 2442 | 190 | 2755 | 196 | 3460-C | 152 | 3662-1 | 109 | X6034 | 112 |
| 1655 | 95 | 2329 | 62 | 2359 | 68 | 2442-C | 189 | X2758 | 103 | 3461 | 154 | 3662-1-C | 109 | 6035 | 197 |
| 1656 | 95 | 2330 | 62 | 2359-C | 67 | 2443 | 190 | 2855 | 196 | 3462 | 104 | 3665 | 110 | 6037 | 137 |
| 1665 | 95 | 2330-C | 40 | 2360 | 68 | 2444 | 190 | 2855-C | 193 | 3462P | 224 | 3665-C | 109 | 6042 | 177 |
| 1666 | 95 | 2330 | 41 | 2360-C | 41 | 2445 | 190 | 2856 | 183 | 3464 | 105 | 3666 | 110 | 6042-125 | 177 |
| 1862 | 96 | 2331 | 62 | 2360-C | 42 | 2445-C | 188 | 2856-C | 184 | 3464-C | 13 | 3672 | 110 | 6044 | 113 |
| 1865 | 188 | 2331-C | 63 | 2360-C | 43 | 2446 | 190 | 2857 | 134 | 3464X | 105 | 3672-79 | 224 | 6044-1X | 113 |
| 1866 | 188 | 2332 | 63 | 2363 | 69 | 2452 | 175 | X2954 | 103 | 3469 | 183 | 3820 | 156 | 6045 | 197 |
| 1872 | 97 | 2332-C | 40 | 2363-C | 35 | 2452X | 176 | 2955 | 196 | 3470 | 154 | 3830 | 156 | 6047 | 137 |
| 1875 | 189 | 2333 | 63 | 3265 | 69 | 2454 | 103 | 2956 | 183 | 3472 | 105 | 3854 | 110 | 6050 | 113 |
| 1875W | 189 | 2333-C | 32 | 2365-C | 67 | 2454-C | 9 | 2956-C | 184 | 3474 | 105 | X3854-C | 105 | 6057 | 137 |
| 1876 | 189 | 2333C | 64 | 2367 | 69 | X2454 | 103 | 2957 | 135 | 3474-C | 13 | 3927 | 70 | 6057-50 | 137 |
| 1877 | 151 | 2334 | 64 | 2367-C | 35 | X2454-C | 105 | 3309 | 151 | 3482 | 105 | 3927-C | 48 | 6058 | 137 |
| 1882 | 97 | 2337 | 64 | 2368 | 69 | 2456 | 183 | 3330 | 151 | 3484 | 105 | 3927 50 | 224 | 6058-C | 132 |
| 1885 | 189 | 2337-C | 61 | 2368-C | 35 | 2457 | 133 | 3330-100 | 223 | 3484-C | 107 | 4357 | 135 | 6059-50 | 137 |
| 1887 | 151 | 2338 | 64 | 2373 | 69 | X2458 | 103 | 3349 | 151 | 3484-25 | 105 | 4452 | 177 | 6059-C | 137 |
| 2003 | 223 | 2338-C | 65 | 2373-C | 36 | X2458-C | 105 | 3356 | 103 | 3484-25-C | 106 | 4454 | 110 | 6059-60 | 137 |
| 2016 | 97 | 2339 | 64 | 2378 | 69 | 2460 | 146 | 3356-150 | 223 | 3484-25-C | 107 | 4457 | 135 | 6062 | 177 |
| 2018 | 97 | 2339-C | 65 | 238-C | 36 | 2460-C | 145 | 3356-C | 106 | 3494-1 | 107 | 4460 | 147 | 6062-50 | 177 |
| 2020 | 97 | 2340 | 64 | 2379 | 69 | 2461 | 151 | 3366-100 | 223 | 3494-1-C | 107 | 4681 | 101 | 6067 | 138 |

| ITEM | PAGE | ITEM | PAGE | ITEM | PAGE | ITEM | PAGE | ITEM | PAGE | ITEM | PAGE | ITEM | PAGE |
|---|---|---|---|---|---|---|---|---|---|---|---|---|---|
| 6076 | 183 | 6264 | 156 | 6427 | 198 | 6463 | 198 | 6464-725 | 127 | 6555-C | 193 | 6826 | 167 |
| 6076 | 184 | 6311 | 157 | 6427-C | 136 | 6464-1 | 120 | 6464-725-C | 124 | 6556 | 129 | 6827 | 167 |
| 6076-75 | 184 | 6315 | 197 | 6427-60 | 142 | 6464-1-C | 116 | 6464-725-C | 125 | 6556-C | 106 | 6827-100 | 225 |
| 6076-100 | 184 | 6315-C | 193 | 6427-500 | 143 | 6464-25 | 121 | 6464-825 | 127 | 6557 | 143 | 6828 | 167 |
| 6110 | 101 | 6315-50 | 197 | 6428 | 114 | 6464-25-C | 116 | 6464-825-C | 125 | 6557-C | 132 | 6828-100 | 225 |
| 6111 | 156 | 6315-60 | 197 | 6429 | 143 | 6464-50 | 121 | 6464-900 | 128 | 6560 | 147 | 6830 | 168 |
| 6111-75 | 156 | 6315-1972 | 197 | 6430 | 161 | 6464-50-C | 116 | 6464-900-C | 125 | 6560 | 148 | 6844 | 168 |
| 6112 | 178 | 6342 | 179 | 6430-C | 152 | 6464-75 | 121 | 6464-TCA | 128 | 6560-C | 145 | 64173 | 133 |
| (6112) | 178 | 6343 | 157 | 6431 | 161 | 6464-75-C | 116 | 6464-1965 | 128 | 6560-25 | 148 | 64273 | 142 |
| 6112-1 | 178 | 6346-56 | 185 | 6434 | 114 | 6464-100 | 121 | 6464-1970 | 128 | 6560-25-C | 145 | 477618 | 133 |
| 6112-25 | 224 | 6346-56-C | 185 | 6436 | 185 | 6464-100 | 116 | 6464-1971 | 128 | 561 | 163 | 477618 | 134 |
| 6112-135 | 178 | 6352-1 | 113 | 6436-C | 185 | 6464-125 | 122 | 6465 | 198 | 6561-C | 161 | 536417 | 141 |
| 6119 | 138 | 6352-1-C | 106 | 6436-1 | 185 | 6464-125-C | 116 | 6465 | 200 | 6562 | 180 | 546446 | 187 |
| 6119-C | 137 | 6356-1 | 114 | 6436-25 | 185 | 6464-150 | 122 | 6465-60 | 200 | 6562-C | 169 | 576427 | 143 |
| 6119-25 | 138 | 6357 | 141 | 6436-100 | 185 | 6464-125-C | 116 | 6467 | 163 | 6572 | 129 | 641751 | 133 |
| 6119-50 | 138 | 6357-25 | 141 | 6436-110 | 185 | 6464-150 | 122 | 6468-1 | 128 | 6572-C | 106 | No-number |  |
| 6119-75 | 138 | 6357-50 | 141 | 6436-500 | 185 | 6464-150-C | 116 | 6468-1-C | 125 | 6630 | 163 | cars: |  |
| 6119-100 | 138 | 6361 | 157 | 6436-1969 | 185 | 6464-175 | 122 | 6468-25 | 128 | 6636 | 187 | Boxcar | 129 |
| 6119-125 | 139 | 6362-55 | 157 | 6437-25 | 143 | 6464-175-C | 120 | 6468-25-C | 125 | 6636-C | 185 | Caboose | 144 |
| 6120 | 139 | 6376 | 114 | 6437-25-C | 136 | 6464-200 | 122 | 6469 | 163 | 6640 | 163 | Flatcar | 168 |
| 6121 | 156 | 6376-C | 106 | 6440 | 162 | 6464-200-C | 120 | 6470 | 129 | 6646 | 129 | Gondola | 180 |
| 6121-25 | 156 | 6401 | 157 | 6440 | 191 | 6464-225 | 123 | 6472 | 129 | 6650 | 163 | Hopper | 187 |
| 6121-60 | 156 | 6401-50 | 158 | 6440-C | 189 | 6464-225-C | 120 | 6473 | 129 | 6650-80 | 224 | A | 225 |
| 6130 | 139 | 6402 | 158 | 6441 | 191 | 6464-250 | 123 | 6475 | 201 | 6651 | 163 | Q | 225 |
| 6130-C | 137 | 6402-50 | 158 | 6441-C | 189 | 6464-250 | 128 | 6476 | 1987 | 6656 | 129 | R | 225 |
| 6142 | 178 | 6404 | 158 | 6442 | 191 | 6464-250-C | 120 | 6476-85 | 187 | 6657 | 144 | S | 226 |
| 6142-50 | 179 | 6405 | 158 | 6443 | 191 | 6464-275 | 123 | 6476-85-C | 187 | 6657-C | 132 | V | 226 |
| 6142-75 | 179 | 6406 | 159 | 6445 | 114 | 6464-275-C | 120 | 6476-125 | 187 | 6660 | 164 | Z | 226 |
| 6142-100 | 179 | 6407 | 159 | 6445-C | 108 | 6464-275-C | 121 | 6476-135 | 187 | 6670 | 164 | KW | 225 |
| 6142-150 | 179 | 6409-25 | 159 | 6446-1 | 185 | 6464-300 | 123 | 6476-160 | 187 | 6672 | 129 | LW | 225 |
| 6142-175 | 179 | 6411 | 159 | 6446-1-C | 185 | 6464-300-C | 121 | 6476-160-C | 187 | 6736 | 187 | RW | 225 |
| 6151 | 156 | 6413 | 159 | 6446-25 | 186 | 6464-325 | 123 | 6476-185 | 187 | 6736-C | 185 | SW | 226 |
| 6157 | 139 | 6414 | 160 | 6446-60 | 186 | 6464-325-C | 121 | 6476-185-C | 187 | 6800 | 164 | TW | 226 |
| 6162 | 179 | 6415 | 198 | 6447 | 143 | 6464-350 | 123 | 6477 | 163 | 6801 | 164 | VW | 226 |
| 6162-60 | 179 | 6415-C | 193 | 6448 | 114 | 6464-350-C | 121 | 6480 | 129 | 6801 | 225 | ZW | 226 |
| 6162-110 | 179 | 6416 | 160 | 6452 | 179 | 6464-375 | 124 | 6482 | 129 | 6802 | 164 | CTC | 225 |
| 6167 | 14 | 6417 | 141 | 6454 | 114 | 6464-375 | 128 | 6500 | 163 | 6803 | 164 | ECU | 225 |
| 6167-25 | 140 | 6417-C | 133 | 6454-C | 12 | 6464-375-C | 121 | 6501 | 163 | 6804 | 165 | LTC | 225 |
| 6167-50 | 140 | 6417-25 | 141 | 6454-C | 16 | 6464-400 | 124 | 6502-50 | 163 | 6805 | 165 | OC | 225 |
| 6167-85 | 140 | 6417-25-C | 133 | X6454 | 105 | 6464-400-C | 121 | 6502-75 | 163 | 6807 | 165 | OC18 | 225 |
| 6167-100 | 140 | 6417-50 | 141 | X6454-C | 114 | 6464-425 | 125 | 6511 | 163 | 6808 | 165 | OC51 | 225 |
| 6167-125 | 140 | 6417-50-C | 133 | 6456 | 184 | 6464-425-C | 121 | 6512 | 163 | 6809 | 165 | OC1/2 | 225 |
| 6167-150 | 140 | 6418 | 161 | 6456 | 186 | 6464-450 | 126 | 6517 | 143 | 6810 | 165 | OTC | 225 |
| 6175 | 156 | 6418 | 224 | 6457 | 143 | 6464-450 | 128 | 6517-C | 137 | 6812 | 165 | RCS | 225 |
| 6176 | 184 | 6418-C | 157 | 6457-C | 132 | 6464-450-C | 124 | 6517-75 | 143 | 6814-1 | 144 | SP | 225 |
| 6176 | 185 | 6419 | 142 | 6460 | 147 | 6464-475 | 126 | 6517-75-C | 137 | 6816 | 165 | T011-43 | 203 |
| 6219 | 140 | 6419-C | 137 | 6460-C | 145 | 6464-475 | 128 | 6517-1966 | 143 | 6816-100 | 225 | T020 | 203 |
| 6219-C | 137 | 6419-25 | 142 | 6460-25 | 147 | 6464-475-C | 124 | 6518 | 163 | 6816-C | 157 | TOC1/2 | 225 |
| 6220 | 71 | 6419-50 | 142 | 6461 | 162 | 6464-500 | 126 | 6518-C | 157 | 6817 | 165 | TOC51 | 225 |
| 6220-C | 51 | 6419-57 | 142 | 6461-C | 161 | 6464-500-C | 124 | 6519 | 163 | 6817-100 | 225 | TOS | 225 |
| 6250 | 71 | 6419-75 | 142 | 6462 | 179 | 6464-510 | 126 | 6520 | 149 | 6818 | 165 | UCS | 225 |
| 6250-C | 51 | 6420 | 142 | 6462-C | 169 | 6464-510-C | 124 | 6527 | 143 | 6819 | 165 | UTC | 225 |
| 6257 | 140 | 6424 | 161 | 6462-25 | 180 | 6464-525 | 127 | 6530 | 129 | 6820 | 165 |  |  |
| 6257-25 | 140 | 6425 | 198 | 6462-75 | 180 | 6464-525 | 128 | 6530-C | 108 | 6821 | 167 |  |  |
| 6257-50 | 141 | 6425-C | 193 | 6462-100 | 180 | 6464-525-C | 124 | 6536 | 187 | 6822 | 149 |  |  |
| 6257-100 | 141 | 6426 | 198 | 6462-125 | 180 | 6464-700 | 127 | 6536-C | 185 | 6823 | 167 |  |  |
| 6257X | 141 | 6427 | 142 | 6462-500 | 180 | 6464-700 | 128 | 6544 | 163 | 6824 | 144 |  |  |
| 6262 | 156 | 6427 | 143 | 6464-0000 | 128 | 6464-700-C | 124 | 6555 | 200 | 6825 | 167 |  |  |